KT-118-177

Time Out Guides Limited
Universal House
251 Tottenham Court Road
London W1T 7AB
Tel + 44 (0)20 7813 3000
Fax + 44 (0)20 7813 6001
Email guides@timeout.com
www.timeout.com

Editorial
Editor Andrew Humphreys
Deputy Editor Simon Coppock
Listings Editors Carol Baker, David Jenkins, Fiona Shield
Proofreader Tamsin Shelton
Indexer Jackie Brind

Editorial/Managing Director Peter Fiennes
Series Editor Ruth Jarvis
Deputy Series Editor Lesley McCave
Financial Director Gareth Garner
Guides Co-ordinator Holly Pick
Accountant Kemi Olufuwa

Design
Art Director Scott Moore
Art Editor Pinelope Kourmouzoglou
Senior Designer Josephine Spencer
Graphic Designer Henry Elphick
Digital Imaging Simon Foster
Ad Make-up Jenni Prichard

Picture Desk
Picture Editor Jael Marschner
Deputy Picture Editor Tracey Kerrigan
Picture Researcher Helen McFarland

Advertising
Sales Director Mark Phillips
Advertising Sales Manager Alison Wallen
Sales Executives Jason Trotman, Ben Holt
Advertising Assistant Kate Staddon
Copy Controller Baris Tosun

Marketing
Group Marketing Director John Luck
Marketing Manager Yvonne Poon
Marketing & Publicity Manager, US Rosella Albanese

Production
Group Production Director Mark Lamond
Production Manager Brendan McKeown
Production Coordinator Caroline Bradford

Time Out Group
Chairman Tony Elliott
Financial Director Richard Waterlow
TO Magazine Ltd MD David Pepper
Group General Manager/Director Nichola Coulthard
MD, Time Out International Cathy Runciman
TO Communications Ltd MD David Pepper
Group Art Director John Oakey
Group IT Director Simon Chappell

Contributors
Introduction Andrew Humphreys. **History** *City chroniclers* Andrew Humphreys. **London Today** Gordon Thomson. **Architecture** Pamela Buxton. **The Director's Cut** Dave Calhoun, Andrew Humphreys. **Capital Records** John Lewis and *Time Out London* magazine music writers. **Where to Stay** Andrew Humphreys; additional reviews by Lesley McCave, Ismay Atkins (*Suite talk, Landmark accommodation* Andrew Humphreys; *You say hotel, I say Yotel* Ismay Atkins). **Sights Introduction** Andrew Humphreys. **The South Bank & Bankside** Andrew Humphreys (*The graveyard express* Peter Watts; *Mash point* Sophie Roberts). **The City** Joe Bindloss. **Holborn & Clerkenwell** Andrew Humphreys. **Bloomsbury & Fitzrovia** Andrew Humphreys. **Covent Garden & the Strand** Andrew Humphreys (*The birth of the beautiful game* Andrew Shields). **Soho & Leicester Square** Andrew Humphreys. **Oxford Street & Marylebone** Andrew Humphreys. **Paddington & Notting Hill** Andrew Humphreys. **Piccadilly & Mayfair** Andrew Humphreys (*Undercover shopping* Kate Riordan). **Westminster & St James's** Andrew Humphreys (*Room for one more on top* Ismay Atkins; *Walk this way* Vesna Maric). **Chelsea** Andrew Humphreys. **Knightsbridge & South Kensington** Andrew Humphreys. **North London** Photini Philippidou. **East London** Simon Coppock (*Oranges are not the only fruit* Lisa Mullen). **South-east London** Peterjon Cresswell. **South-west London** Sharon Lougher (*Tragically underpowered* Andrew Humphreys). **West London** Edoardo Albert. **Restaurants & Cafés** Contributors to *Time Out Eating & Drinking* (*Dimond picks, Good to go* Guy Dimond). **Pubs & Bars** Andrew Humphreys and contributors to *Time Out Bars, Pubs & Clubs* (*I'll have what they're not having, Time at the bar* Andrew Humphreys). **Shops & Services** Jan Fuscoe. **Festivals & Events** David Jenkins (*Air play* Andrew Humphreys, Kathryn Miller). **Children** Cathy Limb. **Comedy** Tracey Graham. **Dance** Allen Robertson. **Film** David Jenkins (*Goodbye NFT, hello BFI* Andrew Humphreys). **Galleries** Martin Coomber. **Gay & Lesbian** Paul Burston. **Music** Will Fulford-Jones. **Nightlife** Simone Baird. **Sport & Fitness** Tom Davies. **Theatre** Natalie Whittle (*Backstage pass* Vesna Maric). **Trips Out of Town** Carol Baker (*Bath time* Andrew Humphreys). **Getting Around** Carol Baker. **Resources A-Z** Fiona Shield.

Maps john@jsgraphics.co.uk.

Photography by Britta Jaschinski, except: pages 3, 7, 43, 55, 57, 58, 59, 60, 61, 64, 72, 73, 79, 126, 128, 130, 131, 149, 151, 154, 181, 182, 189, 190, 191, 242, 270, 308, 314 Olivia Rutherford; pages 12, 32, 106 Matt Carr; pages 15, 21, 28, 31, 35, 140, 276 Jonathan Perugia; page 17 The Bridgeman Art Library; page 18 Topfoto.co.uk; page 20 Corbis; page 23 Scott Wishart; page 24 Rex Features; page 25 Time Life Pictures/Getty Images; pages 30, 89, 134, 337 Rob Grieg; page 37 The Da Vinci code DVD courtesy of Sony Pictures Home Entertainment; page 52 Gautier Deblonde; page 96 Belinda Lawley; page 104 Martin Charles; pages 107, 287, 307 Andrew Brackenbury; pages 112, 320 Angela Moore; page 121 Paul Mattson; page 136 David Purdie; page 187 Andrea Schmidt; page 194 Hadley Kincade; pages 195, 233 Anthony Webb; pages 202, 203, 216, 237, 244, 245, 254, 256, 262, 263, 268, 269 Heloise Bergman; pages 212, 213, 228, 231, 248 Ming Tang Evans; page 221 Kevin Nicholson; page 225 Viktor Pesenti; pages 226, 274, 275 Alys Tomlinson; pages 272, 273 James O'Jenkins; page 279 Tricia de Courcy Ling; page 283 Charlie Hopkinson, 2006; page 284 Michael Franke; page 289 BFI Southbank: Buchanan Associates Architects & The Digital Image Co.; page 290 Dafydd Jones; pages 303, 304 Gordon Rainsford; pages 309, 339 Johan Persson; page 329 Arsenal Football Club; page 335 Haris Artemis; page 341 Joan Marcus; page 345 Adrian Sherratt/Alamy; page 351 Edmund Sumner; page 352 Photolibrary; page 357 4Corners Images.

The following images were provided by the featured establishments/artists: pages 40, 44, 49, 56, 67, 71, 159, 292, 296, 316, 324, 325, 326, 327, 328, 332, 336, 343.

The Editor would like to thank all contributors to previous editions of Time Out London, whose work forms the basis for parts of this book.

Contents

Introduction

For a destination renowned for its history and traditions, London is one rapidly changing city. Don't misunderstand – all the heritage and pomp remains present and correct: the guards still high-step daily at Buckingham Palace; the ravens (and red-costumed Beefeaters) have yet to abandon the Tower; the passing hours continue to be marked by the chimes of Big Ben; and 54 years since it opened Agatha Christie's *The Mousetrap* shows no sign of ending its run at the St Martins Theatre.

But behind the long-established British Museum (founded 1753) and National Gallery (founded 1824), which in 2005 were ranked the two most popular London attractions, are relative newcomers Tate Modern and the British Airways London Eye. Both of these crowd pullers only made their debuts as recently as 2000. Both have contributed to the opening up of a riverside walk along the South Bank that links the Houses of Parliament with Tower Bridge taking in along the way of a clutch of lesser known but equally fascinating attractions. In a similar way, it's hoped that work currently underway in the Kings Cross area (and focused on the magnificent Victorian Gothic St Pancras Chambers building) and at the iconic Battersea Power Station will in the near future add two more landmarks to the tourist map of the city. Meanwhile, opened in the last 12 months are the new Cartoon Art Museum, a brands and packaging museum and the Benjamin Franklin House. Coming in 2007, during the life of this guide, will be a revamped National Film Theatre, Royal Festival Hall and London Transport Museum, plus a new Lord Norman Foster designed national sports stadium at Wembley. Not to mention all the ongoing activity in the east of the city as London continues with its preparations to host the Olympic Games in 2012. The fact is that for all its great age London will always be an unfinished project.

But it's away from the monuments and the museums (wonderful as they are and often free to boot) where London excels. The real joys of the city, the things that make London truly great are the sort of things that you won't find marked on a map. Things like the hotel doormen in their top hats and white gloves. Churches with names like St Andrew's-by-the-Wardrobe and streets such as St Mary Axe. Riding a black cab across a strangely silent West End in the early hours of the morning. Taking a coffee in Soho at 4am and finding it busier than at 4pm. A mug of tea, double bubble, beans, two eggs, bacon and a slice in a traditional London caff. Red double decker buses, red phone boxes, red post boxes. While the city itself may change and grow, all of these things are what keeps it the same – this is the real London.

ABOUT TIME OUT CITY GUIDES

This is the 15th edition of the *Time Out London Guide*, one of an expanding series of Time Out guides produced by the people behind the successful listings magazines in London, New York and Chicago. Our guides are all written by resident experts and, in the case of this guide, largely by journalists and editors who regularly contribute to the weekly *Time Out London* magazine. We have striven to provide you with all the most up-to-date information you'll need to explore the city or read up on its background, whether you're a local or a first-time visitor.

THE LIE OF THE LAND

Thanks to the chaotic street plan – or, rather, the lack of one – London is one of the most complicated of all major world cities to find your way around. To make life a bit easier, we've included an area designation for every venue in this guide. Our area divisions are based on local usage and are clearly marked on the colour-coded map on pages 394-395. Most entries also have a grid reference that points to our street maps at the back of the book (starting on page 396).

ESSENTIAL INFORMATION

For all the practical information you might need for visiting the area – including visa and customs information, details of local transport, a listing of emergency numbers, information on local weather and a selection of useful websites – turn to the Directory at the back of this guide. It begins on page 360.

THE LOWDOWN ON THE LISTINGS

We have tried to make this book as easy to use as possible. Addresses, phone numbers, transport information, opening times and

admission prices are included in the listings. However, businesses can change their arrangements at any time. Before you go out of your way, we strongly advise you to phone ahead to check opening times and other particulars. While every effort has been made to ensure the accuracy of the information contained in this guide, the publishers cannot accept responsibility for any errors it may contain.

PRICES AND PAYMENT

We have noted where venues such as shops, hotels, restaurants and theatres accept the following credit cards: American Express (AmEx), Diners Club (DC), MasterCard (MC) and Visa (V). Some venues also accept other cards, such as Delta, Switch or JCB, and some also take euros (€) as payment.

The prices in this guide should be treated as guidelines, not gospel. If they vary wildly from those we've quoted, ask if there's a good reason. If not, go elsewhere. Then please let us know. We aim to give the most up-to-date advice, and want to know if you've been overcharged.

Advertisers

We would like to stress that no establishment has been included in this guide because it has advertised in any of our publications and no payment of any kind has influenced any review. The opinions given in this book are those of Time Out writers and entirely independent.

TELEPHONE NUMBERS

The area code for London is 020; landlines follow this with eight digits in two groups of four. The 020 code is not used internally within London and is not given in our listings. From abroad, dial your country's exit code (01 in the US), followed by 44 (the international code for the UK), then 20 for London (thereby dropping the first zero of the area code) and the eight-digit number. Mobile phone numbers have a five-digit code, usually starting 07, then a six-digit number. Freephone numbers start 0800, national-rate numbers 0870 and local-rate numbers 0845. For more on telephones and codes, *see p376*.

MAPS

The map section at the back of this book includes orientation and neighbourhood maps of the London area, and street maps of central London, with a comprehensive street index. The street maps start on page 396, and now pinpoint specific locations of hotels (1), restaurants (1) and pubs and bars (1).

LET US KNOW WHAT YOU THINK

We hope you enjoy the *Time Out London Guide*, and we'd like to know what you think of it. We welcome tips for places you consider we should include in future editions and take note of your criticism of our choices. You can email us at guides@timeout.com.

There is an online version of this book, along with guides to over 100 international cities, at **www.timeout.com**.

Time Out Miami
Time Out Milan
Time Out Mumbai & Goa
Time Out Naples
Time Out New Orleans
Time Out New York
Time Out Paris
Time Out Patagonia
Time Out Prague
Time Out Rome
Time Out San Francisco
Time Out Seville & Andalucía
Time Out Shanghai
Time Out Singapore
Time Out South of France
Time Out Stockholm
Time Out Sydney
Time Out Tokyo 東京
Time Out Turin
Time Out Venice
Time Out Vienna
Time Out Washington, DC
Time Out Amsterdam
Time Out Athens
Time Out Bangkok
Time Out Barcelona
Time Out Beijing
Time Out Boston
Time Out Brussels
Time Out Budapest
Time Out Buenos Aires
Time Out California
Time Out Cape Town
Time Out Chicago
Time Out Copenhagen
Time Out Croatia
Time Out Dublin
Time Out Edinburgh
Time Out Florence
Time Out Havana
Time Out Hong Kong
Time Out Istanbul
Time Out Las Vegas
Time Out Lisbon
Time Out London
Time Out Madrid
Time Out Mallorca
Time Out Marrakech
Time Out Miami
Time Out Milan
Time Out Mumbai & Goa
Time Out Naples
Time Out New Orleans
Time Out New York
Time Out Patagonia
Time Out Prague
Time Out Rio de Janeiro
Time Out Rome
Time Out San Francisco
Time Out Seville & Andalucía
Time Out Shanghai
Time Out Singapore
Time Out South of France
Time Out Sydney
Time Out Tokyo 東京
Time Out Toronto
Time Out Turin
Time Out Venice
Time Out Vienna
Time Out Washington, DC
Time Out Amsterdam
Time Out Athens
Time Out Barcelona
Time Out Beijing
Time Out Berlin
Time Out Boston
Time Out Brussels
Time Out Budapest
Time Out Buenos Aires
Time Out California
Time Out Cape Town
Time Out Copenhagen
Time Out Croatia
Time Out Dubai
Time Out Dublin
Time Out Edinburgh
Time Out Florence
Time Out Havana
Time Out Hong Kong
Time Out Istanbul

In Context

Features

St Paul's Cathedral. *See p93.*

Tower of London. *See p13.*

History

Plague, fire, the Blitz, terrorism – we've got the T-shirt.

Peter Ackroyd has said that London is like 'a labyrinth which is constantly expanding, reaching outwards towards infinity'. But while the capital's size and rapid expansion have long fascinated visitors, the city's origins are much less grand. Celtic tribes lived in scattered communities along the banks of the Thames before the Romans arrived in Britain, but no evidence suggests there was a settlement on the site of the future metropolis before the invasion of the Emperor Claudius in AD 43. During the Roman conquest of the country, they forded the Thames at its shallowest point (near today's London Bridge) and, later, built a timber bridge here. A settlement developed on the north side of this crossing over the following decade.

Over the next two centuries, the Romans built roads, towns and forts in the area, and trade flourished. Progress was brought to a halt in AD 61 when Boudicca, the widow of an East Anglian chieftain, rebelled against the Imperial forces who had seized her land, flogged her and raped her daughters. She led the Iceni in a savage revolt, destroying the Roman colony at Colchester and then marching on London. The Roman inhabitants were massacred and their settlement razed to the ground. The following year Boudicca was defeated at the Battle of Watling Street and legend has it that she's buried beneath what's now platform 10 at King's Cross Station.

After order was restored, the town was rebuilt and, around AD 200, a two-mile-long, 18-foot-high wall constructed around it. Chunks of the wall survive today, and early names of the original gates – Ludgate, Newgate, Bishopsgate and Aldgate – are preserved on the map of the modern city. The street known as London Wall traces part of its original course.

By the fourth century, racked by barbarian invasions and internal strife, the Empire was in decline. In 410 the last troops were withdrawn and London became a ghost town. The Roman way of life vanished, their only enduring legacies being roads and early Christianity.

CHRISTIANITY ARRIVES IN LONDON

During the fifth and sixth centuries, history gives way to legend. The Saxons crossed the North Sea and settled in eastern and southern England. Apparently avoiding the ruins of London, they built outside the walls.

Pope Gregory sent Augustine to convert the English to Christianity in 596. Ethelbert, Saxon King of Kent, proved a willing convert, and consequently Augustine was appointed the first Archbishop of Canterbury. Since then, the Kentish city has remained the centre of the English Christian Church. London's first Bishop, though, was Mellitus: one of Augustine's missionaries, he converted the East Saxon King Sebert and, in 604, founded a wooden cathedral dedicated to St Paul inside the old city walls. On Sebert's death, his fickle followers gave up the faith and reverted to paganism, but later generations of Christians rebuilt what is now St Paul's Cathedral.

London, meanwhile, continued to expand. The Venerable Bede, writing in 731, described 'Lundenwic' as 'the mart of many nations resorting to it by land and sea'. This probably refers to a settlement west of the Roman city in the area of today's Aldwych (Old English for 'old town'). During the ninth century the city faced a new danger from across the North Sea: the Vikings. The city was sacked in 841 and, in 851, the Danish raiders returned with 350 ships, leaving London in ruins. It was not until 886 that King Alfred of Wessex – aka Alfred the Great – regained the city, soon re-establishing London as a major trading centre with a merchant navy and new wharfs at Billingsgate and Queenhithe.

Throughout the tenth century the Saxon city prospered. Churches were built, parishes established and markets set up. However, the 11th century brought more harassment from the warlike Vikings, and the English were even forced to accept a Danish king, Cnut (Canute, 1016-35), during whose reign London replaced Winchester as the capital of England.

In 1042 the throne reverted to an Englishman, Edward the Confessor, who devoted himself to building the grandest church in England two miles west of the City at Thorney ('the isle of brambles'). He replaced the timber church of St Peter's with a huge abbey, 'the West Minster' (Westminster Abbey; consecrated in December 1065), and moved his court to the new Palace of Westminster. A week after the consecration, Edward died and was buried in his new church. London now grew around two hubs: Westminster, as the centre for the royal court, government and law, and the City of London, as the commercial centre.

WILLIAM CONQUERS

On Edward's death, there was a succession dispute. William, Duke of Normandy, claimed that the Confessor, his cousin, had promised him the English Crown, but the English instead chose Edward's brother-in-law Harold. Piqued, William gathered an army and invaded; on 14 October 1066 he defeated Harold at the Battle of Hastings in Sussex and marched on London. City elders had little option but to offer William the throne, and the conqueror was crowned in Westminster Abbey on Christmas Day 1066.

'To protect himself "against the fickleness of the vast and fierce population", William ordered the Tower of London built.'

Recognising the need to win over the prosperous City merchants by negotiation rather than force, William granted the Bishop and burgesses of London a charter – still kept at Guildhall – that acknowledged their rights and independence in return for taxes. But, 'against the fickleness of the vast and fierce population', he also ordered strongholds to be built alongside the city wall, including the White Tower (the tallest building in the Tower of London) and the now-lost Baynard's Castle at Blackfriars. The earliest surviving written account of contemporary London was penned 40 years later by a monk, William Fitz Stephen, who conjured up the walled city and the pastures and woodland outside the perimeter.

THE MAYOR AND THE MAGNA CARTA

In the growing city of London, much of the politics of the Middle Ages – the late 12th to the late 15th centuries – revolved around a constant three-way struggle for power between the king and the aristocracy, the Church, and the Lord Mayor and city guilds.

The king and his court frequently travelled the kingdom in the early Middle Ages, however, during the 14th and 15th centuries, the Palace of Westminster became the seat of law and government. The noblemen and bishops who attended court built themselves palatial houses along the Strand from the City to Westminster, with gardens stretching to the river.

The Model Parliament, which agreed the principles of government, was held in Westminster Hall in 1295, presided over by

Edward I and attended by barons, clergy and representatives of knights and burgesses. The first step towards establishing personal rights and political liberty – not to mention curbing the power of the king – had already been taken in 1215 with the signing of the Magna Carta by King John. In the 14th century subsequent assemblies gave rise to the House of Lords (which met at the Palace of Westminster) and the House of Commons (which met in the Chapter House at Westminster Abbey).

Relations between the monarch and the City were never easy. Londoners guarded their privileges with self-righteous intransigence, and resisted all attempts by successive kings to squeeze money out of them to finance wars and building projects. Subsequent kings were forced to turn to Jewish and Lombard moneylenders, but the City merchants were as intolerant of foreigners as of the royals. Rioting, persecution and the occasional lynching and pogrom were all commonplace in medieval London.

The privileges granted to the City merchants under Norman kings, allowing independence and self-regulation, were extended by the monarchs who followed, in return for financial favours. In 1191, during the reign of Richard I, the City of London was formally recognised as a commune – a self-governing community – and in 1197 it won control of the Thames, which included lucrative fishing rights that the City retained until 1857. In 1215 King John confirmed the city's right 'to elect every year a mayor', a position of great authority with power over the Sheriff and the Bishop of London. A month later the Mayor had joined the rebel barons in signing the Magna Carta.

'In the streets around Smithfield, butchers dumped the entrails of slaughtered animals.'

Over the next two centuries, the power and influence of the trade and craft guilds (later known as the City Livery Companies) increased as trade with Europe grew, and the wharfs by London Bridge were crowded with imports such as fine cloth, furs, wine, spices and precious metals. Port dues and taxes were paid to Customs officials, including part-time poet Geoffrey Chaucer, whose *Canterbury Tales* were the first published work of English literature.

The City's markets, already established, drew produce from miles around: livestock at Smithfield, fish at Billingsgate and poultry at Leadenhall. The street markets, or 'cheaps', around Westcheap (now Cheapside) and Eastcheap were crammed with a variety of goods. As commerce increased, foreign traders and craftsmen settled around the port; the population within the city wall grew from about 18,000 in 1100 to well over 50,000 in the 1340s.

THE PEASANTS ARE REVOLTING

Not surprisingly, lack of hygiene became a serious problem in the City. Water was provided in cisterns at Cheapside and elsewhere, but the supply, which came more or less direct from the Thames, was limited and polluted. The street called Houndsditch was so named because Londoners threw their dead animals into the furrow that formed the City's eastern boundary, while in the streets around Smithfield (the Shambles), butchers dumped the entrails of slaughtered beasts in the gutters.

These appalling conditions provided the breeding ground for the greatest catastrophe of the Middle Ages: the Black Death of 1348 and 1349, which killed about 30 per cent of England's population. The plague came to London from Europe, carried by rats on ships. Although the epidemic abated, it was to recur in London several times during the next three centuries, each time devastating the population.

The outbreaks of disease left the labour market short-handed, causing unrest among the overworked peasants. The imposition of a poll tax of a shilling a head proved the final straw, leading to the Peasants' Revolt of 1381. Thousands marched on London, led by Jack Straw from Essex and Wat Tyler from Kent. In the rioting and looting that followed, the Savoy Palace on the Strand was destroyed, the Archbishop of Canterbury was murdered and hundreds of prisoners were set free. When the 14-year-old Richard II rode out to Smithfield to face the rioters, Wat Tyler was fatally stabbed by Lord Mayor William Walworth. The other ringleaders were subsequently rounded up and hanged. But no more poll taxes were imposed.

ROSES, WIVES AND BLOODY MARY

Under the Tudor monarchs (1485-1603) and spurred by the discovery of America and the ocean routes to Africa and the Orient, London became one of Europe's largest cities. The first Tudor monarch, Henry VII, is usually noted for ending the Wars of the Roses, raging in England for many years between the Houses of York and Lancaster. He defeated Richard III at the Battle of Bosworth and married Elizabeth of York. But in London he's also noted for Henry VII's Chapel, the addition he made to the eastern end of Westminster Abbey and a triumph of Renaissance architecture. It was also his eventual resting place.

The reconstructed **Globe** theatre. *See p17.*

Henry VII was succeeded in 1509 by arch wife-collector (and dispatcher) Henry VIII. Henry's first marriage to Catherine of Aragon failed to produce an heir, so in 1527 the King determined the union should be annulled. When the Pope refused to co-operate, Henry defied the Catholic Church, demanding to be recognised as Supreme Head of the Church in England and ordering the execution of anyone who opposed the plan (including his chancellor Sir Thomas More). Thus it was that England began the transition to Protestantism. The subsequent dissolution of the monasteries transformed the face of the medieval city with the confiscation and redevelopment of all property owned by the Catholic Church.

On a more positive note, Henry found time to develop a professional navy, founding the Royal Dockyards at Woolwich in 1512 and at Deptford the following year. He also established palaces at Hampton Court and Whitehall, and built a residence at St James's Palace. Much of the land he annexed for hunting became the Royal Parks, including Greenwich, Hyde, Regent's and Richmond parks.

After Henry, there was a brief Catholic revival under Queen Mary (1553-8), though her marriage to Philip II of Spain met with much opposition in London. She had 300 Protestants burned at the stake at Smithfield, earning her the nickname 'Bloody Mary'.

RENAISSANCE REBIRTH

Elizabeth I's reign (1558-1603) saw a flowering of English commerce and arts. The founding of the Royal Exchange by Sir Thomas Gresham in 1566 gave London its first trading centre, allowing it to emerge as Europe's leading commercial centre. The merchant venturers and the first joint-stock companies (Russia Company and Levant Company) established new trading enterprises, and adventuring seafarers Francis Drake, Walter Raleigh and Richard Hawkins sailed to the New World and beyond. In 1580 Elizabeth knighted Drake on his return from a three-year circumnavigation; eight years later, Drake and Charles Howard defeated the Spanish Armada.

As trade grew, so did London. It was home to some 200,000 people in 1600, many living in dirty, overcrowded conditions; plague and fire were constant, day-to-day hazards. The most complete picture of Tudor London is given in John Stow's *Survey of London* (1598), a fascinating first-hand account by a diligent Londoner whose monument stands in the City church of St Andrew Undershaft.

The glory of the Elizabethan era was the development of English drama, popular with all social classes but treated with disdain by the Corporation of London, which banned theatres from the City in 1575. Two theatres, the Rose (1587) and the Globe (1599, now recreated, *see p15*), were erected on the south bank of the Thames at Bankside, and provided homes for the works of popular playwrights Christopher Marlowe and William Shakespeare. Deemed 'a naughty place' by royal proclamation, 16th-century Bankside was the Soho of its time: home not just to the theatre, but to bear-baiting, cock-fighting, raucous taverns and plenty of 'stewes' (brothels).

The Tudor dynasty ended with Elizabeth's death in 1603. Her successor, the Stuart King James I, narrowly escaped assassination on 5 November 1605, when Guy Fawkes and his gunpowder were discovered underneath the Palace of Westminster. The Gunpowder Plot was hatched in protest at the failure to improve conditions for the persecuted Catholics, but only resulted in an intensification of anti-papist sentiments in London. To this day, 5 November is commemorated with gunpowder-fuelled fireworks as Bonfire Night.

Aside from the Gunpowder Plot, James I deserves to be remembered for hiring Inigo Jones to design court masques (dramas with singing and dancing), and the first – beautiful and highly influential – examples of classical Renaissance style in London, the Queen's House in Greenwich (1616, *see p178*), the Banqueting House in Westminster (1619, *see p140*) and St Paul's Church in Covent Garden (1631, *see p115*).

ROYALISTS AND ROUNDHEADS

Charles I succeeded his father in 1625, but gradually fell out of favour with the City of London (from whose citizens he tried to extort taxes) and an increasingly independent-minded and antagonistic Parliament. The last straw came in 1642 when he intruded on the Houses of Parliament in an attempt to arrest five MPs. The country soon slid into a civil war (1642-9) between the supporters of Parliament (the Roundheads, led by Puritan Oliver Cromwell) and those of the King (the Royalists).

Both sides knew that control of the country's major city and port was vital for victory. London's sympathies were firmly with the Parliamentarians and, in 1642, 24,000 citizens assembled at Turnham Green, west of the City,

City chroniclers Samuel Pepys

'So I rode down to the waterside... and there saw a lamentable fire... Everybody endeavouring to remove their goods, and flinging [them] into the river; poor people staying in their houses as long as till the very fire touched them, and then running into boats. And among other things, the poor pigeons, I perceive, were loth to leave their houses, but hovered about the windows and balconies, till they some of them burned their wings and fell down.'

The pre-eminent diarist of London, Samuel Pepys, was born in Salisbury Court off Fleet Street in the City in 1633 (a blue plaque marks the house). The son of a tailor, he was educated at a school near St Paul's and was working as a lowly paid civil servant when he began writing his diaries on 1 January 1660. Although he only kept it up for nine years, his journal-keeping coincides with two calamitous events: the Plague and the Great Fire. HIs diaries also offer a wealth of detail regarding the daily life of the time ('So to Wilkinson's, the Cook's, to dinner, where we had oysters, the first I have eat this year, and were pretty good') and much of a more personal nature: '[my wife] coming up suddenly, did find me imbracing the girl con my hand sub su coats; and endeed I was with my main in her cunny. I was at a wonderful loss and the girl also...'.

Pepys died in 1703. It seems he knew that one day his journals might be of interest as he had the pages bound in six volumes. Published in 1825 they've remained in print ever since.

to face Charles's army. Fatally, the King lost his nerve and withdrew. He was never seriously to threaten the capital again; eventually, the Royalists were defeated. Charles was tried for treason and, though he denied the legitimacy of the court, he was declared guilty. He was then taken to the Banqueting House in Whitehall on 30 January 1649, and, declaring himself to be a 'martyr of the people', beheaded. To this day, each year a commemorative wreath is laid at the site of the execution (*see p140*) on the last Sunday in January.

For the next 11 years the country was ruled as a Commonwealth by Cromwell, and then for a brief period by his son Richard. The younger Cromwell's inability to continue his father's powerful rule, along with the closing of the theatres, the banning of Christmas (a Catholic superstition), and Puritan strictures on the wickedness of any sort of fun, meant that the restoration of the exiled Charles II in 1660 was greeted with relief and rejoicing by the populace. The Stuart King had Cromwell exhumed from Westminster Abbey and his body hung in chains at Tyburn. His carcass was then thrown into a pit, while his severed head was displayed on a pole outside the abbey until 1685. However, any joy was short lived.

PLAGUE, FIRE AND REVOLUTION

In 1665 the most serious outbreak of bubonic plague since the Black Death killed many of the capital's population. By the time the winter cold had put paid to the epidemic, nearly 100,000 Londoners had died. On 2 September 1666 a second disaster struck. The fire that spread from a carelessly tended oven in Farriner's baking shop on Pudding Lane was to rage for three days and consume four-fifths of the City, including 89 churches, 44 livery company halls and more than 13,000 houses.

The Great Fire at least allowed planners the chance to rebuild London as a rationally planned modern city. Many blueprints were considered, but, in the end, Londoners were so impatient to get on with business that the City

City chroniclers Samuel Johnson

'By seeing London, I have seen as much of life as the world can shew.' The capital's greatest cheerleader was born in 1709 in Staffordshire and it wasn't, in fact, until his 28th year that he arrived in London. He came penniless, a state in which he more or less remained for most of the next 30 years, this despite compiling the hugely influential *A Dictionary of the English Language*. He made his name as a writer of periodical essays on moral and religious topics, published first under the title of *The Rambler* and then in a later series as *The Idler*. He wrote criticism on the plays of Shakespeare and biographies of the lives of English poets, and a satirical novel, reputedly completed in two weeks to raise money for his mother's funeral.

But in large part his reputation rests on the good fortune of possessing two assiduous biographers. In 1763 Johnson met James Boswell, companion and eventual author of *The Life of Samuel Johnson* (1791). The Doctor was also served by the published reminiscences of Hester Thrale, wife of Member of Parliament Henry Thrale, a couple with whom Johnson lodged for 15 years.

Many of Johnson's quotes come not from his own works but from Boswell's recollections. Thank God, then, for Boswell, for where would authors of London books be without him? And without one quote in particular: 'Why, Sir, you find no man, at all intellectual, who is willing to leave London. No, Sir, when a man is tired of London, he is tired of life; for there is in London all that life can afford.'

We also cherish the dictum, 'He who makes a beast of himself gets rid of the pain of being a man', which is a far more useful exhortation to have at the ready when rolling home drunk on a Friday night.

was reconstructed largely on its medieval street plan, albeit in brick and stone rather than wood. The towering figure of the period turned out to be the prolific Sir Christopher Wren, who oversaw work on 51 of the 54 churches rebuilt. Among them was his masterpiece, the new St Paul's, completed in 1710 and, effectively, the world's first Protestant cathedral.

In the wake of the Great Fire, many well-to-do former City dwellers moved to new residential developments west of the old quarters, an area that subsequently became known as the West End. In the City, the Royal Exchange was rebuilt, but merchants increasingly used the new coffeehouses to exchange news. With the expansion of the joint-stock companies and the chance to invest capital, the City emerged as a centre not of manufacturing, but of finance.

Anti-Catholic feeling still ran high. The accession of Catholic James II in 1685 aroused fears of a return to papistry, and resulted in a Dutch Protestant, William of Orange, being invited to take the throne with his wife, Mary Stuart (James's daughter). James fled to France in 1688 in what became known – by its beneficiaries – as the 'Glorious Revolution'. The Bank of England was founded during William III's reign, in 1694, initially to finance the King's wars with France.

CREATION OF THE PRIME MINISTER

After the death of Queen Anne (who, though the daughter of James II, had sided with her sister Mary and brother-in-law William during the Glorious Revolution), the throne passed to George, great-grandson of James I, who had been born and raised in Hanover, Germany. Thus, a German-speaking king – who never learned English – became the first of four long-reigning Georges in the Hanoverian line.

During George I's reign (1714-27), and for several years afterwards, Sir Robert Walpole's Whig party monopolised Parliament. Their opponents, the Tories, supported the Stuarts and had opposed the exclusion of the Catholic James II. On the King's behalf, Walpole chaired a group of ministers (the forerunner of today's Cabinet), becoming, in effect, Britain's first prime minister. Walpole was presented with 10 Downing Street (constructed by Sir George Downing) as a residence; it remains the official home of all serving prime ministers.

During the 18th century London grew with astonishing speed, in terms of both population and construction. New squares and many streets of terraced houses spread across Soho, Bloomsbury, Mayfair and Marylebone, as wealthy landowners and speculative developers who didn't mind taking a risk given the size of the potential rewards, cashed in on the demand for leasehold properties. South London too became more accessible with the opening of the first new bridges for centuries, Westminster Bridge (1750) and Blackfriars Bridge (1769). Until then, London Bridge had been the only bridge over the Thames. The old city gates, most of the Roman Wall and the remaining houses on Old London Bridge were demolished, allowing traffic access to the City.

> **'Public executions at Tyburn were among the most popular events in the social calendar.'**

GIN RUINS POOR, RICH MOCK MAD

In the older districts, however, people were still living in terrible squalor and poverty, far worse than the infamous conditions of Victorian times. Some of the most notorious slums were located around Fleet Street and St Giles's (north of Covent Garden), only a short distance from streets of fashionable residences maintained by large numbers of servants. To make matters worse, gin ('mother's ruin') was readily available at very low prices, and many poor Londoners drank excessive amounts in an attempt to escape the horrors of daily life. The well-off seemed complacent, amusing themselves at the popular Ranelagh and Vauxhall pleasure gardens or with organised trips to Bedlam to mock the mental patients. Similarly, public executions at Tyburn – near today's Marble Arch – were among the most popular events in the social calendar.

The outrageous imbalance in the distribution of wealth encouraged crime, and there were daring daytime robberies in the West End. Reformers were few, though there were exceptions. Henry Fielding, author of the picaresque novel *Tom Jones*, was also an enlightened magistrate at Bow Street Court (*see p116*). In 1751 he and his blind half-brother John set up a volunteer force of 'thief-takers' to back up the often ineffective efforts of the parish constables and watchmen who were the only law-keepers in the city. This crime-busting group of early cops, known as the Bow Street Runners, were the forerunners of today's Metropolitan Police (established in 1829).

Riots were a regular reaction to middlemen charging extortionate prices, or merchants adulterating their food. In June 1780 London was hit by the anti-Catholic Gordon Riots, named after ringleader Lord George Gordon; the worst in the city's violent history, they left 300 people dead.

City chroniclers Charles Dickens

More than any other writer, Charles Dickens (1812-70) was London. In 15 novels and numerous works of short fiction, he captured the sublime chaos of the city: its dark, tight, filthy streets; its crazy, lovely inhabitants; its wealth and poverty, life and death.

Dickens was not a native Londoner: he was born in Portsmouth, Hampshire (and died in Kent) but at the age of ten his family moved to Bayham Street in Camden Town. At 12 he began work in a boot-blacking factory near Charing Cross Station and the money he earned helped to support the family – badly needed given that his father was incarcerated in Marshalsea debtors' prison in Borough. These early experiences informed the semi-autobiographical *David Copperfield*, which sees the hero recalling how he clawed his way from an impoverished, abused childhood to adult success as an author. Well before *Copperfield* Dickens had made his name with the debut novel *The Pickwick Papers*, on the proceeds of which he set up home in Bloomsbury, where his former residence survives as a museum (*see p109*).

All Dickens's books make vivid use of London locations. In *Oliver Twist* there's Smithfield Market 'covered nearly ankle-deep with filth and mire; a thick stream perpetually rising from the reeking bodies of the cattle'. *Our Mutual Friend* contains a lingering description of Mr Venus's Covent Garden taxidermy shop, with its Hindoo baby in a bottle and the corpse of half a Frenchman.

For all that London has changed since Dickens's time, it is still possible to visit his city. If you don't happen to have the complete novels to lead you, you can sign up for one of the guided walks that follow in the footsteps of Little Nell, Pickwick and Mrs Gamp most days of the year (*see p143* **Walk this way**).

Some attempts were made to alleviate the grosser ills of poverty with the founding of five major new hospitals by private philanthropists. St Thomas's and St Bartholomew's were long established as monastic institutions for the care of the sick, but Westminster (1720), Guy's (1725), St George's (1734), London (1740) and the Middlesex (1745) went on to become world-famous teaching hospitals. Thomas Coram's Foundling Hospital (*see p110*) for abandoned children was another remarkable achievement of the time.

INDUSTRY AND CAPITAL-ISM

It wasn't just the indigenous population of London that was on the rise. Country people, whose common land had been replaced by sheep enclosures, were faced with starvation wages or unemployment, and drifted into the towns in large numbers. The East End became the focus for poor immigrant labourers with the building of the docks towards the end of the century. London's population had grown to almost a million by 1801, the largest of any city in Europe. And by 1837, when Queen Victoria came to the throne, five more bridges and the capital's first passenger railway (running from Greenwich to London Bridge) gave hints that a major expansion might be around the corner.

As well as being the administrative and financial capital of the British Empire, which by the end of Victoria's reign spanned a fifth of the globe, London was also its chief port and the world's largest manufacturing centre, with breweries, distilleries, tanneries, shipyards, engineering works and many other grim and grimy industries lining the south bank of the Thames. On the one hand, London boasted splendid buildings, fine shops, theatres and museums; on the other, it was a city of poverty, pollution, disease and prostitution. Residential areas were becoming polarised into districts with fine terraces maintained by squads of servants, and overcrowded, insanitary, disease-ridden slums.

The growth of the metropolis in the century before Victoria came to the throne had been spectacular, but during her reign (1837-1901), thousands more acres were covered with housing, roads and railway lines. If you visit a street within five miles of central London, its houses will be mostly Victorian. By the end of the 19th century, the city's population had swelled to more than six million – an incredible growth of five million in 100 years.

Despite social problems – memorably depicted in the writings of Charles Dickens (*see p20* **City chroniclers**) – major steps were being taken to improve conditions for the majority of Londoners by the turn of the century. The Metropolitan Board of Works installed an efficient sewerage system, street lighting and better roads. The worst slums were replaced by low-cost building schemes funded by philanthropists such as the American George Peabody, who established the Peabody Donation Fund, which continues to this day to provide subsidised housing to the working classes. The London County Council (created in 1888) also helped to house the poor.

The Victorian expansion would not have been possible without an efficient public transport network with which to speed workers into and out of the city from the new suburbs. The horse-drawn bus appeared on London's streets in 1829, but it was the opening of the first passenger railway seven years later that heralded the commuters of the future. The first underground line, which ran between Paddington and Farringdon Road, opened in 1863 and proved an instant success, attracting more than 30,000 travellers on the first day. Soon after, the world's first electric track in a deep tunnel – the 'tube' – opened in 1890 between the City and Stockwell, later becoming part of the Northern Line.

THE CRYSTAL PALACE

If any one event crystallised the Victorian period of industry, science, discovery and invention it was the Great Exhibition of 1851. Prince Albert, the Queen's Consort, helped organise this triumphant event, for which the Crystal Palace, a giant building of iron and glass was erected in Hyde Park. It looked like nothing so much as a giant greenhouse, which is hardly surprising given that it was designed not by a professional architect but by the Duke of Devonshire's gardener, Joseph Paxton. The Palace was condemned by art critic John Ruskin as the model of dehumanisation in design but later came to be presented as the prototype of modern architecture. During the five months it was open, the Exhibition drew six million visitors from Great Britain and abroad. The profits raised from the event were used by the Prince Consort to establish a permanent centre for the study of the applied arts and sciences: the enterprise survives today in the South Kensington museums of natural history, science, and decorative and applied arts, better known as the Victoria & Albert Museum, and in three colleges (of art, music and science; *see*

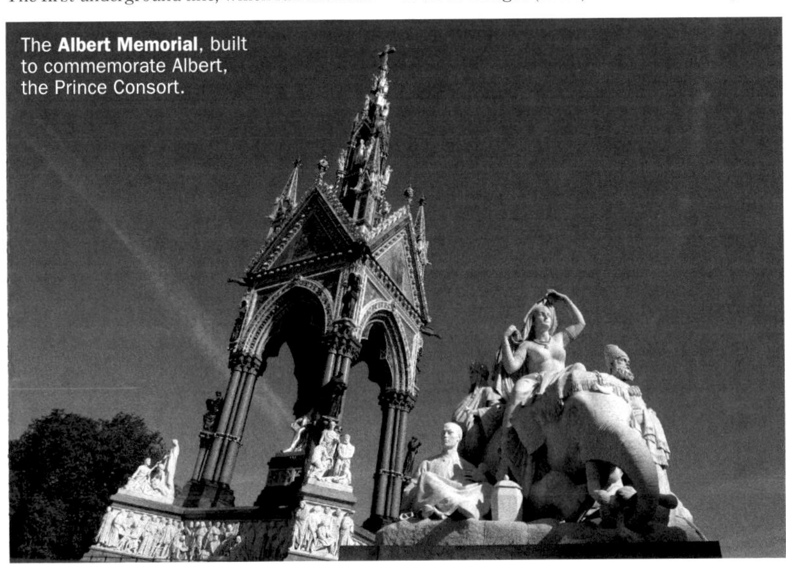

The **Albert Memorial**, built to commemorate Albert, the Prince Consort.

p151). After the Exhibition, the Palace was moved to Sydenham and used as an exhibition centre until it burned down in 1936.

When the Victorians were not colonising, they combined their conquests with scientific developments. The Royal Geographical Society sent navigators to chart unknown waters, botanists to bring back new species and geologists to study the earth. Many of their specimens ended up at the Royal Botanic Gardens at Kew (*see p185*).

ZEPPELINS ATTACK FROM THE SKIES

London entered the 20th century as the capital of the largest empire in history. Its wealth and power were there for all to see, set in stone in grandstanding monuments like Tower Bridge and the Midland Grand Hotel at St Pancras Station, both of which married the retro stylings of High Gothic with modern iron and steel technology. During the brief reign of Edward VII (1901-1910), London regained some of the gaiety and glamour it had lacked in the dour later years of Victoria's reign. A touch of Parisian chic came to London with the opening of the Ritz Hotel in Piccadilly; Regent Street's Café Royal hit the heights of its popularity as a meeting place for artists and writers; and 'luxury catering for the little man' was provided at the new Lyons Corner Houses (the Coventry Street branch, which opened in 1907, could accommodate an incredible 4,500 people).

Road transport too was revolutionised. By 1911 the use of horse-drawn buses had been abandoned, replaced by the motor cars that put-putted around the city's streets, and the motor bus, which was first introduced in 1904. Double-decked electric trams had started running in 1901 (though not through the West End or the City), and continued doing so for 51 years.

Disruption came in the form of devastating air raids during World War I. The first bomb over the city was dropped from a Zeppelin near the Guildhall in September 1915, and was followed by many gruelling nightly raids on the capital; bomb attacks from German Gotha GV bombers began in July 1917. In all, around 650 people lost their lives as a result of Zeppelin raids, but the greater impact was the psychological fear of helplessness.

ROARING BETWEEN THE WARS

Political change happened quickly once the war had ended. David Lloyd George's government averted revolution in 1918-19 by promising (but not delivering) 'homes for heroes' – ie the embittered returning soldiers. But the Liberal Party's days in power were numbered, and in 1924 the Labour Party, led by Ramsay MacDonald, formed its first government.

After the trauma of World War I, a 'live for today' attitude prevailed in the Roaring Twenties among the young upper classes, who flitted from parties in Mayfair to dances

Alexandra Palace, site of the first live telecast. *See p25.*

City chroniclers Peter Ackroyd

You need a bloody big library to accommodate even a fraction of the books that have been published about London. However, if space is limited to the extent that you have to choose just one, then it's an easy choice: Peter Ackroyd's *London: the Biography*.

Born in London in 1949, Ackroyd began his literary career as a poet before becoming a prose writer. One of his lesser-known early works is *Dressing Up*, a history of drag and transvestism. He hit the big time with *Hawksmoor* (1985), a novel intertwining the life and times of a fictionalised version of the 18th-century architect with the investigation of a series of macabre murders on the sites of his churches some 250 years later.

But the book that he was born to write was his city biography. 'London has always provided the landscape for my imagination,' says Ackroyd. 'It becomes a character – a living being – within each of my books.' In his *Biography*, the city is a living organism 'half of stone half of flesh'. Just as his novels are characterised by tripping the switch between past and present (and, incidentally, blurring the lines between the factual and the fictional), so the *Biography* is at its best when sweeping aside centuries to link up the dots. One of his key themes is what he calls the 'territorial imperative' – the idea that the same aura has clung to parts of the city down the years. Take, for instance, St Giles-in-the-Fields, the church behind Centre Point, just off the Charing Cross Road and one of Ackroyd's favourite areas. 'It was the site of an old leper hospital in the Middle Ages, and ever since it has always been a haunt for the vagrant and the outcast,' he told *Time Out*. The area is currently plagued by drug users. The Lloyd's Building is another example – it's on the exact site of the old Maypole, London's tallest structure in the 15th century.

Ackroyd's *Biography* is highly personalised without being self-indulgent. In the centuries to come his collected volume of works on the city, of which this is the keystone, may well be seen as third only to Pepys and Dickens.

at the Ritz. But this meant little to the mass of Londoners, who were suffering greatly in the post-war slump. Civil disturbances, brought on by the high cost of living and rising unemployment, resulted in the nationwide General Strike of 1926, when the working classes downed tools in support of the striking miners. Prime Minister Baldwin encouraged volunteers to take over the public services and the streets teemed with army-escorted food convoys, aristocrats running soup kitchens and students driving buses. After nine days of chaos, the strike was called off by the Trades Union Congress (TUC).

The economic situation only worsened in the early 1930s following the New York Stock Exchange crash of 1929; by 1931 more than three million Britons were jobless. During these years, the London County Council began to have a greater impact on the city's life, undertaking programmes of slum clearance and new housing, creating more parks and taking under its wing education, transport, hospitals, libraries and the fire service.

London's population increased dramatically between the wars too, peaking at nearly 8.7 million in 1939. To accommodate the influx, the suburbs expanded quickly, particularly to the north-west with the extension of the Metropolitan Line to an area that became known as Metroland. Identical, gabled, double-fronted houses sprang up in their hundreds of thousands, from Golders Green to Surbiton.

Londoners were entertained by the new media: film, radio and television. London's first radio broadcast was beamed from the roof of Marconi House in the Strand in 1922, and families were soon gathering around enormous Bakelite wireless sets to hear the British Broadcasting Company (the BBC; from 1927 called the British Broadcasting Corporation). TV broadcasts started on 26 August 1936, when the first telecast went out live from Alexandra Palace (*see p23*). Successful early broadcasts included King George VI's coronation procession on 12 May 1937, the first Wimbledon coverage (June 1937) and the first televised FA Cup Final (30 April 1938).

THE BLITZ

During the 1930s Neville Chamberlain's policy of appeasement towards Hitler's increasingly aggressive Germany collapsed when the Germans invaded Poland, and on 3 September 1939 Britain declared war. The government implemented precautionary measures against the threat of air raids – including the evacuation of 600,000 children and pregnant mothers – but the expected bombing raids did not happen during the autumn and winter of 1939-40, a period that became known as the Phoney War. That came to an abrupt end in September 1940, when hundreds of German bombers dumped their loads of high explosives on east London and the docks, destroying entire streets. The dead and injured numbered more than 2,000. The Blitz had begun. The raids on London continued for 57 consecutive nights, then intermittently for a further six months. Londoners reacted with tremendous bravery and stoicism, a period still nostalgically referred to as 'Britain's finest hour'. After a final massive raid on 10 May 1941, Germany focused its attention elsewhere, but by the end of the war, a third of the City and the East End was in ruins.

From 1942 onwards, the tide of the war began to turn, but Londoners still had a new terror to face: the V1, or 'doodlebug'. Dozens of these deadly, explosive-packed, pilotless planes descended on the city in 1944, causing widespread destruction. Later in the year, the more powerful V2 rocket was launched and, over the winter, 500 of them dropped on London, mostly in the East End. The last fell on 27 March 1945 in Orpington, Kent, around six weeks before Victory in Europe (VE Day) was declared on 8 May 1945.

'YOU HAVE NEVER HAD IT SO GOOD'

World War II left Britain almost as shattered as Germany. Soon after VE Day, a general election was held and Churchill was heavily defeated by the Labour Party under Clement Attlee. The new government established the National Health Service in 1948, and began a massive nationalisation programme that included public transport, electricity, gas, postal and telephone services. For most people, however, life remained regimented and austere.

In war-ravaged London, the most immediate problem faced by local authorities was a critical shortage of housing. Prefabricated bungalows provided a temporary solution for some, but the huge new high-rise housing estates that the planners devised were often badly built and proved to be unpopular with their residents.

> **'The city basked in its new-found reputation as the music and fashion capital of the world.'**

There were bright spots. London hosted the Olympics in 1948; three years later came the Festival of Britain, a celebration of British technology and design. Just as the 1851 Exhibition gifted London several major museums, the 1951 Festival resulted in the redevelopment of its riverside site into the South Bank Centre. As the 1950s progressed, life and prosperity gradually returned, leading Prime Minister Harold Macmillan in 1957 famously to proclaim that 'most of our people have never had it so good'. The coronation of Queen Elizabeth II in 1953 had been the biggest television broadcast in history, and there was the feeling of a new age dawning.

London swings says *Time* in '66. *See p26.*

However, many Londoners were leaving the city. The population dropped by half a million in the late 1950s, causing a labour shortage that prompted huge recruitment drives in Britain's former colonies. London Transport and the National Health Service were particularly active in encouraging West Indians to emigrate to Britain. Unfortunately, as the Notting Hill race riots of 1958 illustrated, the welcome these new immigrants received was rarely friendly. There were several areas of tolerance, among them Soho, which, during the 1950s, became famed for its mix of races and the café and club life they brought with them.

THE SWINGING SIXTIES

By the mid 1960s London had started to swing. The innovative fashions of Mary Quant and others broke Paris's stranglehold on couture: boutiques blossomed along the King's Road, while Biba set the pace in Kensington. Carnaby Street became a byword for hipness as the city basked in its new-found reputation as the music and fashion capital of the world – made official, it seemed, when *Time* magazine devoted its front cover to 'swinging London' in April 1966. The year of student unrest in Europe, 1968, saw the first issue of *Time Out* (a fold-up sheet for 5d) hit the streets in August. The decade ended with the Beatles naming their final album *Abbey Road* after their studios in NW8, and the Rolling Stones playing a free gig in Hyde Park that drew around 500,000 people.

Then the bubble burst. Many Londoners remember the 1970s as a decade of economic strife and the decade in which the IRA began its bombing campaign on mainland Britain. The explosion of punk in the second half of the decade, sartorially inspired by the idiosyncratic genius of Vivienne Westwood, provided some nihilistic colour.

Worse was to come. Historians will regard the 1980s as the decade of Thatcherism. When the Conservatives won the general election in 1979 under Britain's first woman prime minister, Margaret Thatcher, their monetarist economic policy and cuts in public services widened the divide between rich and poor. In London, riots in Brixton (1981) and Tottenham (1985) were linked to unemployment and heavy-handed policing. The Greater London Council (GLC), led by Ken Livingstone, mounted opposition to the government with a series of populist measures. So effective was the GLC, in fact, that Thatcher decided to abolish it in 1986.

The replacement of Thatcher by John Major in October 1990 signalled a shortlived upsurge of hope among Londoners. A riot in Trafalgar Square had helped to see off both Maggie and her inequitable Poll Tax. Yet the early 1990s were scarred by continuing recession and more IRA terrorist attacks. Homelessness in London became an increasing problem and the *Big Issue* was launched in 1991 to give a voice to this socially marginalised group.

THINGS CAN ONLY GET BETTER?

In May 1997 the British people ousted the tired Tories and Tony Blair's Labour Party swept to the first of three general election victories. However, initial enthusiasm didn't last. The government hoped the Millennium Dome, built on a patch of Greenwich wasteland, would be a 21st-century rival to the 1851 Great Exhibition. It wasn't. Badly mismanaged, the Dome ate nearly £1 billion of public money and became a national joke (*see p177*).

The government's plans for Iraq in 2003 generated the largest public demonstration in London's history: over one million participated – to no avail. The new millennium saw Ken Livingstone, former leader of the GLC, become London's first directly elected mayor and head of the new Greater London Assembly (GLA). He was re-elected in 2004 for a second term, a thumbs up for his first term's policies, which included a congestion charge that forces drivers to pay £8 to enter the city centre as a means of easing traffic gridlock.

For a few weeks in the summer of 2005, London was riding the crest of a wave. First came Live8, a star-filled rockfest in Hyde Park watched by nearly ten million people in the UK alone. On the following Wednesday, 6 July, came the announcement that London had won the bid to host the 2012 Olympics. Jubilation turned to horror just one day later, when bombs on tube trains and a bus killed 52 people and injured 700. These were followed two weeks later by similar, though unsuccessful, attacks. In the immediate aftermath of the bombings the number of people travelling on tubes and buses was fewer and more people took to cycling to work, but very quickly the first 'Not Afraid' T-shirts began to appear and London emerged with a revitalised sense of itself – a bloody-minded determination that the river-like flow of the city's existence will not be deflected from its course.

London in 2007 promises much to keep the mood buoyant. Work is ongoing to restore and reinvent two of London's long-neglected architectural jewels, Battersea Power Station (*see p187*) and St Pancras Station (*see p111*), and some use may even finally be found for the beleaguered Dome. Wembley Stadium will be restored to the city too (*see p329*) and come season's end west London's Chelsea FC will most likely top the football league again – but no one said that life in London is perfect.

Key events

AD 43 The Romans invade; a bridge is built on the Thames; Londinium is founded.
61 Boudicca burns Londinium; the city is rebuilt and made the provincial capital.
122 Emperor Hadrian visits Londinium.
200 A city wall is built; Londinium becomes capital of Britannia Superior.
410 Roman troops evacuate Britain.
c600 Saxon London is built to the west.
604 St Paul's is built by King Ethelbert.
841 The Norse raid for the first time.
c871 The Danes occupy London.
886 King Alfred of Wessex takes London.
1013 The Danes take London back.
1042 Edward the Confessor builds a palace and 'West Minster' upstream.
1066 William I is crowned in Westminster Abbey; London is granted a charter.
1067 The Tower of London begun.
1123 St Bartholomew's Hospital founded.
1197 Henry Fitzalwin is the first mayor.
1213 St Thomas's Hospital is founded.
1215 The mayor signs the Magna Carta.
1240 First Parliament sits at Westminster.
1290 Jews are expelled from London.
1348-9 The Black Death.
1381 The Peasants' Revolt.
1388 Tyburn becomes place of execution.
1397 Richard Whittington is Lord Mayor.
1476 William Caxton sets up the first ever printing press at Westminster.
1512-3 Royal Dockyards at Woolwich and Deptford founded by Henry VIII.
1534 Henry VIII cuts off Catholic Church.
1555 Martyrs burned at Smithfield.
1566 Gresham opens the Royal Exchange.
1572 First known map of London printed.
1599 The Globe theatre opens.
1605 Guy Fawkes fails to blow up James I.
1642 The start of the Civil War.
1649 Charles I is executed; Cromwell establishes Commonwealth.
1664-5 The Great Plague.
1666 The Great Fire.
1675 Building starts on the new St Paul's.
1686 The first May Fair takes place.
1694 The Bank of England is established.
1710 St Paul's is completed.
1750 Westminster Bridge is built.
1766 The city wall is demolished.
1769 Blackfriars Bridge opens.
1773 The Stock Exchange is founded.
1780 The Gordon Riots take place.
1784 The first balloon flight over London.
1803 The first horse-drawn railway opens.
1812 PM Spencer Perceval assassinated.
1820 Regent's Canal opens.
1824 The National Gallery is founded.
1827 Regent's Park Zoo opens.
1829 London's first horse-drawn bus runs; the Metropolitan Police Act is passed.
1833 The London Fire Brigade is set up.
1834 Parliament burns down.
1835 Madame Tussaud's opens.
1836 The first passenger railway opens; Charles Dickens publishes his first novel *The Pickwick Papers*.
1843 Trafalgar Square is laid out.
1848-9 Cholera epidemic sweeps London.
1851 The Great Exhibition takes place.
1853 Harrods opens its doors.
1858 The Great Stink: pollution in the Thames reaches hideous levels.
1863 The Metropolitan Line, the world's first underground railway, opens.
1866 London's last major cholera outbreak; the Sanitation Act is passed.
1868 The last public execution is held at Newgate prison.
1884 Greenwich Mean Time established.
1888 Jack the Ripper prowls the East End; London County Council is created.
1890 The Housing Act enables the LCC to clear the slums; the first electric underground railway opens.
1897 Motorised buses introduced.
1915-8 Zeppelins bomb London.
1940-1 The Blitz devastates much of the city.
1948 London hosts the Olympic Games.
1951 The Festival of Britain takes place.
1952 The last London 'pea-souper' smog.
1953 Queen Elizabeth II is crowned.
1966 England win World Cup at Wembley.
1975 Work begins on the Thames Barrier.
1981 Riots in Brixton.
1982 The last of London's docks close.
1986 The GLC is abolished.
1990 Poll Tax protesters riot.
1992 Canary Wharf opens; an IRA bomb hits the Baltic Exchange in the City.
2000 Ken Livingstone is elected mayor; Tate Modern and the London Eye open.
2001 The Labour government re-elected.
2002 Queen Mother dies aged 101.
2003 London's biggest public demonstration ever against the war on Iraq.
2005 London wins bid to host the 2012 Olympics. Suicide bombers kill 52.

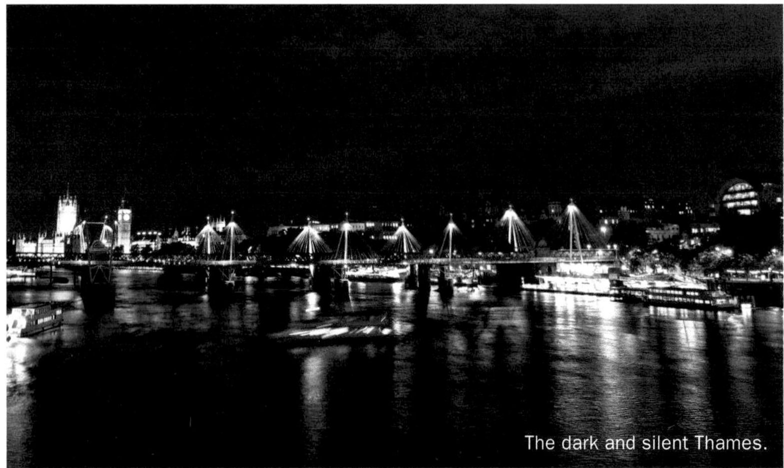
The dark and silent Thames.

London Today

For the editor of the weekly *Time Out London* magazine Gordon Thomson, it all began on the top deck of a bus.

In 1996 I was a PhD student at Glasgow University, billeted in London for six months to complete research on the House of Lords' activities during the Glorious Revolution of 1688 for a doctorate thesis that was never to be completed. I was broke, miserable and, unsurprising given the dryness of the subject matter, thoroughly unconvinced that I was doing the right thing with my life. I spent my first months in London dutifully trundling up the Northern Line from my small flat in Clapham to Tottenham Court Road tube station, from where I would walk to the British Museum, then home to the British Library but also containing the manuscripts office, the spartan common room of British academia and the place where many of the documents I needed to look at were kept. Every other day I would take a different route, catching the 88 bus to Parliament Square, before walking over to the south tower of Westminster Palace, which contains the fantastically arcane House of Lords library. Inspiration was hard to find in these musty old places: the biggest thrill was being allowed entry in the first place, closely followed by being allowed back out again.

I was secretly proud to carry the membership card to the British Library Manuscript Room, knowing that it made me part of a fairly exclusive and often-celebrated club (and, crucially, that it kept my mother happy), but my heart wasn't in the work. Often, after a restless morning spent trying to decipher the handwriting of the Duke of Halifax on some yellowing death warrant or else waiting for documents to be delivered by staff, I would leave my books and notes and wander out into the city. I was, I imagined, like Beckett's Krapp, 'drowned in dreams and burning to be gone'. These were the moments in which I fell for London. Perched at the front of a bus like an excited child on a half-term day trip, I would bunk off from the research and embark on a blind date with the Big Smoke, literally jumping the first double decker I encountered as I left the museum.

It helped that I developed a tube phobia. The city lay above the ground not under it – any time spent in those endless tunnels was precious time wasted. And so it was from on high that I devoured the capital. Westbourne Grove, Clerkenwell Green, Battersea Park Road, Westmoreland Terrace in Pimlico, Brixton

Water Lane, Goswell Road, Honduras Street – I glimpsed all of them for the first time from the top deck of a London bus. Other days I set out on foot, though never with an *A-Z*, determined to map the city with my eyes and mind, spurred on by the ghosts of Samuels Pepys and Johnson but inspired chiefly by my own spontaneity. I would often end up in the corner of a pub, occasionally at lunchtime – deciphering 17th-century shorthand could break the spirit very quickly – but more often than not after I had skulked back to retrieve my bag and books before the library closed for the night. Any guilty feelings quickly evaporated as I nursed my pint in a nook as night fell and tried to piece together the latest fragments of my rapidly expanding London map.

'Nobody can keep up with this city. But Londoners will die trying.'

Though it has now become my paid job to piece together these fragments and make the finished puzzle as enjoyable as possible for other people, I never tire of the task. Historian Geoffrey Fletcher, in his absorbing book *The London Nobody Knows*, said: 'I have no hesitation in admitting that the older I get the more London becomes an obsession with me, so much so that I find myself ill at ease elsewhere.' And so a confession: I moved to London from Glasgow ten years ago and I have no intention or indeed need or desire to ever live anywhere else. This is my city. It is my home. For a Scotsman, this is dangerous talk, but I know for a fact that many of my kinsmen, displaced but now indisputably done-over by London, regularly meet to share the same seditious truth.

Today my London map, along with everyone else's, continues to shift and change as once-imaginary boundaries become real, pushing ever outwards from the old Roman heartland. The landscape may appear more familiar after ten years, but really it is always out of reach. Fifty years, a hundred even, would barely make a difference. Like the water that seeps through sand as it is scooped up by a spade at the seaside, London is permanent and unstoppable.

As the city spreads so too does its vibrant cultural community. Every year it grows. Frequently, I hear it said that there is too much to do in our weekly *Time Out*, too many events to keep up with, 'too much going on'. And it's true. Nobody can keep up with this city. But Londoners will die trying.

September 2006 was a typical month for culture in the capital, perhaps slightly busier than usual, though it's a hectic month by nature. In those four weeks I saw Russia's best male pianist play Mozart at the Barbican (and finally worked out a short cut through its maze-like network of ramps and Orwellian walkways); watched the two finest dancers in the world, Sylvie Guillem and Akram Khan, perform together at Sadler's Wells; saw Stephen Fry introduce the jet-lagged cast of *The History Boys* at the première of Nick Hytner and Alan Bennett's phenomenal play/film. I saw inspirational art by Kandinsky, Bill Viola, Rodin and Holbein; watched teenagers and hippies give Rufus Sewell and Brian Cox six standing ovations at the end of Tom Stoppard's *Rock'n'Roll* at the Duke of York; sat, slightly pissed but much more in awe, as Wynton Marsalis and his band made Ronnie Scott's swoon; ate the best steak I have had in over a year at the new Hawksmoor restaurant in the East End; went to Lady Luck cabaret and watched men in 1950s suits and girls in polka-dots jive and flirt; I walked streets I have never walked before; showed my children the remains of Edward III's palace outside a (very good) pub in Bermondsey; discovered six plaques dedicated to the famous anti-slavery campaigner William Wilberforce; watched a man recreate a medieval lobotomy at the Old Operating Theatre in Southwark; stumbled upon the childhood home of Michael Caine; attended a party at the world's only museum entirely devoted to fans; walked where Caesar walked on Shooters Hill. I ticked off a meagre six places from my 'Must eat here this year' list; visited Charlton Lido and Charlton Athletic FC for the very first time (one only slightly wetter than the other); I worked out, I think, where William Blake saw his vision of angels on Peckham Rye Park. I played 'A Rainy Night in Soho' by the Pogues on my iPod as I walked through Soho… it wasn't raining. I sat on a stationary train in Blackfriars station and looked out over the dark and silent Thames. I lived a full month in this city and yet I barely scratched its surface.

'London has always been an ugly city,' said Peter Ackroyd. 'It is part of its identity. It has always been rebuilt, and demolished, and vandalised. That, too, is part of its history.' Ackroyd is right, in one respect: London is a city of cities, a shape-shifter, a skin-shedder, a layered cake. But it is not ugly. It could never be ugly. Not to me. London is beaten, scarred – unquestionably dirty, noisy, ceaseless, rude and rough as old boots. In other words, London is human. And as it grows yet another year older, and I slope off to a pub near the British Museum to toast this landmark, for old times' sake, its brilliance and beauty remain undiminished.

Ten things to do before you're a proper Londoner

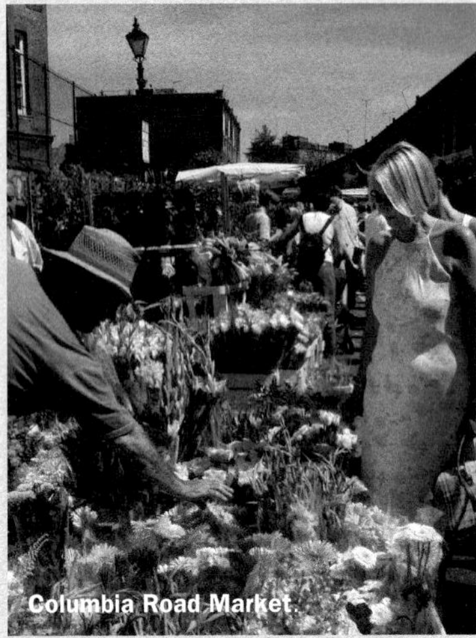
Columbia Road Market.

1. Swim in Hampstead Ponds
There are three bathing ponds (men's, women's and mixed) and a lido. Indoors is for sissies. *See p159.*

2. Eat pie and mash at Manze's
Antique tiles, beat-up trestle tables... and stewed eels. Has to be tried once. *See p89.*

3. Go dahn the dogs
The art deco neon outside, the yelps of the whip-thin dogs inside. A classic night out. Tip: back trap 6 in heavy rain. *See p331.*

4. Make a tomb raid
London has seven Victorian cemeteries, the most famous of which is Highgate, home to Marx and George Eliot. *See p160.*

5. Visit Dennis Severs' House
Take a spooky tour of this former merchant house in Spitalfields and you'll feel like you've just interrupted the guests at dinner. *See p165.*

6. Get sweaty at the Astoria
Nirvana, the Who and, er, Kylie – they've all played at this legendary central London music venue. For an extra gold star seek out the great watching spaces beyond the Keith Moon bar. *See p312.*

7. Pick up a bargain at Bermondsey Market
Set your alarm for this unprepossessing, blink and you'll miss it, full-on cockernee market. Silver, jewellery, books and maybe something for the weekend, sir? *See p88.*

8. Smell the roses at Columbia Road
The best flower market in the world? Go before 8am or after lunch, and stop off at the Royal Oak for a pint or six. *See p259.*

9. Burlesque
Haven't you heard? Tassles and top hats are so this year. Try Lady Luck in Soho and the Bethnal Green Working Men's Club. *See p323.*

10. Nod off at Piccadilly and wake up at Cockfosters
We've all done it.

...and ten things you should never ever do

1. Carry a tube map
2. Make jokes when the carriage is packed
3. Buy a slice of pizza on the street
4. Hail a taxi with its light off
5. Ring in the New Year in Trafalgar Square
6. Arrange to meet mates at the Punch & Judy pub in Covent Garden on a Friday night
7. See *The Mousetrap* or *Blood Brothers*
8. Eat in a Garfunkel's or Angus/Aberdeen Steak House
9. Have your caricature done on Leicester Square
10. Ride in a rickshaw – oh, go on then

Manze's pie and mash.

City Hall. *See p36.*

Architecture

The fusion of old and new makes for exciting results.

Any number of events have left their imprint on the buildings of the city, but the Great Fire of 1666 is a useful marker: it signals the end of medieval London and the start of the city we know today. The fire destroyed five-sixths of the city, burning some 13,200 houses and 89 churches. Its devastation is commemorated by Sir Christopher Wren's 202-foot Monument (*see p100*); beyond the column, much of London as you see it now is a testament to the talents of this man, the architect of the great remodelling, and his successors.

London was a densely populated place built of wood, where fire control was primitive. It was only after the three-day inferno that the authorities felt they could insist on a few basic building regulations. Brick and stone became the construction materials of choice, and key streets were widened to act as firebreaks.

In spite of grand proposals from architects hoping to reconfigure it along classical lines, London reshaped itself around its historic street pattern, with buildings that had survived the Fire standing as monuments to earlier ages. Chief of these was the Norman **Tower of London** (*see p102*), begun soon after William's 1066 conquest and extended over the next 300 years. The Navy cheated the advancing flames of the Great Fire by blowing up the surrounding houses before the inferno could get to it. Then there is **Westminster Abbey** (*see p141*), begun in 1245 when the site lay far outside London's walls and completed in 1745 when the church architect Nicholas Hawksmoor added the west towers. Though the abbey is the most French of England's Gothic churches, deriving its geometry, flying buttresses and rose windows from across the Channel, the chapel, added by Henry VII and completed in 1512, is pure Tudor. Centuries later, Washington Irving gushed: 'Stone seems, by the winning labour of the chisel, to have been robbed of its weight and density, suspended aloft, as if by magic.'

The European Renaissance came late to Britain, making its London debut with Inigo Jones's 1622 **Banqueting House** (*see p140*). The addition of a sumptuously decorated ceiling by Rubens in 1635 made the building a key piece of London's architecture. The following decade, King Charles I provided the public with an even greater spectacle as he was led from the building and beheaded on a stage outside. Tourists also have Jones to thank for

St Paul's Covent Garden (*see p115*) and the **Queen's House** (*see p178*) at Greenwich, but these are not his only legacies. By the 1600s Italian architecture was all the rage, so he mastered the art of piazzas (notably at Covent Garden), porticos and pilasters, changing British architecture forever. His work not only influenced the careers of succeeding generations of architects, but also introduced a habit of venerating the past that caught on in a big way, and would take 300 years to kick.

PHOENIX FROM THE FLAMES

Nothing cheers a builder like a natural disaster, and one can only guess at the relish with which Christopher Wren and co began rebuilding after the Fire. They brandished classicism like a new broom: the pointed arches of English Gothic were rounded off, Corinthian columns made an appearance and church spires became as multi-layered as a baroque wedding cake.

Wren blazed the trail with daring plans for **St Paul's Cathedral** (*see p93*), spending an enormous – for the time – £500 on the oak model of his proposal. But the scheme, incorporating a Catholic dome rather than a Protestant steeple, was too Roman for the reformist establishment and the design was rejected. Wren quickly produced a redesign and gained planning permission by incorporating the much-loved spire, only to set about a series of mischievous U-turns to give us the building – domed and heavily suggestive of an ancient temple – that has survived to this day.

Wren's architectural baton was picked up by Nicholas Hawksmoor and James Gibbs, who benefited from a 1711 decree that 50 extra churches should be built. Gibbs became busy in and around Trafalgar Square, building the steepled Roman temple of **St Martin-in-the-Fields** (*see p138*), as well as the baroque **St Mary-le-Strand** and the tower of **St Clement Danes** (for both, *see p119*).

St George's Bloomsbury.

'St George's was dismissed as the "most pretentious and ugliest edifice in the metropolis".'

Gibbs's work was well received, but the more prolific and experimental Hawksmoor had a rougher ride. His imposing **St Anne** (Commercial Road, Limehouse, E14) proved so costly that the parish couldn't afford a vicar, and **St George's** (*see p109*) in Bloomsbury cost three times its £10,000 budget and took 15 years to build. St George's – dismissed in 1876 as the 'most pretentious and ugliest edifice in the metropolis' – aims to evoke the spirit of the ancients. Rather than a spire, there is a stepped pyramid topped by a statue of George I decked out in a toga, while the interior boasts all the Corinthian columns, round arches and gilding you'd expect from a man steeped in antiquity. Many of these features are repeated in Hawksmoor's rocket-like **Christ Church Spitalfields** (*see p164*).

THE ADAM FAMILY VALUES

One of a large family of Scottish architects, Robert Adam found himself at the forefront of a movement that came to see Italian baroque as a corruption of the real thing. Architectural exuberance was eventually dropped in favour of a simpler interpretation of the ancient forms.

The best surviving work of Adam and his brothers James, John and William can be found in London's great suburban houses **Osterley Park**, **Syon House** (*see p193*) and **Kenwood House** (*see p160*), but the project for which they are most famous no longer stands. In 1768 they embarked on the cripplingly expensive **Adelphi** housing estate off the Strand. Most of the complex was pulled down in the 1930s and replaced by an office block. Only a small part of the original development survives in what is now the **Royal Society of Arts** (8 John Adam Street, Covent Garden, WC2).

Just as the first residents were moving into the Adelphi, a young unknown called John Soane was embarking on a tour of his own. In Rome, Soane met the wealthy Bishop of Derry who persuaded the 25-year-old to accompany him to Ireland in order to build a house. The project came to nothing, so Soane dealt with the setback by working hard and marrying into money. His loss was our gain, as he went on to build the **Bank of England** and **Dulwich Picture Gallery** (*see p175*), recently extended. Regrettably, the Bank was demolished between the wars, leaving nothing but the perimeter walls and depriving London of Soane's masterpiece. A hint of what these bankers might have enjoyed can be gleaned from a visit to Soane's house, now the quirky **Sir John Soane's Museum** (*see p104*), a collection of exquisite architectural experiments with mirrors, coloured glass and folding walls.

A near-contemporary of Soane's, John Nash was arguably a less talented architect, but his contributions to the fabric of London have proved comparable to those of Wren. Among his buildings are **Buckingham Palace** (*see p144*), the **Theatre Royal Haymarket** (Haymarket, SW1) and **Regent Street** (Soho/ Mayfair, W1). The latter began as a proposal to link the West End to the planned park further north, as well as a device to separate the toffs of Mayfair from Soho riff-raff or, in Nash's words, a 'complete separation between the Streets occupied by the Nobility and Gentry, and the narrow Streets and meaner houses occupied by mechanics and the trading part of the community'.

'The new Romantics saw Classicism as foreign and pagan, and favoured Gothic as native and Christian.'

INVASION OF THE GOTHS

By the 1830s the classical form of building had been established in England for some 200 years, but this didn't prevent a handful of upstarts from pressing for change. In 1834 the **Houses of Parliament** (*see p141*) burned down, leading to the construction of Sir Charles Barry's Gothic masterpiece. This was the beginning of the Gothic Revival, a move by the new Romantics to replace what they considered to be foreign and pagan with a style that was native and Christian.

Barry sought out a designer whose name alone makes him worthy of mention: Augustus Welby Northmore Pugin. Working alongside Barry (and not always in agreement – of Barry's symmetrical layout he famously remarked, 'All Grecian, sir. Tudor details on a classic body.'), Pugin created a Victorian fantasy that, while a fine example of the perpendicular form, shows how the Middle Ages had become distorted in the minds of 19th-century architects. The riot of turrets and towers would today be condemned as the Disneyfication of history.

Architects would often decide that buildings weren't Gothic enough; as with the 15th-century **Great Hall** (*see p99*) at the **Guildhall**, which gained its corner turrets and central spire only in 1862. Bombed by the Luftwaffe, the Guildhall was rebuilt largely as the Victorians had left it, apart from the interior statues of Gog and Magog, the protagonists in a legendary battle between ancient Britain and Troy: these two creatures got even uglier.

The argument between classicists and goths erupted in 1857, when the government hired Sir George Gilbert Scott, a leading light of the

Broadcasting House. *See p34.*

Gothic movement, to design a new HQ for the Foreign Office. Scott's design incensed anti-goth Lord Palmerston, then prime minister, whose diktats prevailed. But Scott exacted his revenge by building an office in which everyone hated working, and by going on to construct Gothic edifices all over town, among them the **Albert Memorial** (*see p153*) and **St Pancras Chambers** (*see p110*), the station frontage housing the Midland Grand Hotel.

St Pancras was completed in 1873, after the Midland Railway commissioned Scott to build a London terminus that would dwarf that of its rivals next door at King's Cross. Using the project as an opportunity to show his mastery of the Gothic form, Scott built an asymmetrical castle that obliterated views of the train shed behind, itself an engineering marvel completed earlier by William Barlow. This 'incongruous medievalism' did not go unnoticed by critics; one was prompted to comment, sniffily: 'Their porters might be dressed as javelin men, their guards as beefeaters.'

'Lamentably, the city was little improved by the rebuild, and, in many cases, was worse off.'

Still, the Gothic style was to dominate until the 20th century, leaving London littered with charming and imposing buildings such as the **Royal Courts of Justice** (*see p119*), the **Natural History Museum** (*see p153*), the **Liberty** store (*see p242*) and **Tower Bridge** (*see p102*). World War I and the coming of modernism led to a spirit of tentative renewal. **Freemason's Hall** (*see p116*) and the BBC's **Broadcasting House** (*see p125*) are good examples of the pared-down style of the 1920s and '30s. The latter is currently being extended and modernised with work expected to be completed in 2010.

CONCRETE ISLAND

Perhaps the finest example of between-the-wars modernism can be found at **London Zoo** (*see p128*). Built by Russian émigré Bertold Lubetkin and the Tecton group, the spiral ramps of the Penguin Pool (no longer used by penguins) were a showcase for the possibilities of concrete. The material was also put to good use on the Underground, enabling the quick, cheap building of large, cavernous spaces with sleek lines and curves. The Piccadilly Line was a particular beneficiary: its 1930s expansion yielded the likes of Charles Holden's striking **Arnos Grove** station, the first of many circular station buildings.

There was nothing quick or cheap about the art deco **Daily Express** (*see p90*) building (Fleet Street, the City, EC4). A black glass and chrome structure built in 1931, it is an early example of 'curtain wall' construction where the façade is literally hung on an internal frame. The building has been recently refurbished, but the original deco detailing – crazy flooring, snake handrails and funky lighting – remains intact. Public access is not guaranteed, but it's worth sticking your head around the door of what the *Architects' Journal* has called a 'defining monument of 1930s London'.

TOWER BLOCK-HEADS

The aerial bombing of World War II left large areas of London ruined, providing another opportunity for builders to cash in. Lamentably, the city was little improved by the rebuild; in many cases, it was worse off. The destruction left the capital with a dire housing shortage, so architects were given a chance to demonstrate the efficiency with which they could house large numbers of families in tower blocks.

There were post-war successes, however, including the **Royal Festival Hall** (*see p81*) on the South Bank. The sole survivor of the 1951 Festival of Britain, the RFH was built to celebrate the war's end and the centenary of the Great Exhibition. It can be a crowded and awkward space, but refurbishment work has been restoring what little grandeur the builders of post-war Britain managed to impart. The RFH is now a much-loved piece of London's fabric – unlike the neighbouring **Hayward Gallery** and **Queen Elizabeth Hall**, exemplars of the 1960s vogue for Brutalist experimentation.

But Brutalism couldn't last forever. The 1970s and '80s offered up a pair of architectural replacements: post-modernism and high-tech. The former is represented by Cesar Pelli's **One Canada Water** (*see p170*) at Canary Wharf in Docklands, an oversized obelisk that has become the archetypal expression of 1980s architecture and holds an ambiguous place in the city's affections. Richard Rogers's **Lloyd's of London** building (*see p100*) is London's best-known example of high-tech, in which commercial and industrial aesthetics cleverly combine to produce what is arguably one of the most significant British buildings since the war. Mocked on completion in 1986, the building still manages to outclass newer projects.

Equally ground-breaking is Future Systems' **NatWest Media Centre** at Lord's Cricket Ground (St John's Wood Road, St John's Wood, NW8). Built from aluminium in a boatyard and perched high above the pitch, it's one of London's most daring constructions to date,

The heights of brilliance... and of bad taste

Swiss Re Tower.

In 2005 *Time Out London* magazine asked its readers to vote on their favourite – and least favourite – London buildings.

Love

1. Tate Modern (Sir Giles Gilbert Scott, 1947-63, and Herzog & de Meuron, 2000). *See p85.*
2. Houses of Parliament (Charles Barry and Augustus WN Pugin, 1852, with Big Ben's tower completed 1858). *See p141.*
3. Battersea Power Station (Sir Giles Gilbert Scott, 1935 and 1955). *See p187.*
4. Swiss Re Tower aka 'The Gherkin' (Foster and Partners, 2004). *Photo above.*
5. St Pancras Hotel (Sir George Gilbert Scott, 1866-68). *See p110.*
6. The Great Court, British Museum (Foster & Partners, 2000). *See p109.*
7. Senate House (Charles Holden, 1937). *See p109.*
8. Hoover Building (Wallis Gilbert & Partners, 1932). Stunning art deco factory (5 Western Avenue, Mddsx, UB6 8DW; Perivale tube).
9. St Paul's Cathedral (Sir Christopher Wren, 1714). *See p93.*
10. Mossbourne Academy (Richard Rogers Partnership, 2004). A school described by the architects as 'log cabin meets Lloyd's' (Downs Park Road, Hackney, E5).

Loathe

1. Elephant & Castle Shopping Centre (The Willett Group, 1965). One more reason to avoid south-east London.
2. Guoman Tower Hotel (Renton Howard Wood Partnership, 1973). All the more awful for being sited beside picturesque Tower Bridge.
3. Centre Point (Richard Seifert, 1967). The high-rise at the junction of Oxford Street and Tottenham Court Road. Also London's 16th-placed most-loved building. *Photo below.*
4. Buckingham Palace (John Nash, 1830; Edward Blore, 1847; Sir Aston Webb, 1914). *See p144.*
5. No.1 Poultry (Stirling Wilford Associates, 1998). Crass bit of post-modernism among the elegant Classicism at Bank. *See p98.*
6. Brunswick Centre (Patrick Hodgkinson and Bickerdike Allen, 1973). Ground-breaking but reviled Bloomsbury housing development.
7. Portcullis House (Michael Hopkins & Partners, 2001). *See p140.*
8. National Gallery Sainsbury Wing (Venturi, Scott Brown & Associates, 1991). Does its mediocre best to blend in. *See p137.*
9. National Theatre (Denys Lasdun, 1977). Horizontal concrete bunker. *See p82.*
10. Barbican (Chamberlin, Powell & Bon, 1979). Vertical concrete bunkers. *See p97.*

Centre Point.

especially given the traditional setting. And Will Alsop's multicoloured **Peckham Library** (171 Peckham Hill Street, Peckham, SE15) redefined community architecture so comprehensively that it walked away with the £20,000 Stirling Prize in 2000.

OUTSIDE-IN

With the heritage lobby still strong, much new architecture is to be found cunningly inserted into old buildings. The **National Portrait Gallery** (*see p138*), the **Royal Opera House** (*see p115*) and, in particular, Herzog & de Meuron's fabulous transformation of a power station on Bankside into **Tate Modern** (*see p85*) are good examples of architects adding modern signatures to old buildings, while the **British Museum** (*see p109*), the **National Maritime Museum** (*see p177*) and the **Wallace Collection** (*see p127*) have all gone one better. With the help of large lottery grants, these last three added to their facilities by invading external courtyards. Lord Norman Foster's exercise in complexity at the British Museum, where the £100m Great Court created the largest covered square in Europe, is without doubt the most impressive – every one of its 3,300 triangular glass panels is unique.

'Libeskind's LMU graduate centre is interesting, but not a patch on his extension for the V&A – had it ever gone ahead.'

Any discussion of the city's architecture is, of course, impossible without mention of Foster. Not content with his addition to the British Museum, his new **City Hall** and his already iconic **Swiss Re Tower** (aka 'The Gherkin') at 30 St Mary Axe in the City, his prolific practice is also responsible for the new **Wembley Stadium** – whose soaring arch is sure to become another instantly recognisable symbol of the capital. Beset by delays, the eagerly awaited stadium is nonetheless sure to set new standards in sports design.

Hop on to the DLR and head south to see the other great London building by Tate Modern architects Herzog & de Meuron, Deptford's **Laban** dance centre (Creekside, Deptford, SE8). The capital also has its first building by the acclaimed Daniel Libeskind, who has designed a small graduate centre for the **London Metropolitan University** (Holloway Road, Holloway, N7). Interesting, but not a patch on what his Spiral extension for the V&A Museum would have been if it had ever gone ahead.

But overseas superstar architects aren't snaffling up all the major commissions. Two of the most exciting new buildings in London are by home-grown talent. Will Alsop, architect of the Peckham Library, has designed a stunning £45m medical school building for **Queen Mary, University of London** (Mile End Road, E1). It's highly colourful with projected moving images on the outside; the lively interior includes focal points such as Spikey and Cloud – two distinctive suspended 'pods' containing meeting rooms and seminar space. Nearby on Whitechapel Road, E1, David Adjaye has designed his second new-build **Idea Store** (www.ideastore.co.uk) to follow on from his acclaimed building in Poplar (Chrisp Street, E14). With its sleek and crisp aesthetic, it's a world away from the traditional Victorian library in design as well as name and function, and should confirm Adjaye as a major player on the architectural scene.

Tellingly, these last two new landmarks are in the east. As the capital's focus shifts firmly towards the Olympics-inspired regeneration of east London, they are surely just the fore-runners of a huge period of change that will have a major impact on the capital's built environment. To see where things might be going, visit **New London Architecture** (Building Centre, 26 Store Street, Bloomsbury, WC1, 7692 4000, Goodge Street tube). Opened in 2005, this permanent exhibition aims to provide an overview of the key developments in London for the general visitor and design professional alike. The centre's impressive centrepiece is a 39-foot-long scale model of London, stretching from Battersea Power Station in the south up to King's Cross and out to Docklands and Stratford in the east. It's a fascinating bird's-eye view of what the capital looks like now, and what it might soon become. Currently, there are more than 150 unbuilt schemes on the model, including spectacular 1,000-foot proposals for the City and London Bridge. As jaw-dropping as these are, they represent just a fraction of the £100bn-worth of redevelopment projected for London over the next couple of decades. Especially interesting is the section of the model with the proposed Olympics 2012 facilities, which the bid team used as part of its campaign. Intended to help Londoners and tourists alike orientate themselves, the NLA offers a great way to get an understanding of how different parts of the capital link up, and how big things are. The model is accompanied by a regularly changing exhibition on a specific aspect of the capital's built environments. Content of these displays is updated every three months and there are plans to make the model interactive.

The Da Vinci Code (2006).

The Director's Cut

London has never looked better on the big screen.

Set jetters. They're the new breed of tourist, apparently. 'You've seen the films. Now visit the set.' So runs the tagline for a recent ad campaign that encouraged Britons to hop across the Atlantic to visit the States. An accompanying poster gives us Naomi Watts sitting in the palm of King Kong's hand with a digital New York City spread out below her. It works the other way too. According to a survey conducted jointly by the UK Film Council and FilmLondon, a head-turning one in five foreign visitors to London are here after being inspired by seeing the UK capital up on the big screen.

Not only does that say a lot about modern travel habits, it also says a great deal about how London is portrayed on film. It certainly would not have happened ten years ago. London's filmmakers have traditionally never been keen on polished images of the city. They have variously portrayed it as dark, miserable, tough, squalid and dangerous. Think *Naked* (1993), Mike Leigh's dystopian view of the city as seen through the eyes of the rambling, misanthropic Johnny (David Thewlis). Or *Nil by Mouth* (1997), Gary Oldman's semi-autobiographical tale of abuse and alcoholism on a south London estate. Or Danny Boyle's *Trainspotting* (1995), in which he contrasts the hoary stereotypes of filmic London – red buses, Big Ben, Trafalgar Square – with a piss-stinking squat in Mile End. Imagine the poster: 'You've seen the film. Now visit the set', next to a picture of Bob Hoskins surveying his victims as they hang upside-down on butcher's hooks in *The Long Good Friday* (1979).

How different it is now. Gone is the drab and seedy London of old, replaced by a super-sexy cinematic city inhabited by a host of shaggable types such as Renée Zellweger (albeit slightly fattened up for *Bridget Jones's Diary*; 2001), Scarlett Johansson (in Woody Allen's *Match Point*; 2005), Natalie Portman (in town for *Closer*, 2004 and again for *V for Vendetta*, 2005) and Tom Hanks and Audrey Tatou in *The Da Vinci Code* (2006; *see photo p37*). With them come a whole new set of London clichés: Tate Modern plays host to Rhys Ifans stalking Daniel Craig in *Enduring Love* (2004); Johansson checks out the art in its galleries in *Match Point*; and it's where Ralph Fiennes and Rachel Weisz first meet in Fernando Meirelles's *The Constant Gardener* (2005). The London Eye graces Gurinder Chadha's *Bride and Prejudice* (2004) – in which Bollywood meets Hollywood via the South Bank – and it backdrops some impressive CGI sequences in *Thunderbirds* (2004). The Swiss Re Tower is a suitably phallic office for David Morrissey's character in *Basic Instinct 2* (2006); it's where Jonathan Rhys Meyers works in *Match Point* and turns up again in teen-spy romp *Stormbreaker* (2006).

'To accommodate the shoot for *V for Vendetta*, the Household Cavalry had to be persuaded to postpone its rehearsals for the Queen's Birthday.'

The on-screen makeover is very much an indication of how London itself has changed over the last decade. But it's also evidence of a change in perception on the part of the film-makers. Keenly aware of the multi-billion-pound relationship between film and tourism, London's ruling bodies have been eager to attract movie shoots to the capital. To this end, in 2003 the mayor's office set up FilmLondon to promote the city to the movie-making community. 'We can't pretend London is a cheap place,' says chief executive Adrian Wootton, 'but we can make it a lot cheaper than people think.' His office is also in the business of pulling off the impossible. For *V for Vendetta* FilmLondon managed to shut down Whitehall for one night and fill it with several thousand uniformed extras to march on Parliament – a task that involved gaining permissions from 14 different agencies and persuading the Household Cavalry to postpone its rehearsals for the Queen's Birthday parade. Added to which, Wootton explains, London has the best post-production services outside Hollywood. Then there's the sheer versatility and variety of the city's architecture, which can double for just about anywhere (Paul Schrader recently shot New York and Toronto scenes in London), and the fact that you 'never have to persuade an actor to spend time in London'.

The result is that London is now the third busiest filming production centre in the world, behind Los Angeles and New York. In 2005 there were 12,600 shooting days in London, with on average almost 35 crews busy in the capital every single day of the year. 'Word of mouth is out about how easy it is to film in London,' says Wootton. 'Christopher Nolan said he couldn't have made *Batman Begins* anywhere else. He'll be back for the sequel.'

REEL STREETS

Necktie murderers, werewolves and gangland massacres: London's streets have seen some spectacular moments. Below we list a few choice examples.

Newman Passage, Fitzrovia, W1

Peeping Tom (1960)

Michael Powell's once-vilified psychodrama about a murderously voyeuristic cameraman – now recognised as a masterpiece – may have upset the British press less because of any 'sick' or 'sadistic' violence than because it dared to suggest that London wasn't an entirely respectable place. It opens with a prostitute propositioning the camera and leading her client down the alley (Newman Passage); we soon realise that he will be her killer. Go there now and the alleyway leads not to a knocking shop but to the Pie Shop, a dining room above the Newman Arms pub (*see p229*).

Notting Hill, W11

Performance (1970)

Long before Hugh Grant and Julia Roberts, there was *Performance*, the Notting Hill film par excellence. Two of London's 1960s unseen tectonic plates – the criminal underworld and the bohemian underground – collide in this film in the characters of Chas (James Fox), a violent gangster on the run, and Turner (Mick Jagger), a louche rock star on the slide. The house the two inhabit is referred to as No.81, but the exteriors were of 25 Powis Square, Notting Hill. Fans made pilgrimages to the Electric on Portobello Road (*see p288*), where the film played to packed late shows in the 1970s.

Covent Garden, WC2

Frenzy (1972)

Not the best Hitchcock film, but a great London movie. The long, helicopter shot that opens this murder thriller sweeps under Tower Bridge and along the river westwards before turning and focusing on a crowd of people listening to a politician outside County Hall. It's a striking opening and marks Hitchcock's return to London after many years in Hollywood. Of local interest especially are the scenes in Covent Garden, which was then the city's fruit-and-veg hub. The pub from which the 'wrong man' is fired is the Globe (37 Bow Street), while the murderer's flat, from which the camera recoils and pulls down the stairs and out into the street in one fluid shot, is at 3 Henrietta Street.

Tower Bridge, E1

The Long Good Friday (1979)

Bob Hoskins plays Harold Shand, a savvy London criminal looking to inject a little criminality into the coming regeneration of the

East End by inviting some crooked Americans to invest in the docklands. And how better to woo them than on your yacht as you cruise down the Thames? Tower Bridge forms the perfect backdrop.'Thatcher had just got into power when we made the film,' Hoskins recalled in a *Time Out* interview. 'It was exactly her vision. That's why it was so frightening; a gangster spouting Thatcherism.' There's a sense of prophecy too: not only does the film predict the redevelopment of the docks, but it ties that regeneration into a coming Olympic Games (albeit in 1988).

Tottenham Court Road tube station, W1

American Werewolf in London (1981)
Horror comedy in which two young American hitch-hikers are savagely attacked on the Yorkshire moors. Recuperating in London, David Naughton is visited by his deceased and decomposing pal who keeps popping back to clue him up on what's in store come the full moon. One of the most enduring scenes takes place in the white-tiled subways of Tottenham Court Road tube station. In full-moon mode, the hairy beast scours the tunnels for a late-night bite. So, if you hear a deep snorting sound emanating from a tube stairwell, run like the wind. See also *Death Line* (1972) and *Creep* (2004) for more underground nastiness – although neither comes close to the real-life horror of catching the last tube home from the West End on a Friday night.

Soho, W1

Mona Lisa (1986)
In Neil Jordan's film about an ex-con minder, George (Bob Hoskins), and his hounded prostitute charge, Simone (Cathy Tyson) the developing relationship between the two is played out against the underbelly of 1980s Soho – a world of seedy basement bars, grimy backrooms and stained sheets (the offices of underworld kingpin Mortwell (Michael Caine) are what's now the Soho Revue Bar, *see p326*). It's an unsanitised view of a city and its inhabitants, where beauty and filth co-exist – this is a living, breathing London.

41 Tavistock Crescent, W11

Withnail & I (1986)
Camden Town, the close of the 1960s, and Withnail (Richard E Grant) and 'I' (Paul McGann) are two out-of-work actors, living on a diet of booze and paranoia. Half of Bruce Robinson's semi-autobiographical movie takes place in the rain-soaked Lake District, but there's still a very strong and very real sense of the London of that time: wrecking-balls clear out the vestiges of the post-war city to a tune by Hendrix. Mother Black Cap (41 Tavistock Crescent, Notting Hill, W11) is the pub where 'I' is scared witless by an Irishman and retreats to the toilets – where the graffiti ('I fuck arses') sends him into a fit of paranoia.

Borough Market, SE1

Bridget Jones's Diary (2001)
Of the clutch of recent London-set rom-coms (*Notting Hill, Love Actually, About a Boy*), Bridget does it best. There's no 'ugly duckling blossoms into swan' scenario here. Not only that, but the London she inhabits is believable – well, almost (the last time London saw the sort of snow fall seen in this film, Ebenezer Scrooge was suffering a sleepless night tormented by spirits). Bridget's Borough Market pad is cramped and messy, the publishing company office in which she works is nondescript, and even the use of such a London film convention as Piccadilly Circus is nicely subverted when the illuminated Coca-Cola sign proclaims 'Mark and Bridget: It's the Real Thing'.

Piccadilly Circus, W1

28 Days Later (2002)
Twenty-eight days have passed since the Rage virus was unleashed; four weeks that have decimated the population. When Jim (Cillian Murphy) awakes from a coma it's as if he's still in the throes of some frightening fever dream – the last man alive in London. It's an apocalyptic vision chillingly realised at a still and silent Piccadilly Circus, where hoardings around the statue of Eros are covered with missing person notices, echoing the flyers that appeared around New York in the aftermath of 9/11.

Temple Church, Fleet Street, EC1

The Da Vinci Code (2006)
As the elaborate puzzle surrounding the murder of a Louvre curator and the religious mystery that may not have died with him wends its tourist trail through Paris and London, it hauls in at this Norman and Gothic church (*see p93*). This is where Sophie Neveu (Audrey Tatou) and Robert Langdon (Tom Hanks) search for the next hidden clue that will let them undo the second combination lock of the keystone. Dan Brown imagines the church as a hidden crypt where entombed crusader knights have been keeping the secret of the Holy Grail since the 12th century – and, in fact, there are nine life-size stone effigies of knights in the church. The rest, according to the current Master of the Temple, is 'historical rubbish'. Not that he's complaining. Since the *Code* was published, visitor numbers to the church have gone up 50 per cent and the Master charges £4 a head to deliver a talk on the subject, which he's also expanded into a book of his own.

Capital Records

London has inspired some great songs. Here, in chronological order, is a Time Out top 10.

It's November 1976. The Damned have just beaten fellow Londoners the Sex Pistols in bringing out the first ever English punk single. It's called 'New Rose' and it's delivered in a suitably malevolent mid-Atlantic accent. The Damned huddle around a stereo to hear the Pistols' response, 'Anarchy in the UK'. As the guitar chimes out and Johnny Rotten does his Sid James cackle, their jaws drop.

'We thought they were taking the piss,' says Damned bassist Captain Sensible. 'It sounded like fucking Black Sabbath with Old Man Steptoe wailing away over the top.'

Thirty years ago, pop stars weren't meant to sing like TV's cockney junk collector Albert Steptoe. Not even punks. English bands dutifully sang in an American accent, bowing to its phraseology, its rhythmic cadences and its drawling, rhotic Rrrrrrs.

While many other regional accents of the British Isles were rediscovered in the folk revival of the early 1900s, the London accent remains largely absent from Cecil Sharp's folk archives. Music hall remained the capital's only musical voice: Harry Champion's cockney classics like 'Any Old Iron' and 'Boiled Beef and Carrots' were densely written, filled with innuendo, often alternating between speech and melody. It was a tradition that was sustained right up to World War II and beyond.

But singing in a cockney accent became something of an embarrassment as rock'n'roll swept the nation in the late 1950s. London pop stars like Joe Brown or Tommy Steele would sometimes provide a cheeky nod to music hall – just as Ray Davies of the Kinks or Steve Marriott of the Small Faces would do a few years later – while theatrical songwriter Anthony Newley developed a slightly gentrified cockney accent that plotted a path for David Bowie. But the norm was for born and bred Londoners – Mick Jagger, Rod Stewart, Elton John, Roger Daltrey – to sing like they'd grown up in the backwoods of Louisiana.

By the mid 1970s a few bands started to question that. Chas Hodges from cod-American blues-funk outfit Heads Hands and Feet formed Chas & Dave to explore 'cockney rock'n'roll'. Ian Dury used funk, blues and jazz as a vehicle for surreal, half-spoken cockney doggerel. Robert Wyatt, born in Bristol but brought up in the Home Counties, spoke and sang in an eerily blank estuary English that was to prove highly influential. And, of course, Johnny Rotten was borrowing from such curiously English sources as Max Wall and Laurence Olivier's *Richard III*.

'Before I saw the Clash and the Pistols, I tried to sing like Otis Redding,' says Paul Weller of the Jam. 'After them, I decided to sing as naturally as I talked.'

'There was a definite punk agenda,' says Billy Bragg, 'which was to regionalise yourself, to give yourself a sense of place.'

Bragg acknowledges that a London accent forces a singer to approach melody differently. 'You can't sing something like "Tracks of Your Tears" in a London accent,' he says. 'The cadences are all wrong. It's also difficult to sing harmonies in a London accent. And you can't sustain syllables for long: "Greetings to the New Brunette" starts with that sustained "Shirrrr-LEY!" when I sound like a fucking foghorn. You end up with a higher density of words in a song. It's like those early Jam gigs, where Paul Weller seemed like he could hardly get his words out quick enough, as if he was just bursting with the energy of youth.'

'On "London Boys" Bowie sounds like *My Fair Lady*'s Eliza Doolittle before Henry Higgins put paid to her glottal stops.'

Nowadays the exaggerated sense of regionalism that emerged from punk and received a second wind from Britpop has birthed a host of London-accented artists who follow Weller, Bragg and Blur. Every other indie band from within 500 miles of Bow Bells – being born within earshot of the bells of St Mary-le-Bow church being the traditional criteria of cockneydom – are singing in fluent cockney. And a generation of rappers and MCs who eschew Americanisms aren't far behind.

Here are ten of our all-time favourite London songs, from the birth of English rock'n'roll in Soho to Britpop and beyond.

What a Mouth (1960)

Tommy Steele

Long before the Beatles, Tommy Steele was Britain's first pop idol. During the 1950s a strange rule was enforced that meant that American hits had to undergo a six-month period in quarantine before being released in the UK. Steele was one of a number of artists who launched a career by taking advantage of this quirk to record covers of American songs and pilot them to the top of the charts before the originals saw the light of day. 'What a Mouth' in 1960, however, saw Steele abandon this tactic in favour of ersatz-sounding cockney in order to tell the tale of a chap named Jim whose mouth was so large it was mistaken for a coal cellar. This song saw pop being recalibrated to cater to British audiences and it pointed to the future.

London Boys (1967)

David Bowie

Bowie was born David Robert Jones in Brixton, which is where he lived until, at the age of six, he moved with his family to Bromley in Kent (now part of Greater London). Long before he discovered white soul and Berlin, Bowie was hugely influenced by the vocal stylings of cockney crooner Anthony Newley, no more so than in this 1967 B-side, a paean to the original swinging Londoners, popping pills and dressing dandy – and on which Bowie sounds like *My Fair Lady*'s Eliza Doolittle before Henry Higgins put paid to her glottal stops.

Waterloo Sunset (1967)

The Kinks

Ray Davies has written the songbook of London, covering all its corners. 'Lavender Hill' (it's in Clapham, and not as nice as Davies makes it sound) is pure romance; 'Berkeley Mews' (a quiet Marylebone Street) is romance gone wrong; 'Denmark Street' offers a snapshot of the era when this street on the edge of Soho was home to countless music publishers; while the 'Dedicated Follower of Fashion', a swinging London archetype, is sought in Regent Street and Leicester Square. And then, of course, there's 'Waterloo Sunset', perhaps the London song to end all songs. 'I used to go past Waterloo every day on my way to Croydon Art School,' remembers Davies. 'My first real girlfriend, we walked by the Thames; I was in hospital at the old St Thomas' and my room had a balcony looking out over the river. All the imagery comes from memories like that.'

Primrose Hill (1970)

John & Beverly Martyn

This is one of many tracks inspired by London's second-poshest mount. It keeps good company alongside the Beatles' 'Fool on the Hill' (based on a misty morning encounter with a mysterious disappearing man – absolutely nothing to do with drugs), 'Upfield' by Billy Bragg and 'Primrose Hill' by, variously, Loudon Wainwright III, Saint Etienne, Emiliana Torrini and Madness. The husband-and-wife duo's blissed-up sunset folk-out is, on the surface, a simple tale of the everyday joys of coupledom. To everyone else, it best captures the joy of a summer's evening spent lolling around on the hill, getting good and drunk with friends.

London's Burning (1977)

The Clash

When the Clash performed at Islington's Screen on the Green on 29 August 1976, a new song was unveiled: 'London's Burning', written on the streets of London as Joe Strummer paced the city. 'There was nothing to do in those days,' said Strummer. 'Television stopped at 11pm, all bars stopped at 11pm, and that was it. There was only walking around the street to amuse yourself after that. I was walking around a lot in west London, and "London's Burning" came to me all at once.' And then, of course, there's 'London Calling', which holds a place in many listeners minds as a capital classic. It is quite some battle cry, but it hasn't aged too well: in 2006 it sounds earnest, po-faced and not a little bit wet.

Down in the Tube Station at Midnight (1978)

The Jam

In which the narrator gets beaten, presumably to death, by thugs who 'smelled of pubs and Wormwood Scrubs and too many right-wing meetings'. 'It came about in rehearsals, from my bassline,' remembers Bruce Foxton, 'then Paul put these spasmodic guitar stabs across it, and came in with a fantastic lyric. I think he described it as a short television play transposed into a three-minute pop song. The story is self-explanatory, but it has these evocative images that stay with you – the British Rail posters may have long gone, but violence continues today. It's a very graphic lyric, it's frightening as well.' Similarly bleak in its portrayal of late 1970s London ('My head's been kicked in and blood's started to pour') is '"A" Bomb in Wardour Street', with Paul Weller cursing the violence plaguing the punk scene.

A Rainy Night in Soho (1986)

The Pogues

Soho can be a difficult place to negotiate when you're sober. But when you're drunk, it's even worse. The whole area turns into an emotional minefield, with every neon shopfront or clip joint taking on a profound metaphorical significance. If you want to wallow in boozy heartbreak, Soho's the place for you. Which is probably why this waltzing lament makes so much sense to so many people. See also Al Stewart's 'Soho (Needless to Say)', Kirsty MacColl's 'Soho Square' and Jackie Leven's 'Empty in Soho Square'.

London Belongs To Me (1992)

Saint Etienne

'When we got together we'd all just literally moved to London, out of the suburbs into somewhere more central,' says Bob Stanley. 'Me and Pete [Wiggs] had this basement flat off Dartmouth Park Hill [near Highgate], which was really dark. It wasn't grim, but I'm glad we moved out of it. That was what really inspired the song, just the rush of excitement when you first move to London and get a flat of your own. What it makes me think of is walking the length of Parkway; when you get to the end you're in Regent's Park, and there's a path across the road which has willow trees on it – it's mentioned in the lyrics. Around that time, when the band started, I had this temp job at this boring office block on Marylebone Road, where I was doing photocopies all day. I'd walk across the park to get to work, and I really, really wanted to sit down under one of these trees and just spend the day reading. I still get that feeling walking around London now.'

For Tomorrow (1993)

Blur

London seeps from every grimy pore of Blur's *Modern Life is Rubbish*, but never more so than on this opening track. 'It's about being lost on the Westway,' says Damon Albarn. 'It's a romantic thing, it's hopeful. The nicest thing about that song, that I love, is the bit at the end where it goes on about someone going into a flat, and having a cup of tea in Emperor's Gate. That comes from when my parents first moved to London – they had a flat in Emperor's Gate, right next to the Beatles. For the whole of my life I had this image of my parents living next to the Beatles, so Emperor's Gate, to me, is a romantic thing. Then the person in the song gets in a car and drives all the way up to Primrose Hill and says "It's windy here and the view's so nice".' The following year Blur issued *Parklife* (with Walthamstow dog track cover, *see p40*) and Britpop was born, all Union Jack T-shirts and cocky London attitude.

Has It Come To This? (2001)

The Streets

Mike Skinner was born in London and now lives in Brixton – even if in between he was reared in the Midlands. His 2002 debut *Original Pirate Material* (the cover of which portrays Kestrel House on City Road, EC1, *see p40*) was perhaps the first great London album of the new millennium. This is not a romantic London of sunsets over the river (but then few London songs ever are); it's all about chasing girls, downing brandies, smoking weed and scoffing fry-ups. Released on London's leading garage label of the day, Locked On, the then teenage Skinner's drop-out calls to arms re-energised the capital's music. Rather than trying to compete with the glitzy million-dollar R&B bangers coming over from the States, the Streets' refreshingly low-tech marriage of garage beats, dubwise bass and housey samples reflected the mix of music ruling clubland at that time, and still sounds fresh today. The single broke Skinner as a chart artist in 2001 and set the scene for everything that followed, from grime to dubstep to Lily Allen.

Where to Stay

Features

Where to Stay

Japanese pod? Poet's residence? Berber tent? Take your pick.

With the recent publication of *HIP Hotels: London* and a glossy photo volume from art publishers Taschen also dedicated exclusively to places to stay in the UK capital, what's not in doubt is that this is a city in which there's no shortage of stylish lodgings in which to brush the carmine rose petals from your goose-feather pillow and settle beneath sheets of Egyptian cotton. Which is all well and good if you have the cash to spare (although even the boutique hotels often have good value, cut-rate weekend rates). But what's also encouraging is that London's budget to mid-range hotels have recently raised their game, with lots of sprucing and facility upgrades.

For budget cred there's also the impending arrival of **Yotel** (*see p74* **You say hotel, I say Yotel**), from the people behind the conveyor-belt sushi chain Yo!, and the already established **easyHotel** (*see p72*), both of which offer rooms for less than the price of a hot dinner. The **Hoxton Hotel** (*see p70*), the first hospitality venture from the co-founder of the sandwich-shop chain Pret a Manger, no longer offers rooms for just £1 a night as it did in its opening month, but you can get a very stylish double for under £70 at the weekend.

Now that boutique minimalism and flair have filtered down to corporate digs and even the better mid-range properties offer facilities like CD players and robes as standard, the top end has to offer something special. Few of the newer offerings have enough cachet or have shown sufficient imagination to justify their prices, given that the well-established players generally stay on top of their game. The sector remains in thrall to the rise of hotel queen Kit Kemp, whose new **Haymarket Hotel**, set to open in February 2007, is the next big hospitality news story; see the website www.firmdale.com for the latest on progress.

INFORMATION AND BOOKING

Many of London's swankier hotels are found in Mayfair (W1). Bloomsbury (WC1) is good for mid-priced hotels and B&Bs. For cheap hotels, areas to try include Ebury Street near Victoria (SW1), Gower Street in Bloomsbury, Earl's Court (SW5), Bayswater, Paddington (W2) and South Kensington (SW7).

Unfortunately, there's a lot of dross around, so you should steer clear of booking blind. It is always advisable to book ahead, but if you haven't, the obliging staff at **Visit London** (1 Lower Regent Street, Piccadilly Circus, 0870 156 6366, www.visitlondon.com) will look for a place within your selected area and price range for free. You can also check availability and reserve rooms on its website.

> ❶ Green numbers given in this chapter correspond to the location of each hotel as marked on the street maps. *See pp396-409.*

Malmaison. *See p47.*

PRICES AND CLASSIFICATION

We don't list official star ratings, which tend to reflect facilities rather than quality; instead, we've classified hotels within each area heading according to the price of a double room per night, beginning with the most expensive.

Many high-end hotels sneakily quote room prices exclusive of VAT. Always check. We've included this 17.5 per cent tax in rates listed here; however, room rates change frequently, so verify rates before you book. B&Bs excepted, breakfast isn't usually included.

Hotels are constantly offering special deals, particularly for weekends; check websites or ask for a special rate when booking. Also check discount hotel websites – such as www.alpharooms.com or www.london-discount-hotel.com – for prices that can fall well below the rack rates listed here.

FACILITIES AND ACCESSIBILITY

In this chapter, we have listed the main services offered by each hotel but concierges can often arrange far more, including theatre tickets and meal reservations. We have also tried to note which hotels offer rooms adapted for disabled customers, but it's always best to ring ahead to confirm the precise facilities. Tourism For All (0845 124 9971, www.tourismforall.org.uk) has details of wheelchair-accessible places. We've also stated which hotels offer parking facilities, but it's worth enquiring in advance rather than just pitching up in your car: rates can be high and spaces are sometimes limited.

The South Bank & Bankside

Moderate

Southwark Rose

47 Southwark Bridge Road, SE1 9HH (7015 1480/ www.southwarkrosehotel.co.uk). London Bridge tube/rail. **Rates** £175 double; £215 suite. **Credit** AmEx, MC, V. **Map** p406 P8 1

It may sound like a dodgy faux-Tudor guesthouse, but the Southwark Rose (handily placed for Tate Modern, Borough Market and Shakespeare's Globe) is the antithesis: a purpose-built, budget-conscious and very smart property with the elements that have become shorthand for 'modern luxury hotel'. There's a minimalist lobby with leather armchairs and arty photos, the rooms are dressed in regulation sleek, dark wood and crisp white linen, as well as the obligatory mosaic-tiled bathrooms. Good-value suites are equipped with kitchenettes and an extra sofabed. You can use the gym at Novotel next door.

Bar. Disabled-adapted rooms. Internet (high-speed/ wireless). No-smoking rooms. Parking. Restaurant. TV (pay movies).

Cheap

Premier Travel Inn London County Hall

County Hall, Belvedere Road, SE1 7PB (0870 238 3300/www.premiertravelinn.com). Waterloo tube/rail. **Rates** £92 double. **Credit** AmEx, DC, MC, V. **Map** p403 M9 2

A room in a landmark building on the Thames, next to the London Eye, for less than £100? County Hall's former tenant, the Greater London Council, has been gone for over two decades, but the prices at this outpost of the Premier Travel Inn chain are more in line with the 1980s. Just don't expect the opulence of the exterior to carry on inside. Purple walls and modern prints in the lobby don't dispel the airport check-in feel, and the rooms, while modern and clean, have an institutional feel. Don't expect any Thames views either, as they've all been snaffled by the Marriott that shares the vast building.

Bar. Disabled-adapted rooms. Internet (wireless). No-smoking rooms. Restaurant. TV.

Other locations: throughout the city.

The City

Deluxe

Great Eastern Hotel

40 Liverpool Street, EC2M 7QN (7618 5000/www.great-eastern-hotel.co.uk). Liverpool Street tube/rail. **Rates** £265 single; £335-£394 double; £470-£575 suite. **Credit** AmEx, DC, MC, V. **Map** p407 R6 3

Once a faded railway hotel, the Great Eastern was given a £70m overhaul by Sir Terence Conran in 2000. It's now a mammoth urban style mecca, though

Hotels

For budget boutique style

The **Mayflower Hotel** (*see p71*) and **B&B Belgravia** (*see p63*) are cheap and chic, but for a real designer offering at an off the peg price try the **Hoxton Hotel** (*see p70*).

For period drama

Hazlitt's (*see p53*) and the **Rookery** (*see p47*) evoke 18th-century London, while the **Gore** (*see p69*) is a tribute to the Victorian age.

For afternoon tea

The Lanesborough (*see p66*), **Claridge's** (*see p61*) and **The Dorchester** (*see p61*) all put on an impressive spread, but our favourite has to be **Brown's** (*see p60*).

For evening cocktails

Brasserie Max at the Covent Garden Hotel (*see p62*) buzzes, while the **Long Bar** at the Sanderson (*see p48*) has a famous 80-foot bar, but for sheer class try the **Lobby Bar** at One Aldwych (*see p53*).

For a little peace and quiet

Number Sixteen (*see p69*), the **Academy Hotel** (*see p48*) and **Vancouver Studios** (*see p60*) all have with their own gardens, while the aptly-named **Riverside Hotel** (*see p70*) is practically a country inn.

with a design sympathetic to the glorious Victorian building. The lobby is a showcase for modern art and the six-storey atrium is a showstopper, while the gym occupies a mysterious room in the style of an Egyptian temple. Bedrooms wear the regulation style-mag uniform: Eames chairs, chocolate shagpile rugs and white Frette linens. The hotel has seven restaurants and bars, including the Terminus brasserie; Miyabi, the mandatory Japanese joint; the atmospheric George, a faux-Elizabethan pub; and the Modern European Aurora, with its elegant stained-glass dome. Since 2006 the hotel and its restaurants are no longer Conran owned and run: the Great Eastern is now part of the Hyatt group.
Bar. Bar-restaurants (7). Business centre. Concierge. Disabled-adapted rooms. Gym. Internet (dataport/high-speed/wireless). No-smoking floors. Parking. Room service. TV (pay movies/music/DVD).

Expensive

Threadneedles

5 Threadneedle Street, EC2R 8AY (7657 8080/ www.theetoncollection.com). Bank tube/DLR. **Rates** £183-£288 double; £347-£476 suite. **Credit** AmEx, MC, V. **Map** p407 Q6 ❹
Occupying the former HQ of the Midland Bank, Threadneedles successfully integrates modern design with a monumental space (including a gorgeous stained-glass dome over the lobby). Because of the constraints of developing a listed building, rooms aren't uniform shapes and most have original 19th-century windows. The decor is soothingly neutral, with Korres natural toiletries in the serene limestone bathrooms. Little stress-busting comforts reflect its business-friendly location: fleecy throws, a scented candle lit at turndown, a 'movie treats' menu of pop-corn, ice-cream and Coke (albeit at a price that may raise your blood pressure).
Bar. Concierge. Disabled-adapted rooms. Internet (wireless). No-smoking rooms. Restaurants. Room service. TV (music/DVD).

Holborn & Clerkenwell

Expensive

Rookery

12 Peter's Lane, Cowcross Street, EC1M 6DS (7336 0931/www.rookeryhotel.com). Farringdon tube/rail. **Rates** £205 single; £240 double; £465 Rook's Nest suite. **Credit** AmEx, DC, MC, V. **Map** p404 O5 ❺
Tucked down an alleyway just north of Smithfield Market, the Rookery is straight out of a Dickens novel. The 33-room hotel has been converted from a row of 18th-century buildings and, like its sibling Hazlitt's (*see p53*), it is crammed full of glorious antiques: Gothic oak beds, plaster busts and claw-foot bathtubs. But it's equipped with modern creature comforts too: Egyptian cotton sheets and plush towels draped over heated towel racks; broadband internet and LCD TVs. Rooms vary in size but all are characterful. The star attraction is definitely the Rook's Nest, a huge split-level suite with views over the surrounding area, plus a working Edwardian bathing machine. Judging from the guest book, everyone who stays here falls in love with the place.
Bar. Concierge. Disabled-adapted rooms. Internet (dataport/wireless). No-smoking floors. Room service. TV.

Moderate

Malmaison

Charterhouse Square, EC1M 6AH (7012 3700/ www.malmaison.com). Barbican tube/Farringdon tube/rail. **Rates** £195-£215 double; £265-£395 suite. **Credit** AmEx, DC, MC, V. **Map** p404 O5 ❻
It's part of a UK-wide chain that stretches to nine cities but Malmaison London still manages to feel like a one-off. For a start, the location is an absolute dream – overlooking a semi-private, leafy square next door to Smithfield Market, one of the most exciting parts of town, with its terrific array of restaurants and bars. The decor throughout is striking but comfortable (appealing colour schemes, tactile modern fabrics, lovely specially commissioned photos of London), with lots of distinctive touches, such as black bathrobes instead of the traditional white. Instead of ego-massaging luxuries to bump up the rates, you get stuff you need: 24-hour room service, CD players, free broadband access and bottles of French wine. Clientele are predominantly drawn from the hipper end of City business. Over the weekend rates for a standard double drop to a fantastically desirable £125. **Photo** *p47.*
Bar. Disabled-adapted rooms. Gym. Internet (broadband). No-smoking floors. Parking. Restaurant. Room service. TV (DVD).

Zetter

86-88 Clerkenwell Road, EC1M 5RJ (7324 4444/ www.thezetter.com). Farringdon tube/rail. **Rates** £165-£230 double; £265-£329 suites. **Credit** AmEx, MC, V. **Map** p404 O4 ❼
True to its trendy Clerkenwell location, the Zetter is a bone fide loft hotel in a converted Victorian warehouse, with a soaring atrium, exposed brick and funky 1970s furniture. There's a refreshing lack of attitude – the place is comfortable and fun. Instead of minibars, vending machines in the corridors dispense everything from dental kits to champagne. Rooms are sleek and functional but cosied up with homely comforts like hot-water bottles and old Penguin paperbacks, while walk-in Raindance showers are stocked with Elemis products. The top-floor suites have great rooftop views. Prices beat anything in the West End hands down, and if you don't fancy the buzzing modern Mediterranean house restaurant and bar, the area has a wealth of excellent eating and drinking spots.
Bar. Concierge. Disabled-adapted rooms. Internet (dataport/high-speed/web TV/wireless). No-smoking floors. Restaurant. Room service. TV (pay movies/ music/DVD).

Bloomsbury & Fitzrovia

Deluxe

Sanderson

50 Berners Street, W1T 3NG (7300 1400/ www.morganshotelgroup.com). Oxford Circus tube. **Rates** £310-£500 double; £658 loft studio. **Credit** AmEx, DC, MC, V. **Map** p408 V1 8

Despite looking, from the outside, like a bland 1960s office block, the Sanderson (opened in 2000) is still one of the city's most stylish hotels. A Schrager/ Starck creation, the hotel's sleek design verges on the surreal, starting at the lobby, with its sheer flowing curtains and Salvador Dalí red-lips sofa. The campery continues as you take the purple lift up to the generously sized guest rooms with their silver-leaf sleigh beds, piled high with cushions, and super-modern glassed-in bathroom areas with powerful steam showers and beautiful stand-alone baths. When it's time to mingle, you can slip downstairs to join the A-listers who hang out in the Long Bar and restaurant. Room prices may be out of most people's league, but this is one slick and sexy operation.

Bars (2). Business services. Concierge. Disabled-adapted rooms. Gym. Internet (dataport/wireless). No-smoking floors. Restaurant. Room service. Spa. TV (DVD).

Expensive

Charlotte Street Hotel

15-17 Charlotte Street, W1T 1RJ (7806 2000/ www.firmdale.com). Goodge Street or Tottenham Court Road tube. **Rates** £230 single; £241-£335 double; £400-£1,116 suite. **Credit** AmEx, DC, MC, V. **Map** p400 J5 9

Designer Kit Kemp, doyenne of the city's boutique hotels, pioneered the 'modern English' decorative style sweeping London. This gorgeous hotel – one of seven in Kemp's Firmdale mini-chain – is a fine exponent, fusing traditional English furnishings with avant-garde art. True to the locale, public rooms are adorned with Bloomsbury paintings, by the likes of Duncan Grant and Vanessa Bell. Bedrooms mix English understatement with bold flourishes: soft beiges and greys spiced up with plaid-floral combinations. The huge, ridiculously comfortable beds and trademark Firmdale polished granite and oak bathrooms are wonderfully indulgent. The Oscar restaurant and bar are classy, always busy with a smart crowd from the area's many media and advertising offices. Visit on a Sunday night and you can combine a three-course set meal with a screening of a classic film in the mini-cinema (booking advisable).

Bar. Concierge. Disabled-adapted room. Gym. Internet (high-speed/wireless). No-smoking rooms. Restaurant. Room service. TV (DVD).

myhotel bloomsbury

11-13 Bayley Street, WC1B 3HD (7667 6000/ www.myhotels.co.uk). Goodge Street or Tottenham Court Road tube. **Rates** £205 single; £235-£265 double; £355 suite; myspace £500-£700. **Credit** AmEx, DC, MC, V. **Map** p401 K5 10

Back in 1999 this sleek Conran-designed hotel introduced London to Asian fusion decor and feng shui principles. The aquarium (complete with odd number of fish) and floral arrangements continue to lend the lobby a bit of Zen, and crystals and scented candles are still placed strategically throughout the hotel. Rooms are a stark black (furniture) and white (walls and bed coverings), exoticised with Buddha heads and South-east Asian furnishings, and accessorised with plasma screens, CD players and Aveda products in the bathrooms. Top-floor myspace (*see p52* **Suite talk**) is a self-contained apartment and studio with access to a private rooftop terrace with wonderful views. There's a lovely chilled basement library and a buzzy street-level bar. The adjoining Yo! Sushi restaurant fits nicely with the hotel's East-meets-West theme. The website sometimes offers weekend rates as low as £125. **Photo** *p49.*

Bar. Concierge. Gym. Internet (dataport/wireless). No-smoking floors. Restaurant. Room service. TV (pay movies/DVD).

Moderate

Academy Hotel

21 Gower Street, WC1E 6HG (7631 4115/www.the etoncollection.com). Goodge Street tube. **Rates** £147 single; £170 double; £220 suite. **Credit** AmEx, DC, MC, V. **Map** p401 K5 11

Comprising five Georgian townhouses, the Academy has a tastefully restrained country-house style – most rooms are done up in soft, summery florals and checks, although eight suites have recently been recast in more sophisticated solid colour schemes. Guests are effectively cocooned from busy Bloomsbury – both conservatory and library open on to fragrant walled gardens, where drinks and breakfast are served in summer, and windows are double-glazed to keep out the noise. Great location for the British Museum too.

Bar. Internet (dataport/wireless). No-smoking rooms. Room service. TV.

Harlingford Hotel

61-63 Cartwright Gardens, WC1H 9EL (7387 1551/www.harlingfordhotel.com). Russell Square tube/Euston tube/rail. **Rates** £79 single; £99 double; £110 triple; £115 quad. **Credit** AmEx, MC, V. **Map** p401 L4 12

On the corner of a Georgian crescent lined with cheap hotels, the Harlingford is a stylish trailblazer in this Bloomsbury B&B enclave. The tasteful guests' lounge, scattered with trendy light fittings and modern prints, almost makes you forget this is a budget hotel. But while staff are eager to please, don't expect a porter to carry your bags upstairs, and do turn a blind eye to the odd suitcase scuff on the paintwork. An adjacent garden and tennis court are available to guests.

TV.

myhotel bloomsbury. *See p48.*

Jenkins Hotel

45 Cartwright Gardens, WC1H 9EH (7387 2067/ www.jenkinshotel.demon.co.uk). Russell Square tube/ Euston tube/rail. **Rates** £72 single; £85 double; £105 triple. **Credit** MC, V. **Map** p401 K3 ⑬

In the centre of the same sweeping crescent as the Harlingford (*see p48*), the Jenkins is more traditional – once inside, you could be in a Sussex village guest-house. It has been a hotel since the 1920s, so it's fitting that an episode of Agatha Christie's *Poirot* was filmed in room nine. But don't expect a period look – just tidy, freshly painted en suite rooms with pretty bedspreads, crisp, patterned curtains and a small fridge. Guests have access to a tennis court.

No smoking. TV.

Morgan Hotel

24 Bloomsbury Street, WC1B 3QJ (7636 3735/ www.morganhotel.co.uk). Tottenham Court Road tube. **Rates** £75 single; £95 double; £120 triple. *Flat* £110 1 person; £130 2 people; £160 3 people. **Credit** MC, V. **Map** p401 K5 ⑭

Imagine *EastEnders* transplanted to Bloomsbury. The three Shoreditch-bred Ward siblings have been running this cheap and cheerful hotel since the 1970s, and they're satisfied the upkeep is done well, because they do it themselves. While the place has no aspirations to boutique status, the air-conditioned rooms have extras beyond basic B&B standard: modern headboards with handy inbuilt reading lamps, smart brocade drapes, new bathrooms with granite sinks and – as in the top hotels – a phone by the loo. The cosy, panelled breakfast room, with its framed London memorabilia, is the perfect setting for a 'full English'. The hotel's annexe of spacious flats, equipped with stainless-steel kitchenettes, is one of London's best deals.

No smoking. TV.

Cheap

Arosfa

83 Gower Street, WC1E 6HJ (tel/fax 7636 2115/ www.arosfalondon.com). Goodge Street tube. **Rates** £50 single; £75 double; £88 triple. **Credit** MC, V. **Map** p401 K4 ⑮

Arosfa means 'place to stay' in Welsh, but we reckon this townhouse B&B sells itself short. Yes, the accommodation is fairly spartan, but it's spotless, and all the rooms have en suite shower/WC (albeit tiny). It has a great location – in the heart of Bloomsbury, opposite a huge Waterstone's – and a pleasing walled garden. Broadband internet is available on a shared terminal in the lounge, with wireless access due to be set up as we went to press.

No smoking. TV.

Ashlee House

261-265 Gray's Inn Road, WC1X 8QT (7833 9400/ www.ashleehouse.co.uk). King's Cross tube/rail. **Rates** (per person) £35-£37 single; £23-£25 twin; £21-£23 triple; £9-£22 dorm. **Credit** MC, V. **Map** p401 L3 ⑯

Ashlee House is that rarest of rare beasts: a youth hostel with some panache. The funky lobby is decorated with sheepskin-covered sofas and has wallpaper that is digitally printed with London scenes. The rooms are more basic: each one contains between 2 and 16 beds (there are a total of 170 beds in all) plus a sink and little else besides. But there is a large communal kitchen where a free breakfast is served (a £5 deposit gets you a crockery and cutlery set if you want to do your own cooking), as well as a TV room with nightly film screenings and an Xbox, internet stations, luggage storage, laundry and a payphone. There's no curfew, but the partying doesn't seem quite so relentless as at rival the Generator (*see below*). Early in 2007 the owners will also be opening what promises to be an exceptional new hostel in a former courthouse just up the road: see the Ashlee House website for details.

Internet. Laundry. No smoking. TV.

Generator

37 Tavistock Place, WC1H 9SE (7388 7666/ www.generatorhostels.com). Russell Square tube. **Rates** (per person) £35-£56 single; £25-£28 twin; £17-£23 multi; £12.50-£50 dormitory. **Credit** MC, V. **Map** p401 L4 ⑰

In the cafeteria of the Generator there are posters that advertise drinking contests and breakfast menus entitled 'the Big Hangover Cure'; on the noticeboard you'll see Polaroids of people mooning. Like a London version of a Club 18-30 holiday (strictly no under-18s allowed here), this place is party central for the backpacker brigade. It's got an 'MTV industrial' look: plenty of steel surfaces, exposed pipes and neon signs. There's no curfew, of course, and the massive bar hosts karaoke nights and happy hours galore. There's also a movie lounge. When you've managed to sober up, there's practical stuff: a travel agent, a shop, an internet room, a kitchen and multilingual staff. Oh, we almost forgot – there are beds too, 837 of them, should you ever want to sleep.

Bar.

St Margaret's Hotel

26 Bedford Place, WC1B 5JL (7636 4277/www. stmargaretshotel.co.uk). Holborn or Russell Square tube. **Rates** £55.50-£78 single; £67.50-£103.50 double; £92.50-£125.50 triple. **Credit** MC, V. **Map** p401 L5 ⑱

This sprawling townhouse hotel has 64 rooms, but retains its comfortable feel and welcoming ambience thanks to the Marazzi family, who have run it for the best part of six decades. The rooms are simple, comfy and relatively spacious, with the huge triples being especially good for families. Costs are kept down with shared, scrupulously clean bathrooms (only a dozen are en suite), and cooked breakfasts are served in an old-fashioned chandeliered dining room. Rear rooms have views of two gardens: the Duke of Bedford's formal affair and the hotel's own little green patch.

No smoking. TV.

Suite talk

Sometimes the Holiday Inn just doesn't cut it. It's your honeymoon, an anniversary, his or her birthday... a Lottery win, even. So which are the hotel rooms with the biggest wow factor, the places that can set the scene for the best night money can buy? If money is no object, there are suites at Claridge's that tip the £5,000 a night mark. But excess doesn't have to be only about the green folding stuff. Room 16, for instance, at the far more modestly priced **Portobello Hotel** (*see p59*), has a round bed and a Victorian clawfoot bath in the middle of the room that Johnny Depp allegedly filled with champagne for Kate Moss.

If sharing a mattress with a screen icon (albeit months or years after they slept on it) pushes your buttons, the **Covent Garden Hotel** (*see below*) is where Scarlett Johansson was resident for several months during the filming of *Match Point*. The most luscious room is the Loft Suite (from £950), which has a mezzanine bed space – it's where Liv Tyler always stays. We also like room 110, which has windows on facing walls and so gets flooded with natural light during the day. The **Gore** (*see p69*) offers the chance to sleep in Judy Garland's old bed – adding to the campery, the suite's bathroom has original hand-painted tiles depicting a chariot pulled by winged horses.

Hazlitt's (*see p53*) has a wonderful period piece in its stately Baron Willoughby suite (£300), where the sitting room is graced by original 18th-century Jacobean panelling. We actually prefer the attic rooms, though, with their sloping ceilings (and floors!) and Mary Poppins-esque views across the Soho rooftops. There are more wonderful rooftop views at **myhotel bloomsbury**'s myplace (*see p48*), which is a beautiful studio apartment (£500) with its own roof terrace.

If size matters, the royal suites at **Brown's** (*see p60*) have bedrooms and adjacent reception rooms that even past guests such as Napoleon III must have looked at with envy. The bathtubs are big enough to accommodate several soapy bodies at a time and showers are designed for sharing, with two independent shower heads (two heads, of course, always being better than one).

Capitalising on its connections with French Impressionist Claude Monet, the **Savoy** (*see p53*) offers guests the opportunity to stay in one of the suites in which he painted and create their own interpretation of his views. Art materials are provided, as is tuition from painter and retired art-school lecturer Neil Meacher. For the full two-day package, guests are wined and dined, and get a guided tour of Impressionist paintings at the National Gallery – but you'll pay £2,600 for the experience.

Covent Garden & the Strand

Deluxe

Covent Garden Hotel

10 Monmouth Street, WC2H 9LF (7806 1000/www.firmdale.com). Covent Garden or Leicester Square tube. **Rates** £260 single; £310-£364 double; £412-£1,116 suite. **Credit** AmEx, MC, V. **Map** p409 X2 ⑲

Of all Kit Kemp's gilt-edged portfolio of hotels, the Covent Garden remains most people's favourite. It's snug and it's stylish, and its location on London's sexiest street ensures that it continues to attract far more than its fair share of starry customers. The ground-floor Brasserie Max with its retro zinc bar buzzes like Paris did in the 1920s, although guests who are looking for a bit of privacy have the option of retreating upstairs to the panelled private library or drawing room. In the guest rooms Kemp's distinctive modern English style mixes traditional touches – pinstriped wallpaper, pristine white quilts, floral upholstery – with bold, contemporary elements. Each room is unique but all of them have two Kemp trademarks: upholstered mannequins

and shiny granite and oak bathrooms. The loft suites have high ceilings and exposed beams, while one of the rooms boasts what surely must be London's biggest four-poster.
Bar. Business centre. Concierge. Disabled-adapted rooms. Gym. Internet (dataport). No-smoking rooms. Parking. Restaurant. Room service. TV (DVD).

One Aldwych

1 Aldwych, WC2B 4RH (7300 1000/www.onealdwych.com). Covent Garden/Temple tube/Charing Cross tube/rail. **Rates** £258-£400 single; £258-£423 double; £558-£1,286 suite. **Credit** AmEx, DC, MC, V. **Map** p409 Z3 ⑳

Despite weighty history – the 1907 building is by the architects responsible for the Ritz and was later the HQ of the *Morning Post* – One Aldwych is a thoroughly modern hotel. And a luxury one at that. The beautiful Lobby Bar (as adept at cappuccinos as Caipirinhas) sets the tone, with its dramatic artworks and stunning flower arrangements. Upstairs, everything from the Frette linen, B&B Italia chairs and Bang & Olufsen sound systems in the bedrooms to the environmentally friendly loo-flushing system and chemical-free REN toiletries in the bathrooms has been chosen with care. Flowers and fruit are replenished daily and a card detailing the following day's weather forecast appears at turndown. The location is perfect for Theatreland, but when it comes to dining and entertainment you'll be looking for excuses to avoid setting foot outside: the hotel's intimate screening room has good-value dinner and a movie packages, Axis restaurant serves upmarket Modern Euro fare, while Indigo showcases local seasonal produce. It's worth finding time (and money) for a massage and there's also a gym, a steam room and a swimming pool where classical music provides the soundtrack to accompany your laps.
Bars (2). Business services. Coffee shop. Concierge. Disabled-adapted rooms. Gym. Internet (dataport/wireless). No-smoking floors. Parking. Pool (1 indoor). Restaurants (2). Room service. Spa. TV (pay movies/DVD).

The Savoy

Strand, WC2R 0EU (7836 4343/www.fairmont.com). Covent Garden or Embankment tube/Charing Cross tube/rail. **Rates** £300-£500 double; £546-£1,821 suite. **Credit** AmEx, DC, MC, V. **Map** p409 Z4 ㉑

Built in 1889 to put up theatre-goers from Richard D'Oyly Carte's Gilbert & Sullivan shows next door, the Savoy is London's original grande dame. And what a legacy. Monet painted the river from his room; Noël Coward played in the Thames Foyer; and Vivien Leigh met Laurence Olivier in the Savoy Grill. More importantly, a bartender introduced Londoners to the Martini at the (recently revamped) American Bar. Less ostentatious than the Ritz, the Savoy mixes neo-classical, art deco and gentlemen's club aesthetics. Choose a traditional English or art deco bedroom: all have watering-can showerheads and the latest technology such as internet access. The rooftop gym, with a small pool, is another asset. The hotel has undergone some changes in the past few years: the legendary Savoy Grill was revamped and Banquette, a chi-chi homage to the 1950s American diner, was introduced. Since the property was bought by Fairmont Hotels in 2005, more changes have been wrought, notably the creation of two new signature suites, the Royal Opera House Suite and the Monet Suite (*see p52* **Suite talk**).
Bars (3). Business centre. Concierge. Disabled-adapted rooms. Gym. Internet (dataport/wireless). No-smoking rooms. Pool (1 indoor). Restaurants (3). Spa. TV (pay movies/DVD).

St Martins Lane Hotel

45 St Martin's Lane, WC2N 4HX (7300 5500/ reservations 0800 634 5500/7300 5500/www.morganshotelgroup.com). Leicester Square tube/Charing Cross tube/rail. **Rates** £305-£350 single; £375-£600 double; £1,410-£1,645 penthouse. **Credit** AmEx, DC, MC, V. **Map** p409 X4 ㉒

When it opened in 2000 as a Schrager property, the St Martins was the toast of the town. The flamboyant lobby was always buzzing; the Light Bar was filled with celebrities, and guests giggled at Philippe Starck's playful decor. The novelty has worn off but it remains a bolthole for high-profile guests seeking a high-profile refuge. Although Starck objects – such as the gold tooth stools in the lobby – have become positively mainstream and the space lacks the impact of its heyday, the all-white bedrooms have comfortable minimalism down to a T, with floor-to-ceiling windows, soft throws, gadgetry secreted in sculptural cabinets and modern free-standing tubs in the limestone bathrooms. Asia de Cuba, the only survivor of the hotel's three original eateries, remains consistently excellent.
Bar. Business services. Concierge. Disabled-adapted rooms. Gym. Internet (dataport/high-speed). No-smoking rooms. Parking. Restaurant. Room service. TV (pay movies/DVD).

Soho & Leicester Square

Expensive

Hazlitt's

6 Frith Street, W1D 3JA (7434 1771/www.hazlittshotel.com). Tottenham Court Road tube. **Rates** £205 single; £240-£298 double; £350 suite. **Credit** AmEx, DC, MC, V. **Map** p408 W2 ㉓

This idiosyncratic Georgian townhouse hotel is named after William Hazlitt; friend of Wordsworth, Shelley and Byron, the 18th-century essayist died here. The place maintains an impressive literary pedigree: it was immortalised in Bill Bryson's *Notes from a Small Island* and the library contains signed first editions from such guests as Ted Hughes and JK Rowling. Rooms are as true to period as possible, with fireplaces, carefully researched colour schemes, massive carved wooden beds and clawfoot bathtubs. It gets creakier and more crooked the higher you go, culminating in some enchanting garret rooms with rooftop views. But don't worry, you don't have to

sacrifice 21st-century comforts: air-conditioning, web TV hidden in antique cupboards and triple-glazed windows come as standard. There's no house restaurant or bar but then you've got the whole of Soho just outside the front door.
Business services. Concierge. Internet (dataport/wireless). No-smoking floors. Room service. TV (pay movies/DVD).

Soho Hotel

4 Richmond Mews (off Dean Street), W1D 3DH (7559 3000/www.firmdale.com). Tottenham Court Road tube. **Rates** £282-£346 double; £411-£2,937 suite. Phone for details of the apartment. **Credit** AmEx, DC, MC, V. **Map** p408 W2 24

All eyes might now be on Kit Kemp's upcoming venture the Haymarket, but we're actually still feeling quite dazzled by her 2004 shot at urban hip. Located in the heart of Soho – not that you'd know it once you're inside, it's completely silent – this is her most edgy creation yet. Critics say Kemp brings the country house to the city. Yet the savvy aesthetic here is a very long way indeed from the shires. The new red-brick structure – formerly a multi-storey car park – resembles a converted loft building. Bedrooms exhibit a contemporary edge, with modern furniture, industrial-style windows and all mod cons (Tivoli PAL digital radios, flatscreen TVs), although they're also classically Kemp with bold pinstripes, traditional florals, plump sofas and oversized bedheads. Public spaces feature groovy colours – shocking pinks and acid greens – while Refuel, the predictably pricey loungey bar and restaurant, has an open kitchen and a car-themed mural. It's all very cool, but also thoroughly calming and comfortable.
Bar. Business services. Concierge. Disabled-adapted rooms. Gym. Internet (dataport/high-speed/wireless). No-smoking rooms. Room service. TV (widescreen/DVD).

Cheap

Piccadilly Backpackers

12 Sherwood Street, W1F 7BR (7434 9009/www.piccadillybackpackers.com). Piccadilly Circus tube. **Rates** (per person) £39-£42 single; £29-£32 double; £21-£24 pod; £12-£22 dorms. **Credit** AmEx, MC, V. **Map** p408 V4 25

Piccadilly Backpackers has two great things going for it: impressive rates (from £12 per night) and a terrific location. The accommodation is basic, although graphic art students have painted the rooms on the third floor in an attempt to perk things up a little. Ten rooms feature 'pods' – six beds arranged three up, three down, in pigeonhole fashion. Should you get bored of sightseeing, slob out in the common room, where you can surf 100 channels on the widescreen TV, or get online in the 24-hour internet café. There's also a travel shop and a backpackers' bar a few minutes' walk away (4 Golden Square, 7287 9241).
Disabled-adapted rooms. Laundry. No smoking.

Oxford Street & Marylebone

Expensive

Cumberland

Great Cumberland Place, W1A 4RF (0870 333 9280/www.guoman.com). Marble Arch tube. **Rates** £140-£370 single; £160-£389 double; £340-£458 suite. **Credit** AmEx, DC, MC, V. **Map** p397 F6 26

The sheer scale of this hotel takes your breath. It has 900 rooms (plus another 119 in an annexe down the road) and the echoey lobby, with its arresting, large-scale artworks and panels that change colour through the day, looks like a cross between an airport and a wing of Tate Modern. Rooms are minimalist, with designer bathrooms, huge plasma TVs and a cotton kimono in a mesh zip bag rather than a fluffy robe – however, they're very small. The hotel's Modern British dining room is run by celeb chef Gary Rhodes (*see p207*), with a high-end restaurant, also by Rhodes, due by the end of 2006.
Bars (2). Concierge. Gym. Internet (dataport/high-speed). Restaurants (2). Room service. TV.

Moderate

Montagu Place

2 Montagu Place, W1H 2ER (7467 2778/www.montagu-place.co.uk). Baker Street tube. **Rates** £129-£169 double. **Credit** AmEx, DC, MC, V. **Map** p400 G5 27

Newly opened in summer 2006, the Montagu is a stylish, small hotel in a Grade II-listed Georgian townhouse. Catering primarily for the midweek

Piccadilly Backpackers.

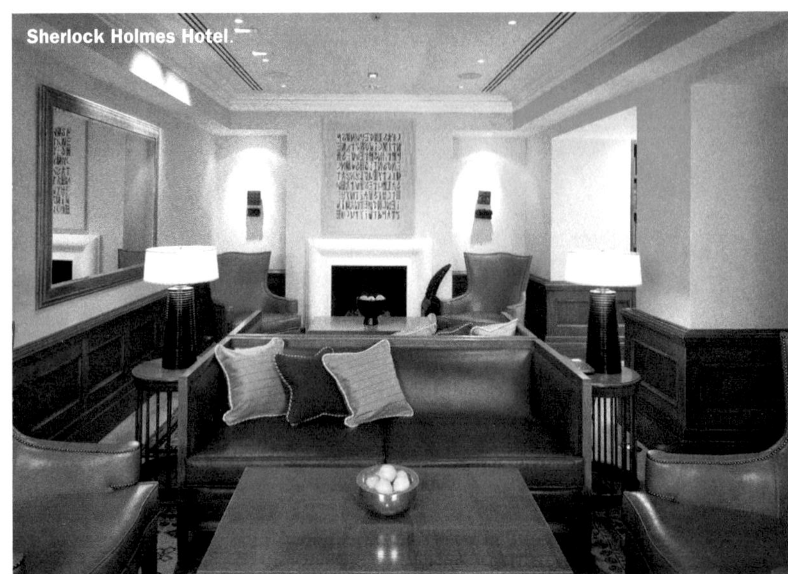
Sherlock Holmes Hotel.

business traveller, its 16 rooms are divided into Comfy, Fancy and Swanky categories, the difference being size – Swanky are the largest, with enormous bathrooms, while Comfy are smallest and at the back of the building with no street views. All rooms have deluxe pocket-sprung beds (queen-size in the smaller rooms, king-size in the two larger categories), as well as cafetières with freshly ground coffee and flatscreen TVs (DVD players are available from reception). The look is boutique-hotel sharp, except in the bar area, which shares space with reception – a mean arrangement that undermines what is otherwise an affordably classy affair.
Bar. TV (widescreen/DVD).

Sherlock Holmes Hotel

108 Baker Street, W1U 6LJ (7486 6161/www.sherlockholmeshotel.com). Baker Street tube. **Rates** (incl breakfast at weekends) £116-£220 double; £450 suite. **Credit** AmEx, DC, MC, V. **Map** p400 G5 ㉘

How do you transform a dreary, chintz-filled Hilton into a hip boutique hotel? It's elementary: hype up the Baker Street address, banish the bland decor and create a sleek lobby bar. That's what the Park Plaza chain did when it snapped up the Sherlock Holmes a few years ago. Guests can mingle with local office workers in the casually chic bar or retreat to the residents-only lounge, which looks like a glossed-up gentlemen's club. The rooms, meanwhile, resemble hip bachelor pads: beige and brown colour scheme, leather headboards, pinstripe scatter cushions and spiffy bathrooms. Split-level 'loft' suites make innovative use of the first floor's double-height ceilings. There's a decent gym with sauna, steam rooms and beauty treatments, and the inevitable memorabilia ranges from expressionist paintings of Holmes and Watson in Sherlock's Grill to magnifying glasses.
Bar. Business centre. Concierge. Disabled-adapted rooms. Gym. Internet (broadband/dataport/wireless). No-smoking rooms. Restaurant. Room service. TV (pay movies).

The Sumner

54 Upper Berkeley Street, W1H 7QR (7723 2244/www.thesumner.com). Marble Arch tube. **Rates** (incl breakfast) £135-£170 double. **Credit** AmEx, DC, MC, V. **Map** p397 F6 ㉙

The end of its lease forced the team behind the highly regarded Five Sumner Place to relocate to this fine old Georgian townhouse just off the Edgware Road and around the corner from Marble Arch, Oxford Street and Hyde Park. Top interior designers have gone to work on the ground-floor public spaces, which are cool and Nordic in shades of slate and grey. Depending on your predilections the results are either hip and minimal or reminiscent of a Harley Street surgery waiting room. The 20 bedrooms are entirely different in feel, being much more like home, although the deluxe options feature custom-designed Ligne Roset furniture. Room sizes vary but are generally spacious, and those at the front are bathed in natural daylight from large (triple-glazed) windows.
Disabled access. Internet (wireless). TV (widescreen).

22 York Street

22-24 York Street, W1U 6PX (7224 2990/www.22yorkstreet.co.uk). Baker Street tube. **Rates** £89 single; £100-£120 double; £141 triple; £188 quad. **Credit** AmEx, MC, V. **Map** p400 G5 ㉚

There's no sign on the door; people usually discover Liz and Michael Callis's immaculately kept B&B by word of mouth. Unpretentious and comfortable, it's perfect for those who loathe hotels and are uncomfortable in designer interiors. The rooms in these two graceful neighbouring Georgian townhouses may not be *Wallpaper** material but they are subtly tasteful, with wooden floorboards, antique pieces and French quilts. Most are en suite; all have an exclusively allocated bathroom. Breakfast is an occasion, served at a huge, curving wooden table in the traditional kitchen, and there's a computer room in the basement with free internet access. It's three minutes' walk to Regent's Park and the shops and restaurants of Marylebone.
Internet (wireless). TV.

Cheap

Weardowney Guesthouse

9 Ashbridge Street, NW8 8DH (7725 9694/ guesthouse@weardowney.com). Marylebone tube/ rail. **Rates** £55-£64 single/double. **Credit** AmEx, DC, MC, V. **Map** p397 E4 ㉛

Amy Wear and Gail Downey are fashion models turned successful knitwear designers. The two recently moved out of the house they'd shared for ten years above their own-label getUp boutique and opened it to paying guests. There are just seven rooms, all of which have either a double bed or twins; only two rooms are en suite, the others share two rooms to one bathroom. Rooms are adorned with hand-knitted throws and curtains, and with prints, art and B&Ws from the pair's creative associates. Guests are free to make use of the downstairs kitchen. It's very cosy and attractive, but a long way from the sort of luxury and comforts you'd expect at a hotel: it really does feel like you're staying over at a friend's house. Lodgers tend to be fellow models, designers and others from the fashion industry. Busy Church Street and Alfies Antique Market are just around the corner and the boutique shopping of Marylebone High Street is ten minutes' walk away.

Paddington & Notting Hill

Deluxe

Hempel

31-35 Craven Hill Gardens, W2 3EA (7298 9000/ www.the-hempel.co.uk). Lancaster Gate or Queensway tube/Paddington tube/rail. **Rates** £346 single/double; £564-£1,580 suite. **Credit** AmEx, DC, MC, V. **Map** p396 C6 ㉜

While pure minimalism may well have been consigned to interior design history, you can't deny the impact of Anouska Hempel's blinding white spaces. The hotel's pristine, Japanesey bedrooms (which look remarkably fresh after more than a decade) exemplify the finest deployment of feng shui principles and they're not as clinical as you might imagine, with touches of oatmeal linen, tactile faux fur and suede. One of the dreamy suites has a bed that hangs from the ceiling. The Hempel was sold in spring 2005 but the new owners have yet to stray far from the original vision.
Bar. Business services. Concierge. Disabled-adapted rooms. Internet (dataport/high-speed/wireless). No-smoking rooms. Restaurant. Room service. TV (pay movies/music/DVD).

Weardowney Guesthouse.

Johnny with Kate, Alice with snake – everyone stays at the **Portobello Hotel**. *See p59.*

Expensive

Guesthouse West

163-165 Westbourne Grove, W11 2RS (7792 9800/ www.guesthousewest.com). Notting Hill Gate tube. **Rates** £176 single/double; £205 terrace. **Credit** AmEx, MC, V. **Map** p396 B6 33

Guesthouse West aims to offer a stylish, affordable antidote to exorbitant hotels by cutting out expensive luxuries such as room service and offering a handy list of local businesses to use. As it's located in the middle of one of London's chicest neighbourhoods, those local businesses are the cat's (designer) pyjamas. The look is pure Notting Hillbilly hip: the retro lobby bar features a changing art display and the front terrace is just made for posing (although the latter is only licensed to serve until 8pm). Minimalist bedrooms have just enough extras to keep hip young things happy: wireless internet access, flatscreen TVs and toiletries from REN.

Bar. Internet (high-speed/wireless). No-smoking rooms. Restaurant. TV (pay movies/music/DVD).

The Lennox

34 Pembridge Gardens, W2 4DX (7229 9977/ www.pemct.co.uk). Notting Hill Gate tube. **Rates** £125-£165 single; £160-£195 double. **Credit** AmEx, DC, MC, V. **Map** p396 A7 34

What do Iggy Pop and this chintz-furnished townhouse hotel have in common? Surprisingly, his band has often put up here in the past, along with numerous other music-biz people, plus the likes of Liz Hurley, Minnie Driver and Paul Gascoigne. Bedrooms are fairly standard traditional English affairs, with walls jazzed up by framed pieces from nearby Portobello Market: Victorian fans, Edwardian christening robes, old school blazers – even a beautiful beaded flapper dress in one room. As we went to press, there was a change of management and name (from the Pembridge Court); phone to check for major changes.

Bar. Business services. Internet (dataport). Parking. Room service. TV (VCR).

Miller's Residence

111A Westbourne Grove, W2 4UW (7243 1024/ www.millersuk.com). Bayswater or Notting Hill Gate tube. **Rates** £150-£230 double/suite. **Credit** AmEx, MC, V. **Map** p396 B6 35

Owned by antiques expert Martin Miller, who set up Miller's Antiques price guides back in the 1960s, this is a one-off. Behind an unmarked door in an unprepossessing side street is a slightly decadent cross between a baronial family pile and a Portobello arcade. Rooms, named after 19th-century poets (Shelley, Wordsworth, Keats et al), are furnished with Miller's finds – some with dramatic four-posters – but balanced out with 21st-century perks such as air-conditioning and DVD players. The drawing room is an Aladdin's cave of ornate candelabra, clocks and curios, plus the odd eastern artefact. It's even more atmospheric in the evenings, when candles are lit, highly conducive to relaxing by the elaborately carved fireplace with a whisky

from the free bar. There's no restaurant, but you've got plenty of choice right on the doorstep.
Internet (wireless). TV.

New Linden

59 Leinster Square, W2 4PS (7221 4321/www.mayflower-group.co.uk). Bayswater tube. **Rates** £90 single; £120 double; £150 triple; £200 quad. **Credit** AmEx, MC, V. **Map** p396 B6 36

The latest addition to the excellent group comprising the Mayflower Hotel (*see p71*) and Twenty Nevern Square (*see p72*), the New Linden was under renovation as we went to press but when finished it should be as much of a bargain showpiece as its sisters. Completed rooms have white walls, wooden floors and streamlined modern and Eastern furnishings. Marble bathrooms (some with deluge shower heads), flatscreen TVs and CD players come as standard. Some of the suites have balconies and one split-level family room retains elaborate period pillars and cornicing. The location – between Notting Hill and Kensington Gardens – is a big plus.
TV.

Portobello Hotel

22 Stanley Gardens, W11 2NG (7727 2777/www.portobello-hotel.co.uk). Holland Park or Notting Hill Gate tube. **Rates** £135 single; £180-£295 double. **Credit** AmEx, MC, V. **Map** p396 A6 37

For three decades this decadent Notting Hill mansion has been the stuff of rock-star fantasies, and has played host to a starry role call of everyone from Kate Moss to Van Morrison. The spectacular beds range from a Balinese four-poster to a ship's bunk and a couple of seductive oriental affairs that resemble Berber tents. In many rooms the Victorian bathtubs take centre stage, including one with a Victorian 'bathing machine'. Alice Cooper used his tub to house his boa constrictor, which he fed with white mice ordered from the local pet shop. Other themed pleasure pads include the seductive Moroccan Room, strewn with carpets and cushions, and serene Japanese Water Garden Room with an elaborate spa bath, Buddhas and its own private grotto. **Photo** *p58.*
Bar. Internet (dataport/wireless). Restaurant. Room service. TV (free in-house movies).

Cheap

Garden Court Hotel

30-31 Kensington Gardens Square, W2 4BG (7229 2553/www.gardencourthotel.co.uk). Bayswater or Queensway tube. **Rates** £40-£65 single; £62-£95 double; £115-£125 triple; £130-£145 family room. **Credit** MC, V. **Map** p396 B6 38

Run by the same family for more than 50 years, this budget hotel has recently been brought bang up to date. It now has a lift and an airy lounge with wooden floors and brown leather sofas facing the fireplace. It also has a bit of character: a giant antique Beefeater statue stands guard in the lobby, and the cheery bedrooms have modish modern wallpaper. As the name suggests, the hotel has a small walled garden; guests have access to the private square too.
Business services. No smoking. TV.

Pavilion

34-36 Sussex Gardens, W2 1UL (7262 0905/www.pavilionhoteluk.com). Edgware Road tube/Marylebone or Paddington tube/rail. **Rates** £60 single; £85-£100 double; £120 triple. **Credit** AmEx, MC, V. **Map** p397 E5 39

Pavilion.

Where to Stay

Brown's.

In a row of dowdy hotels, the Pavilion is a shining star. Or more like a disco ball. When it comes to decor, this hilariously kitsch B&B has tongue firmly planted in cheek. The themed rooms are a riot: the Highland Fling is a tartan theme park, with plaid bedspreads and stag antlers; Better Red Than Dead is a glam extravaganza of crimson, vermilion and burgundy. Rock stars love the place: a favourite shag pad is Honky Tonk Afro, with its mirror ball, fuzzy dice and heart-shaped mirrored headboards. OK, so the location's not exactly rocking and the bathrooms are small, but there's more personality in this humble budget hotel than in many of the capital's big-name boutiques.
Parking. Room service. TV.

Vancouver Studios

30 Prince's Square, W2 4NJ (7243 1270/www.vancouverstudios.co.uk). Bayswater or Queensway tube. **Rates** £75-£79 single; £99-£110 double; £140-£155 triple. **Credit** AmEx, DC, MC, V. **Map** p396 B6 40
Staying here feels more like renting a small flat than putting up in a hotel. The fresh, unfussy studios are equipped with kitchenettes, flatscreen TVs and DVD players. The sitting room, which guests share with the two resident cats, is cosy and funky, with Mexican upholstery, cacti and an old-fashioned gramophone. It opens on to a lush, walled garden with a gurgling fountain. There are also handy on-site facilities such as a laundry room, and free wireless internet access for laptop-carrying guests.
Internet (dataport/shared terminal/wireless). TV (DVD).

Piccadilly & Mayfair

Deluxe

Brown's

33 Albemarle Street, W1S 4BP (7493 6020/www.roccofortehotels.com). Green Park tube.
Rates £345-£696 double; £895-£3,012 suite.
Credit AmEx, DC, MC, V. **Map** p408 U5 41
Brown's was for a long time the quintessential London hotel, having been opened in 1837 by Lord Byron's butler, James Brown. The first ever telephone call was made from the hotel back in 1876, and five years after that Napoleon III and Empress Eugenie took refuge in one of the hotel's suites after fleeing the Third Republic. Franklin Roosevelt, Haile Selassie and Agatha Christie have all been guests. We're not convinced that they'd recognise the place these days, though. In 2003 the Rocco Forte Hotels collection acquired the hotel and shut the front doors for nearly two years as the place underwent a £19m top-to-toe refurbishment. The public spaces remain as gloriously old English as ever they were, particularly the Tea Room (located off the main lobby) with its original wood panelling, fireplaces and Jacobean plaster ceilings (non-residents can visit for afternoon tea, 3-6pm, £29.50 each). The expanded bar – renamed the Donovan Bar in honour of 1960s snapper Terence Donovan – is sheer class. The bedrooms, however, are less impressive. All 117 have been reconfigured and redecorated but, although they are super-large and extremely comfortable, they lack character.

Bar. Business centre. Concierge. Disabled-adapted rooms. Gym. Internet (high-speed/wireless). Restaurant. Room service. Spa. TV (music/pay movies).

Claridge's

55 Brook Street, W1K 4HR (7629 8860/www.claridges.co.uk). Bond Street tube. **Rates** £257-£480 single; £339-£598 double; £480-£3,230 suite; £5,263 penthouse. **Credit** AmEx, DC, MC, V. **Map** p400 H6 42

A favourite with everyone from A-list actors to presidents, prime ministers and even royalty, Claridge's is synonymous with history and class. The hotel dates back in its present form to 1898 and a signature art deco redesign but, despite the place as whole having remained traditional in feel, its bars and restaurant (that man Gordon Ramsay, *see p211*) are actively fashionable. The rooms divide equally between deco original and Victorian, and while both are luxurious, with period touches like deco loo flushes in the swanky marble bathrooms plus mod cons such as bedside panels controlling everything at the touch of a button, you can't help but wonder if they really justify the prices (especially as we've heard, shock horror, tales of less-than-efficient service). The top suites, for instance, clock in at more than £5,000 a night – could a room, albeit one with several bedrooms, bathrooms and a private terrace – ever really be worth that much money? If you want a slice of history without the need for a second mortgage, pop in for afternoon tea or a drink in one of the bars (the profoundly sexy Macanudo Fumoir is our particular favourite). **Photo** *p64.*

Bars (2). Business services. Concierge. Gym. Internet (dataport/high-speed/wireless). No-smoking rooms. Restaurants (3). Room service. TV (DVD/pay movies).

The Dorchester

53 Park Lane, W1A 2HJ (7629 8888/www.thedorchester.com). Hyde Park Corner tube. **Rates** £411 single; £476-£582 double; £740-£1,763 suite. **Credit** AmEx, DC, MC, V. **Map** p402 G7 43

One of the grandes dames of the London hotel scene, the Dorchester is a perennial favourite with celebs. Despite its opulence – it has the grandest lobby in town, complete with Liberace's piano – staff are down to earth, and there's no hint of fustiness. The hotel continually upgrades older rooms to the same high standard as the rest, with floral (but not chintzy) decor, antiques and lavish marble bathrooms; some boast views of Hyde Park. Similarly, it's all change on the food and drink front: within weeks of opening in late 2005, China Tang was the place to be seen, while the newly refurbed Grill Room (*see p211*) is bound to be as popular as its earlier incarnation. Afternoon tea is justly popular, and the revamped spa affordable even for non-residents.

Bar. Concierge. Disabled-adapted rooms. Gym. Internet (dataport/high-speed/web TV). No-smoking rooms/floors. Parking. Restaurants (3). Room service. Spa. TV (pay movies/music/DVD).

Metropolitan

19 Old Park Lane, W1K 1LB (7447 1000/www.metropolitan.como.bz). Hyde Park Corner tube. **Rates** £382-£558 double; £675-£2,935 suite; £3,290-£3,760 apartment. **Credit** AmEx, DC, MC, V. **Map** p402 H8 44

This modern upstart caused quite a stir when it joined the old guard on Park Lane in 1997. The minimalist rooms were an exciting antidote to ostentatious gilt and chintz, and everyone wanted to gain access to the guests- and members-only Met Bar, which heaved nightly with misbehaving celebs. However, now that modern corporate hotels have appropriated its style – blond wood headboards, creamy soft furnishings, suede scatter cushions, marble bathrooms – it doesn't seem so special. The standard doubles are actually quite small, although the hotel has an upgrade policy when larger ones are available. Still, the rooms have recently been refurbished, so everything is pristine, and you can't beat the views on the park side from the floor-to-ceiling windows. Upstairs, Nobu (*see p212*) is an unchallenged destination dining spot and, should you need some proper pampering, massages are available in the elaborately named COMO Shambhala Urban Escape (really just two nice treatment rooms).
Bar. Business centre. Concierge. Gym. Internet (dataport/high-speed/wireless). No-smoking floors. Parking. Restaurant. Room service. Spa. TV (pay movies/DVD).

The Ritz

150 Piccadilly, W1J 9BR (7493 8181/www.theritzlondon.com). Green Park tube. **Rates** £388 single; £470-£588 double; £705-£1,058 suite. **Credit** AmEx, DC, MC, V. **Map** p402 J8 45

The reputation of this lavish establishment precedes it. After all, it's the only London hotel whose name has spawned an adjective meaning 'ostentatiously luxurious and glamorous'. Founded by hotelier extraordinaire César Ritz, the hotel celebrated its centenary in 2006. The high-ceilinged, Louis XVI-style rooms have been painstakingly renovated to their former glory in a range of restrained pastel colours. Less restrained are the swanky 24-carat gold leaf features and the magnificently heavy curtains. The real show-stopper, however, is the ridiculously ornate, vaulted Long Gallery, an orgy of chandeliers, rococo mirrors and marble columns (jackets are compulsory for gentlemen, naturally, although this rule is lifted for breakfast). The overall atmosphere of the Ritz is one of old-world luxury, but mod cons have thankfully slipped through, including wireless internet, large TVs and a gym. In the event that you can't afford a stay at the Ritz, tours are available and a fine afternoon tea is served in the Palm Court.
Bar. Business centre. Concierge. Gym. Internet (dataport/high-speed/wireless). No-smoking floors. Restaurant. Room service. TV (DVD/VCR).

Expensive

No.5 Maddox Street

5 Maddox Street, W1S 2QD (7647 0200/www.living-rooms.co.uk). Oxford Circus tube. **Rates** £290-£423 double suite; £540 2-bed suite; £728 3-bed suite. **Credit** AmEx, DC, MC, V. **Map** p408 U2 46

Blink and you'll miss the entrance of this discreet bolthole just off Regent Street. It's perfect for those visitors who want to pretend they're Londoners, whether for two nights or two months, because it doesn't look like a hotel. Instead of rooms, accommodation is in chic flats, done up in the East-meets-West style that was all the rage when it opened in the late 1990s: bamboo floors and dark wood furniture mixed with sable throws and the obligatory crisp white sheets. There's no bar, but Soho's nearby and there's Patara, a decent Thai restaurant, on the ground floor. Plus the kitchens are stocked with saintly organic as well as naughty treats (room service will shop for you too), so you can whip up dinner and throw your own party.
Business centre. Concierge. Internet (dataport/high-speed/wireless). No-smoking rooms. Private kitchen. Room service. TV (DVD/music).

Westminster & St James's

Deluxe

Trafalgar

2 Spring Gardens, SW1A 2TS (7870 2900/www.hilton.co.uk/trafalgar). Charing Cross tube/rail. **Rates** £340-£398 single/double; £515 suite. **Credit** AmEx, DC, MC, V. **Map** p409 X5 47

Part of the Hilton group, the Trafalgar is its first 'concept' hotel – in other words, it's dropped the branding in favour of funky designer decor. Although it's housed in one of the imposing edifices on the famous square (the former Cunard HQ, in fact, where the ill-fated Titanic was conceived), the mood inside is young and dynamic. The Rockwell Bar, which serves the largest selection of bourbon in London, has a varied programme: it was recently refurbished in a somewhat incongruous style that melds modern chinoiserie with a dash of Edwardian fringing and a black-and-white colour scheme. The rooms have a masculine feel with minimalist walnut furniture and white or chocolate walls, and the bathtubs are made for sharing with the tap in the middle; full-size aromatherapy-based toiletries are a nice touch. The location is its biggest draw – corner rooms overlook the square and the small rooftop bar has panoramic views.
Bars (2). Concierge. Disabled-adapted rooms. Gym. Internet (dataport). No-smoking floors. Restaurant. Room service. TV (CD/DVD/pay movies/games).

Moderate

B&B Belgravia

64-66 Ebury Street, SW1W 9QD (7823 4928/www.bb-belgravia.com). Victoria tube/rail. **Rates** £94 single; £99 double; £105 twin; £125-£170 family room. **Credit** AmEx, MC, V. **Map** p402 H10 48

Opened in September 2004, this is one of the most attractive B&Bs we've seen. Others have been similarly impressed, with the Belgravia winning a gold award at the Visit London Awards 2005. The black

Claridge's. *See p61.*

and white lounge (leather sofa, arty felt cushions, modern fireplace) could be straight out of *Elle Decoration*. But it's not precious: you'll find a laptop equipped with free internet connection and above it games and stuffed toys to keep the kids entertained, plus a collection of DVDs to watch on the flatscreen TV. There's also a high-tech coffee machine, and guests can take their drinks out to tables in the large back garden. The bedrooms are chic and predominantly white, with flatscreen TVs and sleek bathrooms with power showers.
Disabled-adapted rooms. Internet (high-speed). TV.

Windermere Hotel

142-144 Warwick Way, SW1V 4JE (7834 5163/ www.windermere-hotel.co.uk). Victoria tube/rail. **Rates** £89-£99 single; £114-£139 double; £145-£149 family. **Credit** AmEx, MC, V. **Map** p402 H11 (49)
Minutes from Victoria Station, Warwick Way is lined with small hotels and B&Bs. The Windermere edges ahead of the competition with better than expected facilities (including satellite TV, free internet, power showers and its own restaurant), smart rooms light on the chintz and a hospitable atmosphere coupled with terrific levels of service (11 staff for just 20 rooms). Pick of the rooms is No.31, a top-floor double that gets flooded with light from big windows and offers quintessential London rooftop views. Breakfasts are also excellent (included in room rates) and guests get a discount at the neighbouring municipal car park.
Bar. Business services. Internet (dataport). No-smoking floors. Restaurant. Room service. TV.

Cheap

Morgan House

120 Ebury Street, SW1W 9QQ (7730 2384/www. morganhouse.co.uk). Pimlico tube/Victoria tube/rail. **Rates** £52-£82 single; £72-£92 double; £92-£110 triple; £130 quad. **Credit** MC, V. **Map** p402 G10 (50)
The Morgan is an archetypal small English B&B. The passages are narrow and the rooms small. The decor is more serviceable than striking, with pastel walls, traditional iron or wooden beds and print curtains, although framed prints, fireplaces in most rooms and the odd chandelier lend a gracious air. The top-floor rooms are airy and contemporary, including a family room that sleeps four in bunk beds. There's a pleasant patio garden, where guests can chill on a warm evening with a bottle of wine.
No smoking. TV.

Chelsea

Expensive

Cadogan

75 Sloane Street, SW1X 9SG (7235 7141/www. steinhotels.com/cadogan). Sloane Square tube. **Rates** £288-£323 double; £352-£646 suite. **Credit** AmEx, DC, MC, V. **Map** p399 F10 (51)
Louche secrets lurked behind the doors of this terribly British hotel. Edward VII visited his mistress Lillie Langtry here when it was her private home, and poor old Oscar Wilde was arrested in room 118. In recent years the reception's Edwardian tiles have been restored to their original splendour and the stuffy drawing room, bar and restaurant lightened with contemporary colour schemes. Bedrooms boast leather headboards and rich, couture-inspired fabrics. The signature suites are great fun for history buffs – the Oscar Wilde is dressed in crushed velvet and feather prints, the Lillie Langtry is a period cream and pink confection. Guests are permitted access to the secluded Cadogan Place gardens and tennis courts opposite.
Bar. Business centre. Concierge. Gym. Internet (high-speed/wireless). No-smoking floors. Parking. Restaurant. Room service. TV (DVD/pay movies).

myhotel chelsea

35 Ixworth Place, SW3 3QX (7225 7500/www. myhotels.com). South Kensington tube. **Rates** £176-£242 single; £217-£230 double; £305-£423 suite. **Credit** AmEx, DC, MC, V. **Map** p399 E11 (52)
The South Kensington myhotel is a softer, more feminine incarnation of its Bloomsbury sister (*see p48*). Pink walls, a floral sofa and a plate of scones in the lobby offer a posh English foil to feng shui touches such as an aquarium and carefully placed candles. No doubt this is to appeal to a clientele lured by the proximity of prime shopping territory – Brompton Cross is just steps away, while Harrods is a short stroll. The feminine mood continues in the rooms with dusky pink wallpaper, white wicker headboards and velvet cushions, although it's all fresh and modern. Every room has a 21in TV and DVD player. Chill-out places include the white-panelled, Cape Cod-influenced bar and conservatory-style lounge, and pampering is available courtesy of Aveda in the treatment room.
Bar. Business centre. Concierge. Gym. Internet (dataport/wireless). Restaurant. Room service. Spa. TV (pay movies/DVD).

Knightsbridge & South Kensington

Deluxe

Baglioni

60 Hyde Park Gate, SW7 5BB (7368 5700/www. baglionihotellondon.com). High Street Kensington or Gloucester Road tube. **Rates** £370-£400 single/ double; £530-£2,232 suite. **Credit** AmEx, DC, MC, V. **Map** p396 C9 (53)
For a taste of la dolce vita, the Baglioni is hard to beat, displaying exciting designer style that doesn't dip into theatrical excess. Occupying a Victorian mansion opposite Kensington Palace, it has none of the sniffy formality of some of its deluxe English counterparts. The ground-floor Italian restaurant

and bar are part baroque, part Donatella Versace: spidery black chandeliers, burnished gold ceilings, gigantic vases and a truly magnificent mirror from Venice. The chic bedrooms are more subdued: black floorboards, taupe and gold-leaf walls, dark wood furniture enlivened by jewel-coloured cushions and soft throws. Instead of the usual marble, the swanky black-panelled bathrooms have hammered iron sinks imported from Morocco. Health spa treatments range from a four-step anti-ageing itinerary to Botox. A welcome touch of bling on the boutique scene.
Bar. Business centre. Concierge. Disabled-adapted rooms. Gym. Internet (dataport/high-speed/web TV/wireless). No-smoking rooms. Parking. Restaurant. Room service. Spa. TV (DVD/ movies/music).

Blakes

33 Roland Gardens, SW7 3PF (7370 6701/www. blakeshotels.com). South Kensington tube. **Rates** £200-£234 single; £323-£417 double; £664-£1,293 suite. **Credit** AmEx, DC, MC, V. **Map** p398 C11 54
The original London boutique hotel doesn't get that much press any more – and that's exactly how its publicity-shy devotees like it. Opened by Anouska Hempel back in 1983, Blakes has a maximalist decor that has stood the test of time, becoming a sort of living casebook for interior design students. Each room is in a different style, with influences from Italy, India, Turkey and China. Exotic antiques picked up on the designer's travels – intricately carved beds, Chinese birdcages, ancient trunks – are complemented with sweeping drapery and piles of plump cushions. Downstairs is the eclectic, Eastern-influenced restaurant, once described as resembling 'an opium den run by Coco Chanel'. In a bid to stay current, Blakes opened a gym and installed wireless internet. Unsurprisingly, given its discreet off-the-beaten-track location and romantic decor, the hotel's popular for honeymoons; you can get married on site.
Bar. Business services. Concierge. Gym. Internet (dataport/wireless). Parking. Restaurant. Room service. TV (pay movies/DVD).

Halkin

Halkin Street, SW1X 7DJ (7333 1000/www.halkin. como.bz). Hyde Park Corner tube. **Rates** £388-£482 double; £605-£1,410 suite. **Credit** AmEx, DC, MC, V. **Map** p402 G9 55
This gracious, hype-free hideaway is set on a quiet side street near Hyde Park Corner. You'd never guess that the world's only Michelin-starred Thai restaurant, Nahm (*see p217*), lies behind its discreet Georgian-style façade. The first hotel of Singaporean fashion magnate Christina Ong (whose COMO group includes the Metropolitan, *see p61*, among others) was ahead of the East-meets-West design trend when it opened in 1991. Its subtle design – a successful marriage of European luxury and oriental serenity – still looks more current than hotels half its age. The 41 rooms, located off curving black corridors, combine stylish classical sofas with black lacquer tables and South-east Asian artefacts. Each floor's loosely themed by element, note the colour of the carpets and the marble bathrooms. Guest comfort is paramount: using the high-tech touch-screen bedside consoles you can control everything from the 'do not disturb' sign to the air-con, while lolling on the Egyptian cotton sheets.
Bar. Concierge. Disabled-adapted rooms. Internet (high-speed/wireless). No-smoking rooms. Parking. Restaurant. Room service. TV (pay movies/DVD).

The Lanesborough

Lanesborough Place, Hyde Park Corner, SW1X 7TA (7259 5599/www.lanesborough.com). Hyde Park Corner tube. **Rates** £382-£464 single; £523-£640 double; £758-£7,050 suite. **Credit** AmEx, DC, MC, V. **Map** p402 G9 56
That the Lanesborough came late to the ranks of London's historic luxury hotels – in 1991 – has been no bar to its competing at the top level. It occupies an 1820s Greek Revival building by National Gallery designer William Wilkins and its luxurious guest rooms are traditionally decorated, boasting antique furniture and lavish marble bathrooms with customised toiletries. They also venture into the 21st century with electronic keypads that allow you to control everything from the air-conditioning to the 24-hour room service at the touch of a button. There are other well-considered touches that should be, but aren't, regulation at top-end hotels – complimentary high-speed internet access, free movies and personalised business cards. The Library Bar is like a set from *Gosford Park* and, although changes are planned for the old-fashioned Conservatory (where afternoon tea is served), we're assured that none of the ambience will be lost. The hotel is not cheap, but you do get a butler service thrown in.
Bar. Business centre. Concierge. Disabled-adapted rooms. Gym. Internet (dataport/wireless). No-smoking floors. Parking. Restaurant. Room service. Spa. TV (DVD/movies).

Milestone Hotel & Apartments

1 Kensington Court, W8 5DL (7917 1000/www. milestonehotel.com). High Street Kensington tube. **Rates** £300-£390 double; £570-£910 suite; £2,625/wk apartment. **Credit** AmEx, DC, MC, V. **Map** p396 C9 57
Who says traditional equals dull? Rooms in this old-school luxury hotel overlooking Kensington Gardens feature the inspired decor of South African owner Beatrice Tillman. Choose from such sumptuous themes as the floral fecundity of English rose, the masculine clubbiness of Savile Row, or the Safari suite, with its tent-like draperies and leopard-print upholstery. The spectacular Tudor Suite has an elaborate inglenook fireplace, minstrels' gallery and a pouffe concealing a pop-up TV. There's a distinctly British style of service that is rapidly vanishing elsewhere: a tray of sherry and vase of red carnations in reception, butlers on call 24 hours a day to unpack your bag should you require it. No piddling plastic bottles of shampoo here – you get full-sized Penhaligon's toiletries. House restaurant

Milestone Hotel & Apartments. See p66.

Cheneston's serves Modern British cuisine in heritage-listed surrounds with a wine list overseen by the UK's number two sommelier. Modern comforts come in the form of a gym with a resistance pool and treatment room. **Photo** *p67.*
Bar. Business services. Concierge. Disabled-adapted rooms. Gym. Internet (dataport/wireless). No-smoking rooms. Pool (1, indoor). Restaurant. Room service. TV (DVD/pay movies).

Expensive

Bentley Kempinksi

Harrington Gardens, SW7 4JX (7244 5555/www.thebentley-hotel.com). Gloucester Road tube. **Rates** £199-£326 double; £575-£4,000 suite. **Credit** AmEx, DC, MC, V. **Map** p398 C10 58

If you want to put on the glitz, you'll find plenty of chandeliers to swing from at this opulent boutique hotel – in the bedrooms as well as the lobby. Although it has just 64 rooms, the Bentley's style is on a grand scale: Louis XV-style furniture, gilt mirrors, gleaming marble – 600 tons of it, imported from Greece and Italy – and a sweeping circular staircase perfect for making a grand entrance. The bedrooms are pure *Dynasty*: plush carpets, satin bedspreads and dark marble bathrooms with gold fittings and jacuzzi tubs. Next to the glitzy restaurant 1880, the Malachite Bar is a dimly lit, decadent hideaway in deep red, green and leopard-print. But the real showpiece is the classical spa, with gold-laced mosaics and a full-size Turkish hammam.
Bar. Business centre. Concierge. Disabled-adapted rooms. Gym. Internet (dataport/high-speed). No-smoking floors. Restaurants (2). Room service. Spa. TV (pay movies/music/DVD).

Gore

189 Queen's Gate, SW7 5EX (7584 6601/www.gorehotel.com). South Kensington tube. **Rates** £176 single; £212-£330 double; £350 Tudor Room. **Credit** AmEx, DC, MC, V. **Map** p399 D9 59

A stay at the Gore is possibly the next best thing to having a rich and eccentric titled earl as an uncle. It's a classy, creaky period piece housed in a couple of grand Victorian townhouses, one of which served for a spell as the Turkish embassy. The place is crammed with old paintings and antiques, and the bedrooms have fantastic 19th-century carved oak beds (some so high they need library steps), sumptuous drapes and shelves of old books. But it's the suites that steal the show: the Tudor Room has a huge stone-faced fireplace and a minstrels' gallery, while tragedy queens should plump for the Venus room and Judy Garland's old bed. The hotel was recently refurbished and rooms have air-con, wireless internet and high-tech TVs. The casually elegant Bistrot 190 gets good reviews, while the 190 bar is the best drinking den in South Kensington bar none. Hyde Park, the Royal Albert Hall and the museums are all just a few minutes' walk away.
Bar. Concierge. Internet (dataport/wireless). No-smoking floor. Restaurant. Room service. TV.

Number Sixteen

16 Sumner Place, SW7 3EG (7589 5232/www.firmdale.com). South Kensington tube. **Rates** £118-£160 single; £205-£300 double. **Credit** AmEx, MC, V. **Map** p397 D11 60

This may be Kit Kemp's most affordable hotel but there's no slacking in style or comforts. Bedrooms (42 of them, spread over two floors) are generously sized, bright and very light. They are decorated with tasteful floral patterns and muted creams, greens and mauves, making them feminine but far from frilly. In fact, the whole place has an appealing freshness about it, including the drawing room, which is decorated with bird- and butterfly-themed modern art and fresh flowers. Breakfast is served in the conservatory or the lovely, large garden. It's all utterly relaxing and feels like a real retreat from the city. Sumner Place itself is an appealing row of white stucco townhouses a minute away from South Kensington tube station and just around the corner from the museums.
Bar. Business centre. Concierge. Internet (dataport/wireless). No-smoking rooms. Parking. Room service. TV.

Moderate

Aster House

3 Sumner Place, SW7 3EE (7581 5888/www.asterhouse.com). South Kensington tube. **Rates** £125 single; £160 double; £200 deluxe. **Credit** MC, V. **Map** p399 D11 61

This award-winning B&B bravely attempts to live up to its upmarket address. In reality, the lobby – with its pink faux-marble and gold chandeliers – is more kitsch than glam, but the effect is still charming. So is the lush garden, with its pond and ducks. Even lovelier is the palm-filled conservatory, where guests eat breakfast. The bedrooms are comfortable, with traditional floral upholstery, air-conditioning and smart marble bathrooms (ask for one with a power shower). Business travellers take note: staff can lend guests mobile phones during their stay, and the rooms all have wireless internet connectivity. The museums and big-name shops are all close at hand. A good, affordable option.
Business services. Internet (dataport/wireless). No smoking. TV.

Hotel 167

167 Old Brompton Road, SW5 0AN (7373 0672/www.hotel167.com). Gloucester Road or South Kensington tube. **Rates** £72-£79 single; £99-£110 double; £130 triple. **Credit** AmEx, DC, MC, V. **Map** p398 C11 62

It may be located in a Victorian townhouse, but this funky little hotel is no period clone. The lobby makes a bold statement, with its original black-and-white tiled floor and striking abstract art. Upstairs, the bedrooms are a mix of traditional and arty: the odd antique piece, Victorian painting or contemporary print. Run by the affable Irish owner for 30 years, the slightly bohemian (yet well-kept) place has

inspired artists: it was the subject of a song (an unreleased track by the Manic Street Preachers) and a novel (*Hotel 167* by Jane Solomon).
Internet (wireless). No-smoking rooms. TV.

Cheap

Vicarage Hotel

10 Vicarage Gate, W8 4AG (7229 4030/www.londonvicaragehotel.com). High Street Kensington or Notting Hill Gate tube. **Rates** £50-£85 single; £85-£110 double; £105-£140 triple; £112-£155 quad. **Credit** AmEx, MC, V. **Map** p396 B8 63

This Victorian townhouse hotel has a split personality: the lobby is glitzy, with red and gold wallpaper, ornate mirrors and a chandelier, while the rooms are more what you would expect from a traditional B&B, painted in pastels and furnished with faux antiques and floral fabrics. The airy TV lounge is actually very pleasant: you might even consider sitting in it and relaxing. Another bonus: nine of the 17 rooms now have bathrooms.
TV.

North London

Cheap

Hampstead Village Guesthouse

2 Kemplay Road, Hampstead, NW3 1SY (7435 8679/www.hampsteadguesthouse.com). Hampstead tube/Hampstead Heath rail. **Rates** £50-£70 single; £75-£90 double; £95-£170 studio. **Credit** AmEx, MC, V.

Popular with visiting academics and their families, this comfy bed and breakfast is set in a Victorian pile in picturesque Hampstead. This is the place to stay if you hate hotels – the nine guest rooms in hostess Annemarie van der Meer's sprawling home are furnished with an eclectic collection of furniture, paintings and books… it's more like staying in an intellectual relative's spare room than a guesthouse. Space is used to maximum effect, with quirky devices – children love the wardrobe that conceals a fold-out bed. There's a fridge in each room and most of the rooms are en suite (although some bathrooms are tiny); one even has an iron bath in the middle of the floor. There's also a modern studio in a converted garage, sleeping five. Breakfast is served in the kitchen or secluded garden.
Internet (wireless). No smoking. TV.

East London

Moderate

Hoxton Hotel

81 Great Eastern Street, Shoreditch, EC2A 3HU (7550 1000/www.hoxtonhotels.com). Old Street tube/rail. **Rates** Mon-Thur £119-£129; Fri-Sun £59-£69. **Credit** AmEx, MC, V. **Map** p405 Q4 64

With the Hoxton Hotel, Sinclair Beecham – the man behind the Pret a Manger smart sandwich chain – sets out to prove that budget needn't be boring. Opened in September 2006, the first in what promises to be a nationwide chain is a perfect fit for its hip Shoreditch surrounds. The large glass front wall maintains a link between the activity out on the street and the busy double-height foyer with its areas of lounge seating grouped around two fires. A large and well-designed bar and restaurant – visible to passers-by and open to the public – increases the traffic and the buzz. There is a genuine air of excitement about the place. It goes a bit flat upstairs. Rooms are poky and the finishes are cheap, while the pink neon in the corridors makes it feel a bit like the changing rooms at Topshop. However, you do get Frette linen, a flatscreen TV with unlimited movies (and porn) for £5, free Wi-Fi and a free Pret-lite breakfast – all for under £60 at the weekend. It's doubtful you'll get a better deal in London.

South-west London

Moderate

Windmill on the Common

Windmill Drive, Clapham Common Southside, Clapham, SW4 9DE (8673 4578/www.windmillclapham.co.uk). Clapham Common or Clapham South tube. **Rates** £85-£99 single; £95-£115 double; £140 executive. **Credit** AmEx, DC, MC, V.

Perched on the edge of Clapham Common, the Windmill is a pleasant neighbourhood pub in a building dating from 1729. It also boasts one of London's most reasonably priced hotels. In terms of comfort and decor, the bedrooms are superior to most B&Bs in this price bracket. Central London is a short tube journey away, and Clapham is packed with bars and restaurants.
Bar. Disabled-adapted room. Internet (dataport). No-smoking rooms. Parking. Restaurant. Room service. TV.

Cheap

Riverside Hotel

23 Petersham Road, Richmond-upon-Thames, Surrey TW10 6UH (8940 1339/www.riversiderichmond.co.uk). Richmond tube/rail. **Rates** £60-£65 single; £85-£90 double; £115-£125 suite. **Credit** AmEx, DC, MC, V.

A little slice of the country, ten minutes by train from Waterloo, Richmond is a welcome respite from urban grime. This hotel, right on the edge of the Thames, has its own waterfront garden and half of the trad-style rooms have views of the river. It's also near Richmond Park, Kew Gardens and stately homes such as Marble Hill House. The rooms are decorated in trad English style, but the hotel's best feature is proximity to the tranquil Thames Footpath.
Internet (dataport/wireless). No-smoking rooms. Parking. TV.

Landmark accommodation

The Landmark Trust is a building preservation charity, founded in 1965 by Sir John and Lady Smith. It was established to rescue historic and architecturally interesting buildings from neglect and then, when restored, to give them new life by letting them for holidays. Through Landmark you can rent a castle in Scotland or stay in a lighthouse on three-mile-long Lundy Island off the coast of North Devon. There are five properties in London. Two of these are at **Hampton Court Palace** (*see p188*): Fish Court, a small residence that once housed the 'Officers of the Pastry' (Henry VIII's pie-makers) and sleeps six, and the Georgian House, built in 1719 for George, Prince of Wales, which sleeps eight. For three nights over a weekend, you'll pay £859 to £1,927 at the Georgian House or £757 to £1,548 at Fish Court.

Far more central are **Nos.43 & 45A Cloth Fair**, which are enticingly located beside Smithfield Market, EC1 (*see p106*). They are two Georgian houses above shops facing the churchyard of historic St Bartholomew-the-Great (*see p97*). No.43 sleeps two, has a small roof terrace and was from 1955 to 1977 the home of much-loved poet Sir John Betjeman; No.45A sleeps four. Prices for a three-night weekend stay at No.43 range from £546 to £704; at No.45A, from £658 to £923. The remaining London Landmark property is on **Princelet Street** in Spitalfields, just a few doors away from Brick Lane; it's an original 1718 three-storey house that has been lovingly restored and sleeps six.

To book any of these properties you need to purchase the latest edition of the *Landmark Trust Handbook* (£11.50), which comes with a pricelist and set of booking conditions. You can get the Handbook online (www.landmark trust.org.uk) or by phoning the booking office (open 9am-6pm Mon-Fri, 10am-4pm Sat) on 01628 825925.

West London

Moderate

Base2Stay

25 Courtfield Gardens, Earl's Court, SW5 OPG (0845 262 8000/www.base2stay.com). Earl's Court tube. **Rates** £89 single; £99-£119 double; £149-£189 deluxe/superior. **Credit** AmEx, MC, V. **Map** p398 B10 65

The new Base2Stay looks good, with its modernist limestone and taupe tones. It claims to offer 'a synthesis of boutique hotel and serviced apartment' and the prices are certainly agreeable, so where have the corners been cut? The answer is simple: service. Don't expect the receptionists to stir from the reception area as you struggle up the steps with your bag, and certainly don't expect a refund if you're disappointed on inspecting your room – deposits are most definitely not refunded. The so-called 'kitchenette' that supposedly dispenses with the need for a hotel bar or dining area is actually little more than a microwave and sink, squeezed into a cupboard in the bedroom. But as long as you don't mind having to do everything yourself, then Base2Stay is an affordable way to have a clean room less than ten minutes from the tube station (it's emphatically not the 'two minutes' they tell you on the phone, by the way). **Photo** *p73.*

Disabled-adapted rooooms. Internet. No-smoking floors. TV (flatscreen/pay movies).

Mayflower Hotel

26-28 Trebovir Road, Earl's Court, SW5 9NJ (7370 0991/www.mayflower-group.co.uk). Earl's Court tube. **Rates** £65-£79 single; £89-£109 double; £109-£129 triple; £132-£150 quad. **Credit** AmEx, MC, V. **Map** p398 B11 66

At the forefront of the budget-hotel style revolution, the Mayflower Hotel has given Earl's Court – once a far from glamorous B&B wasteland – a kick up the backside. Following a spectacular makeover a couple of years back, the Mayflower proves cheap

really can be chic. The minimalist lobby is dominated by a stainless steel water feature and a gorgeous teak arch that came all the way from Jaipur; there's a fashionably battered leather sofa and even a couple of caged love birds in the juice bar-cum-lounge. The wooden-floored rooms are furnished in an Eastern style with hand-carved beds and sumptuous fabrics or sleek modern headboards and units. Ceiling fans add a tropical feel, which extends to the palm trees in the garden. At such low rates, marble bathrooms, CD players and dataports are hitherto unheard-of luxuries.
Bar (juice bar). Business centre. Internet (wireless). No-smoking rooms. Parking. TV (DVD).

Twenty Nevern Square

20 Nevern Square, Earl's Court, SW5 9PD (7565 9555/www.twentynevernsquare.co.uk). Earl's Court tube. **Rates** £79-£95 single; £90-£150 double; £159-£189 suite. **Credit** AmEx, DC, MC, V. **Map** p398 A11 67

The words 'stylish' and 'Earl's Court' don't usually appear in the same sentence, but it's the less-than-posh location of this immaculate boutique hotel that keeps the place's rates reasonable. Tucked away in a secluded garden square, it feels far away from its less-than-lovely locale. The modern-colonial style was created by its well-travelled owner, who personally sourced many of the exotic furnishings (as well as those in even cheaper sister hotel the Mayflower, *see p71*). Rooms are clad in a mixture of Eastern and European antique furniture and sumptuous silk curtains; in the sleek marble bathrooms, toiletries are tidied away in decorative caskets. The beds are the real stars, though, from elaborately carved four-posters to Egyptian sleigh styles, all with luxurious handmade mattresses. The Far East feel extends into the lounge and the airy conservatory breakfast room, with its white walls, greenery and dark wicker furniture.
Bar. Internet (dataport/wireless). No-smoking floors. Parking. Room service. TV (DVD).

Cheap

easyHotel

14 Lexham Gardens, Earl's Court, W8 5JE (www.easyhotel.com). Earl's Court tube. **Rates** from £20 single/double. **Credit** MC, V. **Map** p398 B10 68

First came easyJet, then easyCar and easyCruise… now let's welcome easyHotel to the fold. Opened in August 2005, the latest venture to which entrepreneur Stelios Haji-Ioannou has applied his no-frills approach is this compact hotel for compact wallets. The 34 rooms come in three sizes – small, really small and tiny. Forget cats, there's not even room to swing a shoulder bag. The rooms come with a bed, a bathroom and that's it. There's no wardrobe, no hairdryer, no lift and no breakfast, and you only get a window if you are prepared to pay extra for it. Just one person mans reception 24 hours a day, and there are no services, food, entertainment or public areas. The rooms, which are bookable online only, start at an admittedly low £20 – but the prices vary according to demand, so expect to pay an average rate of nearer £40. To make a genuine saving, avoid such fripperies as TV (£5) and housekeeping (£10). Check-in and check-out are at a less than generous 4pm and 10am respectively.
TV (£5 supplement).

Apartment rental

The companies we have listed below specialise in holiday lets, although some of them have minimum stay requirements (making this an affordable option only if you're planning a relatively protracted visit to the city). Typical daily rates on a reasonably central property are around £70-£90 for a studio or one-bed, up to £100 for a two-bed, although, as with any aspect of staying in London, the sky's the limit if you want to pay it. Respected all-rounders with properties around the city include **Astons Apartments** (7590 6000, www.astons-apartments.com), **Holiday Serviced Apartments** (0845 060 4477, www.holidayapartments.co.uk) and **Palace Court Holiday Apartments** (7727 3467, www.palacecourt.co.uk). **Accommodation Outlet** (7287 4244, www.outlet4holidays.com) is a recommended lesbian and gay agency that has some excellent properties in Soho, in particular.

Camping & caravanning

If the thought of putting yourself at the mercy of the English weather in some far-flung suburban field doesn't put you off, the transport links into central London might do the job instead. Still, you can't argue with the prices.

Crystal Palace Caravan Club *Crystal Palace Parade, SE19 1UF (8778 7155). Crystal Palace rail/3 bus.* **Open** *Mar-Oct* 8.30am-6pm Mon-Thur, Sat, Sun; 8.30am-8pm Fri. *Nov-Feb* 9am-6pm Mon-Thur, Sat, Sun; 9am-8pm Fri. **Rates** *Caravan* £4.50-£8. *Tent* phone for details. **Credit** MC, V.

Lee Valley Campsite *Sewardstone Road, Chingford, E4 7RA (8529 5689/www.leevalleypark.org.uk). Walthamstow Central tube/rail then 215 bus.* **Open** *Apr-Oct* 8am-9pm daily. **Rates** £6.25; £2.80 under-16s; free under-2s. *Electricity* £2.60 per night. **Credit** MC, V.

Lee Valley Leisure Centre Camping & Caravan Park *Meridian Way, Pickett's Lock, Edmonton, N9 0AS (8803 6900/www.leevalleypark.org.uk). Edmonton Green rail/W8 bus.* **Open** 8am-10pm daily. **Rates** £6.40; £2.90 concs; free under-5s. **Credit** MC, V.

Staying with the locals

Several agencies can arrange for individuals and families to stay in Londoners' homes. Prices for a stay are around £20-£85 for a single and £45-£105 for a double, including breakfast, and depending on the location and degree of comfort. Agencies include **At Home in London** (8748 1943, www.athomeinlondon.co.uk), **Bulldog Club** (0870 803 4414, www.bulldogclub.com), **Host & Guest Service** (7385 9922, www.host-guest.co.uk), **London Bed & Breakfast Agency** (7586 2768, www.londonbb.com) and **London Homestead Services** (7286 5115, www.lhslondon.com). There may be a minimum stay. Alternatively, have a browse around noticeboard-style 'online community' websites such as **Gumtree** (www.gumtree.com).

Base2Stay. *See p71.*

University residences

During the university vacations much of London's dedicated student accommodation is opened up to visitors, providing them with a source of basic but cheap digs.

Goldsmid House *36 North Row, Mayfair, W1K 6DN (7493 8911/uclgoldsmid@studygroup.com). Bond Street or Marble Arch tube.* **Rates** *July, Aug* from £30 single; £20 (per person) twin. *June, Sept* from £25 single; £15 (per person) twin. **Available** 12 June-15 Sept 2007. **Map** p400 G6 (69)

International Students House *229 Great Portland Street, Marylebone, W1W 5PN (7631 8300/www.ish.org.uk). Great Portland Street tube.* **Rates** (per person) £12-£21 dormitory; £34 single; £26.50 (per person) twin. **Available** all year. **Map** p400 H4 (70)

King's College Conference & Vacation Bureau *Strand Bridge House, 138-142 Strand, Covent Garden, WC2R 1HH (7848 1700/www.kcl.ac.uk/kcvb). Temple tube.* **Rates** £19-£39 single; £42-£49.50 twin. **Available** 30 June-11 Sept. **Map** p409 Z3 (71)

Walter Sickert Hall *29 Graham Street, Islington, N1 8LA (7040 8822/www.city.ac.uk/ems). Angel tube.* **Rates** £32-£40 single; £60 twin. **Available** June-Sept (executive rooms available all year). **Map** p404 O3 (72)

Youth hostels

Hostel beds are either in twin rooms or dorms. If you're not a member of the International Youth Hostel Federation (IYHF), you'll pay an extra £3 a night. Alternatively, join the IYHF for £13 (£6.50 for under-18s) at any hostel, or through www.yha.org.uk. The selected hostels include breakfast in the price. All under-18s receive a 25 per cent discount.

Earl's Court *38 Bolton Gardens, SW5 0AQ (7373 7083/www.yha.org.uk). Earl's Court tube.* **Open** *Reception* 7am-11pm daily. *Access* 24hrs daily. **Rates** £13.95-£31.95. **Map** 398 B11 (73)

Holland Park *Holland Walk, W8 7QU (7937 0748/www.yha.org.uk). High Street Kensington tube.* **Open** *Reception* 7am-11pm daily. *Access* 24hrs daily. **Rates** £13.95-£31.95. **Map** p396 A8 (74)

Oxford Street *14 Noel Street, W1F 8GJ (7734 1618/www.yha.org.uk). Oxford Circus tube.* **Open** *Reception* 7am-11pm daily. *Access* 24hrs daily. **Rates** £13.95-£31.95. **Map** p408 V2 (75)

St Pancras *79-81 Euston Road, NW1 2QE (7388 9998/www.yha.org.uk). King's Cross tube/rail.* **Open** *Reception* 7am-11pm daily. *Access* 24hrs daily. **Rates** £13.95-£31.95. **Map** p401 L3 (76)

St Paul's *36 Carter Lane, EC4V 5AB (7236 4965/www.yha.org.uk). St Paul's tube/Blackfriars tube/rail.* **Open** *Reception* 7am-11pm daily. *Access* 24hrs daily. **Rates** £13.95-£31.95. **Map** p406 O6 (77)

Thameside *20 Salter Road, SE16 5PR (0870 770 6010/www.yha.org.uk). Rotherhithe tube.* **Open** *Reception* 7am-11pm daily. *Access* 24hrs daily. **Rates** £13.95-£31.95.

YMCAs

You may need to book months ahead; this Christian organisation is mainly concerned with housing young homeless people. Some hostels open to all are given below (all are unisex), but you can get a full list from the **National Council for YMCAs** (8520 5599, www.ymca.org.uk).

Barbican YMCA *2 Fann Street, EC2Y 8BR (7628 0697/www.ymca.org.uk). Barbican tube/rail.* **Map** p404 P5 (78)

Kingston & Wimbledon YMCA *200 The Broadway, SW19 1RY (8542 9055/www.ymca.org.uk). South Wimbledon tube/Wimbledon tube/rail.*

London City YMCA *8 Errol Street, EC1Y 8SE (7628 8832/www.ymca.org.uk). Barbican or Old Street tube/rail.* **Map** p404 P4 (79)

You say hotel, I say Yotel

Inspired by Japanese capsule hotels, pod-style accommodation is coming to London – or at least to its airports. Claustrophobia notwithstanding, capsule rooms can be a fine way to economise, particularly if you sit in the camp that sees a hotel more as a crashpad than a pamper fest. After all, who needs all those facilities and frills to get a good night's kip? Those allergic to chintz will also be pleased to hear that capsule rooms tend towards a clean, minimalist style, often incorporating design-savvy accents.

Opening in spring 2007, a visionary solution to airport ennui arrives at Heathrow's Terminal 4 and Gatwick's South Terminal when the people behind Japanese-flavoured restaurant chain Yo! Sushi open **Yotel**, 40- and 50-cabin hotels within the respective terminals. 'Cabins' can be booked overnight, or in four-hour blocks (with extensions of one hour available), and you get a clean, crisp room for your money, courtesy of Airbus designers Priestman Goode. For diversion, there's a monsoon shower, 'techno wall' with pull-down desk, universal port, flatscreen TV, free wired and wireless internet, and stacks of movies and CDs. 'Standard cabins' will cost £40 a night, 'Premium class' £70, while four-hour bookings start at £25.

For further details see **www.yotel.com**.

Sightseeing

Features

Covent Garden. *See p113.*

Introduction

A few ideas on where to start.

London is a wonderful place to visit, but its size can also make it overwhelming. With an understanding of its geography and transport, it's a little easier to navigate.

GETTING AROUND

The tube is the most straightforward way to get around, and you are rarely far from a station in central London. Services are frequent and, outside rush hours, you'll usually get a seat. But mix your tube journeys with bus rides to get a handle on London's topography – you can get free bus maps from many large tube stations and from the Britain & London Visitor Centre on Lower Regent Street (*see p377*).

Although the wonderful old hop-on/hop-off Routemaster buses have been withdrawn from general service, two Heritage Routes are run specifically for visitors: *see p140* **Room for one more on top**. It would also be clever to add river services to your transport portfolio (*see p363*). For more information on all methods of transport, *see pp360-365*.

AN OVERVIEW

The **South Bank** (*pp78-81*) is, obviously, the south bank of the Thames but, less obviously, it's also the centre of the nation's arts scene. **Bankside** (*pp82-86*), east of the South Bank and across from the City, has risen to prominence in recent years with the launching of Tate Modern. In the historic **City** (*pp90-101*) reminders of London's ramshackle, though occasionally great, past jostle with today's citadels of high finance. The areas north and east of here, the old warehouse hinterlands of **Shoreditch** and **Hoxton** (for both, *see p166*), are known for their nightlife. Heading back west, **Clerkenwell** (*pp104-106*) used to do the dirty work for the medieval city, but now has some of London's best restaurants and bars, while **Holborn** (*pp103-104*) is the legal quarter; it is also where the City meets the 'West End', which is what would be referred to in America as 'Downtown'. The heart of the West End is **Soho** (*pp120-124*), which – for all that it never quite lives up to its infamy – is fun nevertheless. North are literary **Bloomsbury** (*pp107-110*), home to the British Museum, and **Fitzrovia** (*p112*), which is home to nothing much in particular except a bunch of decent places to eat and drink servicing the many advertising and media agencies of the area.

East of Soho is genuine visitor-magnet **Covent Garden** (*pp113-119*), with its attractive market and Piazza and loads of shopping and theatres.

South of Soho are **Chinatown** (*p124*) and **Leicester Square** (*p124*), the latter useful primarily as a place to buy half-price theatre tickets (*p338*). South again is the official centre of London, **Trafalgar Square** (*p137*), and the officious centre of Britain, **Westminster** (*p137-145*). Bordering the precincts of power is pretty St James's Park, overlooked by **Buckingham Palace** (*p144*), and then to the north aristocratic **St James's** (*p145*), divided from the similarly aristocratic and exclusive area of **Mayfair** (*pp132-136*) by **Piccadilly**.

Piccadilly runs west from **Piccadilly Circus** (*p132*) to Hyde Park Corner and then into **Knightsbridge** (*p150*), home of designer shopping (and Harrods). The similarly privileged areas of **Chelsea** (*pp147-149*) and **South Kensington** (*pp151-154*), location of London's great Victorian museums, lie south and south-west of Knightsbridge.

All of these areas are clearly delineated on our colour-coded map (*see pp394-395*).

PRACTICALITIES

To avoid queues and overcrowding try to avoid weekends. Many attractions are free to enter (all the big museums, for example), so if you're on a budget you can tick off large numbers of places on your must-see list for the price of a bus pass. There is something called a **London Pass** (www.londonpass.com) that gives pre-paid access to more than 50 attractions and sights; however, unless you are prepared to visit several sights a day for four or five days, you are unlikely to get your money's worth.

We've always tried to give last entry times, but don't turn up just before a place closes if you want to appreciate it fully. Some sights close at Christmas and Easter – ring ahead if you are visiting at these times.

Sightseeing tours

By boat

City Cruises *7740 0400/www.citycruises.com.* City Cruises' Rail and River Rover (£10.50; £5.25 concs) combines the facility to hop on and off any of its regular cruises (pick-up points: Westminster, Waterloo, Tower and Greenwich piers) with unlimited travel on the Docklands Light Railway.

London RIB Voyages
7928 2350/www.londonribvoyages.com.
Part speedboat ride, part sightseeing tour, the RIB (Rigid Inflatable Boat) powers up to 12 passengers at a time from Waterloo Pier down to Greenwich and back in a trip lasting an hour. Book in advance by phone or online, or turn up on spec at the booking office beside the London Eye 20 minutes before departure (boats go on the hour every hour, seven days a week).

By bus

Big Bus Company *48 Buckingham Palace Road, Westminster, SW1W 0RN (7233 7797/www.bigbustours.com).* **Open-top bus tours** 2 routes, 2hrs Red tour, 3hrs Blue tour; commentary recorded on Blue route, live on Red. Tickets include river cruise and walking tours. **Departures** every 20-30mins. *Summer* 8.30am-6pm daily. *Winter* 8.30am-4.30pm daily. **Pick-up** any of 20 or more stops incl Haymarket; Green Park (near the Ritz); Marble Arch (Speakers' Corner); Victoria (outside Thistle Victoria Hotel, 48 Buckingham Palace Road). **Fares** £20 (£18 if booked online); £10 concs; free under-5s. Tickets valid for 24hrs, interchangeable between routes. **Credit** AmEx, DC, MC, V.

Original London Sightseeing Tour
8877 1722/www.theoriginaltour.com. **Departures** *Summer* 9am-7pm daily. *Winter* 9am-5.30pm daily. **Pick-up** any of 90 stops. Main departure points are: Grosvenor Gardens; Marble Arch (Speakers' Corner); Baker Street tube (forecourt); Coventry Street; Embankment station; Trafalgar Square. **Fares** £18; £12 5-15s; £72 family (£1.50 discount on individual tickets, £12 on family if booked online); free under-5s. Tickets valid for 24hrs. **Credit** MC, V.

By duck

London Duck Tours *55 York Road, Waterloo, SE1 7NJ (7928 3132/www.londonducktours.co.uk).* **Tours** *Feb-Dec* daily (ring for times). **Pick-up** Chicheley Street (behind the London Eye). **Fares** £17.50; £12-£14 concs; £53 family. **Credit** MC, V.
City of Westminster tours in an amphibious vehicle. The road and river trip, lasting 75 minutes, starts at the London Eye and enters the Thames at Vauxhall.

By bicycle

For more on bike hire, *see p365*.

London Bicycle Tour Company *Gabriel's Wharf, 56 Upper Ground, Waterloo, SE1 9PP (7928 6838/www.londonbicycle.com).* **Open** 10am-6pm daily. **Tours** 2pm Sat, Sun; 3½ hrs (incl pub stop). **Fares** *Bike hire* £3/hr; £16/day; £8 subsequent days; £48/wk. *Bike tours* £16.95/person.

By helicopter

Cabair *Elstree Aerodrome, Borehamwood, Herts, WD6 3AW (8953 4411/www.cabairhelicopters.com).* **Fares** £149/person. **Credit** AmEx, DC, MC, V.
Helicopter tours (30 mins) over London following the course of the Thames. Flights take place Sunday and selected Saturdays. Cabair will collect clients from Edgware station (Northern Line) or Borehamwood (Thameslink from Kings Cross) by pre-arrangement..

By taxi

Black Taxi Tours of London *7935 9363/www.blacktaxitours.co.uk.* **Cost** £85 during day; £90 at night. **No credit cards**.
A tailored two-hour tour for up to five people.

On foot

Numerous companies offer guided walking tours (*see p143* **Walk this way**).

All the best

A purely personal take on the highlights of the city, as relished by the editor of this guide.

Borough Market

Skip breakfast and eat your way round London's best food market (*see p85*), then walk back to central London along the south bank of the river.

British Museum

The riches of the collection are stunning, but it's the drama of the glass-covered Great Court that makes the heart leap, especially on a sunny day. *See p108.*

Portobello Road

Fantastic shops (Travel Bookshop, Books for Cooks, Rough Trade), a lively market, the Electric Cinema and loads of good places to eat. *See p131.*

The Routemaster

London's iconic double-decker bus chugs on along two routes specially devised with the visitor in mind. *See p140* **Room for one more on top**.

St Paul's Cathedral

Specifically, climbing to the top on a crisp, clear morning to look out over London. *See p93.*

Sir John Soane's Museum

London is full of eccentric museums, but this one tops the lot: masses of bits of pilfered antiquity, paintings hidden in the walls, a pharaoh's sarcophagus in the basement and the marble tomb of Fanny the dog. *See p104.*

The Underground

The world's oldest subterranean railway is a place of endless fascination: ride the Circle line and take a look at Baker Street and Gloucester Road stations. It's also really bloody handy for getting around.

The South Bank & Bankside

Gorge yourself on culture and cuisine.

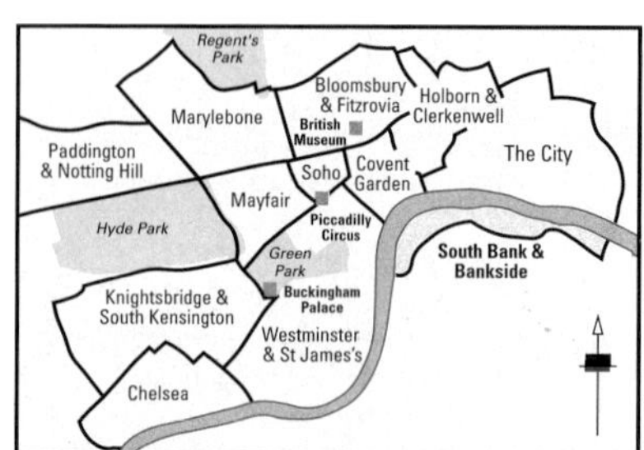

The transformation of the south bank of the Thames has been a work in progress for over 50 years. The Festival of Britain in 1951 opened the way for the building of the blockish South Bank Centre, whose Brutalist design has yet to work its way into most Londoners' affections. The biggest party, however, was linked to the year 2000. Eight years earlier, Marks Barfield architects had taken part in a competition to come up with a millennium structure. Their big wheel, the London Eye, came second. No one remembers what came first. Around the same time, the area gained Tate Modern, plus a graceful new bridge linking it to St Paul's Cathedral. Add to these Shakespeare's Globe and the new City Hall, and a stroll along the river from Westminster Bridge to Tower Bridge is a definite London highlight.

The South Bank

Lambeth Bridge to Hungerford Bridge

Map p403

Embankment or Westminster tube/Waterloo tube/rail.

Lambeth Bridge lands south of the river opposite the Tudor gatehouse of **Lambeth Palace**; this has been the official residence of the Archbishops of Canterbury since the 12th century. The palace is not normally open to the public, except on holidays, but the church next door, St Mary at Lambeth, serves as the **Museum of Garden History** (*see p81*).

Just south of Westminster Bridge is the charming **Florence Nightingale Museum** (*see p79*), part of St Thomas's Hospital; north of the bridge is the start of London's major riverside tourist zone. The **British Airways**

The graveyard express

There are two secrets on Westminster Bridge Road. The first is at No.100, a block of posh flats now inhabited by bankers, Japanese businessmen and Kevin Spacey that used to be MI6 headquarters and is alleged to feature secret prison cells and a secret passage to nearby Lambeth North tube station. The other is a few yards further north on the other side of the road, nestled between a Spar and a Chicken Palace.

No.121's terracotta, mildly Gothic frontage shields the remains of one of London's strangest railway stations – the Waterloo terminus of the **Necropolis Railway**, which took coffins from London to a Surrey graveyard. The line was the brainchild of the London Necropolis Company and, from November 1885, 'the stiffs express' would leave here daily taking corpses to their final resting place in Brookwood Cemetery, 30 miles south-west of London.

The Westminster Bridge Road station had two mortuaries, a chapel and waiting rooms of various classes – the coffins travelled in carriages split into first, second and third class: even in death Londoners were expected to know their place. With the a dvent of the motorised hearse, the railway's popularity declined, but it was still being used twice a week when World War II broke out. However, on 16 April 1941 the station was bombed in an air raid and it never reopened.

You should see the size of the hamster – **British Airways London Eye**.

London Eye (*see below*) packs in the crowds, while in the grand County Hall (once the residence of London's city government) are the **London Aquarium** (*see p81*) and **Dalí Universe** (*see below*).

British Airways London Eye

Riverside Building, next to County Hall, Westminster Bridge Road, SE1 7PB (0870 500 0600/www.ba-londoneye.com). Westminster tube/Waterloo tube/rail. **Open** *Oct-May* 10am-8pm daily. *June-Sept* 10am-9pm daily. **Admission** £13.50; £6.50-£10 concs (only applicable Mon-Fri Sept-June); free under-5s. **Credit** AmEx, MC, V. **Map** p403 M8.

It's hard to believe that this giant wheel was originally intended to turn beside the Thames for only five years. It has proved so popular that no one wants it to come down, and it is now scheduled to keep spinning for another 20 years. The 450ft monster, whose 32 glass capsules each hold 25 people, commands superb views over the heart of London and beyond. A 'flight' takes half an hour, which gives you plenty of time to ogle the Queen's back garden and follow the silver snake of the Thames. You can buy a guide to the landmarks for £2. Some people book in advance (although they take a gamble with the weather), but it is possible to turn up and queue for a ticket on the day. Night flights offer a more twinkly experience. There can be long queues in summer, and security is tight.

Dalí Universe

County Hall Gallery, County Hall, Riverside Building, Queen's Walk, SE1 7PB (7620 2720/www.daliuniverse.com). Westminster tube/Waterloo tube/rail. **Open** 10am-6.30pm daily (last entry 5.30pm). **Admission** *Oct-Apr* £11; £6-£10 concs; £28 family. *May-Sept* £12; £6-£10 concs; £30 family. **Credit** AmEx, DC, MC, V. **Map** p403 M9.

Trademark attractions such as the Mae West Lips sofa and the *Spellbound* painting enhance the main exhibition, curated by long-term Dalí friend Benjamin Levi. There are sculptures, watercolours (including his flamboyant tarot cards), rare etchings and lithographs, all exploring his favourite themes. Don't miss the hyper-surreal Dreams and Fantasy, the exotic and indulgent Femininity and Sensuality, and Religion and Mythology. Be sure to check out too the interesting series of Bible scenes by the Catholic-turned-atheist-turned-Catholic again. The gallery also shows works by new artists.

Florence Nightingale Museum

St Thomas's Hospital, 2 Lambeth Palace Road, SE1 7EW (7620 0374/www.florence-nightingale.co.uk). Westminster tube/Waterloo tube/rail. **Open** 10am-5pm Mon-Fri (last entry 4pm); 10am-4.30pm Sat, Sun (last entry 3.30pm). **Admission** £5.80; £4.80 concs; £16 family; free under-5s. **Credit** AmEx, MC, V. **Map** p403 M9.

The nursing skills and campaigning zeal that made Florence Nightingale's Crimean War work the stuff of legend are honoured here with a chronological tour through her remarkable life. On returning from the battlefields of Scutari she opened the Nightingale Nursing School here in St Thomas's Hospital. Displays of period mementoes – clothing, furniture, books, letters and portraits – include her stuffed pet owl, Athena. Free children's activities take place every other weekend.

Great.
Boys and girls
for lunch.
Hey, and a
grandma too

Come and watch us watching you at the London Aquarium

Tel: 020 7967 8000
londonaquarium.co.uk

London Aquarium

County Hall, Riverside Building, Westminster Bridge Road, SE1 7PB (7967 8000/tours 7967 8007/www.londonaquarium.co.uk). Westminster tube/Waterloo tube/rail. **Open** 10am-6pm daily (last entry 5pm). **Admission** £10.75; £7.25-£8.50 concs; £32 family; free under-3s. (All prices £1 more 1 Apr-3 Sept & school hols; £4 more family.) **Credit** AmEx, MC, V. **Map** p403 M8.

The aquarium, one of Europe's largest, displays its inhabitants according to geographical origin, so there are tanks of bright fish from the coral reefs and the Indian Ocean, temperate freshwater fish from the rivers of Europe and North America, and crustaceans and rockpool plants from shorelines. There are tanks devoted to giant rays, jellyfish, sharks, piranhas and octopuses, and even one containing robotic fish.

Museum of Garden History

Lambeth Palace Road, SE1 7LB (7401 8865/www.museumgardenhistory.org). Waterloo tube/rail. **Open** 10.30am-5pm daily. **Admission** free. *Suggested donation* £3; £2.50 concs. **Credit** AmEx, MC, V. **Map** p403 L10.

John Tradescant, intrepid plant hunter and gardener to Charles I, is buried here at the world's first museum of horticulture. In the graveyard a replica of a 17th-century knot garden has been created in his honour. Topiary and box hedging, old roses, herbaceous perennials and bulbs give all-year interest, and most of the plants are labelled with their country of origin and year of introduction to these islands. A magnificent Coade stone sarcophagus in the graveyard garden contains the remains of William Bligh, captain of the mutinous HMS *Bounty*. Inside are displays of ancient tools, exhibitions about horticulture through the ages, a collection of antique gnomes, a shop and, in the north transept, a wholesome vegetarian café.

Hungerford Bridge to Blackfriars Bridge

Maps p403 & p406

Embankment or Temple tube/Blackfriars or Waterloo tube/rail.

When riverside warehouses were cleared to make way for the **South Bank Centre** in the 1940s, the big concrete boxes that are the Royal Festival Hall, Purcell Room and Queen Elizabeth Hall were hailed as a daring statement of modern architecture. Together with the National Theatre and the Hayward Gallery, they comprise one of the largest and most popular arts centres in the world. The centrepiece, Sir Leslie Martin's **Royal Festival Hall** (1951), is currently being given a £75m overhaul: the improvement of its river frontage has largely been completed, with the arrival of several retail outlets and restaurants (Giraffe, Strada, Wagamama) on the ground floor. The main auditorium will have its acoustics enhanced, remaining closed until summer 2007.

The **Hayward Gallery** (*see p82*) next door is a landmark of Brutalist architecture. Its new pavilion was designed in collaboration with light artist Dan Graham. The gallery's trademark neon-lit tower, designed in 1970 by Phillip Vaughan and Roger Dainton, is a kinetic light sculpture of yellow, red, green and blue tubes controlled by the direction and speed of the wind.

Tucked under Waterloo Bridge is the **National Film Theatre**, the UK's premier cinema centre, also undergoing redevelopment in 2006/7 (*see p289* **Goodbye NFT, hello BFI**). It has an excellent bar-café, while out

Terry meets Julie? **Waterloo Bridge.**

Oxo Tower Wharf from Gabriel's Wharf.

front is a small (unrelated) second-hand book market. **Waterloo Bridge** itself dates from 1942 and was designed by Sir Giles Gilbert Scott to replace an earlier structure. It famously provides some of the finest views of the City, especially at dusk (ideally soundtracked by the Kinks' 'Waterloo Sunset' on your iPod).

East of the bridge is Denys Lasdun's terraced **National Theatre** (*see p339*), which has free outdoor performances in summer, and a little further along the deco tower of the **Oxo Tower Wharf** incorporates covert advertising for the stock cube company that used to own the building. Earmarked for demolition in the 1970s, it was saved by the Coin Street Community Builders, whose exhibition centre on the ground floor tells the full story. It now also provides affordable housing, interesting designer shops and galleries, and a rooftop restaurant, bar and bistro (*see p198*) with more wonderful views.

Hayward Gallery

Belvedere Road, SE1 8XX (information 7921 0813/ box office 0870 169 1000/www.hayward.org.uk). Embankment tube/Waterloo tube/rail. **Open** *During exhibitions* 10am-6pm Mon, Thur, Sat, Sun; 10am-8pm Tue, Wed; 10am-9pm Fri. **Admission** £5; free students & under-16s. Half-price to all Mon. **Credit** AmEx, MC, V. **Map** p403 M8.

In the Hayward's foyer extension and its mirrored, elliptical glass Waterloo Sunset Pavilion, casual visitors can watch cartoons on touch screens as they sip their Starbucks. Art lovers dismayed by the latter nonetheless enjoy the pavilion and the excellent exhibition programme.

Around Waterloo

Map p406

Waterloo tube/rail.

Redevelopment of the Belvedere Road area has improved access to **Waterloo Station**, where Nicholas Grimshaw's glass-roofed terminus for Eurostar trains provides an elegant departure point for travellers bound for Brussels and Paris. Outside, the £20m **BFI IMAX** cinema (*see p291*) was plonked in the middle of the roundabout several years ago, displacing the area's notorious 'cardboard city'.

On the corner of Waterloo Road and the street known as the Cut is the restored Victorian façade of the **Old Vic Theatre** (*see p339*). Known in Victorian times as the 'Bucket of Blood' for its penchant for melodrama, it is now in the hands of Hollywood actor Kevin Spacey. Further down the Cut is the new home of the **Young Vic** (*see p337* **Forever young**), that hotbed of theatrical talent, renovated, rebuilt and due to reopen in autumn 2006. There are some good eateries down here, notably the **Anchor & Hope** gastropub and **Baltic** (for both, *see p197*). North of the Cut, off Cornwall Road, are several atmospheric terraces of early 19th-century artisans' houses that make up part of the Lambeth Preservation Area.

Another place of interest around the station is the **street market** on Lower Marsh (the name originates from the rural village known as Lambeth Marsh until the 18th century). It has a couple of barmy vintage clothing and memorabilia shops – **What the Butler Wore** (No.131) and **Radio Days** (No.87) – and the wonderful **Maries Café** (No.90, 7928 1050).

Bankside

Map p406

Borough or Southwark tube/London Bridge tube/rail.

The area known as Bankside, south of the river between Blackfriars Bridge and London Bridge, was the epicentre of bawdy Southwark in Shakespeare's day. As well as playhouses such as the Globe and the Rose stirring up all sorts of trouble, there were the famous 'stewes' (brothels), seedy inns and other dens of iniquity. Presiding over all this depravity, the Bishops of Winchester made a tidy income from the fines they levied on prostitutes, or 'Winchester Geese' as they were known.

It is no longer 'Geese' that flock to Bankside but culture vultures, drawn in massive numbers to the soaring spaces of **Tate Modern** (*see p85*), the former power station turned gallery. Spanning the river in front of the Tate, the **Millennium Bridge** was the first new Thames crossing in London since Tower Bridge opened in 1894. The bridge opened on 10 June 2000 and promptly closed again two days later because of an excessive swaying motion. After £5m worth of modifications (engineers installed dampers under the deck) it reopened on 27 February 2002. It remains an extremely elegant structure, a 'ribbon of steel' in the words of its conceptualists, architect Sir Norman Foster and sculptor Anthony Caro.

Continuing east, the river walk passes dinky little **Shakespeare's Globe** (*see below*) and, beyond Southwark Bridge, the **Anchor Bankside** pub (34 Park Street, 7407 1577); built in 1775 on the site of an even older inn, the Anchor has been a brothel, a chapel and a ship's chandlers. Dr Johnson is thought to have written his dictionary here and Tom Cruise and Ving Rhames downed a celebratory pint at a table outside after successfully completing 1996's *Mission: Impossible*.

All that's left of the grand Palace of Winchester, home of successive prostitute-fleecing bishops, is the rose window of the Great Hall on Dickensian-looking Clink Street, a short walk from the river, next to the site of the former Clink prison, now the **Clink Prison Museum** (*see below*). Round the corner is the entrance to **Vinopolis, City of Wine** (*see p85*), while at its eastern end Clink Street pulls up short at a small dock containing a terrific replica of Drake's sailing ship, the **Golden Hinde** (*see p83*).

Bankside Gallery

48 Hopton Street, SE1 9JH (7928 7521/www.banksidegallery.com). Southwark tube/Blackfriars tube/rail. **Open** *During exhibitions* 11am-6pm daily. **Admission** free (optional donations). **Credit** DC, MC, V. **Map** p406 O7.

This little gallery is the home of the Royal Watercolour Society and the Royal Society of Painter-Printmakers. Annual shows include the watercolourists in March and October, the painter-printmakers in May, and wood engravers generally every other August. The shop has books and art materials, alongside prints and watercolours.

Clink Prison Museum

1 Clink Street, SE1 9DG (7403 0900/www.clink.co.uk). London Bridge tube/rail. **Open** 10am-6pm Mon-Fri; 10am-9pm Sat, Sun. **Admission** £5; £3.50 concs; £12 family. **Credit** MC, V. **Map** p406 P8.

This small, grisly exhibition looks behind the bars of the hellish prison owned by the Bishops of Winchester from the 12th to the 18th centuries. Thieves, prostitutes and debtors served their sentences within its walls during an era when boiling in oil was legal. On display for the 'hands-on' experience are torture devices and the fetters whose clanking gave the prison its name.

Golden Hinde

St Mary Overie Dock, Cathedral Street, SE1 9DE (0870 011 8700/www.goldenhinde.org). Monument tube/London Bridge tube/rail. **Open** 10am-6pm daily. **Admission** £5.50; £5 children; £18 family. **Credit** MC, V. **Map** p406 P8.

Weekends see this reconstruction of Sir Francis Drake's little 16th-century flagship swarming with children dressed up as pirates for birthday dos. The meticulously recreated ship is fascinating to explore. Thoroughly seaworthy, this replica has even reprised Drake's circumnavigatory voyage. 'Living History Experiences' (some overnight), in which participants dress in period clothes, eat Tudor fare and learn the skills of the Elizabethan seafarer, are a huge hit with the young, as are the pirate parties (book well in advance).

Rose Theatre

56 Park Street, SE1 9AR (7593 0026/www.rosetheatre.org.uk). London Bridge tube/rail. **Open** *May-Sept* by appointment only. **Credit** AmEx, MC, V. **Map** p406 P8.

Built by Philip Henslowe and operational from 1587 until 1606, the Rose was the first playhouse to be erected at Bankside. Funds are currently being sought for new excavation work in search of as yet uncovered portions of the old theatre, which could restore its original ground plan. In the meantime, it is only accessible as part of the guided tour of Shakespeare's Globe (*see below*).

Shakespeare's Globe

21 New Globe Walk, SE1 9DT (7902 1400/box office 7401 9919/www.shakespeares-globe.org). Mansion House or Southwark tube/London Bridge tube/rail. **Open** *Exhibition & tours* 10 Oct-5 May 10am-5pm daily. 6 May-9 Oct 9am-noon Mon-Sat; 9-11.30am Sun. **Admission** £9; £6.50-£7.50 concs; £15 family. **Credit** AmEx, MC, V. **Map** p406 O7.

The original Globe theatre, where many of William Shakespeare's plays were first staged and which he co-owned, burned down in 1613 during a performance of *Henry VIII*. Nearly 400 years later, it was rebuilt not far from its original site under the auspices of actor Sam Wanamaker (who, sadly, didn't live to see it up and running), using construction methods and materials as close to the originals as possible. You can tour the theatre outside the May to September performance season; when the theatre's historically authentic (and frequently very good) performances are staged, the tour is around the Rose Theatre site instead (*see above*). In the UnderGlobe beneath the theatre is a fine exhibition on the history of the reconstruction, Bankside and its Elizabethan theatres, and the London of Shakespeare; it's open year-round. A tour and exhibition visit lasts around 1.5 hours. *See also p340.*

Chelsea Physic Garden
Discover London's
oldest botanic garden
and best-kept secret...
Swan Walk London SW3 ⊖ Sloane Square
www.chelseaphysicgarden.co.uk
Show this advert to save £2 on adult admission
(Valid for up to 4 people. Offer expires 10 Feb 2008)

Tate Modern

Bankside, SE1 9TG (7401 5120/7887 8888/www.tate.org.uk). Blackfriars tube/rail. **Open** 10am-6pm Mon-Thur, Sun; 10am-10pm Fri, Sat. *Tours* 11am, noon, 2pm, 3pm daily. **Admission** free. *Temporary exhibitions* prices vary. **Map** p406 O7.

A powerhouse of modern art, Tate Modern is awe inspiring even before you see anything of the collection thanks to its industrial architecture. It was built as Bankside Power Station and designed by Sir Giles Gilbert Scott, architect of Battersea Power Station (*see p187*) and the designer of the famous British red telephone box. Bankside stopped working in 1981 and opened as an art museum in 2000. The original cavernous turbine hall is used to jaw-dropping effect as the home of large-scale, temporary installations. The permanent collection draws from the Tate organisation's deep reservoir of modern art (international works from 1900 and on) and features heavy-hitters such as Matisse, Rothko, Giacometti and Pollock. In 2006 the galleries were completely rehung, with the artworks grouped according to movement (Surrealism, Minimalism, Post-war abstraction) rather than theme. Almost half of the pieces are new to the museum. Additionally, temporary exhibitions in 2007 will include a major Gilbert & George retrospective (15 Feb-17 May), Dalí & Film (1 June-9 Sept) and Hélio Oiticica (7 June-23 Sept).

If you don't know where to start in all the hugeness, take one of the guided tours (ask at the information desk). There are also various tour packages, some combined with Shakespeare's Globe (*see p83*) and others including lunch or dinner (the café on Level 2 is highly recommended). The Tate to Tate boat service – decor courtesy of Damien Hirst – links with Tate Britain (*see p142*) and runs every 20 minutes, stopping along the way at the London Eye (*see p79*). Tickets are available from ticket desks at the Tates, on board the boat, online or by phone (7887 8888). It costs £4.30 for an adult.

Vinopolis, City of Wine

1 Bank End, SE1 9BU (0870 241 4040/www.vinopolis.co.uk). London Bridge tube/rail. **Open** *Jan-Nov* noon-9pm Mon, Fri, Sat; noon-6pm Tue-Thur, Sun. *Dec* noon-6pm daily. Last entry 2hrs before closing. **Admission** £15, £20, £25 depending on the tour you choose; free under-16s. **Credit** MC, V. **Map** p406 P8.

This glossy attraction is more for wine amateurs than committed oenophiles, but you do need to have some interest to get a kick out it. Participants are furnished with a wine glass and an audio guide. Exhibits are set out by country, with five opportunities to taste wine or champagne from different regions. Gin crashes the party courtesy of a Bombay Sapphire cocktail, and a whisky-tasting area and a micro-brewery (Brew Wharf, *see p224*) were recently added. Highlights include a virtual voyage through Chianti on a Vespa and a virtual flight to the wine-producing regions of Australia. The complex also contains a tourist information centre.

Borough

Map p407

Borough or Southwark tube/London Bridge tube/rail.

At Clink Street the riverside route cuts inland, skirting the edge of the district of Borough. The landmark here is the Anglican **Southwark Cathedral** (*see p88*), formerly St Saviour's and before that the monastic church of St Mary Overie. Shakespeare's brother Edmund was buried in the graveyard here and there's a monument to the playwright inside. Just south of the cathedral is **Borough Market**, a busy food market dating back to the 13th century. It's wholesale only for most of the week but on Fridays and Saturdays it hosts London's best farmers' market (*see p259*). There are several excellent eating options under and around its brick arches including Spanish at **Tapas Brindisa**, seafood at **fish!** and Modern British at **Roast** (for all, *see pp197-198*). There are also a handful of fine pubs including the popular **Market Porter** (*see p225*) and the **Globe** (8 Bedale Street, 7407 0043), which features heavily in the Bridget Jones films – her bachelorette pad is up above the pub. Not far away, at 77 Borough High Street, the **George** (7407 2056) is London's only surviving galleried coaching inn and boasts Dickens as a former regular – but what London pub of age doesn't?

Tate Modern.

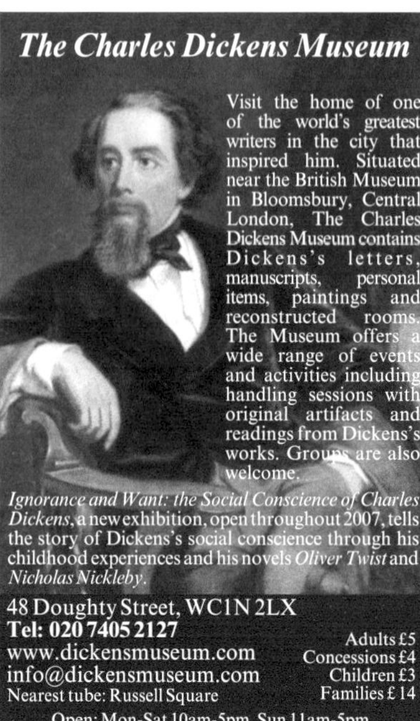
The Charles Dickens Museum
Visit the home of one of the world's greatest writers in the city that inspired him. Situated near the British Museum in Bloomsbury, Central London, The Charles Dickens Museum contains Dickens's letters, manuscripts, personal items, paintings and reconstructed rooms. The Museum offers a wide range of events and activities including handling sessions with original artifacts and readings from Dickens's works. Groups are also welcome.
Ignorance and Want: the Social Conscience of Charles Dickens, a new exhibition, open throughout 2007, tells the story of Dickens's social conscience through his childhood experiences and his novels Oliver Twist and Nicholas Nickleby.
48 Doughty Street, WC1N 2LX
Tel: 020 7405 2127
www.dickensmuseum.com
info@dickensmuseum.com
Nearest tube: Russell Square
Adults £5
Concessions £4
Children £3
Families £ 14
Open: Mon-Sat 10am-5pm. Sun 11am-5pm

V&A
Discover the V&A
The world's greatest museum of art and design
Admission free
South Kensington
www.vam.ac.uk
Dish, Turkey, about 1580 © V&A Images

THE RAGGED SCHOOL MUSEUM
Experience life of the Victorian Poor
Be transported back to 1877, when times were hard for the poor families of East London.
A unique experience for families, schools and groups.
46-50 Copperfield Road, London E3 4RR
Tel: 020 8980 6405
www.raggedschoolmuseum.org.uk
Tube: Mile End
Wheelchair access to ground floor only
Open Wednesday and Thursday 10am-5pm

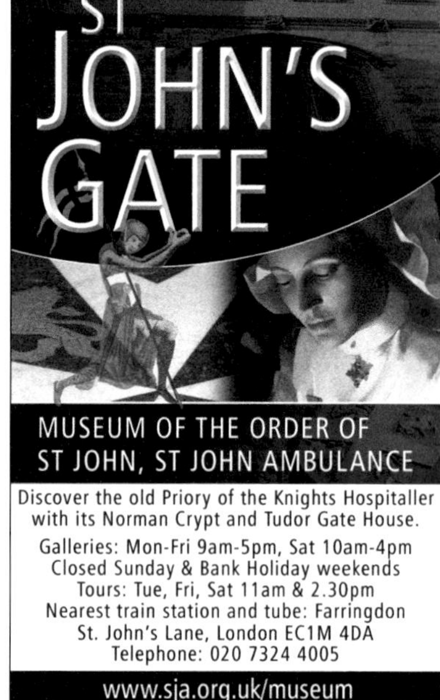
ST JOHN'S GATE
MUSEUM OF THE ORDER OF ST JOHN, ST JOHN AMBULANCE
Discover the old Priory of the Knights Hospitaller with its Norman Crypt and Tudor Gate House.
Galleries: Mon-Fri 9am-5pm, Sat 10am-4pm
Closed Sunday & Bank Holiday weekends
Tours: Tue, Fri, Sat 11am & 2.30pm
Nearest train station and tube: Farringdon
St. John's Lane, London EC1M 4DA
Telephone: 020 7324 4005
www.sja.org.uk/museum

The area around Borough High Street was lively, especially until 1750, because nearby London Bridge was the only dry crossing point on the river below Kingston Bridge, which lies far to the west of the city. There are a couple of small, quirky museums in the area, including the self-explanatory **Bramah Museum of Tea & Coffee** (*see below*) and the **London Fire Brigade Museum** (94A Southwark Bridge Road, 7587 2894, www.london-fire.gov.uk), which traces the history of firefighting in the capital from the Great Fire in 1666 to the present day. Entry to the museum is only possible by guided tour, which must be booked in advance (10.30am, 2pm Mon-Fri, £3, £2 concessions).

Around London Bridge Station tourist attractions clamour for attention. One of the grisliest, with its displays of body parts and surgical implements, is the **Old Operating Theatre, Museum & Herb Garret** (*see below*), although it's the considerably less scary **London Dungeon** (*see below*) that draws the biggest queues at weekends. Competing with the blood-curdling shrieks emanating from its entrance are the dulcet tones of Vera Lyn, broadcast in an attempt to lure visitors into **Winston Churchill's Britain at War Experience** (*see p88*).

Bramah Museum of Tea & Coffee

40 Southwark Street, SE1 1UN (7403 5650/www.bramahmuseum.co.uk). London Bridge tube/rail. **Open** 10am-6pm daily. **Admission** £4; £3.50 concs; £10 family. **Credit** AmEx, DC, MC, V. **Map** p406 P8.

As a nation we get through 100,000 tons of teabags a year, a fact that no doubt appals tea purist Edward Bramah, a former tea taster who set up this museum in the early 1990s. Particularly popular are his regular tours, talks and teas. Bramah's collection displays pots, caddies and ancient coffee makers. They work as visual aids to the history of the beverages and the role they have played in the history of different nations. The exhibition doesn't take long to work round, but it's tempting to linger in the café where a pianist usually tinkles away in the early afternoon. Pre-book for afternoon cream teas (£7).

London Dungeon

28-34 Tooley Street, SE1 2SZ (7403 7221/www.thedungeons.com). London Bridge tube/rail. **Open** *Sept-June* 10.30am-5.30pm daily. *July, Aug* 9.30am-7.30pm daily. **Admission** £16.95; £13.95 concs. **Credit** AmEx, MC, V. **Map** p407 Q8.

A jokey celebration of torture, death and disease under the Victorian railway arches of London Bridge. Visitors are led through a dry-ice fog past gravestones and hideously rotting corpses to experience nasty symptoms from the Great Plague exhibition: an actor-led medley of corpses, boils, projectile vomiting, worm-filled skulls and scuttling rats. Other OTT revisions of horrible London history include the Great Fire and the Judgement Day Barge, where visitors play the part of prisoners (death sentence guaranteed).

Old Operating Theatre, Museum & Herb Garret

9A St Thomas's Street, SE1 9RY (7188 2679/www.thegarret.org.uk). London Bridge tube/rail. **Open** 10.30am-5pm Mon-Wed, Fri-Sun; 10.30am-7pm Thur. **Admission** £4.95; £2.95-£3.95 concs; £12 family; free under-6s. **No credit cards. Map** p407 Q8.

The tower that houses this salutary revelation of antique surgical practice used to be part of the chapel of St Thomas's Hospital, founded on this site in the 12th century. When the hospital was moved to Lambeth in the 1860s most of the buildings were torn down to make way for London Bridge Station and it was not until 1956 that this atmospheric old garret was discovered in the loft of the church. Visitors enter via a vertiginous wooden spiral staircase to view the medicinal herbs on display. Further in is the centrepiece: a pre-anaesthetic Victorian operating theatre dating from 1822, with tiered viewing seats for students. Just as disturbing are the displays of operating equipment that look like torture implements. Other cases hold strangulated hernias, leech jars and amputation knives.

Sightseeing

Borough Market. *See p85.*

Southwark Cathedral

London Bridge, SE1 9DA (7367 6700/tours 7367 6734/www.dswark.org/cathedral). London Bridge tube/rail. **Open** 8am-6pm daily (closing times vary on religious holidays). *Services* 8am, 8.15am, 12.30pm, 12.45pm, 5.30pm Mon-Fri; 9am, 9.15am, 4pm Sat; 8.45am, 9am, 11am, 3pm, 6.30pm Sun. *Choral Evensong* 5.30pm Tue (boys & men), Fri (men only); 5.30pm Mon, Thur (girls). **Admission** (audio tour) £2.50. **Credit** AmEx, MC, V. **Map** p406 P8.

The oldest bits of this building, one of the few places south of the river that Dickens had a good word for, date back more than 800 years. The retro-choir was where the trials of several Protestant martyrs took place during the reign of Mary Tudor. After the Reformation, the church fell into disrepair and parts of it became a bakery and a pigsty; in 1905 it became a cathedral. An interactive museum called the Long View of London, a refectory and a lovely garden are some of the millennial improvements. There are memorials to Shakespeare, John Harvard (benefactor of the US university) and Sam Wanamaker (the force behind Shakespeare's Globe), as well as stained-glass windows with images of Chaucer, who set off on his pilgrimage to Canterbury from a pub on Borough High Street.

Winston Churchill's Britain at War Experience

64-66 Tooley Street, SE1 2TF (7403 3171/www.britainatwar.co.uk). London Bridge tube/rail. **Open** *Apr-Sept* 10am-6pm daily (last entry 5pm). *Oct-Mar* 10am-5pm daily (last entry 4pm). **Admission** £9.50; £4.85-£5.75 concs; £25 family; free under-5s. **Credit** AmEx, MC, V. **Map** p407 Q8.

This old-fashioned exhibition recalls the privations endured by the British during World War II. Visitors descend from street level in an ancient lift to a reconstructed tube station shelter that doubles as a movie theatre showing documentaries from the period. The experience continues with displays about London during the Blitz, including real bombs, rare documents, photos and reconstructed shopfronts. The displays on rationing, food production and Land Girls are fascinating, and the set-piece walk-through bombsite (you enter just after a bomb has dropped on the street) is quite disturbing.

London Bridge to Tower Bridge

Map p407

Bermondsey tube/London Bridge tube/rail.

Across Tooley Street from the London Dungeon and Britain at War Experience pleasures stands a spookily empty mall called **Hay's Galleria**, once an enclosed dock, now dominated by a peculiar sculpture called *The Navigators* (by David Kemp). Here the twinkling **Christmas Shop** (7378 1998, www.thechristmasshop.co.uk) remains doggedly festive, and half-hearted craft stalls await custom. Exiting on the riverside, past the great grey hulk of **HMS Belfast** (*see p89*) – a big hit with children – you can walk east towards Tower Bridge.

Beyond the battleship you pass the pristine environs of **City Hall**, the home of the current London government. Designed by Sir Norman Foster, the eco-friendly rotund glass structure leans squiffily away from the river (to prevent it casting shade on the walkers below – how thoughtful). The building has an exhibition blowing the mayor's trumpet on the ground floor, a café on the lower ground floor and a pleasant outdoor amphitheatre for lunch breaks and sunbathing.

Near Tower Bridge, a noticeboard announces when the bridge is next due to open (which it does about 900 times a year for tall ships to pass through). The bridge is one of the lowest crossings over the Thames, which is why the twin lifting sections (bascules) were designed by architect Horace Jones and engineer John Wolfe Barry. The original steam-driven hydraulic machinery can still be seen at the **Tower Bridge Exhibition** (*see p102*).

Further east, the former warehouses of Butler's Wharf are now mainly about upmarket riverside dining, with a series of Conran restaurants. Shad Thames is the main thoroughfare behind the wharves, where in days long gone dockworkers unloaded tea, coffee and spices into huge warehouses (now pricey apartments and offices, and the **Design Museum**, *see p89*).

Up past the Design Museum across Jamaica Road and down Tanner Street is historic **Bermondsey Street**, site of **Zandra Rhodes' Fashion & Textile Museum** (83 Bermondsey Street, 7407 8664, www.ftmlondon.org), which is currently open by appointment and to groups only. Further south, around Bermondsey Square (where Bermondsey Street meets Tower Bridge Road), it's all Starbucks and delis, new cobbles and hanging baskets, although M Manze (*see p89* **Mash point**), the eel and pie shop, has been here since 1902. The Friday **antiques market** (4am-2pm) here is lovely, though it's well picked over by dealers by the time most of us have had breakfast.

Design Museum

Shad Thames, SE1 2YD (7403 6933/www.designmuseum.org). Tower Hill tube/London Bridge tube/rail. **Open** 10am-5.45pm daily (last entry 5.15pm). **Admission** £7; £4 concs; free under-12s. **Credit** AmEx, MC, V. **Map** p407 S9.

Exhibitions in this white 1930s-style building (a former warehouse) focus on modern and contemporary design. The Tank is a little outdoor gallery of constantly changing installations by leading contemporary designers, while the smart Blueprint Café has a balcony overlooking the Thames. Exhibitions in 2007 include Bruno Manari, Italian Futurist and book designer (13 Jan-6 May 2007).

HMS Belfast

Morgan's Lane, Tooley Street, SE1 2JH (7940 6300/www.iwm.org.uk). London Bridge tube/rail. **Open** *Mar-Oct* 10am-6pm daily. *Nov-Feb* 10am-5pm daily. **Admission** £8.50; £5.25 concs; free under-16s (must be accompanied by an adult). **Credit** MC, V. **Map** p407 R8.

This 11,500-ton battlecruiser, the last surviving big gun World War II ship in Europe, is a floating branch of the Imperial War Museum. It makes an unlikely playground for children, who tear easily around its cramped complex of nine decks, boiler, engine rooms and gun turrets. The *Belfast* was built in 1938, provided cover for convoys to Russia and was instrumental in the Normandy Landings. She also supported UN forces in Korea before being decommissioned in 1965; a special exhibition looks at that 'forgotten war'. Guided tours take in the living quarters, explaining what life was like on board. The ship's guns, incidentally, are trained on London Gateway services on the M1 – a distance of 12.5 miles away.

Mash point

The most modern thing in **Manze's** pie and mash shop is the extractor fan, suspended from the ceiling and gently humming. The rest – the bevelled green tiles and wooden benches – is much as it was when the place was established over 100 years ago. The Tower Bridge Road restaurant is the oldest pie and mash shop still in existence in the capital – a London legend, a last bastion of Britishness. Albeit founded by Italians.

The Manze family left Ravello on the Amalfi Coast in 1878, arriving in Britain with a plan to sell ice-cream. But rainy, industrial London and ice-cream didn't seem such a good match, so they opened the first of their pie shops in 1902 instead. Pies weren't new in London. During the 1700s an army of 'pie men' walked the streets selling their wares to poor families in need of a good, hot but cheap meal. In those days the pies were filled not with beef but with eel, caught in the Thames, and served up with vinegar or pea and mint sauce. The first proper pie shops sprang up in London around 1850, with little stalls outside from which people could buy live eels to take home and cook. The shops tended to be located near markets, mopping up trade from stallholders, dockers and factory workers. By World War I there were 150 pie shops in London and by 1930 the Manze empire had grown to 14 pie, mash and eel shops.

Although only three Manze's shops remain today, the Tower Bridge Road branch still packs them in: young, trendy couples in Campers, shopped-out mums with small kids, and big blokes with tattoos. One of the most impressive aspects of Manze's, apart from the fact that you can still get a meal of two pies, a mountain of mash and a lake of liquor (a thin parsley sauce) for £3.45, is its total resistance to modernisation. The washing up is done by hand behind the counter; the background noise is conversation and the scratch of forks on plates, and the menu, painstakingly spelt out on a peg board by the cash till, never changes: pies, mash, eels, tea, sarsaparilla. 'We did try to change it once,' says current owner Geoff Manze, grandson of the restaurant's founder Michele Manze. 'We introduced baked beans, peas and sausages.' They didn't catch on. 'We threw away more than we sold.'

M Manze

87 Tower Bridge Road, SE1 4TW (7407 2985). London Bridge tube/rail. **Open** 11am-2pm Mon; 10.30am-2.15pm Tue-Thur; 10am-2.15pm Fri; 10am-2.45pm Sat. **Map** p407 Q10.

The City

The cash machine that spawned London.

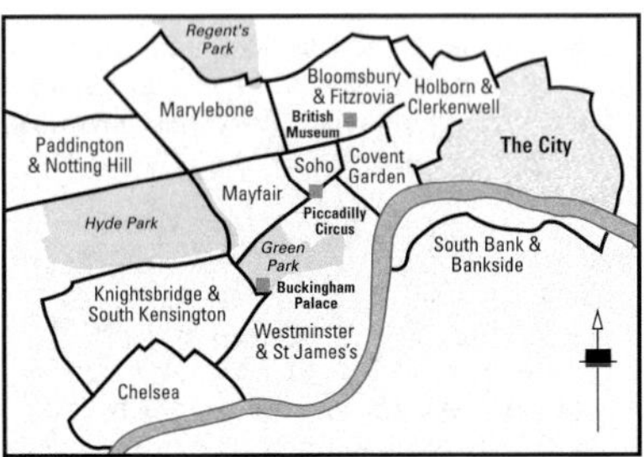

For more than a millennium, the City was London. Only the area bound by the Roman walls – which still broadly define the extent of the City today (*see p97*) – could officially be called 'London' until the City and Westminster joined forces at the end of the medieval period. Enclosing roughly a square mile of land on the north bank of the Thames (hence the term the 'Square Mile', which is sometimes used for the City), the walls protected a fiercely independent population of merchants, who planted the seeds of economic growth that led Britain to become, briefly, the greatest economy on earth. Many of the City's affairs are still run on a profoundly feudal basis, under the auspices of the arcane Corporation of London. It remains the economic heart of the capital, with billions of pounds changing hands every day on the trading floor of the Stock Exchange.

At first glance, the City might not appear to have that much to offer visitors – just ranks of stuffy offices, crowds of office workers in matching suits and shops selling takeaway coffee and sandwiches. But tucked in among the corporations and banking houses are some intriguing titbits of history – the ruins of London's Roman walls; churches from the time of Hawksmoor and Wren; pubs frequented by Dickens and Thackeray; even the former royal palace of the kings and queens of England.

To really understand the City you need to visit on a weekday when the great economic engine is in gear; visit at the weekend and the streets are empty and most places are closed.

City Information Centre

St Paul's Churchyard, EC4M 8BX (7332 1456). St Paul's tube. **Open** *St Paul's* 9.30am-5pm Mon-Sat; noon-6pm Sun. *Oct-Mar* 9.30am-5pm Mon-Fri; 9.30am-12.30pm Sat. **No credit cards. Map** p406 O6.

A helpful source of information on sights, events, walks and talks in the Square Mile, including a guidemap of City churches. At the time of writing the office is closed – instead, there's a temporary information desk inside the shop at St Paul's – but it is due to reopen in 2007.

Fleet Street

Map p406

Temple tube/Blackfriars tube/rail.

Standing on Fleet Street today, it's hard to imagine that this was once the path of a rushing river. In medieval times, the River Fleet was a major artery for the passage of goods into the City, but silt closed the shipping channels in the 19th century and the river was covered over to provide land for construction. It still gurgles somewhere below street level.

Instead Fleet Street is better known for its associations with the press. The history of printing on Fleet Street dates back to 1500, when William Caxton's assistant, Wynkyn de Worde, established the City's first printing press behind **St Bride's Church** (*see p91*). In 1702 London's first daily newspaper, the *Daily Courant*, rolled off the presses, paving the way for the rise of tabloid journalism. By the end of World War II, there were half a dozen newspaper offices churning out scoops and scandals between the Strand and Farringdon Road. Most of the newspapers moved away during Rupert Murdoch's crackdown on the print unions in the 1980s; the last of the news agencies, Reuters, followed suit in 2005. Today the only periodical published on Fleet Street is the *Beano* comic, but you can see some relics from the media days, including the bingo hall-like **Daily Telegraph building** (No.135) and, next door, the sleek, black **Daily Express building** (Nos.121-128). The latter, designed by Owen Williams in the 1930s, is arguably the only real art deco building of note in London.

There are several historic churches around the western end of Fleet Street. At No.184 is **St Dunstan in the West** (7405 1929, www.stdunstaninthewest.org), where the poet John Donne was rector from 1624 until his death in 1631. Next door at No.186 is the house where Sweeney Todd, the 'demon barber of Fleet Street', allegedly murdered his customers before selling their bodies to a local pie shop. Sadly, the legend is a porky pie – Todd was invented by the editors of a Victorian penny dreadful in 1846 and propelled to fame by a stage play and a Stephen Sondheim musical.

While you're here, make time for a pint at one of the pubs that once catered to the hacks – the **Punch Tavern** (No.99, 7353 6170), where satirical magazine *Punch* was launched in 1841 and which is decked out with Victorian finery, or the far older **Old Bell Tavern** (No.95; *see p226*); note, as with so much in the City, both pubs are closed at weekends. Between them on the other side of the road is **Ye Olde Cheshire Cheese** (No.145; *see p225*), a favourite watering hole of both Dickens and Dr Samuel Johnson. At No.66, the **Tipperary** (7583 6470) is the oldest Irish pub outside Ireland – it opened in the 1700s and sold the first pint of Guinness on the British mainland.

Dr Johnson's House

17 Gough Square, off Fleet Street, EC4A 3DE (7353 3745/www.drjohnsonshouse.org). Chancery Lane or Temple tube/Blackfriars tube/rail. **Open** *May-Sept* 11am-5.30pm Mon-Sat. *Oct-Apr* 11am-5pm Mon-Sat. *Tours* by arrangement; groups of 10 or more only. **Admission** £4.50; £1.50-£3.50 concs; £10 family; free under-5s. *Tours* free. **No credit cards. Map** p406 N6.

As well as being the author of the first ever *Dictionary of the English Language*, Dr Samuel Johnson (1709-84) was the pen behind one of the first British travelogues, a mordant account of a tour of the Western Isles with James Boswell. You can tour the stately Georgian townhouse off Fleet Street where Johnson came up with his inspired definitions – 'to make dictionaries is dull work,' he wrote in his definition of the word 'dull'. Johnson shared his house with a cat called Hodge ('a very fine cat'), who is remembered with a bronze statue in the small court in front of the house.

Prince Henry's Room

17 Fleet Street, EC4 (7936 4004). Temple tube. **Open** 11am-2pm Mon-Fri. **Admission** free. **Map** p406 N6.

It's appropriate that London's museum to the great diarist Samuel Pepys (1633-1703) is housed in one of the few buildings still standing from before the Great Fire. Reached through a narrow doorway on Fleet Street, the frontage and parts of the interior date back to the time of James I. Inside you can see an intriguing series of exhibits on the life and times of London's great chronicler.

St Bride's Church

Fleet Street, EC4Y 8AU (7427 0133/www.stbrides.com). Temple tube/Blackfriars tube/rail. **Open** 8am-6pm Mon-Fri; 11am-3pm Sat; 10am-1pm, 5-7.30pm Sun. **Admission** free. **Map** p406 N6.

The newspapers are gone from Fleet Street, but St Bride's is still known as the printers' and journalists' church. Inside is a glorious dark wood reredos (altar-piece) and choir, topped by stern-looking statues of St Paul and St Bride. The Wren-designed spire allegedly provided the inspiration for the traditional tiered wedding cake. Allegedly.

The Temple

Map p406 N5

Temple tube/Blackfriars tube/rail.

South of the western end of Fleet Street are the interlinked courtyards of the **Middle Temple** and **Inner Temple** (7797 8183, www.innertemple.org.uk), two of the Inns of Court that provided training and lodging for London's medieval lawyers. They take their name from the Knights Templar, the body of Crusader monks founded in 1118 to protect pilgrims travelling to the Holy Land. They acquired this land in 1162 and built a church here, the **Temple Church** (*see below*), which is enjoying a sudden surge in public interest since cropping up in *The Da Vinci Code*. Access to the inns is usually reserved for members of the legal profession, but tours of the grandiose and

Hodge the cat outside **Dr Johnson's House**.

St Paul's. *See p93.*

maze-like Inner Temple can be arranged for £10 per person (minimum five people, call 7797 8250 to book).

Temple Church

King's Bench Walk, EC4Y 7BB (7353 8559/ www.templechurch.com). Temple tube. **Open** 11am-12.30pm, 1-4pm Mon, Tue; 2-4pm Wed; 11am-12.30pm, 2-4pm Thur, Fri; 11am-12.30pm Sat, Sun. *Services* 11.15am Sun; 1.15pm Thur. *Organ recital* Wed; call for details. **Admission** free. **Map** p406 N6.

Inspired in its style by Jerusalem's Church of the Holy Sepulchre and consecrated in 1185, the Temple Church was the private chapel of the mystical Knights Templar. It served as their headquarters and the venue for initiation rites until the order was disbanded for heresy, at which point the buildings briefly passed to the Knights of St John of Jerusalem (*see p106*). The church was refurbished in the late seventeenth century by Christopher Wren and suffered bomb damage during the Blitz. The rounded apse contains the worn gravestones of several Crusader knights.

St Paul's & around

Map p406 O6

St Paul's tube.

Although hemmed in by office buildings, the towering dome of **St Paul's Cathedral** (*see below*) still dominates the City, an architectural two fingers up to the Great Fire and the German bombers that tried to bring London down. No other monument captures the resilience of Londoners so adroitly, and few buildings can match it for scale and grandeur. There has been a cathedral to St Paul on Ludgate Hill since 604, but Vikings sacked the first cathedral and its Norman replacement – a magnificent Gothic structure with a 490-foot spire – burned to the ground in the Great Fire of London. The new St Paul's was commissioned from Sir Christopher Wren in 1673 as London re-emerged from the ashes, but Wren had to redesign the building three times before the project was finally given the green light.

Immediately north of the cathedral is the recently redeveloped **Paternoster Square**, a curiously sterile plaza full of corporate art, including a sundial that doesn't tell the time. At the southern entrance to the square stands Christopher Wren's stately **Temple Bar**, which once stood where Fleet Street meets the Strand and marked the historic boundary between the City of London and neighbouring Westminster. In the Middle Ages the monarch needed approval from the Lord Mayor of London to enter the City and the Temple Bar was the gateway through which he or she had to pass. It was also used to display the spiked heads of executed criminals. The archway was dismantled in 1878 and removed to a country estate in Hertfordshire, only returning to its new City site in 2004.

South of St Paul's, a cascade of steps runs down to the **Millennium Bridge**, passing midway the 17th-century **College of Arms** (*see below*), the official seat of heraldry in Great Britain. East of the cathedral is narrow **Bow Lane**, lined with shops, bistros and champagne bars. The lane is bookended by **St Mary-le-Bow**, whose peals once defined a true Cockney, and **St Mary Aldermary**, with its pin-straight steeple, designed by Wren's office. If you've still got the energy for more churches, there are five Wren creations south of St Paul's (St James Garlickhythe, St Mary Somerset, St Nicholas Cole Abbey, St Benet and St Andrew-by-the-Wardrobe) and one to the west (St Martin-within-Ludgate). North-west of the cathedral is the most famous court in the land, the **Old Bailey** (*see below*).

Old Bailey (Central Criminal Court)

Corner of Newgate Street & Old Bailey, EC4M 7EH (7248 3277). St Paul's tube. **Open** *Public gallery* 10.30am-1pm, 2-4.30pm Mon-Fri. **Admission** free. No under-14s; 14-16s accompanied by adults only. **Map** p406 O6.

Be glad that you are visiting the Old Bailey as a tourist, not a defendant. London's most famous criminal court has hosted some of the most controversial trials in British history, from the murder trial of the Kray Twins to the sodomy trial of Oscar Wilde. Members of the public are welcome to attend trials at the courthouse – built in 1907 and topped by a famous gilded statue of blind (meaning impartial) Justice – and join the outcry at the light sentences handed down (a political hot potato for the current government). A list of upcoming trials is displayed by the public entrance but decorum is expected in the public gallery, and bags, cameras, dictaphones, mobile phones and food are strictly prohibited (for security reasons, there are no storage facilities).

College of Arms

130 Queen Victoria Street, EC4V 4BT (7248 2762/www.college-of-arms.gov.uk). St Paul's tube/Blackfriars tube/rail. **Open** 10am-4pm Mon-Fri. *Tours* by arrangement 6.30pm Mon-Fri; prices vary. **Admission** free. **No credit cards**. **Map** p406 O7.

The first coats of arms were created to identify competing knights at medieval jousting tournaments, much like sports uniforms today, but heraldry soon became an integral part of family identity for the British gentry. Visitors interested in finding out about their family arms can consult the official register of arms, held by the heralds at the College of Arms, and arrange tours to view the records.

St Paul's Cathedral

Ludgate Hill, EC4M 8AD (7236 4128/www.stpauls.co.uk). St Paul's tube. **Open** 8.30am-4pm Mon-Sat. *Galleries, crypt & ambulatory* 9.30am-4pm Mon-Sat.

Special events may cause closure; check before visiting. *Tours of cathedral & crypt* 11am, 11.30am, 1.30pm, 2pm Mon-Sat. **Admission** *Cathedral, crypt & gallery* £9; £3.50-£8 concs; £21.50 family; free under-6s. *Tours* £3.50; £1-£3 concs. **Credit** (shop) AmEx, MC, V. **Map** p406 O6.
London's most famous cathedral seems to grow more radiant as it approaches its 300th anniversary. A decade of restoration has stripped most of the Victorian grime from the walls and the extravagant main façade looks as brilliant today as it must have when first unveiled in 1708. Scaffolding still obscures the north wall as restorers remove the last of the soot deposited by the coal-fired power station that now houses Tate Modern, but attention is shifting to the monuments and mausoleums inside.

Sir Christopher Wren had to fight to get his plans for this epic cathedral past the authorities – many dignitaries thought it too large and expensive – and he changed his mind halfway through to create the massive dome for which St Paul's is now famous. In fact, there are three domes – the inner and outer domes are separated by a hidden brick dome that supports the entire structure (believed to weigh 64,000 tons).

Most visitors walk around in wonder at the vast open spaces and memorials to such heroes of empire as Nelson, Wellington, Lawrence of Arabia and General Gordon of Khartoum. You can also look down on it all from the Whispering Gallery inside the dome, reached by 259 steps from the main hall (the acoustics here allow a whisper to be bounced clearly to the other side of the dome). Steps continue to the outdoor Golden Gallery (530 steps), which offers giddying views over the City. Keep an eye out for 18th-century graffiti as you clamber along the narrow stairwells.

Before leaving St Paul's, head down to the maze-like crypt, which contains more memorials to national heroes, including the small, plain tombstone of Christopher Wren, inscribed with the epitaph, 'Reader, if you seek a monument, look around you'. Tours of the Triforium – visiting the library and Wren's 'Great Model' – take place at 11.30am and 2.30pm on Monday and Tuesday and at 2pm on Friday (pre-book on 7246 8357, £14 including admission). **Photo** *p92.*

North to Smithfield

Maps p404 O5 & p406 O5

St Paul's tube/Barbican tube/rail.

From St Paul's, a short walk north across Cheapside takes you to Foster Lane and another elegant Wren church, **St Vedast-alias-Foster** (7606 3998, 8am-6pm Mon-Fri), gutted during World War II but refitted with original trim from other Wren churches. Nearby, off Aldersgate Street, is the delightful **Postman's Park**, with its 'Heroes Wall', a display of Victorian ceramic plaques commemorating fatal acts of bravery. Take the sad story of Sarah Smith, a pantomime artiste at the Prince's Theatre, who received 'terrible injuries when attempting in her inflammable dress to extinguish the flames which had engulfed her companion (1863)'.

St Bartholomew's Hospital. *See p97.*

A few blocks west, on the pleasingly named Little Britain, **St Bartholomew-the-Great** (*see p97*) is the oldest parish church in London and the final resting place of the Augustinian prior who founded St Bartholomew's Hospital. Inside the hospital itself is the interesting **Museum of St Bartholomew's Hospital** (*see p97*). Every Friday at 2pm visitors can take a guided tour (£5, book on 7837 0546) of the museum, St Bartholomew-the-Great, Smithfield and the little church of St Bartholomew-the-Less, which is inside the hospital compound. On the outside wall of the hospital is a monument to the Scots hero William Wallace, who was executed here in 1305; it's still a place of pilgrimage for Scottish nationalists.

For a description of the Smithfield Market area, *see p106.*

Pedalling controversy

For years, they ruled the streets of London: the cycle couriers, self-styled road warriors, willing to jump any red light, mount any curb, speed through any pedestrian crossing to get the package delivered on time. Crossing the road during office hours became a game of Russian roulette – at any moment, a Lycra-clad cyclist could appear from nowhere in a hail of screeching brakes and expletives.

All that may be set to change if a new transport bill, promoted by London mayor Ken Livingstone, is passed by Parliament. Responding to growing tension between cyclists and motorists on London's congested streets, the mayor has proposed a raft of draconian new laws to crack down on cyclists who break the rules. If the government approves the bill, cyclists could face hefty on-the-spot fines or even a two-year jail term for such minor offences as failing to ring their bells at pedestrian crossings.

The plan follows growing concern about the number of pedestrians injured by cyclists on London's roads. In 2005 there were 69 serious collisions, resulting in at least one death. An elite squad of cycle cops has already been sent out to hotspots around the city to warn errant pedallers that their days of cycle crime are numbered. But they face an uphill challenge. According to one survey, more than half of London cyclists routinely ignore traffic rules, while one in five regard red lights as 'optional'.

Adding fuel to the debate, a number of the new proposals have already been dismissed as unworkable. In early 2006 the mayor was forced into an embarrassing U-turn after revealing plans for bicycle 'number plates' on a national radio station. Plans for mandatory cycle helmets have also been knocked back by the publication of a study suggesting that motorists deliberately give less space to cyclists in helmets (the assumption being that helmet-wearers are more experienced and less likely to do anything unpredictable).

Understandably, London's cyclists feel under siege. The CTC, the national organisation of cyclists, launched a scathing attack on the 'Share the Road' scheme, accusing the mayor of painting cyclists as villains instead of victims.

However, the mayor's office can claim some successes. Since 2000 Transport for London has invested more than £50 million in cycling in the capital, creating hundreds of miles of cycle lanes. The number of cycle commuters has almost doubled since the introduction of the congestion charge, although the increase is also partly due to fear of using public transport after the 7 July 2005 bombings.

Still, according to one government report, London bus drivers are almost as likely to jump red lights as cyclists. And the mayor's system of cycle lanes also falls well short of expectations. Only a tiny portion of London's 280 miles of cycle paths are reserved exclusively for bikes – the rest are shared with buses and taxis, the two types of vehicle most likely to pull out unexpectedly into the path of oncoming riders.

Despite these obstacles, the mayor still hopes to transform London into a world-class cycling city to rival Amsterdam or Copenhagen. Transport for London has plans for an extra 250 miles of cycle lanes by 2010, bringing London into the front ranks of cycle-friendly European capitals. In another encouraging development, a chain of cycle shops left a collection of unlocked bikes around the capital in 2006 to be used for free and passed on by public-spirited cyclists (a brave move in a city where 80,000 bikes are stolen every year).

All this may be too little too late for London's besieged pedal-cyclists. With bus and tube fares soaring and traffic congestion in central London set to exceed the levels before the congestion charge, the message from many Londoners to Ken Livingstone at the next mayoral elections may well be 'On yer bike'.

St Bartholomew-the-Great

West Smithfield, EC1A 9DS (7606 5171/www.greatstbarts.com). Barbican or Farringdon tube/rail. **Open** 8.30am-5pm Tue-Fri (until 4pm Nov-Feb); 10.30am-1.30pm Sat; 8.30am-1pm, 2.30-8pm Sun. *Services* 9am, 11am & 6.30pm Sun; 12.30pm Tue; 8.30am Thur. **Admission** free; donations welcome. **Map** p404 O5.

Probably the City's finest medieval church. Parts of the building belong to the 12th-century priory hospital of St Bartholomew, founded by Prior Rahere, a former courtier of Henry I. The church was chopped about during Henry VIII's reign and the interior is now firmly Elizabethan. Benjamin Franklin trained here as a printer in 1724 before launching his political career in America.

Museum of St Bartholomew's Hospital

West Smithfield, EC1A 7BE (7601 8152). Barbican or Farringdon tube/rail. **Open** 10am-4pm Tue-Fri. **Admission** free; donations welcome. **Map** p404 O5.

This small museum is dedicated to the history of London's oldest hospital, with lively displays on medieval surgical techniques that make you glad to be living in the 21st century. If you visit as part of the Friday afternoon tour (*see p95*), you can also view the Hogarth paintings in the Great Hall.

North of London Wall

Map p404 P5

Barbican or Moorgate tube/rail.

London Wall (which is a busy road rather than a vertical barrier) runs east from St Bart's, following the approximate route of the old Roman walls. Although the area has been heavily redeveloped, often to the detriment of pedestrian access, the weathered stones of the Roman wall can still be seen poking up here and there between the office blocks. You can patrol the remaining stretches of the wall on a 1.75-mile walk, with panels (some barely legible) pointing out the highlights. The walk starts near the **Museum of London** (*see below*).

The area north of London Wall was levelled during the Blitz and in 1958 the City of London and London County Council clubbed together to buy land for the construction of 'a genuine residential neighbourhood, with schools, shops, open spaces and amenities'. What Londoners got was the **Barbican**, a vast concrete estate of 2,000 flats that feels a bit like a university campus after the students have all gone home. Design enthusiasts love it, but casual visitors may get the eerie feeling they have somehow been miniaturised, *Betelgeuse*-style, and transported into a giant architect's model.

The main attraction here is the Barbican arts complex, with its library, cinema, theatre and concert hall – each reviewed in the appropriate chapters – plus an art gallery housing a regularly changing collection of conceptual and esoteric art. Just behind is the **Barbican Conservatory** (noon-5pm Sun), a surprisingly pleasant greenhouse, full of exotic ferns and palms. A recent improvement scheme has buffed up many of the public spaces, but finding your way around is still deeply confusing. Marooned amid the concrete towers is the only pre-war building in the vicinity: the heavily restored 16th-century church of **St Giles Cripplegate** (7638 1997, closed Sat), where Oliver Cromwell was married and John Milton buried.

Museum of London

150 London Wall, EC2Y 5HN (0870 444 3851/www.museumoflondon.org.uk). St Paul's tube/Barbican tube/rail. **Open** 10am-5.50pm Mon-Sat; noon-5.50pm Sun. Last entry 5.30pm. **Admission** free; suggested donation £2. **Credit** (shop) AmEx, MC, V. **Map** p404 P5.

Reached through a brick bastion in the middle of a roundabout on London Wall, this expansive museum traces the history of the capital from the earliest settlers to the outbreak of World War I (the Museum in Docklands, *see p170*, fills in some of the gaps). A rolling refurbishment keeps the galleries fresh and interesting, and there are plenty of activities and hands-on exhibits to keep kids entertained. The displays are laid out in chronological order and sound effects add character to the dioramas and displays of ancient artefacts from such surprising sites as the Saxon village under the Savoy Hotel and Julius Caesar's camp at Heathrow. Highlights include a model of the Great Fire, with a narrative from Pepys's diaries, an atmospheric walk-through Victorian shopping street, an outrageous fairytale coach belonging to the Lord Mayor and an original hansom carriage, as patronised by Sherlock Holmes (or at least Conan Doyle). In the central garden is a curious botanical history of the City. The website has details of temporary exhibitions.

Museum of Methodism & John Wesley's House

Wesley's Chapel, 49 City Road, EC1Y 1AU (7253 2262/www.wesleyschapel.org.uk). Moorgate tube/Old Street tube/rail. **Open** 10am-4pm Mon-Sat; after the service-1.45pm Sun. *Tours* arrangements on arrival; groups of 10 or more phone ahead. **Admission** free; donations requested. **Map** p405 Q4.

This quaint museum is set in the former home and chapel of John Wesley (1703-91), the founder of Methodism. The chapel crypt contains some charming displays on Welsey's life and you can tour the minister's slightly austere home, displaying his nightcap, preaching gown and personal experimental electric-shock machine. The chapel is full of memorials to stern-looking Methodist ministers, and downstairs (to the right) are some of the finest public toilets in London – built in 1899 and with original Victorian fittings by Sir Thomas Crapper.

Bank & around

Map p407 Q6

Mansion House tube/Bank tube/DLR.
Seven streets meet at Bank tube station, where the Bank of England, the Royal Exchange and Mansion House mark the symbolic heart of the Square Mile. These towering Portland stone monuments represent the wealth, status and governance of the City of London and most of the important decisions concerning the British economy are made within this small precinct.

Easily the most dramatic building here is the **Bank of England**, founded in 1694 to fund William III's war against the French. Today the bank is responsible for printing the nation's banknotes and setting the base rates for borrowing and lending. Parts of the fortress-like bank – which has no accessible windows and just one public entrance – were constructed by Sir John Soane in 1788, but most of what you see today was built in the 1920s. Access to the inner catacombs is tightly restricted, but members of the public can visit the **Bank of England Museum** (*see below*).

Next door is the Parthenon-like **Royal Exchange**, the former home of the London Stock Exchange. In 1972 the exchange shifted to offices on Threadneedle Street, and later to Paternoster Square. Today the only money changing hands is at the Paul Smith, Prada and de Beers emporiums in the vast central courtyard. Nearby is a statue of James Henry Greathead, who invented the machine that cut the tunnels for the London Underground.

The third historic structure is the Lord Mayor of London's official residence, **Mansion House** (7626 2500, group visits by written application two months in advance to the Diary Office, Mansion House, Walbrook, EC4N 8BH). Designed by George Dance and completed in 1753, it's the only private residence in the UK to have its own court of justice and prison cells. Next door is arguably one of London's worst architectural blunders, **Number 1 Poultry**; the name fits – it's a total turkey, especially as it replaced the beautiful and much-loved Mappin & Webb building.

Fortunately, architectural redemption is close at hand. Immediately south of Mansion House, the charming church of **St Stephen Walbrook** (7283 4444, 9am-4pm Mon-Fri) was built by Wren in 1672. Topped by a coffered dome, the radiant white interior has a wonderful sense of space and tranquillity, but the altar was destroyed by a World War II bomb and replaced by an ugly round blob sculpted by Sir Henry Moore. Back on Queen Victoria Street are the weather-worn remains of the **Temple of Mithras**, constructed by Roman soldiers in AD 240-50. When Rome abandoned paganism in the fourth century, many aspects of Mithras worship were incorporated into modern Christianity. Further south, on Cannon Street, you can observe the **London Stone**, thought to mark the centre point of London or a Roman temple or a druidic altar – or perhaps its just a rock.

On Lombard Street is Hawskmoor's **St Mary Woolnoth** surrounded by 17th-century banking houses with gilded signboards. Other significant churches in the area include Wren's **St Mary Abchurch**, off Abchurch Lane, and **St Clement**, on Clement's Lane, immortalised in the nursery rhyme 'Oranges and Lemons'. Over on Cornhill are two more Wren churches, **St Peter-upon-Cornhill** and **St Michael Cornhill**, the latter containing a bizarre statue of a pelican feeding its young, sculpted by someone who had plainly never seen a pelican.

North-west of the Bank of England is the centre of London's civic life: the **Guildhall**. Here you'll find the headquarters of the Corporation of London, the **Great Hall** (*see p99*), and its associated **Art Gallery** and **Library** (for both, *see p99*), plus the **Clockmakers' Museum** (*see below*), and the church of **St Lawrence Jewry**, another restored Wren construction.

Bank of England Museum

Entrance on Bartholomew Lane, EC2R 8AH (7601 5545/www.bankofengland.co.uk/museum). Bank tube/DLR. **Open** 10am-5pm Mon-Fri. *Tours* by arrangement. **Admission** free. *Tours* free. **Map** p407 Q6.
The bank originally built by Sir John Soane in 1788 has been extensively remodelled over the years, and the restored Stock Office houses an amusing museum on the history of the institution. As well as ancient coins and original artwork for British banknotes, the museum offers a rare chance to lift a real gold bar (closely monitored by CCTV). Since we visited last year, the bar has increased in value from £98,000 to £134,000, which says something about the state of the global gold market.

Clockmakers' Museum

Guildhall Library, Aldermanbury, EC2V 7HH (Guildhall Library 7332 1868/www.clockmakers.org). Mansion House or St Paul's tube/Bank tube/DLR/ Moorgate tube/rail. **Open** 9.30am-4.45pm Mon-Sat. **Admission** free. **Map** p406 P6.
This well-presented horological exhibition gathers hundreds of ticking, chiming clocks and watches, all produced by members of the London Clockmakers' Company. Among other venerable timepieces, you can see the marine chronometers that guided the ships of the British Empire – including examples by John Harrison (1693-1776), who solved the problem of longitude – and the watch Sir Edmund Hillary carried to the top of Everest in 1953.

Leadenhall Market, doing good trade in lattes and Rioja. *See p100.*

Great Hall

Gresham Street, EC2P 2EJ (7606 3030/tours ext 1463/www.corpoflondon.gov.uk). St Paul's tube/Bank tube/DLR. **Open** *May-Sept* 10am-5pm daily. *Oct-Apr* 10am-5pm Mon-Sat. Last entry 4.30pm. *Tours* by arrangement; groups of 10 or more people only. **Admission** free. **Map** p406 P6.

The cathedral-like Great Hall has been the home of the Corporation of London for more than 800 years. Banners and shields of the 100 livery companies grace the walls, and every Lord Mayor since 1189 gets a namecheck on the windows. Around the walls you can see memorials to Pitt the Younger, Pitt the Elder, Nelson, Winston Churchill and the Duke of Wellington. These days the hall mainly serves as the setting for ceremonial events, including meetings of the Court of Common Council (the governing body for the Corporation of London).

Guildhall Art Gallery

Guildhall Yard, off Gresham Street, EC2P 2EJ (7332 3700/www.guildhall-art-gallery.org.uk). Mansion House or St Paul's tube/Bank tube/DLR/ Moorgate tube/rail. **Open** 10am-5pm Mon-Sat (last entry 4.30pm); noon-4pm Sun (last entry 3.45pm). **Admission** £2.50; £1 concs; free under-16s. Free to all after 3.30pm daily, all day Fri. **Credit** (over £5) MC, V. **Map** p406 P6.

As you might expect, most of what's here is stuffy portraiture of royals and politicians, but there are a few surprises, including a delightful collection of Pre-Raphaelite paintings in the basement. The centrepiece of the exhibition is the vast *Siege of Gibraltar* by John Copley – the largest painting in Britain – which spans two floors of the gallery. You can also see works by Constable and Reynolds. Look out for the jug-eared bust of Prince Charles by David Wynne and the life-sized statue of Lady Thatcher, sculpted in appropriately icy white marble. Down in a sub-basement are the ruins of London's Roman amphitheatre, constructed in around AD 70.

Guildhall Library

Aldermanbury, EC2V 7HHJ (7332 1868/www.cityoflondon.gov.uk). St Paul's tube/Bank tube/DLR. **Open** 9.30am-5pm Mon-Sat. **Admission** free. **Map** p406 P6.

An extensive collection of books, manuscripts and prints relating to the history of London. Much of the collection is archived but original works can be requested for browsing, and the library has a regularly changing display of historic books, photographs and prints relating to the history of London. The bookshop has an excellent stock of books on London.

Monument & around

East from Bank along Cornhill is Gracechurch Street and the entrance to one of the most magical corners of the City, **Leadenhall Market**. This delightful Victorian covered market, dating from 1881, features a glorious vaulted ceiling by Horace Jones (who also constructed the market at Smithfield, *see p106*). Its glass-roofed alleys are home to a variety of shops, cafés and restaurants, including the **Lamb Tavern** (*see p226*).

Behind the market is Sir Richard Rogers's high-tech **Lloyd's of London** building, with all its mechanical services (ducts, stairwells, lift shafts and even loos) on the outside. It looks like a disassembled washing machine, but Londoners have come to love it. The original Lloyd's Register of Shipping, decorated with bas-reliefs of sea monsters and nautical scenes, is around the corner on Fenchurch Street.

At its southern end, Gracechurch is just one of six streets that converge in the shadow of the **Monument** (*see below*), the memorial to the Great Fire that engulfed London in 1666. On **Lower Thames Street** you can see several relics from the days when this part of the City was a busy port, including the **old Customs House** and **Billingsgate Market**, London's main fish market until 1982 when the trade moved to the Isle of Dogs. The lanes behind the waterfront are packed with churches, most notably **St Magnus the Martyr** (*see below*).

The Monument

Monument Street, EC3R 8AH (7626 2717/ www.towerbridge.org.uk). Monument tube. **Open** 9.30am-5pm daily. **Admission** £2; £1 concs; free under-5s. **No credit cards. Map** p407 Q7.

Still standing after 330 years, the world's largest free-standing Doric column was constructed by Sir Christopher Wren as a memorial to the Great Fire of London. The 202 feet from the ground to the tip of the golden flame is the distance east to Farriner's bakery in Pudding Lane, where the fire began. Inside, a 311-step spiral staircase winds up to a narrow gallery with views of most of the landmarks in central London.

St Magnus the Martyr

Lower Thames Street, EC3R 6DN (7626 4481/ www.stmagnusmartyr.org.uk). Monument tube. **Open** 10am-4pm Tue-Fri. *Mass* 11am Sun; 12.30pm Tue, Thur; 1.15pm Fri. **Admission** free; donations appreciated. **No credit cards. Map** p407 Q7.

Downhill from the Monument, this solid-looking Wren church marks the entrance to the original London Bridge, which was lined with shops, monuments and fortifications. The bridge was cleared of buildings in 1758, then sold brick and mortar in 1971 to an Arizona millionaire who, so the story goes, believed he was buying Tower Bridge. You can see a scale model of the old bridge inside the church, as well as some fine 18th-century woodcarving and a statue of axe-wielding St Magnus, the 12th-century Earl of Orkney.

Tower of London

Map p407 R7/8

Tower Hill tube/Tower Gateway DLR.

Perched on the riverbank between the City and the Thames, the **Tower of London** (*see p102*) delivers plenty of entertainment for your money and, accordingly, is mobbed all the hours it is open. Nevertheless, it would be extremely bad form to leave without seeing the Crown Jewels, the gruesome medieval weapons in the Royal Armoury and the Bloody Tower, in which Sir Walter Raleigh was imprisoned and the princes Edward V and Richard brutally murdered, allegedly on the orders of Richard III.

Most people detour east to **Tower Bridge** (*see p102*) then move on, but just across Bridge Approach is the tourist-friendly **St Katharine's Docks**. This was one of the first London docks to be formally closed and in 1969 it was sold to the Greater London Council, which demolished the warehouses and drew up plans for the modern development, which now includes a yacht marina, luxury apartments, offices, restaurants, shops and other facilities. Heading in the other direction, west of the Tower, is one

Tower Bridge (*see p102*) as seen from the **Monument** (*see p100*).

of the City's finest Edwardian buildings, the former **Port of London HQ** at 10 Trinity Square, with its towering neo-classical colonnade and gigantic statues of Commerce, Navigation, Export, Produce and Father Thames. In front, the **Trinity Square Gardens** contain a humbling memorial to the tens of thousands of merchant seamen killed in the World Wars. The surrounding streets and alleys have evocative names: Crutched Friars, Savage Gardens and Pepys Street. The famous diarist lived and died in nearby Seething Lane and in 1666 observed the Great Fire of London from **All Hallows by the Tower** (*see below*). Pepys is buried in the church of **St Olave** on Hart Street, nicknamed 'St Ghastly Grim' by Dickens for the leering skulls at the entrance to the churchyard.

More historic churches can be seen north of the Tower, including **St Botolph's-without-Aldgate** (*see p102*) and the tiny church of **St Katharine Cree** (7283 5733) on Leadenhall Street, one of only eight churches to survive the Great Fire. Inside is a memorial to Sir Nicholas Throckmorton, who was twice imprisoned in the Tower of London, despite – or perhaps because of – his close friendship with Queen Elizabeth I. Beside St Katharine is Mitre Street and, off it, **Mitre Square**, the location of the fifth Jack the Ripper murder. Just off Bevis Marks is the oldest synagogue in the country, the superbly preserved **Bevis Marks Synagogue** (7626 1274, closed Thur, Sat), built in 1701 by Sephardic Jews fleeing the Spanish Inquisition. Services are still held in Portuguese as well as Hebrew.

North is **St Mary Axe**, a street that owes its curious name to a long-gone church that is, in its turn, linked with the legend of English princes who travelled overseas only to meet a bloody end at the hands of Attila the Hun. He is said to have killed them with an axe, which was later displayed in the church. The name is now widely known as the address of the Lord Norman Foster-designed **Swiss Re Tower**, arguably London's finest modern building. It's known as the Gherkin for reasons that are obvious once you see it.

One block north, St Mary Axe intersects with **Houndsditch**, which leads to Liverpool Street Station and London Wall (*see p97*). Named after the ditch in which people left their dead dogs in medieval times, it was just inside the walls that divided the City from the East End (*see p163*).

All Hallows by the Tower

Byward Street, EC3R 5BJ (7481 2928/www.allhallowsbythetower.org.uk). Tower Hill tube. **Open** 9am-5.45pm Mon-Fri; 10am-5pm Sat, Sun. *Services* 11am Sun. **Admission** free; donations appreciated. **Map** p407 R7.

Often called London's oldest church, All Hallows is built on the foundations of a 7th-century Saxon church, but much of what you can see was reconstructed after World War II. The main hall contains a Saxon arch and a font cover carved by Grinling Gibbons in 1682; you can view Roman and Saxon relics and a Crusader altar in the undercroft.

St Botolph's-without-Aldgate

Aldgate High Street, EC3N 1AB (7283 1670/ www.stbotolphs.org.uk). Aldgate tube. **Open** 10am-3pm Mon-Fri, Sun. *Eucharist* 1.05pm Mon, Thur. *Prayers* 9am Mon-Fri; 1.05pm Tue, Wed. **Admission** free; donations appreciated. **Map** p407 R6.

The oldest of three surviving churches of St Botolph, this red-brick structure was built at the gates of Roman London as a homage to the patron saint of travellers. Reconstructed by George Dance in 1744, the church is noted for a ceiling beautifully decorated by John Francis Bentley.

St Ethelburga Centre for Reconciliation & Peace

78 Bishopsgate, EC2N 4AG (7496 1610/www.st ethelburgas.org). Bank tube/DLR/Liverpool Street tube/rail. **Open** 11am-3pm Fri, plus other times for events. **Admission** free; donations appreciated. **Map** p407 R6.

Built around 1390, the tiny church of St Ethelburga was almost obliterated by an IRA bomb in 1993, but the chapel has risen from the rubble as a centre for peace and reconciliation. With the progress in Northern Ireland, attention has shifted to promoting dialogue between Christianity and Islam.

St Helen's Bishopsgate

Great St Helen's, off Bishopsgate, EC3A 6AT (7283 2231/www.st-helens.org.uk). Bank tube/DLR/ Liverpool Street tube/rail. **Open** 9.30am-12.30pm Mon-Fri; also open some afternoons by appointment, call for details. *Services* 10.30am, 7pm Sun. **Admission** free. **Map** p407 R6.

Founded in 1210, St Helen's is actually two churches knocked into one, which explains its unusual shape. The church survived the Great Fire and the Blitz, but was badly damaged by IRA bombs in 1992 and 1993. Inside you can see an impressive selection of 16th- and 17th-century memorials, including one to Sir William Pickering, Queen Elizabeth I's ambassador to Spain.

Tower Bridge Exhibition

Tower Bridge, SE1 2UP (7403 3761/www.tower bridge.org.uk). Tower Hill tube. **Open** *Mid Apr-Sept* 10am-6.30pm daily. *Oct-mid Apr* 9.30am-5pm daily. **Admission** £5.50; £3-£4.25 concessions; £14 family; free under-5s. **Credit** AmEx, MC, V. **Map** p407 R8.

Opened in 1894, the steam-powered drawbridge is a triumph of Victorian technology, but these days few big ships venture this far upstream (you can check when the bridge is next due to be raised on the website). Two towers and the west walkway have been converted into an exhibition on the history of the bridge, with stupendous views up and down the river. You also get to visit the rooms in which the steam engines were housed that used to power the bridge lifts. **Photo** *p101.*

Tower of London

Tower Hill, EC3N 4AB (0870 756 6060/www.hrp. org.uk). Tower Hill tube/Fenchurch Street rail. **Open** *Mar-Oct* 10am-6pm Mon, Sun; 9am-6pm Tue-Sat (last entry 5pm). *Nov-Feb* 10am-5pm Mon, Sun; 9am-5pm Tue-Sat (last entry 4pm). **Admission** £15; £9.50-£12 concs; £43 family; free under-5s. **Credit** AmEx, MC, V. **Map** p407 R8.

Over the centuries, the Tower has served as a fortress, a royal palace, a prison and an execution site for traitors to the state – among the unlucky individuals to get the chop here were two of Henry VIII's wives. Despite being insanely crowded and dogged by poor disabled access (an unfortunate consequence of 900 years of fortification), this is one of the best-value attractions in London. There's so much to see that many visitors make a day of it.

Tickets are sold in the modern kiosk just the west of the palace and visitors enter through the Middle Tower, but there's also a free audio-visual display in the modernist Welcome Centre outside the walls. There are two ways to see the Tower: you can go it alone – with or without the audio tour – and stand some chance of having the displays to yourself, or join one of the free hour-long tours led by the Yeoman Warders (Beefeaters), who also care for the Tower's ravens. Kids in particular will love the tours, with gruesome stories of treason, torture and execution delivered by cheery, red-coated former soldiers of the Crown.

The highlight here is almost certainly the Crown Jewels, if only because they occupy such a hallowed position in the British psyche. Numerous films have been made about attempts to steal the jewels, but only one person ever came close – the villainous Colonel Blood in 1671 – and he negotiated a complete pardon! Inside the Jewel House, airport-style travelators glide past such treasures of state as the Monarch's Sceptre, mounted with the Cullinan I diamond, and the Imperial State Crown, worn by the Queen each year for the opening of Parliament. An exhibition in the Martin Tower tells the story of the royal crowns, and how many of the gems were actually borrowed from other European heads of state.

The other big drawcard is the armoury in the White Tower, with its swords and cannons, suits of armour and executioner's axe. Executions were actually carried out on the green in front of the Tower – the site is marked by a glass pillow, sculpted by Brian Catling in 2006. The bodies were buried nearby in the Chapel of St Peter ad Vincula.

New developments for 2007 include an impressive re-creation of Edward I's royal chambers in the Medieval Palace, complete with sound effects and a CGI film of medieval palace life. Ongoing exhibitions include the torture exhibition in the Wakefield Tower and displays on famous prisoners in the Bloody Tower and Beauchamp Tower.

Holborn & Clerkenwell

Where City suits and lawyers meet butchers and clubbers.

Holborn is a buffer between the razzle-dazzle of the West End and the suited institutions of the City. It's bordered by Kingsway to the west, Chancery Lane to the east, and Theobald's Road to the north. Although predominantly characterised by modern office blocks along its main routes, the area derives its essential character from two medieval Inns of Court – Gray's Inn and Lincoln's Inn – tranquil, leafy quadrangles that house the 'chambers' (offices) of barristers. (For London's other two surviving Inns of Court – Middle Temple and Inner Temple – *see p91.*) Clerkenwell is the northern fringe of the City, rich in medieval history and the traditions of monks and craftsmen, recently rediscovered and reborn as a loft-dwelling urban paradise of continental-style delis, gastropubs and all-night super-clubs.

Holborn

Map p401

Holborn tube.

Alighting at busy Holborn tube you'd never guess that just behind it lies the verdant tranquillity of **Lincoln's Inn Fields**, the largest public square in London. The Fields are flanked by a series of historic buildings. On the north side is **Sir John Soane's Museum** (*see p104*); south-west on Portsmouth Street is the **Old Curiosity Shop**, supposedly the oldest extant shop in London (now selling shoes); to the south is the Royal College of Surgeons, which houses the **Hunterian Museum** (*see below*), now open again to the public after an extensive £3m renovation; and south-east is **Lincoln's Inn** (7405 1393, www.lincolns inn.org.uk), the Inn of Court from which the fields take their name. The Inn's various buildings are a historical catalogue of architectures including Gothic, Tudor and Palladian; its Old Hall is more than half a century old. Exiting the Inn via the south gate leads to Carey Street, which runs along the back of the Royal Courts of Justice (*see p119*), and is also the address of one of London's best pubs, the **Seven Stars** (*see p227*).

Heading east along High Holborn takes you past the fine **Pearl Insurance Building**, now a hotel, to the junction with Chancery Lane. Just down Chancery Lane is the underground **London Silver Vaults** (7242 3844, www.thesilvervaults.com), where the goods of over 30 dealers constitute the world's largest 'collection' of antique silver. The vaults first opened in 1876, renting out strong rooms for the wealthy to protect their valuables.

Beside the south exit of Chancery Lane tube is the crooked, half-timbered **Staple Inn**, one of the few buildings to have survived the Great Fire, and one of the only remaining Tudor structures in the capital. Gray's Inn Road, which runs north from here, gives access to **Gray's Inn** (7458 7800, www.graysinn.org.uk). Its gardens, known colloquially as the 'Walks', were laid out in 1606; they are open to the public 10am-2.30pm Monday to Friday.

Further east, **Hatton Garden** is the centre of London's jewellery trade. Running parallel, **Leather Lane** is one of London's oldest street markets (10am-2.30pm Mon-Fri), while east of Hatton Garden **St Etheldreda** (*see p104*) is Britain's oldest Catholic church.

Hunterian Museum

Royal College of Surgeons, 35-43 Lincoln's Inn Fields, WC2A 3PE (7869 6560/www.rcseng.ac.uk/museums). Holborn tube. **Open** 10am-5pm Tue-Sat. **Admission** free. **Map** p401 M6.

John Hunter (1728-93) was a pioneering surgeon and anatomist, appointed physician to King George III. Through his life he amassed a huge collection of many thousands of medical specimens. After he died, the collection was enhanced and expanded by others; today it can be viewed in this recently refurbished museum housed at the Royal College of Surgeons. The bright new space means there is nothing gory about the exhibits – although these do include the brain of 19th-century mathematician Charles Babbage and Winston Churchill's dentures among the displays. There's also a collection of the (non-medical) artworks Hunter gathered.

St Etheldreda

14 Ely Place, EC1N 6RY (7405 1061/www.st etheldreda.com). Chancery Lane tube/Farringdon tube/rail. **Open** 8.30am-7pm daily. **Admission** free; donations appreciated. **Map** p404 N5.

St Etheldreda, which takes its name from an Anglo-Saxon saint, is Britain's oldest Catholic church and London's only surviving example of 13th-century Gothic architecture. Only saved from the Great Fire of London by a change in the wind, this is the last remaining building of the Bishop of Ely's palace. The crypt is dark and atmospheric, untouched by the noise of nearby traffic. The church's stained-glass windows (which, deceptively, are actually from the 1960s) are stunning. As an interesting piece of trivia, the strawberries once grown in the gardens of Ely Place were said to be the finest in the city, even receiving praise in Shakespeare's *Richard III*: 'My lord of Ely, when I was last in Holborn/I saw good strawberries in your garden there.'

Sir John Soane's Museum

13 Lincoln's Inn Fields, WC2A 3BP (7405 2107/ www.soane.org). Holborn tube. **Open** 10am-5pm Tue-Sat; 10am-5pm, 6-9pm 1st Tue of mth. *Tours* 2.30pm Sat. **Admission** free; donations appreciated. *Tours* £3; free concessions. **Map** p401 M5.

A leading architect in his day – he was responsible for the building that houses the Bank of England – Sir John Soane (1753-1837) obsessively collected art, furniture and architectural ornamentation, partly for enjoyment and partly for research. In the early 19th century he turned his house into a museum to which 'amateurs and students' should have access. Much of the museum's appeal derives from its domestic setting. Rooms are modestly sized but modified by Soane with ingenious devices to channel and direct natural daylight and to expand available space, including walls that open out like cabinets to display some of his many paintings (works by Canaletto, Turner and two series by Hogarth). The Breakfast Room has a beautiful and much-imitated domed ceiling inset with convex mirrors, but the real wow is the Monument Court, a multi-storey affair stuffed with an array of sculpted stone detailing that had been removed from ancient and medieval buildings. At the lowest level of the court is a sarcophagus of alabaster that's so thin it's almost translucent. It was carved for the pharaoh Seti I (1291-78 BC) and discovered in his tomb in Egypt's Valley of the Kings, before being removed by 19th-century treasure hunters. Soane bought it after the British Museum declined the opportunity.

Clerkenwell & Farringdon

Map p404

Farringdon tube/rail.

Not that long ago Clerkenwell was just some dilapidated old properties on the main route between the West End and north-east London.

Sir John Soane's Museum, where too much is never enough.

Walk on To market, to market

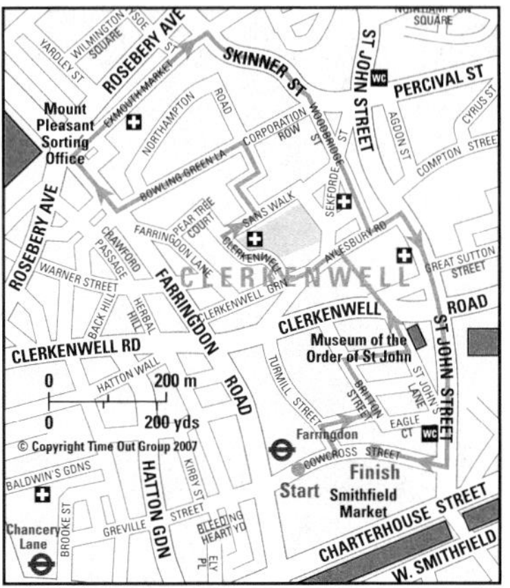

Start/finish: Farringdon tube/rail
Length: 2 miles

Start at **Farringdon station**, one of London's busiest, with a tidal wave of workers that spews out of it at 9am. Go left along Cowcross Street, left up Turnmill Street and then right up a little passage that opens out into Benjamin Street with its tiny gardens, once an overflow burial ground for St John's Church. Turn left up Britton Street and pass some fine 18th-century houses on both sides of the road. Turn right along Briset Street and left into St John's Lane.

Here the **medieval archway** contains a plaque explaining that this was the gateway to the Priory of the Knights of St John and was built in 1504. It's now the **Museum & Library of the Order of St John** (*see p106*). The gate once also housed a coffeehouse, the Old Jerusalem Tavern; a pub on Britton Street has adopted the name (*see p227*).

Across Clerkenwell Road is the **Church of St John**, with a fine Norman crypt. Head up narrow Jerusalem Passage, past the **Dovetail**, purveyor of 101 varieties of Belgium beer, and left at the top for **Clerkenwell Green**, an open space used for public meetings going back centuries. The large Georgian (built 1782) double-fronted mansion on the west end was once Middlesex's county courthouse; now it's the home of the **London Masonic Centre**. Facing you is an imposing grey-green building, dating from 1737 when it was a charity school. These days it's the **Marx Memorial Library** and contains a collection of socialist literature.

Cross the Green and walk up Clerkenwell Close, past the quirky **Three Kings** pub (*see p227*) and **St James Church** (*see p106*). As you carry on up the close, you pass on your right the site of two prisons built in the 17th century. You used to be able to visit some of the cells and see the records of the inmates, who were subsequently sent to Australia. Detour left along Bowling Green Lane. There are two famous architects in the street: Zaha Hadid's office is at No.9 in a converted school and CZWG – Piers Gough's office – is at No.17.

Turn right up Farringdon Road past the **Eagle** (*see p199*), a fine pub serving excellent food. Turn right into **Exmouth Market**, which has turned from a run-down shopping street into a trendy pedestrian zone with bars, cafés and restaurants such as **Ambassador** (*see p199*), **Medcalf** (*see p198*) and **Moro** (*see p199*).

Leave Exmouth Market and turn right down Skinner Street, where in 1390 the Skinners' Livery Company performed for Richard II a play lasting three days. Turn right down **Sekforde Street**, which is easily one of the prettiest streets in Clerkenwell, with its terraces of fine double-fronted Georgian cottages. Take a left-hand fork down Woodbridge Street and head left down Hayward's Place. Here you can still get a real sense of Clerkenwell as a village – until, that is, you emerge on to St John Street.

St John Street was the wide drovers' route for cattle coming into Smithfield Market, which is just to the south. It's one of the capital's most ancient thoroughfares, dating back at least to the 12th century. It's also where the Clerkenwell revival started, with the conversion of its factories and warehouses into smart new offices, apartments, bars and restaurants, including notably the famous **St John** restaurant (No.26; *see p198*), and Vietnamese eateries **Pho** (No.86) and recently opened **Xích Lô** (No.103). There are interesting little courtyards and passageways off St John Street: Passing Alley and Hat and Mitre Court are opposite each other after a few yards.

Once you reach the bottom of the street you have the chance to explore the fine Victorian **Smithfield Market** (*see p106*). Otherwise bear right down Cowcross Street and you're soon back at Farringdon station.

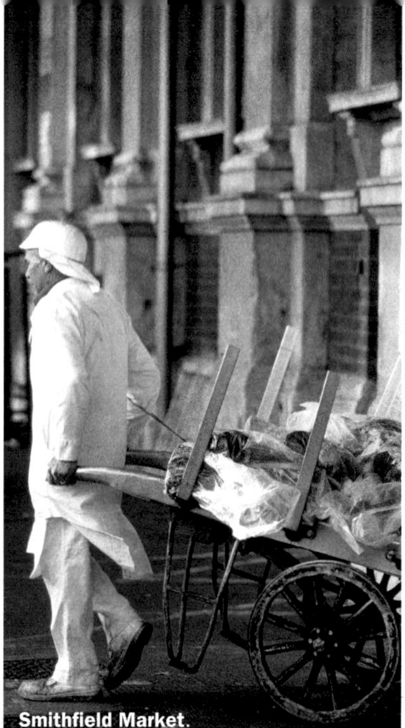
Smithfield Market.

But following decades of general disuse, in the 1980s and '90s the old workshops, warehouses and factories that characterise the area were vacuumed up by property developers and converted into modern flats and lofts. A forgotten and destitute district swiftly became a viable residence for City folk working just to the south, and restaurants, bars, nightclubs and even boutique hotels dutifully followed.

Clerkenwell means 'the clerks' well' – its 'clerks' being indicative of the area's strong monastic links. A community flourished here as early as the 11th century, when the Order of St John of Jerusalem set up its priory near the current St John's Church. The visible reminder of the historic priory is **St John's Gate**, which dates from 1504. It contains the **Museum & Library of the Order of St John** (*see below*), the Order that spawned today's St John Ambulance service.

Clerkenwell Road cuts through the old priory's grounds. North of the modern road, more ecclesiastical history is visible. Just off Clerkenwell Green, the current **St James Church** (Clerkenwell Close, 7251 1190, www.jc-church.org) stands on the former site of the nunnery of St Mary's Clerkenwell. Inside is a memorial to the Protestant martyrs burned at the stake by Mary Tudor, as well as a fine organ. With lots of visible history and some very good places to eat and drink, this is a fascinating area to explore.

Museum & Library of the Order of St John

St John's Gate, St John's Lane, EC1M 4DA (7324 4000/www.sja.org.uk/museum). Farringdon tube/rail.
Open 10am-5pm Mon-Fri; 10am-4pm Sat. *Tours* 11am, 2.30pm Tue, Fri, Sat. **Admission** free. *Tours* free. Suggested donation £5; £4 concessions. **Credit** MC, V. **Map** p404 O4.

Today the Order of St John is best known in London for its provision of ambulance services, but it dates back to early Christian medical practice during the Crusades of the 11th, 12th and 13th centuries. This museum charts the evolution of the medieval Order of Hospitaller Knights into its modern incarnation. There are fascinating collections of objects and artworks relating to this varied history, which visits Jerusalem, Malta and the Ottoman Empire. A separate collection relates specifically to the evolution of the modern ambulance service.

Smithfield

Until World War II, **Smithfield Market** was the main food market in the City, but it was torn apart in the Blitz and today only the meat market survives. It's housed in a lovely bit of Victorian architecture designed by Horace Jones in 1868. The Grand Avenue is particularly photogenic with its family of differently sized, old red phone boxes beneath painted cast-iron arches. The market's solid octagonal corner towers were originally pubs. Early risers (of the non-vegetarian sort) should visit at first light, when the meat trucks start rolling in. The market deals with 85,000 tons of meat and poultry every year – customers can walk through the central avenues, which are lined with individual stalls selling not just wholesale meat, but everything from quails' eggs to cheeses. The **Cock Tavern** (7248 2918), buried beneath the central market building, is licensed to open from 6am weekdays to serve beer and breakfast to market workers.

As in neighbouring Clerkenwell, gentrification stalks Smithfield in the form of an ever-increasing number of style bars and brasseries – but we're not complaining when the venues are as excellent as **Smiths of Smithfield** (*see p199*) and **Cellar Gascon** (*see p199*). Also here is super-club **Fabric** (*see p323*); reeling out at 5am on a Monday morning to weave through armies of white-aproned men carrying raw red carcasses on your way to find a night bus is an essential London experience.

At the north-east corner of the market a small lane leads up to a large grassy square: this is the site of the Carthusian monastery of **Charterhouse**, established in 1370. Its cloisters, 14th-century chapel and 17th-century library survive to this day.

Bloomsbury & Fitzrovia

Two writerly haunts, one of the high-brow, one of the highly intoxicated.

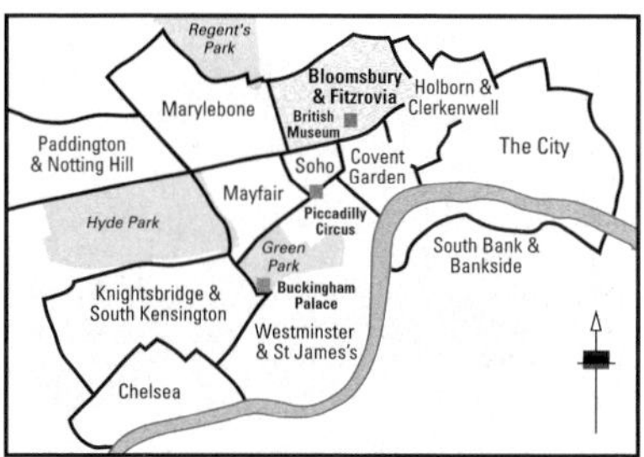

Bloomsbury is characterised by sweeping Georgian terraces and gracious squares, although for visitors its central beacon is the pastiche classicism of the British Museum. The museum's sibling institution, the British Library, is just to the north at King's Cross, which currently offers little else for visitors, although that is changing. Separated from Bloomsbury by Tottenham Court Road, Fitzrovia also lacks for sights but makes up for it with a bohemian recent past that continues to permeate the streets and alleys with a certain appealing louchеness.

Bloomsbury

Map p401

Holborn, Euston Square, Russell Square or Tottenham Court Road tube.

Though often associated with the group of academics, writers and artists who once colonised its townhouses, Bloomsbury hasn't always been a refuge for the high-minded. Its pretty floral name has humdrum origins: it's taken from 'Blemondisberi', or 'the manor of William Blemond', who acquired the area in the early 13th century. It remained rural until the 1660s, when the fourth Earl of Southampton built Bloomsbury Square around his house. The Southamptons intermarried with the Russells, the Dukes of Bedford, and both families developed the area as one of London's first planned suburbs. During the next couple of centuries, they built a series of grand squares and streets, laid out in the classic Georgian grid style: check out **Bedford Square** (1775-80), London's only complete Georgian square, and huge **Russell Square**, now a small but attractive public park.

The area's main charm lies in the sum of its parts, in an afternoon spent meandering through open spaces, browsing Great Russell Street's many **bookshops** and idling in historic pubs. Keep an eye out for the blue plaques, which read like a 'who's who' of English literature: William Butler Yeats once lived at 5 Upper Woburn Place, Edgar Allan Poe at 83 Southampton Row and TS Eliot at 28 Bedford Place; 6 Store Street was the birthplace of Anthony Trollope. Then there's **Dickens' House**, at 48 Doughty Street, now a museum (*see p109*). As for the famous Bloomsbury Group (wonderfully denounced by DH Lawrence as 'this horror of little swarming selves'), its headquarters was at 50 Gordon Square, where EM Forster, Lytton Strachey, John Maynard Keynes, Clive and Vanessa Bell, and Duncan Grant would discuss literature, art and politics. Virginia and Leonard Woolf lived at 52 Tavistock Square. But the real academia is clustered around Bloomsbury's western borders. Here, Malet Street, Gordon Street and Gower Street are dominated by the University of London. The most notable building is

British Museum. *See p109.*

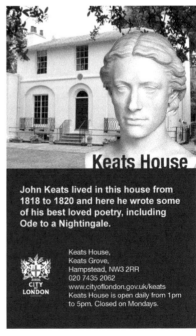

University College, on Gower Street, founded in 1826 and built in the Greek Revival style by William Wilkins, an architect whose name has quite rightly been largely forgotten. Inside lies one of the strangest exhibits in London: the mummified remains of philosopher Jeremy Bentham, who introduced the world to utilitarianism. His preserved remains, stored in a glass-fronted cabinet, are still taken to the weekly board of governors meeting, where he is marked as present but not voting.

The university's main library is housed in towering Gotham City-like **Senate House**, over on Malet Street. It is one of London's most imposing examples of monumental art deco design. Monolithic and brooding, the building was the model for Orwell's Ministry of Truth in his novel *1984*.

South of the university lies the renowned **British Museum** (*see below*), with its collection of the world's riches. Running off Great Russell Street, which is where you find the museum's main entrance, are three attractive parallel streets (Coptic, Museum and Bury), while on a cross-street between them is the new **Cartoon Museum** (*see below*). On Bloomsbury Way **St George's Bloomsbury** (7405 3044, www.stgeorgesbloomsbury.org.uk) is a grand but typically disturbing work by Nicholas Hawksmoor (note the offset spire, which is like a step pyramid), while nearby **Sicilian Avenue** is an Italianate, pedestrian precinct of colonnaded shops that links with Southampton Row. North-east of here is **Lamb's Conduit Street**, a convivial area with interesting shops and one of London's finest old pubs (the **Lamb**, *see p228*). At the top of this street lies wonderful **Coram's Fields** (*see p278*), a children's park (adults are only admitted if accompanied by a child) built on the former grounds of Thomas Coram's Foundling Hospital, which provided for abandoned children. The legacy of the great Coram family is now commemorated in the beautiful **Foundling Museum** (*see p110*).

British Museum

Great Russell Street, WC1B 3DG (7636 1555/ recorded information 7323 8783/www.thebritish museum.ac.uk). Russell Square or Tottenham Court Road tube. **Open** *Galleries* 10am-5.30pm Mon-Wed, Sat, Sun; 10am-8.30pm Thur, Fri. *Great Court* 9am-6pm Mon-Wed, Sun; 9am-11pm Thur-Sat. *Highlights tours* (90mins) 10.30am, 1pm, 3pm daily. *Eye opener tours* (50mins) phone for details. **Admission** free; donations appreciated. *Temporary exhibitions* prices vary. *Highlights tours* £8; £5 concessions. *Eye opener tours* free. **Credit** (shop) DC, MC, V. **Map** p401 K/L5.

Officially London's most popular tourist attraction, the museum is a neo-classical marvel built in 1847 by Robert Smirke, one of the pioneers of the Greek Revival style. Also impressive is Lord Norman Foster's glass-roofed Great Court, the largest covered space in Europe, opened in 2000. This £100m landmark surrounds the domed Reading Room, where Marx, Lenin, Thackeray, Dickens, Hardy and Yeats once worked. Star exhibits include ancient Egyptian artefacts – the Rosetta Stone and statuary on the ground floor, mummies upstairs – and Greek antiquities including the marble freizes from the Parthenon known as the Elgin Marbles. The Celts gallery has the Lindow Man, killed in 300 BC and preserved in peat. The Wellcome Gallery of Ethnography holds an Easter Island statue and regalia from Captain Cook's travels.

The King's Library, which opened in 2004, is the finest neo-classical space in London, and home to a permanent exhibition, 'Enlightenment: Discovering the World in the 18th Century', a 5,000-piece collection devoted to the formative period of the museum. Its remit covers physics, archaeology and the natural world, and it contains objects as diverse as 18th-century Indonesian puppets and a beautiful orrery.

You won't be able to see everything in one day, so buy a souvenir guide and pick out the showstoppers, or plan several visits. The Highlights tours focus on specific aspects of the collection; Eye opener tours are introductions to world cultures. **Photo** *p107.*

Cartoon Museum

35 Little Russell Street, WC1N 2HH (7580 8155/ www.cartoonmuseum.org). Tottenham Court Road tube. **Open** 10.30am-5.30pm Tue-Sat; noon-5.30pm Sun. **Admission** £3; £2-free concessions. **Credit** (shop) AmEx, DC, MC, V. **Map** p409 Y1.

On the ground floor of this transformed former dairy, the very best in British cartoon art is displayed in chronological order, starting with the early 18th century, when high-society types back from the Grand Tour introduced the Italian practice of *caricatura* to polite company. From Hogarth it moves through Britain's cartooning 'golden age' (1770-1830) to examples of wartime cartoons, ending up with modern satirists such as Gerald Scarfe, the wonderfully loopy Ralph Steadman and the *Guardian*'s Steve Bell. Upstairs celebrates UK comic art, with original 1921 Rupert the Bear artwork by Mary Tourtel, Frank Hampson's Dan Dare, Leo Baxendale's Bash Street Kids and a painted Asterix cover by that well-known Brit Albert Uderzo. There is a shop, but it isn't half as good as Gosh!, the comic store just round the corner at 39 Great Russell Street (7636 1011, www.goshlondon.com). **Photo** *p110.*

Dickens' House

48 Doughty Street, WC1N 2LX (7405 2127/www. dickensmuseum.com). Chancery Lane or Russell Square tube. **Open** 10am-5pm Mon-Sat; 11am-5pm Sun. *Tours* by arrangement. **Admission** £5; £4-£3 concessions; £14 family. **Credit** (shop) AmEx, DC, MC, V. **Map** p401 M4.

London is scattered with plaques marking the many addresses where the peripatetic Charles Dickens lived but never quite settled, but this is the only one of the author's many London homes that is still standing. Dickens lived here for three years between 1837 and 1840 while he wrote *Nicholas Nickleby* and *Oliver Twist*. Ring the doorbell to gain access to four floors of Dickensania, from posters advertising his public speaking to personal letters, manuscripts and his writing desk, exhibited in rooms decorated as they would have been at the time of his occupancy.

Foundling Museum

40 Brunswick Square, WC1N 1AZ (7841 3600/ www.foundlingmuseum.org.uk). Russell Square tube. **Open** 10am-6pm Tue-Sat; noon-6pm Sun. **Admission** £5; £4 concessions; free under-16s. **Credit** MC, V. **Map** p401 L4.

This is a child-friendly place in every sense. Opened in 2004, the museum recalls the social history of the Foundling Hospital, set up in 1739 by a compassionate shipwright and sailor, Captain Thomas Coram. Returning to England from America in 1720, he was appalled by the number of abandoned children on the streets. Securing royal patronage, he gained the artist William Hogarth and the composer GF Handel as governors; Hogarth decreed that the building should also be the first public art gallery, and artists including Gainsborough, Reynolds and Wilson donated their work. The museum uses pictures, manuscripts and objects to recount the social changes of the period. There are interactive exhibits, and a case of mementos left by mothers for their babies.

Petrie Museum of Egyptian Archaeology

University College London, Malet Place, WC1E 6BT (7679 2884/www.petrie.ucl.ac.uk). Euston Square, Goodge Street or Warren Street tube. **Open** 1-5pm Tue-Fri; 10am-1pm Sat. **Admission** free; donations appreciated. **Map** p401 K4.

The museum, set up in 1892 by eccentric traveller and diaryist Amelia Edwards (*A Thousand Miles Up the Nile*), is named after Flinders Petrie, one of the most inexhaustible excavators of ancient Egyptian treasures. Where the British Museum's Egyptology collection is strong on the big stuff, the Petrie (pronounced 'pee-tree') focuses on the minutiae of ancient life. Its aged wooden cabinets are filled with pottery shards, grooming accessories, jewellery and primitive tools. Highlights include a small group of Fayoum portraits and artefacts from the heretic pharaoh Akhenaten's short-lived capital Tell el Amarna. Among the oddities are the world's oldest gynaecological papyrus and a 4,000-year-old skeleton of a man who was buried in an earthenware pot. That some corners of this small museum are so gloomy staff offer torches only adds to the fun.

King's Cross & St Pancras

Map p401

King's Cross tube/rail.

In 1835 a monument to the recently deceased King George IV was built at the junction of Pentonville Road, Gray's Inn Road and Euston Road. George had been an unpopular king, and the monument didn't last long. But Georgie had the last laugh: the area formerly known as Battle Bridge was from then on known as King's Cross. Right now, though, its old name seems more apt because the place looks like a warzone with roads ripped up and buildings boarded up. All this is part of an extensive makeover for the area, connected to the new Channel Tunnel Rail Link. **St Pancras Station**, with its gorgeous Victorian glass-and-iron train shed (for many years the largest clear span in the world), will receive international services from Paris and Sir George Gilbert Scott's magnificent Gothic hotel building, which fronts the station, will reopen, with parts given over to commercial and residential use (*see p111* **Station master**).

Bloomsbury's newest draw, the **Cartoon Museum**. *See p109.*

Once all the building work is done, the gaping badlands to the north of St Pancras and King's Cross stations (currently known for drugs and prostitution) will have been transformed into a mixed-use nucleus called King's Cross Central. Until then, there are still a few places to explore: the **London Canal Museum** (*see below*) is secreted north of King's Cross Station, and children will love the wilds of **Camley Street Natural Park** (12 Camley Street, 7833 2311), an unexpected little garden oasis between the stations beside the canal.

British Library

96 Euston Road, NW1 2DB (7412 7332/www.bl.uk). Euston Square tube/Euston or King's Cross tube/rail. **Open** 9.30am-6pm Mon, Wed-Fri; 9.30am-8pm Tue; 9.30am-5pm Sat; 11am-5pm Sun. **Admission** free; donations appreciated. **Map** p401 K/L3.

Opened in 1997, the new British Library went over budget by £350m, took 20 years to complete and was 15 years behind schedule. When it finally opened, architecture critics ripped it to shreds – 'one of the ugliest buildings in the world' in the opinion of a Parliamentary committee. But don't judge a book by its cover: this is still one of the greatest libraries in the world, with 150 million items. Each year, it receives a copy of every publication produced in the UK and Ireland. In the John Ritblat Gallery, the library's main treasures are displayed: the Magna Carta, the Lindisfarne Gospels and original manuscripts from Chaucer. There's fun stuff too: Beatles lyric sheets, first editions of *The Jungle Books* and archive recordings of everyone from James Joyce to Bob Geldof. The library is also famous for its 80,000-strong stamp collection. The focal point of the building is the King's Library, a six-storey glass-walled tower that houses George III's collection.

London Canal Museum

12-13 New Wharf Road, off Wharfdale Road, N1 9RT (7713 0836/www.canalmuseum.org.uk). King's Cross tube/rail. **Open** 10am-4.30pm Tue-Sun. **Admission** £3; £2 concessions; £1.50 children; free under-8s. **Map** p401 M2.

The museum is housed in a former 19th-century ice warehouse, used by Carlo Gatti for his famous ice-cream, and includes an exhibit on the history of the ice trade and ice-cream. This is the most interesting part of the exhibition, as the collection looking at the history of the waterways and those who lived and worked on them is sparse, although there are some moored barges. The canalside walk from here to Camden Town is worth doing if you have the time.

St Pancras Old Church & St Pancras Gardens

St Pancras Road, NW1 1UL (7387 4193). Mornington Crescent tube/King's Cross tube/rail. **Open** *Gardens* 7am-dusk daily. *Services* 9am Mon-Fri; 9.30am Sun; 7pm Tue. **Admission** free. **Map** p401 K2.

Station master

The architectural treasure that is **St Pancras Station** is one of London's best-loved monuments. A riot of Victorian Gothic Revival exuberance, it is a curving cliff-face of red brick topped by massed towers, turrets and spires worthy of the imaginings of the Brothers Grimm. When it opened as the Midland Grand Hotel in the 1870s, it was described as the 'most sumptuous and the best conducted hotel in the whole Empire'. The grand staircase remains one of the finest in the country, and the lofty corridors and chambers of the building have been used as a location for films, pop videos and fashion shoots. It's bizarre, then, that the place has lain empty and decaying since the 1980s. Happily, that's all in the process of change.

A huge £500m project will turn neglected St Pancras into one of Europe's major transport hubs, a landmark station that will see a projected 50 million passengers each year passing beneath its vaulted arches. The roster of transport links is nothing if not impressive: regular, high-speed routes to France and Belgium; the intersection of six London underground lines; high-speed links to Kent (via Stratford in a spry seven minutes). Slick connections are, however, only half the story. The developers envisage St Pancras International as a destination station, a meeting place, somewhere to linger in original, high-end shops, bars and restaurants. It will have the longest champagne bar in Europe, major displays of public art and even – we are promised – a farmers' market. Meanwhile, the innovative Manhattan Loft Corporation is busy transforming the building into a 245-bed five-star hotel and apartments for 2008 (www.stpancraschambers.co.uk).

Those who fear the results of such rapid commercial development will be reassured to hear that English Heritage is involved in the proceedings. The once-fabulous roof, bombed in World War II, will have its glass put back in, and its ironwork will return to its original shade of blue. If the rebirth of St Pancras is successful, the building will be the key to the regeneration of the whole King's Cross area, drawing both Londoners and visitors to a part of town previously best known for its hookers and junkies.

The Old Church, whose site may date back to the fourth century, has been ruined and rebuilt many times. The current structure is handsome, but it's the restored churchyard that delights. Among those buried here are writer William Godwin and his wife, Mary Wollstonecraft; over this grave, their daughter Mary Godwin (author of *Frankenstein*) declared her love for poet Percy Bysshe Shelley. The grave of Sir John Soane is one of only two Grade I-listed tombs (the other is Karl Marx's, in Highgate Cemetery); its dome influenced Gilbert Scott's design for the classic red British phone box.

Fitzrovia

Maps p400 & p401

Tottenham Court Road or Goodge Street tube.
Squeezed in between Tottenham Court Road, Oxford Street, Great Portland Street and Euston Road, Fitzrovia may not be as famous as Bloomsbury but its history is just as rich. The origins of the name are hazy: some believe it comes from Fitzroy Square, which was named after Henry Fitzroy, the son of Charles II; others insist the neighbourhood was named after the famous **Fitzroy Tavern** (16 Charlotte Street, 7580 3714), ground zero for London bohemia of the 1930s and '40s, a favourite with regulars such as Dylan Thomas, George Orwell, 'wickedest man in the world' Aleister Crowley and state hangman Albert Pierrepoint.

Pollock's Toy Museum.

But the neighbourhood's radical roots go back much further. Thomas Paine lived at 154 New Cavendish Street in 1792 – the year he published *The Rights of Man* and incurred governmental wrath. His friend Edmund Burke lived at 18 Charlotte Street. During the early 19th century the district became a hotbed of Chartist activity and working men's clubs. Later, Karl Marx attended Communist meetings in Tottenham Street, Charlotte Street and Rathbone Place.

Fitzrovia's raffish image is now very much a thing of the past. It's better known these days as a high-powered media centre. ITN started broadcasting from 48 Wells Street, and Channel 4's first office was at 60 Charlotte Street from 1982. The area's icon is now the **Telecom Tower**, completed in 1966 as the Post Office Tower. Its revolving restaurant and observation deck were open to the public (it features in the 1967 film *Bedazzled* with Peter Cook and Dudley Moore) until the IRA exploded a bomb in the toilets. **Charlotte Street** and neighbouring byways around remain a good destination for dining and drinking.

All Saints

7 Margaret Street, W1W 8JG (7636 1788/www.allsaintsmargaretstreet.org.uk). Oxford Circus tube.
Open 7am-7pm daily. *Services* 7.30am, 8am, 1.10pm, 6pm, 6.30pm Mon-Fri; 7.30am, 8am, 6pm, 6.30pm Sat; 8am, 10.20am, 11am, 5.15pm, 6pm Sun. **Admission** free. **Map** p408 U1.

This 1850s church was designed by William Butterfield, one of the great Gothic Revivalists. It is squeezed into a tiny site, but its soaring architecture and lofty spire – the second-highest in London – disguise the fact. Behind the striking polychromatic brick façade its shadowy but lavish interior is one of the city's most striking, with rich marble, flamboyant tile work, and glittering stones built into its pillars. British architectural critic Ian Nairn described the church building as an 'orgasm'.

Pollock's Toy Museum

1 Scala Street (entrance on Whitfield Street), W1T 2HL (7636 3452/www.pollockstoymuseum.com). Goodge Street tube. **Open** 10am-5pm Mon-Sat. **Admission** £3; £1.50 concessions; free under-3s. **Credit** (shop) MC, V. **Map** p400 J5.

Housed in a wonderfully creaky Georgian townhouse, Pollock's is named after Benjamin Pollock, the last of the Victorian toy theatre printers. By turns beguiling and creepy, the museum is a nostalgia-fest of old board games, tin trains, porcelain dolls and Robertson's gollies. It's fascinating for adults but possibly less so for children, for whom the displays are a bit static and irrelevant – although confronted with items like the pile of painted woodchips stuffed in a cardboard box and passed off as a 'Build a skyscraper' kit they may gain a bit more of an appreciation for the PlayStation.

Covent Garden & the Strand

A former market and a tax office turned star attractions.

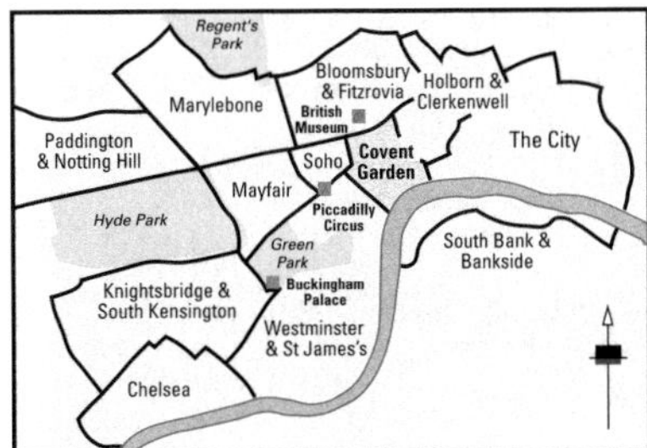

Covent Garden is looked on as a bit touristy by locals, particularly its Piazza. But as the world's tourist honeypots go, it deserves the crowds it attracts. The once-elegant Strand, home of the Savoy, rules off the south side of Covent Garden and in doing so links Trafalgar Square with the Aldwych and Fleet Street.

Covent Garden

Map p409

Covent Garden or Leicester Square tube.

Back in the 13th century this land was indeed, as the name suggests, the site of a convent and its garden, belonging to Westminster Abbey. It came into the hands of John Russell, first Earl of Bedford, in 1552 (the family still owns tracts of land hereabouts) and the following century it was descendants of his who initiated the development of the area. The fourth Earl of Bedford employed the sought-after architect of the day Inigo Jones, who created the Italianate open square that remains the centrepiece of today's Covent Garden. St Paul's Church formed its western boundary and the remaining three sides consisted of tall terraced houses. Fashionable London flocked to the area and paid good money for the privilege of residency.

The first recorded market in Covent Garden appeared on the south side of the square in 1640, selling fruit and vegetables. It attracted coffeehouses and theatres, as well as gambling dens and brothels. During the next three centuries the market grew until it became London's pre-eminent fruit and vegetable wholesaler, employing over 1,000 porters. A flower market was added (where London's Transport Museum now stands) and the market building itself was redesigned by the architect Charles Fowler. It then remained in the Bedfords' hands until 1918, by which time it had been upgraded with new buildings and market halls.

In the second half of the 20th century, it was obvious that the congested streets of central London were unsuitable for market traffic and the decision was taken to move the traders out (for a last look at the market shortly before it closed, watch Alfred Hitchcock's 1972 thriller *Frenzy*). In 1974, with the market gone, property developers loomed over the empty stalls and offices, and it was only through mass squats and demonstrations that the area was saved. Today there exists a thriving residential community alongside a mix of established shops and small enterprises, and a sprinkling of cultural venues carrying on the theatrical heritage. The chain stores may have moved in, but it's still a nice place to stroll.

Covent Garden Piazza

Inigo Jones's Piazza remains an attractive space and Charles Fowler's market hall gets lovelier with age. Visitors flock here for a combination of gentrified shopping, outdoor restaurant and café seating, street artists and classical renditions in the lower courtyard. The majority of the street entertainment takes place under the portico of **St Paul's** (*see p115*). It was here that Samuel Pepys observed what is thought to be Britain's first Punch & Judy show, on 9 May 1662. Maintaining the area's links with the theatre, St Paul's launched its own Avenue of the Stars in September 2005, immortalising British- and Commonwealth-born entertainers. Those honoured so far include Laurence Olivier, Charlie Chaplin and Alec Guinness.

Shoppers favour the **old covered market** (7836 9136, www.coventgardenmarket.co.uk), now a collection of small, sometimes quirky shops, many of them with a twee, touristy appeal, as well as upmarket chain stores such

as Hobbs, Whistles and Crabtree & Evelyn. The Apple Market, in the North Hall, has arts and crafts stalls every Tuesday to Sunday, and antiques on Monday. Across the road, the cheaper, tackier **Jubilee Market** deals mostly in novelty T-shirts and other such tat.

The best view of the Piazza and market is from the Amphitheatre Café Bar terrace loggia at the **Royal Opera House** (*see below*).

London's Transport Museum

39 Wellington Street, WC2E 7BB (7565 7299/ www.ltmuseum.co.uk). Covent Garden tube. **Open/ admission** phone for details. **Map** p409 Z3.

When the renovated museum reopens in July 2007 expect lovingly preserved buses from the horse age to the present day, plus trains, taxis, trams and trolleybuses, not to mention uniforms, models and posters. This is one of London's most joyful museums and we can't wait for its return.

Royal Opera House

Bow Street, WC2E 9DD (7304 4000/www.royal operahouse.org). Covent Garden tube. **Open** 10am-3.30pm Mon-Sat. **Admission** free. *Stage tours* £9; £8/£7 concessions. **Credit** AmEx, DC, MC, V. **Map** p409 Y3.

The Royal Opera House (founded 1732) has witnessed no fewer than three fires in its lifetime. The current building is the third on the site, the second having been sublet in 1855 to John Anderson, who had already seen two theatres burnt down and made this his third – on the final day of his lease. But that's the least of the dramas associated with this stage. Handel premièred *Samson, Judas Maccabaeus* and *Solomon* here, among many other works. Frenzied opera lovers twice rioted against ticket price rises, for 61 nights in 1809, while the 1763 fracas came within an iron pillar of bringing down the galleries. It's possible to explore the building as part of an organised tour, *see p340* **Backstage pass**. Certain parts of the building are also open to the general public, including the glass-roofed Floral Hall, the Crush Bar (so named because in Victorian times the only thing served at the bar during intermissions was orange and lemon crush) and the Amphitheatre Café Bar, with its terrace overlooking the Piazza. Productions for the 2007 season include three complete performances of Wagner's Ring cycle.

St Paul's Covent Garden

Bedford Street, WC2E 9ED (7836 5221/www. actorschurch.org). Leicester Square tube/Charing Cross tube/rail. **Open** 9am-4.30pm Mon-Fri; 9am-12.30pm Sun. *Services* 1.10pm Wed; 11am Sun. *Choral Evensong* 4pm 2nd Sun of mth. **Admission** free; donations appreciated. **Map** p409 Y3.

Known as the Actors' Church for its association with Covent Garden's theatreland, this plain Tuscan pastiche was designed by Inigo Jones in 1631. Actors commemorated on its walls range from those now confined to obscurity – AR Philpott, 'Pantopuck the Puppetman' – to those destined for ambrosian immortality – Vivien Leigh, 'Now boast thee, death, in thy possession lies a lass unparallel'd'. George Bernard Shaw set the first scene of *Pygmalion* under the church's rear portico, and the first known victim of the plague, Margaret Ponteous, is buried in the pleasant churchyard.

Elsewhere in Covent Garden

The area offers a mixed bag of entertainment, eateries and shops. On the area's western border from opposite ends of St Martin's Lane – and the social spectrum – the well-known lap-dancing establishment **Stringfellows** (16-19 Upper Saint Martin's Lane, 7240 5534) faces down the **Coliseum**, the home of the English National Opera. **Brydges Place**, which runs off St Martin's Lane just south of the opera house, is the narrowest alley in London; only one person can walk down it at a time.

Closer to the Piazza, most of the older, more unusual shops have been superseded by a homogeneous mass of cafés. High-profile fashion designers have all but domesticated main shopping street **Long Acre**, although excellent travel bookshop **Stanfords** (*see p238*) still holds out for the independents.

The portico, **St Paul's Covent Garden**.

Sightseeing

The more interesting shopping experiences lie in the streets north of Long Acre, notably the attractive trio of **Neal Street**, **Monmouth Street** and **Earlham Street**. Earlham is home to the **Donmar Warehouse** (*see p344*), a former banana-ripening depot that is now an intimate theatre; Sam Mendes was artistic director here before taking off for Hollywood and fame with *American Beauty*. On Shorts Gardens next door is pungent and wonderful **Neal's Yard Dairy** (No.17, 7240 5700), purveyor of exceptional UK cheeses, while down a little passageway one door along is **Neal's Yard** itself, known for its co-operative cafés, herbalists and head shops.

Where Monmouth and Earlham Streets meet Shorts Gardens is **Seven Dials**, named after the number of sundials incorporated into the central monument (the seventh being formed by the pillar itself). The original pillar, an infamous criminal rendezvous, was torn down in 1773 by a mob who believed that treasure was buried at its base (it wasn't).

South of Long Acre and east of the Piazza, historical depravity is called to account at the former **Bow Street Magistrates Court**, once home to the Bow Street Runners, precursors to the Metropolitan Police, and site of Oscar Wilde's conviction in 1895 for 'indecent acts'. Suffragette Emily Pankhurst and East End mobsters the Kray Twins were also tried here. However, on 14 July 2006 the judge's gavel fell for the last time; the building has been sold and is set to become a boutique hotel.

To the south, Wellington and Catherine Streets mix theatres (including, notably, the grand **Theatre Royal**, where you can join a daily tour; *see p340*) with an excess of small brasseries and restaurants vying for the attention of pre- and post-performance diners.

The **Freemasons' Hall** – the impressive white building at the point where Long Acre becomes Great Queen Street (7831 9811; call for guided tours) – is worth a peek for its solemn, symbolic architecture.

The Strand & Embankment

Map p409

Embankment tube or Charing Cross tube/rail.

Strange to think that until as recently as the 1860s the bustling street known as the Strand ran beside the Thames. In fact, it was originally a bridlepath running alongside the river. As early as the 14th century it was lined with grand residences whose gardens ran down to the water. It wasn't until the 1870s that the Thames was pushed back with the creation of the Embankment and its adjacent gardens. By the time George Newnes's famed *Strand* magazine was introducing its readership to Sherlock Holmes (1891), the street after which the magazine was named boasted the Savoy and its theatre, the Cecil Hotel (long since demolished), Simpson's, King's College and Somerset House (*see p119*), leading the politician Benjamin Disraeli to describe it as 'perhaps the finest street in Europe'.

The birth of the beautiful game

In 26 October 1863 officials from 12 football clubs met at a pub in Covent Garden 'for the purpose of forming an association with the object of establishing a definite code of rules for the regulation of the game'. Those present were Barnes, Blackheath, Blackheath Proprietory School, Charterhouse, Crusaders, Crystal Palace, Forest of Leytonstone, Kensington School, No Names Club of Kilburn, Percival House (Blackheath), Surbiton and the War Office Club.

They were to meet six times in 44 days before announcing the formation of the Football Association, and producing a set of 14 rules that combined dribbling as well as handling. However, there was one point they couldn't agree on: 'hacking' – in other words, kicking an opponent on the shins. Blackheath's representative believed a few bruises were character-building; others thought the practice barbaric. The hackers lost the argument and Blackheath withdrew, taking the concept of handling with them as well – thus creating the game of rugby (which, by the way, outlawed hacking in 1871).

Most football history books insist the pub where the rules were drawn up was the Freemason's Tavern in Great Queen Street. However, the building and those nearby were demolished in the early 20th century to make way for the monolithic Freemasons' Hall I(*see above*). Other sources claim the nearby **Freemasons Arms** (81-82 Long Acre, 7836 3115) is the cradle of the game – something that particular pub is happy to trade on, with its football memorabilia on the walls and plasma screens.

Where better to watch the big match than the pub where football was effectively born? If, indeed, it was.

Seven Dials, site of much infamy and fruitless treasure hunting. *See p116*.

The huge courtyard of **Somerset House**. *See p119.*

Nobody would make any such claims today – there are too many overbearing office blocks and underwhelming restaurants – but there's still plenty of interest. In 1292 the body of Eleanor of Castile, consort to King Edward I, completed its funerary procession from Lincoln to the small hamlet of Charing, which lay at the western end of what's now the Strand, and the occasion was then marked by the last of 12 elaborate crosses. A replica of Eleanor's Cross was erected in 1865 on the forecourt of **Charing Cross Station**, where it remains today, looking like the spire of a sunken cathedral. Across the road is Maggie Hambling's eccentric sarcophagal memorial *A Conversation with Oscar Wilde*.

The Embankment itself can be approached down **Villiers Street**, where at No.43 once lived Rudyard Kipling, author of *The Jungle Book*. Pass through the tube station to where **boat tours** with on-board entertainment embark. Just east stands **Cleopatra's Needle**, an obelisk presented to the British nation by the viceroy of Egypt, Mohammed Ali, in 1820 (although it took another 59 years before it was finally set in place beside the Thames). It was originally erected around 1500 BC by the pharaoh Tuthmosis III at a site near modern-day Cairo, before being moved to Alexandria, Cleopatra's capital, in 10 BC; by this time, however, the great queen was 20 years dead. The plinth contains a full set of British Empire coins, Bibles in various languages, a railway guide and copies of newspapers from 1879, the year it was erected.

Back on the Strand, the majestic **Savoy Hotel** opened in 1889, financed by the profits made by Richard D'Oyly Carte's productions of Gilbert and Sullivan's light operas at the neighbouring Savoy Theatre (which pre-dates the hotel by eight years). Interestingly Savoy Court, which connects the hotel's magnificent deco entrance with the Strand, is the only street in the whole of England where the traffic drives on the right.

Benjamin Franklin House

36 Craven Street, WC2N 5NF (7839 2006/www.benjaminfranklinhouse.org). Charing Cross tube/rail. **Open** pre-book tour by phone or online. **Admission** £8. **Map** p409 Y5.

Restoration of the house where Franklin – scientist, diplomat, philospher, inventor and Founding Father of the United States – lived between 1757 and 1775 was completed in January 2006. It is now open to the public as a centre for academic research concerning Franklin. The house is not a museum in the conventional sense, but it can be explored on well-run, pre-booked tours lasting a short but intense 45 minutes. These are led by an actress in character as Franklin's landlady Margret Stevenson and use projections and sound to conjure up the world of the man and the times in which he lived.

The Aldwych

Map p407

Temple tube (closed Sun).

At the eastern end of the Strand is the Aldwych, a grand crescent that dates back only to 1905, although the name 'ald wic' (old settlement) has its origins in the 14th century. On its south side is the splendidly regal **Somerset House** (*see below*); even if you aren't interested in its galleries, it's worth visiting the fountain courtyard, especially in December and January when it's the venue for a hugely popular open-air ice-skating rink. Beyond Somerset House you pass **King's College**, its 1960s buildings sitting uneasily with Robert Smirke's 1829 originals. In front of the college is **St Mary-le-Strand** (7836 3126, open 11am-4pm Mon-Fri; music recitals 1.05pm Wed, Fri), James Gibbs's first public building, built 1714-17. The church was originally intended to have a statue of Queen Anne on a column beside it, but she died before it could be built and the plan was scrapped. On sinister Strand Lane, reached via Surrey Street, is the so-called **'Roman' bath** where Dickens took many a cold plunge. Back near King's College, on the Strand and on Surrey Street, are entrances to one of London's ghost tube stations: the 1907 Aldwych station (although the signs say 'Strand', the station's earlier name). It has been closed since 1994.

On a traffic island just east of the Aldwych is **St Clement Danes** (7242 8282). It's believed that a church was first built here by the Danish in the ninth century, but the current building is mainly Sir Christopher Wren's handiwork. It's the main church of the RAF. Just beyond the church are the **Royal Courts of Justice** (*see below*) and Temple Bar, which marks the historic boundary of Westminster with the neighbouring City of London.

Turning back towards the Strand, on the north of the Aldwych is a trio of imperial buildings: Australia House, Bush House (home to the BBC's World Service) and India House, offices of the Indian High Commission.

Royal Courts of Justice

Strand, WC2A 2LL (7947 6000/www.courtservice.gov.uk). Temple tube. **Open** 9am-5pm Mon-Fri. **Admission** free. **Map** p401 M6.

The magnificent Royal Courts preside over the most serious civil cases in British law. Members of the public are allowed to attend these trials (with exceptions made for sensitive cases), so if you want to see the British justice system in action, step inside.There are few trials in August and September. Note that cameras and children under 14 are not permitted.

Somerset House

Strand, WC2R 1LA (7845 4600/www.somerset-house.org.uk). Temple tube (closed Sun)/Charing Cross tube/rail. **Open** 10am-6pm daily (last entry 5.15pm). *Tours* phone for details. **Admission** *Courtyard & terrace* free. *Exhibitions* £5; £4 concessions. **Credit** (shop) MC, V. **Map** p403 M7.

The original Somerset House was a Tudor palace commissioned by the Duke of Somerset in 1547. It was extended and refurbished several times over two centuries, but began to suffer from poor maintenance and in 1775 was demolished to make way for an entirely new building. The architect Sir William Chambers spent the last 20 years of his life working on the neo-classical mansion that now peers out over the Thames. It was built to accommodate learned societies such as the Royal Academy; various governmental offices also took up residence, including the Inland Revenue. The taxmen are still here, but the rest of the building is open to the public, and houses three formidable art and museum collections (*see below*), the beautiful fountain court, a little café and a classy restaurant. **Photo** *p118*.

Somerset House museums

Strand, WC2R 0RN. Temple tube (closed Sun)/Charing Cross tube/rail. **Open** 10am-6pm daily (last entry 5.15pm). **Admission** *1 collection* £5; £4 concessions. *2 collections* £8; £7 concessions. *3 collections* £12; £11 concessions. Free students, under-18s; Courtauld Gallery free to all 10am-2pm Mon. *Tours* phone for details. **No credit cards. Map** p407 M7.

Courtauld Institute of Art Gallery

7848 2526/www.courtauld.ac.uk/gallery.

The Courtauld has one of Britain's most important collections of paintings. The gallery is diverse and eclectic, yet on a more manageable scale than, say, the National. Old Masters, Impressionists and Post-Impressionists are here, alongside a range of prints, drawings, sculpture and other pieces. Famous works include Manet's *A Bar at the Folies Bergère*, Van Gogh's *Self-Portrait with Bandaged Ear* and Degas's *Two Dancers on the Stage*. The collection of 20th-century works has been expanded with pieces by Kandinsky, Matisse and Barbara Hepworth. There are regular art-related talks and events.

Gilbert Collection

7420 9400/www.gilbert-collection.org.uk.

In 1949 British-born Sir Arthur Gilbert uprooted to California, where he subsequently made millions in real estate. He developed a predilection for all that glisters, collecting silver, gold and all sorts of gemmed, gilded and shiny objects. In 1996 Britain became the beneficiary of his opulence when he donated his entire collection, saying 'I felt it should return to the country of my birth' – he even continued buying new pieces after the museum had been opened. The dazzling arsenal of objects is now proudly displayed at Somerset House. Two floors are shamelessly bedecked with candelabras, mosaics, vases, urns, plates, mosaics and snuff boxes. The museum holds themed exhibitions throughout the year.

Hermitage Rooms

7845 4630/www.hermitagerooms.co.uk.

The Hermitage Rooms host rotating exhibitions of items belonging to the Winter Palace in St Petersburg; the rooms even recreate in miniature the decor of their Russian twin. New shows arrive twice a year and can include everything from paintings and drawings to decorative art and fine jewellery.

Sightseeing

Soho & Leicester Square

Wilkommen, bienvenue, welcome. Here life is beautiful – but forget about sex.

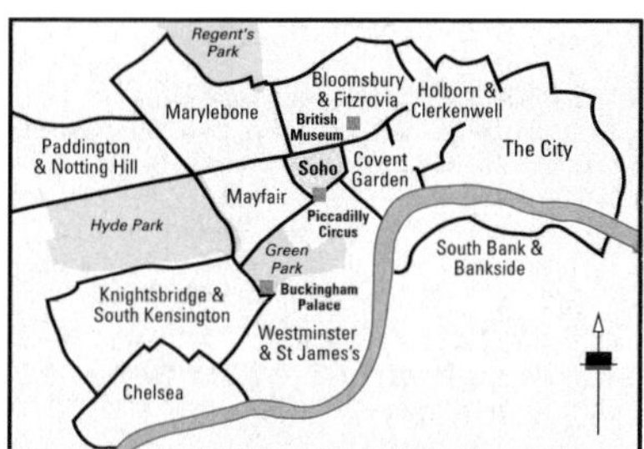

We don't list a single 'sight' in Soho – because there aren't any. It's not that kind of place, and never has been. It swiftly fell from its early status as hunting playground to the aristocracy when refugees made homeless by the Great Fire of London moved in, soon followed by the first of several waves of immigrants. The incomers gave Soho the anarchic, non-conformist and sometimes dangerous character that it hasn't quite lost today. Its streets are home to after-work partiers, media companies, theatre workers, hookers, market traders, tourists and queers, plus the odd hip venture hoping to aquire louche charm by association. It has few chains, character in spades – and it almost never closes.

Bounded by the four Circuses (Oxford, Piccadilly, Cambridge and St Giles's), good places to start exploring Soho's skinny streets are Soho Square, almost impassable for sun-bathing bodies in summer, and Old Compton Street, its main artery. Berwick Street's market is also proper Soho. Leicester Square is really only of any use for going to the cinema, but don't miss Chinatown to its north (the arches are on Gerrard Street): not the world's biggest, but the real thing.

Berwick Street, where West End girls do East End boys. *See p122.*

Soho Square

Map p408

Tottenham Court Road tube.

Soho Square forms the neighbourhood's northern gateway. This tree-lined quadrangle was laid out in 1681 and initially called King's Square – a weather-beaten statue of Charles II stands just north of centre. It's held up pretty well: not as grand as it once was (traffic cruises around it all day and night, waiting for one of the area's few parking bays to become free), but popular with local workers. Its most notable feature is the little, rickety mock Tudor hut in the middle; this houses a lift down to underground shelters, now used to store the gardeners' equipment. Two churches provide spiritual nourishment, but the area is dominated by the advertising and film industries: both the British Board of Film Classification (the censors) and 20th Century Fox have their offices here.

Two streets run south off the square, both rich with history. Serial seducer Casanova and opium-eating writer Thomas de Quincey once lodged on **Greek Street**, though the street is now notable mainly for the gloriously old-fashioned **Gay Hussar** restaurant (No.2, 7437 0973), popular with politicans and political

Soho Square. *See p120.*

journos. In the 1970s writers including Martin Amis, Ian McEwan and Julian Barnes used to meet at the **Pillars of Hercules** (No.7, 7437 1179). Underneath an arch beside the pub, Manette Street links to Charing Cross Road and has a side entrance to **Foyles** (*see p238*), London's best-known bookshop – since modernisation in 1999 it is no longer the wilful eccentric it once was, and it boasts a good first-floor café.

Parallel to Greek Street is **Frith Street**, once home to Mozart (1764-5, No.20), painter John Constable (1810-11, No.49) and essayist William Hazlitt, who lived and died at No.30, now a discreet and charming hotel named in his memory. Opposite the hotel is garlanded new restaurant **Arbutus** (*see p205*) and, a little further down, the legendary **Ronnie Scott's** (*see p316*), Britain's best-known jazz club. Across from Ronnie's is the similarly mythologised all-night café **Bar Italia** (No.22, 7437 4520), which is at its busiest around 3am each morning, when it feels like the whole of the world is revolving around its overworked espresso machine. Similarly when the Italian national football team are playing – for the World Cup final in 2006, in which Italy played France, this half of Soho was closed to traffic because of the crowds gathered outside Bar Italia. And really, who cares whether John Logie Baird first demonstrated television (then called 'noctovision') in 1926 in the rooms above?

Old Compton Street & around

Map p408

Leicester Square or Tottenham Court Road tube.

Soho's main street is also the centre of the city's 'gay village'. Tight T-shirts congregate around **Balans** (No.60; *see p300*), **Compton's** (Nos. 51-53; *see p303*) and the **Admiral Duncan** (No.54; *see p302*). Visit in the morning for a sense of the immigrant Soho of old, with cheeses and cooked meats from **Camisa** (No.61, 7437 7610) and roasting beans from the **Algerian Coffee Stores** (No.52, 7437 2480) scenting the air, and the much-loved **Pâtisserie Valerie** (No.44; *see p203*) doing a brisk trade in buttery croissants. Towards noon the first drinkers turn up for duty at the **French House** (49 Dean Street; *see p230*) and **Coach & Horses** (29 Greek Street, 7437 5920), both just a few doors south of Old Compton Street. The former was a meeting place for the French Resistance during World War II and later became a favourite of painters Francis Bacon and Lucian Freud; it's small, cliquey and only serves beer in half-pint glasses. Until 2006 the Coach was run by Norman Balon, self-proclaimed rudest landlord in Soho. It's best-known regular was the self-destructive and no less rude Jeffrey Bernard, whose column in the *Spectator* magazine was once described as a suicide note in weekly instalments.

A rare quiet moment at 24-hour **Bar Italia**. *See p121.*

Next to the Coach is **Maison Bertaux** (28 Greek Street; *see p203*), another fine old patisserie, and across the road **Kettners** (29 Romilly Street; *see p207*), which majors in the unlikely combination of pizza and champagne.

As well as the French, **Dean Street** is the address of the members-only **Groucho Club** (No.45), once the place that media people prayed they would go to when they died, but now more of a limbo since a corporate takeover in 2006. A few doors along, **Sunset Strip** (No.30) is the sole remaining legitimate strip club in Soho. Hard to believe that Karl Marx, who lived both at No.28 and No.44 from 1850 to 1856, would have approved. Further north is the **Soho Theatre** (No.21; *see p344*), which has fast cemented a reputation for its programme of new plays and comedy.

The buildings on **Wardour Street**, the next street west, largely provide homes to an assortment of film and TV production companies, plus a few good eateries like **Busaba Eathai** (Nos.106-110; *see p205*), **Meza** (No.100; *see p207*) and **Imli** (Nos.167-169, 7287 4243), which peddles a smart modern take on Indian streetfood. One street west again, **Berwick Street** feels like the real Soho deal, a mix of the hip and poncy with the raw and threatening. It's where patrons of hip cafés and independent record shops mix with the East End-accented market traders of Berwick Street **fruit and veg market** (9am-5pm Mon-Sat) and the remnants of the once-infamous Soho sex industry. Doorways down at the southern end of the street still sport hand-lettered signs at the foot of scruffy stairways inviting punters to walk up for 'fresh young models'. Tiny **Walkers Court** (linking Berwick and Brewer Streets) has a squeeze of strip joints and sex shops, while through on Rupert Street are a number of clip joints that lure in the gullible with promises of live sex shows, then follow up with threats of violence when dazed punters decline to cough up for the ridiculously priced drinks. The proliferation of lapdancing clubs and stripper pubs in other parts of town has rendered Soho's sex offerings tame and anachronistic – only the most clueless come here looking for their thrills.

West Soho

Map p408

Piccadilly Circus tube.

Soho gets quieter west of Berwick Street. Brewer Street has a few interesting shops, including the **Vintage Magazine Store** (Nos.39-43, 7439 8525) for everything from retro robots to pre-war issues of *Vogue*. On Great Windmill Street is the **Windmill Theatre** (Nos.17-19), which gained fame in the 1930s and 1940s for its legendary 'revuedeville' shows with erotic 'tableaux' – naked girls who remained stationary in order to stay within the law. The story of the theatre was retold in 2005's *Mrs Henderson Presents*. The place is now a lapdancing joint.

North of Brewer Street is **Golden Square**. Developed in the 1670s it became the political and ambassadorial district of the late 17th and

Walk on Rock routes

Start: Old Compton Street, W1.
Finish: Frith Street, W1.
Length: A mile.

With the honourable exception of a handful of jazz venues, live music has all but abandoned Soho. However, the sheer weight of rock and pop history that permeates its closely knit streets ensures that this is still the beating heart of London's music scene.

It all kicked off on Old Compton Street, at No.59; the **2 i's Coffee Bar** (now Boulevard Bar & Dining Room) was the birthplace of rock 'n'roll in Britain. It started with skiffle in 1956. In 1958 Hank Marvin and Bruce Welch played here and were invited to join Cliff Richard's backing band, the Drifters, who became the Shadows. At around the same time, the **Roundhouse** pub (now the Q Bar) at the corner of Wardour and Brewer Streets hosted Alexis Korner's London Blues and Barrelhouse Club, the country's first blues venue, visited by the likes of Muddy Waters and Big Bill Broonzy.

Jump forward a few years and a few doors down Brewer Street a young David Jones played a gig with the King Bees in 1964 at the Jack of Clubs (No.10, now **Madam Jo Jo's**). The band called off the gig after only two songs. No one was interested. David later changed his surname to Bowie.

Walk on up Wardour Street to what's now Meza (No.90), but which was from 1964 to 1988 the legendary **Marquee**, where Led Zeppelin played their first London gig and Hendrix appeared four times. Here, on 14 February 1976, a journalist from the *NME* saw the Sex Pistols perform and coined the term 'punk rock'. Make a brief detour left down Broadwick Street and then head up Berwick Street to Noel Street; face south to see the scene that graces the cover of the Oasis album *(What's the Story) Morning Glory?*

Back on Wardour Street, look for narrow St Anne's Court, home of **Trident Studios**. Albums recorded here include Lou Reed's *Transformer*, David Bowie's *Hunky Dory* and *Ziggy Stardust*, while the Beatles used the studio to record 'Hey Jude' and several *White Album* tracks. Paul McCartney used to block-book the studio then not turn up; fledgling band Queen used the already paid for time to record their first two albums here for free.

From St Anne's Court turn left, then right and straight on for **Soho Square**, the square where 'the pigeons shiver in the naked trees' in a song by Kirsty MacColl, who now has a bench dedicated to her on its south side. Leave the square and head east, passing by the **Astoria**, which has played host to the Rolling Stones, Nirvana, Oasis and Blur, as well as pop acts performing at the long-running GAY night (Madonna, Kylie Minogue).

A right and a left brings you to **Denmark Street**, London's Tin Pan Alley and the city's most rock-impregnated street. The Beatles and Jimi Hendrix recorded in basements in the street, as did the Stones ('Not Fade Away' was recorded here). It's where Elton John wrote his early classic 'Your Song' and the Sex Pistols recorded their first demo. It is still lined by nothing but instrument sales and repair shops, with the excellent **12 Bar Club** (*see p317*) squeezed in among them.

Return to Soho via Manette Street and make a beeline for Frith Street and **Ronnie Scott's** (No.47; *see p318*). While this classic venue is usually associated with jazz, The Who showcased their rock opera *Tommy* here in 1969, and Jimi Hendrix visited on 16 September 1970, to see the Eric Burdon Band – whom he joined on stage for a jam. The next day Hendrix was dead. Ponder this over a mocha at **Bar Italia** (No.22) 'around the corner in Soho where other broken people go' – this, of course, being the café that lent its name to a song on Pulp's 1995 album *Different Class*.

Forget it, Jake. It's **Chinatown**.

early 18th centuries, and remains home to some of the area's grandest residential buildings – many of which are now filled by media companies. North of the square is **Carnaby Street**: four decades ago the epitome of swinging London and then a rather seamy commercial backwater. It's recently undergone a revival and now boasts a mix of interesting independents and chain shops that trade happily off the area's history.

Chinatown & Leicester Square

Maps p408 & p409

Leicester Square tube.

Shaftesbury Avenue is the heart of Theatreland. The Victorians built seven grand theatres here; six of them still stand. By far the most impressive is the gorgeous **Palace Theatre** on Cambridge Circus. It opened in 1891 as the Royal English Opera House, but grand opera flopped here and the theatre reopened as a music hall two years later. The theatre has been home mostly to musicals, which have included *The Sound of Music* in 1961, *Jesus Christ Superstar* in 1972 and *Les Misérables*, which ran here from 1985 to 2004, racking up 7,602 performances. Opposite the theatre, what's now the Med Kitchen occupies premises that were once home to Marks & Co, the booksellers immortalised in Helene Hanff's *84 Charing Cross Road*.

South of Shaftesbury Avenue is **Chinatown**. The Chinese are relative latecomers to Soho. London's original Chinatown was around Limehouse in east London, but the area suffered heavy bomb damage during World War II so in the 1950s the Chinese migrated west, attracted by the cheap rents along Gerrard and Lisle Streets. The ersatz oriental gates, stone lions and pagoda-topped phone boxes around **Gerrard Street** suggest a Chinese theme park, but this is a close-knit residential and working enclave. The area is crammed with restaurants, Asian grocery stores and a host of small shops selling iced-grass jelly, speciality teas and cheap air tickets to Beijing.

South of Chinatown is **Leicester Square**, reasonably pleasant by day but by night a hellish sinkhole of semi-undressed inebriates out on a big night 'up west'. How different it once was. In the 17th century the square was one of London's most exclusive addresses, and in the 18th century it was home to the royal court of Prince George (later George II). Satirical painter William Hogarth had a studio here (1733-64), as did 18th-century artist Sir Joshua Reynolds; both are commemorated by busts in the small **gardens** that lie at the heart of the square, although it's the statue of a tottering Charlie Chaplin that gets all the attention. There's no particular reason for Chaplin to be here, other than that Leicester Square is considered the home of British film thanks to its numerous cinemas, notably the monolithic **Odeon Leicester Square**. This cinema boasts the UK's largest screen (and possibly also the UK's highest ticket prices). The Odeon and neighbouring Empire are regularly used for movie premières and there's a poor man's version of the Hollywood Walk of Fame here, with the handprints of actors and actresses ringing the square. Unless numbed by alcohol, most Londoners avoid the cheap fast fooderies, expensive cinemas and tacky pavement artists and buskers – so should you. However, there are a couple of bright spots. The south side of the square is where you'll find the **tkts** booth (*see p339*), retailer of cut-price, same-day theatre tickets. North in Leicester Place is the **Prince Charles Cinema** (*see p291*), which screens an eclectic mix of recent movies and cult classics at knockdown prices. Grown men dressed as nuns come here to watch sing-a-long-a-*Sound of Music*. Next to the Prince Charles the French Catholic church of **Notre Dame de France** contains murals by Jean Cocteau.

Oxford Street & Marylebone

Escape from chain-store hell lies close at hand.

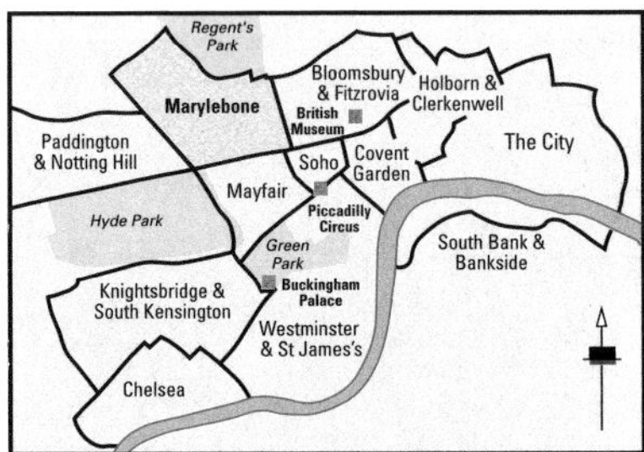

Research carried out by the mayor's office in 2005 revealed that 156 people passed one typical spot on Oxford Street every minute. That's a lot of people. Although increasingly challenged by out-of-town shopping centres, mile-and-a-half-long Oxford Street remains London's favourite spending venue thanks to its line-up of big-name stores and international brands. By contrast, Marylebone, which lies north of Oxford Street between Oxford Circus and Marble Arch, offers excellent boutique shopping, as well as fine dining and drinking options. One of the city's biggest crowd-pullers – Madame Tussauds – is there, with glorious Regent's Park lying a touch further north.

Oxford Street

Map p400

Bond Street, Marble Arch, Oxford Circus or Tottenham Court Road tube.

It may be the busiest shopping street in London, boasting more than 200 million visitors a year and responsible for 10 per cent of retail spending in the capital, but Oxford Street is also one of the city's least loved streets. Many of the grand department stores on which the street's reputation was built (notably John Lewis, Selfridge's and Debenhams, which began as Marshall & Snellgrove) are still commanding presences, but much else is tawdry and second-rate – hence 2006's announcement by London Mayor Ken Livingstone of a £1 billion facelift, including the banning of all traffic and the introduction of trams by 2012. A rare architectural highpoint is **Oxford Circus**, with its four identical convex corners, constructed between 1913 and 1928. We also harbour a soft spot for self-made Chicagoan millionaire Gordon H **Selfridge's** grand store (*see p243*). Opened on 15 March 1909, it has a superb art deco main entrance, helmed by the ornate 3.4-metre (11-foot) bronze *Queen of Time* statue. Almost opposite Bond Street tube station is tiny Gees Court, which leads through to shop- and café-lined pedestrian alley **St Christopher's Place** and its fountain courtyard, which in summer is filled with tables from nearby cafés.

Anchoring the western end of Oxford Street is **Marble Arch**. It was designed by John Nash as a grand gateway to Buckingham Palace, which is where it stood from 1827. It is constructed of white Carrara marble and commemorates Nelson's and Wellington's victories over France. However, when Victoria discovered she couldn't get her new carriage through the central arch, she had the monument removed to this site in 1851, where it now stands forlornly, stranded on a traffic island.

North of Oxford Circus

Map p400

Great Portland Street, Oxford Circus or Regent's Park tube.

Running north from Oxford Circus is Langham Place, which dog-legs to become **Portland Place**, designed by Robert Adam as the glory of 18th-century London. At Langham Place is John Nash's only remaining church, **All Souls** (1822-4), which daringly combines a Gothic spire and classical rotunda. Echoing the curve of its façade is the BBC's newly restored 1932 **Broadcasting House**, featuring external sculptures of Prospero and Ariel by Eric Gill; next door, a new state-of-the-art broadcast centre houses the BBC's national and international news operations. Over on the west side of Langham Place is the **Langham Hotel**, which was the first of London's grand hotels (1865). It was at a dinner here in 1889 that Oscar Wilde was commissioned to write *The Picture of Dorian Gray*.

And none of them will be the one you want – buses on **Oxford Street**. *See p125.*

Originally the residences of aristocrats, the grand houses of Portland Place are now mainly embassies, consulates and prestigious offices. At No.66 is the **Royal Institute of British Architects (RIBA)** with an excellent bookshop and first-floor café. At its northern end, Portland Place forks into the gracefully curving Park Crescent; straight ahead is Regent's Park (*see p127*), while a few blocks west the **Royal Academy of Music** has a small museum (7873 7373, open 11.30-5.30pm Mon-Fri, 12-4pm Sat, Sun). Beyond is Madame Tussauds (*see p127*) and Baker Street (*see p128*).

The next major north–south thoroughfare west of Portland Place is **Harley Street**, which has been associated with highbrow healthcare since the early 19th century. West again is **Wimpole Street**, where at No.57 Paul McCartney lived in a house owned by the parents of then girlfriend Jane Asher. It's here that he wrote the most commercially successful song in the history of recorded music, 'Scrambled Eggs' – which, after a rethink, he retitled 'Yesterday'.

Marylebone

Map p400

Baker Street, Bond Street, Marble Arch, Oxford Circus or Regent's Park tube.

Walk north of Oxford Street and the mood swiftly changes. Instead of jostling crowds and big department stores, there are quiet squares and a pretty high street that looks more like it belongs in an affluent provincial town. Over the past decade, the area that has been rebranded 'Marylebone Village' has become increasingly fashionable.

It has not always been so. The area was once made up of two ancient manors, Lileston (Lisson) and Tyburn (named after a stream – or 'bourn' – that flowed into the Thames). The latter was the site of a famous gallows, a spot marked by a plaque on the traffic island at Marble Arch. The parish church was called St Mary by the Bourne, a name that came to cover the entire village. This was eventually abbreviated to Marylebone.

Not far from the present church (the fourth to be built on the site) on Marylebone Road is tourist attraction extraordinaire **Madame Tussauds** (*see p127*). However, the heart of the area is **Marylebone High Street**, which, with its array of interesting independent retailers, is one of London's most attractive shopping streets. Highlights include the beautiful Edwardian **Daunt Books** (*see p238*) and eclectic clothes boutique **Sixty 6** (No.66, 7224 6066). Neighbouring Marylebone Lane boasts shoe designer **Tracey Neuls** (No.29, 7935 0039) and womenswear label **Saltwater** (No.98, 7935 3336). This winding backstreet retains the neighbourhood's original character; in corner pub the **Golden Eagle** (No.59, 7935 3228) there are nostalgic singalongs around the piano, and 106-year-old lunchroom-deli **Paul**

Rothe & Son (No.35, 7935 6783) is presided over by the original Rothe's grandson and great-grandson. Marylebone is also a magnet for foodies with a clutch of gourmet shops – such as **La Fromagerie** (*see p207*) on Moxon Street, which leads to the site of the weekly farmers' market on Sundays (in the Cramer Street car park behind Waitrose, 10am-2pm). There are also some great restaurants, including the **Providores & Tapa Room** and **FishWorks** (for both, *see p208*).

A little to the south, **St James's Roman Catholic Church** (22 George Street) has a surprisingly soaring Gothic interior (1890). Vivien Leigh wed barrister Leigh Holman here in 1932. South again, Manchester Square is home to the **Wallace Collection** (*see below*) and, in the north-west corner, to the former offices of EMI Records (1960-95), where the photos were taken that adorn the covers of the Beatles' *Blue* and *Red* albums.

Madame Tussauds

Marylebone Road, NW1 5LR (0870 400 3000/ www.madame-tussauds.com). Baker Street tube. **Open** 9.30am-6pm daily (last entry 5pm); times vary during holiday periods. **Admission** *9.30am-5.30pm* £24.99; £15.99-£20.99 concs; £78.00 family (internet booking only). *5.30-6pm* £16.00; £11-£14 concs; £12.99 concs; £50 family. **Credit** MC, V. **Map** p400 G4.

Tussauds compensates for its inherently static attractions with a flurry of attendant activity. As you enter the first room, you're dazzled by fake paparazzi flashbulbs. Starry-eyed kids can take part in a 'Divas' routine with Britney, Beyoncé and Kylie, and Robbie Williams has a hidden sensor activated by kisses to produce a 'twinkle' in his eye. Figures are constantly being added to keep up with new stars, movies and TV shows – the latest are *Little Britain*'s Matt Lucas and David Walliams, in character as wheelchair-bound Andy and his carer Lou. Other rooms contain public figures past and present, from Henry and six of his wives to Blair and Bush, by way of the Fab Four c1964. Below stairs, the Chamber of Horrors surrounds you with hanging corpses and eviscerated victims of torture. For an extra £2 over-12s can be terrorised by serial killers in the Chamber Live. At the kitsch 'Spirit of London Ride', climb aboard a moving black taxi pod for a whirlwind trundle through 400 years of the city's history. What was the Planetarium has gone, to be replaced by more celebrity exhibits.

Wallace Collection

Hertford House, Manchester Square, W1U 3BN (7935 0687/www.wallacecollection.org). Bond Street tube. **Open** 10am-5pm daily. **Admission** free. **Credit** (shop) AmEx, MC, V. **Map** p400 G5.

This handsome late 18th-century house contains a collection of furniture, paintings, armour and objets d'art. It all belonged to Sir Richard Wallace, who, as the illegitimate offspring of the fourth Marquess of Hertford, inherited the treasures his father amassed in the last 30 years of his life. There's room after room of Louis XIV and XV furnishings and Sèvres porcelain, and galleries of lush paintings by Titian, Velázquez, Boucher, Gainsborough and Reynolds; Franz Hals's *Laughing Cavalier* is one of the best-known masterpieces. There are also regular temporary exhibitions. The attractive Café Bagatelle, in the glass-roofed courtyard, ranks among the best London museum eateries.

Regent's Park

Map p400

Baker Street or Regent's Park tube.

With its varied landscape, from formal flowerbeds to extensive playing fields, Regent's Park (open 5am-dusk daily) is one of London's most treasured green spaces. But it wasn't created for public pleasure; indeed, the masses weren't allowed in until 1845. Originally Henry VIII's 'chase', the park was designed in 1811 by John Nash as a private residential estate to raise royal revenue. The Regency terraces of the Outer Circle, the road running around the park, are still Crown property, but of the 56 villas planned, only eight were built. Development of the Royal Park, with its botanic and zoological gardens, took almost two more decades, but rehabilitation after wartime damage and neglect in the mid 20th century was not completed until the late 1970s. As well as

All Souls. *See p125.*

the famous zoo (*see below*), it has a boating lake (home to wildfowl), tennis courts, cafés and a lovely open-air theatre (*see p339*).

To the west of the park is the **London Central Mosque** and the northernmost end of Baker Street where, predictably enough, at No.221B there is the **Sherlock Holmes Museum** (7935 8866, www.sherlock-holmes.co.uk, open 9.30am-6pm daily, admission £6). It contains atmospheric room sets, but serious Sherlockians may want to check out the Sherlock Holmes Collection (books, photos and so on) at **Marylebone Library** (7641 1206, by appointment only) and the **Murder One** bookshop (7539 8820, www.murderone.co.uk) down at 76-78 Charing Cross Road, which has probably the largest collection of Sherlock Holmes-related books for sale anywhere. There's also a **Sherlock Holmes** pub (10 Northumberland Street, 7930 2644), just south of Trafalgar Square, which has a replica of Holmes's study upstairs and endless Basil Rathbone videos on the bar-room TV screens.

Back on Baker Street, No.231 is the **Beatles Store & Gallery** (7935 4464, www.beatlesstorelondon.co.uk, open 10.30am-6pm daily, admission £1), with a basement full of memorabilia including animation cells from *Yellow Submarine* and some sketches by Paul McCartney that show while he could knock out a decent enough tune he couldn't draw for toffee. A short walk south, No.94 was the site of the Beatles-run Apple Boutique, which for seven brief months from December 1967 to July 1968 was a mural-covered Pepperland where, according to McCartney, you could buy 'beautiful things for beautiful people'. The corner building is now tenanted by Reed Employment Services.

London Zoo

Regent's Park, NW1 4RY (7722 3333/www.zsl.org/london-zoo). Baker Street or Camden Town tube then 274, C2 bus. **Open** *Late Oct-mid Mar* 10am-4pm daily. *Mid Mar-late Oct* 10am-5.30pm daily. **Admission** £14.50; £10.75-£12.70 concs; £45 family; free under-3s. **Credit** AmEx, MC, V. **Map** p400 G2.

Opened in 1828, this was the world's first scientific zoo, and today umbrella charity ZSL stresses its commitment to worldwide conservation. The zoo's habitats keep pace with the times – the elephants have been given room to roam at sister-site Whipsnade Wild Animal Park in Bedfordshire, and the penguins have been moved from Lubetkin's famous modernist pool to a more suitable space. The new 1,500sq m (16,000sq ft) walk-through squirrel monkey enclosure allows you to get close to the animals in an open environment based on a Bolivian rainforest, while the African Bird Safari, another new walk-through habitat, has replaced three small, outdated bird enclosures. Opening at Easter 2007 is Gorilla Kingdom, a forest walk to see big apes and the creatures that share their world. It's advisable to follow the recommended route to avoid missing anything; check the daily programme of events to get a good view at feeding times.

Regent's Park – serene and peaceful, but less so for pigeons. *See p127.*

Paddington & Notting Hill

No lost bears, no Hugh Grant, just lots of boutique shopping.

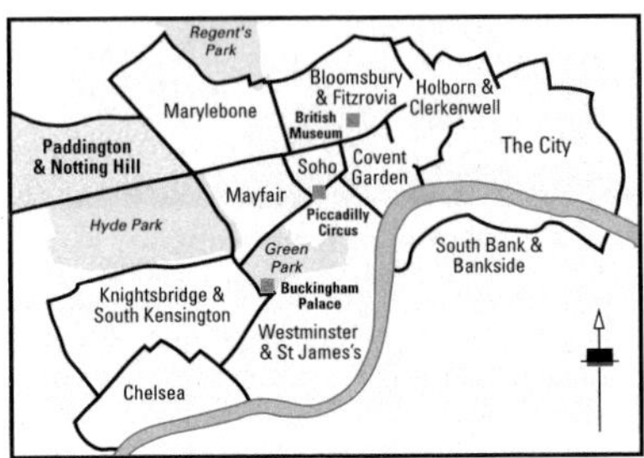

Just west of the city centre and sitting north of Hyde Park, **Paddington** and **Bayswater** occupy the C-list as far as sightseeing goes, although their international – predominantly Middle Eastern – flavour is every bit as representative of London today as other parts of central London. **Notting Hill**, however, is a must, especially on a Saturday when Portobello Market is in full swing.

Edgware Road & Paddington

Maps p397

Edgware Road, Lancaster Gate, Marble Arch or Paddington tube/rail.

Edgware Road rules a very definite north–south line marking where the central West End stops and central west London begins. Its straightness and length give a clue to its origins (it was the main Roman road north out of London) but it is best known these days as the heart of the city's Middle East end. If you want to pick up your copy of the daily *Al Hayat* newspaper, cash a cheque at the Bank of Kuwait or catch some Egyptian league football on TV in a smoke-filled hookah café, then this is the place to come.

North of the Marylebone Road flyover, the landscape bleakens, but it's worth visiting Bell Street, which runs west off Edgware Road, for the cutting-edge **Lisson** gallery (*see p293*). A little further north **Church Street** has a popular local food and general market that is rapidly gentrifying at its eastern end, thanks to the ever fascinating **Alfies Antiques Market** (*see p237*).

The fact that the name Paddington has been immortalised by a certain small, ursine Peruvian émigré is appropriate, given that the area has long served as a home to refugees and immigrants. The district owes its name to an Anglo-Saxon chieftain named Padda. It stayed a country village until the 19th century. Then came the Grand Junction Canal in 1801, linking London to the Midlands, and in 1838 that symbol of Victorian innovation, the railway. The current **Paddington Station** was built in 1851 to the specifications of the great engineer Isambard Kingdom Brunel. The triple roof of iron and glass is a particularly fine example of Victorian engineering.

In the 1950s there was poverty and over-crowding, but the area's proximity to central London meant property developers recognised its potential and the builders duly moved in. The slick **Paddington Central** development east of the station is a case in point, with its 93,000 square metres (about a million square feet) of office space, canalside apartments and health club. Also east of the station is **St Mary's Hospital**, where Alexander Fleming discovered penicillin (*see below*).

Alexander Fleming Laboratory Museum

St Mary's Hospital, Praed Street, W2 1NY (7886 6528/www.st-marys.nhs.uk/about/fleming_museum.htm). Paddington tube/rail. **Open** 10am-1pm Mon-Thur; by appointment 2-5pm Mon-Thur, 10am-5pm Fri. **Admission** £2; £1 concessions; free under-5s. **No credit cards. Map** p397 D5.

When Alexander Fleming noticed the death of staphylococcus bacteria on a discarded petri dish, humanity was handed a powerful weapon against such enemies as pneumonia and tuberculosis. This room, where the ground-breaking 1928 discovery took place, preserves many artefacts from Fleming's day.

Bayswater

Map p396

Bayswater or Queensway tube.

West of Paddington is Bayswater, an area of grand Victorian housing, much of which has been converted into flats and hotels. No.100

Treasures out of the trash at the **Museum of Brands, Packaging & Advertising**.

Bayswater Road, at the junction with Leinster Terrace, is where playwright Sir James Barrie lived from 1902 to 1909 and where he wrote *Peter Pan*. Further up the same side street, 23-24 Leinster Gardens warrants close scrutiny; the façades of these adjacent houses are, in fact, an elaborate bit of set decoration – a painted wall built to hide an opening to the Underground line below, through which early engines would let off steam.

Queensway, the vertical spine of the area, was originally called Black Lion Lane but was later renamed in honour of Queen Victoria. Like Edgware Road, it is now full of Middle Eastern cafés and restaurants. There's a slightly different eastern flavour on Moscow Road, just off Queensway, in the form of the Greek Orthodox **Cathedral of St Sophia** (7229 7260, www.stsophia.org.uk, open 11am-2pm Mon, Wed-Fri, and for services) where Byzantine icons and golden mosaics glow in the candlelight. Near the top end of the street, the bustling **Whiteleys** shopping centre (7229 8844, www.whiteleys.com) was once a grand department store that rivalled Harrods. Its founder, William Whiteley, used to call himself 'the Universal Provider'.

Heading north over the junction with Bishops Bridge Road is the **Porchester Centre** (7792 3980), one of the few surviving examples of the Victorian Turkish baths that once proliferated in Britain. A left at the top of Queensway takes you into **Westbourne Grove**, which starts humble but gets posher the further west you go. Once you cross Chepstow Road you're really into Notting Hill. The shopping is stellar, but you may need to clear purchases with your bank manager. Here you will find **Bill Amberg**'s gorgeous leather accessories (21-22 Chepstow Corner, 7727 3560), and luxury scents and candles at **Maison Diptyque** (195 Westbourne Grove, 7727 8673), while across the street is jet-set holiday boutique **Heidi Klein** (No.174; *see p249*). There are similar riches on **Ledbury Road**, including covetable fashion and home accessories at **Aimé** (*see p244*) and beautiful lingerie at **VPL** (*see p251*). Along with the boutiques are also a handful of tip-top delis including **Tavola** (No.155, 7229 0571), owned by restaurateur Alastair Little, and Tom Conran's celeb-frequented **Tom's** (No.226, 7221 8818). Ledbury Road has a branch of cool deli/ café **Ottolenghi** (No.63, 7727 1121; *see also p218*).

Predictably, the one museum in the area is a homage to consumerism (*see below*).

Museum of Brands, Packaging & Advertising

Colville Mews, Lonsdale Road, W11 2AR (7908 0880/www.museumofbrands.com). Notting Hill Gate tube. **Open** 10am-6pm Tue-Sat; 11am-4pm Sun. **Admission** £5.80; £2-£3.50 concessions; free under-7s. **Credit** MC, V. **Map** p396 A6.

Robert Opie began collecting the things that most of us throw away when he was 16. Over the years the collection has grown to include everything from milk bottles to vacuum cleaners through posters and cereal packets. The emphasis is on British consumerism through the last century or so, though there are items as old as an ancient Egyptian doll. The greatest interest is for British nostalgists who relish the cascading time-travel experience of watching brands such as HP Sauce and Johnson's Baby Powder transmogrify over the years.

Notting Hill

Map p396

Notting Hill Gate, Ladbroke Grove or Westbourne Park tube.

The triangle made by the tube stations of Notting Hill Gate, Ladbroke Grove and Westbourne Park contains some lovely squares, houses and gardens, along with a host of fashionable restaurants, bars and shops, many bent on exploiting the lingering street cred of the rapidly disappearing black and working-class residents.

Notting Hill Gate is not itself an attractive high street, but the leafy avenues south are; so is Pembridge Road, to the north, leading to the boutique-filled streets of Westbourne Grove and Ledbury Road (*see p130*), and more notably to **Portobello Road** and its famed market (*see p263*). The name honours the capture of Puerto Bello from the Spaniards in 1739. Beginning at Pembridge Road, the **Sun in Splendour** (No.7, 7313 9331) is Notting Hill's oldest pub. Over the road is a charming terrace of two-storey cottages: No.22 has a blue plaque commemorating the residency of George Orwell in 1927-8, who began his first book, *Down and Out in Paris and London*, while living here. A little further north, 19 Denbigh Terrace has been home to both Peter Cook and Richard Branson. The **Electric Cinema** (No.191, 7908 9696, www.the-electric.co.uk), built in 1910, is London's oldest surviving movie house. It has a gorgeous façade of cream faience tiles and an equally beautifully maintained interior. Next door, the Electric Brasserie is one of the most fashionable restaurants in Notting Hill.

Blenheim Crescent boasts three notable independent booksellers in **Garden Books** (No.11, 7792 0777), **Books for Cooks** (No.4, 7221 1992; *see also p238*), a cookery book specialist with café attached, and the **Travel Bookshop** (7229 5260; *see also p238*), the store on which Hugh Grant's bookshop was based in the movie *Notting Hill* – a film that did more to undermine the area's bohemian credibility than a fleet of Starbucks. The location of Grant's apartment in the film (actually the then-home of the film's screenwriter Richard Curtis) is one block north at 280 Westbourne Park Road.

Under the Westway, the elevated section of the M40 motorway that links London with the West Country, is small but busy **Portobello Green Market**. Here's where you find the best vintage fashion stalls. Look out for the excellent second-hand boot and shoe stall and the brilliant vintage handbag stall (usually outside the Falafel King café), along with wonderful vintage clothing stall, Sage Femme, which can normally be found outside the Antique Clothing Shop. North of the Westway, Portobello's vitality fizzles out. It sparks back to life at **Golborne Road**, the heartland of London's North African community and the address of the excellent, no-frills **Moroccan Tagine** café (No.95, 8968 8055) and the **Lisboa Pâtisserie**, one of the best Portuguese delis in London (No.57, 8968 5242).

Trellick Tower, the concrete tower at the north-eastern end of Golborne Road, is one of London's most divisive bits of architecture. Love it or hate it, it's a significant piece of modernism. Its designer, Ernö Goldfinger also demolished some fine Victorian properties to make way for his own Hampstead home (*see p160*). A disgusted neighbour sought revenge by using Goldfinger's name as the villain in his latest book. That neighbour was Ian Fleming. Ernö threatened to sue; they settled out of court and the architect was immortalised as the man who 'loves only gold'.

At its western end, Golborne Road connects with Ladbroke Grove, which can be followed north to the famously spooky **Kensal Green Cemetery** (*see below*).

Kensal Green Cemetery

Harrow Road, Kensal Green, W10 4RA (8969 0152/www.kensalgreen.co.uk). Kensal Green tube.
Open *Apr-Sept* 9am-6pm Mon-Sat; 10am-6pm Sun. *Oct-Mar* 9am-5pm Mon-Sat; 10am-5pm Sun. *Tours* 2pm Sun; (incl catacombs) 2pm 1st & 3rd Sun of mth.
Admission free. *Tours* £5 donation; £4 concessions.
No credit cards.

Behind the neo-classical gate is a green oasis of the dead. The resting place of both the Duke of Sussex, sixth son of King George III, and his sister, HRH Princess Sophia, was the place to be buried in the 19th century. Wilkie Collins, Anthony Trollope and William Makepeace Thackeray all lie here, but it is the mausoleums of lesser folk that make the most eye-catching graves.

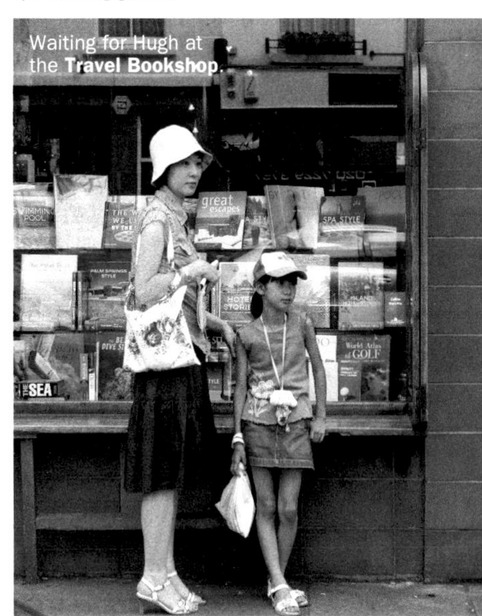

Waiting for Hugh at the **Travel Bookshop**.

Sightseeing

Piccadilly & Mayfair

From the garish to the sublime.

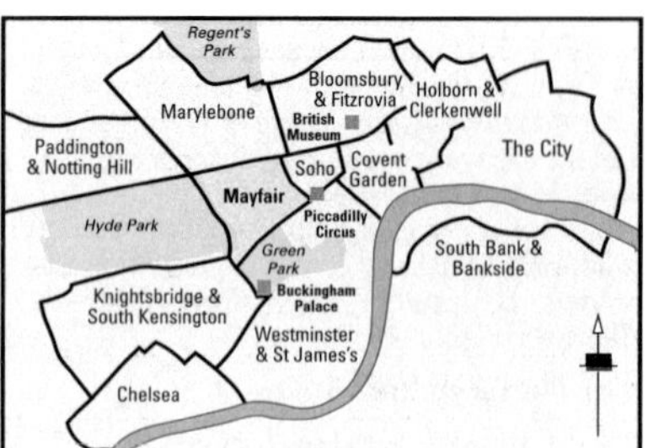

Not for nothing is **Mayfair** the most expensive property on the Monopoly board. Still, it costs nothing to look. Things get a little bit more affordable along **Piccadilly**, which demarcates the southern extent of Mayfair, linking Hyde Park Corner with the world-famous billboard neon of **Piccadilly Circus**.

Piccadilly Circus & Regent Street

Map p408

Oxford Circus or Piccadilly Circus tube.

Undeniable landmark though it is, the **Piccadilly Circus** of today is an uneasy mix of the tawdry and the grandiose. It certainly has little to do with the original vision of its architect John Nash. His 1820s design for the intersection of two of the West End's most elegant streets, Regent Street and Piccadilly, was a harmonious circle of curved frontages. But 60 years later Shaftesbury Avenue muscled its way in, creating the present lopsided and slightly pandemonious traffic junction. In an attempt to add gravitas, a delicate golden statue (since replaced by a lead copy) in honour of child-labour abolitionist Earl Shaftesbury was erected. Its subject was the Angel of Christian Charity, but to critics and public alike it looked like **Eros**, and their judgement has stuck. The illuminated advertising panels first appeared in 1886 and have been present ever since.

Connecting Piccadilly Circus to Oxford Circus to the north and Pall Mall to the south, **Regent Street** is a broad, curving boulevard designed by Nash in the early 1800s to separate the wealthy of Mayfair from the working classes of Soho. The grandeur of the sweeping road is impressive – even if much of Nash's architecture was destroyed in the early 20th century. Halfway up, on the left side, **Heddon Street** is where the iconic photo was taken that graces the cover of David Bowie's album *Ziggy Stardust and the Spiders From Mars* – the building he poses in front of is now the Moroccan-flavoured Mô Tea Room, next door to famed North African eaterie **Momo** (*see p212*). Further north on Regent Street are mammoth children's emporium **Hamleys** (*see p280*) and the landmark **Liberty** store (*see p242*).

Mayfair

Map p402

Bond Street or Green Park tube.

The image of gaiety suggested by its name – deriving from a fair that used to take place here long ago each May – is belied by the staid atmosphere of modern-day Mayfair. It's easy to feel like you don't belong in some of the deadly quiet residential streets that, over the centuries, attracted many of London's biggest wigs. Even on busy shopping streets you are liable to feel out of place without the reassuring heft of a weighty platinum card – if you do have one of those, though, there's no better place in the capital to burn it up.

The Grosvenor and Berkeley families bought the rolling green fields that would become Mayfair in the mid 17th century. In the 1700s they developed the pastures into a posh new neighbourhood. In particular they built a series of squares surrounded by elegant houses. The most famous of these, **Grosvenor Square** (that's 'Grove-ner'), built 1725-31, is now dominated by the supremely inelegant US Embassy. A product of the Cold War era, it takes up one whole side of the square and its only decorative touches are a fierce-looking eagle and a mass of protective barricades. Out front, a big statue of President Dwight Eisenhower has pride of place (Franklin D Roosevelt stands in the park nearby).

When in London, Eisenhower stayed at the exclusive hotel **Claridge's** (*see p61*), a block east on Brook Street. It's still the haunt of the great and the good – we shared a lift with Elvis Costello there recently. **Brook Street** has impressive music credentials: GF Handel lived and died (1759) at No.25, and Jimi Hendrix roomed briefly next door at No.23. These adjacent buildings have been combined into a museum dedicated to Handel's memory (*see p135*). This part of Mayfair, however, is all about shopping. **South Molton Street**, which connects Brook Street with Oxford Street to the north, is no longer the hip enclave it once was, but it still boasts the fabulous boutique-emporium **Browns** (*see p244*), while **New Bond Street** is an A-Z of every top-end, mainstream fashion house you can name.

Beyond New Bond Street, **Hanover Square** is another of the area's big squares, now a busy traffic chicane. Just south is **St George's Church**, built in the 1720s and once everybody's favourite place to get married. Among the luminaries who uttered their vows at the altar were George Eliot and Teddy Roosevelt. Handel, who married nobody, attended services here. South of St George's, salubrious **Conduit Street** is where fashion shocker **Vivienne Westwood** (No.44) faces the more staid **Rigby & Peller** (No.22A), corsetières to the Queen. At No.9 is London's most audacious restaurant, **Sketch** (*see p211*).

Running south off Conduit Street is the most famous Mayfair shopping street of all, **Savile Row**, home of bespoke British tailoring. At No.15 is the estimable **Henry Poole & Co**, which over the years has cut suits for clients including Napoleon Bonaparte, Charles Dickens, Winston Churchill and Charles de Gaulle. No.3 was the home of Apple Records, the Beatles' recording studio. The group famously played their last gig at this address on Thursday 30 January 1969, up on the roof – the set lasted 45 minutes until it was halted by the police following complaints from a local bank manager about 'a breach of the peace'. Two streets west, **Cork Street** is the West End's gallery row and a couple of streets over again is Albemarle Street, where you'll find the Royal Institution (No.21), home to the **Faraday Museum** (7409 2992, www.rigb.org), which is due to reopen in 2007 after refurbishment.

Shepherd Market

The third of Mayfair's famed squares is **Berkeley Square**, which is just west of Albemarle Street. No.44 is one of the square's original houses, built in the 1740s, and once called by noted architectural historian Nikolaus Pevsner 'the finest terrace house of London'. Off the square's north-east corner is Bruton Place, where you'll find the historic **Guinea** (*see p231*), a terrifically unpretentious, no-nonsense drinking den – something all too rare

Piccadilly Circus.

Undercover purchases

Long before Londoners were browsing the high-spec concept shops, superstores and suburban malls, the city's consumate consumers flocked to the select tailors, corsetières and jewellers around Piccadilly. It was here that the city's first shopping centres were built, in the form of genteel and architecturally elegant arcades. They have survived the decades, the chocolate-box shopfronts that line their hushed interiors speaking of a bygone era of 19th-century respectability. However, these are not museum pieces but retail spaces in an area that commands some of the highest rents in the world.

Opened in 1819, skylit **Burlington Arcade** is the most famous of the Piccadilly arcades. It is also the most traditional. According to archaic laws still on the books, it is illegal to sing, whistle or hurry in the arcade, and there are top-hatted 'beadles' on the job to catch anybody doing any of the above. There are a few other eccentric and anachronistic regulations that the beadles let go: it just wouldn't be good for business to exclude unaccompanied women or those with pushchairs. Opposite the Burlington is the opulent **Piccadilly Arcade** (built 1909-10 by G Thrale Jell, whose name can still be seen above the entrance) and its younger, plainer sister, the **Princess Arcade** (1929-33). The latter boasts the royally approved chocolatier Prestat, while the former has Iconastas, which must be the only shop in London where you can buy a verdigrised fifth-century Byzantine cross (£90). The two arcades connect Piccadilly to Jermyn Street (*see p146*), which explains their proliferation of shirtmakers and gentlemen's outfitters.

To the north is Bond Street's 1879 neo-Gothic **Royal Arcade** (*pictured*), with its distinctive peach-coloured mouldings. Inside you'll find the fabulous sparkling costume jewellery of Angela Hale; the best hot chocolate powder, courtesy of Charbonnel et Walker; and Ormonde Jayne, a tiny gem of a perfumery. The oldest of the arcades is hidden away behind Her Majesty's Theatre on Haymarket; the **Royal Opera Arcade** (1816-18) was built by the great Regency architect John Nash, who was also responsible for Regent Street. Originally, the shops went down one side of the arcade only, with access to the theatre on the other. The arcade is now owned by the adjacent New Zealand House and is a sad affair, with a couple of shops aimed at home-sick Kiwis and a number of vacant properties.

Happily, the other arcades continue to flourish and, in fact, Burlington is undergoing a programme of renovation during 2006/7. The aim is to attract a younger, hipper customer by challenging the myth that the arcades are stuffy, snooty and overpriced tourist magnets (in fact, 75 per cent of the arcade trade comes from Londoners). It won't be a case of out with the old and in with the new: heirlooms such as this are worth more if they're meticulously preserved. By the end of the refurb in spring 2007 the arcade should look more 19th century than it does now.

in Mayfair. **Curzon Street**, which runs off the south-west corner of Berkeley Square, was home to MI5, Britain's secret service, from 1945 until the 1990s; it's also the northern boundary of **Shepherd Market**, which is named after a food market set up here by architect Edward Shepherd in the early 18th century, and is perhaps the true heart of the neighbourhood. From 1686 this was where the raucous May Fair was held, until it was shut down for good in the late 18th century after city leaders complained of 'drunkenness, fornication, gaming and lewdness'. Today it seems a pleasant, upscale area with a couple of good pubs (**Ye Grapes** at 16 Shepherd Market and the **Shepherd's Tavern** at 50 Hertford Street) and some of London's most agreeable pavement dining. But, in keeping with tradition, there are still prostitutes working from neighbouring tatty apartment blocks.

Flat 12, 9 Curzon Place, which is just north-west of Shepherd Market, is notable for rock exits. In 1974, after attending Mick Jagger's 32nd birthday party in Chelsea, Mama Cass Elliot of the Mamas and Papas, returned to Curzon Place, went to bed and never woke up. The verdict was heart failure due to obesity. In 1978 the Who's drummer Keith Moon checked out on the same premises, cause of death: an overdose.

Handel House Museum

25 Brook Street (entrance at rear in Lancashire Court), W1K 4HB (7495 1685/www.handelhouse.org). Bond Street tube. **Open** 10am-6pm Tue, Wed, Fri, Sat; 10am-8pm Thur; noon-6pm Sun. **Admission** £5; £2-£4.50 concessions; free under-5s. **Credit** MC, V. **Map** p400 H6.

George Frideric Handel moved to Britain from his native Germany aged 25 and settled in this Mayfair house 12 years later, remaining here until his death in 1759. The house has been beautifully restored with original and recreated furnishings, paintings and a welter of the composer's scores (in the same room as photos of Jimi Hendrix, who lived here rather more recently). The programme of events here is surprisingly dynamic for a museum so small, and includes recitals every Thursday.

Piccadilly & Green Park

Map p402

Green Park, Hyde Park Corner or Piccadilly Circus tube.

Piccadilly's name comes from the fancy suit collars ('picadils') favoured by those posh gentlemen who once paraded down its length. There's not too much parading going on any more, but you can still see remnants of a glossy past in the handful of Regency shopping arcades, designed to protect shoppers from mud and horse manure (*see p134* **Undercover purchases**). High-end retail continues to be represented on Piccadilly by **Fortnum & Mason** (*see p241*), London's most prestigious food store, founded in 1707 by a former footman to Queen Anne. The window displays are a thing of wonder. A couple of doors away at No.187, **Hatchard's** the bookseller dates back to 1801. The simple-looking church at No.197 is **St James's** (*see p136*). This was the personal favourite of its architect Sir Christopher Wren. There's often a market out front, and a handy coffeeshop with outdoor seating is tucked into a corner by a quiet garden.The church also doubles as one of London's most atmospheric music venues – REM played a 'secret' show here in September 2004.

On the north side of Piccadilly, the former Burlington House (1665) is now home to the **Royal Academy of Arts** (*see p136*), which hosts several lavish, crowd-pleasing exhibitions each year and has a pleasant outdoor café in its fountain courtyard.

West down Piccadilly, smartly uniformed doormen mark first the **Wolseley** (*see p211*), a former car showroom reopened in 2004 as an instant classic of a restaurant, followed by the **Ritz** (*see p63*), one of the world's best-known hotels. The simple green expanse just beyond the Ritz is the aptly named **Green Park**. Once a plague pit, where the city's many epidemic victims were buried, it may not be able to match the grandeur of St James's or Regent's parks, but it has its charms, most evident in the spring, when the gentle slopes are covered in bright daffodils (there are no planted flowerbeds here, hence the name). Further along Piccadilly, work your way past the queue (why?) outside the Hard Rock Café to the Duke of Wellington's old homestead, **Apsley House** (*see below*), opposite **Wellington Arch** (*see p136*), both at Hyde Park Corner.

West is Hyde Park itself (*see p154*) and the posh enclave of Belgravia (*see p150*), while south is Buckingham Palace (*see p144*).

Apsley House

149 Piccadilly, W1J 7NT (7499 5676/www.english-heritage.org.uk). Hyde Park Corner tube. **Open** 10am-4pm Tue-Sun. *Tours* by arrangement. **Admission** £4.95; £2.50-£3.70 concessions. *Tours* phone in advance. *Joint ticket with Wellington Arch* £6.30; £3.20-£4.70 concs; £15.80 family. **Credit** MC, V. **Map** p402 G8.

Called No.1 London because it was the first London building one encountered on the road from the village of Kensington, Apsley House was built by Robert Adam in the 1770s. The Duke of Wellington had it as his London residence for 35 years. Although his descendants still live here, some rooms are open to the public and contain interesting trinkets, including extravagant porcelain dinnerware and plates. Ask someone to demonstrate the crafty mirrors in the scarlet and gilt picture gallery, where a fine Velázquez and a Correggio hang near Goya's portrait of the Iron Duke after he defeated the French in 1812 (a last-minute edit, as X-rays revealed that Wellington's head had been brushed over that of Joseph Bonaparte, Napoleon's brother).

Royal Academy of Arts

Burlington House, Piccadilly, W1J 0BD (7300 8000/ www.royalacademy.org.uk). Green Park or Piccadilly Circus tube. **Open** 10am-6pm Mon-Thur, Sat, Sun; 10am-10pm Fri. **Admission** varies. **Credit** AmEx, DC, MC, V. **Map** p408 U4.

Britain's first art school was founded in 1768 and moved to the extravagantly Palladian Burlington House a century later. It's best known these days for its galleries, which stage a roster of populist temporary exhibitions. Those in the John Madejski Fine Rooms are drawn from the RA's holdings – ranging from Constable to Hockney – and are free. The Academy's biggest event is the Summer Exhibition, which for more than two centuries has drawn from works entered by the public.

St James's Piccadilly

197 Piccadilly, W1J 9LL (7734 4511/www.st-james-piccadilly.org). Piccadilly Circus tube. **Open** 8am-7pm daily. *Evening events* times vary. **Admission** free. **Map** p408 V4.

Consecrated in 1684 St James's is the only church Sir Christopher Wren built on an entirely new site. It's a calming building, without architectural airs or graces but not lacking in charm. It was bombed to within an inch of its life in World War II, but later painstakingly reconstructed. Grinling Gibbons's delicate limewood garlanding around the sanctuary survived and is one of the few real frills. This is a busy church as, along with its inclusive ministry, it runs a counselling service, stages regular classical concerts, provides a home for the William Blake Society (the poet was baptised here) and hosts markets in its churchyard: antiques on Tuesday, arts and crafts from Wednesday to Saturday.

Wellington Arch

Hyde Park Corner, W1J 7JZ (7930 2726/www.english-heritage.org.uk). Hyde Park Corner tube. **Open** *Apr-Oct* 10am-5pm Wed-Sun. *Nov-Mar* 10am-4pm Wed-Sun. **Admission** £3; £1.50-£2.30 concessions; free under-5s. *Joint ticket with Apsley House* £6.30; £3.20-£4.70 concessions; £15.80 family. **Credit** MC, V. **Map** p402 G8.

Built in the late 1820s to mark Britain's triumph over Napoleonic France, Decimus Burton's Wellington Arch was shifted from its original location to accommodate traffic at Hyde Park Corner in 1882. It was initially topped by an out-of-proportion equestrian statue of Wellington, but since 1912 Captain Adrian Jones's 38-ton bronze *Peace Descending on the Quadriga of War* has finished it with a flourish. It was restored in 1999 by English Heritage, and has three floors of displays, covering the history of the arch and the Blue Plaques scheme. From the balcony, you can see the Houses of Parliament and Buckingham Palace, though trees obstruct much of the view in summer.

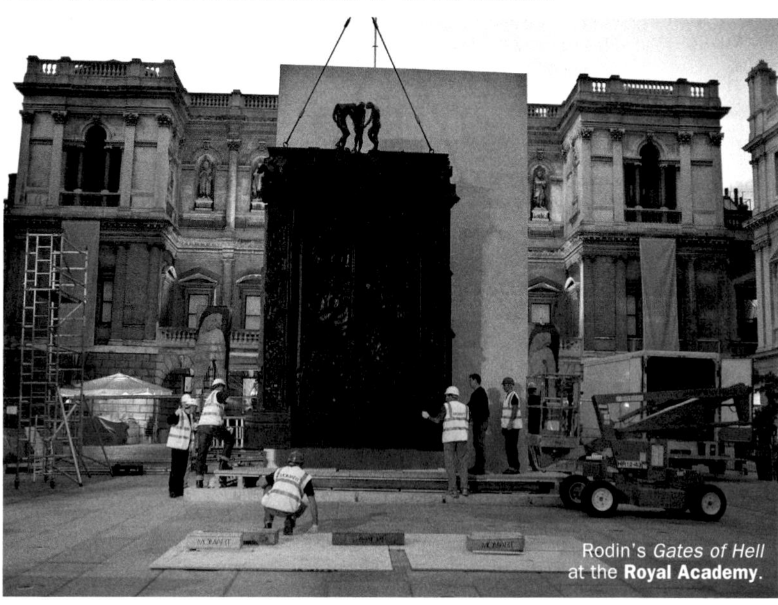

Rodin's *Gates of Hell* at the **Royal Academy**.

Westminster & St James's

Here's where you tick off your list of London's must-see sights.

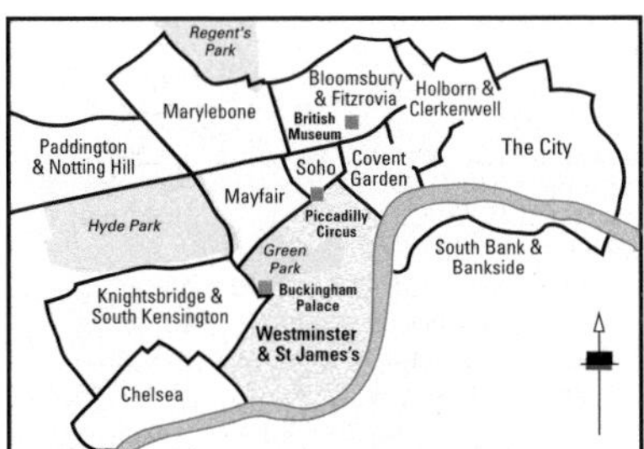

This is the heart of London, if not England. Anchored by three centres of power – the **Houses of Parliament** (governmental), **Buckingham Palace** (royal) and **Trafalgar Square** (a place for mass civic gatherings) – it has been pivotal for almost 1,000 years, since Edward the Confessor built his 'West Minster' and palace on marshy Thorney Island. By its nature, Westminster is imposing rather than atmospheric, although it does contain many of the city's unmissable sights, including the **National Gallery**, **Westminster Abbey** and **Tate Britain**. St James's, particularly the very lovely park, has more charm – in a very stately fashion, of course.

Trafalgar Square

Map p409

Leicester Square tube or Charing Cross tube/rail.

The centrepiece of London, Trafalgar Square has always been a natural gathering point, even more so since it was semi-pedestrianised in 2003. Protest marches start and finish here, and it is a venue for concerts and festivals, as well as impromptu demonstrations and celebrations. The piazza was conceived by the Prince Regent, later George IV, who was obsessed with building monuments. He commissioned John Nash to create a grand square to pay homage to Britain's naval power. It wasn't fully laid out until 1840, after the King's death, but Nash certainly did as he was told. The focal point is **Nelson's Column**, a tribute to the heroic Horatio, who died during the Battle of Trafalgar in 1805. This Corinthian column, designed by William Railton, is topped by a statue of Nelson by neo-classical architect Charles Barry. The granite fountains were added in 1845 (then redesigned by Lutyens in 1939) and the bronze lions – the work of Sir Edwin Landseer – in 1867. Statues of George IV and a couple of Victorian military heroes anchor three of the square's corners; modern sculpture takes up the fourth plinth: Marc Quinn's statue of a pregnant woman who was born with no arms and shortened legs will be replaced in April 2007 with Thomas Schütte's perspex acrylic structure *Hotel for the Birds*.

On the south side of the square a **statue of Charles I**, dating from the 1630s, faces down Whitehall. Immediately behind the statue, which was the first equestrian bronze in England, a plaque set in the pavement marks the original site of Eleanor's Cross (*see p118*); it is from here that all mileages from London are measured – in other words, this is taken to be the city's exact geographical centrepoint.

Neo-classical buildings overlook the square: James Gibbs's **St Martin-in-the-Fields** (*see p138*) and one of the world's great art museums, the **National Gallery** (*see below*). Don't miss the smaller but equally impressive **National Portrait Gallery** (*see p138*).

National Gallery

Trafalgar Square, WC2N 5DN (7747 2885/ www.nationalgallery.org.uk). Leicester Square tube/ Charing Cross tube/rail. **Open** (incl Sainsbury Wing) 10am-6pm Mon, Tue, Thur-Sun; 10am-9pm Wed. *Tours* 11.30am, 2.30pm daily; additionally 6pm, 6.30pm Wed; 12.30pm, 3.30pm Sat. **Admission** free. *Special exhibitions* prices vary. **Credit** (shop) MC, V. **Map** p409 X5.

Founded in 1824, the collection has grown from a mere 38 paintings into one of the greatest in the world, with more than 2,000 Western European pieces. There are masterpieces from virtually every school of art, starting with 13th-century religious works and culminating in Van Gogh. The modern Sainsbury Wing (1991) concentrates on the early Renaissance period, with an emphasis on Italian and Dutch painters. In the North Wing, look out for masterpieces by Rubens, Rembrandt and Vermeer. The East Wing has a strong collection of English paintings, including Constable's *The Hay Wain*, Turner's Romantic watercolours and works by Hogarth, Gainsborough and Reynolds. The real big-ticket items, however, are the Impressionist paintings: Monet's *Water Lilies* series, Van Gogh's *Chair* and Seurat's *Bathers at Asnières* are the stars. You can't see everything in one visit, but guided tours take in the major works and there are excellent free audio guides. There's also a fine café-restaurant in the National Dining Rooms (*see p213*).

Forthcoming major exhibitions include 'Manet to Picasso' (until May), 'Renoir landscapes 1865-1883' (21 Feb-20 May), Leon Kossof (14 Mar-1 July), 'Dutch Portraits: the Age of Rembrandt and Frans Hals' (27 June-16 Sept) and 'Renaissance Siena: Art for a City' (24 Oct 2007-13 Jan 2008).

National Portrait Gallery

2 St Martin's Place, WC2H 0HE (7306 0055/ www.npg.org.uk). Leicester Square tube/Charing Cross tube/rail. **Open** 10am-6pm Mon-Wed, Sat, Sun; 10am-9pm Thur, Fri. **Admission** free. *Special exhibitions* prices vary. **Credit** AmEx, MC, V. **Map** p409 X4.

Subjects of the portraits hanging here range from Tudor royalty to present-day celebs, of interest for contributions not only to history but to culture, sport, science and government. The exhibits are organised chronologically from top to bottom: start on the second floor and work your way down. One of the gallery's most prized possessions is the only known contemporary portrait of William Shakespeare. The gallery has a wonderfully personal feel (a result of the subject matter, its manageable size and its attractive design) and a lovely restaurant on the top floor.

Exhibitions for 2007 include David Hockney's portraits (until 21 Jan 2007), including new works specially created for the show, and 'Portraits in Fashion' (22 Feb-28 May).

St Martin-in-the-Fields

Trafalgar Square, WC2N 4JJ (7766 1100/Brass Rubbing Centre 7766 1122/box office evening concerts 7839 8362/www.stmartin-in-the-fields.org). Leicester Square tube/Charing Cross tube/rail. **Open** *Church* 8am-6pm daily. *Services* 8am, 5.30pm Mon-Fri; 1pm, 5pm, 6pm Wed; 9am Sat; 8am, 10am, 2.15pm (in Chinese), 5pm, 6.30pm Sun. *Brass Rubbing Centre* 10am-6pm Mon-Sat; noon-6pm Sun. *Evening concerts* 7.30pm Thur-Sat & alternate Tue. *Free concerts* 1pm Mon, Tue, Fri. **Admission** free. *Brass rubbing* £3-£15. *Evening concerts* prices vary. **Credit** MC, V. **Map** p409 X4.

A church has stood on this site since the 13th century, 'in the fields' between Westminster and the City; this one was built in 1726 by James Gibbs, who designed it in a curious combination of neo-classical and baroque styles. This is the parish church for Buckingham Palace (note the royal box to the left of the gallery), but it is perhaps best known for its classical music concerts (*see p307*). It also has a good café, a small gallery and the London Brass Rubbing Centre. The church is in the middle of a £34m refurbishment project, due for completion around Easter 2007; improved underground spaces will be entered through a new glazed pavilion.

Whitehall to Parliament Square

Map p403

Westminster tube or Charing Cross tube/rail.

Lined with government buildings, the long, gentle curve of **Whitehall** is named after Henry VIII's magnificent palace, which burned to the ground in 1698. The street is still home to the Ministry of Defence, the Foreign Office and the Treasury among other government buildings. They're closed to the public, but pop into the **Whitehall Theatre** (No.14) for a peek at its gorgeous art nouveau interior. Halfway down the street, the **Horse Guards** building faces the **Banqueting House** (*see p140*), London's first entirely Italianate building.

Nearby is Sir Edwin Lutyens's plain memorial to the dead of both world wars, the **Cenotaph**, and **Downing Street** with the equally plain homes of the prime minister and chancellor at Nos.10 and 11. Until 1989 members of the public could enter the street and deliver petitions to the prime minister's door, but Margaret Thatcher put a stop to that when she had the way closed off by iron security gates. At the end of King Charles Street, home of the Foreign Office, sit the **Cabinet War Rooms** (*see p141*), the operations centre used by Churchill during World War II air raids, along with the new **Churchill Museum**.

A few hundred feet from the Cenotaph stands the new **memorial to the women of World War II**. The bronze monument features 17 sets of work clothes hanging on pegs; it was designed by the sculptor John Mills, inspired by the advice given in 1945 to the seven million or so women who had contributed to the war effort: 'hang up your uniforms and overalls and go home – the job is done.'

At the end of Whitehall, neat grassy **Parliament Square**, laid out in 1868, is surrounded by architecture on an appropriately grand scale. It's overlooked by the fantastical, neo-Gothic **Middlesex Guildhall** (1906-13) on the west side, while to the south are **Westminster Abbey** (*see p141*), the most venerable ancient building in central London, and the smaller **St Margaret's Church** (*see p141*), where Samuel Pepys and Churchill were each married. It's still a favourite for society weddings. The square itself is dotted with statues of British politicians, such as Disraeli and Churchill, and one outsider, Abraham Lincoln, who sits sombrely to one side.

Trafalgar Square – designated riot and party zone. *See p137.*

Room for one more on top

For over 50 years the conductor-operated Routemaster bus served London both as a uniquely practical means of travel and an international symbol of the capital. At the start of 2006 the red double-deckers headed a list of the nation's most popular icons, along with Stonehenge and the FA Cup. Enduringly popular for their open design, which allowed passengers to hop on or off whenever they liked, the model was finally withdrawn from service in December 2005, despite prior assurance from Mayor Ken Livingstone that this would not happen (to wit: 'only a ghastly dehumanised moron would want to get rid of the Routemaster').

Slightly happier news for Routemaster lovers arrived when Transport for London announced that the bus would live on along two 'heritage' routes. Beautifully refurbished Routemasters now run through the central London sections of routes 9 and 15. The vehicles used first went into service between 1960 and 1964. They have been lovingly repainted in their original colour scheme, complete with a cream-coloured horizontal stripe, and fitted with new engines that meet European emission standards.

The buses run daily every 15 minutes from 9.30am to 6.30pm, supplementing the normal bus services. Route 9 runs from the Aldwych via the Strand, Trafalgar Square and Piccadilly Circus to the Royal Albert Hall; Route 15 runs from Trafalgar Square to Tower Hill and allows passengers to glimpse the Strand, Fleet Street and St Paul's Cathedral.

Routemaster fares match the rest of the bus network (£1.50, less with an Oyster card; *see p361*), and Travelcards are accepted. Note you must buy tickets or cards before you board.

If it is true, as some say, that few buildings in London really dazzle, the extravagant **Houses of Parliament** (*see p141*) are an exception. Although formally still known as the Palace of Westminster, the only surviving part of the medieval royal palace is Westminster Hall (and the **Jewel Tower**, just south of Westminster Abbey, *see p141*). One note: the legendary **Big Ben** is actually the name of the bell, not the clock tower that houses it. Opposite Big Ben is **Portcullis House**, an office block for MPs completed in 2000 by architect Michael Hopkins – he also designed the high-tech Westminster tube station that sits underneath the building. At the end of Westminster Bridge stands a statue of the warrior queen Boudicca and her daughters gesticulating toward Parliament.

Banqueting House

Whitehall, SW1A 2ER (0870 751 5178/www.hrp.org.uk). Westminster tube/Charing Cross tube/rail. **Open** 10am-5pm Mon-Sat. **Admission** £4.50; £3-£3.50 concessions; free under-5s. **Credit** MC, V. **Map** p403 L8.

Designed by the great neo-classicist Inigo Jones in 1622, this was the first Palladian building in London. The austere simplicity of the exterior belies the sumptuous ceiling in the beautifully proportioned first-floor hall, painted by Rubens no less. Charles I commissioned the Flemish artist to glorify his father James I, 'the wisest fool in Christendom', and celebrate the Divine Right of the Stuart kings. A bust over the entrance commemorates the fact that Charles was beheaded just outside in 1649. The event is marked annually on 31 January with a small ceremony. Call to check the hall is open before you visit: the building sometimes closes for corporate and government functions. Lunchtime concerts are held here on the first Monday of every month except August.

Cabinet War Rooms & Churchill Museum

Clive Steps, King Charles Street, SW1A 2AQ (7930 6961/www.iwm.org.uk). St James's Park or Westminster tube. **Open** 9.30am-6pm daily (last entry 5pm). **Admission** £11; £8.50 concs; free under-15s. **Credit** MC, V. **Map** p403 K9.

This small underground set of rooms was Churchill's bunker during World War II. Almost nothing has been changed since it was closed on 16 August 1945: every book, chart and pin in the map room remains in place, as does the BBC microphone he used when making his famous addresses. The furnishings are spartan, vividly evoking the wartime atmosphere, and the audio guide's sound effects – wailing sirens, Churchill's wartime speeches – add to the nostalgia. Occupying an underground space adjoining the War Rooms is the Churchill Museum, which provides an in-depth look at the great man's life and times.

Houses of Parliament

Parliament Square, SW1A 0AA (Commons information 7219 4272/Lords information 7219 3107/tours information 0870 906 3773/www.parliament.uk). Westminster tube. **Open** (when in session) *House of Commons Visitors' Gallery* 2.30-10.30pm Mon, Tue; 11.30am-7.30pm Wed; 10.30am-6.30pm Thur; 9.30am-3pm Fri. *House of Lords Visitors' Gallery* from 2.30pm Mon, Tue; from 3pm Wed; from 11am Thur; occasional Fri. *Tours* summer recess only; phone for details. **Admission** *Visitors' Gallery* free. *Tours* £7; £5 concs; free under-5s. **Credit** MC, V. **Map** p403 L9.

The ornate architecture here is the ultimate expression of Victorian self-confidence, even if its style was a throwback to the Middle Ages. Completed in 1860, it was the creation of architect Charles Barry, who won the architectural competition to replace the original Houses of Parliament, which were destroyed by fire in 1834. Barry was assisted on the interiors by Augustus Pugin. The original palace was home to the young Henry VIII, until he upped sticks to Whitehall in 1532. Although the first Parliament was held here in 1275, Westminster did not become its permanent home until Henry moved out. Parliament was originally housed in the choir stalls of St Stephen's Chapel, where members sat facing each other from opposite sides, and the tradition continues today. The only remaining parts of the original palace are the Jewel Tower (*see below*) and the almost mythically historic Westminster Hall, one of the finest medieval buildings in Europe.

In all there are 1,000 rooms, 100 staircases, 11 courtyards, eight bars and six restaurants (plus a visitors' cafeteria). None of them is open to the public, but you can watch the Commons or Lords in session from the galleries. In truth there's not much to see: most debates are sparsely attended and unenthusiastically conducted. Visitors queue at St Stephen's Entrance (it's well signposted) and, in high season, may have to wait a couple of hours. The best spectacle is Prime Minister's Question Time at noon on Wednesday, but you need to book advance tickets through your embassy or MP, who can also arrange tours. Parliament goes into recess in summer, at which times tours of the main ceremonial rooms, including Westminster Hall and the two houses, are available to the general public.

Jewel Tower

Abingdon Street, SW1P 3JY (7222 2219/www.english-heritage.org.uk). Westminster tube. **Open** *Apr-Oct* 10am-5pm daily. *Nov-Mar* 10am-4pm daily. **Admission** (EH) £2.70; £1.40-£2 concs; free under-5s. **Credit** MC, V. **Map** p403 L9.

Emphatically not the home of the Crown Jewels, this old stone tower was built in 1365 to house Edward III's gold and silver plate. Along with Westminster Hall, it is one of only two surviving parts of the medieval Palace of Westminster. From 1621 to 1864 the tower stored Parliamentary records, and it contains an exhibition on Parliament's past.

St Margaret's Church

Parliament Square, SW1P 3JX (7654 4840/www.westminster-abbey.org/stmargarets). St James's Park or Westminster tube. **Open** 9.30am-3.45pm Mon-Fri; 9.30am-1.45pm Sat; 2-5pm Sun (times may change at short notice due to services). *Services* 11am Sun; phone to check for other days. **Admission** free. **Map** p403 L9.

Some of the most impressive pre-Reformation stained glass in London can be found here. The east window (1509) commemorates the marriage of Henry VIII and Catherine of Aragon. Later windows celebrate Britain's first printer, William Caxton, buried here in 1491; explorer Sir Walter Raleigh, executed in Old Palace Yard; and writer John Milton (1608-74), who married his second wife, Katherine Woodcock, here. Founded in the 12th century, this historic church was demolished in the reign of Edward III, but rebuilt from 1486 to 1523. Since then it has been restored many times. It has been the official church of the House of Commons since 1614, so the bells are rung when a new Speaker is chosen.

Westminster Abbey

20 Dean's Yard, SW1P 3PA (7222 5152/tours 7654 4900/www.westminster-abbey.org). St James's Park or Westminster tube. **Open** *Chapter House, Nave & Royal Chapels* 9.30am-3.45pm Mon, Tue, Thur, Fri; 9.30am-7pm Wed; 9.30am-1.45pm Sat. *Abbey Museum* 10.30am-4pm Mon-Sat. *Cloisters* 8am-6pm Mon-Sat. *Garden* Apr-Sept 10am-6pm Tue-Thur. Oct-Mar 10am-4pm Tue-Thur. Last entry 1hr before closing. *Services* 7.30am, 8am, 12.30pm, 5pm Mon-

Fri; 8am, 9am, 3pm Sat; 8am, 10am, 11.15am, 3pm, 5.45pm, 6.30pm Sun. **Admission** £10, £6 concs; £22 family; free under-11s with paying adult. **Credit** MC, V. **Map** p403 K9.

Westminster Abbey has been synonymous with British royalty since 1066, when Edward the Confessor built a church on the site just in time for his own funeral (it was consecrated eight days before he died). Since then a 'who's who' of the monarchy has been buried here and, with two exceptions (Edwards V and VIII), every ruler since William the Conqueror (1066) has been crowned in the abbey. Of the original abbey, only the Pyx Chamber (the one-time royal treasury) and the Norman undercroft remain. The Gothic nave and choir were rebuilt in the 13th century; the Henry VII Chapel, with its spectacular fan vaulting, was added in 1503-12, and Nicholas Hawksmoor's west towers completed the building in 1745.

The interior is cluttered with monuments to statesmen, scientists, musicians and poets. Poets' Corner contains the graves of Dryden, Samuel Johnson, Browning and Tennyson – although it has plaques for many more, most are buried elsewhere. The centrepiece of the octagonal Chapter House is its faded 13th-century tiled floor, while the Little Cloister, with its pretty garden, offers respite from the crowds, especially during free lunchtime concerts.

Millbank

Map p403

Pimlico or Westminster tube.

Millbank runs along the river from Parliament to Vauxhall Bridge; you walk this way to get to Tate Britain. Immediately south of the Houses of Parliament are the **Victoria Tower Gardens**, which contain a statue of suffragette leader Emmeline Pankhurst, a cast of Rodin's glum-looking *Burghers of Calais* and the Buxton Drinking Fountain commemorating the emancipation of slaves. On the other side of the road, Dean Stanley Street leads to **Smith Square**, home to **St John's, Smith Square**, an exuberant baroque fantasy built as a church in 1713-28 but now a venue for classical music (*see p307*). **Lord North Street**, which runs north from the square, is one of the best-preserved Georgian streets in London in addition to being one of the city's most prestigious addresses.

Further along the river, just north of Vauxhall Bridge, stands the **Tate Britain** gallery (*see below*), with its excellent collection of British art. It occupies the former site of the Millbank Penitentiary, one of Britain's fouler Victorian prisons, eventually demolished in 1890. (The ghost of a past inmate is supposed to haunt the cellars of the nearby **Morpeth Arms**, 55 Millbank, 7834 6442.) Across the river, the curious cream and green-glass post-modernist block is the highly conspicuous HQ of the Secret Intelligence Service (SIS), which people more commonly refer to as MI6.

Tate Britain

Millbank, SW1P 4RG (7887 8000/www.tate.org.uk). Pimlico tube. **Open** 10am-5.50pm daily. *Tours* 11am, noon, 2pm, 3pm Mon-Fri; noon, 3pm Sat, Sun. **Admission** free. *Special exhibitions* prices vary. **Credit** (shop) MC, V. **Map** p403 K11.

Tate Modern (*see p85*), its younger, sexier sibling, seems to get all the attention, but we think the collection at the TB is far stronger. It contains London's second great collection of historical art, after the National Gallery. With the opening of the Modern, plenty of space was freed up to accommodate the collection of British art from the 16th century to the present day. The collection more than fills the 'something for everyone' remit that you'd hope for from a gallery whose exhibits span five centuries. It takes in works by artists such as Hogarth, the Blakes (William and Peter), Gainsborough, Constable (who gets three rooms all to himself), Reynolds, Bacon and Moore. Turner is particularly well represented, even more so since 2003 when the gallery recovered two classics – *Shade and Darkness: The Evening of the Deluge* and *Light and Colour (Goethe's Theory)* – that had been stolen in 1994. Tate Modern doesn't have a monopoly on contemporary artists, either: there are works here by Howard Hodgkin, Lucian Freud and David Hockney. The shop is well stocked with posters and art books, and the restaurant is highly regarded. You can also have the best of both art worlds, thanks to the Tate-to-Tate boat service (*see p85*).

Exhibitions planned for 2007 include 'East–West: Objects between Cultures' (until 18 Feb 2007). The annual – and always headline-grabbing – Turner Prize exhibition for contemporary artists runs from October to January. **Photo** *p145.*

Victoria

Map p402

Pimlico tube or Victoria tube/rail.

Victoria Street, stretching from Parliament Square to Victoria Station, links political London with a rather more colourful and chaotic backpackers' London. Victoria Coach Station, one of the city's main arrival terminuses for visitors from the rest of Europe, is a short distance away in Buckingham Palace Road; Belgrave Road provides an almost unbroken line of cheap (and often grim) hotels.

Not to be confused with the abbey in Parliament Square, **Westminster Cathedral** (*see p143*) is partly hidden by office blocks, and comes as a pleasant surprise. The striking, red-brick Byzantine church was built between 1895 and 1903, although its interior decoration is still unfinished. North of Victoria Street back towards Parliament Square is **Christchurch Gardens**, burial site of Thomas ('Colonel')

Blood, the 17th-century rogue who nearly got away with stealing the Crown Jewels in 1671. Nearby is **New Scotland Yard**, with its famous revolving sign and, just north of that, **55 Broadway**, home of London Underground.

Westminster Cathedral

42 Francis Street, SW1P 1QW (7798 9055/www.westminstercathedral.org.uk). Victoria tube/rail. **Open** 7am-7pm Mon-Fri, Sun; 8am-7pm Sat. *Services* 7am, 8am, 10.30am, 12.30pm, 1.05pm, 5.30pm Mon-Fri; 8am, 9am, 10.30am, 12.30pm, 6pm Sat; 8am, 9am, 10.30am, noon, 5.30pm, 7pm Sun. **Admission** free; donations appreciated. *Campanile* £3; £1.50 concs. **No credit cards.** **Map** p402 J10.

Westminster Abbey might be more famous, but Westminster Cathedral is spectacular in its own bizarre way. Part wedding cake, part sweet stick, this neo-Byzantine confection is Britain's premier Catholic cathedral, built between 1895 and 1903 by John Francis Bentley, who was inspired by the Hagia Sophia in Istanbul. The land on which it is built had formerly been a bull-baiting ring and a pleasure garden before being bought by the Catholic Church in 1884. With such a festive exterior, you'd expect an equally ornate interior. Not so: the inside has yet to be finished. Even so, you can get a taste of what the faithful will eventually achieve from the magnificent columns and mosaics (made from more than 100 kinds of marble). Eric Gill's sculptures of the Stations of the Cross (1914-18) are world renowned. Simple and objective, they were controversial at the time of installation, labelled Babylonian and crude by critics. The nave of Westminster Cathedral is the broadest in England, and dark wood floors and flickering candles add to the drama. The view from the 273ft bell tower is superb: best of all, it's got a lift.

St James's Park

Map p402 & p403

St James's Park tube.

Originally a royal deer park for St James's Palace, the park's pastoral landscape owes its influence to John Nash, who redesigned it in the early 19th century under the orders of George IV. The view of **Buckingham Palace** (*see p144*) from the bridge over the lake is wonderful, especially at night when the palace is floodlit. The lake is now a sanctuary for wildfowl, among them pelicans (fed at 3pm daily) and Australian black swans.

Walk this way

Apparently, before he took to writing, Charles Dickens nearly became an actor. Spurred on by encouraging remarks, he arranged an audition but on the day in question suffered a terrible head cold and couldn't make it. In the words of the lovely and arthritic Judy, a tour guide with **Original London Walks** (7624 3978, www.walks.com), we may owe some of our greatest works of literature to a bit of a temperature and a runny nose.

It's appropriate that the name of Dickens comes up, as back in the 1860s he had already cottoned on to one of the greatest joys that London has to offer: 'Whenever I think I deserve particularly well of myself, and have earned the right to enjoy a little treat, I stroll from Covent Garden into the City of London and roam about its deserted nooks and corners.' Unlike New York or Paris, London has never been subjected to logical planning, but has grown organically out of a thick mulch of story and experience. What better way to explore, then, than as part of a guided walking tour led by a local expert, who showers his or her charges with historical detail, trivia and anecdote at every concealed alley and hidden courtyard. Judy leads a 'Shakespeare's & Dickens's London' walk, one of an astonishing 140 walks the company runs each week, from 'Ghosts of the Old City' to 'The Beatles "In My Life" Walk'.

In the drizzle outside Tower Hill tube station a small crowd slowly assembles for one of the most popular outings, gravitating to a gentleman shouting 'This way for Jack the Ripper'. It's amazing how many people are keen to be regaled with all the details of these most infamous of murders, but as the streets narrow, the evening darkens and the guide dwells on the slaughter, you might begin to appreciate safety in numbers.

More tales of east London violence are related in the sensationally titled 'Evil East End' walk (call 07913 253242 for details), which follows the careers of the Kray twins. Walkers are invited to down a pint in the Blind Beggar where Ronnie Kray shot and killed fellow gangster George Cornell.

Other notable walking companies include **Citisights** (8806 4325, www.chr.org.uk), **Performing London** (01234 404774, www.performinglondon.co.uk) and **Silvercane Tours** (07720 715295, www.silvercanetours.com), which also does movie location walks including the 'Big Knickers Tour' (*Bridget Jones's Diary*) and a *Da Vinci Code* walk.

On the south side of the park, the Wellington Barracks, home of the Foot Guards, contains the **Guards' Museum** (*see below*). Running along the north side is the grand processional route of the **Mall**, which connects Buckingham Palace with Trafalgar Square. However, the Mall was not designed with its current purpose in mind (despite being tarmacked in pink to match the Queen's forecourt): Charles II had it laid out before the palace was even a royal residence. He wanted a new pitch for 'pallemaille', a popular game that involved hitting a ball through a hoop at the end of a long alley. Nearby Pall Mall, his favourite pitch, had become too crowded for the sport.

On the north side of the Mall is **Carlton House Terrace**, the last project completed by John Nash before his death in 1835. It was built on the site of Carlton House, which was George IV's home until he decided it wasn't fit for a king and enlarged Buckingham House into a palace to replace it. Part of the terrace now houses the **Institute of Contemporary Arts** (ICA; *see below*). The steps beside the ICA lead up to the **Duke of York column**, which commemorates Prince Frederick, Duke of York, commander-in-chief of the British Army during the wars with the French and the 'Grand old Duke of York' of the nursery rhyme. When he died in 1827, the entire British Army had to forfeit a day's wages in order to pay for his extravagent monument.

Changing of the Guard

A Foot Guards regiment (scarlet coats and bearskin hats) lines up in the forecourt of Wellington Barracks, just off Birdcage Walk, from 10.45am; at 11.27am the soldiers march, accompanied by their regimental band, to Buckingham Palace to relieve the sentries in the forecourt in an impressive 45-minute ceremony. If there are four guards at the front rather than two, it means that Her Majesty is in residence. In another bit of daily pomp, at Horse Guards Parade in Whitehall, the Household Cavalry mount the guard (10am-4pm daily) then ride to Whitehall via the Mall from Hyde Park for the changeover.

The schedule is subject to change: see www.changing-the-guard.com/sched.htm.

Ceremonies *Dec-Aug* 11.30am daily. *Sept, Oct* 11.30am even numbered dates. *Nov* 11.30am odd numbered dates.
Horse Guards ceremonies 11am Mon-Sat; 10am Sun.

Buckingham Palace & Royal Mews

The Mall, SW1A 1AA (7766 7300/Royal Mews 7766 7302/www.royalcollection.org.uk). Green Park or St James's Park tube/Victoria tube/rail. **Open** *State Rooms* mid July-Sept 9.45am-5.30pm daily. *Queen's Gallery* 10am-5.30pm daily. *Royal Mews* Oct-July 11am-4pm daily. Aug, Sept 10am-5pm daily. Last entry 45mins before closing. **Admission** *Palace* £14; £8-£12.50 concs; £36 family; free under-5s. *Queen's Gallery* £7.50; £4-£6.50 concs; £19 family; free under-5s. *Royal Mews* £6.50; £4-£5.50 concs; £17.50 family; free under-5s. **Credit** AmEx, MC, V. **Map** p402 H9.

The world's most famous palace, built in 1703, started life as a grand house for the Duke of Buckingham, but George III liked it so much he bought it, in 1761, for his young bride Charlotte. It became known as the Queen's House and 14 of their 15 children were born here. His son, George IV, hired John Nash to convert it into a palace. Thus construction on the 600-room palace began in 1825. But the project was beset with disaster from the start. Nash was fired after George IV's death – he was too flighty, apparently – and the reliable but unimaginative Edward Blore was hired to finish the job. After critics saw the result, they dubbed him 'Blore the Bore'. What's more, Queen Victoria, who was the first royal to live here, hated the place, calling it 'a disgrace to the country'.

Judge for yourself. In August and September, while the Windsors are off on their holidays, the ostentatious State Apartments – used for banquets and investitures – are open to the public. The Queen's Gallery, which is open for most of the year, contains highlights of Elizabeth's decorative and fine art collection: Old Masters, Sèvres porcelain, ornately inlaid cabinets and the Diamond Diadem (familiar from millions of postage stamps). Further along Buckingham Palace Road, the Royal Mews holds horses (when they're not out trooping the colour) and royal carriages.

Guards' Museum

Wellington Barracks, Birdcage Walk, SW1E 6HQ (7414 3428/www.theguardsmuseum.com). St James's Park tube. **Open** 10am-4pm daily (last entry 3.30pm). **Admission** £3; £2 concs; free under-16s. **Credit** (shop) AmEx, MC, V. **Map** p402 J9.

This small, immaculately maintained museum, founded in the 17th century under Charles II, records the history of the British Army's five Guards regiments. It contains mainly uniforms, some important paintings, intriguing memorabilia and medals, including the first ever minted for the army, for its victory over the Scots at the Battle of Dunbar in the 17th century.

Institute of Contemporary Arts

The Mall, SW1Y 5AH (box office 7930 3647/ www.ica.org.uk). Piccadilly Circus tube/Charing Cross tube/rail. **Open** *Galleries* noon-7.30pm daily.

Tate Britain, whose classical façade fronts four centuries of Brit art. *See p142*.

Membership *Daily* £2, £1.50 concs Mon-Fri; £3, £2 concs Sat, Sun; free under-14s. *Annual* £35; £25 concs. **Credit** AmEx, DC, MC, V. **Map** p403 K8.

Founded in 1948 by the anarchist Herbert Read, the Institute of Contemporary Arts still revels in a remit that challenges traditional notions of art from its incongruously establishment-looking home. Scores of challengers have held their first exhibitions here, including Henry Moore, Picasso, Max Ernst, Damien Hirst, Helen Chadwick and Gary Hume. Its cinema (*see p288*) shows London's artiest films (and is the venue for the annual onedotzero digital film festival, *see p291*), its theatre stages performance art and quality gigs, and its exhibitions are always talking points. There's also a bar and café, and a small, selectively stocked book and DVD shop.

St James's

Maps p408 & p402

Green Park or Piccadilly Circus tube.

One of central London's quietest and most exclusive areas, St James's does not get many visitors. Bordered by Piccadilly, Haymarket, the Mall and Green Park, it was laid out in the 1660s and has long been associated with the aristocracy who wanted to be close to the royal palaces. This is a London that has remained unchanged for centuries: its squares and hushed streets are all very charming, although it all remains resolutely rich and gently conceited all the same.

The area is typified by **Pall Mall**, which is lined by stately gentleman's clubs (think drawing rooms and open fires rather than thongs and pole dancing); these include the **Reform Club** (Nos.104-105), where Phileas Fogg takes on the bet that results in him travelling around the world in 80 days in the Jules Verne novel, and the **Athenaeum** (No.107), founded in 1824 as the leading intellectual club of St James's. All are, unfortunately, members-only.

North of Pall Mall, **St James's Square** was the most fashionable address in London for the 50 years after it was laid out in the 1670s: some seven dukes and seven earls were residents by the 1720s. Alas, no private houses survive on the square today. Among the current occupants is the prestigious **London Library**, founded by Thomas Carlyle in 1841 in disgust at the inefficiency of the British Library. It's the world's largest independent lending library but, as with much in St James's, it's members only. However, the grassy enclosure at the centre of the square is a pleasant place to take lunch: bring your own sandwiches.

The material needs of the gents who habituate clubland are met by the anachronistic retailers and restaurants of **Jermyn Street**, such as old-fashioned shirt shop **Harvie & Hudson** (Nos.96-97) and classic British dining room **Wiltons** (No.55, 7692 9955), which originally opened in 1742 as a stall selling oysters, shrimps and cockles. There's more of the same round the corner on St James's Street.

Just off St James's Street is the Queen Mother's old residence, **Clarence House** (*see below*). Now the official London home of Prince Charles, his sons Harry and William, and his wife Camilla, it is open to the public in summer. Adjacent to Clarence House, **St James's Palace** was originally built for Henry VIII in the 1530s. It has remained the official residence of the sovereign throughout the centuries, despite the fact that since 1837 the monarchs have all actually lived at nearby Buckingham Palace. It has great historic significance to the monarchy: Mary Tudor surrendered Calais here, Elizabeth I lived here during the campaign against the Spanish Armada, and Charles I was confined here before his execution in 1649.

Today St James's Palace is used by the Princess Royal (the title given to the monarch's eldest daughter, which is Princess Anne) and various minor royals. Tradition still dictates that foreign ambassadors to the UK are officially known as 'Ambassadors to the Court of St James's'. Although the palace is closed to the public, you can attend Sunday services at the palace's historic **Chapel Royal** (1st Sun of mth, Oct-Easter Sunday; 8.30am, 11.15am).

Across Marlborough Road lies the **Queen's Chapel**, which was the first classical church to be built in England. Designed by the mighty and prolific Inigo Jones in the 1620s for Charles I's intended bride of the time, the Infanta of Castile, the chapel now stands in the grounds of **Marlborough House** and is only open to the public during Sunday services (Easter-July; 8.30am, 11.15am). The house itself was built by Sir Christopher Wren.

Two other notable St James's mansions stand nearby and overlook Green Park (from which they're visible). The neo-classical **Lancaster House** was rebuilt in the 1820s by Benjamin Dean Wyatt for Frederick, Duke of York, and impressed Queen Victoria with its splendour. Closed to the public, it's now used mainly for government receptions and conferences. A little further north, on St James's Place, is the beautiful, 18th-century **Spencer House** (*see below*), ancestral townhouse of the late Princess Diana's family and now infrequently open as a museum and art gallery.

Clarence House

The Mall, SW1A 1AA (7766 7303/www.royal collection.org.uk). Green Park tube. **Open** *Aug-mid Oct* 10am-4.30pm daily. **Admission** £7; £4 under-17s; free under-5s. *Tours* all tickets must be pre-booked. **Credit** AmEx, MC, V. **Map** p402 J8.

Standing austerely beside St James's Palace, Clarence House was erected between 1825 and 1827, based on designs by John Nash. It was built for Prince William Henry, Duke of Clarence, who lived there as King William IV until 1837. The house has been much altered by its many royal inhabitants, the most recent of whom was the Queen Mother, who lived here until she died in 2002. Prince Charles and his two sons have since moved in, but parts of the house are open to the public in summer: five receiving rooms and the small but significant art collection accumulated by the Queen Mother. Among the art on display is a lovely 1945 portrait of her by Sir James Gunn. There are also works by John Piper, WS Sickert and Augustus John. Tickets are hard to come by and tend to sell out by the end of August.

Spencer House

27 St James's Place, SW1A 1NR (7499 8620/ www.spencerhouse.co.uk). Green Park tube. **Open** *House* Feb-July, Sept-Dec 10.30am-5.45pm Sun (last entry 4.45pm). *Gardens* spring,summer (phone to check). **Admission** *Tours* £9; £7 concs. Under-10s not allowed. **No credit cards. Map** p402 J8.

Designed by John Vardy and built for John Spencer, who became Earl Spencer the year before his house was completed, this 1756-66 construction is one of the capital's finest examples of a Palladian mansion. The eponymous Spencers moved out just over a century ago and the lavishly restored building is now used chiefly as offices and for corporate entertaining, hence the limited access.

Chelsea

It wasn't always all about José Mourinho and footballing prima donnas.

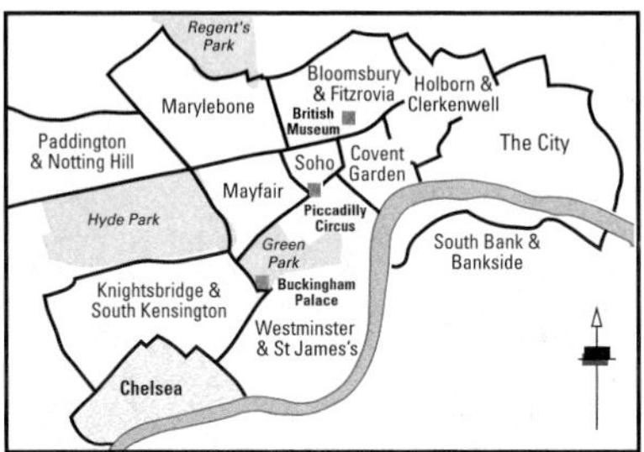

When the cover of the 15 April 1966 issue of *Time* magazine informed its international readership that London was 'swinging', Chelsea's King's Road was described as the swingingest place of all. It was where the Rolling Stones began and the miniskirt was first worn. Not much later it was also where the Sex Pistols exploded and bondage trousers got their first airing. In the 1960s and '70s Chelsea groovers were at the forefront of music, theatre, fashion and art. Chelsea was where the image of modern London was cemented. That was then. Now, like some ageing rocker, Chelsea's very comfortably off, thank you – the torn trousers exchanged for tailored suits, the speedball cocktails for vintage Bordeaux. Get off the King's Road, though, and it can still surprise with displays of raffish charm.

Sloane Square & the King's Road

Maps p398 & p399

Sloane Square tube then various buses.

Chelsea proper begins with Sloane Square, spoiled by circling traffic but redeemed by the noble artistic venue that is the **Royal Court Theatre** (*see p340*). This modest playhouse sent shockwaves around the world in 1956 with the première of John Osborne's *Look Back in Anger*. It boasts two wonderfully intimate auditoriums and, with tickets costing as little as £10, it's well worth a punt whatever's showing. On the opposite side of the square is **Peter Jones** (7730 3434, www.peterjones.co.uk), a polished department store in a beautiful 1930s building – recently successfully refurbished – with fine views from the top-floor café.

Running south-west from Sloane Square is the **King's Road**, Chelsea's high street. The name reflects its origins as a highway built for Charles II to facilitate his travels between the palaces of Hampton Court and Whitehall. Off the top end is **Duke of York Square**, an upmarket shopping development that includes a branch of **Pâtisserie Valerie** (*see p203*), plus summer fountains much loved by over-heated children. In fact, kids actually do better than adults for King's Road shopping these days – unless the adult happens to be a fan of posh chain stores. Places of note include **Antiquarius** (Nos.131-141; *see p237*) for antiques; childrenswear shop **Daisy & Tom** (Nos.181-183; *see p247*); **Austique** (No.330; *see p244*) for sexy womens' wear and lingerie; and the **Organic Pharmacy** (No.369; *see p260*) for all-natural brands. Eateries include Terence Conran's **Bluebird Dining Rooms** (No.350; *see p214*), which also has a great deli (*see p257*); both are housed in a gorgeous original 1920s garage.

Beyond Bluebird, at No.430, is the site of Vivienne Westwood's shop, a punk pilgrimage in the early 1980s, when it was called, simply, SEX. It's now a boutique called World's End.

The pretty streets that branch off the King's Road are the nicest. Sydney Street takes you to **St Luke's Church**, a vast place of worship where Charles Dickens was married in 1836. Tucked-away crescents and streets to the south are beautiful – **Glebe Place** has a little children's nursery, while at Nos.49 and 50 is a mansion covered in statuary and climbers.

Cheyne Walk & Chelsea Embankment

Map p399

Sloane Square tube then various buses.

As early as the 15th century the fishing village of Chelsea was earning itself a fashionable reputation. Aristocrats built country manors in the area. Its grandeur was further enhanced when Sir Thomas More, Lord Chancellor to Henry VIII, came to live here in 1520. Other bigwigs followed, including the King himself, whose lofty presence endowed Chelsea with the title 'Village of Palaces'. Elizabeth I also lived in the area for a spell in the late 1540s.

The **King's Road**. *See p147.*

The grandest areas lie south of Sloane Square, between the King's Road and the river. Also in this area are the grounds of the **Royal Hospital Chelsea** (*see p149*) and Ranelagh Gardens, best known these days as the site of the **Chelsea Flower Show** (*see p267*), but for most of the year the area is peaceful, as befits a place of sanctuary for retired soldiers. Next door is the **National Army Museum** (*see p149*).

Chelsea's idyllic riverside location also attracted writers and intellectuals, although Thomas Carlyle was in two minds about moving there in 1834, because at that time the area was still separated from civilised Westminster by the type of marshy common land beloved of criminals. The surrounding countryside was built over during his lifetime, which disturbed him even more. His house is preserved at 24 Cheyne Row (*see below*).

Artists and sculptors were drawn by the area's reputation for creativity. This was enhanced by the presence of the Chelsea Porcelain Works, which operated in Lawrence Street from 1745 to 1784, and the restorative **Chelsea Physic Garden** (*see p149*), founded by the Apothecaries' Company in 1676.

Chelsea's bohemian reputation lasted well into the 20th century. Between the wars Dylan Thomas was the local celeb – he drank in the nearby pubs, and made derisory comments about the trendy set of **Cheyne Walk** (George Eliot, Dante Gabriel Rossetti, and later Henry James and TS Eliot, had all lived on this pleasant riverside road).

These days the artistic presence is reduced to a vast number of blue plaques, while Cheyne Walk, although still attractive, is marred by thundering embankment traffic. The western end of this famous street becomes **Cremorne Road**, whose well-kept riverside park, though a far cry from the rowdy pleasure gardens of its Victorian heyday, affords uplifting views east to Old Ferry Wharf and west to **Chelsea Harbour**, which has been transformed from industrial wasteland into opulent offices, swish hotels, shops, restaurants and a marina to make it a playground for the rich and famous (including the players of Chelsea FC, whose ground, **Stamford Bridge**, is a few minutes' drive away on Fulham Road; *see p331*).

The oldest street in Chelsea, **Old Church Street**, provides some relief from the traffic. The church in question (*see p149*) was founded in the 13th century but largely destroyed in World War II. Sir Thomas More sang in the choir here and there's a river-facing statue to his memory nearby. At No.143 the private **Chelsea Arts Club** is another relic of the area's artistic heritage. It was founded in 1891 on the suggestion of Whistler, and its members number hundreds of painters, sculptors, designers and writers.

Carlyle's House

24 Cheyne Row, SW3 5HL (7352 7087/www.nationaltrust.org.uk). Sloane Square tube/11, 19, 22, 49, 211, 319 bus. **Open** 2-5pm Wed-Fri; 11am-5pm Sat, Sun. Closed Nov-Mar. **Admission** £4.50; £2.30 concs; £11.30 family. **Map** p399 E12.

Thomas Carlyle and his wife Jane, both towering intellects, moved to this four-storey, Queen Anne house in 1834. In 1896, 15 years after Carlyle's death, the house was preserved as a museum, offering an intriguing snapshot of Victorian life. From the stone-flagged basement kitchen, with its little bed for the maid, up several flights of stairs to Carlyle's attic office, the atmosphere is lent authenticity by the creaking floorboards. Evidence of the writer's desperate quest for peace and quiet strikes a chord today – there is much information on Carlyle's attempts to soundproof the attic; he was plagued by the sound of fireworks and revelry from nearby Cremorne Pleasure Gardens and by the clucking of next door's poultry.

Chelsea Old Church

Cheyne Walk, Old Church Street, SW3 5DQ (7795 1019/www.chelseaoldchurch.org.uk). Sloane Square tube/11, 19, 22, 49, 319 bus. **Open** 2-4pm Tue-Thur; 1.30-5pm Sun. *Sun services* 8am, 10am, 11am, 12.15pm. *Evensong* 6pm. Guides available Sun. **Admission** free; donations appreciated.

Most of the ancient church, which dates back to the 13th century, was destroyed by a bomb in 1941. The Thomas More Chapel remains on the south side, and legend has it that his headless body is buried somewhere under the walls (his head, after being spiked on London Bridge, was 'rescued' and buried in a family vault in St Dunstan's Church, Canterbury).

Chelsea Physic Garden

66 Royal Hospital Road (entrance on Swan Walk), SW3 4HS (7352 5646/www.chelseaphysicgarden.co.uk). Sloane Square tube/11, 19, 239 bus. **Open** *Apr-Oct* noon-dusk Wed; noon-5pm Thur, Fri; noon-6pm Sun & bank hols. *Tours* times vary; phone to check. **Admission** £7; £4 concs; free under-5s. *Tours* free. **Credit** (shop) AmEx, MC, V. **Map** p399 F12.

The garden was set up in 1673, but the key phase of development was under Sir Hans Sloane in the 18th century. The 165,000sq ft grounds are filled with beds containing healing herbs and rare trees, dye plants and medicinal vegetables. The world's first rock garden was built here in 1772, using bits of old stone from the Tower of London. The physic garden opened to the public in 1893, but nowadays hours are restricted. Free tours conducted by entertaining volunteers trace the history of the medicinal beds, where herbs are grown for their efficacy in treating illness.

National Army Museum

Royal Hospital Road, SW3 4HT (7730 0717/www.national-army-museum.ac.uk). Sloane Square tube/11, 137, 239 bus. **Open** 10am-5.30pm daily. **Admission** free. **Credit** (shop) AmEx, MC, V. **Map** p399 F12.

Some eccentric exhibits and displays make this museum dedicated to the history of the British Army far more entertaining than the modern exterior might suggest. The collection kicks off with Redcoats, a gallery that starts at Agincourt in 1415 and ends with the American War of Independence. Upstairs, the Road to Waterloo marches through the 20-year struggle against the French, featuring 70,000 model soldiers and bloodstained souvenirs of Waterloo. The experiences of the Victorian soldier, army life during the two world wars and a gallery devoted to National Service bring the soldier's life right up to date. On display upstairs is the kit of Olympic medal winner Kelly Holmes (an ex-army athlete), while Major Michael 'Bronco' Lane, conqueror of Mount Everest, has kindly donated his frostbitten fingertips.

Royal Hospital Chelsea

Royal Hospital Road, SW3 4SR (7881 5200/www.chelsea-pensioners.org.uk). Sloane Square tube/11, 19, 22, 137, 211, 239 bus. **Open** *Oct-Apr* 10am-noon, 2-4pm Mon-Sat. *May-Sept* 10am-noon, 2-4pm Mon-Sat; 2-4pm Sun. **Admission** free. **Map** p399 F12.

About 350 Chelsea Pensioners (retired soldiers) live here. Their quarters, the Royal Hospital, was founded in 1682 by Charles II, and the building was designed by Sir Christopher Wren, with later adjustments added by Robert Adam and Sir John Soane. Retired soldiers are eligible to apply for a final posting here if they are over 65 and in receipt of an Army or War Disability Pension for Army Service. The in-pensioners (as opposed to the Chelsea Pensioners who live elsewhere) are organised into companies, along military lines, with a governor and other officers. They have their own club room, bowling green and gardens. The museum (open at the same times as the Hospital) has more about their life.

Royal Court Theatre. *See p147.*

Knightsbridge & South Kensington

The museums and park are free but otherwise it's all about money.

Knightsbridge is where the money comes out to play: in strings of designer shops and fashionable restaurants where your credit card had better be gold. For all that, the area is neither hip nor particularly stylish – the money is largely old-school, which makes for great people-watching. South Kensington offers more of the same, with a slightly lower stuffiness rating and three of the capital's biggest-hitting museums.

Knightsbridge

Map p399

Knightsbridge tube.

Knightsbridge in the 11th century was a village celebrated for its taverns, highwaymen and the legend that two knights once fought to the death on the bridge that spanned the Westbourne River (later dammed to form Hyde Park's Serpentine). Nowadays, urban princesses are too busy unsheathing their credit cards to look out for duelling knights. Modern Knightsbridge is a shopper's paradise, with the voguish **Harvey Nichols** (*see p242*) holding sway at the top of **Sloane Street**, which leads down to Sloane Square and Chelsea (*see p147*). Expensive brands dominate this otherwise unremarkable road – Gucci, Prada, Chanel and Christian Dior are all present.

East of Sloane Street is Belgravia, characterised by a cluster of foreign embassies around imposing **Belgrave Square**. Hidden behind the stucco-clad parades fronting the square are numerous tiny mews well worth exploring if only for the wonderful pubs they conceal, notably the delightfully nostalgic **Nag's Head**, the shabbily grand **Grenadier**, Madonna's local when she was living in Belgravia back in the late 1990s, and the **Star Tavern**, which in the 1960s was where gangsters and Great Train Robbers mixed with movie stars such as Elizabeth Taylor (for all three pubs, *see p231*). **St Paul's Knightsbridge** on Wilton Place is an appealing Victorian church, with scenes from the life of Jesus in ceramics tiling the nave, and a wonderful wood-beamed ceiling.

For tourists, Knightsbridge means one thing: **Harrods** (*see p242*). From its tan bricks and olive green awning to its green-coated doormen, it is an instantly recognisable retailing legend – all the more so at night when it's lit up like a Vegas casino. Originally a family grocer's, it is now the world's most famous department store, employing about 5,000 people. Owner Mohammed Al Fayed continues to add to the richness of eccentricity that characterises the place, notably with his Egyptian Hall and memorial to son Dodi and Princess Diana, but he'll have to go some to match extravagences of the past – for example the sale made in 1967, when the Prince of Albania purchased a baby elephant from here for Ronald Reagan.

The western end of Knightsbridge is dominated by the imposing mass of **Brompton Oratory** (*see below*), a church of suitably lavish proportions for a part of town long associated with extravagant displays of wealth. To really see how the rich live, wander behind the Oratory and north through the small park to emerge on Ennismore Garden Mews, one of the loveliest streets in London; actors Michael Caine and Terence Stamp shared a flat here in the late 1950s.

Brompton Oratory

Thurloe Place, Brompton Road, SW7 2RP (7808 0900/www.bromptonoratory.com). South Kensington tube. **Open** 6.30am-8pm daily. *Services* 7am, 10am, 12.30pm, 6pm Mon-Fri; 7am, 8.30am, 10am, 6pm Sat; 7am, 8am, 9am, 10am, 11am, 12.30pm, 4.30pm, 7pm Sun. **Admission** free; donations appreciated. **Map** p399 E10.

One of the food halls at London's third most popular tourist sight, **Harrods**. *See p150.*

The second-biggest Catholic church in the country (after Westminster Cathedral), the London Oratory of St Philip of Neri is awesome. Completed in 1884, it feels older – partly because of its baroque Italianate style, but also because many of its marbles, mosaics and statuary pre-date the structure. Mazzuoli's late 17th-century apostle statues, for example, were once in Siena's cathedral. The vast main space culminates in a magnificent Italian altarpiece, and a number of ornate confessionals stand in the several chapels flanking the nave. The 11am Solemn Mass sung in Latin on Sundays is enchanting. During the Cold War, the church was used by the KGB as a dead-letter box.

South Kensington

Map p399

Gloucester Road or South Kensington tube.

This is the land of plenty, as far as cultural and academic institutions are concerned. Three heavyweight museums, three lofty colleges and one landmark concert hall dominate the area once known as Albertopolis, in honour of the prince who oversaw the inception of all the above. Today £186,000 won't buy much, but back in the 1850s this sum, the profits of the 1851 Great Exhibition, bought the 350,000 square metres (3,789,000 square feet) of land for the building of institutions to 'extend the influence of Science and Art upon Productive Industry'. Prince Albert did not survive to see the resulting oasis of learning, which includes the **Natural History Museum** (*see p153*), the **Science Museum** (*see p154*) and the **Victoria & Albert Museum** (*see p154*). Don't be tempted to try to see all three on the same day; each contains an encyclopaedia's worth of content and rewards multiple visits.

The three colleges in question are **Imperial College**, the **Royal College of Art** and the **Royal College of Music** (Prince Consort Road, 7589 3643; call for details of concerts and Wednesday openings of the musical instrument museum), which forms a unity with the **Royal Albert Hall**, the great, rotund performance space inaugurated in 1871 and since used for boxing bouts, motor shows, marathons (524 circuits of the arena adds up to 26 miles), table tennis championships, the Eurovision Song Contest, Miss World, sumo wrestling, rock and pop concerts (including an annual season by Eric Clapton), and whose murky acoustics test conductors and musicians during the world-famous summer Proms concerts (*see p307*). Looking out across Kensington Gore from the Hall gives a great view of the golden tribute to the royal benefactor, the **Albert Memorial** (*see p153*).

South of the museums, around the lovely tube station with its small arcade, is the heart of South Kensington. Outside the station at the junction of Old Brompton Road and Onslow Square is a coppery statue of Hungarian composer Béla Bartók, who used to stay at nearby Sydney Place whenever he was performing in London. Just north of the station is Cromwell Place where, at No.7, Francis Bacon

kept a studio in the 1940s before relocating 100 metres west along Harrington Road to 7 Reece Mews, where he lived and worked from 1961 until his death in 1992.

Albert Memorial

Kensington Gardens (opposite Royal Albert Hall), SW7 (tours 7495 0916). South Kensington tube. **Tours** 2pm, 3pm 1st Sun of mth. **Admission** free. *Tours* £4.50; £4 concs. **No credit cards.** **Map** p397 D8.

'I would rather not be made the prominent feature of such a monument,' was Prince Albert's reported response when the subject of commemoration came up. Quite what he would have made of this overblown memorial, unveiled 15 years after his death, is hard to imagine. It is, however, one of the great sculptural achievements of the Victorian period. Created by Sir George Gilbert Scott, it centres around a gilded Prince Albert holding a catalogue of the Great Exhibition of 1851. He's guarded on four outer corners by massive representations of the continents of Africa, America, Asia and Europe, and sits enshrined in a white marble frieze of poets and painters; pillars are crowned with bronze statues representing the sciences, and the arts are shown in a series of intricate mosaics. The dramatic 55m (180ft) spire is inlaid with semi-precious stones.

Natural History Museum

Cromwell Road, SW7 5BD (information 7942 5725/switchboard 7942 5000/www.nhm.ac.uk). South Kensington tube. **Open** 10am-5.50pm daily; **Admission** free; charges apply for special exhibitions. *Tours* free. **Credit** (shop) MC, V. **Map** p399 D10.

This cathedral to the Victorian mania for collecting and cataloguing its empire was designed by Alfred Waterhouse. The building is every bit as impressive as the giant cast of a Diplodocus skeleton in the main hall, and frequently overwhelms the exhibits. If you've come with children, you may not see much more than the Dinosaur gallery, with its star turn, the animatronic Tyrannosaurus rex. But there's much more – 70 million plants, animals, fossils, rocks and minerals, to be exact. Some of the galleries are static and dry; others, like Creepy Crawlies, so beloved of children you can hardly get near the exhibits. Entry to the Earth Galleries is portentous: you travel via an escalator, passing through a giant suspended globe and twinkling images of the star system. A gallery called Restless Surface has a mock-up of a Kobe supermarket, where the floor shakes to video coverage of the 1995 earthquake.

Outside, the Wildlife Garden (open Apr-Oct, £1.50) is the museum's living exhibition, with a range of British lowland habitats.

The joy of sheds

In front of the Victoria & Albert Museum in the middle of the road is a small, jolly green shed. It's one of a handful of functioning cabmen's shelters, where London's taxi drivers can pull in for a tea and a bacon sarnie. The shelters belong to the Cabmen's Shelter Fund, founded in 1874 by Sir George Armstrong, a newspaper publisher who got fed up waiting for cabs on rainy days when the drivers had decamped to the nearest pub. He started a fund to supply drivers with a place to get out of the cold and have a cheap meal without having to stray too far from the cab stand. Because the shelters stood on public highways, they were not allowed to take up more space than a horse and cart. At their peak, there were more than 60 shelters in London, but the number declined after World War II as they fell victim to bombs and road-widening. Thirteen shelters still exist, complete with tables, benches and a small kitchen, and they are still run by the Fund. All are Grade II-listed buildings. Members of the public are allowed to drop in for a cuppa but cabbies get priority. Some shelters are friendlier than others; some serve drinks and food from a serving hatch for the less bold. In addition to the one by the V&A, there are central London shelters at Embankment Place by the Millennium Bridge; on Grosvenor Gardens in Victoria; on the west side of Hanover Square, W1; on Russell Square; and on Temple Place, WC2.

Royal Albert Hall – nice shape, shame about the sound. *See p151.*

Science Museum

Exhibition Road, SW7 2DD (7942 4000/booking & information 0870 870 4868/www.sciencemuseum.org.uk). South Kensington tube. **Open** 10am-5.45pm daily. **Admission** free; charges apply for special exhibitions. **Credit** AmEx, MC, V. **Map** p399 D9.

The Science Museum demonstrates with great aplomb how science filters down through myriad elements of daily life, with displays on engines, cars, aeroplanes, ships, the home, medicine and computers. Landmark inventions such as Stephenson's Rocket, Whittle's turbojet engine, Arkwright's spinning machine and the Apollo 10 command module are celebrated in the Making the Modern World gallery. The Wellcome Wing consists of four storeys of discovery, from the IMAX cinema on the ground, upstairs to the Who Am I? gallery, which explores human characteristics and discoveries in genetics, brain science and psychology, up to In Future, where visitors choose how much they'll allow science to affect their fates. The new-look Energy Hall on the ground floor now includes a hands-on gallery all about power and saving energy.

Victoria & Albert Museum

Cromwell Road, SW7 2RL (7942 2000/www.vam.ac.uk). South Kensington tube. **Open** 10am-5.45pm Mon, Tue, Thur-Sun; 10am-10pm Wed & last Fri of mth. *Tours* daily, phone for details. **Admission** free; charges apply for special exhibitions. **Credit** (shop) MC, V. **Map** p399 E10.

The 150-year-old V&A dazzles: its grand galleries contain about four million pieces of furniture, textiles, ceramics, sculpture, paintings, posters, jewellery, glass and metalwork from cultures across the world. Items are grouped by theme, origin or age. The museum boasts the finest collection of Italian Renaissance sculpture outside Italy, while home-grown treasures – including the Great Bed of Ware, Canova's *The Three Graces* and Henry VIII's writing desk – are housed in the British Galleries, where you'll find a range of interactive exhibits for children. Take time to admire the Fashion galleries, which run from 18th-century court dress right up to a summer chiffon number for 2005. The Architecture gallery has videos, models, plans and descriptions of various architectural styles, and the museum's famous Photography collection holds over 500,000 images. Opened in 2006, the Jameel Gallery is dedicated to Islamic art from the seventh century to the fall of the Ottoman empire in the last century. Its centrepiece is the massive Ardabil carpet, the world's oldest and arguably most splendid floor covering.

Exhibitions for 2007 include 'Surreal Things: Surrealism and Design' (29 Mar-22 July), 'Lee Miller' (2 Aug 2007-6 Jan 2008) and 'The Golden Age of Couture 1947-1957' (27 Sept 2007-6 Jan 2008).

Hyde Park & Kensington Gardens

Maps p396 & p397

Hyde Park Corner, Knightsbridge, Lancaster Gate or Queensway tube.

At 1.5 miles long and about a mile wide, **Hyde Park** (7298 2100, www.royalparks.gov.uk) is the largest of London's Royal Parks. The land was once part of a medieval manor, before being bequeathed to the monks of Westminster

Abbey. In 1536 it was appropriated by Henry VIII for hunting deer. Despite opening to the public in the early 1600s, the parks were only frequented by the upper echelons of society. At the end of the 17th century William III, averse to the dank air of Whitehall Palace, relocated to **Kensington Palace** (*see below*). A corner of Hyde Park was sectioned off to make grounds for the palace and, although today the two merge, Kensington Gardens was closed to the public until King George II opened it on Sundays to those in formal dress only. Nowadays the best element of Kensington Gardens, if you're a child, is the **Diana, Princess of Wales Memorial Playground** (*see p278*). Adults may prefer the **Serpentine Gallery** (*see below*). Across the road is the ring-shaped **Princess Diana Memorial Fountain**, created by US architect Kathryn Gustafson. Almost as soon as it had been unveiled by the Queen, in July 2004, the fountain (more of a babbling moat) was in the headlines for the wrong reasons: people slipping on the granite while paddling.

Back across the road and further north, by the Long Water, is a bronze statue of **Peter Pan** by Sir George Frampton, erected in 1912: it was beside Hyde Park's Round Pond eight years earlier that playwright JM Barrie met Jack Lewellyn Davies, the boy who became the inspiration for Peter. Other sculptures of note include GF Watts's violently animated *Physical Energy* and Jacob Epstein's *Rima, Spirit of Nature*.

Hyde Park has long been a focal point for freedom of speech. It became a hotspot for mass demonstrations in the 19th century and remains so today – a march against war in Iraq in 2003 was (according to police) the largest in British history, and the Live8 concert of July 2005 was attended by lucky thousands who sent a text to Sir Bob Geldof. The legalisation of public assembly in the park led to the establishment of **Speakers' Corner** in 1872 (close by Marblke Arch tube), where ranters both sane and bonkers – and predominantly these days Middle Eastern and African – have the floor. This isn't the place to come for balanced political debate, but Marx, Engels, Lenin, Orwell and the Pankhursts have all attended.

A rather more orderly entertainment takes place at 10.30am every morning (9.30am on Sundays), when you can watch the Household Cavalry emerge smartly from their barracks on South Carriage Drive. They ride across the park to Horse Guards Parade, prior to the **Changing of the Guard** (*see p144*). Year-round the park's perimeter is popular with both inline- and roller-skaters, as well as with bike- and horse-riders (for the riding school, *see p334*).

If you're exploring on foot and the vast expanses defeat you, look out for the Liberty Drives electric buggies (May to October). Driven by cheerful volunteers (there's no fare, but a donation is appreciated), these pick up and deposit groups of sightseers around the park. Cyclists should stick to the designated tracks; only under-tens are allowed to ride on the footpaths.

At the western side of the park is the **Serpentine**, London's oldest boating lake and home to ducks, coots, swans and tufty-headed grebes. You can rent rowing boats and pedalos from March to October.

Kensington Palace

Kensington Gardens, W8 4PX (7937 9561/booking line 0870 751 5180/www.hrp.org.uk). Bayswater, High Street Kensington or Queensway tube. **Open** *Mar-Oct* 10am-5pm daily. *Nov-Feb* 10am-4pm daily. Last entry 1hr before closing. **Admission** £11.50; £9.00, £7.50 concs; £34 family; free under-5s. **Credit** MC, V. **Map** p396 B8.

Sir Christopher Wren extended this Jacobean mansion to palatial proportions on the instructions of William III, who afterwards moved in with his wife Mary II. The asthmatic king considered the countryside location would be better for his health. The sections of the palace that the public are allowed to see give the impression of intimacy, although the King's Apartments, which you enter via Wren's lofty King's Staircase, are pretty grandiose. In the King's Gallery hang portraits of the first glamorous royals to live here. It appears from the Queen's Apartments, however, that William and Mary lived quite simply in these smaller rooms. The Royal Ceremonial Dress Collection is a fascinating display of the tailor's and dressmaker's art, with lavish ensembles worn for state occasions and a permanent collection of 14 dresses worn by Diana, Princess of Wales, the palace's most famous resident. Make time for tea in Queen Anne's Orangery (built 1704-5) and admire – through the hedge – the piece of horticultural perfection that is the Sunken Garden.

Serpentine Gallery

Kensington Gardens (nr Albert Memorial), W2 3XA (7402 6075/www.serpentinegallery.org). Lancaster Gate or South Kensington tube. **Open** 10am-6pm daily. **Admission** free; donations appreciated. **Credit** AmEx, MC, V. **Map** p397 D8.

Its secluded location, sitting pretty to the west of the Long Water, makes this light and airy gallery for contemporary art an attractive place for a visit while walking in the park. A rolling two-monthly programme of often-challenging exhibitions keeps the Serpentine in the arts news, as does the annual Serpentine Pavilion commission. Every spring an internationally renowned architect, who has never built in the UK before, is commissioned to design and build a new pavilion, which is open to visitors from June until September; in 2006 the honour fell to Rem Koolhaas. **Photo** *p270*.

North London

A bastion of the middle classes but agreeably rough around the edges.

North London's a mixed bag. Camden, which is just a couple of tube or bus stops out of central London, is the indie-kid hangout, a Disneyland for disaffected teen goths, grounded backpackers and an international jamboree of strapped-for-cash students. Further out, Belsize Park, Hampstead, Highgate, St John's Wood and Islington are all well-looked-after sorts of places with leafy streets of bijou eateries and boutiques, and worthy cultural institutions, such as the Freud Museum and Estorick Collection. It's worth visiting for the many green open spaces, notably Hampstead Heath, which is a genuinely unmanicured piece of wild woodland, and also Primrose Hill, a pretty, grassy rise north of Regent's Park. Beyond the middle-class belt are the rows and rows of terraced houses of Finchley, Tottenham and Muswell Hill – the places where Londoners live. There's little of beauty until you get up to Alexandra Palace and the ribbed patterns of rooftops below ripple into the distance to mesmerising effect.

Camden

Camden Town or Chalk Farm tube.

Camden has long been associated with the rougher side of life. Cheap lodging houses dominated the area around the time when the Regent's Canal was being dug out in 1816. It was rough in Victorian times too, according to Charles Dickens, who grew up in Bayham Street. In the mid 1800s Irish and Greek immigrants put down roots here, many of them working on the new railways. The area has largely remained working class until today, while the low rents have attracted a sizeable student community since the 1960s – hence the indie music scene for which the area's known.

Of course, there are pockets of wealth and gentrification: the tall, spacious houses around Albert Street and Camden Square, in particular, have long since been colonised by white-collar professionals. Today parts of Camden have a decidedly middle-class flavour and many residents shun the markets and buy their provisions from Nicholas Grimshaw's high-tech Sainsbury's supermarket on Camden Road.

There are also signs that Camden may be about to enjoy something of a renaissance, with the recent revivals of two major music and arts venues at the northern (the **Roundhouse**, *see p159* **Right round, baby, right round**) and southern (**Koko**, *see p313*) ends of Camden High Street. Otherwise, traditional sights are few, but there's no lack of colour and clamour – every night Camden Town tube is garlanded with exotica, whether punks and goths in full regalia, vocal street preachers or the less photogenic junkies. Opposite the tube newly repaved **Inverness Street** is a fruit market by day (8.30am-5pm daily) and a hub of activity by night, teeming with bars banging out anything from dirty electro and Latin house to flat-out rock'n'roll. At the top end of the street, the **Good Mixer** (No.30, 7916 7929) is where Blur, Oasis and other musical luminaries drank before Britpop hyped itself to death.

Most visit for the various sites collectively known as **Camden Market** (*see p157*), which stretches from the tube station north along the alt-retail experience that is Camden High Street to the canal, its locks and beyond. No longer just a hangout for students and teens, this is now one of London's big tourist attractions, particularly at weekends when crowds can be unbearable. Better to explore on weekdays.

Cutting through the market is **Regent's Canal**, which opened in 1820 to provide a link between east and west London. The route was opened to the public as a scenic path in 1968, and the canal's industrial trappings have been transformed over the decades since. Any stretch of the canal is worth a stroll, but the most popular patch is from Camden Lock west to Little Venice, passing Regent's Park and **London Zoo** (*see p128*). You can also peel off the canal into Primrose Hill (*see p157*), where you'll find some decent eating and drinking venues. Narrowboat cruises travel the route in summer and on winter weekends, departing from Camden Lock (Jason's Canal Boat Trip, 7286 3428; Jenny Wren, 7485 4433; London Waterbus Company, 7482 2660).

Away from the High Street to the west of Camden Town tube station, just off Parkway, is the lovely **Jewish Museum** (*see p157*), a reflection of the area's cultural diversity.

By night, Camden is still a great place to catch a gig. It has far more than its fair share of excellent small venues, including the legendary **Dublin Castle** (94 Parkway, 7485 1773), where the likes of Madness, Travis and Blur first cut their teeth (signed posters adorn the walls), as well as **Barfly**, **Dingwalls**, **Green Note**, the **Jazz Café** and **Underworld** (for all, *see pp314-317*). But the place is poorly furnished with eating and drinking options. You could try the ever-reliable **Wagamama** (*see p218*), or **Fresh & Wild** (49 Parkway, 7428 7575) offers organic snacks, or there's excellent tapas at **Jamon Jamon** (38 Parkway, 7284 0606). Camden Lock's newly-opened enormous pan-Asian restaurant **Gilgamesh** (7482 5757, www.gilgameshbar.com, open evenings only) is worth a look if only to have your mind seriously boggled by the riotously OTT ancient Babylon-meets-Ibiza decor.

Camden Market

Camden Canal Market *off Chalk Farm Road, south of the junction with Castlehaven Road, NW1 9XJ (7485 8355/www.camdenlock.net).* **Open** 10am-6pm daily.
Camden Lock *Camden Lock Place, off Chalk Farm Road, NW1 8AF (7485 3459/www.camdenlock market.com).* **Open** 10am-6pm Mon-Wed, Fri-Sun; 10am-7pm Thur.
Camden Market *Camden High Street, junction with Buck Street, NW1 (7278 4444).* **Open** 9.30am-5.30pm daily.
Electric Ballroom *184 Camden High Street, NW1 8QP (7485 9006/www.electric-ballroom.co.uk).* **Open** 10.30am-3.30pm Fri; 10am-6pm Sat, Sun (markets); record & film fairs occasional Sats throughout the year.

Dublin Castle. *See p156.*

Stables *off Chalk Farm Road, opposite junction with Hartland Road, NW1 8AH (7485 5511/www. camdenlock.net).* **Open** 10am-6pm daily (reduced stalls Mon-Fri).
All *Camden Town or Chalk Farm tube.*
Camden Market (formerly Buck Street Market), just next to the tube station, flogs cheap sunglasses and cut-price interpretations of current fashions. The Electric Ballroom sells second-hand clothes and young designers' wares; while it's neither cheap nor particularly exciting, it does have cheap CDs. Both are fairly negligible, but Camden Lock market has the advantage of being very attractive thanks to a courtyard setting beside the Regent's Canal. There are pleasant cafés, a couple of good bars and shops selling things you might actually want to buy. Crafty stalls sell largely decorative items from funky lighting to ethnic homeware, art and antiques. North of the courtyard that contains Gilgamesh (*see above*) is the Stables area, with more permanent stalls and food huts. Some of Camden's best shopping is here, with a whole row of vintage clothing and clubwear shops housed underneath the railway arches, including boutique sneaker store TRAINERd (*see p257*). Even better are the antiques and contemporary designer furniture sold at the very north of the site at the part of the market known as the Horse Hospital (which once cared for horses injured while pulling canal barges).

Jewish Museum (Camden)

Raymond Burton House, 129-131 Albert Street, NW1 7NB (7284 1997/www.jewishmuseum.org.uk). Camden Town tube. **Open** 10am-4pm Mon-Thur; 10am-5pm Sun. **Admission** £3.50; £1.50-£2.50 concs; free under-5s. **Credit** MC, V.
One of a pair (its sister is in Finchley, *see p162*), Camden's Jewish Museum provides a fascinating insight into one of Britain's oldest immigrant communities. Jewish life over three and a half centuries is illustrated through oil paintings, artefacts from a tailor's 'sweatshop', silver and chinaware, photographs and passports. The museum also has one of the world's finest collections of Jewish ceremonial art, including a collection of silver Hanukkah candlesticks, spice boxes and an amazing 17th-century Venetian synagogue ark, brought to Britain in the 1800s. Temporary exhibitions in 2007 include 'Ghetto Warriors', exploring minority boxing in Britain, and 'The Last Goodbye', focusing on the rescue of children from Nazi Europe (until 2 Sept).

Around Camden

Primrose Hill, to the west of Camden Town, with its elegant terraces, is as pretty as the actors and pop stars who live here (look out for Supernova Heights, former residence of Noel Gallagher, now home to David Walliams). Past the park and its namesake hill (with grand views over London), **Regent's Park Road** becomes a pleasant mix of independent cafés, restaurants and smart shops. There are also a couple of quality gastropubs on Gloucester Avenue: the **Engineer** (No.65, 7722 0950) and the **Lansdowne** (No.90, 7483 0409).

St John's Wood

St John's Wood or Swiss Cottage tube.

Rural calm prevailed in St John's Wood until well into the 19th century, when the only developments around the wooded hills and meadows were smart stucco villas. The pure air attracted artists, scientists and writers: George Eliot often held receptions at her house (The Priory, North Bank). A blue plaque marks the house at 44 Grove End Road once owned by the artist Sir Lawrence Alma-Tadema; sadly, the house is closed to the public.

In the 19th century the inexpensive but pretty dwellings suited rich men, who often used them to house their mistresses, until building work by the Great Central Railway in 1894 destroyed the lubricious rural idyll. Sensitive redevelopment during the 1950s has left the area smart, desirable and fabulously expensive – just take a look at the chic boutiques of the exceedingly couth High Street. **Lord's**, the world's most famous cricket ground (*see p330*), is the reason why most people visit. However, Beatles fans have their own motives: Grove End Road leads to **Abbey Road**, made famous by the Fab Four when its recording facility was still called EMI Studios (No.3). And, of course, it's the site of London's most photographed zebra crossing.

Up the Finchley Road from St John's Wood, you'll find that a Swiss Cottage actually exists over the station of the same name – it's a loosely Swiss-style tavern, which stands where the Junction Road Toll Gate once stood. The excitement stops at the entrance so, instead of having a pint, sample the cakes at nearby **Louis Hungarian Pâtisserie** (12 Harben Parade, 7722 8100).

Lord's Tour & MCC Museum

St John's Wood Road, NW8 8QN (7616 8595/ www.lords.org). St John's Wood tube. **Tours** *Oct-Mar* noon, 2pm daily. *Apr-Sept* 10am, noon, 2pm daily. **Admission** £10; £7-£6 concs; £25 family; free under-5s. **Credit** MC, V.

The wearers of the famous egg-and-bacon striped tie have come to love the NatWest Media Centre, the funky raised pod that dominates the self-proclaimed home of cricket. The centre joins the portrait-bedecked Long Room on the guided tour (you'll need to book), along with the expected collection of battered bats, photos and blazers. There's plenty of WG Grace ephemera, a stuffed sparrow with the ball that killed it and, of course, the urn that contains the Ashes, cricket's greatest prize.

Hampstead

Golders Green or Hampstead tube/Gospel Oak or Hampstead Heath rail.

Exclusive Hampstead was a popular retreat in times of plague and remains a delightful place for a restorative wander. It has long been the favoured roosting place for literary and artistic bigwigs; Keats and Constable called it home in the 19th century, while the modern British sculptors Barbara Hepworth and Henry Moore lived the London village idyll here in the 1930s.

Hampstead tube station stands at the top of the steep High Street. The Georgian terraces that make up nearby **Church Row**, one of Hampstead's most beautiful streets, lead down to **St John at Downshire Hill** (7794 5808), whose cemetery is less ostentatious than near-neighbour Highgate, but it is just as restfully bucolic. Among the notables buried here are Constable and the comedian Peter Cook.

On Holly Mount is Hampstead's antique **Holly Bush** pub (*see p232*), which was painter George Romney's stable block (his house still stands on Holly Bush Hill). A minute's climb will bring you to **Fenton House** (*see p159*), while the celestially inclined should potter up to the **Hampstead Scientific Society Observatory** (Hampstead Grove, 8346 1056).

East of Heath Street, a maze of attractive streets shelters **Burgh House** on New End Square (7431 0144), a Queen Anne house that contains a small local history museum and gallery space, and **2 Willow Road** (*see p160*), the residence that Hungarian architect Ernö Goldfinger built for himself in the 1930s. Nearby, off Keats Grove, is **Keats House** (*see p160*), where the poet wrote many of his best poems. Just by the station, the bullet-marked **Magdala** pub (2A South Hill Park, 7435 2503) is where Ruth Ellis shot and killed her former boyfriend in 1955, an act for which she was sentenced to death, thereby becoming the last woman to be hanged in Britain.

Hampstead Heath is some of the city's finest countryside. Its charming contours and woodlands conspire to make it feel far larger and more rural than it is (something over a mile in each direction). The views of London from the top of **Parliament Hill** are wonderful and on hot days the murky bathing ponds (men's, women's and mixed, open daily all year) are a godsend. (There's also a great lido at Gospel Oak; call 7485 5757.) The heath is popular for flying kites and sailing model boats too. Pick up a map from one of the information points on the heath, which can advise you of concerts held at the two bandstands on Sundays during the summer. At the north end of the park is **Kenwood House** (*see p160*).

Right round, baby, right round

Arguably the single best thing about Camden is the **Roundhouse** (Chalk Farm Road, NW1 8EH, 7424 9991, www.roundhouse.org.uk), which from industrial beginnings has served on and off for four decades as a magnet for radical art and raving lunacy. The building started life in 1846 as a railway engine shed, but within 20 years locomotives had become too large for it to handle. It was subsequently used for a while as a store for gin makers W&A Gilbey Limited, but no real purpose was found for it until 1966, when the then Greater London Council bought the freehold and turned it into an arts venue.

The Doors, Jimi Hendrix and Pink Floyd all famously played here, while Peter Brook used the place as a backdrop for his great experimental version of *The Tempest* and radical playwright Arnold Wesker ran it as the arts forum Centre 42. When lack of funds in the 1980s saw the demise of Centre 42, the Roundhouse's days as a legendary performance venue seemed numbered and for many years the buiding was empty. Local businessman Torquil Norman came to the rescue in 1996, reopening the venue and causing a huge sensation with a phenomenal season by Argentinian performance group De La Guarda ('It's as good as sex,' gasped one critic). Then in 2004 the Roundhouse closed its doors again. Happily, this time it was only briefly.

As part of a £30m refit, the Roundhouse has had its lower passageways perked up and its auditorium restyled, while the exterior has been granted an expensive facelift. Downstairs, the new black-box theatre has been named Studio 42 in recognition of Wesker's work, while a maze of spaces has been turned into rehearsal rooms, recording studios and production suites. New bars and a ground-floor café have opened to the public. The building is now an incredible resource, not least through the practical emphasis it places on encouraging younger people to sign up and take advantage of its facilities.

Tucked in among the handsome residential streets in south-west Hampstead is the former home (and now museum) of Sigmund Freud (*see p160*). Nearby, the innovative **Camden Arts Centre** (Arkwright Road, corner of Finchley Road, 7472 5500) has a reputation for hosting distinctive shows by contemporary artists. The centre also boasts landscaped gardens and a café that hosts themed food evenings and a Wednesday evening programme of film screenings and live performances.

Fenton House

3 Hampstead Grove, NW3 6RT (7435 3471/www.nationaltrust.org.uk). Hampstead tube. **Open** *Mar* 2-5pm Sat, Sun. *Apr-Oct* 2-5pm Wed-Fri; 11am-5pm Sat, Sun. *Tours* phone for details. **Admission** *House & gardens* £5.20; £2.60 concs; free under-5s. *Joint ticket with 2 Willow Road £7. Gardens only* £1; free concs. **No credit cards**.

Devotees of early music will be impressed by the collection of harpsichords, clavichords, virginals and spinets in this late 17th-century house. The bequest

Hampstead Heath. See p158.

was made on condition that qualified musicians be allowed to play them, so you might be lucky enough to hear them in action (otherwise phone for details of the lunchtime and evening concerts held during the summer). The porcelain collection won't appeal to everyone – the 'curious grotesque teapot' certainly lives up to its billing – but, for fans, there's work by Meissen and Rockingham. The maze-like series of sunken gardens is a delight, with the small orchard coming into its own for October's Apple Day celebration. Out of season (Nov-early Mar), you can only see the exterior or join the 'Heights of Hampstead' walking tour, which takes in grand houses of various periods and ends up here (£6; 01494 755572).

Freud Museum

20 Maresfield Gardens, NW3 5SX (7435 2002/www.freud.org.uk). Finchley Road tube. **Open** noon-5pm Wed-Sun. **Admission** £5; £3 concs; free under-12s. **Credit** AmEx, MC, V.

After Anna Freud's death in 1982, the house she and her father Sigmund shared for the last year of his life became a museum. The analyst's couch sits in the study, round glasses and unsmoked cigars setting the scene, and the copious library is impressive, but more intellectual or biographical context would be appreciated. Upstairs is Anna's room – with another couch – and a gallery. This is one of the few buildings in London to have two blue plaques: commemorating both father and daughter (she was a pioneer in child psychiatry), they were unveiled by comedian John Cleese in 2002.

Keats House

Keats Grove, NW3 2RR (7435 2062). Hampstead tube/Hampstead Heath rail/24, 46, 168 bus. **Open** 1-5pm Tue-Sun. *Tours* 3pm Sat, Sun. **Admission** £3.50; £1.75 concs; free under-16s. **Credit** MC, V.

The Romantic poet made his home here from 1818 to 1820, when he left for Rome in hopes of alleviating his tuberculosis (sadly, he died of the disease the following year, aged only 25). As well as mooching through the rooms, you can attend events and talks in the poetry reading room and see a display on Keats's sweetheart, Fanny Brawne, who lived next door. The industrial carpets ruin the overall ambience – something that may be corrected if an application for money for renovations get the OK. The garden, in which Keats wrote 'Ode to a Nightingale', is a particularly pleasant spot.

Kenwood House/Iveagh Bequest

Hampstead Lane, NW3 7JR (8348 1286/www.english-heritage.org.uk). Hampstead tube/Golders Green tube then 210 bus. **Open** *Apr-Sept* 11am-5pm daily. *Nov-Mar* 11am-4pm daily. *Tours* by appointment only. **Admission** free; donations appreciated. *Tours* £5; £4-£3 concs. **Credit** MC, V.

Built in 1616, Kenwood House was remodelled (1764-79) by Robert Adam for William Murray, first Earl of Mansfield (it was Murray's decision as Chief Justice in a test case in 1772 that made it illegal to own slaves in England). Brewing magnate Edward Guinness bought the property in 1925, filling it with his art collection. Now English Heritage is in charge, endorsing Guinness's wish 'that the atmosphere of a gentleman's private park should be preserved'. Art includes Vermeer's *The Guitar Player*, a Rembrandt self-portrait, works by Hals and Van Dyck, and Gainsborough's *Countess Howe*. Outside, Humphrey Repton's landscape remains mostly unchanged from its creation in 1793. An ivy tunnel leads from the flower garden to a raised terrace with lovely views over the lakes – one of Repton's famous 'surprises'. Part of Kenwood's grounds is now listed as a Site of Special Scientific Interest for its four species of bat and nine Nationally Scarce invertebrates. People too are scarce on what feel like country lanes, winding through the middle of the woods, whereas seats are the rarity at the café adjacent to Kenwood House, which does a terrific breakfast. In July and August there are concerts by the lake.

2 Willow Road

2 Willow Road, NW3 1TH (7435 6166/www.nationaltrust.org.uk). Hampstead tube/Hampstead Heath rail. **Open** *Mar, Nov* noon-5pm Sat. *Apr-Oct* noon-5pm Thur-Sat; 5-9pm 1st Thur of mth. *Tours* noon, 1pm, 2pm. **Admission** £4.90; £2.50 concs; £12.30 family; free under-5s. *Joint ticket with Fenton House* £7. **No credit cards**.

This strange and atmospheric 1939 building is the National Trust's only example of international modernism. It's the centre residence in a terrace of three houses designed by Hungarian-born émigré architect Ernö Goldfinger (also responsible for Notting Hill's Trellick Tower, *see p131*). The house was designed to be flexible with movable partitions and folding doors, and a spiral staircase between levels that is both elegant and space-saving, removing the need for large landing spaces. The palette of colours grows lighter and brighter progressing upwards through the house. The house served as home to the architect and his wife until their deaths, and contains artworks by Max Ernst and Henry Moore.

Highgate

Archway or Highgate tube.

The name comes from a tollgate that once stood on the site of the Gate House pub on the High Street. Legend has it that Dick Whittington, having walked away from the city as far as the foot of Highgate Hill, heard the Bow Bells peal out 'Turn again Whittington, thrice Mayor of London.' The event is commemorated on the Whittington Stone (topped with a statue of Whittington's cat), near the hospital. The area is today best known for the burial grounds of **Highgate Cemetery** (*see below*), last resting place of such important figures as Karl Marx. Adjoining is the beautiful **Waterlow Park**, donated to Londoners by low-cost housing pioneer Sir Sydney Waterlow in 1889. The park has terrific views, ponds, a mini-aviary, tennis courts and, in 16th-century **Lauderdale House**, a garden café. Swains Lane leads down to **Hampstead Heath** (*see p158*): pass the mock-Tudor flats built to house single women in the 1920s, peep through the Gothic entrance to **Holly Village**, a private village built in 1865 by heiress Angela Burdett Coutts, or grab a pavement table at the lovely **Kalendar** café (No.15A, 8348 8300).

A little east of Highgate Hill is **Archway**, so-named because of the Victorian viaduct high over the road. This has long been famous among Londoners as 'Suicide Bridge' – the first recorded jumper had taken the plunge as early as 1908 – but the addition of fencing has put a stop to the leaping. East again down Hornsey Lane is comfortable, middle-class **Crouch End**, presided over by an 1895 clock tower and Hornsey Town Hall. The High Street houses an appealing mix of boutiques and restaurants.

North of Highgate tube, shady **Highgate Woods** were mentioned (under another name) in the Domesday Book. Much of the ancient woodland remains as a conservation area with a nature trail, an adventure playground and a café that hosts live jazz during the summer.

Highgate Cemetery

Swains Lane, N6 6PJ (8340 1834/www.highgate-cemetery.org). Highgate tube. **Open** *East Cemetery* Apr-Oct 10am-4.30pm Mon-Fri; 11am-4.30pm Sat, Sun. Nov-Mar 10am-3.30pm Mon-Fri; 11am-3.30pm Sat, Sun. *West Cemetery* by tour only. *Tours* 11am, noon, 1pm, 2pm, 3pm, 4pm Sat, Sun; Mar-Nov 2pm Mon-Fri. No under-8s. **Admission** £2. *Tours* £5. **No credit cards**.

With its dramatic tombs topped by towering angels, shrouded urns and broken columns, Highgate exudes a romantic atmosphere of ivy-covered neglect. The original 1839 West Cemetery (visitable by tour only; book ahead at weekends) is breathtaking: long pathways wind through gloomy catacombs and the graves of notables such as Christina Rossetti and chemist Michael Faraday. Prize sites include the tombs lining Egyptian Avenue (pharaonic styling being all the rage in the 1830s) and the ring of neo-classical tombs known as the Lebanon Circle. Not quite as atmospheric, the East Cemetery, added just 15 years later, allows you to wander freely as you seek the memorials to Marx and George Eliot. The cemetery closes during burials, so call ahead.

Islington

Map p404

Angel tube/Highbury & Islington tube/rail.

Henry VIII owned houses for hunting in this once-idyllic village, but by the 19th century it was already known for its shops, theatres and music halls. The new Regent's Canal meant the arrival of industrial slums from 1820, and Islington declined into one of London's poorest boroughs. However, its Georgian squares and Victorian terraces have been gentrified in recent decades. These days, despite stubborn pockets of poverty, this is a wealthy middle-class area.

Emerge from Angel tube and walk north along **Upper Street**, past hoary old **Camden Passage** antiques market (*see p237*) on the right and the glass façade of the Business Design Centre on the left, alongside the triangle of Islington Green and up towards **Highbury**. En route, you'll take in countless boutiques, the excellently named **Screen on the Green** cinema (*see p289*), the **Almeida Theatre** (*see p343*) and the often-raucous **King's Head** theatre pub (*see p233*).

Taking this route you'll graze the south entrance of the N1 Centre shopping mall, near the Angel, which includes a music venue (the **Carling Academy Islington**, *see p311*), a Vue cineplex and lots of chain stores. This behemoth is a symptom of the increasing influx of high-street names into the area, turning a unique locale into something more standard issue. But for every Starbucks, newcomers such as the pleasingly minimalist **Ottolenghi** café-deli (*see p218*) offer some compensation.

On the way along Upper Street take a detour east to **Canonbury Square**, a Regency creation that was once home to George Orwell (No.27) and Evelyn Waugh (No.17A). It is now the address of the **Estorick Collection of Modern Italian Art** (*see below*).

Just beyond the end of Upper Street is **Highbury Fields**, to which 200,000 Londoners fled in 1666 to escape the Great Fire. Smart Highbury is best known as home to Arsenal football club, which moved from its small but perfectly formed art deco Highbury Stadium to the new 60,000-capacity Emirates Stadium down the road in time for the 2006/7 season. There are occasional 90-minute guided tours of the new stadium, which end at the **Arsenal Museum** (call 7704 4504 to book).

Sightseeing

Estorick Collection of Modern Italian Art

39A Canonbury Square, N1 2AN (7704 9522/ www.estorickcollection.com). Highbury & Islington tube/rail/271 bus. **Open** 11am-6pm Wed-Sat; noon-5pm Sun. **Admission** £3.50; £2.50 concs; free under-16s, students. **Credit** AmEx, MC, V.

Britain's only gallery devoted to modern Italian art. Eric Estorick was a US political scientist, writer and art collector whose collection includes some fine work by Italian Futurists such as Balla's *Hand of the Violinist* and Boccioni's *Modern Idol*, as well as pieces by Carra, Russolo and Severini. The museum has a library with over 2,000 modern Italian art books , a shop and a café. Exhibitions in 2007 include 'Italian Satire of the Great War' (until 19 Mar).

Screen on the Green. *See p161.*

Further north

Dalston's immigrant communities are chiefly Afro-Caribbean and Turkish, and their influence can be seen in the area's cafés and clubs. The tidy suburban streets at north London's perimeter are also enlivened by the immigrant communities that have made them their home. **Golders Green**, **Hendon** and **Finchley** have large Jewish communities; the last of these is the location of north London's second **Jewish Museum** (80 East End Road, 8349 1143, *see also p157*). There's been a **Jewish cemetery** on Hoop Lane since 1895; cellist Jacqueline du Pré is buried here. TS Eliot, Marc Bolan and Anna Pavlova ended up at **Golders Green Crematorium** (8455 2374).

The neighbourhoods of **Tottenham** and **Haringey** have sizeable Greek Cypriot, Turkish Cypriot and Kurdish communities. The groups live side by side in **Green Lanes**, where food-related business success is evident in the thriving kebab shops, supermarkets and bakeries. However, the real draw up here is **Alexandra Palace** (*see below*).

Alexandra Park & Palace

Alexandra Palace Way, N22 7AY (park 8444 7696/ information 8365 2121/boating 8889 9089/www. alexandrapalace.com). Wood Green tube/Alexandra Palace rail/W3, W7, 84A, 144, 144A bus. **Open** *Park* 24hrs daily. *Palace* times vary.

'The People's Palace', when it opened in 1873, was supposed to provide affordable entertainment for all. It burned to the ground just 16 days later. Rebuilt, it became the site of the first TV broadcasts by the BBC in 1936, but in 1980 was destroyed by fire once more. The born-yet-again palace has remained upright for the past 25 years and yields panoramic views of London. Its grounds provide ice skating and boating, while the entertainment and exhibition centre hosts fairs, concerts and events.

Royal Air Force Museum Hendon

Grahame Park Way, NW9 5LL (8205 2266/www. rafmuseum.org). Colindale tube/Mill Hill Broadway rail/32, 226, 292, 303 bus. **Open** 10am-6pm daily. *Tours* times vary. **Admission** free. **Credit** AmEx, MC, V.

There's been an airfield at Hendon since 1910, hence its claims to be the birthplace of aviation in Britain. These days the Aerodrome houses more than 80 historic aircraft – among them World War I Fokkers, World War II Spitfires and a state-of-the-art Eurofighter Typhoon – in World War I hangars and a listed aircraft factory building. A new structure, part of an £11m redevelopment, houses the Milestones of Flight exhibition, which traces a century of aviation history. Other attractions include an interactive Battle of Britain show, a Red Arrows flight simulator and a 'touch and try' Jet Provost cockpit. Phone for details of specialist tours.

East London

Adventurousness is richly rewarded in the edgy east.

Spitalfields Market.

Right on the City's doorstep, the East End has a reputation for overcrowding, poverty and criminality that goes back hundreds of years. It's where London's foul-smelling and fire-prone industry thrived, and where the proximity of London's huge, international docks created a population that was a hotch-potch of cultures, united by a physical lack of living space, shared privations and the toughness necessary to survive those rigours.

Even today nearly half of the population of ceertain east London boroughs is from non-white ethnic groups, reflecting a centuries-long history of immigration into the area. This is most apparent in that part of east London closest to the City – the areas of Spitalfields, Brick Lane and Whitechapel – which are best known as home to the city's Bangladeshi community. Immediately north, Shoreditch and Hoxton couldn't be more different in character: back in the 1980s artists and designers broke ground among the area's old factories and the trendy bars, cafés and restaurants have followed.

Docklands, the name bestowed on the area around London's last working docks at the time of their initially catastrophic 1980s redevelopment, holds plenty of interest for visitors. Attention is inevitably grabbed by the skyscrapers of Canary Wharf at the northern end of the Isle of Dogs, but parts of Thames-side Wapping and Limehouse maintain a pleasingly dark Victorian atmosphere.

Further east, despite recently being singled out by a Channel 4 TV property show as the worst place in the UK to live, Hackney is, in fact, becoming increasingly desirable as a residential area, and beginning to exploit enough of its cultural diversity to tempt visitors. To the north, villagey Walthamstow benefits from having the ancient woods of Epping Forest on its doorstep.

Spitalfields

Maps p405 & p407

Aldgate East tube or Liverpool Street tube/rail.

Spitalfields, famous for its covered market, is best approached from Liverpool Street Station up Brushfield Street. You'll know you're on the right track when you are confronted by the dramatic frontage of **Christ Church Spitalfields** (*see p164*) visible at the end of the street. Before the market is new shopping area Crispin Place, announced by a courtyard shaded by a sail-like curved awning. The slick shops here sell upmarket clothes, cosmetics, homeware and gourmet olive oil, while excellent new Brit restaurant **Canteen** (No.2, *see p219*) presides over the cluster of eating options.

Also on Brushfield Street are boutique grocers **Verde & Co** (No.40, 7247 1924), opened by author Jeanette Winterson, and **A Gold** (*see p257*). The adjacent **Old Spitalfields Market** is a beautiful structure with shops open seven days a week (*see also p164* **Oranges are not the only fruit**). Enter from Crispin Place and you'll see the brand new glass-walled **Kinetica** (7392 9674), a gallery that focuses on new media and kinetic art – at the time of writing this takes the form of a bunch of industrial robots. Also within the market building is the **Spitz** (*see p317*), a combined art gallery, music venue and bistro, and the redoubtable barbecue joint **Arkansas Café** (*see p219*).

Oranges are not the only fruit

The redevelopment of Spitalfields has hardly been a rapid process. The uncharitable could alight on 1991 when, just like London's other old central markets, the original Spitalfields fruit and veg traders were banished to more traffic-accessible suburbs – in this instance, further east to Temple Mills. The developers then sought to demolish the handsome covered-market building, last modernised by the City of London Corporation for a meagre £2m back in 1928. However, thanks to an impassioned campaign by locals, the bulldozers were kept at bay.

When redevelopment began in earnest in 2002, vigorous campaigns were launched to preserve the market's character. The fear was that the area would become a recreational retail opportunity for a well-heeled elite, driving up rents and driving out the small stalls that gave the place its character. Certainly, the Norman Foster-designed, plate-glass office of corporate lawyers Allen & Overy could be anywhere in the City. And the banners that flutter – at least as long as the scaffolding remains – above each entrance to the market and declare 'Open. Since 1887' are rather too evidently the work of a snappy PR organisation. Even shops that appear to have been here since Dickens's day are recent inventions, like the charming grocery shop A Gold, which was a run-down dwelling when it was lovingly restored six years ago, or the Market Coffee House, whose wood panelling and creaky furniture are reclaimed materials put into what was until recently an empty shell. The deli Verde & Co was opened by its owner, author Jeanette Winterson, after she was inspired by the local food shops she found in – whisper it – France.

Yet the Friday fashion market and main Sunday market thrive. Stallholders may bridle at the disruption and uncertainty of continuing development, but the idea that a precious fragment of 'real' London is fighting for its life in an area sandwiched between the Rolexed wheeler-dealing of the City and the self-conscious trendiness of Brick Lane isn't the whole truth. For Halil Koch, who's spent the last decade running an old-school health food shop beside the market (Spitalfields Organic, 103 Commercial Street, 7377 8909), gentrification began long ago. 'This area has been getting very expensive for a while,' he claims. 'There used to be a big community of artists here at one time, but that's all gone now.'

As you drool over the luxury chocolate and Somerset-made Very Lemon Curd it may prove hard to mourn their passing.

Just a street to the north is **Dennis Severs' House** (*see p165*), an atmospherically restaged Huguenot dwelling, while across from the market, on the east side of Commercial Street in the shadow of Christ Church, the **Ten Bells** (84 Commercial Street, 7366 1721) is where one of Jack the Ripper's prostitute victims drank her last gin; it's now a pleasant and lively pub with a lounge vibe. The streets between here and Brick Lane to the east are dourly impressive, lined with tall, shuttered Huguenot houses; **19 Princelet Street** is sometimes open to the public. This unrestored 18th-century house was home first to French silk merchants and later Polish Jews who built a synagogue in the garden. Because of the fragile state of the Grade II-listed house, it only opens a dozen days a year (see www.19princeletstreet. org.uk). **Story** (4 Wilkes Street, 7377 0313) has exquisite vintage and reclaimed clothing, displayed in a bare white space.

If you are in the area on Sunday, pay a visit to the famously salt-of-the-earth **Petticoat Lane Market**, which centres on Middlesex Street. During the week, pop into the Wash House Café upstairs at the **Women's Library** (Old Castle Street, 7320 2222, www.thewomens library.ac.uk) or sample a very different kind of culture at the foot of parallel Goulston Street: **Tubby Isaacs** seafood stall has been selling whelks, cockles and crab to Cockneys since 1919.

Christ Church Spitalfields

Commercial Street, E1 6QE (7247 7202/www.christ churchspitalfields.org). Liverpool Street tube/rail.
Open 11am-4pm Tue; 1-4pm Sun. **Admission** free.
Map p403 S5.

Built in 1729 by architect Nicholas Hawksmoor, Christ Church Spitalfields has in recent years been cleaned to pristine whiteness and restored to its original state having been tastelessly altered in the mid 19th century. Most tourists get no further than cowering before the overbearing spire, but the revived interior is one of Hawksmoor's most detailed and impressive. The formidable 1735 Richard Bridge organ – subject of ongoing restoration work – is almost as old as the church. The internationally renowned Gabrieli Consort & Players are resident at the church and give regular performances.

Dennis Severs' House

18 Folgate Street, E1 6BX (7247 4013/www.dennissevershouse.co.uk). Liverpool Street tube/rail. **Open** 2-5pm 1st & 3rd Sun of mth; noon-2pm Mon following 1st & 3rd Sun of mth; Mon eves (times vary). **Admission** £8 Sun; £5 noon-2pm Mon; £12 Mon eves. **Credit** MC, V. **Map** p405 R5.

The ten rooms of this original Huguenot house have been decked out to recreate, down to the smallest detail, snapshots of life in Spitalfields between 1724 and 1914. A tour through this compelling 'still-life drama', as American creator Dennis Severs dubbed it, takes you through the cellar, kitchen, dining room, smoking room and upstairs to the bedrooms. With hearth and candles burning, smells lingering and objects scattered haphazardly, it is as if the inhabitants only deserted the rooms just moments before.

Brick Lane

Maps p405 & p407

Aldgate East tube.

Irony of ironies: tatty old **Brick Lane** is world-famous for its curries (there's now a Brick Lane restaurant in Manhattan and a namesake street in Dhaka) but the rise in reputation has been mirrored by an equally sharp decline in quality. Nowadays Brick Lane is the last place you'd go in London for a decent Indian meal. It does, however, sell brilliant Bengali sweets (drop in on Madhubon Sweet Centre at No.42 to prove the case) and all manner of rare groceries.

The building that houses the **Jamme Masjid Mosque**, towards the south end of Brick Lane, is often pointed to as symbolic of the area's hybridity: it began life as a Huguenot chapel and was later used as a synagogue before being converted, in 1976, into a mosque. Despite this ward officially taking the name 'Banglatown' in 2002, gentrification has put a new layer on the Brick Lane experience: it's now more about young urban bohemians than Bangladeshis. Sunday is the day to visit for the busy local **market**, which makes the place irresistibly lively.

The other side of the Brick Lane experience is the cutting-edge street culture. Once a major local employer, the **Old Truman Brewery** (No.91) is now an artistic and creative hub, and a focal point for small, hip businesses: **Story Deli** (*see p219*) sells organic edibles such as pizzas, while the **Big Chill Bar** (*see p326*) is an excellent DJ space with a popular street-side terrace and shares its clientele with the long-established **Vibe Bar** (*see p328*) and gig venue **93 Feet East** (*see p324*). Fashion-heads will enjoy the retro fare at **Gloria's** (6 Dray Walk, 7700 6222, www.superdeluxe.net), although all our needless spends take place at the classic clothing emporium **A Butcher of Distinction** (*see p243*).

North of the brewery are more quirky cafés and clothes shops, including the divine **Luna & Curious** (*see p245*) and the unique jewellery of the **@work gallery** (No.156, 7377 0597, www.atworkgallery.co.uk). Second-hand clothing emporium **Rokit** (Nos.101 & 107, 7375 3864, 7247 3777) is also always good for a rummage. A lingering remnant of the area's

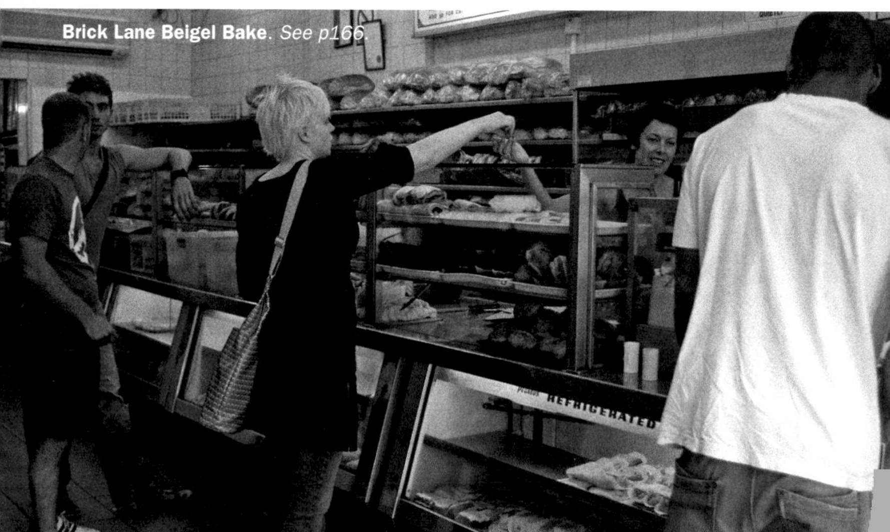

Brick Lane Beigel Bake. *See p166.*

Jewish heritage is to be found at the northern end of the street in the form of the unmissable 24-hour **Brick Lane Beigel Bake** (*see p220*), favourite of old residents, tea-breaking taxi drivers and raddled clubbers alike.

For more excellent shopping, detour east along Cheshire Street for everything from rare vinyl at **Search & Destroy** (No.1, 7613 5604) to Serbian designed garments in silk, cashmere and organza (**Dragana Perisic**, No.30), and London's biggest, baddest retro shop, **Beyond Retro** (*see p251*).

Whitechapel

Maps p407

Aldgate East or Whitechapel tube.

Not one of the prettier parts of London, the district that takes its name from the white stones used to build a now demolished church centres on busy but anonymous Whitechapel Road. It's somehow still quite fitting that the majority of visitors who do venture here come as part of a Jack the Ripper tour (*see p143* **Walk this way**). One of the rare bright spots is the **Whitechapel Art Gallery** (*see below*), which is certainly worth travelling for – except that it is closed for all of 2007. Its neighbouring alley has a wall of anarchists' portraits and the **Freedom Press Bookshop** (7247 9249), on the first floor just round the corner, should you need to bone up on the Situationists or some radical ecology.

A little to the east, the **Whitechapel Bell Foundry** (Nos.80-82, 7247 2599, www.whitechapelbellfoundry.co.uk) has been knocking out bells since 1570, most famously Big Ben. You can visit the displays in the foyer 9am-4.15pm Mon-Fri (Big Ben's frame surrounds the door), but to see the foundry itself it is necessary to reserve a place on one of the scheduled Saturday tours.

Bells are not required at Whitechapel's current foremost place of worship; the **East London Mosque** is the focal point for Britain's largest Muslim community and can accommodate an impressive 10,000 worshippers. Behind the mosque is Fieldgate Street and the dark mass of **Tower House**, an enormous former doss house whose 700 rooms are currently being redeveloped. Joseph Stalin and George Orwell (researching his *Down and Out in Paris and London*) were former tenants. The red-brick alleys around here give a good sense of Victorian Whitechapel. Fieldgate Street is also the address of the superb **New Tayyab** (Nos.83-89, 7247 9543, open 5.30-11pm daily), which does the best seekh kebabs this side of Lahore: impeccably lamby, aggressively spiced and phenomenally cheap.

East again is the Royal London Hospital and its small **Royal London Hospital Archives & Museum** (7377 7608, closed Sat, Sun), which is several streets back on Newark Street, in a former church crypt. Inside are reproduction letters from Jack the Ripper (including the notorious missive 'From Hell', which was delivered with a piece of human kidney) and information on Joseph Merrick, the so-called 'Elephant Man', so named for his fearsome congenital deformities. Rescued by surgeon Sir Frederick Treves, Merrick was given his own room in the Royal London Hospital.

Back on Whitechapel Road, you can stock up on standard **street market** miscellanea (household goods, clothes, Bangladeshi fruit and veg, knock-off batteries and cigarettes from the roaming derelicts) or, at the corner of Whitechapel Road and Cambridge Heath Road, drop into the **Blind Beggar** (337 Whitechapel Road, 7247 6195) where on 9 March 1966 notorious East End gangster Ronnie Kray shot George Cornell dead.

Whitechapel Art Gallery

80-82 Whitechapel High Street, E1 7QX (7522 7888/www.whitechapel.org). Aldgate East tube. **Open** gallery closed until 2008; see website for events. **Map** p407 S6.

Whitechapel's architecturally impressive art gallery has always been an unexpected cultural treat between the tatty clothing wholesalers, stripper pubs and the other flotsam that washes along Whitechapel Road. An east London institution, founded by a Victorian philanthropist to bring art to the working classes, it has presented contemporary, forward-thinking exhibitions for over a century (Picasso's *Guernica*, for example, was shown here in 1939). The good news is that the gallery is about to enjoy an impressively thoroughgoing renovation as it expands into the historic former library next door. The bad news? It closed at the end of 2006 and won't open again until summer 2008. In the meantime check the website for ongoing evening events.

Shoreditch & Hoxton

Map p405

Old Street tube/rail.

Small in area, Hoxton and Shoreditch exert a disproportionately large influence on London life thanks to a reputation as a hip arts and clubbing nexus. The heart of all of this is a triangle formed by Old Street to the north, Shoreditch High Street (east) and Great Eastern Street (south-west). Anchoring the southernmost point of the triangle is the huge **Tea Building**, on the corner of Shoreditch High Street and Bethnal Green Road, a former tea warehouse that's now a hive of small creative studios plus a fine bar in the **T Bar**

Banksy on it

It's a rainy Sunday afternoon in Shoreditch and two workmen in fluorescent vests are working in the Ridgeway Place car park. Working on a Sunday? It isn't until they hump their ladders, their gear and themselves over the fence to zoom off in an anonymous flatbed truck that the onlookers' suspicions are confirmed: they're not workmen at all, they are graffiti artists.

When it comes to east London, there's a lot of them about. The most famous of their number may come from Bristol and may have risen to international notoriety for high-profile pranks like placing a dummy dressed in a Guantanamo Bay jumpsuit on a Disneyland ride, but Banksy's main stenciling grounds are round Hoxton and Shoreditch. If, unlike Angelina Jolie, you don't have £200k to splash on his work (as she did in September 2006), you can always head to Rivington Street instead. There, at the Old Street Station end, the aforementioned Ridgeway Place car park is currently decorated with two Banksy pieces: a trademark giant rat and a TV being thrown out of a window.

Over on Curtain Road beside a bus stand is a boy in trendy beach cut-offs ruminating over a lit match and a burning schooner. Back on Rivington Street and, in the car park opposite the Comedy Café is stecilled 'DESIGNATED PICNIC AREA' – with an arrow pointing down to the tarmac. The wall opposite the club Cargo, a regular Banksy canvas, has a boy wielding paintbrush and pot, while a copper and his red-nosed poodle police the courtyard of the club's Street Food Café: 'BY ORDER NATIONAL HIGHWAYS AGENCY: THIS WALL IS A DESIGNATED GRAFFITI AREA'.

Of course, this being graffiti all that we describe may be gone by the time you read this. (Banksy's stencils of snogging and cocaine-snorting policemen seem especially prone to swift obliteration.) The line of yellow Smiley-faced riot police that for the longest time stretched across the bridge over Old Street is no more. The army of rats on the viaduct over Kingsland Road is currently sheathed in plastic sheeting, presumably while it's being scrubbed clean.

Other more permanent forms of street art have appeared around town in recent years. Renegade tiling, for instance, which chimes with a current London vogue for handicrafts (there are Space Invaders in pretty colours high on an alley wall beside the Dragon Bar on Leonard Street and beside St Anne's churchyard in Soho, and a tiled Johnny Rotten on Hanway Street, off Oxford Street). Hip-hop nostalgists who crave the full-colour 'filled-in throw-ups' can still get their kicks on Sclater Street, between Shoreditch High Street and Brick Lane, and Grimsby Street, just off Brick Lane, the latter a grim and threatening alley only partly brightened by the vibrant Fabulous Furry Freak Brothers artwork. But stencilling remains popular because it allows sophisticated designs, prepared off-site, to be applied to a wall in a matter of seconds – a huge advantage for an illegal pastime.

Back on Brick Lane, the local authorities tried to pre-empt the graffiti-ists by supplying official street decoration in the form of green boarding and some yin-yang designs. It wasn't long before it was topped by the street artist's piss-takingly official response 'TO ADVERTISE HERE CALL 0800 BANKSY'.

(7729 2973, www.tbarlondon.com), galleries and a restaurant. The real landmark venues of the neighbourhood, though, are places like **333** (*see p325*), **Cargo** (*see p321*) and **Plastic People** (*see p325*), plus a bunch of venues on and around Hoxton Square, including the **Hoxton Square Bar & Grill** (*see p234*).

It was artists who sparked the Hoxton resurgence; they took advantage of the area's large light industrial spaces and cheap rents to set up their studios here in the 1980s. That legacy is at its most high profile at the **White Cube** (*see p297*) on Hoxton Square, where openings rarely fail to draw a gossip column's worth of celebs. These days, City workers happy to pay serious money for some street cred have driven rents through the roof. The impecunious artists have moved east into Hackney and Bethnal Green, leaving the bars and clubs to fight a valiant rearguard action, vainly insisting 'No ties please'.

The area's sole bona fide tourist attraction is the exquisite **Geffrye Museum** (*see below*), which is a short walk north up Kingsland Road. The surrounding area is dense with Vietnamese cafés and restaurants, some of which are excellent, notably **Sông Quê** (*see p220*).

Geffrye Museum

Kingsland Road, E2 8EA (7739 9893/recorded information 7739 8543/www.geffrye-museum.org.uk). Liverpool Street tube/rail then 149, 242 bus/ Old Street tube/rail then 243 bus. **Open** *Museum*

Sightseeing

10am-5pm Tue-Sat; noon-5pm Sun. *Almshouse tours* 1st Sat of mth & 1st & 3rd Wed of mth – call for times. **Admission** *Museum* free; donations appreciated. *Almshouse tours* £2; free under-16s. **Credit** (shop) MC, V. **Map** p405 R3.

The Geffrye Museum is a quite marvellous physical history of the English interior, housed in a set of converted almshouses. It recreates typical English living rooms from the 17th century to the present, and has a series of lovely gardens designed on similar chronological lines. There's an airy restaurant and special exhibitions are mounted throughout the year in a purpose-built downstairs space.

Bethnal Green

Bethnal Green tube/rail, Cambridge Heath rail or Mile End tube.

Once a suburb of spacious townhouses and gardens, by the mid 1900s Bethnal Green had become one of London's poorest neighbourhoods – and so it remained until very recently. As in neighbouring Hoxton, the changes are to an extent occasioned by the choice of Bethnal Green as home by a new generation of artists. That, and the fact that the area is now the cheapest closest place to the City for low-wage home buyers. The new Bethnal Green is typified by the gallery **Between Bridges** (223 Cambridge Heath Road, 7729 8599), which occupies the entrance space to celebrated artist-photographer Wolfgang Tillmans's studio. The old Bethnal Green is best experienced through a trip to **E Pellicci** (*see p213*), a traditional café that has been serving tea and fry-ups to locals for the last 105 years.

The area's other attraction is the famous **Columbia Road flower market**, held every Sunday morning (*see p259* **Top five**), which is well worth attending. A microcosmic retail community has grown up around the market: **Treacle** (No.160, 7729 5657) is the place for groovy pieces of crockery and dinky cup cakes; **Angela Flanders** (No.96, 7739 7555) is a lovely perfume shop; **Marcos & Trump** (No.146, 7739 9008) is a treasure trove for vintage fashion and assorted covetables.

White Cube. *See p167.*

Bethnal Green Museum of Childhood

Cambridge Heath Road, E2 9PA (8983 5200/ recorded information 8980 2415/www.museumofchildhood.org.uk). Bethnal Green tube/rail/ Cambridge Heath rail. **Open** 10am-5.45pm daily. **Admission** free; donations appreciated; *workshops* small charge. **Credit** MC, V.

Officially part of the Victoria & Albert Museum (*see p154*), the Museum of Childhood has amassed a huge collection of children's toys, dolls' houses, games and costumes since it opened in 1872. The museum presents plenty of hands-on activities for kids, including dressing-up boxes and a zoëtrope, and runs free drop-ins and regular workshops. A £4.7m, five-year refurbishment was coming to an end as we went to press, but the museum should have opened its splendid new entrance for the first time in December 2006. Internal improvements include a new community art gallery, learning centre and exhibition of moving toys.

Ragged School Museum

46-50 Copperfield Road, E3 4RR (8980 6405/www.raggedschoolmuseum.org.uk). Mile End tube. **Open** 10am-5pm Wed, Thur; 2-5pm 1st Sun of mth. *Tours* by arrangement; phone for details. **Admission** free; donations appreciated.

Ragged schools were an early experiment in public education: they provided tuition as well as food and clothing for destitute children. The Copperfield Road Ragged School was the largest in London, and it was here that the famous Dr Barnardo taught. It's now a fascinating museum that contains a complete mock-up of a ragged classroom, where historical re-enactments are staged for schoolchildren, as well as an Edwardian kitchen. There are also displays on local history and industry in a downstairs room.

Docklands

London's docks were fundamental to the long prosperity of the British Empire. Between 1802 and 1921, ten separate docks were built between Tower Bridge in the west and Woolwich in the east employing tens of thousands of people. Yet by the 1960s the shipping industry was changing irrevocably. The new 'container' system of cargo demanded larger, deep-draught ships, which the existing set-up could not accommodate. The result was that the work moved out to Tilbury and by 1980 the London docks had all closed.

The London Docklands Development Corporation (LDDC), founded in 1981, spent £790m of public money on redevelopment during the following decade, only for a country-wide property slump in the early 1990s to leave the shiny new high-rise offices and luxury flats unoccupied. Nowadays that's just so much old history. As a financial hub, Docklands is now a booming rival to the City of London, with an estimated 90,000 workers commuting to the area each day. Regular **Thames Clippers** (0870 781 5049, www.thamesclippers.com) boat connections between Docklands and central London and eastward extensions to the Docklands Light Railway (DLR) have made the area ever more accessible.

Wapping & Limehouse

Wapping tube or Limehouse DLR/rail.

The Saxon settlement of Wapping has a maritime history extending back centuries. In 1598 John Stowe described Wapping High Street as 'a filthy strait passage, with alleys of small tenements or cottages, inhabited by sailors' victuallers'. A number of these historic pubs survive, including the 1545 **Town of Ramsgate** (No.62, 7481 8000), where 'hanging judge' George Jeffreys was captured in 1688 while trying to escape to Europe disguised as a woman. Privateer Captain William Kidd was executed in 1701 at Execution Dock, a gruesome spot near **Wapping New Stairs** where the bodies of pirates were hanged from a gibbet until seven tides had washed over them. Further east, the **Prospect of Whitby** (*see p235*) dates from 1520 and in its time has counted Samuel Pepys and Charles Dickens among its regulars. Opposite sits a more modern breed of 'victualler': the **Wapping Food** (*see p220*), a restaurant and gallery in an ivy-clad Victorian hydraulic power station.

A riverpath connecting Wapping to easterly neighbour Limehouse offers a decent stroll during daylight hours (not at night, when one essential gate is locked). Dickens knew the way – and it is said that he based the Six Jolly Fellowship Porters tavern from *Our Mutual Friend* on the **Grapes** (*see p234*). Britain's first wave of Chinese immigrants, mostly seafarers, settled in Limehouse in the 19th century to create London's original Chinatown. Canton, Nankin and Pekin Streets are all nearby, and

Canary Wharf Station.

the city's first Chinese restaurant is thought to have been on Commercial Road just above **Limehouse Basin**. This glossy marina is enlivened by some narrowboats, but luxury flats and a sense of self-satisfaction prevail.

Visible from the Basin is the white clock tower of **St Anne's Church**, an impressive Hawksmoor construction. The gloomily pleasing churchyard has a narrow pyramid in its north-west corner that's taller than a man.

Isle of Dogs

West India Quay, Mudchute or Island Gardens DLR/Canary Wharf tube/DLR.

The origin of the name 'Isle of Dogs' remains uncertain, but the first known use is on a 1588 map; one popular theory claims Henry VIII kept hunting dogs here. It isn't strictly an island, but rather a peninsula that extends to create the prominent loop in the river that has been immortalised in the title sequence of the indefatigable soap opera *EastEnders*. In the 19th century a huge system of docks completely transformed what had previously been no more than drained marshland; in fact, the West India Docks cut right across the peninsula so as to finally make it into some sort of island.

The natural isolation of the area and the formerly thriving docklands industry conspired to create a strong, compact community, one that took a heavy beating over the course of the 20th century – during World War II, this was one of the hardest hit parts of London. At the height of the Blitz, the docks were bombarded on 57 consecutive nights. Yet as late as 1970 the community was cohesive enough to block the two entry roads to the Isle of Dogs and declare itself independent of the rest of Great Britain.

Almost all the interest for visitors is to be found in the vicinity of Cesar Pelli's dramatic **One Canada Water**, Britain's tallest habitable building since 1991. The only slightly shorter HSBC and Citygroup towers recently joined it, and clones are springing up thick and fast. Shopping options are limited to the mall beneath the towers (www.mycanarywharf.com), but there's a soothing if rather too crisp **Japanese garden** beside Canary Wharf tube station. Sit out front of **Carluccio's Caffè** (Nash Court, 7719 1749) beneath Pelli's tower to sip an espresso among the clocks – more sculpture, not functional timepieces – or splash out on a seriously luxury feed at Conran's glass-walled, space-age French restaurant **Plateau** (4th floor, Canada Place, Canada Square, 7715 7100, www.conran.com). Alternatively, head east on West India Avenue to the Thames for a row of well situated riverbank eateries, which includes a branch of the excellent **Royal China** (30 Westferry Circus, 7719 0888, www.royalchinagroup.co.uk).

At the foot of One Canada Water a central fountain bubbles in Cabot Square. Steps lead north down to a floating bridge. On the far side, within a warehouse, is the splendid **Museum in Docklands** (*see below*).

It's also well worth hopping back on the DLR and heading to **Island Gardens** at the southerly tip of the Isle of Dogs. There are great views across the river to Greenwich. You can cross under the river through the Victorian pedestrian **tunnel** (lift service 7am-7pm Mon-Sat, 10am-5.30pm Sun).

Museum in Docklands

No.1 Warehouse, West India Quay, Hertsmere Road, E14 4AL (recorded information 0870 444 3856/ box office 0870 444 3857/www.museumindocklands.org.uk). West India Quay DLR/Canary Wharf tube. **Open** 10am-6pm daily. Last entry 5.30pm. **Admission** (unlimited entrance for 1yr) £5; £3 concs; free under-16s. **Credit** MC, V.

This huge museum explores the long and diverse history of London's docklands over two millennia. Many exhibits are narrated by people who saw the changes for themselves; the Docklands at War section is particularly moving. There are also full-scale mock-ups of a quayside and a dingy riverfront alley. A new permanent gallery explores links between the slave trade and sugar imports, with particular attention to the role of West India Dock. **Photo** *p171*.

Further east

Pontoon Dock or King George V DLR.

Pontoon Dock is the stop for the beautiful **Thames Barrier Park** (www.thamesbarrierpark.org.uk). Opened in 2001, this was London's first new park in half a century. It has a lush sunken garden of waggly hedges and offers perhaps the best views of the Thames Barrier (*see p179*). Head to the terminus of this branch of the DLR at King George V for ready access to the jolly little **North Woolwich Old Station Museum** (Pier Road, 7474 7244, open 1-5pm Sat, Sun, 1-5pm Mon-Fri during school hols, closed Dec) and the ramshackle free ferry (every 15mins daily, 8921 5786) that chugs pedestrians and cars to Woolwich (*see p179*).

Hackney

London Fields or Hackney Central rail.

Few tourists ever make it out to this tube-less, north-eastern district of London – nobody is missing anything, there's nothing to see. However, in anticipation of an East London Line extension and the arrival of Crossrail, which will finally connect Hackney with the rest of the city, the borough has begun to pull together its cultural assets. The core of these are the refurbished 1901 **Hackney Empire** (291 Mare Street, 8985 2424, www.hackneyempire.co.uk), together with the art deco **town hall** and impressive little **Hackney Museum** (1 Reading Lane, 8356 3500, www.hackney.gov. uk/museum). Just to the east, **Sutton House** (*see below*) is the oldest house in the East End.

A belwether for ongoing changes, **Broadway Market** (*see p259* **Top five**) has a suddenly thriving market, a wonderful deli, an inspiring independent bookshop and two mighty fine pubs – gastropub the **Cat & Mutton** (No.76, 7254 5599, www.catandmutton.co.uk) and, for a brilliant selection of Belgian beers, the **Dove** (Nos.24-28, 7275 7617, www.belgianbars.com). New and old east London are represented by two Broadway market eateries: the nouveau Argentinian grill of **Santa Maria de Buen Ayre** (No.50, 7275 9900) or traditional pie and mash at **F Cooke** (No.9, 7254 6458), present since the early 1900s.

Sutton House

2-4 Homerton High Street, E9 6JQ (8986 2264/ www.nationaltrust.org.uk). Bethnal Green tube then 254, 106, D6 bus/Hackney Central rail. **Open** *Early Feb-late Dec* Historic rooms 12.30-4.30pm Thur-Sun. Café, gallery, shop noon-4.30pm Thur-Sun. Closed Jan. *Tours* group tours phone for details; free tours on 1st Sun of mth. **Admission** £2.70; 60p 5-16s; free under-5s; £6 family; £2.20 group. **Credit** MC, V.

Built in 1535 for Henry VIII's first secretary of state, Sir Ralph Sadleir, this red-brick Tudor mansion is east London's oldest home. Miraculously, it has survived waves of development – as well as squatters in the 1980s. Now beautifully restored in authentic original decor, with a real Tudor kitchen to boot, it makes no secret of its history of neglect. Special events and activities are often held (check the website); there's also an art gallery exhibiting contemporary work by local artists.

Lea Valley Park

Fight the boredom for long enough as you head east and Mile End Road will become Bow Road. Where it crosses the River Lea, easily accessible by tube, is the delightful **Three Mills Island** (*see below*). A short walk north-east up the canal-like tributary brings you to **Stratford**, nucleus of the transformation for the 2012 Olympics (*see below*).

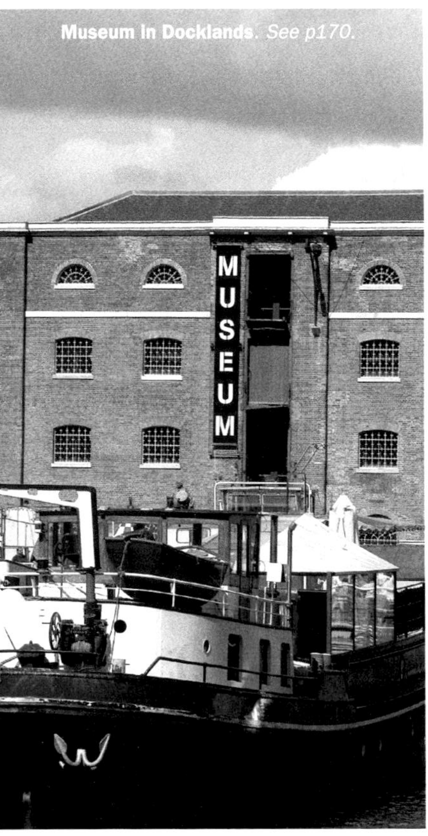

Museum in Docklands. *See p170.*

Otherwise, the River Lea wriggles north-west from Three Mills Island past the scrubby flats of Hackney Marsh and, either side of horrible Lea Bridge Road, an ice rink, riding stables and the **WaterWorks Nature Reserve** (Lammas Road, 8988 7566, open April-Sept 8am-dusk daily, Oct-Mar 9am-6pm daily). A touchingly odd combination of golf course and nature reserve, these water-filter beds were built in 1849 to purify water during a cholera epidemic. The WaterWorks now house 322 species of plant and 25 species of breeding birds, observable from easily accessible hides. Further north are off-road cycle tracks, boating lakes and even an area where you can watch (or more likely hear) rare bitterns.

Olympic Park

Stratford, E15 (www.london2012.org). Stratford tube/rail/DLR/West Ham tube/rail/Pudding Mill DLR/Hackney Wick rail.

London is gearing up to host the 2012 Olympics, having pipped Paris with its bid in 2005. Different venues will be used across London, including the All England Tennis Club at Wimbledon and Lord's Cricket Ground, but the main events will take place at the new Olympic site in Stratford, currently under construction. The Olympic Park will eventually include an 80,000-capacity stadium, an aquatic centre, a velopark, a hockey centre and the Olympic village, located east of Victoria Park, around the western fringe of Stratford and north of Three Mills Island. Go East London has been running an occasional Routemaster bus tour of the Olympic sites from Stratford; check www.goeastlondon.co.uk for details of any upcoming tours.

Three Mills Island

Three Mill Lane, E3 3DU (8980 4626/www.housemill.org.uk). Bromley-by-Bow tube. **Tours** *May-Dec* 1-4pm Sun. **Admission** £3; £1.50 concs; free under-16s. **No credit cards**.

This large island in the River Lea takes its name from the three mills that, until the 18th century, ground flour and gunpowder here. The House Mill, built in 1776, is the oldest and largest tidal mill in Britain and, though out of service, is occasionally opened to the public. The island offers pleasant walks, which can feel surprisingly rural once you're among the undergrowth. There's also a small café, a crafts market on the first Sunday of the month and, to puncture the idyll, part of the site is a TV studio.

Walthamstow to Epping Forest

Walthamstow Central tube/rail or Loughton/Theydon Bois tube.

Apart from the famous Walthamstow Stadium greyhound track (*see p331*), this area's best asset is quaint little **Walthamstow Village**, just a few minutes' walk east of the tube station. At the top of Orford Road is an ancient timber-framed cottage, relic of a settlement that stood here long before the Victorian terraces sprung up. Just opposite is **St Mary's Church**, parts of which date back to the 16th century although there's been a church on the site since the 1100s. Across Vinegar Alley – so named because it was once a vinegar-filled ditch, intended as protection against plague – are the Monoux Almshouses. Further almshouses lead back along Church End to the modest **Vestry House Museum** (Vestry Road, 8509 1917, closed Sun & bank holidays), with its lovely garden and the reconstructed Bremer Car, London's first petrol-driven vehicle.

North of Walthamstow Central is the daily **market**, which spans the length of Walthamstow High Street and is reputed to be the longest street market in Europe. Pie and mash shop **L Manze** (No.76, 8520 2855) retains its original decor from 1929. Further north, near the junction of Hoe Street and Forest Road, is peaceful **Lloyd Park**; the grand Georgian house at its entrance is home to the **William Morris Gallery** (*see below*) – the Arts and Crafts pioneer was a Walthamstow boy.

Forest Road is justly named. Follow it east past the extraordinary art deco **town hall** and it does indeed bring you to the southerly part of a long finger of ancient woodland. **Epping Forest** extends nearly eight miles north, its existence guaranteed by the Victorians: in 1878 Parliament granted the City of London the power to buy land within 25 miles of the city centre to be used for the recreation of city dwellers. Dedicated ramblers might stumble across the faint remains of two Iron Age forts, but Queen Elizabeth I's **hunting lodge**, now a free museum (8529 6681, 1-4pm Sat, Sun), is easier to find. Drivers will want to stop at the High Beach visitors' centre (8508 0028) for information and maps. The self-propelled can get information from Guildhall Library before taking the Central Line to Loughton or Theydon Bois stations, either of which will bring you within striking distance of the forest's edge.

William Morris Gallery

Lloyd Park, Forest Road, E17 4PP (8527 3782/www.lbwf.gov.uk/wmg). Walthamstow Central tube/rail/34, 97 bus. **Open** 10am-1pm, 2-5pm Tue-Sat, 1st Sun of mth. *Tours* phone for details. **Admission** free; donations appreciated. **Credit** (shop) MC, V.

Artist, socialist and source of all that wallpaper, William Morris lived here between 1848 and 1856. There are plenty of wonderful designs – in fabric, stained glass and ceramic – on show here, produced not only by Morris but also by his acolytes. There's even a medieval-style helmet and sword, props for Pre-Raphaelite paintings. Yet we prefer the humbler domestic objects: Morris's coffee cup and the satchel he used to carry his radical pamphlets.

William Morris Gallery.

South-east London

Royal riverside recreation and a little urban grit.

Howzat! Kennington's **Brit Oval**.

Sightseeing

Ever since 16th-century dramatist Christopher Marlowe was stabbed to death in these parts, south-east London has had a bit of an unsavoury reputation. Even today, it's one of the poorer parts of town, with high streets that empty after dark, and side streets and estates that are roamed by ruthless teenage gangs. But there are bright spots. Greenwich is simply lovely and makes for a great one-day excursion from central London, especially if you make the trip by boat. The wonderfully eccentric Horniman Museum and similarly eclectic Eltham Palace are both well worth the effort it takes to get to them, while the ever-excellent Imperial War Museum is, in fact, just a short walk from Westminster Bridge and the South Bank.

Kennington & the Elephant

Kennington tube/Elephant & Castle tube/rail.
Now an inner-city mishmash of decrepit Irish pubs, late-night drinking holes and lively enclaves of Portuguese and South Americans, Kennington has an equally colourful history. Once owned by the Duchy of Cornwall, Kennington Common (now **Kennington Park**) was the main place of execution for the county of Surrey. During the 17th and 18th centuries, preachers, notably John Wesley (*see p97*), addressed audiences here. By the 19th century the area had become polluted. The transformation of the present park ensured it a significant footnote in sporting history. The end to local cricket matches saw the founding of the Oval Cricket Club, the home of Surrey County Cricket, today the dreadfully-prefixed **Brit Oval** (*see p330*). In 1872 it staged football's first FA Cup final and, a year later, the first England–Scotland international.

Just across from Kennington tube station is the **Black Cultural Archives** (Othello Close, 7582 8516), which charts the history of black people in London and holds interesting historic exhibitions and art displays. A short walk north takes you to the **Imperial War Museum** (*see p174*), beyond which lies the shambolic **Elephant & Castle**. The Elephant and Castle Regeneration scheme has earmarked £1.5bn to transform this area into a smart new town centre by 2014, though some campaigners fear

that the current diverse range of market traders and stallholders will be lost to a 'clone town' of chain stores and cafés.

Imperial War Museum

Lambeth Road, SE1 6HZ (7416 5320/www.iwm.org.uk). Lambeth North tube/Elephant & Castle tube/rail. **Open** 10am-6pm daily. **Admission** free. *Special exhibitions* prices vary. **Credit** MC, V. **Map** p406 N10.

In 1936 the central wing of the old Bethlehem Royal Hospital (Bedlam) became the Imperial War Museum. Its collection covers conflicts, especially those involving Britain and the Commonwealth, from World War I to the present day. The exhibits range from tanks, aircraft and big guns to photographs and personal letters. There are also film and sound recordings, and some of the 20th century's best-known paintings, among them John Singer Sargent's *Gassed*.

The lower-ground floor has both the smelly World War I Trench Experience and the teeth-chattering Blitz Experience. The Holocaust Exhibition, on the third floor, traces the history of anti-Semitism and the rise of Hitler: the vast collection of salvaged shoes, clothes, spectacles and testimonials from survivors breaks the heart. The fourth floor's Crimes Against Humanity exhibit, covering genocide and ethnic violence in our time, is for over-16s only. Temporary exhibitions include Children's War, which runs until 2008.

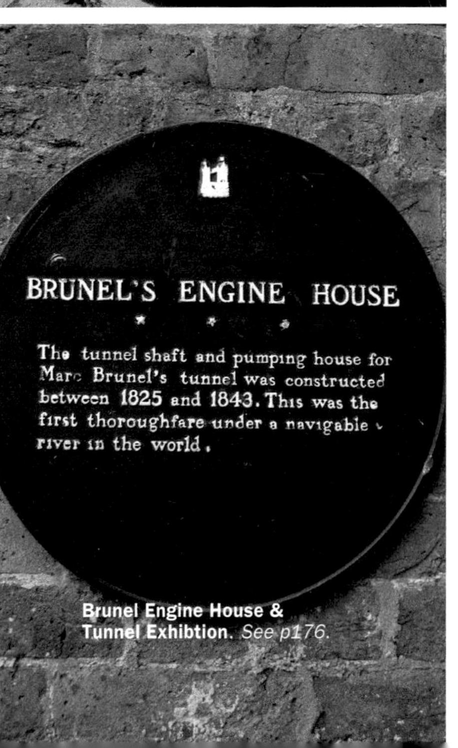

BRUNEL'S ENGINE HOUSE
The tunnel shaft and pumping house for
Marc Brunel's tunnel was constructed
between 1825 and 1843. This was the
first thoroughfare under a navigable
river in the world.

Brunel Engine House & Tunnel Exhibtion. *See p176.*

Camberwell & Peckham

Denmark Hill or Peckham Rye rail.

Camberwell Green is a rather frantic bus junction linking Kennington, Elephant, Peckham and points south-east. Choose east and you pass **St Giles's Church**, an imposing early Victorian structure by Sir George Gilbert Scott, renowned as the designer of St Pancras Station and Bankside and Battersea power stations. Further towards Peckham lies **Camberwell College of Arts** (Peckham Road, 7514 6300), London's oldest art college, and the **South London Gallery** (*see p298*). Social life revolves around pubs such as Funky Munky (No.25, 7277 1806) and the Hermit's Cave (No.28, 7703 3188) on Camberwell Church Street and sundry DJ bars, filled with art students and arty wanabees – a kind of poor man's Shoreditch.

Linking Camberwell to Peckham, **Burgess Park** was created by filling in the Grand Surrey Canal and razing rows of houses. The nicest bit of the park is **Chumleigh Gardens**, where there are picturesque almshouses, gardens and a pleasant café (7525 1070, www.chumleigh gardens.co.uk). Walking through it to **Peckham** takes you to a canal-path cycle route that runs past the increasingly tatty-looking, but much-lauded **Peckham Library** (122 Peckham Hill Street, 7525 2000), designed by Will Alsop.

Follow chaotic Rye Lane south to the recently smartened **Peckham Rye Common**, an airy stretch with ornamental gardens. At the top, Honor Oak and Forest Hill look down over suburban south-east London and Kent. The **Horniman Museum** (*see below*) is the best reason for taking to these hills.

Horniman Museum

100 London Road, SE23 3PQ (8699 1872/www.horniman.ac.uk). Forest Hill rail/363, 122, 176, 185, 312, 356, P4, P13 bus. **Open** 10.30am-5.30pm daily. **Admission** free; donations appreciated. **Credit** MC, V.

Tea trader Frederick J Horniman assembled a great number of curiosities in this culturally active art nouveau museum, left to the people of London in 1901. In the main collection, in the Natural History Gallery, skeletons, pickled animals, stuffed birds and insect models in old-fashioned glass cases are all presided over by a plump stuffed walrus on a centre plinth. The African Worlds Gallery has Egyptian mummies, ceremonial masks and a huge Ijele masquerade costume. Be sure to visit the fabulous Apostle clock on the gallery above the Natural History collection; when it chimes four o'clock, 11 apostles come out and bow to the central Jesus,while the 12th, Judas, turns away. Newly opened in 2006 is a £1.5m basement aquarium with more than 250 different species of animals and plants in seven distinctive zones. The collections are complemented by a regular programme of films, concerts, talks and children's workshops. Outside, there is a spacious café and lovely gardens with an animal enclosure.

Dulwich & Crystal Palace

Crystal Palace, East Dulwich, Herne Hill, North Dulwich or West Dulwich rail.

Upscale **Dulwich Village**, with its pretty park (once a favourite duelling spot), is home to a historic boys' public school, founded by the actor Edward Alleyn in 1616, and the **Dulwich Picture Gallery** (*see below*). West of it, Herne Hill is like a halfway point between posh, smug Dulwich and multicultural **Brixton** (*see p181*).

The **Crystal Palace**, built by Joseph Paxton for the Great Exhibition in Hyde Park in 1851, was subsequently moved here, and made Sydenham a tourist attraction – until the glittering structure burned down in 1936. The original terrace arches and the sphinx from the exhibition's Egyptian-themed area can still be seen. When **Crystal Palace Park** was laid out in the 1860s, part of it was given over to the world's first **Dinosaur Park**, created by Benjamin Waterhouse-Hawkins and depicting a journey through prehistory via life-size dinosaur statues. Restored in 2003, these prehistoric beasts pose menacingly around a freshly landscaped tidal lake, not far from the replanted **Hornbeam Maze**. The **Crystal Palace Museum** (Anerley Hill, SE19 2BA, 8676 0700, www.crystalpalacemuseum.org.co.uk), opened by volunteers each weekend, has a display on the 1851 Great Exhibition. A small John Logie Baird display marks its status as the birthplace of television. Its display on the Great Exhibition includes Victorian artefacts from the original Hyde Park production, as well as video and audio presentations about the great glass building and the Baird Television Company, which had studios at Crystal Palace.

Dulwich Picture Gallery

Gallery Road, SE21 7AD (8693 5254/www.dulwichpicturegallery.org.uk). North Dulwich or West Dulwich rail. **Open** 10am-5pm Tue-Fri; 11am-5pm Sat, Sun. **Admission** £4; £3 concs; free under-16s, students, unemployed, disabled. **Credit** MC, V.

Described by the *Sunday Telegraph* as the 'most beautiful small art gallery in the world'. Sir John Soane's neo-classical building, which inspired the National Gallery's Sainsbury Wing and the Getty Museum in Los Angeles, was England's first public art gallery (1814). Inside is a roll-call of the greats: Rubens, Van Dyck, Cuyp, Poussin, Rembrandt, Gainsborough, Raphael and Reynolds. Shows for 2007 include 'Canaletto in England' (until 15 April), with many loans from private collections.

Rotherhithe

Rotherhithe tube.

Nestling in the loop of the Thames opposite Wapping and the Isle of Dogs, Rotherhithe was a shipbuilding village, with the mariners' church of **St Mary's Rotherhithe** (*see p176*) at its heart. The Pilgrim ship, the *Mayflower*, sailed from here in 1620. Today the filled-in docks contain smart homes – a proposed development in Downtown Road is currently causing political controversy – but an atmospheric slice of old Rotherhithe remains in the conservation area and its rickety waterside pubs such as the Mayflower. Here you'll find St Mary's and the **Brunel Engine House & Tunnel Exhibition** (*see p176*).

The **Norwegian Church & Seaman's Mission** lie at the mouth of Rotherhithe's road tunnel, not completed until 1908, many years after Brunel's successful excavations. The number of Scandinavian churches, including a Finnish one with a sauna at 33 Albion Street (7237 1261), is a relic of Rotherhithe's links with Nordic sailors dating back to the Vikings. Across Jamaica Road, **Southwark Park**, London's oldest municipal park, has a community art gallery (7237 1230, www.cafegalleryprojects.com, open 11am-4pm Wed-Sun), an old bandstand, a landscaped lake and playgrounds.

Brunel Engine House & Tunnel Exhibition

Brunel Engine House, Railway Avenue, SE16 4LF (7231 3840/www.brunelenginehouse.org.uk). Rotherhithe tube. **Open** 11am-5pm daily. *Tours* by appointment only. **Admission** £2; £1 concs; £5 family; free under-5s. **No credit cards**.

This exhibition, refurbished for the bicentenary of Isambard Kingdom Brunel in 2006, describes the joint venture between father Marc Isambard Brunel and son to build the first ever tunnel under a river. All is set in the original red-brick engine house, under which the tunnel is still in use – as part of the London Underground. The guided tour is certainly worthwhile. By the river, an award-winning sculpture garden is the scene of a popular annual summer playscheme and just a few hundred yards across the river from Millwall, the launch site of Brunel's last project, the monster ship *Great Eastern*. **Photo** *p174*.

St Mary's Rotherhithe

St Marychurch Street, SE16 4JE (7967 0518). Rotherhithe tube. **Open** by appointment. **Admission** free.

Unless you're attending a service, all St Mary's treasures have to be viewed through the glass door. This beloved community church, completed in 1715, was built by the sailors and watermen of the parish. The style of the church, with wooden frame and barrel roof, suggests it was built by a shipwright, and all over are reminders of the area's links with the sea. *Mayflower* captain Christopher Jones was buried here in 1622. Grinling Gibbons contributed work to the beautifully carved reredos in the sanctuary, while the communion table in the Lady Chapel is made from timber salvaged from the warship *Fighting Temeraire*, the painting of which, by Turner, hangs in the National Gallery.

Greenwich

Cutty Sark DLR for Maritime Greenwich or Greenwich DLR/rail.

Greenwich welcomes visitors with a wealth of maritime attractions and one of the most wonderfully sited parks in London. As well as the **Royal Observatory** (*see p178*) and the **Ranger's House** (*see p178*), with the unusual **Fan Museum** nearby (*see p177*), **Greenwich Park** offers a sweeping panoramic view. Up at the Wolfe Monument you can take in **Queen's House** (*see p178*), the **National Maritime Museum** (*see p177*) and the Old Royal Naval College.

Greenwich earned its reputation when it was a playground for Tudor royalty. Henry VIII and his daughters Mary I and Elizabeth I were born here – Greenwich Palace was Henry's favourite residence. It fell into disrepair under Oliver Cromwell, then William and Mary designated it the Royal Naval Hospital. It is now the **Old Royal Naval College** (*see p178*).

Walking past it, keeping the river to your left, you reach the Thames-lapped **Trafalgar Tavern** (*see p234*), haunt of Thackeray, Dickens and Wilkie Collins, and the **Cutty Sark Tavern** (4-6 Ballast Quay, 8858 3146), which dates to 1695. Near the DLR stop, its station revamped with a new Novotel hotel and cocktail bar on the forecourt, is Greenwich Pier. Every 15 minutes at peak times the Thames Clipper commuter boat (0870 781 5049, www.thamesclippers.com) shuttles to central London. Nearby, in the shadow of the **Cutty Sark** (*see below*), the **Greenwich Tourist Information Centre** (0870 608 2000, www.greenwich.whs.org.uk) is a useful port of call.

A short walk away, shoppers swarm round **Greenwich Market** and film buffs head for the plush **Greenwich Picturehouse Cinema** (180 Greenwich High Road, 0870 755 0065), with its members' screening room.

To the north sits the forlorn **Millennium Dome**, slated for sport and leisure development (*see p177* **Doh!me**). To the south lie the grassy expanses of upmarket **Blackheath**. Smart restored Georgian homes and stately pubs surround the heath, where some of the world's earliest sports clubs started: Royal Blackheath Golf in 1745, Blackheath Hockey in 1861 and Blackheath Football (actually rugby) in 1862. Down the slope cluster the bars, shops and restaurants comprising Blackheath Village, the focus for social activity.

Cutty Sark

King William Walk, SE10 9HT (www.cuttysark.org.uk). Cutty Sark DLR/Greenwich DLR/rail.

Built to last 30 years when launched on the Clyde in 1869, the world's last surviving tea clipper went some 130 years before almost collapsing completely. Sat for decades in Greenwich dry dock as a tourist sight after record-breaking service on the South China Seas, the *Cutty Sark* will be enjoying a complete overhaul until October 2008 after a long campaign to save her. During the £25m, two-year restoration, the ship will be suspended 10ft off the ground for visitors to see shipwrights and their trainees at work. For much of this time (from April 2007) an exhibition centre will detail the history and revamping of the ship, with live webcams focused on the work next door. Hard-hat tours will be available on request. A café and restaurant are being set up too. Once reopened 5ft from the ground, the ship will have a new keel and main deck, accessed by lift, with a small auditorium for concerts. Below will be an exhibition space and gallery. The main attraction, though, remains the ship herself, an icon from the age of sail. Along with the captain's original navigational instruments and memorabilia related to Robert Burns, whose poem gave her her name, is a colourful collection of merchant figureheads donated when she opened to the public in 1957.

Fan Museum

12 Crooms Hill, SE10 8ER (8305 1441/8293 1889/ www.fan-museum.org). Cutty Sark DLR/ Greenwich DLR/rail. **Open** 11am-5pm Tue-Sat; noon-5pm Sun. **Admission** £4; £3 concs; £10 family; free under-7s; OAPs, disabled free 2-5pm Tue. **Credit** MC, V.

The world's most important single collection of fans is housed in a pair of restored Georgian townhouses dating back to 1721. It features more than 3,500 hand-held folding fans from every period from the 11th century on, although the permanent collection contains only a fraction; rarer items are put on display in themed exhibitions rotating every four months. You can also wander around the beautiful Orangery with its murals and exquisite furnishings, overlooking a Japanese garden.

National Maritime Museum

Romney Road, SE10 9NF (8858 4422/information 8312 6565/tours 8312 6608/www.nmm.ac.uk). Cutty Sark DLR/Greenwich DLR/rail. **Open** *July, Aug* 10am-6pm daily. *Sept-June* 10am-5pm daily. *Tours* phone for details. **Admission** free; donations appreciated. **Credit** (shop) MC, V.

Opened in 1937, this colonnaded complex comprises the National Maritime Museum, Queen's House (*see p178*) and Royal Observatory and Planetarium (*see p178*), and a collection of some two million items. The nation's seafaring history is covered in great depth over three floors, including the world's largest store of maritime art, cartography, ship's models, flags, instruments and costumes. Of the permanent galleries, 'Explorers' is devoted to pioneers of sea travel and includes a chilling *Titanic* display,

Doh!me

A dictionary definition of the phrase 'white elephant', stuck out on the Greenwich peninsula, the Dome is as controversial now as it was when the green light was given for the millennial project by the then Conservative government in 1996. The Tories envisioned a showcase structure in which to celebrate 2000, perhaps on similar lines to their happy memories of the post-war Festival of Britain and its regeneration of the South Bank. Then they lost the election the following year.

Incoming prime minister Tony Blair, despite pleading from several of his leading MPs, took the ball and ran with it – right out of the ballpark. The world's largest single-roofed structure, 365 metres (around 1,200 feet) in diameter, one for every day of the year (wasn't 2000 a leap year?). Yellow support towers, 12 in number, of similar temporal significance. What were they thinking?

What it all meant was a bloody big place with nothing to put in it once the party hats had been swept away and half the estimated number of 12 million visitors had attended incongruous, ill-conceived exhibits over the 12 months thereafter. On 31 December 2000, the Dome closed.

Since then, little – on home soil at least – has been of such costly embarrassment to the Labour government as the Dome. Every political figure that goes near ends up coated in doo-doo thicker than the toxic sludge that once covered the former gasworks site. Deputy PM John Prescott, chairman of the committee that oversaw the sale of the Dome to a consortium including the Anschutz Entertainment Group, had to 'fess up to 'conflict-of-interest' socialisings with billionaire boss Philip Anschutz on his Colorado ranch – dressed in his newly gifted £600 cowboy suit. Anschutz has made no secret of its desire to build a supercasino on the site.

Also with its hat in the ring is O_2, the UK mobile phone company that bought the naming rights from Anschutz. Its plan is to transform the Dome into a 20,000-capacity indoor sports arena. The scheduled opening date for O_2 is late 2007, the first event pencilled in being the Festival of Scouting (100 years, folks!). The funding and underwriting for a perhaps more attractive proposition, the treasures of King Tutankhamen – the last time they will ever leave Egypt – is dependent on Anschutz's riches. The Egyptians won't be losing sleep if it doesn't happen: in the only memorable event to have taken place here in 2000, thieves tried to steal an exhibition of precious diamonds. On the agenda thereafter are gymnastics, for the 2012 Olympic Games and the 2009 World Championships, as well as the basketball and trampolining elements of the 2012 Games.

Meanwhile, the Greenwich peninsula, whose redevelopment was the very reason for the go-ahead ten years ago, is at last under scrutiny. Greenwich Council has so far pencilled in some £600m of funding to develop the half square mile site, claiming it will create 24,000 jobs in the next 18 years. As well as the sports arena, it plans a waterfront leisure complex and large-scale conference centre. Central to such a budget, again, is the casino. Without it, the council's plans shrink considerably.

Eltham Palace. *See p180.*

where grainy launch footage is juxtaposed with ghostly wreck images; 'Passengers' is a history of the cruise holiday, with a cabin mock-up and hilarious old footage of luxury ocean travel. Upstairs, the 'All Hands' gallery provides interactive fun.

Old Royal Naval College

Greenwich, SE10 (8269 4747/group tours 8269 4791/www.oldroyalnavalcollege.org.uk). Cutty Sark DLR/Greenwich DLR/rail. **Open** 10am-5pm daily. *Tours* by arrangement. **Admission** free. **Credit** (shop) MC, V.

Sir Christopher Wren's 1696 neo-classical buildings were originally a hospital, then a naval college and are now part of the University of Greenwich and Trinity College of Music. The public are allowed into the rococo chapel and Painted Hall – a tribute to William and Mary that took Sir James Thornhill 19 years to complete. The chapel has free organ recitals on the first Sunday of each month. A modest visitor centre features an exhibition on Greenwich history and the story of the naval hospital. The college runs events and there's an ice rink outside in winter.

Queen's House

Romney Road, SE10 9NF (8312 6565/www.nmm.ac.uk). Cutty Sark DLR/Greenwich DLR/rail. **Open** 10am-5pm daily (last entry 4.30pm). *Tours* noon, 2.30pm. **Admission** free; occasional charge for temporary exhibitions. *Tours* free. **Credit** (over £5) MC, V.

This handsome Palladian abode, intended for James I's wife and passed on, unfinished, to Charles I's queen, Henrietta Maria, was a labour of love for Inigo Jones. It was completed in 1640. The beautiful, square entrance hall, with its gallery, elaborate painted ceiling and panels, and the elegant, spiral Tulip Staircase segue into the Orangery, which affords sweeping views over undulating Greenwich Park. Today the house is mainly a showcase for the National Maritime Museum's fine-art collection, with paintings by Gainsborough, Hogarth and Reynolds. In the Tudor Room is a display of items – thimbles, a syringe and leather shoe – salvaged from Henry VIII's doomed ship the *Mary Rose*.

Ranger's House

Chesterfield Walk, SE10 8QX (8853 0035/www.english-heritage.org.uk). Blackheath rail or Cutty Sark DLR/53 bus. **Open** *Mar-Sept* 10am-5pm Mon-Wed, Sun. *Oct-Dec* group bookings only. **Admission** £5.30; £2.70-£4 concs; free under-5s. **Credit** MC, V.

This Georgian villa dating back to 1723, occupied by aristocrats and minor royals, became the official residence of the Greenwich Park Ranger in 1815. Today it houses the treasures of diamond magnate Julius Wernher, 12 rooms of sculpture, tapestries, paintings and Renaissance jewellery.

Royal Observatory & Planetarium

Greenwich Park, SE10 9NF (8312 6565/www.rog.nmm.ac.uk). Cutty Sark DLR/Greenwich DLR/rail. **Open** 10am-5pm daily (last entry 4.30pm). *Tours* phone for details. **Admission** free. *Tours* free. **Credit** MC, V.

This Observatory – built by Christopher Wren for Charles II in 1675 – straddles the Prime Meridian Line, with one foot in each hemisphere. The exhibition in this historic building is a history of celestial study and its relation to sea travel, part of a £15m project entitled 'Time and Space', launched in 2006. Among the astrolabes, sextants and hourglasses are

timepieces belonging to John Harrison, who discovered accurate measurement of longitude thanks to work here with Astronomer Royal Edmund Halley, of comet fame. A new, state-of-the-art planetarium opens in spring 2007, with an education centre, a gallery dedicated to space and, still in place, the largest refracting telescope in the country.

Charlton & Woolwich

Charlton, Woolwich Arsenal or Woolwich Dockyard rail.

Until 1872 Charlton was famous for the rowdy Charlton Horn Fair – a gift to the people from King John as recompense for seducing a local miller's wife. Today Horn Fair Park boasts historic manor **Charlton House** (*see below*) and a lido, one of the few 50-metre open-air swimming pools in London. Further north, Maryon Park takes you up towards Woolwich and the **Thames Barrier** (*see below*).

Woolwich may soon enjoy a revival thanks to improved transport connections: the terminus for the Thames Clipper riverline service into town, a DLR station by 2008 and, after a long public campaign, a station on the high-speed Crosslink service slated for 2015. Many still use the free Woolwich car ferry (8921 5786); on the north shore, you'll find **North Woolwich Old Station Museum** (*see p170*).

Established in Tudor times as the country's main source of munitions, the **Woolwich Arsenal** stretched 32 miles along the river by World War I; by then it employed 72,000 people and had its own internal railway system. Much of the land was sold off during the 1960s, but thankfully the main section, with its beautiful cluster of Georgian buildings, has been preserved and is now open to the public as **Firepower**, the impressive artillery museum (*see below*). For more on the arsenal, visit the **Greenwich Heritage Centre** (Artillery Square, Royal Arsenal, SE18 4DX, 8854 2452; closed Mon, Sun).

Charlton House

Charlton Road, SE7 8RE (8856 3951/www.greenwich.gov.uk). Charlton rail/53, 54, 380, 422 bus. **Open** *Library* 2-7pm Mon, Thur; 10am-12.30pm, 1.30-5.30pm Tue, Fri; 10am-12.30pm, 1.30-5pm Sat. *Toy library* 10.30am-12.30pm, 1.30-3.30pm Mon, Tue, Fri. *Tearooms* 9am-5pm Mon-Fri. **Admission** free.

From the outside, this Jacobean manor house looks like the grandest of stately homes – which it once was. Built in 1612, it housed the tutor of Henry, eldest son of James I. These days it's a library and community centre, but glimpses of its glorious past can be seen in the creaky oak staircase, marble fireplaces and its mulberry tree, which dates back to 1608. It overlooks Charlton Park and two walled gardens, including the recently opened Peace Garden with its centrepiece sculpture, *The Portage*.

Firepower

Royal Arsenal, SE18 6ST (8855 7755/www.firepower.org.uk). Woolwich Arsenal rail. **Open** *Nov-Mar* 10.30am-5pm Fri-Sun (last entry 3.30pm). *Apr-Oct* 10.30am-5pm Wed-Sun (last entry 3.30pm). **Admission** £5; £2.50-£4.50 concs; free under-5s; £12 family; group rates available on request. **Credit** MC, V.

This Royal Artillery Museum is the first attraction in the development of the large former Royal Arsenal site. It's an entertaining introduction to the Gunners, ranging from primitive catapults to nuclear warheads. Visitors are treated to a short film in the Breech Cinema, before being bombarded by the sounds, smoke and searchlights of multimedia presentation 'Fields of Fire'. In the Gunnery Hall, you can get up close to all sorts of artillery, including anti-aircraft guns, anti-tank weapons and missile launchers. The Real Weapons gallery has an interactive exhibition on how guns work, which uses ammo such as table tennis balls. Kids love the first-floor Command Post, with its climbing wall, air-raid shelters and paintball gallery. Special events take place throughout the year, including a grand display on Bonfire Night.

Thames Barrier Information & Learning Centre

1 Unity Way, SE18 5NJ (8305 4188/www.environment-agency.gov.uk). North Greenwich tube/Charlton rail/180 bus. **Open** *Apr-Sept* 10.30am-4.30pm daily. *Oct-Mar* 11am-3.30pm daily. **Admission** *Exhibition* £1.50; 75p-£1 concs; free under-5s. **Credit** MC, V.

The key player in London's flood defence system looks like a row of giant metallic shark's fins spanning the 1,700ft of Woolwich Reach. The barrier is the world's largest adjustable dam and was built in 1982 at a cost of £535m; since then it has saved London from flooding 95 times. The small Learning Centre shows which parts of London would be submerged if it stopped working. Time your visit to see the barrier in action: every September there's a full-scale testing, with a partial test closure once a month (ring for dates). The best way to see the barrier is by boat (trips from Greenwich can be booked all year round on 8305 0300 or 8858 3996), although there are also great views from Thames Barrier Park (*see p170*) on the other side of the river, which is easily reached by public transport (it's right by Pontoon Dock station on the Docklands Light Railway).

Further afield

Watling Street, the old pilgrims' road out of London en route to Canterbury, is now the A207 and the villages it once passed through are London suburbs, such as **Bexleyheath**. This was where artist, writer and socialist William Morris (1834-96) chose to settle in **Red House** (*see below*), the home designed for him by young architect Philip Webb. A short walk from Red House, in gracious Danson Park, lies **Danson Mansion**, an 18th-century Palladian villa, restored by the Bexley Heritage Trust (01322 526574) and open to visitors at certain times. More award-winning gardens, this time containing a Tudor mansion, are at nearby **Hall Place** (Bourne Road, Bexley, Kent, DA5 1PQ, 01322 526574, www.hallplace.com).

South of the pilgrims' way, **Eltham** was known to Geoffrey Chaucer, who served as the clerk of works during improvements to **Eltham Palace** (*see below*) in the reign of Richard II. The poor clerk was mugged on his way to work there. Today there is white, working-class Eltham, marked by the infamous racially motivated murder of Stephen Lawrence in 1993, and historic Eltham, in which the Eltham Society endeavours to renovate attractions such as the award-winning grounds of **Well Hall Pleasaunce**, with its centrepiece Tudor barn restaurant (Well Hall Road, 8850 5145), formal gardens and waterfall.

Paths in the area link with the **Green Chain Walk** (8921 5028, www.greenchain.com), a 40-mile network of walking and cycling routes starting near the **Thames Barrier** (*see p179*) and ending at **Crystal Palace** (*see p175*), taking in ancient woodland along the way. Heading further south into Kent, the village of **Chislehurst** has Druids' caves (8467 3264, www.chislehurst caves.co.uk) to tempt day-trippers underground.

Eltham Palace

Court Yard, SE9 5QE (8294 2548/www.elthampalace.org.uk). Eltham rail. **Open** *Apr-Oct* 10am-5pm Mon-Wed, Sun. *Nov-Dec* 10am-4pm Mon-Wed, Sun. *Feb-Mar* 10am-4pm Mon-Wed, Sun. Closed week before Christmas-end of Jan. **Admission** *House & grounds* (incl audio tour) £7.60; £3.80-£5.70 concessions; £19 family; free under-5s. *Grounds only* £4.80; £2.40-£3.60 concs; free under-5s. **Credit** MC, V.

The palace was acquired by Edward II in 1305 and was home to kings and queens, including a young Henry VIII, until the royal party decamped to Greenwich in the 15th century. But the palace's draw lies in the 1930s additions, a country residence commissioned by super-rich society couple Stephen and Virginia Courtauld to complement their Grosvenor Square townhouse. Though the palace is often cited as one of London's art deco gems, influences include Venetian palaces, classical temples, Parisian salons and Swedish modernism. The Courtaulds also took advantage of all the latest technological gadgetry: a clock that received a time signal direct from Greenwich, loudspeakers that could pipe music throughout the ground floor and a centralised vacuum cleaner system. Decorative highlights include the block-printed wallpaper featuring Kew Gardens in the master bedroom, the black-and-white laquerwork in the art deco dining room and the caged sleeping quarters decorated with bamboo forest murals of Mah-Jongg, the Courtauld's pet ring-tailed lemur, bought from Harrods.

Of the original royal building, the Great Hall, with stained glass and hammer-beam roof, remains. In the grounds there is also a beautiful 15th-century stone bridge over a moat, probably built by Edward IV, and further medieval ruins. The extensive grounds have been carefully restored to a 1930s design, complete with a sunken rose garden and rock garden with water cascades. The traditional tearoom and shop also have a 1930s flavour. **Photo** *p178*.

Red House

Red House Lane, Bexleyheath, Kent DA6 8JF (8304 9878/www.nationaltrust.org.uk). Bexleyheath rail then 15min walk or taxi from station. **Open** (pre-booked guided tour only) 11am-4.15pm Wed-Sun & bank holiday Mondays (last tour 3.30pm). Closed 13 Jan-14 Feb. **Admission** £6; £3 concs; £15 family; National Trust members free.

This handsome red-brick house was purchased by the National Trust in 2003. It was built for William Morris, whose Society for the Protection of Ancient Buildings in 1877 eventually gave rise to the Trust itself. In furnishing Red House, Morris sought to combine his taste for Gothic romanticism with the need for practical domesticity. Beautifully detailed stained glass, tiling, paintings and items of furniture remain in the house, but there is plenty being uncovered in the continuing restoration work. Fundraising is an ongoing concern if Red House is to become once more 'the beautifullest place on earth', as Sir Edward Burne-Jones so clumsily put it.

South-west London

Mighty palaces, beautiful gardens and a dilapidated power station.

The Palm House at **Kew**. *See p185.*

The area embraced by the title south-west London is geographically vast and ethnically diverse. It takes in inner-city neighbourhoods such as Stockwell and Brixton, both best known for the colour brought by waves of immigration in the latter half of the twentieth century, and extends to the semi-rural, white and wealthy fringes of Richmond and Twickenham, with their stately homes and public-school sporting associations of boating, cricket and rugby.

Vauxhall, Stockwell & Brixton

Brixton or Vauxhall tube/rail/Stockwell tube.

The area now known as Vauxhall was, in the 13th century, home to a big house owned by one Falkes de Bréauté, a soldier rewarded for carrying out King John's dirtier military deeds. Over time Falkes' Hall became Fox Hall, Vaux Hall and finally Vauxhall.

Vauxhall's heyday was in the 18th century when the infamous Pleasure Gardens, built back in 1661, reached the height of their popularity. William Thackeray touched on the place's titillations in *Vanity Fair*, describing how the wealthy mingled briefly with the not-so-wealthy, getting into all kinds of trouble on so-dark-anything-could-happen 'lovers' walks.

The Gardens closed in 1859, and the area became reasonably respectable – all that remains is Spring Garden, behind popular gay haunt the **Royal Vauxhall Tavern** (372 Kennington Lane, 7737 4043). For a glimpse of old Vauxhall head to lovely, leafy **Bonnington Square**, a bohemian enclave thanks to squatter heritage. Down on the river, the benign-looking cream and emerald HQ of the Secret Intelligence Service (still almost universally referred to by its old title: MI6) dominates the waterfront, along with the green apartment towers at the adjacent St George's Wharf – a glitzy complex justifiably nicknamed the 'five ugly sisters'.

Hitting the headlines as the place where Jean Charles de Menezes was mistakenly shot by police in 2005, **Stockwell** – to the south of Vauxhall – is prime commuter territory, with little to lure visitors except some charming Victorian backstreets: Albert Square, Durand Gardens, Stockwell Park Crescent. Van Gogh lived briefly at 87 Hackford Road, but South Lambeth Road's **Little Portugal**, where Portuguese cafés, shops and tapas bars cluster, is a more rewarding destination.

South of Stockwell is **Brixton**, a lively hub of clubs and music, with a vibrant Afro-Caribbean community. It's an interesting, unpredictable area, with a vast street market, late-night clubs and live music venues. The main streets are modern and filled with chain stores, but attractive architecture is dotted here and there – check out the splendid 1911 **Ritzy Cinema** (*see p290*). Brixton's best-known street, **Electric Avenue**, was immortalised during the 1980s by Eddy Grant's eponymous song – it got its name when, in 1880, it became one of the first shopping streets to get electric lights. Other well-known songs provide potted histories of a more recent Brixton: the Clash's 'Guns of Brixton' and the Specials' 'Ghost Town' both recall the rage that swept through the area in the 1980s, 30 years after immigrants arrived from the West Indies at the government's

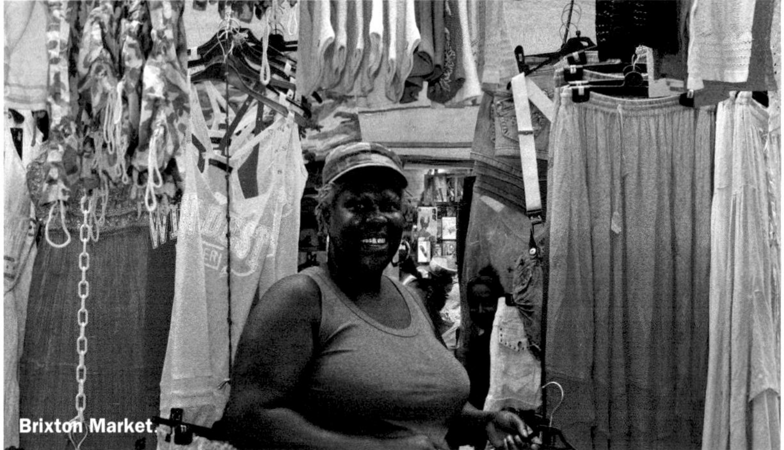

Brixton Market.

invitation only to find employment limited and their faces often unwelcome.

The riots of 1981 and 1985 around Railton Road and Coldharbour Lane left the area scarred for years. Start your Brixton wandering near the chaos of Brixton station, at the 21-year-old **Brixton Art Gallery** (35 Brixton Station Road, www.brixtonartgallery.co.uk), which has an excellent and constantly changing collection of contemporary art, in particular ethnic works. Turn a corner from the station and you're in the extended, colourful and noisy mess of **Brixton Market**, which sells everything from kebabs to jewellery and bright African clothes. Watch your handbag as you stroll – purse snatchers and pickpockets are a problem here – and always take a cab at night. Gentrification is under way, and the fringes of Brixton hold some pricey housing, but that hasn't pushed out the anarchists, criminals and artists that give the place its buzz and its edge.

Battersea

Battersea Park or Clapham Junction rail.

Battersea started life as an island in the Thames, before it was reclaimed by draining the marshes. Huguenots settled here from the 16th century and, prior to the Industrial Revolution, the area was mostly farmland. Today its dominant site is Sir Giles Gilbert Scott's magnificent four-chimneyed **Battersea Power Station**, which can be seen close up from all trains leaving Victoria station. Work started on it in 1929, and it closed in 1983. Too impressive to be destroyed, the power station is to become an entertainment complex, with controversy finally subsiding sufficiently to allow the developers to begin work in late 2006 (*see p187* **Tragically underpowered**).

Rather less industrial is nearby **Battersea Park**, with beautiful fountains, ponds and boating lakes. In 2004 it was relandscaped according to the original 19th-century plans, albeit with some modern additions left in place: a Peace Pagoda (built in 1985 to commemorate Hiroshima Day), a small zoo (7924 5826) and a tiny art gallery (the Pumphouse, 7350 0523) within a Grade II-listed building. The park extends to the Thames; from the wide riverside walk you can see both the elaborate **Albert Bridge** and the simpler, but lovely, **Battersea Bridge**, which was rebuilt in 1886-90 to designs by the man who solved London's sewage problems, Joseph Bazalgette.

Further along the river, west of the bridges, and adjacent to a development of high-tech luxury flats by architect Richard Rogers is **St Mary's Battersea** (Battersea Church Road), which oozes historical grace; here William Blake was married, American traitor Benedict Arnold was buried and JMW Turner came to paint the river.

Clapham & Wandsworth

Clapham Common tube/Wandsworth Common or Wandsworth Town rail.

In the 18th and 19th centuries Clapham had calmed down after the plague and became home to the wealthy upper classes and social reformers. But the coming of the railways meant that the posh folk upped sticks, and from 1900 the area fell into decline.

Nowadays the area is once again one of the capital's desirable addresses. **Clapham Common** provides an oasis of peace amid busy traffic, with **Holy Trinity Church**, which dates from 1776, at its perimeter. During the summer, the common switches into music festival mode, attracting thousands to a series of high-profile events. From Clapham Common station, turn north into the street called **The Pavement** – it leads to the pubs and shops of Clapham Old Town. Alternatively, head south to Abbeville Road, the centre of **Abbeville Village**, with its array of smart shops and cafés. The area to the west of the common is known as 'Nappy Valley', because of the many young middle-class families who reside there. They're out in force at weekends, pushing their prams. If you can fight your way between the baby carriages, head for the appealing shops, bars and restaurants along **Northcote Road**.

It's a short stroll from Northcote Road to **Wandsworth Common**, arguably prettier than Clapham Common. The north-west side is dominated by a Grade II-listed Victorian heap, the Gothic **Royal Victoria Patriotic Building**. Originally an asylum for orphans of the Crimean War, it became a POW camp during World War II; now it contains flats, workshops and a drama school.

Putney & Barnes

East Putney or Putney Bridge tube/Barnes or Putney rail.

If you want proof of an area's well-to-do credentials, count the rowing clubs: Putney has a couple of dozen. Putney Bridge is partly to blame, as its buttresses made it difficult for large boats to continue upstream, creating a stretch of water conducive to rowing. The Varsity Boat Race (*see p267*) has started in Putney since 1845.

Putney was chic in Tudor times, when it was home to Thomas Cromwell. In 1647 another Cromwell – Oliver – chaired the Putney Debates in **St Mary's Church**, at which the establishment of an English constitution was discussed. The river has good paths in either direction; heading west along the Putney side of the river will take you past the **WWT Wetland Centre** (*see below*), which lies alongside **Barnes Common**. The main road across the expanse, Queen's Ride, humpbacks over the railway line below. It was here, on 16 September 1977, that singer Gloria Jones drove her Mini off the road, killing her passenger (and boyfriend) T-Rex singer Marc Bolan. The slim trunk of the sycamore tree hit by the car is covered with notes, poems and declarations of love; steps lead to a bronze bust.

WWT Wetland Centre

Queen Elizabeth's Walk, SW13 9WT (8409 4400/ www.wwt.org.uk). Hammersmith tube then 283 bus/ Barnes rail/33, 72 bus. **Open** *Mar-Oct* 9.30am-6pm daily (last entry 5pm). *Nov-Feb* 9.30am-5pm daily (last entry 4pm). **Admission** £7.25; £4.50-£6 concessions; £18.50 family; free under-4s. **Credit** MC, V.

The trust that owns the Wetland Centre celebrates its 60th anniversary this year. Long may it continue: a mere four miles from central London, the WWT Wetland Centre feels worlds away. Quiet ponds, rushes, rustling reeds and wildflower gardens teem with bird life – some 150 species. Naturalists ponder its 27,000 trees and 300,000 aquatic plants, swoon over 300 varieties of butterfly, 20 types of dragonfly, four species of bat and the rare water vole. The site wasn't always this pretty. Until 1989 it consisted of four huge concrete reservoirs owned by the local water company. Then Sir Peter Scott transformed the marshy space into a unique wildlife habitat. There are weekly activities here virtually year-round, and the attractive visitors' centre has a decent café with an outdoor terrace.

Kew & Richmond

Kew Gardens or Richmond tube/rail/Kew Bridge rail.

Kew's big appeal is its vast and glorious **Royal Botanic Gardens** (*see p185*), whose peace is only disturbed by the planes that fly over en

route to Heathrow. The **National Archives** – formerly the Public Records Office – are housed here too, a repository for everything from the Domesday Book to recently released government documents. The place is always full of people researching family trees.

Kew itself has a rarified air, with leafy streets that lead you into a quaint world of teashops, tiny bookstores and gift shops, a sweet village green, ancient pubs and pleasant riverpaths.

Originally known as the Shene, the wealthy area of **Richmond** about 15 minutes' walk west down Kew Road, has been linked with royalty for centuries: Edward III had a palace here in the 1300s, and Henry VII loved it so much he built a palace here in 1501, naming it Richmond after his favourite earldom. Elizabeth I spent her last summers here too. Ultimately, the whole neighbourhood took the palace's name, although the building itself is long gone – all that's left is a gateway on **Richmond Green**. Once the site of royal jousting tournaments, the green is less noble now, but it's still surrounded by gorgeous pre-Victorian architecture.

On its east side medieval alleys (such as Brewer's Lane) with ancient pubs tucked into every corner lead to the traffic-choked high street. The **Church of St Mary Magdalene**, on Paradise Road, is a blend of architectural styles from 1507 to 1904. A short walk away in Richmond's Old Town Hall, the small **Museum of Richmond** (Whittaker Avenue, 8332 1141, www.museumofrichmond.com, closed Mon & Sun) has exhibits on the town's development. Nearby, the riverside promenade is eminently strollable and dotted with pubs; the **White Cross** (*see p236*), which has been here since 1835, has a special 'entrance at high tide' – the river floods regularly. The 13 arches of **Richmond Bridge** date from 1774 – this is the oldest surviving crossing over the Thames. The bridge has fine sweeping river views.

Royal heritage invariably means parkland, and the four square miles of **Richmond Park** make it London's largest park, a vestige of the area's once-dominant oak woodland. The park provides a natural habitat for free-roaming herds of red and fallow deer. Within its bounds are the fine Pembroke Lodge, childhood home to philosopher Bertrand Russell and now a café, and the Palladian splendour of White Lodge.

Royal Botanic Gardens (Kew Gardens)

Kew, Richmond, Surrey TW9 3AB (8332 5655/ information 8940 1171/www.kew.org). Kew Gardens tube/rail/Kew Bridge rail/riverboat to Kew Pier. **Open** *Late Mar-Aug* 9.30am-6.30pm Mon-Fri; 9.30am-7.30pm Sat, Sun. *Sept-late Oct* 9.30am-6pm daily. *Late Oct-early Feb* 9.30am-4.15pm daily. *Early Feb-late Mar* 9.30am-5.30pm daily. **Admission** £11.75; £8.75 concessions; free under-16s. **Credit** AmEx, MC, V.

Kew's lush, landscaped beauty represents the pinnacle of our national gardening obsession. From the early 1700s until 1840, when the gardens were given to the nation, these were the grounds for two royal residences – the White House and Richmond Lodge. The 18th-century residents Henry II and Queen

The Buddhists of suburbia

Wimbledon has invariably been a stamping ground for high-rolling Londoners looking for a bit of peace and quiet. But in 1982 the area found itself at a different point on the karmic wheel when the gorgeous **Buddhapadipa Temple** (14 Calonne Road, Wimbledon Parkside, SW19 5HJ, 8946 1357, www.buddhapadipa.org) was formally recognised as a temple in the Thai Buddhist tradition.

It was designed by Praves Limparangsi, then an architect in the fine arts department of Thailand's Ministry of Education. It took three years to build, and its inauguration ceremony was hosted by the elder sister of the Thai king. At the time, it was the only Thai temple to have been built in Europe.

The peaceful, pretty Uposotha Hall, with its four gabled roofs, is a treat to visit. The warm and sweet-smelling Shrine Room is dominated by a golden statue of Buddha, a copy of the Buddhasihing in Bangkok's National Museum. Other Buddha statues, presented to the temple and Queen Elizabeth II, also reside here. Brightly coloured murals depicting the life of the Buddha, painted by 14 artists from Thailand, also dominate the gaze in this room.

Visitors are welcome to look around when the hall is not in use, but should be mindful of a few rules of etiquette: shoes must be removed before entering the temple (leave them outside), visitors are not permitted to touch the monks and the soles of your feet must never face the Buddha. After you've had a peek inside, it's worth wandering around the hall's landscaped grounds and ornamental lake, flower garden, orchard and grove.

The temple also runs a number of intriguing classes, courses and meditative retreats.

Caroline were enthusiastic gardeners; Caroline was particularly fond of exotic plants brought back by voyaging botanists. In the mid 1700s Lancelot 'Capability' Brown began designing an organised layout for the property, using the plants Caroline had collected. Thus began the extraordinary collection that today attracts hundreds of thousands of visitors every year. Covering more than half a square mile, Kew feels surprisingly big – pick up a map at the ticket office and follow the handy signs. Any visit to Kew should take in the two huge 19th-century greenhouses, filled to the roof with plants – some of which have been here as long as the fanciful glass structures. The sultry Palm House holds tropical plants: palms, bamboo, tamarind, mango and fig trees, not to mention fragrant hibiscus and frangipani. The Temperate House features *Pendiculata sanderina*, the Holy Grail for orchid hunters, with petals 3ft long. Also of note is the Princess of Wales Conservatory, which houses ten climate zones under one roof. For an interesting perspective on 17th-century life, head to Kew Palace – the smallest royal palace in Britain. Once little more than an addition on the now-gone White House, it's a lovely structure that is now open after years of renovation. Also open 'for the first time in recent memory' is the 163ft pagoda, completed in 1762. Those who climb the 253 steps (it costs £3) are rewarded with views of Battersea Power Station and, to the far east and north respectively, Canary Wharf and Wembley Stadium. Queen Charlotte's Cottage, with its dazzling springtime bluebell garden, repays return visits year after year. The Rose Garden and Woodland Garden are the stuff of fairytales, while Redwood Grove has a treetop walkway 33ft off the ground. Hungry from all the walking? There are tearooms scattered throughout. **Photo** *p181*.

Wimbledon

Wimbledon tube/rail.

Beyond the world-famous tennis tournament, Wimbledon is little but a wealthy and genteel suburb. Turn left out of the station on to the uninspiring **Broadway**, and you'll wonder why you bothered. So turn right instead, climbing a steep hill lined with huge houses. At the top is **Wimbledon Village**, a trendy little enclave of posh shops, eateries and some decent pubs.

From here you can hardly miss **Wimbledon Common**, a huge, wild, partly wooded park, criss-crossed by paths and horse tracks. In an eccentric touch, the common has a **windmill** (Windmill Road, 8947 2825) that houses a tearoom and hands-on milling museum. If tea doesn't meet your needs, there are two decent pubs close to the common: the **Fox & Grapes** (9 Camp Road, 8946 5599) and **Hand in Hand** (6 Crooked Billet, 8946 5720). East of the common lies **Wimbledon Park**, with its boating lake and the All England Lawn Tennis Club and **Wimbledon Lawn Tennis Museum** (*see below*). Two other attractions should be visited while you're here – pleasant **Cannizaro Park** and the mesmerising **Buddhist temple** on Parkside (*see p185* **The Buddhists of suburbia**).

Wimbledon Lawn Tennis Museum

Centre Court, All England Lawn Tennis Club, Church Road, SW19 5AE (8946 6131/www.wimbledon.org/museum). Southfields tube/39, 93, 200, 493 bus. **Open** 10.30am-5pm daily; ticket holders only during championships. **Admission** (incl tour) £14.50; £11-£13 concessions; free under-5s. **Credit** AmEx, MC, V.

Highlights at this popular museum on the history of tennis include a 200° cinema screen that allows you to find out what it's like to play on Centre Court and a re-creation of a 1980s men's dressing room, complete with a 'ghost' of John McEnroe. Visitors can also get to grips with rackets, check changing tennis fashions and enjoy a behind-the-scenes tour.

Further south-west

If the water level allows, follow the river from Richmond on a pastoral walk west to **Petersham**, home to Petersham Nurseries with its brilliant café (Church Lane, off Petersham Road, 8605 3627, www.petershamnurseries.com), or take in one of the grand country mansions, among them **Ham House** (*see below*) and, in Marble Hill Park, **Marble Hill House** (*see p188*). Next to the park stands **Orleans House Gallery** (*see p188*).

Further along, the river meanders around Twickenham (home to **Twickenham Stadium**, *see p188*) to the evocatively named **Strawberry Hill** (8240 4114), home of Horace Walpole, who pretty much invented the Gothic novel with *The Castle of Otranto* in 1764. Several miles further along, after a leisurely trip through suburban Kingston, the river arrives at the splendid **Hampton Court Palace** (*see p188*) – but if you want to head this far, you'd be better taking the train from Waterloo or, for that extra fillip of adventure, the boat.

Ham House

Ham, Richmond, Surrey TW10 7RS (8940 1950/www.nationaltrust.org.uk/hamhouse). Richmond tube/rail then 371 bus. **Open** *Gardens* 11am-6pm or dusk if earlier Mon-Wed, Sat, Sun. *House* 1-5pm Mon-Wed, Sat, Sun. Closed Nov-Mar. **Admission** *House & Gardens* £8; £4 concessions; £19 family; free under-5s. *Gardens only* £4; £2 concessions; £9 family; free under-5s. **Credit** MC, V.

Built in 1610 for one of James I's courtiers, Thomas Vavasour, this lavish red-brick mansion is full of period furnishings, rococo mirrors and ornate tapestries. Detailing is exquisite, down to a table in the dairy with sculpted cows' legs. The restored formal

Tragically underpowered

Forget the Houses of Parliament, St Paul's or Tower Bridge – if there's one iconic building that perfectly represents London, it is Battersea Power Station. It has graced album covers (notably Pink Floyd's *Animals*), vodka ads and films (Ian McKellen's *Richard III*, Monty Python's *The Meaning Of Life*, Michael Radford's *1984*), and its instantly recognisable silhouette repeatedly pops up as you move around the capital.

The first half of the power station was completed in 1933, the second half followed in 1953. The architect was the already famous Sir Giles Gilbert Scott, designer of the Bankside power station that eventually became Tate Modern. When Battersea was complete it was reckoned to be the largest brick building in Europe. It provided 20 per cent of the capital's electricity – until it closed on 31 October 1983.

Since being decommissioned, the power station has lain vacant. In the 1980s there was a scheme to turn the place into a Disneyland-style attraction; the place was gutted, the east wall demolished and the roof removed. Then work stopped. Since 1983 the building has sat roofless and rain-lashed, held up with a rusting framework of iron and surrounded by a windswept wasteland.

At present all 1.6 million square feet of it are in the hands of Hong Kong Chinese property company Parkview International who are to subject the site to a £1.5bn transformation into what their brochure describes as 'a major international meeting place, a creative hub and a place of celebration, fun and entertainment'. This means the usual moneyspinners: offices, apartments, hotels, subterranean auditorium, public park, piazzas and conference facilities. The main work is being masterminded by Nicholas Grimshaw, famous for his graceful glass canopy at Waterloo International.

Critics decry the plans as uninspired and inappropriate. Battersea is in the middle of nowhere and it's going to take more than a few high-end high-street retailers and hotel rooms to tempt anybody to make the trek. Compared to the singular vision that transformed sister power station Bankside into one of London's major tourist attractions, Parkview's proposal is underwhelming, if not tragically inadequate. However, there may be little point fretting about the plans as there have been so many aborted projects and promises since 1983 that it's almost too radical to imagine that something might one day be done with Battersea.

grounds attract the most attention: there's a lovely trellised Cherry Garden dominated by a statue of Bacchus. The tearoom in the old orangery turns out historic dishes (lavender syllabub, for instance) using ingredients from the Kitchen Gardens.

Hampton Court Palace

East Molesey, Surrey KT8 9AU (0870 751 5175/ 24hr information 0870 752 7777/advance tickets 0870 753 7777/www.hrp.org.uk). Hampton Court rail/riverboat from Westminster or Richmond to Hampton Court Pier (Apr-Oct). **Open** *Palace* Apr-Oct 10am-6pm daily. Nov-Mar 10am-4.30pm daily (last entry 1hr before closing). *Park* dawn-dusk daily. **Admission** *Palace, courtyard, cloister & maze* £12.30; £8-£10 concessions; £36.40 family; free under-5s. *Maze only* £3.50; £2.50 concessions. *Gardens only* £4; £2.50-£3 concessions. **Credit** AmEx, MC, V.

It may be a 30min train ride from central London, but this spectacular palace, once owned by Henry VIII, is well worth the trek. It was built in 1514 by Cardinal Wolsey, the high-flying lord chancellor, but Henry liked it so much he seized it for himself in 1528. For the next 200 years it was the focal point of English history: Elizabeth I was imprisoned in a tower here by her jealous and fearful elder sister Mary I; Shakespeare gave his first performance to James I here in 1604; and, after the Civil War, Lord Protector Oliver Cromwell was so besotted by the building he ditched his puritanical principles and moved in to enjoy its luxuries.

Centuries later, the rosy walls of the palace still dazzle. Its vast size can be daunting, so it's a good idea to take advantage of the costumed guided tours. If you decide to go it alone, start with King Henry VIII's State Apartments, which include the Great Hall, noted for its splendid hammer-beam roof, beautiful stained-glass windows and elaborate religious tapestries; in the Haunted Gallery, the ghost of Catherine Howard – Henry's fifth wife, executed for adultery in 1542 – can reputedly be heard shrieking. The King's Apartments, added in 1689 by Sir Christopher Wren, are notable for a splendid mural of Alexander the Great, painted by Antonio Verrio. The Queen's Apartments and Georgian Rooms feature similarly elaborate paintings, chandeliers and tapestries. The Tudor Kitchens are great fun, with their giant cauldrons, fake pies and blood-spattered walls (no vegetarians in those days). More spectacular sights await outside, where the exquisitely landscaped gardens include perfectly sculpted trees, peaceful Thames views, and the famous Hampton Court maze (in which, incidentally, it's virtually impossible to get lost).

Marble Hill House

Richmond Road, Twickenham, Middx TW1 2NL (8892 5115/www.english-heritage.org.uk). Richmond tube/rail/St Margaret's rail/33, 90, 490, H22, R70 bus. **Open** *Apr-Sept* 10am-2pm Sat; 10am-5pm Sun; group visits Mon-Fri by request. *Oct* 10am-4pm daily. *Nov-Mar* by request. **Admission** £4; £2-£3 concessions; free under-5s. **Credit** MC, V.

King George II spared no expense to please his mistress, Henrietta Howard. Not only did he build this perfect Palladian house (1724) for his lover, he almost dragged Britain into a war while doing so: by using Honduran mahogany to construct the grand staircase, he sparked a diplomatic row with Spain. It was worth it. Over the centuries, luminaries such as Alexander Pope, Jonathan Swift and Horace Walpole have been entertained in the Great Room; Pope and Swift are said to have drunk the cellar dry. Picnic parties are welcome, as are sporty types (there are tennis, putting and cricket facilities). A programme of concerts and events keeps things busy in the summer. Ferries regularly cross the river to neighbouring Ham House (*see p186*).

Museum of Rugby/ Twickenham Stadium

Twickenham Rugby Stadium, Rugby Road, Twickenham, Middx TW1 1DZ (8892 8877/ www.rfu.com). Hounslow East tube then 281 bus/Twickenham rail. **Open** *Museum* 10am-5pm Tue-Sat; 11am-5pm Sun (last entry 4.30pm). *Tours* 10.30am, noon, 1.30pm, 3pm Tue-Sat; 1pm, 3pm Sun. **Admission** £10; £7 concessions; £34 family. **Credit** AmEx, MC, V.

The impressive Twickenham Stadium is the home of English rugby union. Tickets for international matches are extremely hard to come by (*see p332* **Getting in**), but the Museum of Rugby offers some compensation. Tours take in the England dressing room, the players' tunnel and the Royal Box. A permanent collection of memorabilia, selected from 10,000 pieces that make up the museum's collection, charts the game's development from the late 19th century. It includes the oldest surviving international rugby jersey, the Calcutta Cup (awarded annually to the winners of the Scotland–England match) and the recently acquired Melrose Winners Medal – awarded to one of the winners of the first ever seven-a-side contest at Melrose in 1883. Until 1 April 2007 is a special exhibition, 'From War To Tour', a look at how South Africa went from warring nation to a rugby tour de force in just five years.

Orleans House Gallery

Riverside, Twickenham, Middx TW1 3DJ (8831 6000/www.richmond.gov.uk/orleans_house_gallery). Richmond tube then 33, 490, H22, R68, R70 bus/ St Margaret's or Twickenham rail. **Open** *Apr-Sept* 1-5.30pm Tue-Sat; 2-5.30pm Sun. *Oct-Mar* 1-4.30pm Tue-Sat; 2-4.30pm Sun. **Admission** free.

Secluded in pretty gardens, this Grade I-listed riverside house was constructed in 1710. It was built for James Johnson, Secretary of State for Scotland, and named after the Duke of Orleans, Louis-Philippe, who lived in exile here between 1800 and 1817, before returning to post-Napoleonic France to claim the throne. The house was partially demolished in 1926, but the building retains James Gibbs's neo-classical Octagon Room, which houses the Richmond-upon-Thames collection, a soothing pictorial record of the local countryside since the early 1700s.

West London

Riverside walks, high-end shops and a surprising garden.

Fine houses on **Kensington Square**.

London's wealthy have always favoured the west; it is upwind and upriver, which is no small attraction when you think that London was the world's most populous city from 1831, yet it had only 15 miles of sewers even by mid-century. In 1858 a combination of a hot, dry summer and new sewers discharging directly into the Thames caused the Great Stink, a smell so bad that Parliament covered its windows with sheets soaked in lime chloride. So it is that the rich built where the air was cleaner and, for these were the days when river traffic was still important, the water was cleaner as well. And there the rich remain – Kensington and Holland Park probably still boast more millionaires per square mile than any other part of London, while Fulham is home to newer money. No one could accuse Hammersmith of being wealthy but it is well worth a visit for the riverside walk west toward Chiswick, location of more fine old country mansions.

Kensington & Holland Park

Maps p396 & p398

High Street Kensington or Holland Park tube.

Kensington makes an appearance in the Domesday survey of 1086 as Chenesit and the earliest settlement was, most likely, around the still existing but often rebuilt St Mary Abbots Church. For the next 800 years the area remained rural, and the rich and the noble began to build grand retreats that offered an escape to the country without the tiresome necessity of days spent travelling to a far-off estate. Despite these aristocratic residences, the population at the start of the 19th century was less than 10,000. Dramatic growth occurred during the next century: by 1901 there were 176,628 residents.

Today **Kensington High Street** is one of London's main shopping streets, although not one suited to tight purses. Off the High Street are streets and squares lined with handsome 19th-century houses, most of which remain homes. Linking with Notting Hill to the north (*see p130*), **Kensington Church Street** has many antiques shops selling furniture so fine you could probably never use what you'd bought. **St Mary Abbots**, at the junction of Church Street and High Street, is a wonderful Victorian neo-Gothic church, built by Sir George Gilbert Scott in 1869-72 on the site of the original 12th-century church. Past worshippers include Sir Isaac Newton and William Wilberforce. As well as beautiful stained-glass windows, it has London's tallest spire (278 feet).

Across the road is the striking art deco ex-department store **Barkers** (63 Kensington High Street), now an outlet for fashion brands such as Karen Millen and Monsoon. South down Derry Street, past the entrance to the **Roof Gardens** (*see p191*) six storeys above, is **Kensington Square**, which boasts one of London's highest concentrations of blue plaques. The writer William Thackeray lived at No.16, the painter Edward Burne-Jones at No.41 and at No.18 John Stuart Mill's maid made her bid for 'man from Porlock' status by using Carlyle's manuscript of *The French Revolution* to start the fire. Mrs Patrick Campbell, actress and famous beauty, resided at No.33. She was as well known for her exploits off stage as on, but eventually settled into 'the deep peace of the

Leighton House.

double bed as opposed to the hurly burly of the chaise longue'. The houses here, though much altered, date from when the square was developed in 1685, and – hard to believe now – were until 1840 surrounded by fields.

Further to the west is one of London's finest green spaces, **Holland Park**; Holland Walk, which runs along the eastern edge of the park between Holland Park Avenue and Kensington High Street, is one of the most pleasant paths in central London. At the heart of the park is **Holland House**, originally built in 1606. Six years later, King James complained after a stay that he had been kept up by the wind blowing through the walls; the house was more seriously ventilated by World War II bombs. Left derelict, it was bought by the London County Council in 1952 and the east wing now houses the most exclusively sited youth hostel in town. In summer you can watch open-air theatre and opera on the front terrace of the house, while the garden ballroom houses the Belvedere, a Marco Pierre White restaurant.

There are three lovely formal gardens near the house and, a little further away, the Japanese-style Kyoto Garden. It has huge koi carp sucking noisily at the pool's surface and a bridge at the foot of a waterfall. Elsewhere rabbits hop about (dogs must be kept on the lead) and peacocks stroll with the confidence of all beautiful creatures. Weary parents can let their under-fives roll around a safe playground, while older siblings get to enjoy the adventure playground with its various tree walks and rope swings.

Near Holland Park are two more historic houses: **Leighton House** and **Linley Sambourne House** (for both, *see below*).

Leighton House

12 Holland Park Road, W14 8LZ (7602 3316/ www.rbkc.gov.uk/leightonhousemuseum). High Street Kensington tube. **Open** 11am-5.30pm Mon, Wed-Sun. *Tours* 2.30pm Wed, Thur; by appointment other times (min group of 12). **Admission** £3; £1 concessions. **Credit** MC, V. **Map** p398 A9.

From without, the house of the artist Frederic, Lord Leighton (1830-96), presents a sternly Victorian façade of red-brick respectability. But inside it's like a scene from *The Arabian Nights*, complete with tinkling fountain, oriental mosaics and a golden mosaic frieze. Instead of a kohl-eyed Scheherazade, visitors must make do with Lord Leighton's classical paintings, which are scattered through the house, along with those of contemporaries Edward Burne-Jones, John Everett Millais and Sir Lawrence Alma-Tadema. The garden offers a serene resting place, and an incongruous statue of a horseback American Indian spearing a rearing serpent.

Linley Sambourne House

18 Stafford Terrace, W8 7BH (Mon-Fri 7602 3316 ext 300/Sat, Sun 7938 1295/www.rbkc.gov.uk/linley sambournehouse). High Street Kensington tube. **Open** *18 Mar-10 Dec* by appointment only. **Admission** £6; £4 concessions; £1 children. **Credit** MC, V. **Map** p398 A9.

The home of cartoonist Edward Linley Sambourne was built in the 1870s and has almost all of its original fittings and furniture. Tours must be booked in advance; they last 90mins, with weekend tours led by an actor in period costume.

Roof Gardens

99 Kensington High Street, W8 5SA (7937 7994/ www.virgin.com/roofgardens). High Street Kensington tube. **Admission** free. **Map** p398 B9.

Babylon had its Hanging Gardens and in 1936 the vice-president of Barkers, Trevor Bowen, determined that Kensington should have its Roof Gardens. Despite being 70 years old, the gardens have remained largely unknown outside the world of corporate entertaining. However, so long as they are not booked for an event (telephone first), the gardens are open to all: simply take the lift up six storeys and emerge to find water gurgling into a brook. Follow the stream through a woodland garden, complete with trees rooted 100ft above the ground, past pools and over bridges, and round to formal Tudor and Spanish gardens. To complete the exotic scene a pair of Lesser Chilean flamingos sieve for crustaceans alongside a pair of pochards and Piers the pintail (ducks for the non-birders).

Earl's Court & Fulham

Maps p398

Earl's Court, Fulham Broadway or West Brompton tube.

Earl's Court sells itself short, grammatically speaking. Once the site of the courthouse of both the Earl of Warwick and the Earl of Holland, it should be Earls' Court. The 1860s saw Earl's Court move from rural hamlet to investment opportunity as the Metropolitan Railway arrived. Twenty years later it was much as we see today, except for the fast-food joints. The terraces of grand old houses are mostly subdivided into bedsits and cheap hotels, many inhabited by returning descendants of those once sentenced to deportation by their Lordships' court, hence the area's old nickname: Kangaroo Valley. These days the transient population is more weighted towards Eastern Europe and South America.

In 1937 the **Earl's Court Exhibition Centre** was built, at the time the largest reinforced concrete building in Europe – a phrase that surely makes one's heart sing. The centre hosts a year-round calendar of events, from trade shows, pop concerts (Pink Floyd built and then tore down *The Wall* here) to the Ideal Home Show. Two minutes south down Warwick Road is an altogether different venue, with an equally impressive pedigree: the **Troubadour** (263-267 Old Brompton Road, 7370 1434, www.troubadour.co.uk) is a 1950s coffeehouse, whose downstairs club hosted Jimi Hendrix, Joni Mitchell, Bob Dylan and Paul Simon in the 1960s. It still has a full programme of live music, poetry and comedy, plus an excellent deli and gallery on the ground floor.

West along Warwick Road are the gates of **Brompton Cemetery**. It's full of magnificent monuments commemorating the famous and infamous, including suffragette Emmeline Pankhurst, shipping magnate Sir Samuel Cunard and, his grave marked by a lion, boxer 'Gentleman' John Jackson who taught Lord Byron to box. Sioux chief Long Wolf was buried here in 1892; he died touring with Buffalo Bill's Wild West Show. His body was moved back to Pine Ridge, South Dakota, in 1997. The quiet of the cemetery is regularly disturbed at its southern end by neighbouring **Stamford Bridge**, home of Chelsea FC. Craven Cottage, the home of west London's other Premiership football team, Fulham FC, is west of here, at the northern end of the park that surrounds **Fulham Palace** (*see below*), once the Bishop of London's official residence.

Fulham Palace & Museum

Bishop's Avenue, off Fulham Palace Road, SW6 6EA (7736 3233). Putney Bridge tube/14, 74, 220, 414, 430 bus. **Open** noon-4pm Mon, Tue; 11am-2pm Sat; 11.30am-3.30pm Sun. **Tours** 2pm 2nd & 4th Sun of mth. **Admission** free; under-16s must be accompanied by an adult. *Tours* £4; free under-16s. **No credit cards**.

The Bishop of London first had a residence in Fulham in the 11th century (when it must have counted as his country retreat), but the present building was built in the early 16th century, with later additions. After the bishop moved out in 1973 the local council took over the running and maintenance of the building, keeping some of the palace as offices but also opening a museum. The Heritage Lottery Fund contributed a £2.5m grant and by the start of 2007 the refurbished museum should be open for

Sightseeing

visitors. The botanical gardens, planted with rare and exotic trees, are open to all except dogs and those wanting to kick a football.

Shepherd's Bush & Hammersmith

Goldhawk Road, Hammersmith or Shepherd's Bush tube.

Shepherd's Bush and its central green do not offer much in the way of sights to visitors – the green being a fairly nondescript triangular patch of grass hemmed in by traffic. However, the **Bush** (*see p343*) and **Shepherd's Bush Empire** (*see p313*), a fine theatre and music venue respectively, might make a visit worthwhile depending on what's playing. Just to the north, in **White City**, is what was once a home of British excellence and is now the centre of the British mediacrity, the BBC. Further up the road is the expansive green space of Wormwood Scrubs and the rather more restrictive confines of its prison.

Walk south down Shepherd's Bush Road and you'll see Hammersmith's dominating architectural feature: the grey concrete of the flyover. The A4 – the Great West Road – is one of the main trunk routes into London, with thousands of cars and lorries thundering along it each day. In the flyover's shadow, Hammersmith Broadway was once a bus garage but has had the obligatory multi-million-pound redevelopment. Make it over the road and you'll find one of London's most notable rock venues, the **Hammersmith Apollo**, which was immortalised in the title of Motörhead's 1981 live album *No Sleep 'til Hammersmith*. The Apollo started life in 1932 as the Gaumont Palace Hammersmith, became legendary as the Hammersmith Odeon (where Bowie killed off Ziggy), turned into the Labatt's Apollo, teased us as the Hammersmith Apollo, flirted with another brewer as the Carling Apollo, then settled back down with its current name.

Not far away, **Hammersmith Bridge**, the city's oldest suspension bridge, is a green and gold hymn to the strength of Victorian ironwork. Had a pedestrian not thrown the bomb in the river, the IRA might have succeeded in blowing the bridge up in 1939. They tried again in 2000, but all the explosion achieved was further snarling up local traffic for the months it took for the bridge to be repaired. There's a lovely walk west along the Thames Path that takes in a clutch of historic pubs including the **Blue Anchor** and the **Dove** (for both, *see p236*); walking in the opposite direction leads to the **Riverside Studios** (*see p291*), a cinema, theatre and arts venue, and to the endlessly excellent **River Café** (*see p223*).

BBC Television Centre Tours

Wood Lane, W12 7RJ (0870 603 0304/www.bbc.co.uk/tours). White City tube. **Tours** by appointment only Mon-Sat. **Admission** £8.95; £7.95 concessions; £6.50 10-16s, students; £25 family. No under-9s. **Credit** MC, V.

Tours of the BBC include visits to the news desk, the TV studios and the Weather Centre, though you must book ahead to secure a place. To be part of a TV audience, apply for free tickets at www.bbc.co.uk/whatson/tickets. Which is about the only thing that comes free from the BBC. According to its 2005 report, the Corporation costs British taxpayers £2.9bn annually in licence fees, plus a further £225m via Foreign Office grants.

Chiswick

Turnham Green tube/Chiswick rail.

To walk the riverside path from Hammersmith to Chiswick is to learn a lesson in transport history. To your left the Thames would once have resounded with the swearing of boatmen – it is now quiet apart from the occasional rowing eight. To your right is the Great West Road and its constant stream of traffic. Above there's the main flight path into Heathrow Airport. And finally you, on foot. Should walking produce a thirst, never fear. As Benjamin Franklin said, 'Beer is proof that God loves us and wants us to be happy' and just off Chiswick Mall on Chiswick Lane South is the **Fuller's Brewery**. There's been a brewery here since Elizabethan times, so the brewers have had some time to get things right: the London Pride is always a winner. Tours of the brewery can be arranged by calling 8996 2063.

After refreshments, cross (under) the A4 to **Hogarth's House** (*see p193*) and the rather grander **Chiswick House** (*see below*). A bus might be necessary to reach **Kew Bridge Steam Museum** (*see p193*), although it is possible to return to the river path after visiting Chiswick House; the wonderful **Kew Gardens** (*see p185*) are just over the bridge. Further yet upstream is **Syon House** (*see p193*), which is situated in Syon Park. If you make the journey out here, the park has more than enough attractions to fill an expensive day: in addition to the house itself, you can visit the **Tropical Forest** animal sanctuary (8847 4730, £3.75-£5) and the **Butterfly House** (8560 7272, www.londonbutterflyhouse.com, £3.95-£5).

Chiswick House

Burlington Lane, W4 2RP (8995 0508/www.english-heritage.org.uk). Turnham Green tube then E3 bus to Edensor Road/Hammersmith tube/rail then 190

The Great Conservatory at **Syon House**.

bus/Chiswick rail. **Open** *Apr-Oct* 10am-5pm Wed-Fri, Sun; 10am-2pm Sat. Closed Nov-Mar. **Admission** £4; £3 concessions; £2 5-16s; free under-5s. **Credit** MC, V.

Richard Boyle, third Earl of Burlington, designed this lovely Palladian villa in 1725 as a place to entertain the artistic and philosophical luminaries of his day, including Alexander Pope, Jonathan Swift, George Frideric Handel and Bishop Berkeley. The grounds contain many stately cedars of Lebanon in a fine 18th-century design.

Hogarth's House

Hogarth Lane, Great West Road, W4 2QN (8994 6757). Turnham Green tube/Chiswick rail. **Open** *Apr-Oct* 1-5pm Tue-Fri; 1-6pm Sat, Sun. *Nov, Dec, Feb, Mar* 1-4pm Tue-Fri; 1-5pm Sat, Sun. **Admission** free; donations appreciated. **No credit cards**.

From the garden (a tranquil island next to the A4) you can still appreciate this place as the country retreat of the 18th-century painter, engraver and social commentator, William Hogarth. On display are most of his engravings, including *Gin Lane*, *Marriage à la Mode* and a copy of *Rake's Progress*.

Kew Bridge Steam Museum

Green Dragon Lane, Brentford, Middx TW8 0EN (8568 4757/www.kbsm.org). Gunnersbury tube/ Kew Bridge rail/65, 237, 267, 391 bus. **Open** 11am-5pm Tue-Sun. **Admission** *Tue-Fri* £4.25; £3.25 concessions; £2 5-15s; free under-5s; £10 family. *Sat, Sun* £6.50; £5.50 concessions; free under-15s. **Credit** MC, V.

Housed in a Victorian pumping station, the Steam Museum explores the city's use of water. For some, the highlight is a walk through a section of the London ring-main waterpipe; for others it's when the engines are in steam (weekends, 11am-5pm).

Syon House

Syon Park, Brentford, Middx TW8 8JF (8560 0883/ www.syonpark.co.uk). Gunnersbury tube/rail then 237, 267 bus. **Open** *House* (24 Mar-31 Oct only) 11am-5pm Wed, Thur, Sun. *Gardens* (year-round) 10.30am-dusk daily. *Tours* by arrangement. **Admission** *House & gardens* £8; £4-£7 concessions; £18 family. *Gardens only* £4; £2.50 concessions; £9 family. *Tours* free. **Credit** MC, V.

The Percys, Dukes of Northumberland, were once known as 'the Kings of the North'. Syon House is their southern pad, sufficiently effete to have starred in Robert Altman's *Gosford Park*. The house stands on the site of a Bridgettine monastery, suppressed by Henry VIII in 1534. The nun's father confessor, Richard Reynolds, refused to accept the king as head of the Church and was executed. Perhaps he had the last laugh: when Henry died, his body was brought here en route to Windsor. During the night the coffin burst open and in the morning it was discovered dogs had been busy with the royal corpse. The building was converted into a house in 1547 for the Duke of Northumberland, its neo-classical interior created by Robert Adam in 1761; there's an outstanding collection of Regency portraits by the likes of Gainsborough. The gardens, by Capability Brown, are enhanced by the splendid Great Conservatory.

Sikh-ing a bargain? **Southall Market**.

Southall

Southall rail.

Head west to go east. A stroll up Southall's South Road (which runs north from the railway station) and along the Broadway might have you wondering if some unsuspected wormhole has deposited you in Chennai: honking car horns, blaring Bollywood music, open shopfronts disgorging vibrant rolls of cloth and shimmering saris, and the air heavy with the pungent smell of spices. All that's missing are wandering cows and persistent flies. This is London's Little India where, according to a study by the research organisation OriginsInfo, only 17.8 per cent of the areas's 70,000 residents have English names, the lowest proportion in the country.

Asians first started settling in the area, which is conveniently close to Heathrow, in the 1950s, although this first wave was composed mostly of men. Wives and families started arriving in the 1960s, mostly from the Punjab, and Sikhs still comprise the largest group in Southall, although there are also many Hindus and Muslims.

If the **Broadway** isn't subcontinental enough for you, then try **Southall Market**, off the High Street and opposite North Road. What's on sale varies by the day, from squawking poultry on Tuesday, to horses (honestly) on Wednesday, general bric-a-brac on Friday and then, on Saturday, pretty well everything else. Equally unmissable is to attend a show at the three-screen **Himalaya Palace** (*see p291*), a beautifully restored old movie house dedicated to Bollywood epics.

But it's the food that makes Southall special. **Madhu's** (39 South Road, 8574 1897) is one of the area's stars, with an Indo-Kenyan menu of food that's boldly spiced and expertly char-grilled. The best kebabs and superb yoghurt-based snacks can be had at the **New Asian Tandoori Centre** (114-118 The Green, 8574 2597), which is south of the station. Here the wholesome food is not only astonishingly cheap, but also as authentic as can be. There's even a Punjabi pub, the **Glassy Junction** (97 South Road, 8574 1626): all the trappings of a white working men's club – patterned carpet, pints of keg beer – plus the considerable boon of hot parathas. It's the only pub in the UK that accepts payment in rupees.

A short walk south of Southall railway station, the **Gurdwara Sri Guru Singh Sabha Southall** (Havelock Road, 8574 4311, www.sgsss.org) is the largest Sikh place of worship outside India. Its golden dome is visible from the London Eye in the east and Windsor Castle to the west; it also provides vegetarian food from the *langar*, communal kitchen, free to all visitors. Non-Sikh visitors are welcome, but must take off their shoes before entering and women must wear a headscarf – provided if you don't have one to hand. Enthroned within is the Guru Granth Sahib, the Sikh scripture and supreme spiritual authority of Sikhism; most unusually, the Guru Granth Sahib contains, in addition to the writings of the ten Sikh Gurus, extracts from other religions.

The suburb of Neasden, six miles north-east of Southall, has its own claim to British Asian fame. It is the site of the **Shri Swaminarayan Mandir temple** (105-119 Brentfield Road, 8965 2651, www.mandir.org), which is the largest Hindu temple outside India to have been built using traditional methods. To this end, nearly 5,000 tons of stone and marble were shipped out to India, where craftsmen carved it into the intricate designs that make up the temple. Then the temple was shipped, piece by piece, to England, where the gigantic jigsaw was assembled on site. The shining marble temple now stands incongruously close to one of IKEA's giant blue boxes.

Eat, Drink, Shop

Features

Restaurants & Cafés

Dine often and dine well – London is one of the world's best food cities. Really.

Roast, serving great British meals in the city's foodie heartland. *See p197.*

London still has its share of dowdy restaurants with indifferent food and sullen service, but you have to be very complacent or very unlucky to eat badly in London these days. The most welcome trend is the resurgence of pride in British ingredients and cooking. It all started with the **St John** (*see p198*), which opened in 1994; since then, various St John alumni have left to set up their own places, from gastropubs (**Anchor & Hope**, *see p197*) to DJ bars (**Medcalf**, *see p198*), all serving modern versions of British cooking. In the last year alone we've seen the excellent **Roast** (*see p197*), **National Dining Rooms** (*see p213*) and **Canteen** (*see p219*) open. Yes, over the past couple of years British food has become cool.

❶ Purple numbers given in this chapter correspond to the location of each restaurant and café as marked on the street maps. *See pp396-409.*

Other recent trends have been the surge of interest in steakhouses (exemplified by Piccadilly's **Gaucho**, *see p209*) and bistros, and a huge growth in the number of low-budget Korean restaurants. Asian food in general continues to improve and move upmarket.

The gastropub movement continues apace too – that is pubs that put as much emphasis on food as on drink. In fact, many gastropubs are restaurants with a big bar counter rather than anything resembling a traditional boozer. This is confirmed by the news that the UK's most over-exposed chef, Gordon Ramsay, is to open a restaurant in a pub in Limehouse, east London.

DOS AND DON'TS

It's always best to book in advance. At many places it's absolutely essential and at a select few (notably the Ivy, Nobu and anything connected with Gordon Ramsay) you're going to have to book weeks in advance. Some places are entirely non-smoking and others allow smoking anywhere, although this will change in summer

2007 when smoking will be banned in all public places. Tipping is standard practice: ten to 15 per cent is usual. Many restaurants now add this automatically to your bill, so check to avoid double-tipping.

We've listed a range of meal prices for each place. However, restaurants often change their menus, so these prices are only guidelines.

For the best places to eat with children, *see pp275-277*; for more on eating out in London, pick up the annual *Time Out London Eating & Drinking Guide* (£10.99) and *Time Out Cheap Eats in London* (£6.99).

The South Bank & Bankside

The best place to eat in London is **Borough Market** (*see p259* **Top five**), which is filled with stalls selling all kinds of wonderful food – shame that it's only open Friday and Saturday.

Fish

fish!

Cathedral Street, Borough Market, SE1 9AL (7407 3803/www.fishdiner.co.uk). London Bridge tube/rail. **Open** 11.30am-11pm Mon-Thur; noon-11pm Fri, Sat; noon-10.30pm Sun. **Main courses** £9.95-£19.95. **Credit** AmEx, DC, MC, V. **Map** p406 P8 ❶

Gleaming in glass and steel, fish! does very well out of affluent Borough Market food shoppers. The provenance of your dinner is indicated (the cod's Icelandic, the salmon organic, the vegetables come from the market over the road), the mode of preparation – battered, steamed, grilled – is up to you.

Fish & chips

Masters Super Fish

See p221 **Fish and chips**.

Gastropubs

Anchor & Hope

36 The Cut, SE1 8LP (7928 9898). Southwark or Waterloo tube/rail. **Open** 5-11pm Mon; 11am-11pm Tue-Sat; noon-5pm Sun. **Main courses** £9.80-£12.80. **Credit** MC, V. **Map** p406 N8 ❷

There are two problems: the A&H doesn't take bookings and it's always full. But persist: it is full because the food (seasonal British classics) is extremely good and the bar treats real ales and classic cocktails with appropriate respect. Come at 2pm or after 8.30pm and the crowds might have thinned.

Global

Baltic

74 Blackfriars Road, SE1 8HA (7928 1111/www.balticrestaurant.co.uk). Southwark tube/rail. **Open** noon-11pm Mon-Sat; noon-10.30pm Sun. **Main courses** *Bar* £3-£8. *Restaurant* £9-£15. **Credit** AmEx, MC, V. **Map** p406 N8 ❸

Thousands of amber shards aglow in a spectacular chandelier reference one of the Baltic region's major mineral exports, as well as providing a serious wow factor. Food is a modern take on central and eastern European cuisine, which means blinis, pickled and sozzled fish, and dumplings. The bar has a vast array of vodkas.

Modern British

Roast

The Floral Hall, Borough Market, Stoney Street, SE1 1TL (7940 1300/www.roast-restaurant.com). London Bridge tube/rail. **Open** 7-9.30am, noon-2.30pm, 5.30-10.30pm Mon-Fri; 8-10.30am, 11.30am-3.30pm, 6-10.30pm Sat; 9-11am, noon-3.30pm Sun. **Main courses** £13.50-£25. **Credit** AmEx, MC, V. **Map** p406 P8 ❹

The location is terrific – a big, airy atrium of a room with views of Borough Market below and trains passing above. The food also deserves wholehearted enthusiasm (predominantly well sourced meat and fish), and it's accompanied by an intriguing range of drinks, many of them also British. Breakfast here is a treat. **Photo** *p196*.

For here and now

Ambassador (*see p199*); **Arbutus** (*see p205*); **National Dining Rooms** (*see p213*); **Maze** (*see p211*).

For old-school dining

Simpson's Tavern (*see p198*); **Sweetings** (*see p198*); **Kettners** (*see p207*).

For drop-dead design

Hakkasan (*see p201*); **Yauatcha** (*see p207*); **Sketch** (*see p211*); **Amaya** (*see p215*).

For cheap but stylish

Canela (*see p202*); **Masala Zone** (*see p203*); **Busaba Eathai** (*see p205*); **Abeno Too** (*see p203*).

For eating where the locals eat

Carluccio's Caffè (*see p201*); **Inside** (*see p220*); **Wagamama** (*see p218*). *See also p216* **Good to go**.

For star-spotting

J Sheekey (*see p202*); **The Ivy** (*see p202*); **The Wolseley** (*see p211*); **Zuma** (*see p217*); **Sketch** (*see p211*).

Modern European

Oxo Tower Restaurant, Bar & Brasserie

Eighth floor, Oxo Tower Wharf, Barge House Street, SE1 9PH (7803 3888/www.harveynichols.com). Blackfriars or Waterloo tube/rail. **Open** 11am-11pm Mon-Sat; noon-10.30pm Sun. **Main courses** *Bar/brasserie* £10.25-£17. *Restaurant* £17.50-£26. **Credit** AmEx, DC, MC, V. **Map** p406 N7 5

This landmark venue commands striking views across the Thames – reserve a seat on the terrace if you want to make the most of it. Dinner times are very busy, but for lunch you can often book the same day. Food is of a high standard, although not especially ambitious.

Spanish

Tapas Brindisa

18-20 Southwark Street, SE1 1TJ (7357 8880/www.brindisa.com). London Bridge tube/rail. **Open** noon-11pm Mon-Thur; 9am-11am, noon-11pm Fri, Sat. **Tapas** £3-£8. **Credit** MC, V. **Map** p406 P8 6

The interior is basic, and you can't book ahead, but this class act beside Borough Market packs in the punters. Quality imported Spanish ingredients make for superb food and there's a sound selection of sherry and Spanish wine. For the associated Brindisa delis, *see p258.*

The City

British

Simpson's Tavern

382 Cornhill, EC3V 9DR (7626 9985). Bank tube/DLR. **Open** 11.30am-5pm Mon-Fri. *Food served* noon-3pm Mon-Fri. **Main courses** £6.50-£12.50. **Credit** AmEx, DC, MC, V. **Map** p407 Q6 7

A venerable City tavern (established 1757) in a tiny courtyard. The upstairs dining room, with its waft of Dickensian vittles from the smoky grill, has communal tables packed with former public schoolboys eager to remind themselves of what they used to eat. An essential City experience.

Fish

Sweetings

39 Queen Victoria Street, EC4N 4SA (7248 3062). Mansion House tube. **Open** 11.30am-3pm Mon-Fri. **Main courses** £10.50-£25.50. **Credit** AmEx, MC, V. **Map** p406 P6 8

In business since 1830 and settled on this site for a century, Sweetings is a City institution. Exceedingly popular with Square Mile suits (mainly male), it has a charmingly shabby and cramped interior. Scoff potted shrimps or fish pie from your stool at one of the high counters, washed down with a silver tankard of ale.

French

1 Lombard Street

1 Lombard Street, EC3V 9AA (7929 6611/www.1lombardstreet.com). Bank tube/DLR. **Open** 11am-11pm Mon-Fri. *Lunch served* noon-3pm, *dinner served* 6-10pm Mon-Fri. **Main courses** *Brasserie* £14.50-£27.50. *Restaurant* £27.50-£29.50. **Credit** AmEx, DC, MC, V. **Map** p407 Q6 9

By no means the only former banking hall to have been remodelled into a restaurant, 1 Lombard Street is set apart by its Michelin star. The rear restaurant is calm and secluded; the larger front brasserie more approachable and anchored by a circular bar benaeth a domed skylight. Food is terrific in both.

Mediterranean

Royal Exchange Grand Café & Bar

The Royal Exchange, EC3V 3LR (7618 2480/www.conran.com). Bank tube/DLR. **Open** 8-11am, 11.30am-10pm Mon-Fri. **Main courses** £6.50-£14.50. **Credit** AmEx, DC, MC, V. **Map** p407 Q6 10

Hidden from the street, this smart Conran venture mutates from calm breakfast haunt to lively cocktail bar. A mezzanine looks down on the action in the grand concourse with its oval bar. The food can be workaday, but the premises are among the grandest in London. Conran's understated and excellent new French restaurant Sauterelle (7618 2483) is also here.

Holborn & Clerkenwell

British

Medcalf

40 Exmouth Market, EC1R 4QE (7833 3533/www.medcalfbar.co.uk). Angel tube/Farringdon tube/rail/19, 38 bus. **Open** noon-11pm Mon-Thur, Sat; noon-12.30am Fri; noon-5pm Sun. **Main courses** £9.50-£14.50. **Credit** MC, V. **Map** p404 N4 11

Medcalf occupies long thin premises that used to be a butcher's. The very focused kitchen turns out a short, top-quality, regularly changing menu. Save room for dessert, and be sure to book: Exmouth Market is a gastro destination these days.

St John

26 St John Street, EC1M 4AY (7251 0848/4998/www.stjohnrestaurant.com). Farringdon tube/rail. **Open** 11am-11pm Mon-Fri; 6-11pm Sat. **Main courses** *Bar* £4-£15. *Restaurant* £12.70-£21.50. **Credit** AmEx, MC, V. **Map** p404 O5 12

The look of the internationally renowned home of 'nose to tail' dining is quite basic, but it is all in keeping with the ethos of the menu: simply described British dishes, incorporating all manner of offal, beautifully cooked. A more snacky version of the menu is served in the affable ground-floor bar.
Other locations: St John Bread & Wine, 94-96 Commercial Street, Spitalfields, E1 6LZ (7251 0848/www.stjohnbreadandwine.com).

Fish & chips

Fryer's Delight

See p221 **Fish and chips**.

French

Club Gascon

57 West Smithfield, EC1A 9DS (7796 0600). Barbican tube/Farringdon tube/rail. **Open** noon-2pm, 7-10pm Mon-Thur; noon-2pm, 7-10.30pm Fri; 7-10.30pm Sat. **Main courses** £8.30-£20. **Tapas** £6-£16.50. **Credit** AmEx, MC, V. **Map** p404 O5 ⓭

Club Gascon has quietly become one of London's consistently great restaurants. Sure, it has spun off a neighbouring wine bar (Cellar Gascon) and a deli-restaurant (Le Comptoir Gascon, 61-63 Charterhouse Street), but it remains low-key. The room is atmospheric, and the food artistically conceived and beautifully presented. Foie gras is the house speciality.

Gastropubs

Coach & Horses

26-28 Ray Street, EC1R 3DJ (7278 8990/www.thecoachandhorses.com). Farringdon tube/rail. **Open** 11am-11pm Mon-Fri; 6-11pm Sat; noon-4pm Sun. **Main courses** £10-£14. **Credit** AmEx, MC, V. **Map** p404 N4 ⓮

There's a gastropub on virtually every street in this part of town, but this congenial and thoughtfully updated old corner boozer (a former *Time Out* award winner) is a cut above the competition. It is as popular with after-work beer-hounds, as it is with diners sampling the daily changing, but always-appetising full menu.

Eagle

159 Farringdon Road, EC1R 3AL (7837 1353). Farringdon tube/rail. **Open** noon-11pm Mon-Sat; noon-5pm Sun. **Main courses** £8-£15. **Credit** MC, V. **Map** p404 N4 ⓯

It's the grandaddy of all gastropubs, regarded as having kicked off the radical notion of good food in pubs, but there's no suggestion the Eagle is shuffling into retirement. The place buzzes, with the chefs in the tiny kitchen area behind the bar kept busy delivering from a daily changing, blackboard menu of hob- and grill-based Med dishes. There's a good selection of beer, decent wines by the glass and bottle, and a laid-back vibe. Popular with staff at the *Guardian*, whose offices are just down the hill.

Modern European

Ambassador

55 Exmouth Market, EC1R 4QL (7837 0009/www.theambassadorcafe.co.uk). Angel tube/Farringdon tube/rail/19, 38 bus. **Open** 8.30am-10.15pm Mon-Fri; 11am-4pm Sat, Sun. **Main courses** £9.50-£17. **Credit** AmEx, MC, V. **Map** p404 N4 ⓰

This easygoing incarnation of an idealised bistro was a worthy runner-up for *Time Out*'s Best New Restaurant of 2006. You can just have a drink, or add a bar plate or two, or order a full meal from a short but tempting menu that is matched by an interesting wine list (with plenty by the glass). Breakfast is also served, plus brunch at weekends. When the weather permits, the restaurant spills out on to the pavement, continental style.

Smiths of Smithfield

67-77 Charterhouse Street, EC1M 6HJ (7251 7950/www.smithsofsmithfield.co.uk). Farringdon tube/rail. **Open** *Ground-floor bar/café* 7am-4.30pm Mon; 7am-5pm Tue-Fri; 10am-5pm Sat; 9.30am-5pm Sun. *Dining Room* noon-2.45pm, 6-10.45pm Mon-Fri; 6-10.45pm Sat. *Top Floor* noon-3pm, 6.30-10.45pm Mon-Fri; 6.30-10.45pm Sat; noon-3.45pm, 6.30-10.30pm Sun. **Main courses** £11.50. *Top Floor* £17-£28. **Credit** AmEx, DC, MC, V. **Map** p404 O5 ⓱

These four floors and 15,000sq ft (1,400sq m) of converted warehouse are unstoppable: the ground-floor bar (*see p227*) is said to serve more beer per square foot than any other in London (you can also eat breakfast, brunch and lunch down here). Like the spaces below it, the second-floor Dining Room carries an artfully industrial look, while the British-slanted Top Floor is quieter, calmer, classier. Expert cooking allows first-rate ingredients – meats, particularly – to shine.

North American

The Bar & Grill

2-3 West Smithfield, EC1A 9JX (7246 0900/www.barandgrill.co.uk). Farringdon tube/rail. **Open** noon-11pm daily. **Main courses** £6.75-£50. **Credit** AmEx, MC, V. **Map** p404 O5 ⓲

The Bar & Grill opened in 2005 with a rush of publicity for its 'Kobe' beef and big steaks. It offers all the usual cuts plus the fabled wagyu steak (£50 for 8oz – you can cheat and have a £16.95 wagyu steak burger). On Friday evenings, the cocktail bar is full-to-bursting with men slackening off their ties and women who've brought their heels to change into.

Spanish

Moro

34-36 Exmouth Market, EC1R 4QE (7833 8336/www.moro.co.uk). Farringdon tube/rail/19, 38 bus. **Open** 12.30-11.45pm Mon-Sat (last entry 10.30pm). **Tapas** £2.50-£12. **Main courses** £13.50-£17.50. **Credit** AmEx, DC, MC, V. **Map** p404 N4 ⓳

Having made its Spanish–North African food part of London's restaurant lexicon over the last ten years, Moro is still going strong. Expect to wait up to three weeks for a booking, although if you're prepared to settle for tapas at the long zinc bar you may be able to get a seat on the night. Note too that Moro is now open on Saturday lunchtimes, offering tasting menus with matching sherries.

Bloomsbury & Fitzrovia

Italian

Carluccio's Caffè

8 Market Place, W1W 8AG (7636 2228/www.carluccios.com). Oxford Circus tube. **Open** 7.30am-11pm Mon-Fri; 10am-11pm Sat; 10am-10pm Sun. **Main courses** £5.95-£12.95. **Credit** AmEx, MC, V. **Map** p408 U1 ⑳

With 15 branches around town this New York-style Italian deli chain may feel a bit more chain-like than it did a few years ago but it still pushes all the right buttons. The menu blends classic and innovative regional Italian food, plus a few daily specials. Eat inside, where pasta, wines and deli produce are for sale, or outside where there are plenty of pavement tables, weather permitting.

Other locations: throughout the city.

Sardo

45 Grafton Way, W1T 5DQ (7387 2521/www.sardo-restaurant.com). Warren Street tube. **Open** noon-3pm, 6-11pm Mon-Fri; 6-11pm Sat. **Main courses** £8.90-£18. **Credit** AmEx, MC, V. **Map** p400 J4 ㉑

Although it observes mainstream Italian aesthetics, there's an air of Sardinian separatism in this charming restaurant. Regional dishes such as spaghetti bottarga – a rich classic of fish roe and extra-virgin oil – are enhanced by an almost Greek array of grilled fish and lamb. There's an intriguing selection of good Sardinian wine, temptingly priced.

Other locations: Sardo Canale, 42 Gloucester Avenue, Camden, NW1 8JD (7722 2800).

Modern European

Villandry

170 Great Portland Street, W1W 5QB (7631 3131/www.villandry.com). Great Portland Street tube. **Open** *Bar* 8am-11pm Mon-Fri; 9am-11pm Sat. *Restaurant* noon-3pm, 6-10.30pm Mon-Fri; 11.30am-4pm, 6-10.30pm Sat; 11.30am-4pm Sun. **Main courses** *Bar* £9.50-£17.50. *Restaurant* £9-£19.50. **Credit** AmEx, MC, V. **Map** p400 H5 ㉒

Bar, restaurant, shop and lunch takeaway rolled into one: bustling Villandry has been a welcome breath of life in an otherwise dead part of town for a decade. Ingredients are carefully sourced and high quality, with decent choice for vegetarians.

Oriental

Hakkasan

8 Hanway Place, W1T 1HD (7907 1888). Tottenham Court Road tube. **Open** noon-12.30am Mon-Wed; noon-1.30am Thur-Sat; noon-midnight Sun. **Dim sum** £3.50-£16. **Main courses** £12.50-£48. **Credit** AmEx, MC, V. **Map** p408 W1 ㉓

We love the startingly beautiful Hakkasan, which remains one of London's best-looking restaurants. For dinner, you need to book well in advance, but for lunch on a weekday you can explore the innovative dim sum menu and spend a mere £15 per head. From the food to a cutting-edge cocktail list, this is a seminal London experience.

Roka

37 Charlotte Street, W1T 1RR (7580 6464/www.rokarestaurant.com). Goodge Street or Tottenham Court Road tube. **Open** noon-11pm Mon-Fri; 12.30-11pm Sat; 12.30-10.30pm Sun. **Main courses** £3.60-£21. **Credit** AmEx, DC, MC, V. **Map** p400 J5 ㉔

What started life as baby Zuma (*see p217*) has grown into a confident, vital operation serving some of London's best modern Japanese food. From a central grill kitchen surrounded by brown wooden benching, head chef Nic Watts and his team serve the likes of succulent chicken wings or expertly charred sea bream. Desserts are fun.

Spanish

Cigala

54 Lamb's Conduit Street, WC1N 3LW (7405 1717/www.cigala.co.uk). Holborn or Russell Square tube. **Open** noon-10.45pm Mon-Fri; 12.30-10.45pm Sat; noon-9.45pm Sun. **Main courses** £11-£19.50. **Tapas** £2-£8. **Credit** AmEx, DC, MC, V. **Map** p401 M4 ㉕

Chef-proprietor Jeff Hodges is an aficionado of classic Spanish cooking and it shows on the plate – although not in the clean-lined decor, which is blissfully free of Costa memorabilia. Fish and meat dishes are the stars, some served simply, others getting a twist of innovation. The wine list goes well beyond Rioja, with fine examples from regions on the rise.

Fino

33 Charlotte Street, entrance on Rathbone Street, W1T 1RR (7813 8010/www.finorestaurant.com). Goodge Street or Tottenham Court Road tube. **Open** noon-2.30pm, 6-10.30pm Mon-Fri; 12.30-2.30pm, 6-10.30pm Sat. **Tapas** £4-£15.50. **Credit** AmEx, MC, V. **Map** p400 J5 ㉖

One of a growing army of restaurants serving updated Spanish food in chic settings, Fino serves a bountiful, daily changing tapas menu in a smart, buzzing basement setting. Prices edge towards £10 for all but the most basic tapas, but you can expect an impeccable dining experience. **Photo** *p202.*

Salt Yard

54 Goodge Street, W1T 4NA (7637 0657/www.saltyard.co.uk). Goodge Street tube. **Open** noon-11pm Mon-Fri; 5-11pm Sat. **Tapas** £2.75-£8.50. **Credit** AmEx, MC, V. **Map** p400 J5 ㉗

This compact space is deftly furnished with a sleek, pared-down aesthetic of steely greys and chocolatey browns. The brief menu – divided into cold meats, bar snacks and tapas – and wine list demonstrate superb attention to detail, gathering the very best of Spain and Italy – corn-fed jamón ibérico and tangy chorizos meet delicate prosciuttos and herb-flecked salami. Continuously busy, for all the right reasons.

Covent Garden & the Strand

Cafés & brasseries

Canela

Thomas Neal Building, 33 Earlham Street, WC2H 9LS (7240 6926/www.canelacafe.com). Covent Garden tube. **Open** 9.30am-10pm Mon-Sat; 10am-8pm Sun. **Main courses** £6.50-£7.90. **Credit** MC, V. **Map** p409 X2 ㉘

Covent Garden doesn't have many interesting cafés, so Canela's worth seeking out. The high-ceilinged room with lots of natural light is an attractive showcase for an compelling mix of Portuguese and Brazilian snacks and baked dishes, such as *bacalhau à bràs* (made with salt cod, potatoes, eggs, onion and parsley) or *feijoada* (Brazilian black bean and pork stew). The cakes are a high point.

Fish

J Sheekey

28-32 St Martin's Court, WC2N 4AL (7240 2565/ www.caprice-holdings.co.uk). Leicester Square tube. **Open** noon-3pm, 5.30pm-midnight Mon-Sat; noon-3.30pm, 6pm-midnight Sun. **Main courses** £10.75-£35. **Credit** AmEx, DC, MC, V. **Map** p409 X4 ㉙

Sheekey's continues to earn its renown as London's star fish restaurant. Choose between immaculate restaurant rooms or a stool at the very handsome bar to peruse a plain-speaking menu, egalitarian enough to sit caviar beside jellied eels. The honeycomb ice-cream is one of the city's must-scoff desserts and service strikes the perfect balance of formality and friendliness. Book well in advance.

Fish & chips

Rock & Sole Plaice

See p221 **Fish and chips**.

Modern American

Joe Allen

13 Exeter Street, WC2E 7DT (7836 0651/ www.joeallen.co.uk). Covent Garden tube. **Meals served** noon-12.45am Mon-Fri; 11.30am-12.45am Sat; 11.30am-11.30pm Sun. **Main courses** £8-£16. **Set brunch** £18.50 2 courses, £20.50 3 courses incl drink. **Set meal** (noon-3pm Mon-Fri, 5-6.45pm Sat) £15 2 courses, £17 3 courses incl coffee. **Credit** AmEx, MC, V. **Map** p409 Z3 ㉚

A true West End institution and the prime spot for pre- and post-theatre dining. Not just audience members, but cast and crew gather here nightly. Food often seems an afterthought and it sometimes can feel as though the waiters are just killing time between auditions but the buzz is infectious.

Modern European

The Ivy

1 West Street, WC2H 9NQ (7836 4751/www. caprice-holdings.co.uk). Leicester Square tube. **Open** noon-3pm, 5.30pm-midnight Mon-Sat; noon-3.30pm, 5.30pm-midnight Sun. **Main courses** £9.75-£38.50. **Credit** AmEx, DC, MC, V. **Map** p409 X3 ㉛

Behind its old-fashioned latticed windows and the legend of impossible-to-book tables groaning with celebs, the Ivy is elegant and vivacious, serving mainstream Mod European classics augmented by

a satisfying dose of earthiness and laudable seasonality. Expect to book weeks ahead, although – with a bit of phone patience – you might nab same-day seats for lunch.

Oriental

Abeno Too

17-18 Great Newport Street, WC2H 7JE (7379 1160/www.abeno.co.uk). Leicester Square tube. **Open** noon-11pm Mon-Sat; noon-10.30pm Sun. **Main courses** £6.95-£18.50. **Credit** AmEx, DC, MC, V. **Map** p409 X3 32

Its discreet exterior makes it easy to miss, but this modest little Japanese restaurant is always packed with those lucky enough to have stumbled across it. Furnishings are simple, staff are polite and efficient, and the food is delicious. Pride of place on the menu goes to *okonomiyaki*, the Japanese equivalent of a Spanish omelette. There are rice and noodle dishes too, as well as teppanyaki and salads.

Other locations: Abeno, 47 Museum Street, Bloomsbury, WC1A 1LY (7405 3211).

Vegetarian & organic

Food for Thought

31 Neal Street, WC2H 9PR (7836 9072). Covent Garden tube. **Open** noon-8.30pm Mon-Sat; noon-5pm Sun. **Main courses** £3-£6.70. **No credit cards. Map** p409 Y2 33

A compact subterranean café, Food for Thought is furnished with chunky wooden furniture and a small service counter crammed with friendly staff. Loyal customers munch old-school veggie and vegan food.

Fino. *See p201.*

Soho & Chinatown

Cafés & brasseries

Maison Bertaux

28 Greek Street, W1D 5DQ (7437 6007). Leicester Square tube. **Open** 8.30am-11pm daily. **Main courses** £1.50-£4.50. **No credit cards. Map** p409 X3 34

Opened in 1871, Maison Bertaux's charms have remained unchanged for decades, with an interior and eccentric staff straight out of *Monsieur Hulot's Holiday*. With no espresso machine, the main alternative to café crème is pots of tea, and the savoury pastries aren't terribly good. Happily, the pâtisserie saves the day: lemon and fruit tarts, éclairs and various permutations of cream and choux pastry.

Pâtisserie Valerie

44 Old Compton Street, W1D 4TY (7437 3466/ www.patisserie-valerie.co.uk). Leicester Square, Piccadilly Circus or Tottenham Court Road tube. **Open** 7.30am-8.30pm Mon, Tue; 7.30am-9pm Wed-Fri; 8am-9pm Sat; 9.30am-7pm Sun. **Main courses** £3.75-£8.25. Licensed. **Credit** (over £5) AmEx, DC, MC, V. **Map** p408 W3 35

We keep returning to this branch of Pâtisserie Valerie for its quirky atmosphere and the views of Soho streetlife from the bright and breezy first floor; the ground floor tends to be a bit gloomy. Decor is an appealing tribute to 1920s Parisian café culture, and breakfast is served until 4pm.

Other locations: throughout the city.

New Piccadilly

See p212 **Caffs with class**.

Indian

Masala Zone

9 Marshall Street, W1F 7ER (7287 9966/www. realindianfood.com). Oxford Circus tube. **Open** 12.30am-3.30am, 5pm-11pm Mon-Fri; 12.30-11pm Sat; 12.30pm-3.30pm; 5.30-10.30pm Sun. **Main courses** £6.50-£9. **Credit** MC, V. **Map** p408 V2 36

Indian street snacks are the latest food fashion to hit London, and few spice it up better than Masala Zone. It serves homey and affordable grub to trendy office wallahs who have more taste than spare cash. In addition to standard tikkas, samosas and bhajias, there's a wide range of regional dishes prepared in the open kitchen. Not every dish is perfect, but you can expect quick service and good value for money.

Other locations: 80 Upper Street, Islington, N1 0NU (7359 3399); 147 Earl's Court Road, Earl's Court, SW5 9RQ (7373 0220).

Red Fort

77 Dean Street, W1D 3SH (7437 2115/www.redfort. co.uk). Leicester Square or Tottenham Court Road tube. **Open** noon-2.15pm, 5.45-11pm Mon-Fri; 5.45-11pm Sat; 5.30-10pm Sun. **Main courses** £12.50-£20. **Credit** AmEx, MC, V. **Map** p408 W2 37

Palms of Goa

SWAGATHAM (Welcome)

South indian cuisine in the heart of London
A new benchmark in Indian dining has been reached.

Eugine Dias teamed up with Shabdin Gharuk and opened the first Goan restaurant in central London, 1994. With their vast experience in cooking together they offered authentic and unheard of dishes that were not seen in other restaurant menus.

That is what we call The Palms of Goa Experience.

You are invited to share that experience with us.

"The tarka dal and the breads we tried were carefully prepared. Service led by Mr Dias is courteous and responsive to an interest in the food."
- Evening Standard

"be prepared for the appeal of lamb xacutti, 'a very famous Goan dish prepared with coconuts, vinegar and hot spices' that's all the more welcome because it's not actually famous enough to have found its way onto the menu of most curry houses."
- Time Out

"(apart from Palms of Goa) most Indian restaurants have failed to realise that taste should go hand in hand with more healthy and reduced-fat dishes"
- Tandoori Magazine

PALMS OF GOA . FITZROVIA
160 New Cavendish Street, London W1W 6YR
T: 020 7580 6125

Underground: Gt Portland St (Bakerloo, Circle Hammersmith & City) Warren Street (Northern & Victoria) Goodge Street (Northern)

Palms of Goa Opening Times
Monday-Saturday 12.00pm-3.00pm & 6.00pm-11.00pm
Sunday - Closed

---

www.palmsofgoa.com

Providing rich pickings for smart young media types, the classy Red Fort is a calming place, with a sleek water feature and antique artefacts. Its largely north Indian cooking is legendary for its blends of spices. Booking advisable.

Modern European

Alastair Little

49 Frith Street, W1D 4SG (7734 5183). Leicester Square or Tottenham Court Road tube. **Open** noon-3pm, 6-11.30pm Mon-Fri; 6-11.30pm Sat. **Main courses** £19.50-£24.50. **Credit** AmEx, MC, V. **Map** p408 W2 38

As much a Soho fixture as its neighbour, jazz club Ronnie Scott's, this unassuming little restaurant was at the forefront of the British cooking revolution that introduced Modern European food. Little has departed, but you'll still eat high-quality seasonal ingredients cooked simply and with aplomb. Well worth the high prices.

Arbutus

63-64 Frith Street, W1D 3JW (7734 4545/www.arbutusrestaurant.co.uk). Tottenham Court Road tube. **Open** noon-2.30pm, 5-11pm Mon-Sat; 12.30-3.30pm, 6.30-9.30pm Sun. **Main courses** £12-£15.50. **Credit** AmEx, MC, V. **Map** p408 W2 39

For the prices alone, *Time Out*'s Best Restaurant of 2006 deserves to succeed. The set lunch/pre-theatre menu (£13.50 2 courses, £15.50 3 courses) is a steal for cooking of this imagination and flair, and the wine prices (a choice of around 60 wines by 250ml carafe) are almost shockingly diner-friendly. The room is attarctive and it's an impressive operation, with real heart and verve. Be sure to book.

Oriental

Bar Shu

28 Frith Street, W1D 5LF (7287 6688). Leicester Square tube. **Open** noon-11am daily. **Main courses** £7-£30. **Credit** AmEx, MC, V. **Map** p408 W3 40

Bar Shu isn't London's first Sichuan restaurant, but it is the city's most successful re-creation of the cuisine, using no fewer than six Sichuanese chefs – and plenty of the extraordinary numbing peppers for which the cuisine is renowned. Best dish is the 'fire-exploded kidney flowers' – pigs' kidneys cross-hatched before being fried at high temperature so they 'flower'. The smart three-storey site is an appealing mix of dark stone, carved wood, blue lighting and bold graphics using Sichuan opera masks. Service can be chaotic, but this is a must-visit for fans of Chinese food.

Busaba Eathai

106-110 Wardour Street, W1F 0TR (7255 8686). Oxford Circus, Tottenham Court Road or Leicester Square tube. **Open** noon-11pm Mon-Thur; noon-11.30pm Fri, Sat; noon-10pm Sun. **Main courses** £5.50-£9. **Credit** AmEx, MC, V. **Map** p408 W2 41

Style is paramount at this Thai mini-chain, with chunky, dark wood tables bathed in pools of light from huge lanterns. Food arrives in a trice and is consumed quickly, then customers move on to make space for the next wave, as theatrical waiters buzz around. The cooking is sometimes rushed, but more often is subtle and inspired; pick of the dishes is the kwaiteow pad thai, with smoked chicken and basil. **Other locations**: 8-13 Bird Street, Marylebone, W1U 1BU (7518 8080); 22 Store Street, Bloomsbury, WC1E 7DS (7299 7900).

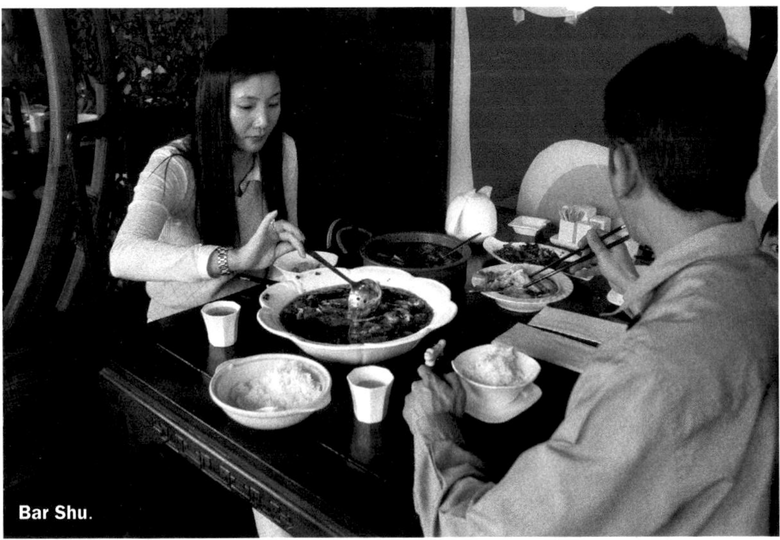

Bar Shu.

Dimond picks

I often have discerning, food-loving friends visit me in London; the onus is then on me to dazzle them with what my city can offer that other cities can't. The trump card, the thing that distinguishes London from other culinary capitals, is diversity. Of all the world's big cities, only New York comes close for its range of types of food and variety of places to eat. For example, London is the best city in the world for upmarket Indian restaurants; there are several that excel, but for sheer wow factor **Amaya** (*see p215*) takes some beating. The same could be said of **Hakkasan** (*see p201*) and **Yauatcha** (*see p207*), two restaurants where the design is simply stunning, yet it's bettered by the achievements of the kitchen; go to Hakkasan for the dim sum lunch (which is excellent, affordable and you can always get a table) and to Yauatcha's ground-floor tea room for Chinese teas and pâtisserie. Both these restaurants were created by Alan Yau, London's most innovative and foremost restaurateur.

Gallery at Sketch (*see p211*) raises the eyebrows of even the most sophisticated (or blasé) of my friends. I always insist that they visit the bejewelled upstairs loos, then take a peek at the fine-dining restaurant on the uppermost floor. The food is an eclectic car-crash of styles and ingredients, masterminded by Parisian superchef Pierre Gagnaire, and can leave you feeling as if you've participated in a laboratory experiment.

Sketch is renowned for its 'scene', but if I'm looking to impress with simple but delicious food I head for **Zuma** (*see p217*) in Knightsbridge. The bar is a hoot, full of dodgy men with offshore bank accounts and girls who have had too much plastic surgery, but watching the international jet trash is only incidental to the enjoyment of the restaurant's new-style Japanese dishes, which are very good indeed.

Apart from over-the-top design and culinary risk-taking, London is also a great place to eat history. I always include a trip to Brick Lane – not for the Indian food, which is of a tragically poor standard, but to visit the **Brick Lane Beigel Bake** (*see p220*). Open 24 hours daily, this takeaway joint is at its liveliest in the early hours of the morning, and is one of the few traces left of the Jewish East End. Just around the corner from Brick Lane, **St John Bread & Wine** (*see p198*) is a piece of history in the making. This younger sibling of the legendary Clerkenwell restaurant also has an unusual, retro-modern take on what great British food currently is, or perhaps should be. On a similar theme but at vastly reduced cost, the **Square Pie Company** in Old Spitalfields Market serves the traditional dish of Cockney pie and mash, but in a top-quality version.

Britain doesn't really share the all-day café society found on the Continent, so it may not come as a surprise that London's open-all-day brasseries mimic their European counterparts. The example par excellence of this is the **Wolseley** (*see p211*), a wonderfully retro-styled place that's great for breakfast or snacks – but it's an even better place for that most British of rituals, afternoon tea. If the Wolseley's take on elevenses and the Full English is a bit too stiff, then **Ottolenghi** (*see p218*) in Islington is its opposite: ultra-modern, laid-back, chic, convivial and with stunning dishes that borrow from colourful Mediterranean and Levantine traditions; the breads and pastries are also quite sublime.

Guy Dimond is the award-winning Food & Drink Editor of *Time Out London* magazine.

Imperial China

White Bear Yard, 25A Lisle Street, WC2H 7BA (7734 3388/www.imperial-china.co.uk). Leicester Square tube. **Open** noon-11.30pm Mon-Sat; 11.30am-10.30pm Sun. **Main courses** £6-£24. **Credit** AmEx, MC, V. **Map** p409 X3 42

Menus here are now fully translated, so even non-speakers of Chinese can try rarities such as baked lobster with salted duck egg-yolk. Be bold also with the dim sum list: items marked 'not recommended' are expected to be popular only with Chinese diners, but congee with sliced fish, for example, isn't too challenging. Smarter than most Chinatown eateries, although service can be shambolic.

Mr Kong

21 Lisle Street, WC2H 7BA (7437 7341/7437 9679). Leicester Square. **Open** noon-2.45am Mon-Sat; noon-1.45am Sun. **Main courses** £5.90-£26. **Credit** AmEx, DC, MC, V. **Map** p409 X3 43

A Chinatown old-hand whose long and confusing menu demands careful scrutiny – see 'chef's specials', 'manager's recommendations' and 'miscellaneous dishes' for the most alluring options, with plenty of classics alongside the more innovative dishes. Service improves markedly if you avoid the set meals. Although many tourists eat here, so too do Chinese Londoners, who know how to winkle out some of Chinatown's best food from the menu.

New Mayflower

68-70 Shaftesbury Avenue, W1D 6LY (7734 9207). Leicester Square or Piccadilly Circus tube. **Open** 5pm-4am daily. **Main courses** £6.80-£45. **Credit** MC, V. **Map** 408 W3 44

Not even a booking can ensure you slip past the perpetual queue just inside, but it is fast-moving, and once you're seated service is eager and attentive. The Cantonese cooking here is excellent and interesting. The menu (or rather three menus – English, Chinese and specials) is full of surprises.

New World

1 Gerrard Place, W1D 5PA (7734 0396). Leicester Square tube. **Open** 11am-11.45pm Mon-Sat; 11am-11pm Sun. *Dim sum served* 11am-6pm daily. **Main courses** £4.90-£10.50. *Dim sum* £2-£5. **Credit** AmEx, DC, MC, V. **Map** p408 W3 45

One of the very few London dim sum restaurants with service from trolleys. Turn up when the doors first open to guarantee you get the freshest food (and expect to queue for at least half an hour at weekends). Dining is on three floors, although the ground floor is the liveliest.

Wong Kei

41-43 Wardour Street, W1D 6PY (0871 332 8296). Leicester Square or Piccadilly Circus tube. **Open** noon-11.30pm Mon-Sat; noon-10.30pm Sun. **Main courses** £2.50-£8. **No credit cards**. **Map** p408 W3 46

This Chinatown stalwart draws an eclectic set of diners, all curious to experience Wong Kei's legendary reputation for rudeness – only to find that it's no longer deserved. Ignore the conversation-drowning noise levels and lack of privacy caused by table-sharing, and just get stuck in to the huge portions (dishes are large enough to share) at low prices.

Yauatcha

15 Broadwick Street, W1F 0DL (7494 8888). Leicester Square, Oxford Circus or Tottenham Court Road tube. **Open** *Tea house* noon-11pm Mon-Fri; 11.45am-11pm Sat; 11.45am-10.30pm Sun. *Restaurant* noon-midnight Mon-Sat; noon-10.30pm Sun. **Main courses** *Dim sum* £3-£14.50. *Set tea* £19-£26.50. **Credit** AmEx, MC, V. **Map** p408 V2 47

Within Richard Rogers' glassy Ingeni building designer Christian Liagre has created a ground-floor tea room (for exquisite east-meets-west cakes and 150 varieties of tea) and a large, buzzing basement restaurant where lights twinkle from a black ceiling, a fish tank runs the length of the bar, and fastidious staff flit among the plain wooden tables and turquoise banquettes. A broad range of innovative dim sum is served into the night.

Pizza

Kettners

29 Romilly Street, W1D 5HP (7734 6112/www.kettners.com). Leicester Square or Piccadilly Circus tube. **Open** *Bar* 11am-midnight Mon-Wed; 11am-1am Thur-Sat; 11am-10.30pm Sun. *Restaurant* noon-midnight Mon-Wed; noon-1am Thur-Sat. **Main courses** £8.95-£16. **Credit** AmEx, DC, MC, V. **Map** p408 W3 48

Kettners was founded in 1867 as a highfalutin French restaurant by the former chef to Napoleon III, Auguste Kettner. By the 1970s it had been taken over by Pizza Express; the result was like a pizzeria wearing a posh but tattered frock. A refurb in 2002 spruced it up considerably but, despite the addition of grills and contemporary Italian dishes such as lemon polenta cake, the pizzas are still the big draw. The champagne list is vast.

Spanish

Meza

100 Wardour Street, W1F 0TN (7314 4002/www.conran.com). Tottenham Court Road or Leicester Square tube. **Open** noon-2.30pm, 5pm-2am Mon-Thur; noon-2.30pm, 5pm-3am Fri, Sat. **Tapas** £1.50-£8.50. **Credit** AmEx, MC, V. **Map** p408 W2 49

Upmarket Meza, in a space as big and sleek as you'd expect from a Conran restaurant, is on the upper floor of the building whose basement is Cuban-themed bar Floridita (*see p229*). Waiters are charming and very professional, and the classic Spanish tapas simply and stylishly prepared, using first-rate ingredients. The sherry selection would appease a connoisseur.

Oxford Street & Marylebone

British

Rhodes W1

The Cumberland, Great Cumberland Place, W1A 4RF (7479 3838/www.garyrhodes.co.uk). Marble Arch tube. **Open** 11am-11pm Mon-Sat; 11am-10.30pm Sun. **Main courses** £11.90-£23. **Credit** AmEx, MC, V. **Map** p397 F6 50

The Cumberland's dining room is resolutely modern, but with a great sense of space. The looks won't be to everyone's taste, but the food is a more certain bet. Everything we tried left us wanting more and, unlike many upmarket British restaurants, there's no dress code or stiff atmosphere.

Other locations: Rhodes Twenty Four, Tower 42, Old Broad Street, the City, EC2N 1HQ (7877 7703/www.rhodes24.co.uk).

Cafés & brasseries

La Fromagerie

2-4 Moxon Street, W1U 4EW (7935 0341/www.lafromagerie.co.uk). Baker Street or Bond Street tube. **Open** 10.30am-7.30pm Mon; 8am-7.30pm Tue-Fri; 9am-7pm Sat; 10am-6pm Sun. **Main courses** £6.50-£13.50. **Credit** AmEx, MC, V. **Map** p400 G5 51

The 'tasting café' in the back of this popular, rustic-style deli is a simple set-up: one communal wooden table and three small satellite tables. The daily cheese plate takes centre stage (the cheese room stocks over 100 varieties), but the exemplary ploughman's lunch and fish plate are as carefully sourced; superior cakes are served for tea.

Fish

FishWorks

89 Marylebone High Street, W1U 4QW (7935 9796/ www.fishworks.co.uk). Baker Street tube. **Open** noon-2.30pm, 6-10.30pm Tue-Fri; noon-10.30pm Sat, Sun. **Main courses** £9.50-£26. **Credit** AmEx, DC, MC, V. **Map** p400 G5 52

Each branch of this Bath-based chain combines fishmonger and restaurant, and all are casual and relaxed. The menu offers 'classic' dishes and specials that vary according to the day's catch. Expect super-fresh ingredients, simply cooked.

Other locations: throughout the city.

Fish & chips

Golden Hind

See p221 **Fish and chips**.

Global

The Providores & Tapa Room

109 Marylebone High Street, W1U 4RX (7935 6175/ www.theprovidores.co.uk). Baker Street or Bond Street tube. **Open** *The Providores* noon-2.45pm, 6-10.30pm Mon-Sat; noon-2.45pm, 6-10pm Sun. *Tapa Room* 9-10.30pm Mon-Fri; 10am-10.30pm Sat; 10am-10pm Sun. **Main courses** £18-£24.50. *Tapas* £2-£13.40. **Credit** AmEx, MC, V. **Map** p400 G5 53

The buzzy street-level Tapa Room on Marylebone High Street is frequently packed to capacity, the crowds attracted by the exquisite global tapas and breakfasts. Upstairs, the restaurant part of the operation is small and refined, offering dishes that are a rarefied fusion of mainly Asian and Middle Eastern ingredients. The cooking is exceptional, a fact that's reflected in the prices.

Italian

Locanda Locatelli

8 Seymour Street, W1H 7JZ (7935 9088/www. locandalocatelli.com). Marble Arch tube. **Open** noon-3pm, 6.45-11pm Mon-Thur; noon-3pm, 6.45-11.30pm Fri; noon-3.30pm, 6.45-11.30pm Sat; noon-3.30pm, 6.45-10pm Sun. **Main courses** £19.50-£29.50. **Credit** AmEx, MC, V. **Map** p400 G6 54

The permanently darkened interior of wood veneer, convex mirrors and expansive tan leather lounges suggests sleazy Saturday nights rather than sunny Sunday lunchtimes; however, Sunday lunch is one of the easiest times to get a table at this smart and notoriously popular venue. At £12 a bottle the pleasant house white might be the only bargain on offer, but the food is carefully considered – often exquisite – and delicious.

Modern European

Orrery

55 Marylebone High Street, W1U 5RB (7616 8000/ www.orrery.co.uk). Baker Street tube. **Open** *Bar* 11am-11pm daily. *Restaurant* noon-2.30pm, 6.30-10.30pm Mon-Wed, Sun; noon-2.30pm, 6.30-11pm Thur-Sat. **Main courses** £16-£28. **Credit** AmEx, DC, MC, V. **Map** p400 G4 55

The most ambitious restaurant in the Conran group, Orrery can feel as sombre as a church. Still, staff generally warm up if you show an interest in the food, which remains excellent under new chef Allan Pickett. The three-course set lunch is stupendously good value at £23.50 a head. Be sure to book.

Oriental

Eat-Thai.net

22 St Christopher's Place, W1U 1NP (7486 0777/ www.eatthai.net). Bond Street tube. **Open** noon-3pm, 6-10.30pm daily. **Main courses** £8.25-£15.95. *Set lunch* £8.95 2 courses. *Set dinner* £25-£35 per person (minimum 2) 3 courses. **Credit** AmEx, MC, V. **Map** p400 G6 56

Hidden on a tiny alley off Oxford Street, this has to be one of our favourite Thai restaurants for sheer consistency. Nipon Senkaewsai, a former five-star hotel chef, has produced a huge menu of royal Thai classics, Esarn dishes from north-east Thailand and intriguing Thai-fusion creations. Service is prompt and presentation faultless.

Paddington & Notting Hill

Cafés & brasseries

Notting Hill Brasserie

92 Kensington Park Road, W11 2PN (7229 4481). Notting Hill Gate tube. **Open** noon-3pm, 7-11pm Mon-Sat; noon-3pm Sun. **Main courses** £18.50-£23.50. **Credit** AmEx, MC, V. **Map** p396 A6 57

NHB's casual-posh style is bang on for Notting Hill's ever-more chi-chi bohemianism. The elegant cuisine offers sensitively cooked fish mains and some marvellous roast meats, at prices that discourage the riff-raff. There's live jazz in the bar nightly.

French

The Ledbury

127 Ledbury Road, W11 2AQ (7792 9090/ www.theledbury.com). Westbourne Park tube. **Open** noon-2pm, 6.30-10.15pm Mon-Fri; noon-2.30pm, 6.30-10.15pm Sat, Sun. **Set meals** £24.50 2 courses, £30 3 courses. **Credit** AmEx, MC, V. **Map** p396 A6 58

Everything about the Ledbury is delightful. The staff are unfailingly pleasant and helpful. The dining room is smart without being intimidating. And the food, cooked by Australian Brett Graham, is exceptional – fine seasonal ingredients; a few dashes of Ferran Adria-style technology; ravishing presentation; sublime tastes and textures.

Gastropubs

Cow

89 Westbourne Park Road, W2 5QH (7221 0021). Royal Oak or Westbourne Park tube. **Open** noon-11pm Mon-Thur; noon-midnight Fri, Sat; noon-10.30pm Sun. **Main courses** £15.50-£19. **Credit** MC, V. **Map** p396 A5 (59)

We can't fault the Cow, still among the most popular noshing shops in its field. Upstairs from one of the best pubs in London, the dining room has a menu that's simple, inventive and deftly dispatched. Like the bar, the restaurant is compact, squeezing into an awkward trapezium-shaped room with a 1950s, retro feel. Oysters are a speciality and the global wine list is strong (and doesn't exceed £50 a bottle).

Global

Mandalay

444 Edgware Road, W2 1EG (7258 3696/ www.mandalayway.com). Edgware Road tube. **Open** noon-2.30pm, 6-10.30pm Mon-Sat. **Main courses** £3.90-£6.90. **Credit** AmEx, DC, MC, V. **Map** p397 D4 (60)

Modest, family-run Mandalay is London's only Burmese restaurant – and it's a gem. Look beyond the drab location and easy-wipe tablecloths to focus on the cooking, with its Thai, Indian and Chinese influences. Expect plenty of fish and seafood, fragrant rice and noodles, and light aromatic curries.

Italian

Assaggi

First floor, 39 Chepstow Place, W2 4TS (7792 5501). Bayswater, Queensway or Notting Hill Gate tube. **Open** 12.30-2.30pm, 7.30-11pm Mon-Fri; 1-2.30pm, 7.30-11pm Sat. **Main courses** £16.95-£19.50. **Credit** MC, V. **Map** p396 B6 (61)

Assaggi is tucked above a pub on a residential street near the highly fashionable stores of Westbourne Grove, yet it's one of London's premier destinations for authentic Italian dining. Staff are young but experienced, and the menu is purist, offering just a brief list of simply cooked dishes using fine seasonal ingredients. Excellent.

Middle Eastern

Maroush Gardens

1-3 Connaught Street, W2 2DH (7262 0222/ www.maroush.com). Marble Arch tube. **Open** noon-midnight daily. **Main courses** £13-£16. **Credit** AmEx, DC, MC, V. **Map** p397 F6 (62)

Marouf Abouzaki launched the original Maroush (21 Edgware Road) in 1981, and since then has opened a further five Lebanese restaurants. We like the atmosphere at this branch, just a few doors up from the original; its airy dining room buzzes like a train station with troops of waiters ferrying laden platters to dozens of big round tables. The menu runs to about 60 meze plus mixed grills.

Other locations: throughout the city.

Oriental

E&O

14 Blenheim Crescent, W11 1NN (7229 5454/ www.eando.nu). Ladbroke Grove or Notting Hill Gate tube. **Open** noon-3pm, 6-10.30pm Mon-Sat; 12.30-3.30pm, 6-10pm Sun. *Dim sum served* noon-midnight Mon-Sat; noon-11.30pm Sun. **Main courses** £6-£21.50. *Dim sum* £3-£6.50. **Credit** AmEx, DC, MC, V.

Often lauded as the star among Will Ricker's restaurants – also including the Great Eastern Dining Room (*see p220*) – E&O boasts a dark wood and fuchsia-walled bar full of gorgeous people sipping delicious cocktails and nibbling dim sum. The calmer, cream-walled dining room offers a pan-Asian fusion menu so full of exotic names that a glossary is enclosed.

Spanish

Café García

248-250 Portobello Road, W11 1LL (7221 6119). Ladbroke Grove tube. **Open** 9am-5pm Mon-Thur; 8am-11pm Fri, Sat; 10am-7pm Sun. **Tapas** £1.50-£5. **Credit** AmEx, MC, V.

Annexed to veteran Spanish supermarket/importers R García & Son, this place is basic. There is no table service: you point out your tapas choices from under the glass counters and take a seat. The selection isn't huge, but everything is freshly prepared and it's just perfect for refuelling on market day.

Piccadilly & Mayfair

The Americas

Gaucho Piccadilly

25 Swallow Street, W1B 4QR (7734 4040/ www.gaucho-grill.com). Piccadilly Circus tube. **Open** noon-1am Wed-Sat; noon-midnight Sun-Tue. **Main courses** £15-£20. **Credit** AmEx, DC, MC, V. **Map** p408 V4 (63)

This refurbished flagship branch stretches over four floors and its cowhide decor is less camp than you'd think. The steaks – rump, sirloin, fillet, ribeye and churrasco de lomo (a fillet that is cut open and turned out, the better to soak up its olive oil and garlic marinade) – are just fabulous: flavoursome and so tender you could cut them with a spoon (no steak knives are even offered). Enjoy with great thin chips, spicy sweetcorn, steaming balls of cheese bread and a bottle of pocket-friendly malbec.

British

Dorchester Grill Room

The Dorchester, 53 Park Lane, W1A 2HJ (7317 6336/www.dorchesterhotel.com). Hyde Park Corner tube. **Open** 7-11am, noon-2.30pm, 6-11pm Mon-Sat; 8-11am, 12.30-3pm, 7-10.30pm Sun. **Main courses** £14-£30. **Credit** AmEx, DC, MC, V. **Map** p402 G7 64

Redecoration has left the Grill Room a riot of red and green tartans; almost as striking a sight as the murals of rugged, larger-than-life Highlanders. Staff are welcoming and, for all that lunch and dinner remain a serious business (with wine list to match), the menu has moved with the times: the likes of venison burger with quail's egg, griottine cherries, parsnips and port appear with traditional grills. Dress smart casual and, if you're planning a weekend visit, be sure to book.

Fish

Green's

36 Duke Street, SW1Y 6DF (7930 4566/www.greens.org.uk). Green Park or Piccadilly Circus tube. **Open** *Sept-Apr* 11.30am-3pm, 5.30-11pm Mon-Sat; noon-3pm, 5.30-9pm Sun. *May-Aug* 11.30am-3pm, 5.30-11pm Mon-Sat. **Main courses** £11-£40. **Credit** AmEx, DC, MC, V. **Map** p408 V5 65

Despite opening in the 1980s, Green's harks back to an older era with its racing green banquettes, mahogany panelling and a marble oyster bar. Service is formal, but surprisingly warm, and lovers of meat are almost as well catered for as lovers of seafood. No jeans or trainers.

Indian

Tamarind

20-22 Queen Street, W1J 5PR (7629 3561/www.tamarindrestaurant.com). Green Park tube. **Open** noon-3pm, 6-11.30pm Mon-Fri; 6-11.30pm Sat; noon-3pm, 6-10.30pm Sun. **Main courses** £14.50-£26. **Credit** AmEx, DC, MC, V. **Map** p402 H7 66

This well-established fine-dining restaurant is popular with deep-pocketed, well-travelled business folks. The awkward basement space is enlivened with mirrors and the sight of chefs working at their clay ovens in the open kitchen. Celebrating authenticity over new-wave presentations, the food focuses on earthy, mainly north Indian dishes – the makhani dahl must be the best in London.

Modern European

Gordon Ramsay at Claridge's

Claridge's, 55 Brook Street, W1K 4HR (7499 0099/www.gordonramsay.com). Bond Street tube. **Open** noon-2.45pm, 5.45-11pm Mon-Fri; noon-3pm, 5.45-11pm Sat; noon-3pm, 6-11pm Sun. **Set meals** £30-£60 3 courses, £75 6 courses. **Credit** AmEx, DC, MC, V. **Map** p400 H6 67

The setting is impressively vintage-luxe, but the restaurant is buzzy and more relaxed than the other Gordon Ramsay (*see p214*). The menu is exciting without resorting to whimsy, and satisfyingly seasonal. Dress up and enjoy an exceptional restaurant experience, but only if you arrive shortly after midday on a Monday to Thursday are you likely to secure a precious table; otherwise, a tedious telephone booking system awaits.

Maze

10-13 Grosvenor Square, W1K 6JP (7107 0000/www.gordonramsay.com). Bond Street tube. **Open** noon-midnight daily. **Main courses** £14-£20. **Tapas** £6-£9. **Credit** AmEx, DC, MC, V. **Map** p402 G7 68

Maze has repackaged Ramsay in a bid to tempt younger diners into fine dining and to keep pace with the trend for smaller portions of more daring combinations. Head chef Jason Atherton brings Asian-French know-how from Spain's famous El Bulli, but the food is pure Ramsay – haute cuisine courses rather than punchy bursts of tapas. The expensively reared protein is prepared and cooked to perfection, flavours are intense, sauces essence-like, the presentation finely tuned.

Sketch

9 Conduit Street, W1S 2XZ (0870 777 4488/www.sketch.uk.com). Oxford Circus tube. The Lecture Room **Open** noon-2.30pm, 7-10.30pm Tue-Fri; 7-10.30pm Sat. **Main courses** £45-£59. *The Gallery* **Open** 7-11pm Mon-Sat. **Main courses** £12-£24. *The Glade* **Open** noon-3.30pm Mon-Sat. **Main courses** £9-£24. **Credit** AmEx, DC, MC, V. **Map** p408 U3 69

Greeters at the entrance lead you down to the Gallery (Louis XIV meets IMAX theatre) or up to the legendarily expensive Lecture Room ('Pierre Gagnaire's fine dining experience'). Food is designed to challenge culinary preconceptions, with technically brilliant nibbles (all the pastry work is superb) giving way to exotic tasting menus. Specify which venue you want when booking, and expect a time-limit and to have to leave your credit card number. A pâtisserie, the Parlour, resides on the ground floor and, in autumn 2005, the fun, quirky and amusingly pretentious Glade opened. Here, a large starter or small main (also under the supervision of Gagnaire) costs a comparatively proletarian £9. **Photo** *p215*.

The Wolseley

160 Piccadilly, W1J 9EB (7499 6996/www.thewolseley.com). Green Park tube. **Open** 7-11.30am, noon-3pm, 5.30pm-midnight Mon-Fri; 9-11.30am, noon-3pm, 5.30pm-midnight Sat; 9-11.30am, noon-3pm, 5.30-11pm Sun. *Tea served* 3-5.30pm Mon-Fri; 3.30-6pm Sat, Sun. **Main courses** £6.75-£28.50. **Credit** AmEx, DC, MC, V. **Map** p408 U5 70

One of the city's loveliest-looking restaurants, the Wolseley has a high, multi-domed ceiling, a sleek black and cream colour scheme, and loads of old-fashioned charm. The inspiration is grand Viennese café, so wiener schnitzel and soufflé suisse sit beside

Caffs with class

The handful of British working men's cafés left in London that retain some of their mid 20th-century Formica fittings are often dismissed as mere greasy spoons. But for a country that faced the collapse of long-held social and political certainties after World War II, these cafés became forcing houses for London's cultural advance guard of the time.

Within a decade of the Moka, Soho's first espresso bar, opening at 29 Frith Street in 1953, London had become the world's hippest city: a ferment of music, fashion, film, sex, scandal and avant-gardism. The of-the-moment design of the cafés and their Populuxe youth appeal galvanised British cultural life, incubating a generation of writers, artists, musicians and crime lords.

Most of these cafés are now vanishing in a flurry of redevelopment and refitting, and the architecture and ambience of those that remain fast being levelled by mega-coffee combines. But for their cultural impact, we owe these classic cafés an immense debt of gratitude and a serious duty of care. And for their decently priced menus and hearty fare, we also owe them our custom. Help keep 'em classic by visiting the following fine survivors.

Alpino

97 Chapel Market, Islington, N1 9EY (7837 8330). Angel tube. **Meals served** 6.30am-4pm Mon-Fri; 6.30am-5pm Sat. **Main courses** £4-£5. **No credit cards. Map** p404 N2 ⓻⓵

Founded in 1959, this popular local has held on to every ounce of its character. The plum-patterned cup and saucer sets alone are ceramic perfection, but the fine booth seating, teak-veneer Formica and glorious lamp holders make the place a stone classic. All the liver/bacon/sausage combinations come highly recommended, especially in an area that's been Starbucked in particularly comprehensive fashion.

Frank's

Addison Bridge Place, Kensington, W14 8XP (7603 4121). Kensington (Olympia) tube/rail. **Meals served** 6am-3pm Mon-Fri; 6-11am Sat. **Main courses** £2-£4.50. **No credit cards.**

Constructed out of an abandoned signal box, this is a superb old diner-style place with a crumbling interior, single-stool seating and a

steak tartare, omelettes and a superlative mix of English cakes and French pâtisserie. Teatime is possibly the most relaxed hour to experience the Wolseley; lunchtime bookings are now likely to have a 90-minute limit, but walk-ins are still welcomed.

North African

Momo

25 Heddon Street, W1B 4BH (7434 4040/www.momoresto.com). Piccadilly Circus tube. **Open** noon-2.30pm, 6.30-11.30pm Mon-Sat; 6.30-11pm Sun. **Main courses** £9.75-£19.50. **Credit** AmEx, DC, MC, V. **Map** p408 U3 ⓻⓶

We've heard of diners being hurried to vacate tables and of haphazard service from those oh-so attractive waiting staff, but where else is dancing on the table chic? Dining à deux, it's hard not to make new friends as you cosy up on long canteen-like tables and, every so often, the fine mix of North African sounds ratchets up and you're encouraged to down cutlery and get grooving.

Oriental

Nobu

First floor, The Metropolitan, 19 Old Park Lane, W1K 1LB (7447 4747/www.noburestaurants.com). Hyde Park Corner tube. **Open** noon-2.15pm, 6-10.15pm Mon-Thur; noon-2.15pm, 6-11pm Fri; 12.30-2.30pm, 6-11pm Sat; 12.30-2.30pm, 6-9.30pm Sun. **Main courses** £3.50-£27.50. **Credit** AmEx, DC, MC, V. **Map** p402 H8 ⓻⓷

The Nobu chain extends from the US to Tokyo, with three Nobus in London alone. Here at the Met, you still get great Hyde Park views and a substantial picturesque art deco counter area. Nosh-wise, stick with the bacon roll variants favoured by the rambunctious cabbies who fill the place.

Harris' Café Rest

39 Goldhawk Road, Shepherd's Bush, W12 8QQ (8743 1753). Goldhawk Road tube. **Meals served** 11.30am-9.30pm Mon-Sat; 11.30am-8.45pm Sun. **Main courses** £3-£7. **No credit cards.**

This is the dowager on Goldhawk Road. In 1951 Loizos Prodromou came to London from Cyprus to take over Harris'. The same Greek Cypriots have been running the place ever since. The beautiful signage, fluted wall panelling, net curtains, sun-ray relief designs and solicitous waitresses make this a real home from home. The immense portions and solid Sunday roast options are a big draw.

New Piccadilly

8 Denman Street, Soho, W1D 7HQ (7437 8530). Piccadilly Circus tube. **Meals served** noon-8.30pm daily. **Main courses** £4-£7.50. **No credit cards. Map** p408 V4 74

This cathedral among caffs (*pictured*) revels in Festival of Britain glory. Despite criticism of its 'tinned' dishes, the kitchen serves up pretty good house risottos and canellonis. Great tea is served in proper Pyrex cups underneath wall-to-wall yellow Formica; the menus have even become collector's items. Cravated proprietor Lorenzo Marioni is fast passing into Soho legend.

E Pellicci

332 Bethnal Green Road, Bethnal Green, E2 0AG (7739 4873). Bethnal Green tube/rail/8 bus. **Meals served** 6.15am-4.45pm Mon-Sat. **Main courses** £4.80-£7.80. **No credit cards.**

This 105-year-old East End masterpiece, with a primrose Vitrolite frontage and a rich, art deco-style interior, now has Grade II-listed status. Owner Nevio was born above the shop; his mother Elide supervised the marquetry Empire State-style panelling, crafted in 1946. These days, Maria Pellicci makes the grub, and her range of own-cooked Italian specials is unrivalled. Sample the liver and bacon butties and own-made steak pie.

waiting list, but Nobu Matsuhisa's signature dishes – rock shrimp tempura with spicy sauce, new-style sashimi, black cod with miso – no longer hold the same wow factor.

Other locations: 15 Berkeley Street, Mayfair, W1J 8DY (7290 9222); Ubon, 34 Westferry Circus, Canary Wharf, Docklands, E14 8RR (7719 7800).

Westminster & St James's

British

Inn the Park

St James's Park, SW1A 2BJ (7451 9999/www.innthepark.co.uk). St James's Park tube. **Open** 8-11am, noon-3pm, 5-9.45pm Mon-Fri; 9-11am, noon-4pm, 5-9.45pm Sat, Sun. **Main courses** £13.50-£22. **Credit** AmEx, MC, V. **Map** p403 K8 75

This is one of the best-located restaurants in London. The modern wooden structure fits perfectly into a lakeside slot, and every table has a water view. Good for families, it's also a romantic night-time haunt. Food runs from breakfasts through sandwiches to full meals, with attention paid to British sourcing.

National Dining Rooms

Sainsbury Wing, National Gallery, Trafalgar Square, WC2N 5DN (7747 2525/www.nationalgallery.co.uk). Charing Cross tube/rail. **Open** *Bakery* 10am-5.30pm Mon, Tue, Thur-Sun; 10am-8.30pm Wed. *Restaurant* noon-3.30pm Mon, Tue, Thur-Sun; 5-7.15pm Wed. **Main courses** £13.50-£18.50. **Credit** AmEx, MC, V. **Map** p409 X5 76

Three cheers for Oliver Peyton (who runs a growing number of eateries in attractions around town, including Inn the Park, *see above*) – and for the National Gallery for choosing him over some corporate catering option. This is fine British food, in a modern setting, at a reasonable price – especially in the café area, where a raised pork pie is £4.50 and scones with Cornish clotted cream cost £3.50. There's an interesting drinks list, with more than 20 teas, plus ales and ciders. The only shame is the limited opening times.

Indian

Cinnamon Club

The Old Westminster Library, 30-32 Great Smith Street, SW1P 3BU (7222 2555/www.cinnamonclub.com). St James's Park or Westminster tube. **Open** 7.30-9.30am, noon-2.30pm, 6-10.45pm Mon-Fri; 6-10.45pm Sat. **Main courses** £12-£26. **Credit** AmEx, DC, MC, V. **Map** p403 K9 77

Housed in a spacious former Victorian library, the Cinnamon Club makes much of its colonial club atmosphere and proximity to Parliament. It's a prime destination for politicians and power brokers. Executive chef Vivek Singh's menu isn't for timid palates – expect fiery flavours and robust masalas rather than delicate notes, along with innovation aplenty. Indian breakfasts are also offered.

Italian

Quirinale

North Court, 1 Great Peter Street, SW1P 3LL (7222 7080). St James's Park or Westminster tube. **Open** noon-2.30pm, 6-10.30pm Mon-Fri. **Main courses** £12.50-£17. **Credit** AmEx, DC, MC, V. **Map** p403 L10 78

A creamy stone stairway leads guests into an interior where glass brickwork and neat sliding doors make a small basement seem spacious and full of light. The menu emphasises seasonal ingredients and tempting combinations. Pasta courses are generously portioned, there's a good array of antipasti and the sizeable cheese list is most impressive. Service is formal but friendly.

Chelsea

Gastropubs

Lots Road Pub & Dining Room

114 Lots Road, SW10 0RJ (7352 6645/www.thespiritgroup.com). Fulham Broadway tube then 11 bus/Sloane Square tube then 11, 19, 22 bus. **Open** 11am-11pm Mon-Thur; 11am-midnight Fri, Sat; noon-10.30pm Sun. **Main courses** £8.50-£14. **Credit** MC, V. **Map** p398 C13 79

The food here is terrific: even basic dishes such as cod or steak are cooked with precision, inventiveness and considerable flair. Such is the quality of the presentation that you feel like photographing the dishes before you tuck in. Other pluses include well-kept real ales and a commendably broad range of wines by the glass. Beware drunken Chelsea fans on match days.

Indian

Chutney Mary

535 King's Road, SW10 0SZ (7351 3113/www.realindianfood.com). Fulham Broadway tube/11, 22 bus. **Open** 6.30-11pm Mon-Fri; 12.30-2.30pm, 6.30-11pm Sat; 12.30-3pm, 6.30-10.30pm Sun. **Main courses** £16-£29.75. **Credit** AmEx, DC, MC, V. **Map** p398 C13 80

Though perhaps no longer London's most fashionable Indian restaurant, Chutney Mary remains a top-drawer affair. It is run by the Panjabi sisters, who are also behind Amaya (*see p215*) and Masala Zone (*see p203*). The kitchen specialises in modern Indian cuisine, with elements of Anglo-Indian and regional styles. Main courses include luxury ingredients such as lobster, but we recommend the tasting curry platter and the Punjabi vegetable selection (a fine thali). Puddings hsould not be overlooked either, particularly the dark chocolate fondant with orange blossom lassi.

Modern European

Gordon Ramsay

68 Royal Hospital Road, SW3 4HP (7352 4441/www.gordonramsay.com). Sloane Square tube. **Open** noon-2pm, 6.30-11pm Mon-Fri. **Set meals** £40-£70 3 courses, £90 tasting menu. **Credit** AmEx, DC, MC, V. **Map** p399 F12 81

TV presenter, author, entrepreneur, tableware designer… with Gordon Ramsay so busy at the moment, it's just as well the staff in Royal Hospital Road are able to keep the hallowed place humming. Executive chef Mark Askew and restaurant director Jean-Claude Breton know all about sublime food and subliminal service. Booking a table is nigh-on impossible, but if you do manage it then the reward is amazing examples of British ingredients and French know-how at their best. Expect the likes of braised belly of pork with baby langoustines or pan-fried john dory wth Cromer crab and cavier.

Knightsbridge & South Kensington

British

Bluebird Dining Rooms

350 King's Road, entrance in Beaufort Street, SW3 5UU (7559 1129/www.conran.com). Sloane Square tube then 11, 19, 22, 49, 319 bus. **Open** 7-10.45pm Mon-Sat. **Set meal** £30 3 courses. **Credit** AmEx, DC, MC, V. **Map** p399 D12 82

A vision of 1930s masculine glamour, right down to the bar filled with leather armchairs, this place always seems quiet. Perhaps people are deterred by the £30 set meal, yet the seasonally based menu is an assured, inventive roam around the country. A shining example of ambitious British cooking.

If you like the Parlour at **Sketch**, just wait till you see the rest of the place. *See p211.*

French

Racine

239 Brompton Road, SW3 2EP (7584 4477). Knightsbridge or South Kensington tube/14, 74 bus. **Open** noon-3pm, 6-10.30pm Mon-Fri; noon-3.30pm, 6-10.30pm Sat; noon-3.30pm, 6-10pm Sun. **Main courses** £12.50-£20.75. **Credit** AmEx, MC, V. **Map** p399 E10 83

Enter through curtains into one of London's most consistently enjoyable restaurants. Tables, placed convivially close together, are filled with families, bon vivants from the French Embassy, and fathers treating their student daughters. The food is a mix of modern and retro bistro classics, the staff focused and French. Chef Henry Harris has been teased for creating a place too retro even for France; to our minds though, this is a thoroughly vibrant restaurant that knows how to inovate and delight.

Global

Lundum's

117-119 Old Brompton Road, SW7 3RN (7373 7774/www.lundums.com). Gloucester Road or South Kensington tube. **Open** 9am-4pm, 6-11pm Mon-Sat; noon-1.30pm Sun. **Main courses** £13.50-£27.25. **Credit** AmEx, DC, MC, V. **Map** p399 D11 84

Lundum's loyal clientele of monied professionals delight in simply prepared Scandinavian dishes executed with a light touch. The chefs are renowned for their fish, but the menu also includes meatballs, stroganoff and cured roast duck. There's a cosy lounge by the entrance, alcoves for secluded eating and spacious dining areas, with service slick but a little austere. The Sunday brunch is a big draw.

Indian

Amaya

Halkin Arcade, Motcomb Street, SW1X 8JT (7823 1166/www.realindianfood.com). Knightsbridge tube. **Open** 12.30-2.15pm, 6.30-11.15pm Mon-Fri; 12.30-2.30pm, 6.30-11.15pm Sat; 12.45-2.45pm, 6.30-10.15pm Sun. **Main courses** £8.50-£25. **Credit** AmEx, DC, MC, V. **Map** p402 G9 85

Amaya opened in 2004 in a blaze of publicity thanks to its innovative grazing menu of kebabs and birianis, and its beautifully smart decor of rosewood panels, terracotta ornamentation and twinkling chandeliers. Our dining experiences have been mixed: some dishes so good they left us speechless, others not so good. There's a notable list of fabulous sugar-free desserts.

Italian

Daphne's

112 Draycott Avenue, SW3 3AE (7589 4257/www.daphnes-restaurant.co.uk). South Kensington tube. **Open** noon-3pm, 5.30-11.30pm Mon-Fri; noon-3.30pm, 5.30-11.30pm Sat; 12.30-4pm, 5.30-10.30pm Sun. **Main courses** £12.25-£22.75. **Credit** AmEx, MC, V. **Map** p399 E10 86

Don't be fooled by the old-fashioned name and crusty location: Daphne's is an impressive operation, run by the folks behind the Ivy (*see p202*). From the

Good to go

Globalisation may have given KFC, Subway and McDonald's an unwelcome express route into our city, but London's fast-food chains aren't all of the type to spur independent filmmakers to vomit-inducing outrage. Happily, some of the better and more popular to-go outlets are refreshingly home-grown. So while we have Domino's and Pizza Hut, they don't arouse the same loyalty, affection and debate as **Pizza Express** (*pictured*; 96 branches across town, visit www.pizzaexpress.co.uk for details). Established in 1965 in Wardour Street, Soho, there are now around 300 branches in the UK and Ireland; fans defend its honour from those who accuse the pizzas of getting smaller and the company of selling out because its pizzas now appear on supermarket shelves. Whatever the case, Pizza Express is still, for many, the standard by which others are measured.

A more authentically Italian experience can be had at the **Carluccio's Caffè** (*see p201*) chain. Avuncular Italian and TV star Antonio is the front man, but it's wife Priscilla (sister of Terence Conran) who is the driving force of the business. The secret of their success? Proper Italian ingredients and dishes, served up in simple but appealing surroundings.

It's a similar formula that has underpinned the prolific rise of the **Wagamama** (*see p218*) chain, only in this case the flavours are all Asian. Cheap and cheerful, these good-looking oriental noodle bars are a huge asset if you're on a low budget but don't want to compromise on style. Kids and vegetarians are also amply catered for.

Gourmet burger bars have been a recent success. Previous quality burger bars such as Ed's Easy Diner were unapologetically US-themed, but the first branch of the **Gourmet Burger Kitchen** (now 11 branches across town, see www.gbkinfo.com), which opened in Battersea in 2001, was conceived and run by Kiwis; more significantly, the burgers taste out of this world, using prime-quality ingredients and many succulent toppings and flavour combinations. The most recent branch to open is on Frith Street in Soho.

For a home-grown take on meaty snacks there's one name worth seeking out: the **S&M Café**. The chortlesome name is a reference to sausage and mash, served in a variety of flavours with mushy peas or gravy or sauce. There are three branches, but the best-looking and most historic is in Islington (4-6 Essex Road, 7359 5361). It has a carefully restored wood and Formica interior dating back to the golden age of the British caff.

Sandwiches are a traditional part of the British diet which is in no danger of becoming extinct. The 4th Earl of Sandwich set a trend for eating filled bread in the 18th century, and sandwiches are now a billion-pound industry. The market leaders are **Marks & Spencer**, better known for reliably good underwear, but also top of the charts when it comes to volume of sandwich sales nationally, thanks to premium-quality fillings. However, in London **Pret a Manger** (branches throughout London, www.pret.com) is the iconic sarnie shop for most office workers. Established in 1986, Pret made waves for its refusal to use preservatives, and by seeking out organic and free-range produce. It lost some of its wholesome kudos in 2001 when McDonald's bought a 33 per cent stake in the company, but for most Londoners it is still the benchmark sandwich bar. Curiously, the attempt at expansion in Manhattan has never taken off; New Yorkers like to see their sandwiches made to order, while Londoners like theirs to take away in under two minutes.

courtyard-like entrance, you enter a soothing split-level section divided by a sculpted stone balustrade, then an airy, simply decorated room with glass ceiling. The rustic cooking makes the best of seasonal produce and, in true Italian style, favours first-rate local (that is, British) ingredients.

Modern European

Bibendum

Michelin House, 81 Fulham Road, SW3 6RD (7581 5817/www.bibendum.co.uk). South Kensington tube. **Open** noon-2.30pm, 6.30-11.30pm Mon-Fri; 12.30-3pm, 7-11.30pm Sat; 12.30-3pm, 7-10.30pm Sun. **Main courses** £19-£42. **Credit** AmEx, DC, MC, V. **Map** p399 E10 87

Never mind an odd entrance through the ground-floor Oyster Bar in the art deco Michelin building, with its stunning stained-glass windows of the tyre-clad one – Bibendum is one of the classiest joints in town. Chef Matthew Harris gives clever spins on the pan-European dishes familiar from many a Conran outlet, including meat dishs as imaginative as desserts. Service is excellent: a waiter for every course, neither too stuffy nor too casual. The 23-page wine list is a corker too and includes a house Burgundy that's as good a house wine as you'll get anywhere – and very reasonable at £18. Allow a fortnight if you want to book dinner.

Oriental

Nahm

The Halkin, Halkin Street, SW1X 7DJ (7333 1234/ www.nahm.como.bz). Hyde Park Corner tube. **Open** noon-2.30pm, 7-11pm Mon-Fri; 7-11pm Sat; 7-10pm Sun. **Main courses** £11-£16.50. **Credit** AmEx, DC, MC, V. **Map** p402 G9 88

Nahm's Australian-born founder David Thompson is the world's most renowned Thai chef, so well regarded in Bangkok that he teaches Thai cooking to chefs there, and every dish from this menu of recreated Thai courtly cooking is faultless. Patient waiters steer you through a menu that strays far from the familiar. The dining room, a sophisticated, stone-lined space in Belgravia's sleek Halkin hotel, has annoying acoustics, but then you're here for the food. Book for dinner.

Zuma

5 Raphael Street, SW7 1DL (7584 1010/www. zumarestaurant.com). Knightsbridge tube. **Open** *Bar* noon-11pm Mon-Fri; 12.30-11pm Sat; noon-10pm Sun. *Restaurant* noon-2.15pm, 6-10.45pm Mon-Fri; 12.30-3.15pm, 6-10.45pm Sat; 12.30-2.45pm, 6-10.15pm Sun. **Main courses** £3.80-£65. **Credit** AmEx, DC, MC, V. **Map** p399 F9 89

No longer new, Zuma has retained its glamorous sheen: *The Flintstones*-chic interior is a hoot and the food as good as ever. New-style sushi and sashimi are just the ticket (seared miso-marinated foie gras or wagyu beef with shoyu and wasabi) and the saké list is amazing. Seats at the sushi bar, the grill or in the slickly designed main dining area still require a week or two's wait – and then expect to be informed that the table is yours for just two hours.

North London

African/Caribbean

Cottons

55 Chalk Farm Road, Camden, NW1 8AN (7485 8388/www.cottons-restaurant.co.uk). Chalk Farm tube. **Open** 6pm-midnight Mon-Thur; 6pm-1am Fri; noon-4pm, 6pm-1am Sat; noon-midnight Sun. **Main courses** £10.25-£14.50. **Credit** AmEx, MC, V.

Cottons does classic Caribbean dishes (saltfish, curried goat), in large portions and with the occasional twist, and excellent cocktails. The wood-lined interior is comfortable and cosy. There are DJs and jazz bands at the weekend, when it is essential to book.

Other locations: 70 Exmouth Market, Clerkenwell, EC1R 4QP (7833 3332).

Lalibela

137 Fortess Road, Tufnell Park, NW5 2HR (7284 0600). Tufnell Park tube/134 bus. **Open** 6pm-midnight daily. **Main courses** £7.50-£8.95. **Credit** MC, V.

The capital's most beautiful Ethiopian restaurant, bedecked with East African artefacts, has a lengthy menu including stir-fried dishes and classic hot and spicy stews. A good place to start if you've never tried Ethiopian food.

Cafés & brasseries

Alpino

See p212 **Caffs with class**.

Fish & chips

Fish Central

See p221 **Fish and chips**.

French

Morgan M

489 Liverpool Road, Highbury, N7 8NS (7609 3560/ www.morganm.com). Highbury & Islington tube/rail. **Open** 7-10pm Tue, Sat; noon-2.30pm, 7-10pm Wed-Fri; noon-2.30pm Sun. **Set meals** £19.50 2 courses, £23.50-£32 3 courses, £36-£39 tasting menu. **Credit** DC, MC, V.

Chef-proprietor Morgan Meunier's ambitious venture is renowned for its vegetarian food: perhaps an intense gazpacho with just a single croûton topped with aubergine pâté and a scoop of tomato and olive oil sorbet. The hushed cream and green decor, a grown-up wine list, and seriously accented and attired staff all add up to a somewhat reverential dining experience. Be certain to book.

Gastropubs

Marquess Tavern

32 Canonbury Street, Islington, N1 2TB (7354 2975). Angel tube/Highbury & Islington tube/rail. **Open** noon-11pm, 12.30-10pm Mon-Thur, Sun; noon-midnight Fri, Sat. **Main courses** £8-£18. **Credit** AmEx, MC, V.

It rapidly becomes clear why the Marquess won *Time Out*'s Best Gastropub award for 2006. The fare, served in the airy and attractive open dining room at the rear, is a superb take on English food of the 1940s: potted salmon, sardines on toast, whole crab. All this is prepared without fuss or frippery by kitchen staff drawn from the Ivy and St John. The wine list is inspiring, highlights being some English sparkling wines (really!), while the fridges in the gorgeous, meandering bar area are stuffed with more than 40 exotic bottled ales. There's even a bar billiards room. Exemplary.

International

Ottolenghi

287 Upper Street, Islington, N1 2TZ (7288 1454/www.ottolenghi.co.uk). Angel tube/Highbury & Islington tube/rail. **Open** 8am-11pm Mon-Sat; 9am-7pm Sun. **Main courses** £4.90-£11.50. *Meze* £5.50-£9. **Credit** MC, V. **Map** p404 O1 90

Simple but not plain, Ottolenghi looks stunning. The entrance area, which doubles as a bakery shop and deli, leads into a stunning long, brightly white room with long tables, white Panton chairs and clever art. At night, it shifts emphasis from café to restaurant, with a daily changing menu of small dishes that imaginatively combine modern Mediterranean flavours. More than just somewhere for terrific food, Ottolenghi is also huge fun as the shared tables encourage cross-party chat.

Other locations: 63 Ledbury Road, Notting Hill, W11 2AD (7727 1121); 1 Holland Street, Kensington, W8 4NA (7937 0003).

Oriental

Isarn

119 Upper Street, Islington, N1 1QP (7424 5153). Angel tube/Highbury & Islington tube/rail. **Open** noon-3pm, 6-11pm Mon-Fri; noon-11pm Sat; noon-10.30pm Sun. **Main courses** £6.50-£14.50. **Credit** AmEx, MC, V. **Map** p404 O1 91

This elegant restaurant only opened in 2005 but it's already turning out imaginative food with more confidence and flair than many of London's longer established Thai names. It offers a boutique dining experience in surroundings that are futuristic without being spartan – dark wood, cloth canopies and giant lampshades. A real find.

Wagamama

11 Jamestown Road, Camden, NW1 7BW (7428 0800/www.wagamama.com). Camden Town tube. **Open** noon-11pm Mon-Sat; noon-10pm Sun. **Main courses** £5.95-£9.95. **Credit** AmEx, DC, MC, V.

Wagamama has stood the test of time, staying close to its original ethos of providing wholesome fast food at a fair price. Although the menu has broadened over the years, it is still focused on Japanese-style noodle dishes, served by perky staff to communal tables with bench seating.

Other locations: throughout the city.

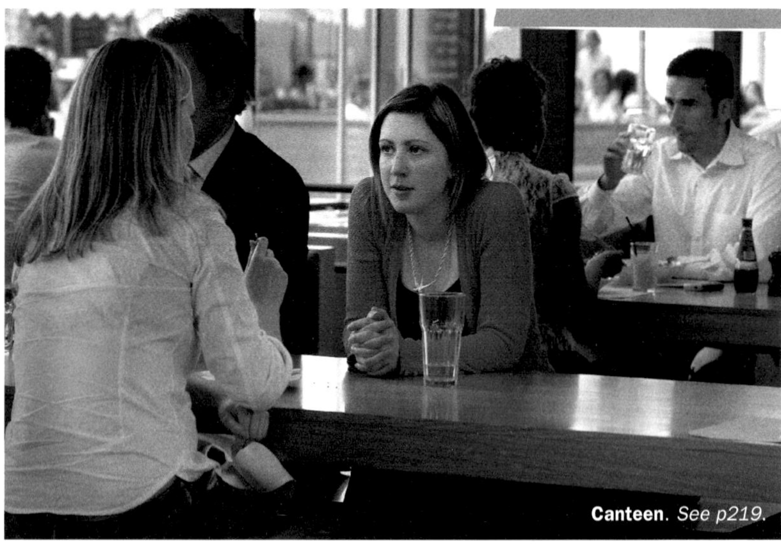

Canteen. *See p219.*

Eat, Drink, Shop

Vegetarian & organic

Manna

4 Erskine Road, Primrose Hill, NW3 3AJ (7722 8028/www.manna-veg.com). Chalk Farm tube. **Open** 6.30-11pm Mon-Sat; 12.30-3pm, 6.30-11pm Sun. **Main courses** £9.50-£12.95. **Credit** MC, V.
Smart and spacious, yet still intimate, Manna serves food that's modern and imaginative, using fashionable ingredients little seen in London's other vegetarian restaurants. You might find celeriac and blue cheese roulade with watercress pesto, or nettle ravioli with wild garlic pesto. An impressive range of organic options on the drinks list too.

East London

Cafés & brasseries

Canteen

2 Crispin Place, off Brushfield Street, Spitalfields, E1 6DW (0845 686 1122/www.canteen.co.uk). Liverpool Street tube/rail. **Open** 11am-10pm Mon-Fri; 9am-10pm Sat, Sun. **Main courses** £7-£12.50. **Credit** AmEx, MC, V. **Map** p405 R5 92
Neat, functional and streamlined, Canteen has utilitarian yet elegant communal oak tables and diner-like booths, with a glazed canopy outside sheltering a busy alfresco space, all attended to by lovely staff. The food covers breakfast (toasted crumpets, bacon sandwiches), light lunches (potted duck with piccalilli), well priced stomach fillers (a £7 macaroni cheese) and cakes. And best of all, it's bang in the new bit of Spitalfields Market. **Photo** *p218.*

E Pellicci

See p212 **Caffs with class**.

Story Deli

3 Dray Walk, The Old Truman Brewery, 91 Brick Lane, E1 6QL (7247 3137). Liverpool Street tube/rail. **Open** 9am-6pm daily. **Main courses** £6.50-£9.50. **Credit** AmEx, MC, V. **Map** p405 S5 93
With its huge butcher-block tables and cardboard packing-case seats creating a strangely uncafé-like appearance, you could easily overlook this 100% organic café and pizzeria. But the food is amazing – running from thin-crust pizzas to prawn kebabs or steak sandwiches. Often packed.

French

Plateau

Canada Place, Canada Square, Docklands, E14 5ER (7715 7100/www.conran.com). Canary Wharf tube/DLR. **Open** *Bar & grill* noon-10.45pm Mon-Sat; noon-4pm Sun. *Restaurant* noon-3pm, 6-10.15pm Mon-Fri; 6-10.15pm Sat. **Main courses** £10-£27.50. **Credit** AmEx, DC, MC, V.
Dramatic floor-to-ceiling windows run the length of the fourth floor of Canada Place, where white curves and statement lighting beautifully complement the views across Canada Square. Conran's Plateau is vast, with restaurant, bar-grill and open-roofed terrace at various degrees of formality, but none very casual. Super-attentive service, rigorous attention to detail and an economically unfettered menu.

Rosemary Lane

61 Royal Mint Street, Whitechapel, E1 8LG (7481 2602/www.rosemarylane.btinternet.co.uk). Tower Hill tube/Fenchurch Street rail/Tower Gateway DLR. **Open** noon-2.30pm, 5.30-10pm Mon-Fri; 6-10pm Sat. **Main courses** £13-£19. **Credit** AmEx, MC, V. **Map** p407 S7 94
The gentrification of the East End has yet to spread to run-down Royal Mint Street – until, that is, you get inside this upmarket, organic 'French fusion' restaurant. Hush-inducing curtains and friendly service set the scene for unusual combinations of French basics and enthusiastic New World experimentation, with a globalised wine list to match.

Les Trois Garçons

1 Club Row, Brick Lane, E1 6JX (7613 1924/www.lestroisgarcons.com). Liverpool Street tube/rail/8, 388 bus. **Open** 7-10.30pm Mon-Thur; 7-11pm Fri, Sat. **Main courses** £18-£32. **Credit** AmEx, DC, MC, V. **Map** p405 S4 95
This former corner pub is now a stupendously theatrical mix of antique bar fittings, vintage handbags (dangling from the ceiling) and ornamental taxidermy. However, it's far from a case of style over content: the kitchen delivers an immaculate French-slanted menu to Shoreditch sophisticates. It isn't cheap, but from dazzling decor to fabulous food, you get what you pay for.

Gastropubs

Gun

27 Coldharbour, Docklands, E14 9NS (7515 5222/www.thegundocklands.com). Canary Wharf tube/DLR/South Quay DLR. **Open** 11am-midnight Mon-Sat; noon-11pm Sun. **Main courses** £9.50-£21.50. **Credit** AmEx, MC, V.
In a pretty little residential area that hardly feels like Docklands, the Gun has a bright front bar/dining room, and terrace tables (with an intimate view of the Dome) and riverside rooms at the back. The kitchen offers great food, usually with a seasonal or British slant. Service is friendly and practised.

Global

Arkansas Café

Unit 12, Old Spitalfields Market, Spitalfields, E1 6AA (7377 6999). Liverpool Street tube/rail. **Open** noon-2.30pm Mon-Fri; noon-4pm Sun. **Main courses** £7-£16. **Credit** MC, V. **Map** p405 R5 96
If you want a real barbecue, this is where to go. Seating is ramshackle and service can be abrupt, but the food is huge portions of well-sourced, freshly grilled meats. All platters come with potatoes, 'slaw, purple cabbage and beans (cooked from scratch).

Italian

Fifteen

15 Westland Place, Old Street, Hoxton, N1 7LP (0871 330 1515/www.fifteenrestaurant.com). Old Street tube/rail. **Open** *Trattoria* 7.30-11am, noon-3pm, 6-10pm Mon-Sat; 9-11am, noon-3.30pm Sun. *Restaurant* noon-2.30pm, 6.30-9.30pm daily. **Main courses** £11-£24. **Credit** AmEx, MC, V. **Map** p405 Q3 97

With offshoots in Amsterdam and Cornwall, Fifteen continues as promised in founder Jamie Oliver's ground-breaking TV series: to provide disadvantaged young people with an opportunity to learn the restaurant trade. Prices are high and the quality of the cooking is variable, but booking is still essential.

Jewish

Brick Lane Beigel Bake

159 Brick Lane, E1 6SB (7729 0616). Liverpool Street tube/rail/8 bus. **Open** 24hrs daily. **No credit cards. Map** p405 S4 98

A charismatic East End institution rolling out perfect bagels, both plain and filled (egg, cream cheese, herring, moutains of salt beef), superb breads and magnificently moreish cakes, including what many rate as London's best cheesecake.

Mediterranean

Eyre Brothers

70 Leonard Street, Shoreditch, EC2A 4QX (7613 5346/www.eyrebrothers.co.uk). Old Street tube/rail. **Open** noon-3pm Mon-Fri. **Open** 6.30-11pm Mon-Sat. **Main courses** £13-£22. **Credit** AmEx, DC, MC, V. **Map** p405 Q4 99

Eyre Brothers is entirely contemporary – sleek dark woods, deep-brown leather banquettes – but feels utterly comfortable. Essential to this is the service: friendly, knowledgeable and attentive. The food – a mix of Spanish and Portuguese influences – has just the right blend of strength and subtlety.

Modern European

Wapping Food

Wapping Hydraulic Power Station, Wapping Wall, Docklands, E1W 3ST (7680 2080/www.thewapping project.com). Wapping tube/Shadwell DLR. **Open** noon-3.30pm, 6.30-11pm Mon-Fri; 10am-4pm, 7-11pm Sat; 10am-4pm Sun. **Main courses** £11-£19. **Credit** AmEx, MC, V.

There can be few more unusual spots in London to eat: a former hydraulic power station dramatically converted into a restaurant/gallery, with trendy orange chairs, silver chandeliers and crisp white linen alongside a hall of rusting pumps, chains and giant hooks. The menu changes daily and the staff strike the right note between casual and formal. Art expos next door add to the experience. **Photo** *p223.*

Oriental

Great Eastern Dining Room

54-56 Great Eastern Street, Shoreditch, EC2A 3QR (7613 4545/www.greateasterndining.co.uk). Old Street tube/rail/55 bus. **Open** *Bar* noon-midnight Mon-Fri; 6pm-midnight Sat. *Restaurant* 12.30-3pm, 6.30-10.45pm Mon-Fri; 6.30-10.45pm Sat. **Main courses** £6.50-£18.50. **Credit** AmEx, DC, MC, V. **Map** p405 R4 100

What's not to like about a place that serves beautifully presented pan-Asian fusion food in comfortable, cool surroundings? Start with a seductively strong cocktail before moving on to a menu full of tempting dishes that arrive looking like jewels. Part of the Will Ricker group, along with E&O (*see p209*). Book for Friday or Saturday, when DJs play.

Sông Quê

134 Kingsland Road, Hoxton, E2 8DY (7613 3222). Old Street tube/rail/26, 48, 55, 67, 149, 242, 243 bus. **Open** noon-3pm, 5.30-11pm Mon-Sat; noon-11pm Sun. **Main courses** £4.40-£5.60. **Credit** AmEx, MC, V. **Map** p405 R3 101

The interior of Sông Quê may be kitsch – flaky pale green paint, plastic lobsters, fake ivy – but the food is delicious and authentic Vietnamese. The menu lists an overwhelming 170 dishes, including a couple of dozen varieties of pho (noodle soup).

South-east London

Modern European

Inside

19 Greenwich South Street, Greenwich, SE10 8NW (8265 5060/www.insiderestaurant.co.uk). Greenwich rail/DLR. **Open** noon-2.30pm, 6.30-11pm Tue-Fri; 11am-2.30pm, 6.30-11pm Sat; noon-3pm Sun. **Main courses** £10.95-£16. **Credit** AmEx, MC, V.

Set among run-down shops near the station, Inside is a little gem. Service from the sole waitress is faultlessly attentive and the menu offers plenty of spring-like flavours alongside Middle Eastern influences. Classic brunch dishes available on Saturday.

South-west London

Cafés & brasseries

Crumpet

66 Northcote Road, Clapham, SW11 6QL (7924 1117/www.crumpet.biz). Clapham Junction rail. **Open** 9am-6pm Mon-Sat; 10am-6pm Sun. **Main courses** £3.95-£14.95. **Credit** AmEx, MC, V.

Bright, airy and uncluttered, Crumpet has a tempting assortment of old-fashioned cakes, hand-cut sandwiches, salads and snacks, as well as smoothies and a long list of teas. There's a separate children's menu full of healthy options. Fantastic for families, pointless for those without small children.

Fish and chips

The exact origins of this peculiarly British ensemble – fried fish with chipped potatoes – have been all but lost in the murk of myriad deep-fat fryers. In London it's likely that the eat-in chippie began life in the mid 19th century, propelled into being by the same imperative that helped create pie and mash shops (*see p89* **Mash point**): a vast increase of the urban working class, whose members needed a cheap, filling lunch.

Despite a lengthy heritage of fish frying, you should choose your chippie with care. Timing, oil temperature and ultra-fresh ingredients are needed to produce fragile, crisp batter; flaky, succulent fish; and golden-brown chips.

Strangely, given that fish and chips are still a core part of the London diet, few chains have been successful and almost all of the best chippies are one-offs.

Fish Central

149-155 Central Street, Clerkenwell, EC1V 8AP (7253 4970/www.fishcentral.co.uk). Angel tube/Old Street tube/rail/55 bus. **Open** 11am-2.30pm, 5-10.30pm Mon-Thur; 11am-2.30pm, 5-11pm Fri, Sat. **Credit** AmEx, MC, V. **Map** p404 P3 102

Miles from anywhere, this place is nonetheless constantly packed by Londoners who travel from all over for what they reckon is the best chippie in town.

Fryer's Delight

19 Theobald's Road, Holborn, WC1X 8SL (7405 4114). Chancery Lane or Holborn tube. **Open** noon-10pm Mon-Sat. **No credit cards. Map** p401 M5 103

Long a cabbies' favourite, this no-frills Formica-clad chippie comes with low-wattage lighting and unforgiving bench seating. The menu is short but sweet: fish, chips and the relevant accompaniments, plus sausages.

Golden Hind

73 Marylebone Lane, Marylebone, W1U 2PN (7486 3644). Bond Street tube. **Open** noon-3pm, 6-10pm Mon-Fri; 6-10pm Sat. **Credit** AmEx, MC, V. **Map** p400 G5 104

The fish here is as fresh as you'll find anywhere. Chips – the colour of proper lager – are done to a turn, and the mushy peas are excellent, but the biggest draw for fish and chips fans is the decommissioned art deco fryer displayed in the dining room.

Masters Super Fish

191 Waterloo Road, South Bank, SE1 8UX (7928 6924). Waterloo tube/rail. **Open** noon-3pm, 5.30-10.30pm Mon; noon-3pm, 4.30-10.30pm Tue-Thur, Sat; noon-3pm, 4.30-11pm Fri. **Credit** MC, V. **Map** p406 N8 105

It ain't sophisticated, but the food here's great. Takeaway or sit down, the menu offers everything from hamburgers to dressed Cromer crab, whitebait and calamares, as well as own-made pickles and puddings.

Rock & Sole Plaice

47 Endell Street, Covent Garden, WC2H 9AJ (7836 3785). Covent Garden tube. **Open** 11.30am-11pm Mon-Sat; noon-10pm Sun. **Credit** MC, V. **Map** p409 Y2 106

There has been a chippie on this site since 1871. In clement weather the outside seats get thronged – and the waiting staff shoo off takeaway customers hoping to rest their legs.

Sea Cow

57 Clapham High Street, Clapham, SW4 7TG (7622 1537). Clapham Common or Clapham North tube. **Open** noon-11pm Tue-Sat; noon-9pm Sun. **Credit** JCB, MC, V.

Part of a small south London chain and one of the very few chippies to offer organic food. Trendy minimal design complements unusual fish options such as swordfish, red snapper and a daily special. The future of the chippie?

Other locations: 37 Lordship Lane, Dulwich, SE22 8EW (8693 3111); 78 Fulham Road, Fulham, SW6 5SA (7610 8020).

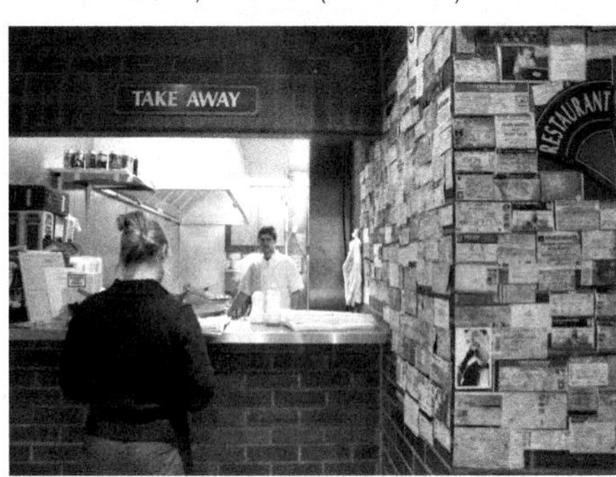

Fish & chips

Sea Cow

See p221 **Fish and chips**.

French

Le Bouchon Bordelais

5-9 Battersea Rise, Battersea, SW11 1HG (7738 0307/www.lebouchon.co.uk). Clapham Junction rail/35, 37 bus. **Open** *Brasserie* 10am-1am Mon-Sat; 10am-11pm Sun. *Restaurant* noon-3pm, 6-11pm Mon-Fri; noon-11pm Sat; 12.30-11pm Sun. **Main courses** £14.50-£19.50. **Credit** AmEx, MC, V.

A classic French brasserie: heavy accents at the zinc bar, whirring ceiling fans, loud music, Ricard ashtrays, a serious coffee machine and a competent bar menu. Most of the classics are present, with lovers of French desserts likely to be thrilled. The more staid restaurant dispenses digestifs and brasserie fare to an older clientele. Service is supercilious and/or charmingly knowledgeable.

Chez Bruce

2 Bellevue Road, Wandsworth, SW17 7EG (8672 0114/www.chezbruce.co.uk). Wandsworth Common rail. **Open** noon-2pm, 6.30-10.30pm Mon-Fri; 12.30-2.30pm, 6.30-10.30pm Sat; noon-3pm, 7-10pm Sun. **Set meals** £23.50-£37.50 3 courses. **Credit** AmEx, DC, MC, V.

It's remarkable to find a Michelin-starred restaurant this far from the centre of town. Bruce Poole's classy modern French cuisine hits the heights, and his wondrous sommelier presides over one of London's finest lists. Ignore the puddings, because you *must* try the cheeseboard. It's a lovely setting too, overlooking the Common. Be certain to book.

Gastropubs

Inn at Kew Gardens

292 Sandycombe Road, Kew, Surrey TW9 3NG (8940 2220/www.theinnatkewgardens.com). Kew Gardens tube. **Open** 11am-11pm Mon-Thur, Sun; 11am-midnight Fri, Sat. **Main courses** £9.50-£13.50. **Credit** AmEx, MC, V.

A rustic bistro feel dominates the main dining room at the back of this tastefully refurbished boozer. The menu features confidently executed gastropub classics (ribeye, Toulouse sausages) and sensational fish and charcuterie platters. Well-kept draught beer and a notable wine list complete the picture.

Modern European

The Glasshouse

14 Station Parade, Kew, Surrey TW9 3PZ (8940 6777/www.glasshouserestaurant.co.uk). Kew Gardens tube/rail. **Open** noon-2.30pm, 7-10.30pm Mon-Thur; noon-2.30pm, 6.30-10.30pm Fri, Sat; 12.30-2.45pm, 7.30-10pm Sun. **Set meals** £23.50-£35 3 courses, £50 7 courses. **Credit** AmEx, MC, V.

A light, bright, wedge-shaped room in the middle of Kew village, the Glasshouse continues to be a major local attraction. You can expect excellent food – it's owned by the people behind Chez Bruce (*see p222*) – with some dishes having been evolving on the menu for years. Book for dinner and Sunday lunch.

Oriental

Tsunami

5-7 Voltaire Road, Clapham, SW4 6DQ (7978 1610). Clapham North tube. **Open** 6-11pm Mon-Fri; 12.30-11.30pm Sat; 1-9.30pm Sun. **Main courses** £6.95-£20. **Credit** AmEx, MC, V.

When Tsunami opened in 2001, chef Singi Nakamura was hailed by critics as the new saviour of Japanese food. Nakamura has long since moved on, but the menu still has that Nobu-esque blend of old and new, and the food is as fantastic as ever.

West London

Cafés & brasseries

Frank's

See p212 **Caffs with class**.

Harris' Café Rest

See p212 **Caffs with class**.

French

Chez Kristof

111 Hammersmith Grove, Hammersmith, W6 0NQ (8741 1177/www.chezkristof.co.uk). Goldhawk Road or Hammersmith tube. **Open** *Deli* 8am-8pm Mon-Fri; 8.30am-7pm Sat; 9am-6pm Sun. *Restaurant* noon-3pm, 6-11.15pm Mon-Fri; noon-4pm, 6-11.15pm Sat; noon-4pm, 6-10.30pm Sun. **Main courses** £12.50-£17. **Credit** AmEx, MC, V.

Light and airy by day, intimate at night, Chez Kristof was created by owner Jan Woroniecki (also behind Baltic, *see p197*) as a space where dining is a social event, with informal staff who could as easily be customers and a buzzy, party atmosphere.

Indian

Sagar

157 King Street, Hammersmith, W6 9JT (8741 8563). Hammersmith tube/266 bus. **Open** noon-2.45pm, 5.30-10.45pm Mon-Thur; noon-2.45pm, 5.30-11.30pm Fri; noon-11.30pm Sat; noon-10.45pm Sun. **Main courses** £5-£10. *Thalis* £8.95-£11.45. **Credit** AmEx, DC, MC, V.

We've had consistently fabulous meals at Sagar, which specialises in Udupi cuisine, the natural, additive-free, vegetarian temple-style cooking from the southern Indian coastal region Karnataka. Expect subtle, sophisticated and distinctive flavours, and friendly and professional service.

Zaika

1 Kensington High Street, Kensington, W8 5NP (7795 6533/www.zaika-restaurant.co.uk). High Street Kensington tube. **Open** noon-2.45pm, 6.30-10.45pm Mon-Fri; 6.30-10.45pm Sat; noon-2.45pm, 6.30-9.45pm Sun. **Main courses** £12.50-£19.50. **Credit** AmEx, DC, MC, V. **Map** p396 C8 107

Zaika's substantial antiques, sweeping silken drapes and artful flower arrangements help transform this former bank into a theatrical setting. Chef Sanjay Dwivedi's delectable modern Indian cooking produces plenty of drama on the plates too.

Italian

River Café

Thames Wharf, Rainville Road, Hammersmith, W6 9HA (7386 4200/www.rivercafe.co.uk). Hammersmith tube. **Open** 12.30-3pm, 7-9.30pm Mon-Sat; 12.30-3pm Sun. **Main courses** £23-£32. **Credit** AmEx, DC, MC, V.

High summer is the best time to visit the hip and terrific River Café: it's easier to get a table and the table is likely to be in the pretty courtyard. You'll encounter exquisite ingredients (at premium prices) and a sensibly priced wine list that makes other establishments look greedy. Chocolate fans should opt for the famous Nemesis.

Timo

343 Kensington High Street, Kensington, W8 6NW (7603 3888/www.timorestaurant.net). High Street Kensington tube. **Open** noon-2.30pm, 7-11pm Mon-Fri; 7-11pm Sat; 7-10.30pm Sun. **Main courses** £13.50-£21.95. **Credit** AmEx, MC, V. **Map** p398 A9 108

This is a highly polished operation, with the food a tempting mixture of the innovative and the familiar. The interior is stylish and serene, and there's an enchanting walled garden.

Modern European

Clarke's

124 Kensington Church Street, Kensington, W8 4BH (7221 9225/www.sallyclarke.com). Notting Hill Gate tube. **Open** 12.30-2pm Mon; 12.30-2pm, 7-10pm Tue-Fri; 11am-2pm, 7-10pm Sat. **Main courses** *Lunch* £14-£16. *Dinner* £39.75 3 courses, £49.50 4 courses. **Credit** AmEx, MC, V. **Map** p396 B7 109

Sally Clarke has stayed at the cutting edge of culinary trends since the 1980s with her no-choice evening menu: three courses of char-grills and salads, using seasonal ingredients, carefully sourced. The drinks list has one of Europe's best selections of unusual New World wines. Book for weekends.

Vegetarian & organic

The Gate

51 Queen Caroline Street, Hammersmith, W6 9QL (8748 6932/www.thegate.tv). Hammersmith tube. **Open** noon-2.45pm, 6-10.45pm Mon-Fri; 6-10.45pm Sat. **Main courses** £8.50-£13.50. **Credit** AmEx, MC, V.

This well-heeled, artistically decorated venue is one of the capital's leading vegetarian restaurants. Food is based on the Mediterranean repertoire, but incorporates exotica such as Caribbean curry or aubergine teriyaki. Be sure to book.

Wapping Food. *See p220.*

Eat, Drink, Shop

Pubs & Bars

The cause of all life's problems – and the solution.

The citizens of London have been boozing in taverns and alehouses for centuries. With all that tradition and experience, you'd think that finding a convivial little pub for a pint and a bit of hospitality would be a pretty straightforward affair. We're sorry to say, it's not. Following years of intensive research into the subject, we can confidently – if somewhat regretfully – pronounce that four out of five London pubs are just dire. Too many are owned by massive conglomerates that treat their premises purely as retail outlets run by transient landlords who are encouraged to cultivate spreadsheets rather than customers.

That's the bad news. The good news is that the one out of five pubs that are good are very good indeed. In fact, in recent years the London pub has been given a new lease of life by a new (and often young) generation of entrepreneurial landlords (and landladies). Across town, neglected or ailing pubs are being given radical makeovers typically involving exciting drinks selections, good food and a concerted pitch for the affections of the locals, whether that be through regular DJ sessions, singalongs round the piano or providing family corners.

Despite the continuing restlessness of a drinking scene that has been thriving and shape-shifting for many centuries, there remains a solid anchor of tradition. You can still find the London Pub of traditional lore, with its low beams and wonky floors and the thick-glassed little windows that ensure it's always 10pm at night no matter the time outside. Be warned, though: any pub that actually advertises itself as 'traditional' almost certainly dates back no further than the late 1990s (for the real lowdown on London's historic taverns, *see p234* **Time at the bar**).

In fact, there are a handful of other rules worth observing that will make your drinking experience in London a happier one. Avoid any pub where the beers are all 'lite', 'ice' or 'smooth' and where the staff sport logo-ed T-shirts. Offers of 2-for-1s and similar drink deals are the hallmark of the pub chain – if you're OK with mass-produced brands and staff who have all the motivation of an employee of a fast-food franchise, then please do take a seat. If a pub bears the same name as a remarkably similar-looking establishment you saw a couple of streets back, avoid – although this rule does not necessarily hold true for names such as the Blue Posts, Coach & Horses and Red Lion, all of which are attached to multiple pubs in central London, none of which have anything to do with each other.

One bane of drinking in London that is much harder to avoid is the ringing bell and cry of 'Time, please!' Despite new licensing laws introduced in November 2005 that allow pubs and bars to extend the hours they serve alcohol (they can stay open round the clock in theory), in practice this has made little difference. Almost no venues in central London have been given permission to stay open late. For a drink beyond 11pm (10.30pm on Sunday) you have to pay for entry to a DJ bar or club (*see pp319-328*). A more wide-reaching change is due for summer 2007, in the form of a ban on smoking in all public places, including pubs and bars.

But the best advice we can give is to start the night with a tube ticket: the days of the West End being home to the best bars are over. Try Hoxton and Shoreditch in the east, Notting Hill and Westbourne Grove in the west, and Brixton in the south. You'll not only find great venues, but also see London at its most cosmopolitan.

For a full survey of London drinking options, pick up a copy of the annual *Time Out Bars, Pubs & Clubs* guide (£8.99).

> ❶ Pink numbers given in this chapter correspond to the location of each pub and bar as marked on the street maps. *See pp396-409.*

The South Bank & Bankside

Archduke

Concert Hall Approach, SE1 8XU (7928 9370). Waterloo tube/rail. **Open** 8.30am-11pm Mon-Fri; 11am-11pm Sat. **Credit** AmEx, DC, MC, V. **Map** p403 M8 ❶

En route between Waterloo station and the South Bank Centre, this relaxed split-level bar sits beneath the Victorian railway arches, beguiling visitors with live jazz (8.30pm Tue-Sat) and amiable chatter.

Brew Wharf

Brew Wharf Yard, Stoney Street, SE1 9AD (7378 6601/www.brewwharf.com). London Bridge tube/rail. **Open** 11am-11pm Mon-Sat; 11am-4pm Sun. **Credit** MC, V. **Map** p406 P8 ❷

Beer + table football = **Café Kick**. The winning formula. *See p227.*

Housed in huge warehouse arches, the smart and sophisticated Brew Wharf boasts its own micro-brewery (a rarity in London). It shares a kitchen with the neighbouring Wine Wharf, where enthusiastic staff help you negotiate a vast array of viniculture. **Other locations**: Wine Wharf, Stoney Street (7940 8335/www.winewharf.com).

Fire Station

150 Waterloo Road, SE1 8SB (7620 2226). Waterloo tube/rail. **Open** 11am-11pm Mon, Sat; 11am-midnight Tue-Fri; noon-10.30pm Sun. **Credit** AmEx, MC, V. **Map** p406 N8 ❸

The shell of a fire station, built in 1910, is packed inside with long wooden tables, typically filled with boozy thirty-year-olds. The back restaurant does steady business, and there's a long wine list chalked up above the bar and a healthy range of hand-pumped beers. Very handy for Waterloo station.

George Inn

77 Borough High Street, SE1 1NH (7407 2056). London Bridge tube/rail. **Open** 11am-11pm Mon-Sat; noon-10.30pm Sun. **Credit** MC, V. **Map** p406 P8 ❹

See p234 **Time at the bar**.

Market Porter

9 Stoney Street, SE1 9AA (7407 2495). London Bridge tube/rail. **Open** 6-8.30am, 11am-11pm Mon-Fri; noon-11pm Sat; noon-10.30pm Sun. **Credit** AmEx, MC, V. **Map** p406 P8 ❺

Alongside Borough Market, the Market Porter cheerfully serves ludicrously monikered beer to lovers of real ale all day long; the early opening time is a historical anomaly, allowing thirsty porters to satisfy their thirst. In the evenings, no matter the weather, customers spill out from among the solid tables and barrels to drink on the pavements.

For merry olde England

See p234 **Time at the bar**.

For riverside views

Prospect of Whitby (*see p235*); **Trafalgar Tavern** (*see p235*); **White Cross** (*see p236*); **Blue Anchor** (*see p236*); **City Barge** (*see p236*); **Dove** (*see p236*).

For the talk of the town

Annex 3 (*see p227*); **Crazy Bear** (*see p228*); **Floridita** (*see p229*); **Milk & Honey** (*see p230*); **Cow** (*see p230*); **Apartment 195** (*see p232*).

For character and eccentricity

Black Friar (*see p226*); **Jerusalem Tavern** (*see p227*); **Seven Stars** (*see p227*); **Gordon's** (*see p229*); **Windsor Castle** (*see p230*); **Nag's Head** (*see p232*).

For great beer

See p228 **I'll have what they're not having**.

For great food

Seven Stars (*see p227*); **Smiths of Smithfield** (*see p227*); **Newman Arms** (*see p229*); **French House** (*see p230*); **Cow** (*see p230*); **Guinea** (*see p231*); **Anglesea Arms** (*see p232*); **Queens** (*see p233*).

Seven Stars. See p227.

The City

Black Friar

174 Queen Victoria Street, EC4V 4EG (7236 5474). Blackfriars tube/rail. **Open** 11am-11pm Mon-Wed, Sat; 11am-11.30pm Thur, Fri; noon-10.30pm Sun. **Credit** AmEx, MC, V. **Map** p406 O5 ❻

Built in 1875, the Black Friar was remodelled by Arts and Crafts Movement devotees in 1905. The result is a pale green mosaic exterior, a billowing white marble-topped bar and an odd anteroom with glorious lush carpet and gold and jade mosaic ceiling. Possibly London's most beautiful pub – and it serves a good selection of real ales.

Lamb Tavern

10-12 Leadenhall Market, EC3V 1LR (7626 2454). Monument tube/Bank tube/DLR. **Open** 11am-midnight Mon-Fri. **Credit** AmEx, DC, MC, V. **Map** p407 Q6 ❼

In the 18th-century glory days of this photogenic pub, it kept the market's meat, fish and fruit stallholders properly lubricated. These days most local traders deal only in stocks and shares. The matey main space is little more than a room with a bar in it, but there are tables on the gallery above, and a restaurant at the top.

Old Bell Tavern

95 Fleet Street, EC4Y 1DH (7583 0216). Blackfriars tube/rail. **Open** 11am-11.30pm Mon-Fri. **Credit** (over £10) AmEx, MC, V. **Map** p406 N6 ❽

See p234 **Time at the bar**.

Vertigo 42

Tower 42, 25 Old Broad Street, EC2N 1HQ (7877 7842/www.vertigo42.co.uk). Bank tube/DLR/Liverpool Street tube/rail. **Open** noon-3pm, 5-11pm Mon-Fri. **Credit** AmEx, DC, MC, V. **Map** p407 Q6 ❾

Check in at reception, pass through X-ray machines and metal detectors, and take a neon-illuminated express lift up 42 floors to the champagne bar. The decor is reminiscent of an airport executive lounge and the cocktails unimpressive, but the 360° views of London through floor-to-ceiling windows are everything you might hope for.

Ye Olde Cheshire Cheese

145 Fleet Street, EC4A 2BU (7353 6170). Blackfriars tube/rail. **Open** 11am-11pm Mon-Sat; noon-3pm Sun. **Credit** AmEx, DC, MC, V. **Map** p406 N6 ❿

This huge and gloomy 17th-century chophouse has serious literary pedigree (Dr Johnson, Dickens and Yeats are among those who got squiffy here). A cosy side bar by the alley entrance is the most appealing, although the cellared antechambers on several levels beneath are also atmospheric. Run by Yorkshire's Sam Smith brewery, so expect a short range of keenly priced ales.

Ye Old Watling

29 Watling Street, EC4M 9BR (7653 9971). Mansion House tube. **Open** 11am-11pm Mon-Fri. **Credit** AmEx, MC, V. **Map** p406 P6 ⓫

See p234 **Time at the bar**.

Holborn & Clerkenwell

Café Kick

43 Exmouth Market, EC1R 4QL (7837 8077/ www.cafekick.co.uk). Angel tube/Farringdon tube/rail/19, 38 bus. **Open** noon-11pm Mon-Thur; noon-midnight Fri, Sat; 4-10.30pm Sun (spring/summer only). **Credit** MC, V. **Map** p404 N4 ⓬

Enjoyably boisterous, Café Kick has three babyfoot tables at the front of a narrow bar. It stocks an excellent range of international bottled beers. A great destination at any time of the year, but especially so in summer when the bay doors open to the street. **Photo** *p225.*

Other locations: Bar Kick, 127 Shoreditch High Street, Shoreditch (7739 8700).

Cittie of York

22 High Holborn, WC1V 6BN (7242 7670). Chancery Lane or Holborn tube. **Open** 11.30am-11pm Mon-Sat. **Credit** (over £10) AmEx, MC, V. **Map** p401 M5 ⓭

See p234 **Time at the bar.**

Jerusalem Tavern

55 Britton Street, EC1M 5UQ (7490 4281/ www.stpetersbrewery.co.uk). Farringdon tube/rail. **Open** 11am-11pm Mon-Fri. **Credit** MC, V. **Map** p404 O4 ⓮

This former coffeehouse serves exemplary and often extraordinary booze from St Peter's Brewery in a fabulously wonky setting. Behind a shopfront dating to 1810, the interior is tight and cosy, with green-painted wood, chipped walls and candles complementing original tilework.

Match

45-47 Clerkenwell Road, EC1M 5RS (7250 4002/ www.matchbar.com). Farringdon tube/rail. **Open** 11am-midnight Mon-Fri; 5pm-midnight Sat. **Credit** AmEx, DC, MC, V. **Map** p404 O4 ⓯

Match is one of the the old guard of Clerkenwell bars, and much of its continuing success is down to Dale DeGroff's definitive and frequently changing cocktail list – prices of drinks can reach £12, but you get what you pay for. The space consists of a table-lined balcony overlooking a sunken standing and dancing space, which faces the excellently stoked and styled bar.

Babies and children admitted (before 5pm). Disabled: toilet. Tables outdoors (4, pavement).

Seven Stars

53 Carey Street, WC2A 2JB (7242 8521). Chancery Lane or Temple tube. **Open** 11am-11pm Mon-Fri; noon-11pm Sat; noon-10.30pm Sun. **Credit** AmEx, MC, V. **Map** p401 M6 ⓰

A fabulous little pub that squeezes the best ales, wines and food into a tiny, impressively narrow interior. It's low-ceilinged and cramped, but nobody minds. There's a blackboard of gastronomic fare prepared by proprietress, raconteur and TV chef Rosie Beaujolais. **Photo** *p226.*

Smiths of Smithfield

67-77 Charterhouse Street, EC1M 6HJ (7251 7950/ www.smithsofsmithfield.co.uk). Farringdon tube/rail. **Open** *Ground-floor bar/café* 7am-11pm Mon-Wed; 7am-12.30am Thur, Fri; 10am-12.30am Sat; 9.30am-10.30pm Sun. *Cocktail bar* 5.30-10.30pm Mon-Wed; 5.30pm-1am Thur-Sat. **Credit** AmEx, DC, MC, V. **Map** p404 O5 ⓱

Vibrant and roomy, SOS sprawls over four floors of a listed building right opposite Smithfield Market. The ground floor is where the buzzy after-work crowd drink and eat, but there's also a small red cocktail bar on the first floor. DJs play at 8pm Wednesday to Saturday; the decor is industrial warehouse chic.

Three Kings of Clerkenwell

7 Clerkenwell Close, EC1R 0DY (7253 0483). Farringdon tube/rail. **Open** noon-11pm Mon-Fri; 7-11pm Sat. **No credit cards. Map** p404 N4 ⓲

Welcome to slacker HQ, where shambling, creative souls congregate for happy pints under the watchful eye of a papier-mâché rhino head thrusting out over the open fire. Decorations run to glitter balls, fairy lights and candles, with a glass cabinet of snowdomes and a mighty Prestige jukebox in the slightly grungy upstairs rooms.

Ye Old Mitre

1 Ely Court, Ely Place, at the side of 8 Hatton Gardens, EC1N 6SJ (7405 4751). Chancery Lane tube/Farringdon tube/rail. **Open** 11am-11pm Mon-Fri. **Credit** AmEx, MC, V. **Map** p404 N5 ⓳

A gruffly cheerful and efficient Scottish barman pulls quality pints amid the wood panels and exposed beams of this deliciously hidden pub (it's down a tiny alley, marked only by a little pub sign between jewellers' shops). There's even a snug sized for half a dozen close friends. The upstairs room has least character and is thus usually less busy.

Bloomsbury & Fitzrovia

Annex 3

6 Little Portland Street, W1W 7JE (7631 0700). Oxford Circus tube. **Open** 5pm-midnight Mon-Fri; 6pm-midnight Sat. **Credit** AmEx, MC, V. **Map** p408 U1 ⓴

A maximalist, bad-taste chic informs the design at Annex 3, with an abundance of kitsch art, elaborate furniture and bin-end wallpapers, truly a junk-store muddle of styles. It can feel like you're moving around inside a pinball machine, but the extensive cocktail list is one of the most interesting in the West End. From the people behind fabulously camp Loungelover (*see p235*).

Bradley's Spanish Bar

42-44 Hanway Street, W1T 1UT (7636 0359). Tottenham Court Road tube. **Open** noon-11pm Mon-Sat; noon-10.30pm Sun. **Credit** MC, V. **Map** p408 W1 ㉑

This off-Oxford Street landmark is still a Spanish colony, even though a new generation (dreadlocked

I'll have what they're not having

Budweiser? Foster's? Carlsberg? Just say no. You are discerning enough to be consulting this particular guidebook, so apply that same well-honed level of discrimination when it comes to ordering a beer at the pub of your choice. What you want is a beer that is made of malt, yeast, hops and water, stored lovingly in a nice pub cellar and served fresh – what's known as a 'real ale', a living, breathing entity that's the beer drinker's equivalent of a decent farmhouse cheese. This being London, you also preferably want a London beer. That means Fuller's (producer of London Pride, as well as ESB, Chiswick and a few others) or Young's (Ordinary or Special). Except that Young's was recently bought out by a regional brewer and is set soon to leave its traditional south-west London home, but never mind. Both breweries have their own pubs (Fuller's pubs include the Dove, *see p236*, and the Star Tavern, *see p232*; Young's pubs include the Lamb, *see below*, the Lamb Tavern, *see p226*, and the Lamb & Flag, *see p229*), which are the best places to drink their beers.

But the range of good beers available in London goes well beyond that. Brews that we particularly like include Timothy Taylor's Landlord (served all over the place, but notably at Soho's Dog & Duck, *see p229*) and anything by south-coast brewer Harvey's (try it at the Seven Stars in Holborn, *see p227*). Any half-decent pub will have at least three real ales on draught and quite a few have considerably more. Brick Lane's Pride of Spitalfields (*see p235*) and the Fire Station in Waterloo (*see p225*) both offer a wide choice of real ales; the Market Porter (*see p225*) at Borough Market has a regularly changing roster of around eight, and the White Horse (*see p236*), way out west in Parsons Green (a lengthy trip but worth it), keeps up to 20.

For something truly unusual, visit the Jerusalem Tavern in Clerkenwell (*see p227*). This is the solitary London representative of Suffolk's St Peter's Brewery; its beers are dispensed in marsh-green bottles and come in combinations such as lemon and ginger or cinnamon and apple or, in the case of King Cnut Ale (dyslexics beware), barley, nettles and juniper.

Just one more thing: don't look to your fellow London drinkers for approval of your sophisticated and knowing choice. In England 75 per cent of the beer market is cornered by just five brands of heavily advertised, typically foreign, mass market, 'premium' lagers. Please don't let that put you off – real ale needs all the help it can get, and one day London's drinkers will thank you for it.

and/or pierced) mans pricey pumps of Spanish lager in the cramped, creaking, two-floor casket of velour. Punters spill on to the street in taxi-blocking bonhomie on summer nights. Top-quality jukeboxes.

Crazy Bear

26-28 Whitfield Street, W1T 2RG (7631 0088/ www.crazybeargroup.co.uk). Goodge Street tube. **Open** noon-11pm Mon-Fri; 6-11pm Sat. **Credit** AmEx, MC, V. **Map** p401 K5 22

Über-stylish yet supremely comfortable. Ignore the upstairs restaurant and head down an ornate staircase to the opulent bar of cowhide swivel stools and red padded alcoves. There's one menu for cigars, another for 'dim sum and drinks' which offers ace all-day £4 nibbles and stunningly good cocktails.

Lamb

94 Lamb's Conduit Street, WC1N 3LZ (7405 0713/ www.lambtavern.co.uk). Holborn or Russell Square tube. **Open** 11am-midnight Mon-Sat; noon-10.30pm Sun. **Credit** AmEx, MC, V. **Map** p401 M4 23

Founded in 1729, this beautifully restored etched glass and mahogany masterpiece is sheer class. Today the snob screens have a decorative role above the horseshoe island bar, but, back in the days when music hall stars were regulars here, they were used to deflect unwanted attention. The Pit, a sunken back area, gives access to a summer patio.

Museum Tavern

49 Great Russell Street, WC1B 3BA (7242 8987). Holborn or Tottenham Court Road tube. **Open** 11am-11.30pm Mon-Thur; 11am-midnight Fri, Sat; noon-10.30pm Sun. **Credit** AmEx, DC, MC, V. **Map** p401 L5 ㉔

While cagouled Italian kids crocodile into the main entrance to the British Museum, canny drinkers can be found in the pub opposite. Former haunt of Orwell and Marx, the Museum Tavern has been a handsome beast ever since its sumptuous mid 19th-century refurb. Tourists come for tradition; locals for the splendid range of ales.

Newman Arms

23 Rathbone Street, W1T 1NG (7636 1127/www.newmanarms.co.uk). Goodge Street or Tottenham Court Road tube. **Open** noon-midnight Mon-Fri. **Credit** MC, V. **Map** p400 J5 ㉕

The narrow alley beside this former brothel was splendidly sinister in the 1960 film *Peeping Tom*, but don't expect maverick Fitzrovia bohemians these days. The poky downstairs bar is patronised by chuckling nine-to-fivers, and upstairs duvet-sized puffs of pastry cover any number of creative fillings in the Famous Pie Room.

Covent Garden & the Strand

Coach & Horses

42 Wellington Street, WC2E 7BD (7240 0553). Covent Garden tube. **Open** 11am-11pm Mon-Sat; noon-10.30pm Sun. **Credit** MC, V. **Map** p409 Z3 ㉖

The closest decent boozer to the Piazza, the Coach is a genuine, expat Irish pub. Well-pulled black stuff is, of course, dispensed in the tiny bar area, as well as more than 70 whiskies from either side of the Irish Sea. The kind of place that could make a fortune from tourism, but doesn't feel it has to.

Gordon's

47 Villiers Street, WC2N 6NE (7930 1408/www.gordonswinebar.com). Embankment tube/Charing Cross tube/rail. **Open** 11am-11pm Mon-Sat; noon-10pm Sun. **Credit** AmEx, MC, V. **Map** p409 Y5 ㉗

A candelit warren of a cellar wine bar – the oldest in London, established in 1890 – where schooners of sherry are still dispensed from the ageing barrels behind the bar. And it's only a minute from Charing Cross station.

Lamb & Flag

33 Rose Street, WC2E 9EB (7497 9504). Covent Garden tube. **Open** 11am-11pm Mon-Sat; noon-10.30pm Sun. **Credit** MC, V. **Map** p409 Y3 ㉘

The Lamb & Flag is by far the best pub in the Covent Garden area. Consequently, most evenings, especially in warmer weather, you'll be hard pushed to get anywhere near its 350-year-old (or more) interior. The location is picture-perfect, at the head of a cobbled lane, with an ancient tunnelled passageway down one side. Elderly musos play trad jazz on a Sunday evening.

Lowlander

36 Drury Lane, WC2B 5RR (7379 7446/www.lowlander.com). Covent Garden or Holborn tube. **Open** noon-11pm Mon-Sat; noon-10.30pm Sun. **Credit** AmEx, MC, V. **Map** p409 Z2 ㉙

The bar counter is a vision: no fewer than 15 tall, gleaming chrome beer taps line up behind a twinkling array of upturned beer glasses of all shapes and sizes. Not enough? Then try one of the 40 bottled beers. A bit too much? Wait staff in white pinnies are ready to steady you with moules-frites.

Nell Gwynne

2 Bull Inn Court, WC2R 0NP (7240 5579). Covent Garden tube/Charing Cross tube/rail. **Open** 11am-11pm Mon-Sat. **No credit cards**. **Map** p409 Y4 ㉚

The West End's friendliest and, surely, its smallest pub. A short, tiled passageway leads to a cubbyhole, just large enough to accommodate a few tables. The historic connection dates from when King Charles II's mistress trod the boards of the theatres nearby, and the cosy interior is dark enough to imagine all kinds of liaisons taking place in a hidden corner.

Soho & Leicester Square

Cork & Bottle

44-46 Cranbourn Street, WC2H 7AN (7734 7807/www.donhewitson.com). Leicester Square tube. **Open** 11am-11.30pm Mon-Sat; noon-11pm Sun. **Credit** AmEx, DC, MC, V. **Map** p409 X4 ㉛

People have been celebrating fine wine here, between a sex shop and a cheap pizza place, for more than three decades. A 28-page list testifies to Don Hewitson's unpretentious, enthusiastic oenophilia; the bar food is exemplary.

Dog & Duck

18 Bateman Street, W1D 3AJ (7494 0697). Tottenham Court Road tube. **Open** noon-11pm Mon-Thur; noon-midnight Fri, Sat; noon-10.30pm Sun. **Credit** AmEx, MC, V. **Map** p408 W2 ㉜

Built in 1734, the Dog & Duck is traditional as can be, although the carved wood and glazed tiles date to the fin-de-siècle. Past guests include Orwell, who gives his name to the wine bar upstairs. Downstairs, in the tiny bar area and cosy back room, ale rules.

Floridita

100 Wardour Street, W1F 0TN (7314 4000/www.floriditalondon.com). Tottenham Court Road tube. **Open** 5.30pm-2am Mon-Wed; 5.30pm-3am Thur-Sat. **Admission** £10 after 7.30pm Thur-Sat. **Credit** AmEx, DC, MC, V. **Map** p408 W2 ㉝

Floridita recreates the glitz and gluttony of pre-Castro Cuba, concocting faithful Daiquiris in an expansive, sparkling basement space. An array of Cuban musicians and dancers provide entertainment after midnight, and there's an extensive cigar menu and fabulous bar snacks.

French House

49 Dean Street, W1D 5BG (7437 2799). Leicester Square or Piccadilly Circus tube. **Open** noon-11pm Mon-Sat; noon-10.30pm Sun. **Credit** AmEx, DC, MC, V. **Map** p408 W3 ㉞

The French House began between the wars; owner Victor Berlemont invited cabaret stars such as Maurice Chevalier here, creating a French connection strengthened when De Gaulle and his Free French had their office upstairs. The post-war era saw legendary boozers Brendan Behan, Dylan Thomas and Francis Bacon let rip. Today, with a restaurant uptairs, French House lager on tap and John Claridge's black-and-white photographs, it's all a bit more civilised.

Milk & Honey

(7292 9949/0700 655 469/www.mlkhny.com). Oxford Circus tube. **Open** *Non-members* 6-11pm Mon-Fri; 7-11pm Sat. **Credit** AmEx, DC, MC, V. **Map** p408 V2 ㉟

Milk & Honey has the cachet of a members' bar, without the pretension of complete exclusivity. The London incarnation of Manhattan's legendary referral-only destination is a total triumph. It isn't just the 40-odd cocktails (although they are exquisite and reasonably priced), it's the service that ushers them to your own snug booth. Numbers of punters are kept comfortable by the house policy of booking in a limited number of non-members, generally at the start of the week and always before 11pm – phone ahead.

Sun & Thirteen Cantons

21 Great Pulteney Street, W1F 9NG (7734 0934). Oxford Circus or Piccadilly Circus tube. **Open** noon-11pm Mon-Fri; 6-11pm Sat. **Credit** AmEx, DC, MC, V. **Map** p408 V3 ㊱

A pleasant mix of corner pub and clubby bar, this once-traditional tavern is a smart alternative to either. Etched glass and dark wood provide a pleasing backdrop to the main bar, adjoined by an understatedly stylish dining area. This being Soho, the clientele is an appealing social jumble.

Oxford Street & Marylebone

Prince Regent

71 Marylebone High Street, W1U 5JN (7467 3811). Baker Street tube. **Open** noon-11pm Mon-Sat; noon-10.30pm Sun. **Credit** AmEx, MC, V. **Map** p400 G4 ㊲

Giant pink fluffy umbrellas here are a touch of flamboyance in a well-thought-out pub. The food is a touch short of bona fide gastro, but everything else makes the grade: dark wood, lots of comfy seating, extensive blackboard wine list and a very impressive selection of wheat beers. An instant favourite with younger locals and often very busy.

Windsor Castle

29 Crawford Place, W1H 4LJ (7723 4371). Edgware Road tube. **Open** 11am-11pm Mon-Sat; noon-10.30pm Sun. **Credit** MC, V. **Map** p397 E5 ㊳

A festival of patriotism awaits the visitor to this diminutive traditional boozer. Every wall, shelf and corner is crammed full of relics of the royal family, past and present, and there's even a beefeater who presides over the entrance from his sentry box. A lively pub with a loyal local following.

Paddington & Notting Hill

Churchill Arms

119 Kensington Church Street, W8 7LN (7727 4242). Notting Hill Gate tube. **Open** 11am-11pm Mon-Wed; 11am-midnight Thur-Sat; noon-10.30pm Sun. **Credit** AmEx, MC, V. **Map** p396 B8 ㊴

Halfway between High Street Ken and Notting Hill, the Churchill has an interior that is filled with Davy lamps, musical instruments and a variety of copper knick-knacks. Despite the fine English beer and Winston-abilia, there's a definite Irish tinge to the place, with *Cead Mille Failte* signs and photos of the Clare hurling team.

Cow

89 Westbourne Park Road, W2 5QH (7221 0021). Royal Oak or Westbourne Park tube. **Open** noon-11pm Mon-Thur; noon-midnight Fri, Sat; noon-10.30pm Sun. **Credit** MC, V. **Map** p396 A5 ㊵

Tom Conran's take on the Irish pub is renowned for its oysters and Guinness. The pub part of the operation is located on the ground floor, with a dining area at the back that serves a well-executed seafood-oriented menu; the more expensive dining room upstairs is popular for Sunday roasts. It's a bona fide celeb haunt.

Lonsdale

44-48 Lonsdale Road, W11 2DE (7727 4080/www.thelonsdale.co.uk). Ladbroke Grove or Notting Hill Gate tube. **Open** 6pm-midnight Mon-Thur, Sun; 6pm-1am Fri, Sat. **Credit** AmEx, MC, V. **Map** p396 A6 ㊶

The space-age decor seems less enticing than when the Lonsdale was *Time Out*'s Bar of the Year back in 2003 and the clientele no longer solely comprises the beautiful people, but the cocktail list remains long and imaginative (it was conceived by London mixmaster Dick Bradsell). DJs play on Friday and Saturday nights.

Portobello Gold

95-97 Portobello Road, W11 2QB (7460 4900/www.portobellogold.com). Notting Hill Gate tube. **Open** 10am-midnight Mon-Thur; 10am-12.30am Fri; 9am-12.30am Sat; 10am-11.30pm Sun. **Credit** AmEx, DC, MC, V. **Map** p396 A6 ㊷

At the hilly end of Portobello Road, the Gold is an undeniable treasure. The small bar is well stocked with wine and both draught and bottled beer, there's a restaurant at the back that serves seafood (including fine oysters), and live music events are put on each Wednesday night. The pub also hires itself out as a gallery, and there are a cybercafé and small hotel upstairs.

Tom & Dick's

30 Alexander Street, W2 5NU (7229 7711/www.tomanddicks.com). Royal Oak tube. **Open** 6.30pm-midnight Tue-Sat. **Credit** AmEx, MC, V. **Map** p396 B5 43

Part French boudoir, part multimedia venue, this quirky place hovers between art deco and the 21st century, just managing to stay on the cool side of camp. Service is slick but friendly, and the cocktail-led drinks list achieves a good balance between classics and innovations.

Trailer Happiness

177 Portobello Road, W11 2DY (7727 2700/www.trailerh.com). Ladbroke Grove or Notting Hill Gate tube. **Open** 5-10pm 1st Mon of mth; 5-11pm Tue-Fri; 6-11pm Sat; 6-10.30pm Sun. **Credit** AmEx, MC, V.

A cosy little basement bar that resembles an Austin Powers shag pad. The good range of cocktails include authentic 1950s-style Tikis – the Zombie (five rums, absinthe) is limited to two per person, for obvious reasons. 'TV Dinners' run from finger food to lamb and lemon racks. DJs play most nights.

Windsor Castle

114 Campden Hill Road, W8 7AR (7243 9551/www.windsorcastlepub.co.uk). Notting Hill Gate tube. **Open** noon-11pm Mon-Sat; noon-10.30pm Sun. **Credit** AmEx, MC, V. **Map** p396 A8 44

The layout of the Windsor Castle is as it was when the place was built in 1835, with the Campden, Private and Sherry Rooms filled with wooden pews and booths. Food is as important as the real ale and wines. There are seats outside in summer, and a warming fire in winter.

Piccadilly & Mayfair

Guinea

30 Bruton Place, W1J 6NL (7499 1210/www.theguinea.co.uk). Bond Street or Green Park tube. **Open** 11am-11pm Mon-Fri; 6-11pm Sat. **Credit** AmEx, DC, MC, V. **Map** p402 H7 45

In stark contrast to the English sophistication of the Restaurant & Grill that lurks at the back, the pub is fairly rough and ready, with slightly unruly customers kept in check by stern, elegant women who operate the bar with speed and efficiency.

Red Lion

1 Waverton Street, W1J 5QN (7499 1307). Green Park tube. **Open** 11.30am-11pm Mon-Fri; 6-11pm Sat; 6-10.30pm Sun. **Credit** AmEx, MC, V. **Map** p402 H7 46

Hidden in the back streets, the pub has an intimate, front-room feel with its miniature tables and toby jugs. The landlord is always hospitable, pulling pints with a cheeky wink. There's honest, unpretentious pub fare too.

Westminster & St James's

Red Lion

2 Duke of York Street, SW1Y 6JP (7321 0782). Piccadilly Circus tube. **Open** noon-11pm Mon-Sat. **Credit** MC, V. **Map** p408 V5 47

Just behind Piccadilly stands yet another of London's many Red Lions, renamed in the early 1600s, like hundreds of others, in honour of King James I. Many, such as this one, were later given

The **Golden Heart**, home-from-home for Young British Artists. *See p234.*

an ornate Victorian makeover, hence the delicately carved woodwork and etched glass that enliven the compact bar to this day.

Red Lion

48 Parliament Street, SW1A 2NH (7930 5826). Westminster tube. **Open** 11am-11pm Mon-Fri; 11am-9.30pm Sat; noon-8pm Sun. **Credit** AmEx, MC, V. **Map** p403 L9 48

No bar – or, at least, no public bar – sums up Westminster as well as this famous boozer yards from the Houses of Parliament. The skinny main bar (there's also a cellar bar and an upstairs grill room) has wooden alcoves full of chatter, a division bell and TVs screening BBC Parliament, all of them haughtily overseen by sideburned ministers in Empire-era portraits.

Chelsea

Apartment 195

195 King's Road, SW3 5ED (7351 5195/www.apartment195.co.uk). Sloane Square tube/11, 19, 22, 211 bus. **Open** 4-11pm Mon-Sat. **Credit** AmEx, MC, V. **Map** p399 E12 49

Despite buzzed-in access via an ominous black door, this upmarket cocktail bar is very welcoming. In a setting reminiscent of the tasteful mansion of a glam rock star you get to browse a little flip-book menu of fine cocktails (the Mojitos are renowned) mixed for you by an all-female corps of bartenders.

Fox & Hounds

29 Passmore Street, SW1W 8HR (7730 6367). Sloane Square tube. **Open** 11am-11pm Mon-Sat; noon-10.30pm Sun. **Credit** MC, V. **Map** p402 G11 50

This minuscule pub is like a village local that has been flown in and dumped near Sloane Square. It could be someone's living room, with well-used armchairs, bookcases and paintings. The clientele is to match: guffawing blokes supping their ale out of old-style beer mugs.

Knightsbridge & South Kensington

Anglesea Arms

15 Selwood Terrace, SW7 3QG (7373 7960). South Kensington tube. **Open** 11am-11pm Mon-Sat; noon-10.30pm Sun. **Credit** AmEx, MC, V. **Map** p399 D11 51

This is a cheerful, unpretentious free house: the day's papers, polite and cheery regulars, staff of like demeanour… Interior decoration comes in the form of William Morris wallpaper, wood panelling and a discreetly erotic semi-nude. It's even got a colourful legend: Bruce Reynolds is said to have planned the Great Train Robbery here.

The Grenadier

18 Wilton Row, SW1X 7NR (7235 3074). Hyde Park Corner tube. **Open** noon-11pm Mon-Sat; noon-10.30pm Sun. **Credit** AmEx, DC, MC, V. **Map** p402 G9 52

Centuries old, this grand pub was originally the mess for Wellington's men; it's said that one soldier, beaten to death for cheating at cards, still haunts the place. The tiny front bar is packed nightly with a mix of toffee-nosed locals and tourists eyeing up the souvenir tankards.

Nag's Head

53 Kinnerton Street, SW1X 8ED (7235 1135). Hyde Park Corner or Knightsbridge tube. **Open** 11am-11pm Mon-Sat; noon-10.30pm Sun. **No credit cards. Map** p402 G9 53

In this winningly eccentric pub, the floor of the main bar is a foot lower behind the counter, rendering staff in curious miniature; conversely, from the downstairs room, you can see bartenders' feet as they pour perfect pints. The place is cluttered with all sorts of relics (including a what-the-butler-saw kiosk) and, best of all, mobile phones are banned.

Star Tavern

6 Belgrave Mews West, SW1X 8HT (7235 3019/www.fullers.co.uk). Hyde Park Corner or Knightsbridge tube/Victoria tube/rail. **Open** 11am-11pm Mon-Sat; noon-10.30pm Sun. **Credit** AmEx, MC, V. **Map** p402 G9 54

Back in the 1960s, the centuries-old Star Tavern was favoured by some of London's more raffish drinkers: actors, models and even Great Train Robbers. The ale is in excellent nick, the food is decent and there's no piped music. It can be a bugger to find, but once you're in, you won't be in any hurry to leave.

Townhouse

31 Beauchamp Place, SW3 1NU (7589 5080/www.lab-townhouse.com). Knightsbridge tube. **Open** 4pm-midnight Mon-Sat; 4-11.30pm Sun. **Credit** AmEx, MC, V. **Map** p399 F10 55

From the street the Townhouse is little more than a discreet sign and a doorway – and even that is hidden behind a meaty bouncer. Get past him and you'll find a sleek, narrow bar, with leather sofas in the tiny seating area at the back. The place is pleasantly chic, the bar staff are lovely and the cocktail list as big as a phonebook.

North London

Camden Head

2 Camden Walk, Islington, N1 8DY (7359 0851). Angel tube. **Open** 11am-11pm Mon, Tue; 11am-midnight Wed, Thur; 11am-1am Fri, Sat; noon-11pm Sun. **Credit** MC, V. **Map** p404 O2 56

Away from the frantic activity of Upper Street, the Head feels like a proper Victorian pub: frosted glass, working fireplace, gaslight fittings, banquettes. The indie-heavy jukebox plays at a sensible volume and a performance space upstairs hosts comedy nights.

Holly Bush

22 Holly Mount, Hampstead, NW3 6SG (7435 2892/www.hollybushpub.com). Hampstead tube.

Open noon-11pm Mon-Sat; noon-10.30pm Sun. **Credit** MC, V.
The Holly Bush can be a bugger to find, tucked away from Hampstead's main drag up a hill and off a gorgeous, almost rural residential road, but it's terrific. Dating to the 1800s, it has capacious, dim-lit front rooms (you could sit on on a beer barrel by the real fire) and lighter but no less charming rooms out back. Additional bonuses? No music, no fruit machine, splendid pies.

King's Head

115 Upper Street, Islington, N1 1QN (7226 0364/ www.kingsheadtheatre.org). Angel tube/Highbury & Islington tube/rail. **Open** 11am-1am Mon-Thur; 11am-2am Fri, Sat; noon-1am Sun. **No credit cards. Map** p404 O1 57
Legendary for its in-house theatre, where several British stars have cut their teeth, the King's Head is also a good place for a pint. The atmosphere is friendly and relaxed, bands play after the show each night, and the pub opens late.

Lockside Lounge

75-89 West Yard, Camden Lock Place, Camden, NW1 8AF (7284 0007/www.locksidelounge.com). Camden Town tube. **Open** noon-midnight Mon-Thur, Sun; noon-1am Fri, Sat. **Credit** AmEx, MC, V.
Assuredly Lockside, the Lounge is more like a trendily converted boathouse, with wooden tables strung along a narrow slice of a room, and refreshingly free of leather sofas. Tattooed and pierced bar staff serve up great tapas and bottled beers, plus decent cocktails. Around the outside is one of the best decks in Camden. Unpleasantly busy in summer.

Lock Tavern

35 Chalk Farm Road, Camden, NW1 8AJ (7482 7163/www.lock-tavern.co.uk). Camden Town or Chalk Farm tube. **Open** noon-midnight Mon-Thur; noon-1am Fri, Sat; noon-11pm Sun. **Credit** MC, V.
Don't be intimidated by the fiercely fashionable punters and the icily gorgeous staff, this is a brilliant boozer in a prime location. DJ sessions (*see p327*) guarantee a full house from Thursday to Sunday, but the media types are happy to spill out into the beer garden; upstairs is a more intimate space, with a quiet roof terrace. Be sure to wear your finest jeans and trainers.

Queens

49 Regent's Park Road, Primrose Hill, NW1 8XD (7586 0408/www.geronimo-inns.co.uk). Chalk Farm tube. **Open** 11am-11pm Mon-Thur; 11am-midnight Fri, Sat; noon-10.30pm Sun. **Credit** AmEx, MC, V.
Queens is two parts faded country boozer to one part London gastropub. The bar stretches down a long corridor-like space, with banquettes at one end and a curved window seat at the other.

Spaniards Inn

Spaniards Road, Hampstead, NW3 7JJ (8731 6571). Hampstead or Archway tube/210 bus. **Open** 11am-11pm Mon-Fri; 10am-11pm Sat, Sun. **Credit** AmEx, MC, V.
The Spaniards dates to the 16th century and has murky connections with highwayman Dick Turpin. It looks the part, with dim lantern lighting and galleon-style windows, and has a perfect location across the road from Hampstead Heath.

East London

Big Chill Bar

Old Truman Brewery, off Brick Lane, Spitalfields, E1 6QL (7392 9180/www.bigchill.net). Aldgate East tube/Liverpool Street tube/rail. **Open** noon-midnight Mon-Thur; noon-1am Fri, Sat; 11am-11.30pm Sun. **Credit** DC, MC, V. **Map** p405 S5 58
On the hip, pedestrianised area between Brick Lane and Commercial Street, this place teems with drinkers every night. Low-slung leather seating, patterned drapes, a chandelier and an incongruous bison head add to its allure. There's a cider menu, plus the usual beers and cocktails, and DJs play nightly (*see p327*).
Other locations: Big Chill House, 257-259 Pentonville Road, King's Cross (7427 2540).

dreambagsjaguarshoes

34-36 Kingsland Road, Hoxton, E2 8DA (7729 5830/www.dreambagsjaguarshoes.com). Old Street tube/rail. **Open** 5pm-midnight Mon; noon-1am Tue-Fri; 5pm-1am Sat; noon-12.30am Sun. **Credit** MC, V. **Map** p405 R3 59
This bar was once two retail outlets (hence the odd name), but there's little left of them except the old signs. Now concrete walls are softened by mellow

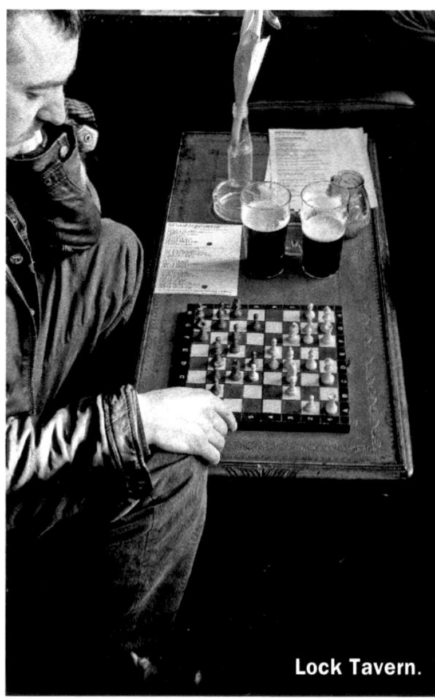
Lock Tavern.

Eat, Drink, Shop

Time at the bar

Age is always a thorny subject for conversation, so it's no surprise that there is such contention over the question of which London pub can call itself the city's oldest. There are as many candidates as there are criteria. Is it the **Lamb & Flag** (*see p229*), which occupies a building said to date to Tudor times but has only (only!) been a licensed premises since 1623? Or the **Cittie of York** (*see p227*), which has been the site of an inn since 1420, even if the building itself dates to around 1645 and was almost completely rebuilt in the 1890s, with the name pinched from an older tavern that used to sit across the road? Then there's the **Angel** (*see p235*), which since the 15th century was a pub kept by monks at the nearby 11th-century monastery, but was rebuilt in the 19th century. And the Thames-side **Prospect of Whitby** (*see p235*), which dates back to 1520, when it was known as the Devil's Tavern. Yet even this pub burnt down in the 18th century when the current, historically appealing structure went up in its place.

London lost lots of pubs in the Great Fire, which is why so many of the city's oldest pubs date to 1667 or thereabouts. In fact, **Ye Old Watling** (*see p226*) and the **Old Bell** (*see p226*) both claim to have been built by Sir Christopher Wren himself for the use of post-blaze rebuilders working at nearby churches. Modifications in the intervening centuries mean that neither pub appears particularly old. At least **Ye Olde Cheshire Cheese** (*see p226*) looks the part; it was built in 1667 but there was a pub here called the Horn in 1538 and the cellar dates to a 13th-century monastery. Also visually impressive is the **George Inn** (*see p225*), London's last galleried coaching inn, complete with fabulous black and white frontage, wonky beams aplenty and a full complement of lattice windows. Unfortunately (and the same is true of the Cheshire Cheese) the pub is packaged and marketed with a pack-'em-in mentality that borders on crass.

Such a confusion of name, location, licence and architecture makes finding London's definitive oldest pub almost impossible. With age and history being attractions in their own right, enterprising landlords will always be happy to muddy the waters in an attempt to gain custom. Our personal favourite, for which we make no claims (although the date on the sign says 1542), is **Ye Old Mitre** (*see p227*), which if not the city's oldest pub is certainly its best hidden.

lighting and a changing array of graffiti, manga figures or giant tattoos. DJs play everything from soft metal to rockabilly, and the place is reliably packed at the weekends.

Florist

255 Globe Road, Bethnal Green, E2 0JD (8981 1100/ www.thefloristE2.co.uk). Bethnal Green tube/rail/8 bus. **Open** 2.30-11pm Mon-Fri; noon-11pm Sat; noon-10.30pm Sun. **Credit** MC, V.

From the floral stained-glass over the door to the upright piano at the back this is a comfy East End local, but sofas, low tables and odd artwork indicate a bar, complete with diffident DJ. Come summer, you can sit on a bench-shelf outdoors. The beautifully tiled Camel (No.277, 8983 9888) just up the road is run by the same people – and serves terrific gourmet pies, mash 'n' mushy peas.

Golden Heart

110 Commercial Street, Spitalfields, E1 6LZ (7247 2158). Liverpool Street tube/rail. **Open** 11am-11pm Mon-Sat; 11am-10.30pm Sun. **Credit** AmEx, MC, V. **Map** p405 S5 (60)

The Golden Heart is a trad, dark wood boozer with a roaring fire in the saloon bar. Its enduring popularity is due to landlady Sandra Esquilant, confidante and surrogate mother of many BritArt enfants terribles (locals include Tracey Emin and Gilbert & George). With Spitalfields Market opposite, things are always busy: it's also worth dropping by the scruffy Ten Bells (No.84, 7366 1721) and the flamboyant and often unhinged Commercial Tavern (No.142, 7247 1888). **Photo** *p231.*

Grapes

76 Narrow Street, Limehouse, E14 8BP (7987 4396). Limehouse or Westferry DLR. **Open** noon-3pm, 5.30-11pm Mon-Fri; noon-11pm Sat; noon-10.30pm Sun. **Credit** AmEx, MC, V.

Imagine a historic riverside pub and it looks like this: handsome etched glass and greenery frontage; a wood-beams interior on the small side of cosy; model ships and sea charts; old-fashioned Sunday roasts and quality beer. It's believed this was the model for the Six Jolly Fellowship Porters in Dickens's *Our Mutual Friend.* A rickety balcony extends over the Thames.

Hoxton Square Bar & Kitchen

2-4 Hoxton Square, Hoxton, N1 6NU (7613 0709). Old Street tube/rail. **Open** 11am-1am Mon-Thur, Sun; 11am-2am Fri, Sat. **Credit** AmEx, MC, V. **Map** p405 R3 (61)

This is a fine space – huge front windows looking out on to patio seating, acres of leather sofas and swivel chairs – but timing is key. At weekends, it attracts noisy throngs of identikit drinkers, so weekday early evenings and Sunday afternoons are best. There's an adjoining restaurant, and DJs and bands play out back at weekends.

Loungelover

1 Whitby Street, Spitalfields, E2 7DP (7012 1234/ www.loungelover.co.uk). Liverpool Street tube/rail. **Open** 6pm-midnight Tue-Thur; 6pm-1am Fri; 7pm-1am Sat; 6pm-midnight Sun. **Credit** AmEx, DC, MC, V. **Map** p405 S5 ㉜

London's campest and most divinely decadent bar, swish Loungelover has a wealth of extravagantly theatrical fixtures, fittings and accessories – hippo's head, religious fresco, coloured perspex lighting, faux Regency chairs, fabulous chandeliers. You'll need to book to bag a seat in any of the nooks; otherwise, there's only the tiny space by the bar.

Pride of Spitalfields

3 Heneage Street, Spitalfields, E1 5LJ (7247 8933). Aldgate East tube. **Open** 11am-11pm Mon-Sat; noon-10.30pm Sun. **Credit** MC, V. **Map** p405 S5 ㉝

It's a relief to know there's a dyed-in-the-wool boozer just off Brick Lane, complete with pull-down screen for the football and quality ales on tap. The clientele successfully mixes old East Enders and middle-class bohemians.

Prospect of Whitby

57 Wapping Wall, Wapping, E1W 3SH (7481 1095). Wapping tube. **Open** noon-11pm Mon-Fri; noon-midnight Sat; noon-10.30pm Sun. **Credit** AmEx, DC, MC, V.

See p234 **Time at the bar**.

Royal Oak

73 Columbia Road, Bethnal Green, E2 7RG (7729 2220). Old Street tube/rail/Bethnal Green tube/26, 48, 55 bus. **Open** 6-11pm Mon; noon-11pm Tue-Thur; 6pm-midnight Fri; noon-midnight Sat; noon-11pm Sun. **Credit** AmEx, MC, V. **Map** p405 S3 ㉞

Another old-fashioned pub taken over by trendy locals, but the feel is casually welcoming rather than posey. An extensive wine list is chalked on the wooden beams, and the menu boasts mussels with parmesan and oysters in cider. The upstairs dining area is a less crowded space for feasting.

South-east London

Angel

101 Bermondsey Wall East, Rotherhithe, SE16 4NB (7394 3214). Bermondsey or Rotherhithe tube. **Open** noon-11pm Mon-Sat; noon-10.30pm Sun. **Credit** MC, V.

See p234 **Time at the bar**.

Ashburnham Arms

25 Ashburnham Grove, Greenwich, SE10 8UH (8692 2007). Greenwich rail/DLR. **Open** noon-11pm Mon, Wed, Sun; noon-midnight Tue, Thur-Sat. **Credit** MC, V.

A lovely neighbourhood pub, this, well run, well staffed, well stocked. Shepherd Neame beers and Oranjeboom lager are quietly consumed in the compact main bar, while a narrow corridor and conservatory lend themselves to convivial dining.

Liquorish

123 Lordship Lane, Dulwich, SE22 8HU (8693 7744/www.liquorish.com). East Dulwich rail/40, 176, P13 bus. **Open** 5pm-midnight Mon-Thur; 5pm-1am Fri; 11am-1am Sat; 11am-11.30pm Sun. **Credit** AmEx, MC, V.

This popular sliver of space somehow manages to be split into two, one part a sleek cocktail bar, the other a simple diner. DJ decks are discreetly positioned at the back for after-dark vibe control, when bare bulbs illuminate primary-coloured walls and bar stools apparently fashioned by Henry Moore.

Trafalgar Tavern

Park Row, Greenwich, SE10 9NW (8858 2909/ www.trafalgartavern.co.uk). Cutty Sark DLR/Maze Hill rail. **Open** noon-11pm Mon-Thur; noon-1am Fri, Sat; noon-10.30pm Sun. **Credit** MC, V.

Still 'home to the famous whitebait dinners', the Tavern trendified its food offerings for the bicentenary of the eponymous battle but the three-space candlelit bar remains as ever it was. The Thames laps against its wall and tourist trade (it's handy for the *Cutty Sark*) keeps things busy.

South-west London

Bread & Roses

68 Clapham Manor Street, Clapham, SW4 6DZ (7498 1779/www.breadandrosespub.com). Clapham Common or Clapham North tube. **Open** noon-11pm Mon-Thur; noon-midnight Fri; noon-midnight Sat; 11am-10.30pm Sun. **Credit** MC, V.

The Bread & Roses attracts a mixed and charming clientele because it's one of the city's best pubs – simple as that. The decor is simple, but enhanced by thoughtful additions such as the comical jelly bean machine. Entertainment includes live music and stand-up, and there's wireless internet access.

Cricketers

The Green, Richmond, TW9 1LX (8940 4372). Richmond tube/rail. **Open** noon-11pm Mon-Sat; noon-10.30pm Sun. **Credit** AmEx, MC, V.

Not many pubs boast a cricket team that plays outside their front door. In summer, even when not hosting a game, the Green often teems with punters wielding plastic glasses. Inside, the place combines traditional pub with wine bar, catering to a diverse crowd. There's comedy on a Wednesday.

Duke's Head

8 Lower Richmond Road, Putney, SW15 1JN (8788 2552). Putney Bridge tube/22, 265 bus. **Open** 11am-midnight Mon-Thur; 11am-1am Fri, Sat; noon-midnight Sun. **Credit** AmEx, MC, V.

This is a grand Victorian pub, set right on the bank of the Thames. The public bar is ideal for watching rugby matches; the larger saloon, with its fine open fire, is reminiscent of a country manor's drawing room, and the dining room offers wonderful views across the river, perfect for watching the annual Oxford–Cambridge Boat Race.

Living

443 Coldharbour Lane, Brixton, SW9 8LN (7326 4040/www.livingbar.co.uk). Brixton tube/rail. **Open** noon-2am Mon-Thur, Sun; noon-4am Fri, Sat. **Admission** £5 after 10pm Fri, Sat. **Credit** AmEx, MC, V.

If you're looking for a lively, up-for-it bar bang in the centre of Brixton, this two-floor venue delivers the goods. The atmosphere is pretty raucous on Friday and Saturday nights. Bhangra, Cuban or house DJs play out every night; there are also pole-dancing classes.

Prince of Wales

38 Old Town, Clapham, SW4 0LB (7622 3530). Clapham Common tube. **Open** 5-11pm Mon-Wed; 5pm-midnight Thur; 5pm-1am Fri; 1pm-1am Sat; 1-11pm Sun. **Credit** AmEx, MC, V.

Pots hang from the ceiling, a surfboard juts towards one of the small windows, a sofa is backed with skis and halberds, and the toilets are neighboured by a statuette and a mounted deer's head, but this pub's an amiable mess – the clientele just get on with their boozing and chatter.

White Cross

Water Lane, Richmond, TW9 1TH (8940 6844). Richmond tube/rail. **Open** 11am-midnight Mon-Sat; noon-10.30pm Sun. **Credit** MC, V.

Recalling the monastery that was this site's previous occupant, the White Cross's huge illuminated sign towers over the river. There are separate entrances for low and high tide, but during the spring you'll occasionally have to wade in anyway. A fire in winter and a secluded upstairs lounge make the place perfect for a mollifying drink.

White Horse

94 Brixton Hill, Brixton, SW2 1QN (8678 6666/www.whitehorsebrixton.com). Brixton tube/rail then 59, 118, 133, 159, 250 bus. **Open** 5pm-midnight Mon-Thur; 4pm-3am Fri; noon-3am Sat; noon-1am Sun. **Credit** AmEx, MC, V.

Part scruffy boozer, part style bar and part rave, the White Horse is a likeably mixed-up beast. The pleasant, open interior is perfect for munching Jamaican jerk chicken or playing pool during the day; things get louder and more riotous with DJs playing until late on Fridays and Saturdays.

West London

Blue Anchor

13 Lower Mall, Hammersmith, W6 9DJ (8748 5774). Hammersmith tube. **Open** 11am-11pm Mon-Sat; noon-11pm Sun. **Credit** MC, V.

Dating from 1722, the sleepy riverside boozer where Gustav Holst allegedly penned his *Hammersmith* is a mere blade-length from the Thames – and an unashamedly boaty establishment. On cold days, the upstairs function room is a lovely spot, with views of Hammersmith Bridge; in warm weather, there are the tables outside, which make another fine vantage for the annual Varsity Boat Race.

City Barge

27 Strand-on-the-Green, Kew, W4 3PH (8994 2148). Gunnersbury tube/rail/Kew Bridge rail. **Open** 11am-11pm Mon-Sat; noon-10.30pm Sun. **Credit** AmEx, DC, MC, V.

This place isn't a barge at all – but it is on the river and it has been the site of a pub since medieval times. The several different bars are characterised by tiled floors and open fires, with the low-ceilinged downstairs bar the most atmospheric (and the most popular). A handful of tables overlook the river on the waterside terrace.

Defectors Weld

170 Uxbridge Road, Shepherd's Bush, W12 8AA (8749 0008/www.defectors-weld.com). Shepherd's Bush tube. **Open** noon-midnight Mon-Thur; noon-1am Fri, Sat; noon-11.30pm Sun. **Credit** MC, V.

This large, brown-fronted, two-storey corner pub is lively, modern and stylish. The front has leather seats, fresh flowers and an open fire; the back is more intimate, with candlelit seating, exceptionally soft armchairs and small wooden booths, and upstairs is a smart cocktail lounge with table service. A commendable music policy is not confined to the DJs at weekends.

Dove

19 Upper Mall, Hammersmith, W6 9TA (8748 5405). Hammersmith or Ravenscourt Park tube. **Open** 11am-11pm Mon-Sat; noon-10.30pm Sun. **Credit** AmEx, MC, V.

Selling drinks since Hammersmith was a dozy hamlet, this 17th-century masterpiece started as a coffee shop before moving on to bigger things. William Morris lived next door, Hemingway and Graham Greene both drank here, and the *Guinness Book of Records* bestowed an award on the microscopic front bar (50in x 94cm) back in 1989. In addition to some lovely river views from within, the Dove has a Thames-side terrace.

White Horse

1-3 Parsons Green, Parsons Green, SW6 4UL (7736 2115/www.whitehorsesw6.com). Parsons Green tube. **Open** 11am-midnight Mon-Sat; 11am-11pm Sun. **Credit** AmEx, MC, V.

Large and generally very crowded, the White Horse merits some waiting time at the bar: it has 20 beers on draught, another 75 British and international ales in bottles. Food is also a strong point, with emphasis on British fare like hot smoked pheasant or steak and ale pie. No wonder it has been voted best UK pub two years running by trade mag *The Morning Advertiser*.

Shops & Services

Whatever you want, you'll find it here.

James Smith & Sons. *See p254.*

Multicultural street markets and deluxe department stores, mould-breaking fashion designers and traditional tailors who still stitch suits by hand, flashy modern furniture flagships and dusty antiquarian dens – not to mention a cornucopia of local and globe-spanning foodstuffs and some of the best places on the planet to buy books, records and vintage clothes… The sheer breadth of choice can be overwhelming, but we've taken pains to root out obscure gems as well as the pick of the latest openings.

Central London shops are open late one night a week, usually till 7pm or 8pm. Those in the West End (Oxford Street to Covent Garden) are open until late on Thursdays, while Wednesday is late opening in Chelsea and Knightsbridge.

For more listings, reviews pick up the annual *Time Out Shops & Services* (£9.99).

Antiques

Islington, Kensington and Chelsea are the three antiques centres in London. *Antiques Trade Gazette* (www.antiquestradegazette.com), the *Collector* (www.artefact.co.uk) and *Antique Collecting* (www.antique-acc.com) have listings on dealers, plus details of auctions. **Greenwich Market** has a sizeable antiques section, as does **Portobello Road** (for both, *see p263*).

Alfies Antique Market

13-25 Church Street, Marylebone, NW8 8DT (7723 6066/www.alfiesantiques.com). Edgware Road tube/Marylebone tube/rail. **Open** 10am-6pm Tue-Sat. **Credit** varies. **Map** p397 E4.
Vintage furniture and fashion. *See also p256* **Get thee to Church**.

Antiquarius

131-141 King's Road, Chelsea, SW3 5PH (7351 5353/www.antiquarius.co.uk). Sloane Square tube then 11, 19, 22, 319, 211 bus. **Open** 10am-6pm Mon-Sat. **Credit** varies. **Map** p399 E12.
Around 120 dealers with specialisms from vintage trunks to original film art.

Camden Passage

Camden Passage, off Upper Street, Islington, N1 5ED (7359 0190/www.antiquesnews.co.uk/camden passage). Angel tube. **Open** *General market* 7am-6pm Wed, Sat. *Book market* 8.30am-6pm Thur. *Vintage clothing* noon-7pm Sun. **Credit** varies. **Map** p404 O2.
Boutiques are encroaching on this once-thriving antiques enclave, but plenty of dealers remain.

Grays Antique Market & Grays in the Mews

58 Davies Street, Mayfair, W1K 5LP & 1-7 Davies Mews, Mayfair, W1K 5AB (7629 7034/www.grays antiques.com). Bond Street tube. **Open** 10am-6pm Mon-Fri. **Credit** varies. **Map** p400 H6.
Stalls in this smart covered market sell everything from jewellery to rare books. More than 200 dealers.

Books

Branches of the big chains can be found on Oxford Street, including **Borders** (No.203, 7292 1600, www.borders.co.uk) and **Waterstone's** (No.311, 7499 6100, www.waterstones.co.uk), while **Blackwells** is on Charing Cross Road (No.100, 7292 5100, www.blackwell.co.uk). For local bookshops, *see p241* **Fully booked**.

Books for Cooks

4 Blenheim Crescent, Notting Hill, W11 1NN (7221 1992/www.booksforcooks.com). Ladbroke Grove tube. **Open** 10am-6pm Tue-Sat. **Credit** MC, V.
Books in this much-celebrated shop cover hundreds of cuisines, chefs and cookery techniques. Even better, the shop's kitchen-café tests a different recipe every day.

Daunt Books

83-84 Marylebone High Street, Marylebone, W1U 4QW (7224 2295/www.dauntbooks.co.uk). Baker Street tube. **Open** 9am-7.30pm Mon-Sat; 11am-6pm Sun. **Credit** MC, V. **Map** p400 G5.
Our favourite place in town for travel guides and literature, plus a well-selected array of general fiction and non-fiction. The shop itself is gorgeous, with a galleried area illuminated by a vast fan light.
Other locations: 193 Haverstock Hill, Belsize Park, NW3 4QL (7794 4006); 51 South End Road, Hampstead, NW3 2QB (7794 8206); 112-114 Holland Park Avenue, Holland Park, W11 4UA (7727 7022).

Foyles

113-119 Charing Cross Road, Soho, WC2H 0EB (7437 5660/www.foyles.co.uk). Tottenham Court Road tube. **Open** 9.30am-9pm Mon-Sat; noon-6pm Sun. **Credit** AmEx, MC, V. **Map** p409 X2.
Independently owned and open since 1906, Foyles is London's best-known bookshop, revered for the sheer volume of its stock, which is spread over five floors. Ray's Jazz (*see p239*) and attached café are on the first floor.
Other locations: Riverside, Level 1, Royal Festival Hall, South Bank, SE1 8XX (7440 3212).

Hatchards

187 Piccadilly, St James's, W1J 9LE (7439 9921/ www.hatchards.co.uk). Piccadilly Circus tube. **Open** 9.30am-7pm Mon-Sat; noon-6pm Sun. **Credit** AmEx, DC, MC, V. **Map** p408 V5.
London's oldest bookshop (established 1797) is spread over five floors; former shoppers include Disraeli, Byron and Wilde; an 18-year-old Noël Coward was once caught shoplifting here.

The exquisite **Daunt Books**.

Stanfords

12-14 Long Acre, Covent Garden, WC2E 9LP (7836 1321/www.stanfords.co.uk). Covent Garden or Leicester Square tube. **Open** 9am-7.30pm Mon, Wed, Fri; 9.30am-7.30pm Tue; 9am-8pm Thur; 10am-7pm Sat; noon-6pm Sun. **Credit** MC, V. **Map** p409 Y3.
Three floors of travel guides, travel literature, maps, language guides, atlases, globes and magazines. There's a Trailfinders concession and a select range of equipment. The basement houses the full range of British Ordnance Survey maps.

Travel Bookshop

13-15 Blenheim Crescent, Notting Hill, W11 2EE (7229 5260/www.thetravelbookshop.com). Ladbroke Grove or Notting Hill Gate tube. **Open** 10am-6pm Mon-Sat; noon-5pm Sun. **Credit** AmEx, MC, V.
Focused as much on travel literature as guides, with well-informed staff. Stock spans travelogues, history books, biographies, photographic titles – even children's travel books. Cabinets of antiquarian and rare books provide a taste of travel in times past.

CDs & records

HMV (www.hmv.co.uk) and the **Virgin Megastore** (www.virgin.com) are the most prominent high-street chains, but newcomer **Fopp** (*see p239*) has the lowest prices. Serious browsers should head for Soho's Berwick Street for **Reckless Records** (Nos.26 & 30, 7434 3362, www.reckless.co.uk), **Sister Ray** (Nos.34-35, 7734 3297, www.sisterray.co.uk), **CD City** (No.42, 7287 2272), **Mr CD** (No.80, 7439 1097, www.mrcd. co.uk) and **Vinyl Junkies** (No.94, 7439 2923, www.vinyl-junkies.co.uk). For rare vinyl, try **Hanway Street**, which is just off the western end of Oxford Street.

Brill

27 Exmouth Market, Clerkenwell, EC1R 4QL (7833 9757). Angel tube/Farringdon tube/rail. **Open** 10.30am-6.30pm Mon-Fri; 10.30am-5.30pm Sat. **Credit** AmEx, MC, V. **Map** p404 N4.
A record shop-cum-café, Brill uses its small size selectively: if it's stocked here, it's going to be good. If there were any prizes going for friendly and well-informed staff, then this place would be guaranteed a podium finish.

Flashback

50 Essex Road, Islington, N1 8LR (7354 9356/ www.flashback.co.uk). Angel tube. **Open** 10am-7pm Mon-Sat; noon-6pm Sun. **Credit** AmEx, MC, V. **Map** p404 O1.
This second-hand treasure trove has been stacking them high and selling them cheap for almost a decade. The CD selection is particularly strong for indie and rock, but there are also 99p singles, Xbox and PS2 games and the coolest rarities in town.

Fopp

220-224 Tottenham Court Road, Fitzrovia, W1T 7PZ (7299 1640/www.fopp.co.uk). Goodge Street tube. **Open** 10am-10pm Mon-Sat; noon-6pm Sun. **Credit** AmEx, MC, V. **Map** p401 K5.
Fast-growing independent chain store that amazes with low prices. Latest releases are just £10 and masses of back catalogue at £7 and £5. Books and DVDs retail at similarly low prices. It's impossible to visit without filling a basket.
Other locations: 1 Earlham Street, Covent Garden, WC2H 9LL (7379 0883); 18-24 Westbourne Grove, Bayswater, W2 5RH (7985 7470); 285 Camden High Street, Camden, NW1 7BX (7482 8960).

Harold Moores Records

2 Great Marlborough Street, Soho, W1F 7HQ (7437 1576/www.hmrecords.co.uk). Oxford Circus tube. **Open** 10am-6.30pm Mon-Sat; noon-6pm Sun. **Credit** AmEx, DC, MC, V. **Map** p408 V2.
The astonishing basement vinyl collection has perhaps 90,000 records, extending into all reaches of classical music.

Honest Jon's

278 Portobello Road, Notting Hill, W10 5TE (8969 9822/www.honestjons.com). Ladbroke Grove tube. **Open** 10am-6pm Mon-Sat; 11am-5pm Sun. **Credit** AmEx, MC, V.
Honest Jon's found its way here in 1979, where it was reportedly the first place in London to employ a Rastafarian. You'll find jazz, hip hop, soul, broken beat, reggae and Brazilian music on the shelves.

Ray's Jazz at Foyles

1st floor, Foyles Bookshop, 113-119 Charing Cross Road, Soho, WC2H 0EB (7440 3205/www.foyles. co.uk). Tottenham Court Road tube. **Open** 9.30am-9pm Mon-Sat; noon-6pm Sun. **Credit** AmEx, MC, V. **Map** p409 X2.
Modern jazz is best represented of the myriad sub-genres on display, even though it constitutes less than half the selection, which begins with 1920s trad jazz and doesn't stop until it reaches contemporary avant-garde. Second-hand jazz books too.

Museum gifts

Design Museum

Cool gifts with impeccable design credentials, such as Tord Boontje's ceramics (£10-£30), Jamie Hewlett's Designer of the Year posters (with characters from Gorillaz, £6) and the Nabaztag Wi-Fi rabbit (£80). *See p88.*

Museum of London

Anything and everything to do with London, from the new cockney rhyming slang range to handmade gifts and jewellery by local designers. *See p97.*

National Portrait Gallery

Books, postcards, slides and posters with faces of the famous are the thing here: Churchill playing cards, Shakespeare chocolates, Gunpowder Plot leather-bound notebooks. *See p138.*

Science Museum

A one-stop shop for gadgets and gizmos: plasma balls, model planes, space ice-cream (from £3), chemistry sets (£29.99) and an insect exploring kit (£9.99). *See p154.*

Tate Modern

A huge range of postcards, posters and books, as well as Orly Kiely laptop cases and Ally Capellino accessories. *See p85.*

Victoria & Albert Museum

In addition to the jewellery, furniture and books on fashion and textiles, there are one-off items, the 'Cherry on the Cake' collection, including two-tone flock wallpaper by Timorous Beasties (£120 per roll), and fake diamond rings (£8) by Alissia Melka-Teichrow. *See p154.*

Fully booked

There is currently a vogue across London for smaller, independently owned shops, a fashion that happily extends to local bookshops. They can't compete with the chains on price, but they often provide a better informed service and more select titles, reintroducing casual shoppers to the pleasure of browsing a curated collection of books that shows the personality of the selector. From **Bookseller Crow on the Hill** (50 Westow Street, SE19 3AF, 8771 8831, www.booksellercrow.com) in Crystal Palace and **John Sandoe** (10 Blacklands Terrace, SW3 2SR, 7589 9473, www.johnsandoe.com) in Chelsea to the **Owl Bookshop** (209 Kentish Town Road, NW5 2JU, 7485 7793) in Kentish Town and **Primrose Hill Books** (134 Regent's Park Road, Primrose Hill, NW1 8XL, 7586 2022, www.primrosehillbooks.co.uk), small bookshops across London have integrated into their communities by organising regular events and showing commitment to promoting local authors.

In Waterloo **Crockatt & Powell** (119-120 Lower Marsh, SE1 7AE, 7928 0234, www.crockattpowell.com) runs a book club and regular readings, while Hackney's **Broadway Books** (6 Broadway Market, E8 4QJ, 7241 1626) has cemented an enthusiastically loyal clientele simply by its responsiveness to local readers' preferences. Shops like **Metropolitan Books** (49 Exmouth Market, Clerkenwell, EC1R 4QL, 7278 6900, www.metropolitanbooks.co.uk) on Exmouth Market and **Blenheim Books** (11 Blenheim Crescent, W11 2EE, 7792 0777) in chi-chi Notting Hill have focused on creating spaces that people enjoy spending time in, while other independents have worked hard to develop specialisms that suit their particular locale: **Kilburn Bookshop** (8 Kilburn Bridge, Kilburn High Road, NW6 6HT, 7328 7071) is good for Irish and Caribbean literature, for example, whereas **Bolingbroke Bookshop** (147 Northcote Road, SW11 6QB, 7223 9344) in family-friendly Clapham is strong on children's fiction.

Rough Trade

130 Talbot Road, Notting Hill, W11 1JA (7229 8541/www.roughtrade.com). Ladbroke Grove tube. **Open** 10am-6.30pm Mon-Sat; noon-5pm Sun. **Credit** AmEx, DC, MC, V.

When the first CDs to jump out at you are Built to Spill, Fugazi and Thurston Moore, you know Rough Trade still has its radar set to 'quality control: maximum'. Its taste is impeccable, whether CD or vinyl. Here's to another 30 years in business.

Department stores

High-street fave for undies and ready meals, **Marks & Spencer** (www.marksandspencer.co.uk) also houses a designer Autograph collection for men and women. Its George Davis's Per Una fashion line has won fans too.

Fenwick

63 New Bond Street, Mayfair, W1A 3BS (7629 9161/www.fenwick.co.uk). Bond Street tube. **Open** 10am-6.30pm Mon-Wed, Fri, Sat; 10am-8pm Thur. **Credit** AmEx, MC, V. **Map** p400 H6.

If you appreciate having everything under one roof, but cower before the leviathans of Knightsbridge and Oxford Street, Fenwick offers a far more sedate shopping experience. Founded in 1891, it remains a family-run business, and the company prides itself on showcasing new labels alongside well-known designers. Accessories are a particular strength.

Fortnum & Mason

181 Piccadilly, St James's, W1A 1ER (7734 8040/ www.fortnumandmason.co.uk). Green Park or Piccadilly Circus tube. **Open** 10am-6.30pm Mon-Sat; noon-6pm Sun (food hall only). **Credit** AmEx, DC, MC, V. **Map** p408 V4.

Celebrating its tercentenary in 2007, London's oldest department store has remained resolutely old-fashioned, right down to its courtly tail-coated staff. The famed over-the-top food hall – marbled pillars and chandeliers – holds a wonderful range of confectionery, biscuits, jams and preserves, coffee and tea, as well as a bakery, although it can get as packed as a tin of Portuguese Sardines Picante (£2.25). Downstairs you'll find fresh meat, game and fish, traiteur dishes and a wine bar designed by the man behind the Wolseley (*see p211*). The upper floors are essentially a very large, classy gift shop – antique china teacups, bags by Lulu Guinness, leather backgammon sets and select perfumes (Miller Harris, Clive Christian).

Harrods

87-135 Brompton Road, Knightsbridge, SW1X 7XL (7730 1234/www.harrods.com). Knightsbridge tube. **Open** 10am-8pm Mon-Sat; noon-6pm Sun. **Credit** AmEx, DC, MC, V. **Map** p399 F9.

By turns tasteful (the unrivalled food halls, the fifth-floor perfumerie curated by renowned 'nose' Roja Dove) and tacky (the life-size waxwork of owner Mohammad Al Fayed in menswear; the mawkish shrine to Dodi and Di in the basement), this exuberant cathedral to consumerism has long been one of London's top tourist attractions. The food halls are spectacular – chandeliers drip with ornamental grapes in fruit and veg, while the meat and game room retains its original Edwardian tiling. The two Rooms of Luxury, plus the Egyptian Room with its friezes and a 10ft-high gold Ramses II pharoah, cover luxury accessories by the likes of Louis Vuitton, Valextra and Chloé. The main beauty hall includes a sizeable Chantecaille counter (*see p248* **Top five**), but there's also a Lifestyle Beauty room showcasing Kiehl's and MAC. Across the street Harrods 102 is a luxury version of a convenience store, offering takeaway food, dry cleaning and alternative remedies.

Harvey Nichols

109-125 Knightsbridge, SW1X 7RJ (7235 5000/ www.harveynichols.com). Knightsbridge tube. **Open** *Store* 10am-8pm Mon-Sat; noon-6pm Sun. *Café* 8am-10pm Mon-Sat; 8am-6pm Sun. *Restaurant* 10am-11pm Mon-Sat; 10am-6pm Sun. **Credit** AmEx, DC, MC, V. **Map** p399 F9.

Harvey Nicks is a stylish receptacle of well sourced labels and a restaurant (Fifth Floor, 7235 5250) that knocks spots off every other department store eaterie. The ground-floor beauty hall has exclusives such as make-up artist Sue Devitt's line. You'll find oversized 'it' bags from Chloé and Balenciaga, and slick suits alongside über-cool Fair Isle knits from California design collective Trovata. The third floor boasts one of the best denim ranges in London. The home department has a concession of Italian luxury brand Culti and there are pitstop beauty treatments courtesy of an Elemis SpaPod (*see p248* **Top five**).

John Lewis

278-306 Oxford Street, Marylebone, W1A 1EX (7629 7711/www.johnlewis.co.uk). Bond Street or Oxford Circus tube. **Open** 9.30am-7pm Mon-Wed, Fri, Sat; 9.30am-8pm Thur; noon-6pm Sun. **Credit** AmEx,MC, V. **Map** p400 H6.

Renowned for solid reliability and the courtesy of its staff, John Lewis also deserves a medal for its breadth of stock. Dressmakers usually find the material of their choice and knitters are impressed by a range of yarns that covers basics and posher Rowan and Debbie Bliss wools. Major renovations, due to be unveiled in spring 2007, will include two new transparent-sided banks of escalators and a partly glazed roof that will flood the store with natural light, as well as a new brasserie and restaurant.

Liberty

Regent Street, Soho, W1B 5AH (7734 1234/www.liberty.co.uk). Oxford Circus tube. **Open** 10am-7pm Mon-Wed, Fri, Sat; 10am-8pm Thur; noon-6pm Sun. **Credit** AmEx, DC, MC, V. **Map** p408 U2.

Charmingly idiosyncratic, Liberty is housed in a 1920s mock Tudor structure on Great Marlborough Street. It might not be the most dynamic department store but it is the most attractive. The gift room is in the middle of a soaring, galleried atrium, with the store's characteristic art nouveau prints adorning everything from lingerie (own-label silk print camisoles and French knickers) to stamped-leather handbags. Take time out in the lovely tearoom or the café, with its sweet collection of mismatched chairs and tables. The fourth-floor furniture really dazzles, spanning 20th-century classics, one-off reconditioned vintage pieces and an impressive array of Arts and Crafts furniture.

Harrods. *See p241.*

Selfridges

400 Oxford Street, Marylebone, W1A 1AB (0870 837 7377/www.selfridges.com). Bond Street or Marble Arch tube. **Open** 9.30am-8pm Mon-Sat; noon-6pm Sun. **Credit** AmEx, DC, MC, V. **Map** p400 G6.

Selfridges' innovative displays, mini-me concession boutiques and themed events bring a sense of theatre to shopping. The designer accessory department has a new section devoted to keenly priced and highly covetable bags. Spirit, which houses a good-sized Topshop outpost among its high-street concessions, has recently upped its fashion cred with hip diffusion lines. Menswear covers everything from high-street staples to 'Superbrands'. The second floor's nine mini-boutiques of hot international labels for women have almost been eclipsed by the elegant new designer room, showcasing labels including Missoni and Roland Mouret.

Electronics

Tottenham Court Road (map p401 K5) has the city's main concentration of electronics and computer shops, but for good prices, expert advice and no hardsell **John Lewis** (*see p242*) is always a good option.

Ask

248 Tottenham Court Road, Fitzrovia, W1T 7QZ (7637 0353/www.askdirect.co.uk). Tottenham Court Road tube. **Open** 10am-7pm Mon-Wed, Fri, Sat; 10am-8pm Thur; noon-6pm Sun. **Credit** AmEx, DC, MC, V. **Map** p401 K5.

Some TCR shops feel gloomy and claustrophobic, but Ask has four capacious, well-organised floors that give customers space to browse. Stock concentrates on the major consumer brands, with a couple of more obscure, high-end manufacturers represented. Prices are fairly competitive.

Other locations: throughout the city.

Computers

CeX is good for accessories (*see below*).

Apple Store

235 Regent Street, Mayfair, W1B 2EL (7153 9000/ www.apple.com). Oxford Circus tube. **Open** 10am-9pm Mon-Sat; noon-6pm Sun. **Credit** AmEx, MC, V. **Map** p408 U2.

This trail-blazing, squeaky-clean concept store is always bustling with shoppers after the newest thing. Don't miss the bargain bins to the right of the stairs (which sometimes even include discount laptops). Book an appointment at the 'Genius Bar' to receive one-on-one technical support.

Micro Anvika

245 Tottenham Court Road, Fitzrovia, W1T 7QT (7467 6000/www.microanvika.co.uk). Goodge Street or Tottenham Court Road tube. **Open** 9.30am-6pm Mon-Wed, Fri, Sat; 9.30am-6.30pm Thur; 11am-5pm Sun. **Credit** AmEx, MC, V. **Map** p401 K5.

With three shops on Tottenham Court Road (plus a fourth just off it, and branches in Harrods and Selfridges), Micro Anvika is hard to avoid. We aren't enamoured of the overall vibe or the in-your-face service, but it occupies a specific market niche that leaves the chain few competitors. Stocking both the full range of Apple computers and a detailed selection of quality PCs (Toshiba, Sony, Fujitsu, HP), Micro Anvika is one of the few genuine one-stop computer shops in the centre of town. Also sells digital cameras and MP3 players.

Other locations: throughout the city.

Computer games

CeX

32 Rathbone Place, Fitzrovia, W1T 1JJ (0845 345 1664/www.cex.co.uk). Tottenham Court Road tube. **Open** 10am-7.30pm Mon-Wed, Sat; 10am-8pm Thur, Fri; 11am-7pm Sun. **Credit** MC, V. **Map** p401 K5.

With stores right across the UK, the CeX chain specialises in video games and DVDs on the one hand, computer equipment, peripherals and other electronics on the other. The Rathbone Place flagship focuses on games and DVDs, with staff who really know (and care) about what they are selling and stock that is bang up to date. The electronics side of the business is covered at 70 Tottenham Court Road.

Eat, Drink, Shop

Photography

For film processing, there are citywide branches of **Jessops** (www.jessops.com) and **Jacobs Photo & Digital** (www.jacobsdigital.co.uk).

Calumet

93-103 Drummond Street, Somers Town, NW1 2HJ (7380 1144/www.calumetphoto.com). Euston tube/rail. **Open** 8.30am-5.30pm Mon-Fri; 8.30am-5.30pm Sat. **Credit** AmEx, MC, V. **Map** p400 J3.

Caters mainly for professional snappers, students and darkroom workers. Lights, power packs, gels, tripods, printing and storage stock complement top-end digital gear. Also does repairs and rental.

Other locations: 175 Wardour Street, Soho, W1F 3WU (7434 1848).

Fashion

For shoes and other accessories, *see pp251-257*; for spectacles, *see p261*.

Boutiques

A Butcher of Distinction

11 Dray Walk, Old Truman Brewery, off Brick Lane, Spitalfields, E1 6QL (7770 6111/www.butcherof distinction.com). Liverpool Street tube/rail. **Open** 10am-7pm daily. **Credit** AmEx, MC, V. **Map** p405 S5.

In contrast to the area's more experimental retail spaces, this is a haven of impeccable, traditional fashion. The clean-lined butcher theme (meat hooks, beautifully framed joint charts, porcelain tiles) offsets the clothes to perfection; labels are a successful mix of old and new, embracing Levi's Vintage, Loomstate, Ralph Lauren and Tricker's shoes.

Aimé

32 Ledbury Road, Notting Hill, W11 2AB (7221 7070/www.aimelondon.com). Notting Hill Gate tube. **Open** 10.30am-7pm Mon-Sat. **Credit** AmEx, MC, V. **Map** p396 A6.

French-Cambodian sisters Val and Vanda Heng-Vong have brought understated Parisian cool to Notting Hill. Inside their airy, two-floor shop, you'll find casual separates, nostalgic Repetto ballet flats and romantic silver jewellery, inscribed with lines of French poetry. There are also delicately packaged bath products and hard-to-resist home accessories, including Aimé's own-brand scented candles.

Austique

330 King's Road, Chelsea, SW3 5UR (7376 3663/ www.austique.co.uk). Bus 11, 22. **Open** 10.30am-6.30pm Mon-Sat; noon-5pm Sun. **Credit** AmEx, MC, V. **Map** p399 D12.

Austique stocks super-feminine clothes, lingerie and accessories in a light space. Find sexy cashmere sweaters and party dresses, as well as great denim from not-yet-ubiquitous names. Rising British star Alice McCall's saucy-sweet pieces have been hot sellers. Upstairs you'll find everything for the boudoir.

Browns

24-27 South Molton Street, Mayfair, W1K 5RD (7514 0000/www.brownsfashion.com). Bond Street tube. **Open** 10am-6.30pm Mon-Wed, Fri, Sat; 10am-7pm Thur. **Credit** AmEx, MC, V. **Map** p400 H6.

Joan Burstein's venerable store has reigned supreme for over 35 years. Among the 100-odd designers jostling for attention among its five interconnecting shops are Chloé, Dries Van Noten and Balenciaga, with an entire floor devoted to Jil Sander. As well as the superstars, there are up-and-coming designers such as Marios Schwab. A new women's shoe salon showcases footwear from the likes of Christian Louboutin, Biba and Yves Saint Laurent. Browns Focus is younger and edgier, while Browns Labels for Less is loaded with the leftovers from the previous season.

Other locations: Browns Men, 23 South Molton Street, Mayfair, W1K 5RD (7514 0038); Browns Focus, 38-39 South Molton Street, Mayfair, W1K 5RN (7514 0063); Browns Labels for Less, 50 South Molton Street, Mayfair, W1K 5SB (7514 0052); Browns Bride, 59 Brook Street, Mayfair, W1K 4HS (7514 0056); 6C Sloane Street, Chelsea, SW1X 9LE (7514 0040).

b store

24A Savile Row, Mayfair, W1S 3PR (7734 6846/ www.bstorelondon.com). Oxford Circus tube. **Open** 10.30am-6.30pm Mon-Fri; 10am-6pm Sat. **Credit** AmEx, MC, V. **Map** p408 U3.

To preview the UK's hottest up and coming designers, this is the place. New names include Alex Foxton, Ehud Joseph and Carola Euler, who provide

modern men's tailoring. b store continues to champion Peter Jensen's offbeat mens- and womenswear, as well as Bernhard Willhelm's eye-catching designs; footwear from Eley Kishimoto and b store's own Buddhahood label is another draw, as are the Judy Blame accessories.

Comfort & Joy

109 Essex Road, Islington, N1 2SL (7359 3898). Angel tube. **Open** 10.30am-6pm Tue-Sat. **Credit** MC, V. **Map** p404 P1.

Bored with identikit brands but lack the funds for niche designer gear? Comfort & Joy is a great source of unusual, good-quality clothes at high-street prices. Most of the unique garments sold here are made by partners Ruth and Anthony Wilson.

The Cross

141 Portland Road, Notting Hill, W11 4LR (7727 6760/www.thecrossshop.co.uk). Holland Park tube. **Open** 11am-5.30pm Mon-Sat. **Credit** AmEx, MC, V.

With consistently strong fashion and choice accessories, not to mention an A-list following, the Cross remains one of the capital's most successful boutiques. Upstairs, a range of Missoni womenswear is juxtaposed with kids' clothes and toys. The downstairs takes in Easton Pearson, Betty Jackson, Clements Ribeiro and oriental-influenced Dosa.

Koh Samui

65-67 Monmouth Street, Covent Garden, WC2H 9DG (7240 4280/www.kohsamui.co.uk). Covent Garden tube. **Open** 10.30am-6.30pm Mon-Wed, Fri, Sat; 10.30am-7pm Thur; noon-5.30pm Sun. **Credit** AmEx, DC, MC, V. **Map** p409 X3.

b store. *See p244.*

Koh Samui is a well-established name in any serious London shopper's black book. Alongside an eclectic mix of heavyweight labels like Marc Jacobs and Chloé (including their diffusion lines) are hand-picked vintage finds. As well as securing the season's must-haves, buyer Mark Sexton prides himself on his ability to root out new and exciting designers, many exclusive to the store. There's a massive display of beautiful jewellery and accessories.

The Library

268 Brompton Road, South Kensington, SW3 2AS (7589 6569). South Kensington tube. **Open** 10am-6.30pm Mon, Tue, Thur-Sat; 10am-7pm Wed; 12.30-5.30pm Sun. **Credit** AmEx, DC, MC, V. **Map** p399 E10.

Designer labels and literature may seem an unlikely combination, but this fantastic emporium convinces otherwise. Stock from seasoned greats like McQueen and Westwood hangs alongside that of newer stars like Kris Van Assche, whose suits are well worth a visit alone. There's a small selection of gift-friendly womenswear (cashmere, Balenciaga bags).

Luna & Curious

198 Brick Lane, Spitalfields, E1 6SA (mobile 07977 440212/www.lunaandcurious.com). Aldgate East tube/Liverpool Street tube/rail. **Open** noon-7pm daily. **Credit** MC, V. **Map** p405 S4.

Brick Lane's latest groovacious shop is this collective of jewellers, illustrators, ceramicists, textile and fashion designers whose beautiful arts are displayed within an exquisite boutique adorned by Natasha Lawes's strangely dark but intriguing masks and ornamental objects. Susie Coulthard specialises in the restoration of special vintage pieces, at very reasonable prices: a 1950s cocktail dress accessorised with matching necklace goes for just £65. Home furnishings and boudoir attire sit alongside Rachel Spencer's Heirloom Couture and Rheanna Lingham's individual jewellery and textiles.

RelaxGarden

40 Kingsland Road, Hoxton, E2 8DA (7033 1881/ www.relaxgarden.com). Old Street tube/rail. **Open** 1-7pm Mon-Wed; 1-8pm Thur, Fri; noon-6pm Sat, Sun. **Credit** MC, V. **Map** p405 R3.

Until you've paid a visit to Shinya Abe's tiny boutique, it's hard to imagine that such an oasis of calm could exist on edgy Kingsland Road. Buyer Eriko Nagata sources most of the stock in Japan and Italy, and also co-designs the shop's own label, which is the real highlight here: simple, feminine separates that are fantastic value. The collection is being expanded to include bags and other accessories.

Saloon

23 Arlington Way, Finsbury, EC1R 1UY (7278 4497/www.saloonshop.co.uk). Angel tube. **Open** 11am-7pm Mon, Wed-Fri; 11am-6pm Tue; noon-6pm Sat. **Credit** AmEx, MC, V. **Map** p404 N3.

Tucked behind Sadler's Wells, Keiko Kim-Hindley's sweet little shop combines fashion with interior items, stationery and a bit of art. Her excellent eye for pieces that are original but wearable takes in established names like Ginka by Neisha Crosland and Erotokritos, but also less familiar finds such as Finnish label Ivana Helsinki and Parisian chic courtesy of Néologie. There's a small selection of casual menswear and also an array of fantastic jewellery by independent designers.

Santos & Mowen

10 Earlham Street, Covent Garden, WC2H 9LN (7836 4365/www.santosandmowen.com). Covent Garden or Leicester Square tube. **Open** 11am-7pm Mon-Sat. **Credit** AmEx, MC, V. **Map** p409 X2.

Principally stocking DSquared and Dolce & Gabbana, alongside comparable niche brands, this small boutique avoids Eurotrash accusations by careful selection. The store layout is clever too. The large range of clothes – from leather trousers through preppy, checked chinos to monochrome T-shirts – throws up something for everyone.

Sefton

196 Upper Street, Islington, N1 1RQ (7226 7076). Highbury & Islington tube/rail. **Open** 10am-6.30pm Mon-Wed; 10am-7pm Thur, Fri; 10am-6.30pm Sat; noon-6pm Sun. **Credit** MC, V.

If you like your clothes high-end but don't have the energy for big-hitters like Harvey Nichols or Selfridges, Sefton could be the answer. Costume National, Miu Miu and Comme des Garçons are prominent and a good selection of Junk de Luxe and Yohji Yamamoto pleases those of quieter taste and slimmer wallet. Accessories include skinny, knitted block-colour ties, cufflinks and sunnies. The store is well thought out: the relatively small space feels neither cramped nor labyrinthine.

High street

Reiss

Kent House, 14-17 Market Place, Marylebone, W1H 7AJ (7637 9112/www.reiss.co.uk). Oxford Circus tube. **Open** 10am-6.30pm Mon-Wed, Fri, Sat; 10am-7.30pm Thur; noon-6pm Sun. **Credit** AmEx, MC, V. **Map** p400 H6.

While much of the high street continues to complain that trade is slow, sales are up at Reiss – proving that if you do something consistently well, you reap the rewards. Reiss sits somewhere between high street and high-end, delivering quality mens- and womenswear aimed at the mid-20s to mid-30s market. Womenswear looks youthful yet classy, and menswear runs from suits to chunky knitwear.

Other locations: throughout the city.

Topshop

214 Oxford Street, Marylebone, W1N 9DF (0845 121 4519/www.topshop.com). Oxford Circus tube. **Open** 9am-8pm Mon-Wed, Fri, Sat; 9am-9pm Thur; noon-6pm Sun. **Credit** AmEx, MC, V. **Map** p408 U2.

There aren't many shops that can keep everyone from teenies to 40-year-old fashion editors happy, but Topshop does so with seeming ease. The renovated London flagship accommodates an even bigger shoe department, a dedicated denim section and a brilliant maternity shop. Following in the strides of its older sister's success, Topman (www.topman.com) has acquired cult status leaps ahead of its high-street rivals. For affordable, directional casualwear, there is no competition. And with the introduction of Topman Design, fashionistas on the most shoe-string of budgets can look every inch the seasoned Hoxtonite. **Photo** *p249.*

Other locations: throughout the city.

Babies & children

The first stop for all things infant-related is **Mothercare** (www.mothercare.com). **John Lewis**, **Harrods** and **Selfridges** all have great kids' departments; for all three, *see p241* **Department stores**. The several London branches of the **Early Learning Centre** (www.elc.co.uk) are all dedicated to imaginative play for babies and little ones. And if pictures of Madonna's daughter Lourdes in a beautiful, hand-sewn dress from **Bunny London** (7627 2318, www.bunnylondon.com) caught your eye, there's a concession at Harvey Nichols (*see p242*). *See also p280* **Tot shops**.

Bob & Blossom

140 Columbia Road, Bethnal Green, E2 7RG (7739 4737/www.bobandblossom.com). Old Street tube/rail/55 bus. **Open** 9am-3pm Sun. **Credit** MC, V. **Map** p405 S3.

Not quite a toy shop – Bob & Blossom does those distinctive baby clothes with cheeky mottos ('The Boss') – here you'll also find beautiful wooden and knitted playthings, Mexican jumping beans and spinning tops. Classic toy cars and musical instruments have won the outlet many fans.

Boomerang

69 Blythe Road, Kensington, W14 0HP (7610 5232). Kensington (Olympia) tube/rail. **Open** 10am-6pm Tue-Sat. **Credit** MC, V.

Top-quality children's clothes are made to last, which is a shame if your child can only fit those Diesel trousers for one season, but a boon if you're sensible enough to check out Boomerang's nearly new range. There's a huge selection of new and second-hand sleepsuits and Grobags, kids' separates and shoes, and loads of baby paraphernalia.

Caramel Baby & Child

291 Brompton Road, South Kensington, SW3 2DY (7589 7001/www.caramel-shop.co.uk). South Kensington tube. **Open** 10am-6pm Mon-Sat; noon-5pm Sun. **Credit** AmEx, MC, V. **Map** p399 E10.

High-end children's fashion for lovers of labels. Delight in the tiny Prada leather pram shoes, little girls' linen sundresses and boys' striped pullovers in cashmere for those chilly Knightsbridge autumns. Rompers, skirts and trousers for ages up to ten, plus sweet soft stuffed rabbits and other trinkets for new babies widen the store's appeal.

Daisy & Tom

181-183 King's Road, Chelsea, SW3 5EB (7352 5000/www.daisyandtom.com). Sloane Square tube then 11, 19, 22 bus/49 bus. **Open** 9.30am-6pm Mon, Tue, Thur, Fri; 10am-7pm Wed, Sat; noon-6pm Sun. **Credit** AmEx, MC, V. **Map** p399 E12.

Top five

In-store treatments

Chantecaille

Following on from its Healing Spa (a slightly overblown name for the small room on the top floor of Fenwick, *see p241*), Chantecaille has brought Flower Facial to **Harrods** (*see p241*) to complement its new beauty counter. The 45-minute treatment (£75) feels longer because of the high massage quotient, using custom-blended organic oils. Attention to detail is impressive, from the rose petals and candles that create a soothing ambience to your own personal cotton robe. After a double-cleanse and spritz with pure rose water, the gorgeous-smelling Lily & Jasmine Healing Mask – warmed before application – is applied to face, neck and décolletage and topped off with a garnish of fresh rose petals. The facial left us destressed and dewy-skinned. Call 7225 5758 for appointments.

Elemis

British brand Elemis has a luxurious holistic spa in Mayfair but, if you don't have the time or money for a four-and-a-half-hour ritual, its SpaPod in **Harvey Nichols** (*see p242, pictured below*) offers a condensed version of the full spa experience. The treatment kicks off with a relaxing hot stone massage. As in the full spa version, the collagen mask is applied over silk, which is said to aid penetration. While your face is being tended to, the chair is working your body – pummelling, pulsating and vibrating while squeezing your legs to promote lymphatic drainage. Although it doesn't quite measure up to a spa treatment, you'll leave feeling revitalised and with a glowing complexion – not bad for £45. Call 7201 8585 for appointments.

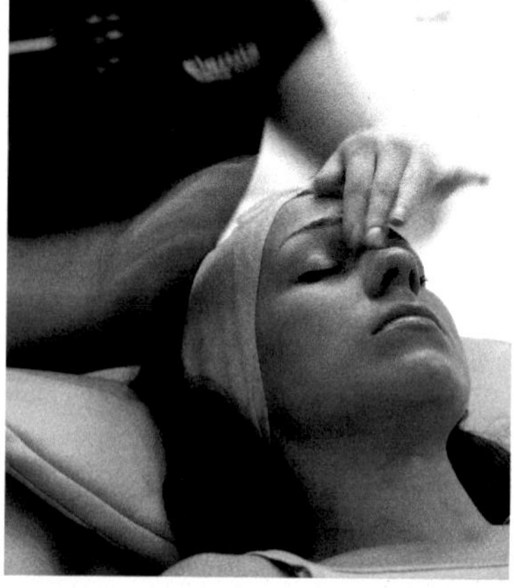

Fresh

It is surprisingly little known that all the treatments at Marylebone's **Fresh** shop (*see p260*) are redeemable against its covetable products, used throughout. Essentially, this boils down to free pampering, which takes some of the sting out of this premium skincare line's high prices. The menu majors in facials (£35-£65) and extravagant body rituals. The most popular is the elaborate Sake and Rice Body Treatment (£95 for 90 minutes); using the Rice range, it includes a full-body cleanse, exfoliation and massage, plus a mini- facial and foot soak. The chic, white treatment room is wonderfully calm and, unlike many in-store spaces, sound-insulated. Call 7486 4100 for appointments.

Groom

Hot on the heels of Knightsbridge's stand-alone Groom salon, this smart new **Selfridges** (*see p243*) outpost is already doing a busy trade in speedy beauty treatments for time-starved shoppers. These include the Weekly Groom (£105), a beauty MOT including a facial, mani, pedi and brow tidy; the latter can be swapped for a head massage if you prefer pampering to plucking. Although you can hear clients in the next treatment area, the super-comfy leather chairs tilt back properly, and having two therapists working on you in tandem feels highly indulgent. Call 7499 1199 for appointments.

Jo Malone

Despite the cachet of this exclusive brand, the Jo Malone therapists are personable and down to earth. The treatment room at the back of the flagship store (150 Sloane Street, 7730 2100, www.jomalone.co.uk) is serene, silent and candlelit. The treatment itself is gorgeous, using massage techniques to help the serums and moisturisers sink in properly, and your skin will be left glowing. The therapist even applies a touch of JM's make-up afterwards, which means you don't have to rush home but can carry right on with your shopping. The full-length 75-minute facial (plus a 15-minute consultation) costs £125. Call 7730 2100 for appointments.

Four times a day there's a call to the children to gather at the ground-floor carousel for a gentle spin. The toy selection is vast, everything from Lego kits to £2,000-plus handmade rocking horses. The clothing department carries its own Daisy & Tom label, plus Timberland, Elle, Catimini and more.

Green Baby

345 Upper Street, Islington, N1 0PD (7359 7037/ www.greenbaby.co.uk). Angel tube. **Open** 9.30am-5.30pm Mon-Fri; 9.30am-6pm Sat; 11am-5pm Sun. **Credit** MC, V. **Map** p404 N2.

Come here for adorable clothing basics for the newborn. Baby clothing is made in South India, as part of a community project that supports young girls.

Other locations: 5 Elgin Crescent, Notting Hill, W11 2JA (7792 8140).

Igloo

300 Upper Street, Islington, N1 2TU (7354 7300/ www.iglookids.co.uk). Angel tube/Highbury & Islington tube/rail. **Open** 10am-6.30pm Mon-Wed; 9.30am-7pm Thur-Sat; 11am-5.30pm Sun. **Credit** AmEx, DC, MC, V. **Map** p404 O1.

An imaginatively stocked and carefully thought-out one-stop shop for parents of babies and children aged up to eight. There are soft and pretty essentials by Petit Bateau, IKKS and Mitty James, and trendy shirts for boys by His Nibs. A haircutting station (fringe trim, £5) and shoe corner are also on site.

Trendys

72 Chapel Market, Islington, N1 9ER (7837 9070). Angel tube. **Open** 10am-6pm Mon-Sat; 11.30am-4.30pm Sun. **Credit** AmEx, MC, V. **Map** p404 N2.

An excellent source of affordable designerwear for babies and children, with frequent sales: for girls, half-price Converse All Stars at half price or Diesel jeans for £30, perhaps, and, for boys, affordable Bench workwear and Timberland boots.

Lingerie & swimwear

Agent Provocateur

6 Broadwick Street, Soho, W1V 1FH (7439 0229/ www.agentprovocateur.com). Oxford Circus or Tottenham Court Road tube. **Open** 11am-7pm Mon-Wed, Fri, Sat; 11am-8pm Thur; noon-5pm Sun. **Credit** AmEx, MC, V. **Map** p408 V2.

A leader in the luxury lingerie market: expect anything from transparent slips of near-nothingness to sculptured bras, from full-on corsets to half-cup peepholes. Brand staples include decadent, pure silk PJs and the tulle-lined, lacy Love range.

Other locations: throughout the city.

Alice & Astrid

30 Artesian Road, Notting Hill, W2 5DD (7985 0888/www.aliceandastrid.com). Notting Hill Gate tube. **Open** 11am-6pm Mon-Sat. **Credit** AmEx, DC, MC, V. **Map** p396 A6.

Girlishness is embraced at this compact boutique, with delicate but wholesome lingerie and nightwear – lots of cotton alongside flimsier silks. Camisoles are particularly strong, and knickers are often of the laid-back French variety, made with lounging more in mind than overt sexuality.

Good gear, great price: **Topshop**. *See p247.*

Heidi Klein

174 Westbourne Grove, Notting Hill, W11 2RW (7243 5665/www.heidiklein.com). Notting Hill Gate tube. **Open** 10am-6pm Mon-Sat; noon-5pm Sun. **Credit** AmEx, MC, V. **Map** p396 A6.

A year-round, one-stop holiday shop. Head to the back for tanning, tinting and waxing, then show off your beach-ready body in own-label swimsuits, hats and wraps, plus Michael Kors and Eres swimwear, Lenny kaftans, and Tom Ford sunglasses.

Other locations: 257 Pavilion Road, Chelsea, SW1X 0BP (7259 9418).

Miss Lala's Boudoir

148 Gloucester Avenue, Primrose Hill, NW1 8JA (7483 1888). Chalk Farm tube. **Open** 10am-6pm Mon-Wed, Fri, Sat; 10am-7pm Thur; 11am-4pm Sun. **Credit** DC, MC, V.

This cute dressing-up box of a shop is brimming with eclectic unmentionables – vividly hued bikinis, prettily printed pants, frilly undies – and sundresses. There's also a modest range of vintage jewellery.

Rigby & Peller

22A Conduit Street, W1S 2XT (7491 2200/www.rigbyandpeller.com). Oxford Circus tube. **Open** 9.30am-6pm Mon-Wed, Fri, Sat; 9.30am-7pm Thur. **Credit** AmEx, MC, V. **Map** p402 H7.

The corsetier to the Queen offers own-brand styl that are surprisingly modern and cost from a ve reasonable £25. A wide assortment of other mak is stocked, including predictably high-end play such as La Perla and Aubade, as well as classics l the Berlei shock absorber sports bra (£28). T made to measure service for which the family-r company is famed costs from £250.
Other locations: 2 Hans Road, Chelsea, SW3 (08 076 5545).

VPL

61A Ledbury Road, Notting Hill, W11 2AA (722 6644/www.vpl-london.co.uk). Notting Hill Gate tub **Open** 10am-6pm Mon-Sat; noon 5pm Sun. **Credit** AmEx, DC, MC, V. **Map** p396 A6.
This small but perfectly formed boutique st well-sourced lingerie, sleepwear and beautiful th to lounge in that you'd be hard-pressed to find where. The lingerie includes jewel-coloured sets by Frankly Darling in luscious hues of ruby and jade, and more casual cotton, broderie anglaise babydolls.

Tailors

Eddie Kerr

52 Berwick Street, Soho, W1F 8SL (7437 3727/ www.eddiekerr.co.uk). Oxford Circus tube. **Open** 8am-5.30pm Mon-Fri; 8.30am-1pm Sat. **Credit** MC, V. **Map** p408 V2.
A Soho institution since the early 1960s, Eddie Kerr turns out sharp bespoke gear in friendly, unostentatious surroundings. Suits cost from around £950. **Photo** *p252*.

Timothy Everest

32 Elder Street, Spitalfields, E1 6BT (7377 5770/ www.timothyeverest.co.uk). Liverpool Street tube/rail. **Open** 9am-6pm Mon-Fri; 9am-4pm alternate Sat. **Credit** AmEx, MC, V. **Map** p405 R5.
One-time apprentice to the legendary Tommy Nutter, Everest is a star of the latest generation of London tailors and known for his more relaxed 21st-century definition of style.
Other locations: 35 Bruton Place, Mayfair, W1J 6NS (7629 6236).

Tony Lutwyche

83 Berwick Street, Soho, W1F 8TS (7292 0640/ www.lutwyche.co.uk). Leicester Square or Tottenham Court Road tube. **Open** by appointment 9am-6pm Mon-Fri. **Credit** MC, V. **Map** p408 V2.
A career in the army helped Lutwyche develop his keen eye for sharpness, as well as the toughness to deal with customers like the fiery Gordon Ramsay. A bespoke two-piece can be yours from £800.

Vintage & second-hand

Luna & Curious (*see p245*) boasts an impressive and reasonably priced selection of reconditioned pieces. For the city's many markets, *see p259* **Top five**.

stylist, thrifter ... mega-bargains and inspiration. The 10,000 items on the warehouse floor include 1950s dresses, cowboy boots and denim hot pants, all for under £20.

British Red Cross Shop

67 Old Church Street, Chelsea, SW3 5BS (7351 3206). Sloane Square tube then 11, 19, 22 bus. **Open** 10am-5pm Mon-Sat. **Credit** MC, V. **Map** p399 E12.
Buying from charity shops is all about location: the more affluent the area, the better the stock. This happens to be the place where many designer neighbours – Manolo Blahnik, Catherine Walker – donate unwanted items. A recent look uncovered a fabulous Chanel bag, an Yves Saint Laurent shirt and a Catherine Walker wedding dress at bargain prices.
Other locations: throughout the city.

Twinkled

Unit 1.5, Kingly Court, Carnaby Street, Soho, W1B 5PW (7734 1978/www.twinkled.net). Oxford Circus tube. **Open** 11am-7pm Mon-Wed, Sat; 11am-8pm Thur, Fri; noon-6pm Sun. **Credit** AmEx, MC, V. **Map** p408 U3.
Combining vintage clothes and furniture, this is the place to come for Stepford Wives teasets, cocktail kits and petit four moulds. There's a very large selection of dresses from the 1930s to the '80s, airline-logo flight bags and even a selection of original patterns.

Fashion accessories & services

Accessories

The many citywide branches of **Accessorize** (www. accessorize.co.uk) provide decent quality at low prices.

The Jacksons

5 All Saints Road, Notting Hill, W11 1HA (7792 8336/www.thejacksons.co.uk). Notting Hill Gate tube. **Open** 10am-6pm Mon-Fri; 11am-6.30pm Sat. **Credit** AmEx, DC, MC, V.

Eddie Kerr. See p251.

The Jacksons sells standout shoes, bags and hats. The cowskin bag, brightened with a beaded handle, is a signature piece, but less expensive choices include a deep suede tote with studded handles.

Mimi

40 Cheshire Street, Spitalfields, E2 6EH (7729 6699/www.mimimika.com). Liverpool Street tube/ rail. **Open** by appointment only Tue-Thur; 10.30am-6pm Fri-Sat; 11am-6pm Sun. **Credit** MC, V. **Map** p405 S4.

Mimi Berry has been designing and crafting leather bags and purses since 2001. Her work has a girlie bent, evident in squishy, prettily dyed clutches and purses. All styles are beautifully lined in a variety of printed and multicoloured fabrics.

T Fox & Co

118 London Wall, City, EC2Y 5JA (7628 1868/ www.tfox.co.uk). Moorgate tube. **Open** 9am-6pm Mon-Fri. **Credit** AmEx, MC, V. **Map** p406 P5.

This independent company started out as an umbrella-maker in 1868, and today has widened its remit to include leather goods and workwear for the smart businessman.

Jewellery

Angela Hale

5 Royal Arcade, 28 Old Bond Street, W1S 4SE (7495 1920/www.angela-hale.co.uk). Green Park tube. **Open** 10am-6pm Mon-Sat. **Credit** AmEx, MC, V. **Map** p408 U4.

The destination for those in search of retro glamour. Edwardian styles are a recurring influence on the handmade costume jewellery, which is based on hypoallergenic bronze and prettified with Swarovski crystals. Achieve that vampish look with a jet on bronze, film noir-ish choker.

ec one

41 Exmouth Market, Clerkenwell, EC1R 4QL (7713 6185/www.econe.co.uk). Farringdon tube/rail. **Open** 10am-6pm Mon-Wed, Fri; 11am-7pm Thur; 10.30am-6pm Sat. **Credit** AmEx, MC, V. **Map** p404 N4.

Jos and Alison Skeates showcase jewellery from more than 50 designers. Jos Skeates's own designs are serious statement pieces, while Emma Craig makes impossibly delicate rings and bangles. There's also a dazzling array of Niessing and Henrich & Denzel engagement and wedding rings. **Other locations**: Notting Hill Showroom, 184 Westbourne Grove, W11 2RH (7243 8811).

Electrum Gallery

21 South Molton Street, Mayfair, W1K 5QZ (7629 6325). Bond Street tube. **Open** 10am-6pm Mon-Fri; 10am-5pm Sat. **Credit** AmEx, DC, MC, V. **Map** p400 H6.

This establishment is at the forefront of fresh, exciting jewellery design. Some of its newest arrivals are straight out of the Royal College of Art, but there are also established names such as Wendy Ramshaw and Tom Munsteiner among the 100 designers.

Garrard

24 Albemarle Street, Mayfair, W1S 4HT (7758 8520/www.garrard.com). Bond Street or Green Park tube. **Open** 10am-6pm Mon-Sat. **Credit** AmEx, DC, MC, V. **Map** p408 U5.

The crown jewellers' flirtation with cool flourishes, thanks to Jade Jagger. Her input as creative director modernised Garrard's designs to such an extent that Missy Elliott has been sparkling in its bling-tastic creations. But those with traditional tastes still pay stratospheric prices for classic diamond jewellery.

Lesley Craze Gallery

33-35A Clerkenwell Green, EC1R 0DU (7608 0393/ www.lesleycrazegallery.co.uk). Farringdon tube/rail. **Open** 10am-5.30pm Tue-Sat. **Credit** AmEx, DC, MC, V. **Map** p404 N4.

This multi-arts emporium is a gallery for work by regularly changing designers. The bulk is jewellery, augmented by metalsmithing and textiles. The most unusual pieces are to be found in the mixed-media section, which gives free rein to the unexpected and experimental. Prices start from £15.

Made in London

Open studio weekends, when artists and artisans throw open the doors of their private work spaces, provide a great opportunity to get your finger on London's creative pulse. Most venues hold open studio weekends twice a year, typically in early December and late spring or early summer.

Studios tend to be in former factories, with sweet factories seeming a particular favourite. You're more likely to see paintings than toffees, but the good news is it's all for sale. However, the real value of open studios – for artists and visitors alike – is making contact with an eye to future commissions. That could be anything from a bespoke hat to a vast painting.

Arts Unwrapped (www.creativelondon.org.uk/artsunwrapped) organises Europe's biggest open-studios event, which involves 2,000 London artists in November/December every year. To encourage visitors, a free shuttle service ferries you between premises. Also check out **Hidden Art** (7729 3800, www.hiddenart.com), a not-for-profit organisation that supports designer-makers working on a small or large scale. It holds open studio events in a series of locations around Holborn and Clerkenwell; see the website for details for 2007.

Clerkenwell Green Association

Pennybank Chambers, 33-35 St John's Square, Clerkenwell, EC1M 4DS (7251 0276/www.cga.org.uk). Barbican tube/ Farringdon tube/rail. **Dates** May or June 2007. **Admission** £2.50; free under-16s. **Map** p404 O4.

Supporting over 300 designer-makers, the Clerkenwell Green Association aims to sustain the fine craft skills that are in danger of being lost to Clerkenwell – an area where they have thrived for centuries. Every summer and winter, the association invites the general public to view work from more than 70 designer-makers; goods encompass jewellery, fashion accessories, textiles, homeware, ceramics, glass engravings, fresco and mural work, and photographs.

Cockpit Arts

Bloomsbury *Cockpit Yard, Northington Street, WC1N 2NP (7419 1959/www.cockpitarts.com). Chancery Lane tube.* **Dates** late May-early June 2007. **Admission** £5 (incl entry to Deptford site). **Map** p401 M4.

Deptford *Deptford Centre, 18-22 Creek Side, SE8 3DZ (8692 4463). Deptford or Greenwich rail.* **Dates** mid-late May 2007. **Admission** free-£2.

There are 100 designer-makers at Cockpit's Holborn studios and a further 65 at its Deptford arm. The variety of disciplines and wealth of talent mean that their open weekends are a craft-buyer's dream. Aline Johnson's candy-striped glass (tableware, vases, lighting) is particularly popular.

Great Western Studios

The Lost Goods Building, Paddington New Yard, Great Western Road, Bayswater, W9 3NY (7221 0100/www.greatwesternstudios.com). Westbourne Park tube. **Dates** late May 2007. **Admission** free. **Map** p396 A4.

A former British Rail building in the shadow of the Westway might seem an unlikely location for a hotbed of creativity, but the 140 artists and designers who work here don't seem too distracted by the sounds of buses, trains and automobiles. Central Saint Martins graduate Justin Hibbs creates urban landscapes in oil on board; Claudia Carr does micro-landscapes inspired by 14th-century Italian painting. You'll also find hand-painted wallpaper by Fromental. Lisa Campbell (actually Lady Lisa), author of the 2006 memoir *Title Deeds* about growing up in Cawdor Castle, has a studio here; her collages are fascinating and beautiful.

Wint & Kidd

237 Westbourne Grove, Notting Hill, W11 2SE (7908 9990/www.wintandkidd.com). Notting Hill Gate tube. **Open** 10.30am-5.30pm Mon-Wed, Fri, Sat; 10.30am-6.30pm Thur. **Credit** AmEx, MC, V. **Map** p396 A6.

Named after the villains in *Diamonds Are Forever*, Wint & Kidd deals exclusively in diamonds. There's a vast selection of stones and help is at hand for deciding how to wear your gem. Bespoke service is the focus, although there are ready-to-wear pieces. **Other locations**: The Courtyard, Royal Exchange, the City (EC3V 3LQ).

Shoes

Among the best shoe chains are **Aldo** (3-7 Neal Street, WC2, 7836 7692, www.aldoshoes. com), **Bertie** (36 South Molton Street, W1, 7493 5033, www.theshoestudio.com), **Birkenstock** (70 Neal Street, WC2, 7240 2783, www.birkenstock.co.uk), **Camper** (8-11 Royal Arcade, 28 Old Bond Street, W1, 7629 2722, www.camper.com), **Clarks** (476 Oxford Street, W1, 7629 9609, www.clarks.co.uk) and **Shellys** (266 Regent Street, W1, 7287 0939, www.shellys.co.uk).

It's trad, dad

James Smith & Sons.

Fancy a side order of history with your London purchases? Although, sadly, the traditional butcher, baker and fishmonger may not be a fixture of the city's high streets for much longer, for the moment at least, London retains some wonderful traditional old shops, in full working order. Here is a selection of our favourite survivors, all combining characterful atmosphere with fine wares.

Bates the Hatter

21A Jermyn Street, St James's, SW1Y 6HP (7734 2722/www.bates-hats.co.uk). Piccadilly Circus tube. **Open** 9am-5.15pm Mon-Fri; 9.30am-4pm Sat. **Credit** AmEx, DC, MC, V. **Map** p408 V4.

Sporting its iconic, topper-shaped sign outside, Bates has been equipping the Jermyn Street gent with classy headwear for more than 100 years. Hats and hatboxes line the cramped space. Even today you'll find impeccably crafted traditional toppers, bowlers and homburgs. Less anachronistic, a wide-brimmed fedora goes for £150, while a dapper grey trilby in Harris tweed is £63.50.

G Smith & Sons

74 Charing Cross Road, Covent Garden, WC2H 0BG (7836 7422). Leicester Square tube. **Open** 9am-6pm Mon-Fri; 9.30am-5.30pm Sat. **Credit** AmEx, DC, MC, V. **Map** p409 X3.

Established in 1869, G Smith was the first licensed tobacconist on Charing Cross Road and holds a condition of lease that states the site can only house a tobacconist. Which is good news for the many tobacco, pipe and cigar buffs who travel miles to visit this unique shop, virtually unchanged thanks to its status as a listed building. G Smith also has a natty line in lighters, cutters, ashtrays, pipes and snuff.

James Smith & Sons

53 New Oxford Street, Fitzrovia, WC1A 1BL (7836 4731/www.james-smith.co.uk). Holborn or Tottenham Court Road tube. **Open** 9.30am-5.25pm Mon-Fri; 10am-5.25pm Sat. **Credit** AmEx, MC, V. **Map** p409 X1.

A family umbrella business that has been on this site since 1830, James Smith (*photo left*) still boasts charming Victorian fittings that were made by the brolly craftsmen themselves. As well as umbrellas, there's an excellent range of walking sticks and canes – from shepherds' crooks to expensive South American snake-wood sticks with silver tops.

Church's Shoes

201 Regent Street, Mayfair, W1B 4NA (7734 2438). Oxford Circus tube. **Open** 10am-6.30pm Mon-Wed, Sat; 10am-7pm Thur, Fri; noon-6pm Sun. **Credit** AmEx, MC, V. **Map** p408 U3.

Church's formal men's shoes are world-renowned. Brogues, Oxfords and loafers start at around £265.

Other locations: throughout the city.

Office

57 Neal Street, Covent Garden, WC2H 9PP (7379 1896/www.office.co.uk). Covent Garden tube. **Open** 10am-8pm Mon-Fri; 10am-7pm Sat; 11am-6pm Sun. **Credit** AmEx, DC, MC, V. **Map** p409 Y2.

Office has yet to take its finger off the fashion-pulse, offering excellent catwalk-led designs at high-street prices. The chain's trademark retro focus shows no signs of abating, with high-heeled T-bar styles alongside 1970s-vibe Mary Janes, ballerina pumps and ankle boots.

Other locations: throughout the city.

Sniff

1 Great Titchfield Street, Fitzrovia, W1W 8AU (7299 3560/www.sniff.co.uk). Oxford Circus tube. **Open** 10am-7pm Mon-Wed; 10am-8pm Thur; 10am-6.30pm Fri, Sat; noon-6pm Sun. **Credit** AmEx, MC, V. **Map** p408 U1.

L Cornelissen & Son

105 Great Russell Street, Fitzrovia, WC1B 3RY (7636 1045/www.cornelissen.com). Tottenham Court Road tube. **Open** 9.30am-5.30pm Mon-Fri; 9.30am-5pm Sat. **Credit** MC, V. **Map** p409 X1.

This delightful art shop – which recently celebrated its 150th year of trading – has to be one of the loveliest around. The window displays are fascinating, with traditional flat-topped, glass-stoppered regent jars filled with rainbow-coloured pigments (vermilion, azurite, verdigris, malachite, lapis lazuli) that are sold by the bag. These sit alongside wooden cases of coloured pastels and pencils, while the shelves inside heave under an array of brushes, gilding and restoration tools, waxes and gums, as well as calligraphy equipment.

Melrose & Morgan

42 Gloucester Avenue, Primrose Hill, NW1 8JD (7722 0011/www.melroseandmorgan.com). Chalk Farm tube. **Open** 8am-8pm Tue-Fri; 9am-6pm Sat; 10am-6pm Sun. **Credit** (over £7.50) AmEx, MC, V.

Melrose & Morgan (*photo right*) is a glass-fronted Primrose Hill deli that fits in perfectly with the laid-back affluence of the locale. Both the shop and the wares look gorgeous and, more importantly, foodstuffs have been sourced and prepared with painstaking care. There are old-fashioned sweets, breads, cheeses, chocolates, English wines and ales, condiments, teas and coffees, and limited-edition honey from hives in Regent's Park.

Paxton & Whitfield

93 Jermyn Street, St James's, SW1Y 6JE (7930 0259/www.paxtonandwhitfield.co.uk). Green Park tube. **Open** 9.30am-6pm Mon-Sat. **Credit** MC, V. **Map** p408 V5.

According to Winston Churchill, 'a gentleman only buys his cheese from Paxton & Whitfield'. The shop's roots stretch all the way back to 1742, when it was Sam Cullen's cheese stall in Aldwych market. It opened on Jermyn Street in 1797, Britain's oldest cheese-monger stocks a range of artisan cheeses from the UK, France and Italy, such as Cornish capra, brillat-savarin, epoisses de Bourgogne, Celtic promise and ticklemore. Charcuterie, condiments and preserves, biscuits and wines are also sold, as are cheese knives, boards and tableware. The friendly staff's knowledge is second to none.

Melrose & Morgan.

Get thee to Church

Church Street has always held an attraction of one sort or another for Londoners. By 1880 the street even had its own department store – Jordan's. You can still shop there, perhaps even buy some Victorian goods. The only difference is that now Jordan's is **Alfies Antique Market** (Nos.13-25; *see p237*). Although antiques – in the technically correct sense of objects over 100 years old – are slowly being replaced by shiny (and pricey) 20th-century furniture and lighting, there are still plenty of treasures. **The Girl Can't Help It** (7724 8984, www.thegirlcanthelpit.com), run by platinum-maned burlesque artist Sparkle Moore, stocks 1940s dresses and corsets, 1950s bikinis and some divine shoes (*photo below*), while **Biba Lives** (7258 7999, www.bibalives.com) covers everything from 1930s evening wear to minis from the '60s and '70s. **Dodo Posters** (7706 1545, www.dodoposters.com) on the first floor, has a huge collection of ads from the 1920s and 1930s. For all things silver, stop off at **Goldsmith & Perris** (7724 7051, www.goldsmithandperris.com). For a respite from shopping, Alfies pleasant rooftop café has views over the roofs to the BT Tower and does a good line in toasted sandwiches. Once refreshed head back on to Church Street for some individual shops.

Andrew Nebbett Antiques (Nos.35-37, 7723 2303, www.andrewnebbett.com) has a penchant for large pieces with wow factor (such as a set of massive Victorian fairground distorting mirrors). Just across the street **Cristobal** (No.26, 7724 7230, www.cristobal.co.uk) is crammed with collectable costume jewellery; if you like Cristobal's deco style, you'll love **Susie Cooper Ceramics** (Gallery 1930, 7723 1555, www.susiecooperceramics.com) further along at No.18. **Bloch Antiques** (No.22, 7723 6575) offers big, good-quality furniture and hefty objects that will impress even the most macho anti-shopper; Andrew Angell, who shares Bloch's space, specialises in vintage advertising signs and tins. At **D&A Binder** (No.34, 7723 0542, www.dandabinder.co.uk) you can catch a glimpse of what Alfies might have looked like a century ago when it was a department store. Binder deals in lovely old shop fittings, from vast mahogany display cabinets down to individual hat stands, objects that are given a second shot at life as retro fittings in smart new stores.

Other shops to dip into include **North West Eight** (No.36, 7723 9337) for decorative antiques, and **James Worrall** (No.2, 7563 7181, www.jamesworrall.com) for furniture, leather chairs and kitchenalia.

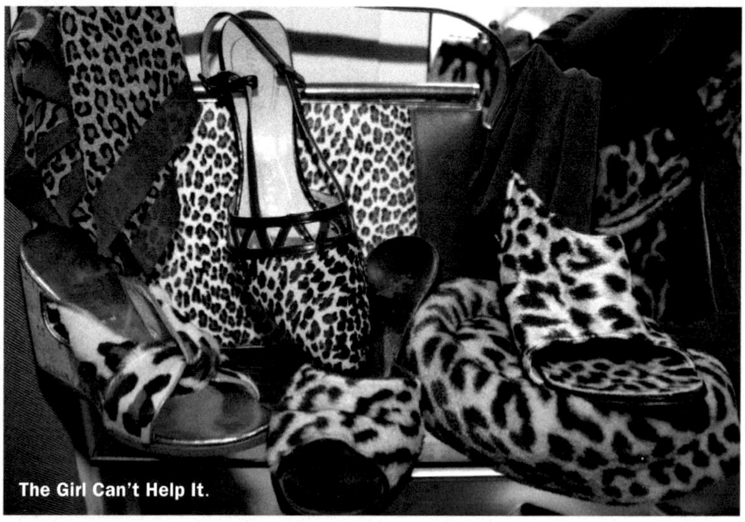

The Girl Can't Help It.

Conceived as an antidote to identikit high-street shoes, Sniff stocks established brands (Repetto, Chie Mihara, French Sole, Paco Gil) but also pushes the eye-catching and adventurous including Victorian styles from British designer Miss L Fire and Sniff's own 1940s-inspired peep- and closed-toe wedges, fitted stilettos and platform boots.

Terra Plana

64 Neal Street, Covent Garden, WC2H 9PA (7379 5959/www.terraplana.com). Covent Garden tube. **Open** 10am-8pm Mon-Sat; noon-6pm Sun. **Credit** AmEx, MC, V. **Map** p409 Y2.

Terra Plana is on a mission to revive artisan shoemaking, producing eco-friendly shoes that are stitched rather than glued. Choose from the likes of the stylish lace-up Aveiro kitten-heeled shoe, made with nubuck leather and wood from sustainable forests, or for men the ergonomic Stankonia range, with recycled rubber soles.

TRAINERd

Unit 539, Stables Market, Chalk Farm Road, Camden, NW1 8AH (mobile 07786 026486). Chalk Farm tube. **Open** 11am-7pm daily. **No credit cards**.

Tucked in under the railway arches, TRAINERd is the latest in a wave of trainer boutiques to open in London. Shoes are imported from the US, Europe and Asia, with the spotlights on rare Nike, Adidas and Pumas. Jedi Rifts, Denim Dunks, Nike SB styles and the original 1987 Air Max model are regular features, but the place's old-school ethos keeps it all affordable – expect to pay £25 to £100.

Food & drink

Bakeries & pâtisseries

& Clarke's

122 Kensington Church Street, Kensington, W8 4BU (7229 2190/www.sallyclarke.com). Notting Hill Gate tube. **Open** 8am-8pm Mon-Fri; 8am-4pm Sat. **Credit** AmEx, DC, MC, V. **Map** p396 B8.

Sally Clarke's renowned shop sells aromatic and voluptuous breads, pastries and cakes baked without artificial colours and preservatives. The casual, prettily laid-out shop also stocks Neal's Yard cheeses, Monmouth Coffee House coffee, fruit and veg, olive oils, chocolates, and own-made pickles, jams and chutneys – all enticingly packaged.

Pôilane

46 Elizabeth Street, SW1W 9PA (7808 4910/www.poilane.fr). Sloane Square tube/Victoria tube/rail. **Open** 7.30am-7.30pm Mon-Fri; 7.30am-6pm Sat. **Credit** MC, V. **Map** p402 G10.

A national institution in France, Parisian Left Bank bakery Poilâne is best known for its round sourdough loaves – the Rolls Royce of breads. Now available in London, the bread's made from pesticide-free, stone-ground wheat and spelt flour, using a modernised version of an ancestral recipe.

Berry Bros & Rudd. See p258.

Delicatessens

Planet Organic (www.planetorganic.com) is an excellent organic supermarket that has grown into a mini-chain. The deli-café chain **Carluccio's** (www.carluccios.com), which sells a broad range of foodstuffs sourced direct from Italy, is another good choice.

A Gold

42 Brushfield Street, Spitalfields, E1 6AG (7247 2487/www.agold.co.uk). Liverpool Street tube/rail. **Open** 11am-8pm Mon-Fri; 10am-6pm Sat; 11am-6pm Sun. **Credit** AmEx, MC, V. **Map** p405 R5.

A Dickensian den of forgotten treasures and the finest artisan revivalist fare, Amelia Gold's French milliners opposite Spitalfields market is the adopted home of Safia and Ian Thomas's tiny shop showcasing the traditional foods of Britain. You'll find Cornish saffron bread, Yorkshire brack, Shrewsbury biscuits, plus Welsh, Banbury and Eccles cakes.

Bluebird Epicerie

350 King's Road, Chelsea, SW3 5UU (7559 1140/www.conran.com). Sloane Square tube then 11, 19, 22, 319 bus/49 bus. **Open** 8am-9pm Mon-Fri; 9am-8pm Sat; 9am-6pm Sun. **Credit** AmEx, MC, V. **Map** p399 D12.

This deli and continental-style traiteur recently joined Conran's foodie complex in the art deco Bluebird garage. A must-visit destination for loaded gourmands, it has a great selection: some of the more unusual items include Corsican cured meats, Alsatian lard fumé and Morteau sausages, fresh choucroute and Ketchoupade – a Basque 'ketchup'.

Brindisa

32 Exmouth Market, Clerkenwell, EC1R 4QE (7713 1666/www.brindisa.com). Angel tube/Farringdon tube/rail. **Open** 10am-6pm Mon; 9.30am-6pm Tue-Sat. **Credit** MC, V. **Map** p404 N4.

Brindisa imports foods from some of Spain's best producers. Wooden shelves are stacked with chocolates, wine, sherry, paella pans and cookery books. There's an unrivalled selection of Iberico and Serrano hams, which can be carved on site. For the tapas restaurant, *see p198*.

Other locations: Stoney Street, Borough Market, SE1 (7407 1036).

Flâneur Food Hall

41 Farringdon Road, Clerkenwell, EC1M 3JB (7404 4422/www.flaneur.com). Farringdon tube/rail. **Open** 8.30am-10pm Mon-Sat; 10am-6pm Sun. **Credit** AmEx, MC, V. **Map** p404 N5.

Deli and restaurant elements merge into each other at idiosyncratic Flâneur. Floor-to-ceiling shelves are stacked with food sourced from small artisans in the UK, France, Italy, Spain and the US, but includes vegetables from Secretts Farm, smoked wild venison, and English and continental cheeses.

Drink

Bedales

5 Bedale Street, Bankside, SE1 9AL (7403 8853/ www.bedalestreet.com). London Bridge tube/rail. **Open** 11.30am-8.30pm Mon-Thur; 11am-9.30pm Fri; 9am-5pm Sat. **Credit** AmEx, DC, MC, V. **Map** p406 P8.

This shop is packed with bottles from around the world: not just Bordeaux and Burgundy, but Tuscany, Spain, some great New World bottles, fabulous kosher wines, and a few of Luxembourg's best. Weekly wine tastings cost £35-£50, with food.

Berry Bros & Rudd

3 St James's Street, St James's, SW1A 1EG (7396 9600/www.bbr.com). Green Park tube. **Open** 10am-6pm Mon-Fri; 10am-4pm Sat. **Credit** AmEx, DC, MC, V. **Map** p402 J8.

Britain's oldest wine merchant has been trading on the same premises since 1698 and its heritage is reflected in its panelled sales and tasting rooms. There are some 20,000 bottles in the cellars and occasionally pompous yet indisputably knowledgeable staff on hand to advise. **Photo** *p257*.

Cadenhead's Covent Garden Whisky Shop

3 Russell Street, Covent Garden, WC2B 5JD (7379 4640/www.coventgardenwhiskyshop.co.uk). Covent Garden tube. **Open** 11am-6.30pm Mon, Sat; 11am-7pm Tue-Fri; noon-4.30pm Sun. **Credit** DC, MC, V. **Map** p409 Z3.

There are four casks of pure malt whisky in store, plus one of rum, from which three bottle sizes (20cl, 35cl and 70cl) are dispensed. There are also around 800 pre-bottled single malts.

Gerry's

74 Old Compton Street, Soho, W1D 4UW (7734 4215). Leicester Square or Piccadilly Circus tube. **Open** 9am-6.30pm Mon-Fri; 9am-5.30pm Sat. **No credit cards. Map** p408 W3.

Gerry's lays claim to the widest range of spirits in London. It offers 150 different vodkas – including cannabis flavour and a bottle containing a whole scorpion – and no fewer than 90 tequilas and 80 rums, plus various absinthes.

Milroy's of Soho

3 Greek Street, Soho, W1D 4NX (7437 9311/www.milroys.co.uk). Tottenham Court Road tube. **Open** 10am-8pm Mon-Fri; 10am-7pm Sat. **Credit** AmEx, MC, V. **Map** p408 W2.

Milroy's reckons to stock over 600 different types of whiskies including its own-brand and examples from around the world – Scotland and Ireland, of course, but also Japan, Canada and India. The shop also hosts an ongoing evening programme in its tasting cellar.

Health & beauty

Department stores are a good bet for upmarket make-up brands and treatments. Several hotels, including the **Sanderson** (*see p48*) and the **Dorchester** (*see p63*), have excellent spa facilities that are open to the public. For everyday needs, there is a branch of **Boots** (www.boots.com) on most high streets. *See also p248* **Top five**.

Aveda Lifestyle Institute

174 High Holborn, Covent Garden, WC1V 7AA (7759 7355/www.aveda.com). Covent Garden tube. **Open** 9.30am-7pm Mon-Fri; 9am-6.30pm Sat. **Credit** AmEx, MC, V. **Map** p409 Y2.

Aveda has been fine-tuning its environmentally sensitive hair and beauty lines for over 25 years – and the results are impressive, with products covering hair, body and face, make-up, tea and perfumes.

Benefit

227 Westbourne Grove, Notting Hill, W11 2SE (7243 7800/www.benefitcosmetics.com). Notting Hill Gate tube. **Open** 10am-6pm Mon-Sat; noon-5pm Sun. **Credit** AmEx, MC, V. **Map** p396 A6.

San Francisco-based retro-kitsch beauty brand Benefit opened its first London boutique in 2005. The highlight of the collection is the 'Fake-Its', including our old fave Benetint, the waterproof, stay-rosy tint for cheeks and lips, and You're Bluffing, a redness-concealing wand. **Photo** *p260*.

Other locations: 49 Brushfield Street, Spitalfields, E1 6AA (7377 2684).

Crabtree & Evelyn

6 Kensington Church Street, Kensington, W8 4EP (7937 9335/www.crabtree-evelyn.co.uk). High Street Kensington tube. **Open** 10am-6pm Mon-Wed, Fri, Sat; 10am-7pm Thur; 11am-5pm Sun. **Credit** AmEx, MC, V. **Map** p396 B8.

Top five Markets

London has a large number of colourful and fascinating markets (*see p262*), but a handful stand out above all the others.

Borough Market

Southwark Street, Borough. SE1 (7407 1002/www.boroughmarket.org.uk). London Bridge tube/rail. **Open** noon-6pm Fri; 9am-4pm Sat. **Map** p406 P8.

Borough (*photo below*) offers a deliciously rich mix of fine foods. The selection of meat encompasses everything from Iberian acorn-fed ham to free-range chicken, and on Saturdays lengthy queues wait patiently for a chorizo and rocket roll from the Brindisa stall. Add fruit and veg, organic cakes and breads, exotic teas, olive oil, dairy (cheeses, yoghurts), fish and oysters, beers, ciders and wines and you've got the makings of a feast.

Broadway Market

Broadway Market, Hackney, E8 (07709 311 869/www.broadwaymarket.co.uk). London Fields rail/236, 394 bus. **Open** 8am-5pm Sat.

Revived a mere two years ago, one of London's oldest markets has stalls selling vintage and new designer threads, old *Vogue* patterns, flowers and hand-knits. You'll also find great cheeses, breads, rare-breed meats, organic vegetables, chocolate treats, luscious tarts and cakes. Alongside the stalls are boutiques: Black Truffle for handmade shoes and La Vie Boutique for vintage fashion. Eat Ghanaian jolloff, Gujarati veg curry and French crêpes, or check out L'Eau à la Bouche deli (No.49, 7923 0600, www.labouche.co.uk).

Columbia Road Market

Columbia Road, Bethnal Green, E2. Liverpool Street tube/rail then 26, 48, bus/Old Street tube/rail then 55, 243 bus. **Open** 8.30am-2pm Sun. **Map** p405 S3.

This Sunday morning fixture has blossomed into one of London's loveliest markets. It overflows with buckets full of every kind and colour of bloom. Alongside the market is a host of independent galleries and shops selling groovy furniture, pottery, antiques, trendy lampshades, hats, baby togs and toys. Refuel at Jones Dairy (23 Ezra Street, 7739 5372, www.jonesdairy.co.uk) for artisanal cheeses, bagels and coffee, or, on Columbia Road, Laxeiro (No.93, 7729 1147) for tapas and Fleapit (No.49, 7033 9986, www.thefleapit.com) for cakes.

Spitalfields Market

Commercial Street, E1 (7247 8556/www.visit spitalfields.com). Liverpool Street tube/rail. **Open** *General* 10.30am-4.30pm Mon-Fri; 9.30am-5pm Sun. *Antiques* 8am-3.30pm Thur. *Food* 10am-5pm Thur, Fri, Sun. *Fashion* 10am-4pm Fri. *Records & books* 10am-4pm 1st & 3rd Wed of mth. **Map** p405 R5.

Though a third of its original size, following redevelopment (*see p164* **Oranges are not the only fruit**), Spitalfields is well worth a visit. Clothes range from creations by up and coming designers to second-hand glad rags. Also in the mix are crafts, jewellery and antiques. Around the edge of the market, stands sell grub from around the world. The thrice-weekly food market is now enhanced by a cluster of gourmet food shops.

Shepherd's Bush Market

East side of railway viaduct between Uxbridge Road & Goldhawk Road, W12. Goldhawk Road or Shepherd's Bush tube. **Open** 8.30am-6pm Tue, Wed, Fri, Sat; 8.30am-1pm Thur.

There's a fantastic range of ethnic treats (Indian, Caribbean, African and Polish) with stalls selling sweet potatoes, yams, coconuts, cassava, okra, falafel, rice, mangoes and some of the freshest fish in the capital. You'll also find vivid print fabrics, goatskin rugs and saris, plus jewellery, scarves, hats, toys, kitchenware, sweets, CDs and DVDs.

Overcoming its twee country image, Crabtree & Evelyn has won over a younger fan base in recent years, attracted by newer lines such as the retro crockery collection, cutesy baby toiletries, gardeners' and cooks' products, spa collection and best-selling hand and foot therapy ranges.
Other locations: throughout the city.

Fresh

92 Marylebone High Street, Marylebone, W1U 4RD (7486 4100/www.fresh.com). Baker Street tube. **Open** 10am-7pm Mon-Wed, Fri, Sat; 10am-8pm Thur; noon-5pm Sun. **Credit** AmEx, MC, V. **Map** p400 G5.
Made with ingredients such as soy, milk, rice and sugar, these exquisitely packaged American skin-, body- and haircare products smell good enough to eat. The most indulgent purchase is Crème Ancienne at £155 for 100g; it is made by hand in a Czech monastery. The budget-conscious take note: the cost of a mini-treatment is redeemable against products (*see p248* **Top five**).

HQ hair & beautystore

2 New Burlington Street, Mayfair, W1S 2JE (0871 220 4141/www.hqhair.com). Oxford Circus tube. **Open** 10am-6pm Mon, Sat; 10am-7pm Tue, Fri; 10am-8pm Wed, Thur. **Credit** AmEx, MC, V. **Map** p408 U3.
The small storefront gives no clue as to the beauty bounty inside: from hair products and skincare to make-up and tools of the trade, HQ has it covered. As well as hairdressing, the salon offers brand-name facials, massages, waxing, manicures and pedicures, and Fantasy Tans.

Organic Pharmacy

369 King's Road, Chelsea, SW10 0LN (7351 2232/www.theorganicpharmacy.com). Sloane Square tube then 11, 22 bus. **Open** 9.30am-6pm Mon-Sat; noon-6pm Sun. **Credit** AmEx, MC, V. **Map** p399 D12.
Natural/organic brands sold here include Weleda, Dr Hauschka and Green People, and make-up by Logona and Jane Iredale. But it's the company's own brand – free of artificial preservatives, petrochemicals and harsh detergents – that takes centre stage.

This Works

18 Cale Street, Chelsea, SW3 3QU (7584 1887/www.thisworks.com). Sloane Square tube. **Open** 10am-6pm Mon-Sat. **Credit** MC, V. **Map** p399 E11.
This sleek, white haven stocks sleek, white This Works lines: the Enjoy Really Rich Lotion, the best-selling Skin Deep Dry Leg Oil and the In the Zone Shower Oil work particularly well on dry skin.

Hairdressers

If the options we list below are out of your range, then you can get a great-value cut (£6 men; £10 women) at the nearest **Mr Topper's** (7631 3233).

Daniel Hersheson

45 Conduit Street, Mayfair, W1S 2YN (7434 1747/www.danielhersheson.com). Oxford Circus tube. **Open** 9am-6pm Mon-Wed; 9am-8pm Thur, Fri; 9am-6pm Sat. **Credit** AmEx, MC, V. **Map** p408 U3.
Despite its upmarket location, this modern two-storey salon isn't at all snooty, with a staff of very talented cutters and colourists. Prices start at £55,

The face place: **Benefit**. *See p258.*

though you'll pay £250 for a cut with Daniel. There's also a menu of therapies; the swish Harvey Nichols (*see p242*) branch has a dedicated spa.

Fish

30 D'Arblay Street, Soho, W1F 8ER (7494 2398/ www.fishweb.co.uk). Leicester Square tube. **Open** 10am-7pm Mon-Wed, Fri; 10am-8pm Thur; 10am-5pm Sat. **Credit** MC, V. **Map** p408 V2.

This relaxed and buzzing salon was a fishmonger's, hence the name. Staff are understatedly stylish and laid-back, offering a good mix of classic and fashion cuts for men and women, as well as own-brand hair products. Prices are reasonable.

4th Floor

4 Northington Street, Bloomsbury, WC1N 2JG (7405 6011/www.4thfloor.co.uk). Chancery Lane tube. **Open** 9am-7pm Mon-Fri; 9am-6pm Sat. **Credit** AmEx, MC, V. **Map** p401 M4.

This well-established studio-style salon is light and airy, the atmosphere cool and contemporary without being intimidating. Stylists cut hair with impressive attention to detail, leaving realistic, manageable cuts tailored to your hair type and lifestyle.

Jo Hansford

19 Mount Street, Mayfair, W1K 2RN (7495 7774/ www.johansford.com). Bond Street or Green Park tube. **Open** 8.30am-6pm Tue-Sat. **Credit** MC, V. **Map** p402 G7.

Hailed as 'the best tinter on the planet', Jo Hansford has built up a starry clientele: Yasmin Le Bon, Elizabeth Jagger, Camilla Parker Bowles. If you want Jo's personal touch (she works three days a week), it's £275 for a half head of highlights.

Nyumba

6-7 Mount Street, Mayfair, W1K 3EH (7408 1489/ www.nyumbasalon.com). Bond Street or Green Park tube. **Open** 9am-6pm Tue, Wed, Fri, Sat; 9am-8pm Thur. **Credit** AmEx, MC, V. **Map** p402 H7.

Michael Charalambous will tell you straight (but politely) if your current haircut doesn't suit you, and name-drop anyone famous who's been by. Word of mouth keeps this place vital and fully booked, with cuts that are designed to last and strong colouring.

Opticians

Boots (www.boots.com/opticians), **David Clulow** (www.davidclulow.com), **Dollond & Aitchison** (www.danda.co.uk) and **Specsavers** (www.specsavers.com) have branches on most high streets.

Cutler & Gross

16 Knightsbridge Green, Knightsbridge, SW1X 7QL (7581 2250/www.cutlerandgross.com). Knightsbridge tube. **Open** 9.30am-7pm Mon-Sat; noon-4pm Sun. **Credit** AmEx, DC, MC, V. **Map** p399 F9.

C&G's stock of handmade frames runs from Andy Warhol-inspired glasses to naturally light buffalo-horn frames.

Mallon & Taub

35D Marylebone High Street, Marylebone, W1U 4QB (7935 8200/www.mallonandtaub.com). Baker Street or Regent's Park tube. **Open** 10am-6.30pm Mon-Wed, Fri, Sat; 10am-7pm Thur; noon-6pm Sun. **Credit** AmEx, MC, V. **Map** p400 G5.

This simple, airy and award-winning independent stocks original, funky, sculptural and cutting-edge specs and sunglasses. Service is excellent.

Michel Guillon Vision Clinic & Eye Boutique

35 Duke of York Square, Chelsea, SW3 4LY (7730 2142/www.michelguillon.com). Sloane Square tube. **Open** 10am-7pm Mon-Sat; noon-5pm Sun. **Credit** AmEx, MC, V. **Map** p399 F11.

The first thing you notice about this Abe (son of architect Richard) Rogers-designed shop is that the display cabinets are constantly on the move. In fact, nothing is static for long here, including the excellent range of frames.

Opera Opera

98 Long Acre, Covent Garden, WC2E 9NR (7836 9246/www.operaopera.net). Covent Garden tube. **Open** 10am-6pm Mon-Sat. **Credit** MC, V. **Map** p409 Y2.

Trading for 25 years, and with over 3,000 pairs of frames in stock, Opera Opera is the place to head if you're looking for something a bit different. This may also be the only place in London to find a pair of old-fashioned driving goggles (by Barufaldi).

Homeware

The Regent Street **Zara Home** (Nos.127-131, www.zarahome.com) is a stylish addition to central London's high-street homeware options.

Aria

295-297 Upper Street, Islington, N1 2TU (7704 1999/www.ariashop.co.uk). Angel tube/Highbury & Islington tube/rail. **Open** 10am-7pm Mon-Fri; 10am-6.30pm Sat; noon-5pm Sun. **Credit** AmEx, DC, MC, V. **Map** p404 O1.

Aria is a great place for browsing. As well as furniture, lighting and a wide Alessi range, you'll find Nigella Lawson's cookware, scented candles and Cowshed skincare.

The Conran Shop

Michelin House, 81 Fulham Road, Fulham, SW3 6RD (7589 7401/www.conran.com). South Kensington tube. **Open** 10am-6pm Mon, Tue, Fri; 10am-7pm Wed, Thur; 10am-6.30pm Sat; noon-6pm Sun. **Credit** AmEx, MC, V. **Map** p399 E10.

Terrrence Conran's flagship Fulham Road store is elegantly packed with a beautifully arranged selection of design treats, be they modern classics, vintage finds or contemporary pieces. Deeply satisfying and something of a one-stop design destination, whatever your budget.

Other locations: 55 Marylebone High Street, W1U 5HS (7723 2223).

Ella Doran Design

46 Cheshire Street, Spitalfields, E2 6EH (7613 0782/www.elladoran.co.uk). Bethnal Green tube/ Liverpool Street tube/rail. **Open** by appointment only Mon; 10am-6pm Tue-Fri; noon-5pm Sat; 11am-6pm Sun. **Credit** AmEx, MC, V. **Map** p405 S4.

Ella Doran's iconic kitsch placemats and coasters featuring striking photographic images (a kiwi fruit, artichokes, a Tokyo street scene) are all available in this showroom-cum-studio. But other objects also get the Doran treatment including cushions, purses and notebooks, well priced at £10-£65.

Marimekko

16-17 St Christopher's Place, Marylebone, W1U 1NZ (7486 6454/www.marimekko.co.uk). Bond Street tube. **Open** 10am-6.30pm Mon-Wed, Fri, Sat; 10am-7pm Thur; noon-5pm Sun. **Credit** AmEx, DC, MC, V. **Map** p400 H6.

Founded in 1951 by Finn Armi Raita, Marimekko took an experimental approach to textile design from the start, inviting young graphic designers to apply bold graphics and bright colours to fabric. As well as the textiles and clothes, you can now buy bags and tableware.

Mint

70 Wigmore Street, Marylebone, W1U 2SF (7224 4406/www.mintshop.co.uk). Bond Street tube. **Open** 10.30am-6.30pm Mon-Wed, Fri, Sat; 10.30am-7.30pm Thur. **Credit** MC, V. **Map** p400 G6.

Surprising and inspirational, Mint is a compact two-level space full of globally sourced pieces from established designers and recent graduates alike. One-off items might include illustrated plates and striking pieces of furniture, cushions by Hella Jongerius or sleek-with-a-twist Italian brushed-steel cutlery. Although the store specialises in statement pieces, there are plenty of smaller more affordable items.

Nicole Farhi Home

17 Clifford Street, Mayfair, W1S 3RQ (7494 9051/ www.nicolefarhi.com). Green Park or Piccadilly Circus tube. **Open** 10am-6pm Mon-Wed, Fri, Sat; 10am-7pm Thur. **Credit** AmEx, DC, MC, V. **Map** p408 U4.

Nicole Farhi Home emanates a laid-back, luxurious feel and, although the stunning one-off antiques gathered from Farhi's world travels may be expensive (a French dining table for £4,000), the simple yet original ceramics, glass, tableware, candles and furniture in natural hues are generally good value.

Markets

Vibrant, bustling and culturally rich, the city's local markets are unique social spaces that offer a microcosm of London life – as well as a great place to pick up cheap produce and unusual goods. For the best, *see p259* **Top five**.

Berwick Street Market

Berwick Street, Soho, W1. Piccadilly Circus tube. **Open** 9am-5pm Mon-Sat. **Map** p408 V2.

Seasonal produce, particularly fruit and veg.

Brick Lane Market

Brick Lane (north of railway bridge), Cygnet Street, Sclater Street, E1; Bacon Street, Cheshire Street, E2 (information 7364 1717). Aldgate East tube. **Open** 8am-2pm Sun. **Map** p405 S5.

Flea market, surrounded by trendy clothes boutiques and chic home accessories shops.

Brixton Market

Electric Avenue, Pope's Road, Brixton Station Road, Atlantic Road, SW9. Brixton tube/rail. **Open** 8am-6pm Mon, Tue, Thur-Sat; 8am-3pm Wed.

Caribbean fruit and veg, halal meat, fish, clothes, fabrics, reggae music, crafts and wigs.

Mint (because you never know when you might need a wind-up chicken).

Camden

Various sites, see p157.
Sprawling collection of markets offering a smörgåsbord of street culture; goods run the gamut from crafts to vintage clothes.

Greenwich Market

Off College Approach, SE10 (Mon-Fri 7515 7153/ Sat, Sun 8293 3110/www.greenwichmarket.net). Greenwich rail/Cutty Sark DLR. **Open** *Antiques & collectibles* 6.30am-5pm Thur, Fri. *Village Market (Stockwell Street)* 8am-5pm Sat, Sun. *Arts & crafts* 9.30am-5.30pm Sat, Sun.
Bric-a-brac, second-hand clothes, ethnic ornaments, CDs, jewellery and plenty of accessories.

Leather Lane

Leather Lane (between Greville Street & Clerkenwell Road), Holborn, EC4. Chancery Lane tube. **Open** 10.30am-2pm Mon-Fri. **Map** p404 N5.
Busy lunchtime market selling cut-price clothing (skirts from a fiver), flowers, fruit and veg.

Petticoat Lane Market

Middlesex Street, Goulston Street and around, E1 (information 7364 1717). Aldgate East tube. **Open** 8am-4pm Mon-Fri; 9am-2pm Sun. **Map** p407 S6.
Mainly tat (cheap clothes, leather luggage, toys and electronic goods) but good for the odd bargain.

Portobello Road Market

Portobello Road, W10 & W11 (7229 8354/www.portobelloroad.co.uk). Ladbroke Grove or Notting Hill Gate tube. **Open** *General* 8am-6pm Mon-Wed; 9am-1pm Thur; 7am-7pm Fri, Sat. *Antiques* 4am-4pm Sat. **Map** p396 A6.
Several markets rolled into one: antiques start at the Notting Hill end; further up are food stalls; under the Westway and along the walkway to Ladbroke Grove are emerging designer and vintage clothes.

Ridley Road Market

Ridley Road, off Kingsland High Street, E8. Dalston Kingsland rail/30, 38, 56, 67, 76, 149, 236, 242, 243, 277 bus. **Open** 8.30am-5.30pm Mon-Sat.
Everything from domestic and exotic fruit, veg, fish and meat to clothes, household goods, toys, African and Indian fabrics.

Sunday (Up)Market

The Old Truman Brewery (entrances on Brick Lane & Hanbury Street, E1 (7720 6100/www.sundayupmarket.co.uk). Liverpool Street tube/rail. **Open** 10am-5pm Sun. **Map** p405 S5.
140 stalls of new designer and vintage fashion, accessories and collectibles.

Sport & fitness

John Lewis (*see p242*) own-brand goods are competitively priced, while **Selfridges** (*see p243*) has specialist concessions such as Cycle Surgery. **Topshop** (*see p247*) does seasonal surf- and skiwear. For trainers **JD Sports** (www.jdsports.co.uk) has branches all over town, and there's also **NikeTown** (236 Oxford Street, W1W 8LG, 7612 0800, www.nike.com).

Ellis Brigham

Tower House, 3-11 Southampton Street, Covent Garden, WC2E 7HA (7395 1010/www.ellis-brigham.com). Covent Garden tube. **Open** 10am-7pm Mon-Wed, Fri; 10am-7.30pm Thur; 9.30am-6.30pm Sat; 11.30am-5.30pm Sun. **Credit** AmEx, MC, V. **Map** p409 Z4.
Two spacious floors lined with polished glass cabinets parading GPS systems and Oakley glasses. Climbing equipment, tents, outdoor wear and luggage are in-store year-round, as is London's only ice-climbing wall, 26ft high and refrigerated to -15°C.

Arts & Entertainment

Features

Festivals & Events

So much to do, so little time.

If you find yourself at a loose end during a weekend or you've just got a bit of spare time, chances are there's a festival of some sort taking place somewhere in London. Recent years have seen an increase in outdoor festivals, particularly during the summer, as well as some imaginative sponsored seasons and one-off events.

We've included as many regular events as we can here, but keep an eye on *Time Out* magazine for events that crop up at short notice. Also note that, if you're going out of your way to attend any festival or event, it's always a good idea to confirm details nearer the time.

All year

For the **Changing of the Guard**, which takes place at Horse Guards Parade and Buckingham Palace, *see p144*.

Ceremony of the Keys

Tower of London, Tower Hill, the City, EC3N 4AB (0870 751 5177/www.hrp.org.uk). Tower Hill tube/ Tower Gateway DLR. **Date** daily. *Apr-Oct* max party of 7. *Nov-Mar* max party of 15. **Map** p407 R7.

As part of this 700-year-old ceremony, the Yeoman Warders lock the entrances to the Tower at 9.53pm every evening. Assemble at the West Gate at 9pm, and it's all over by 10pm, when the last post sounds. Details of the ticket-application procedure are on the website – you need to apply at least two months before your visit.

Gun Salutes

Green Park, Mayfair & St James's, W1, & Tower of London, the City, EC3. **Dates** 6 Feb (Accession Day); 21 Apr & 17 June (Queen's birthdays); 2 June (Coronation Day); 10 June (Duke of Edinburgh's birthday); 17 June (Trooping the Colour); State Opening of Parliament (*see p273*); 11 Nov (Lord Mayor's Show); 11 Nov (Remembrance Sunday); & for state visits. **Map** p402 H8.

The King's Troop Royal Horse Artillery makes a mounted charge through Hyde Park, sets up the guns and fires a 41-gun salute (at noon, except on the occasion of the State Opening of Parliament) opposite the Dorchester Hotel. Not to be outdone, the Honourable Artillery Company fires a 62-gun salute at the Tower of London at 1pm.

> ▶ For more festivals, see our specialist Arts & Entertainment chapters. For a list of public holidays, *see p377*.

January-March 2007

London International Mime Festival

Various venues across London (7637 5661/ www.mimefest.co.uk). **Date** 12-28 Jan.

Proving that mime isn't all black and white face paint and Marcel Marceau impressions, the LIMF brings together companies from the UK and abroad to perform a variety of innovative shows for all ages. Highlights at last year's festival included a performance from garish British mime troupe Faulty Optic and aerialist Matilda Leyser. Free brochures are available via the website or by telephone.

London Art Fair

Business Design Centre, 52 Upper Street, Islington, N1 0QH (0870 126 1783/www.londonartfair.co.uk). Angel tube. **Date** 17-21 Jan. **Map** p404 N2.

At this large-scale art sale millions of pounds are spent by collectors on modern British and contemporary works from such artists as Ben Nicholson, William Scott and LS Lowry, as well as on a range of exceptional contemporary pieces from the likes of Keith Coventry, Paula Rego and Lucian Freud. More than 100 galleries participate. *See also p297* **Beyond the galleries**.

Chinese New Year Festival

Around Gerrard Street, Chinatown, W1, Leicester Square, WC2 & Trafalgar Square, WC2 (7851 6686/www.chinatownchinese.com). Leicester Square or Piccadilly Circus tube. **Date** 18 Feb. **Map** p408 W3.

In 2007 the Year of the Pig will take over from the Year of the Dog. Celebrations begin at 11am with a children's parade from Leicester Square gardens south to Trafalgar Square, where the traditional lion and dragon dance teams perform. There are, of course, firework displays (both at lunchtime and at 5pm). About 200,000 people attended the Chinese New Year celebrations in 2006 (which is 150,000 more than was reported in 2005), so expect dense crowds – especially at the hub of the party on Gerrard Street. **Photo** *p268*.

Great Spitalfields Pancake Race

Dray Walk, Brick Lane, E1 6QL (7375 0441). Liverpool Street tube/rail. **Date** 20 Feb (Shrove Tuesday). **Map** p405 S5.

Think of this as a high-brow alternative to school sports day. Teams of four run a relay race while simultaneously tossing pancakes. Festivities kick off at around 12.30pm. Call in advance if you want to take part; just show up if all you're after is seeing the 'cakes hit the deck.

National Science Week

Various venues across London (www.the-ba.net). **Date** 9-18 Mar.

A week of scientific shenanigans across the capital, ranging from hands-on shows for youngsters to in-depth discussions for adults. Each event celebrates different aspects of science, engineering and technology.

St Patrick's Day Parade & Festival

Various venues across London (7983 4100/ www.london.gov.uk). **Date** 18 Mar.

Supported by the mayor, this popular, thousands-strong parade through central London is followed by a free party. Expect plenty of Irish music and dancing, arts and crafts, and activities for all ages.

April-June 2007

For **Royal Ascot**, *see p331.*

Oxford & Cambridge Boat Race

Thames, from Putney to Mortlake (01225 383483/ www.theboatrace.org). Putney Bridge tube/Putney, Barnes Bridge or Mortlake rail. **Date** 7 Apr.

Some 250,000 people are expected to line the Thames from Putney to Mortlake for the 153rd edition of this annual elitist grudge match (flag down at 4.30pm). Oxford, kitted out in dark blue, won the 2006 Boat Race in a time of 18 minutes and 26 seconds by a margin of five lengths; Cambridge wear light blue. The riverside pubs in Mortlake and Hammersmith are the most popular vantage points (read: obscenely crowded and packed with toffs).

London Marathon

Greenwich Park to the Mall via the Isle of Dogs, Victoria Embankment & St James's Park (7902 0200/www.london-marathon.co.uk). Maze Hill rail or Charing Cross tube/rail. **Date** 22 Apr.

Brush down your banana costume and fill up on pasta for one of the biggest metropolitan marathons in the world. It usually attracts some 35,000 starters, all of whom must have applied by the previous October, and spectators line most of the route. Front runners reach the 13-mile mark near the Tower of London at around 10am.

May Fayre & Puppet Festival

St Paul's Church Garden, Bedford Street, Covent Garden, WC2E 9ED (7375 0441/www.alternative arts.co.uk). Covent Garden tube. **Date** 13 May. **Map** p409 Y4.

Commemorating the first recorded sighting of Mr Punch in England (by diarist Samuel Pepys in 1662, here in Covent Garden), this free event offers puppetry galore from 10.30am to 5.30pm.

Playtex Moonwalk

Start & finish at Hyde Park, W1 (01483 741 430/ www.walkthewalk.org). **Date** 19 May. **Map** p397 F7.

Power walk through the night in your best bra to raise money for breast cancer research. Last year's event attracted around 15,000 participants, men included. Choose either the marathon (26.2 mile) or half-marathon (13.1 mile) route.

Chelsea Flower Show

Grounds of Royal Hospital, Royal Hospital Road, Chelsea, SW3 4SR (7649 1885/www.rhs.org.uk). Sloane Square tube. **Date** 22-26 May. **Map** p399 F12.

The hysteria that builds up around this annual flower show has to be seen to be believed. Fight your way past the rich old ladies to see perfect roses bred by experts, or to get ideas for your own humble plot. Tickets go on sale for the event from 30 October 2006, but be quick as they sell out fast; the first two days are reserved for Royal Horticultural Society members. The show closes at 5.30pm on the final day, with display plants sold off from 4.30pm.

Kew Summer Festival

Royal Botanic Gardens, Kew, Richmond, Surrey TW9 3AB (8332 5655/www.kew.org). Kew Gardens tube/rail/Kew Bridge rail. **Date** 26 May-Sept.

Each season at the botanical gardens brings its own programme of events, with the summer one lasting the longest. In summer 2007 the spotlight is on the flora of the Mediterranean region. At King William's Temple a planting depicting a typical Mediterranean natural habitat will comprise cork oaks, stone pines and Tuscan olive trees. There will be a Kew-grown chilli display in the Waterlily House, and in the Princess of Wales Conservatory a section of a Spanish-style olive grove.

Don't miss Festivals

Brick Lane Festival

Low-key and loads of fun, the Brick Lane Festival has food, music, dance and more. *See p271.*

Mayor's Thames Festival

A winning combination of events on the South Bank, plus spectacular fireworks over the river. *See p271.*

London Film Festival

Even if you don't get to watch any of the movies you can join in the rubbernecking of the stars at Leicester Square. *See p272.*

Remembrance Sunday Ceremony

A sombre, moving affair, headed by the Queen, dedicated to those who have lost their lives in conflict. *See p273.*

Ice-skating at Somerset House

The setting is a flood-lit court with Christmas tree and flaming braziers. If you don't skate, at least watch. *See p270* **Air play**.

Chinese New Year Festival. See p266.

Jazz Plus

Victoria Embankment Gardens, Villiers Street, Westminster, WC2R 2PY (7375 0441/www.alternativearts.co.uk). Embankment tube. **Date** June-July. **Map** p409 Y5.

Free lunchtime concerts are performed by a variety of contemporary jazz musicians on Tuesdays and Thursdays.

Coin Street Festival

Bernie Spain Gardens (next to Oxo Tower Wharf), South Bank, SE1 9PH (7401 3610/www.coinstreet.org). Southwark tube/Waterloo tube/rail. **Date** June-Aug. **Map** p406 N8.

A series of themed weekend and occasional weekday events celebrating cultural diversity in the capital. These take place on the South Bank and chiefly centre on live music performances, with some dance and theatre events thrown in. There are also food, drink and craft stalls in the gardens. All of the entertainment is free; check the website for details of the festivities nearer the time.

Royal National Theatre Watch This Space Festival

South Bank, SE1 9PX (7452 3400/www.nationaltheatre.org.uk). Waterloo tube/rail. **Date** June-Aug. **Map** p403 M7.

A lively free festival of music, street theatre and films taking place on Theatre Square outside the National Theatre.

Derby Day

Epsom Downs Racecourse, Epsom Downs, Surrey KT18 5LQ (01372 470 047/www.epsomderby.co.uk). Epsom rail then shuttle bus. **Date** 2 June.

One of the most important flat races of the season. You'll find a carnival mood whatever part of the course you're in, but if you want comfort or a good view be prepared to pay for it. Preceding Derby Day on 1 June, Ladies Day is the occasion for donning your most flamboyant hat.

Beating Retreat

Horse Guards Parade, Whitehall, Westminster, SW1A 2AX (bookings 7414 2271). Westminster tube/Charing Cross tube/rail. **Date** 7-8 June. **Map** p403 K8.

This patriotic 'spectacle of sound and colour' begins at 7pm, with the 'Retreat' beaten on drums by the Mounted Bands of the Household Cavalry and the Massed Bands of the Guards Division.

Open Garden Squares Weekend

Various venues across London (www.opensquares.org). **Date** 9-10 June.

Ever wondered what it's like in those enchanting little private parks dotted around the wealthy parts of town? Each year the London Parks and Gardens Trust opens up many posh garden squares and roof gardens to allow visitors a peek inside. Gardens vary from Japanese-style retreats to secret 'children-only' play areas.

Meltdown

South Bank Centre, Belvedere Road, South Bank, SE1 8XX (0870 380 0400/www.rfh.org.uk). Embankment tube/Waterloo tube/rail. **Date** last 2wks in June. **Map** p403 M8.

A no-show in 2006 due to the redevelopment of the Royal Festival Hall, this hugely successful festival of personally curated contemporary culture should be back in 2007. Patti Smith and Scott Walker are among those whose tastes have roamed free in past years, so expect the brilliantly unpredictable.

Architecture Week

Various venues across London (www.architectureweek.co.uk). **Date** mid June.

Celebrates contemporary architecture with a programme of events, exhibitions, talks and tours, plus an open-practice initiative that allows the public into selected architecture practices.

Trooping the Colour

Horse Guards Parade, Whitehall, Westminster, SW1A 2AX (7414 2479/www.trooping-the-colour.co.uk). Westminster tube/Charing Cross tube/rail. **Date** 16 June. **Map** p403 K8.

Though the Queen was born on 21 April, this is her official birthday celebration. At 10.45am she makes the 15-minute journey from Buckingham Palace to Horse Guards Parade, then scurries back home to watch a midday Royal Air Force flypast and receive a formal gun salute from Green Park.

Pride London

Parade from Oxford Street, to Victoria Embankment (7164 2182/www.pridelondon.org). Hyde Park Corner or Marble Arch tube/Charing Cross tube/rail. **Date** *Festival* 16-30 June. *Parade & rally* 30 June.

In 2006 this annual free bash thrown by London's proud-to-be-gays and -lesbians became even bigger, when Pride combined with EuroPride. Always colourful, the Parade – 2007 theme Icons – heads down Oxford Street, Regent Street, Piccadilly and Whitehall, ending up at Victoria Embankment, and is followed by a Trafalgar Square rally. Last year Soho was closed to traffic for the day to make room for dance stages, market stalls and a food festival. Down the road, Leicester Square hosted cabaret and 'Drag Idol'. The two weeks leading up to the Pride rally are Festival Fortnight, a mix of cultural performances in various venues. Red Hot Christmas Pride (7-14 Dec) is primarily a fundraiser for the main event.

Wimbledon Lawn Tennis Championships

PO Box 98, Church Road, Wimbledon, SW19 5AE (8944 1066/recorded information 8946 2244/www.wimbledon.org). Southfields tube/Wimbledon tube/rail. **Date** 25 June-8 July.

The world's most prestigious tennis tournament. For more information, including how to get hold of those coveted tickets, *see p332*.

City of London Festival

Various venues across the City, EC2-EC4 (box office 0845 120 7502/information 7796 4949/www.colf.org). Bank, Barbican, Moorgate & St Paul's tube/Blackfriars, Cannon Street & Farringdon tube/rail. **Date** 25 June-12 July.

Now in its 45th year, the City of London Festival takes place in some of the finest buildings in the Square Mile, among them Guildhall and St Paul's Cathedral. The programme comprises traditional classical music, such as concerts from the London Symphony Orchestra, and more unusual offerings from the worlds of jazz, dance, visual art, literature and theatre, as well as outdoor and free events. This year takes a French theme, but also with work focused on the abolition of the slave trade.

July-September 2007

Henley Royal Regatta

Henley Reach, Henley-on-Thames, Oxon RG9 2LY (01491 572153/www.hrr.co.uk). Henley-on-Thames rail. **Date** 4-8 July.

First held in 1839 – and under royal patronage since 1851 – Henley is now a five-day affair. Boat races range from open events for men and women through student crews to junior boys. As posh as can be.

Rhythm Sticks

South Bank Centre, Belvedere Road, South Bank, SE1 8XX (0870 380 0400/www.rfh.org.uk). Embankment tube/Waterloo tube/rail. **Date** July. **Map** p403 M8.

Air play

In recent years a combination of warm summers, patio heaters and rejuvenated outdoor public spaces has successfully lured Londoners out of doors in their masses. Suddenly it seems as if the capital has gone all Mediterranean. Nowhere is this more apparent than Trafalgar Square where, since the pedestrianisation of the north side transformed it into a pleasant piazza, there's hardly a weekend goes by without some open-air event. The annual **Summer in the Square** (www.london.gov.uk) is a popular programme of free cultural events organised there by the Mayor of London, which includes gigs, live dance and street theatre performances for all ages. At other times of the year the square is used for more free concerts, Diwali celebrations, St Patrick's Day raucousness and spontaneous celebrations by supporters of whatever team of any nationality has just triumphed in some sporting event anywhere else in the world.

The Serpentine Gallery's **Summer Pavilion** events programme of talks and film screenings may be highbrow, but it's also well attended. Each year the gallery (*see p154*) commissions a world-class architect who has not previously built anything in the UK to construct a pavilion, which sits on the lawn outside the gallery from July to September. In 2006 it was Rem Koolhaas, but the plans for the structure are not normally confirmed until early in the year.

The South Bank's **National Theatre** (*see p339*) has created a space especially for outdoor events: from June through August, Theatre Square hosts all manner of unstuffy entertainments, from acrobatics to outdoor film screenings. Another summer highlight is **Somerset House** (*see p119*), where a welcome oasis of calm can be found in the large fountained courtyard – except during the weeks in July when it hosts a series of concerts.

Londoners love a picnic, more so when combined with a concert in the setting of a stately home. English Heritage's **Kenwood House** (*see p160*) and **Marble Hill House** (*see p188*) both host annual open-air concerts throughout July and August which always make a grand day out. Just be prepared: pack a brolly along with your rug.

Ironically, recent mild winters have coincided with an increase in outdoor ice rinks in the capital. One old favourite, round the back of Liverpool Street Station, is **Broadgate Circle** (7505 4068, www.broadgateice.co.uk), which has the longest period of operation (from late October to early April). An especially lovely setting for an ice rink is the courtyard of **Somerset House** (late Nov-late Jan; *see p119*). Other venues include **Hampton Court Palace** (Dec-mid Jan; 0870 060 1778; *see p188*), **Duke of York Square** on the King's Road (early Dec-early Jan; 7730 7978), the **Tower of London** (late Nov-early Jan; 0870 602 1100; *see p100*), the **Old Royal Naval College** in Greenwich (early Dec-mid Jan; 0870 169 0101; *see p178*), **Kew Gardens** (Dec-early Jan; www.kewgardensicerink.com; *see p185*) and the **Natural History Museum** (Nov-Jan; www.nhm.ac.uk; *see p153*).

Each year Rhythm Sticks fills a week with a celebration of all that bangs, crashes and pings. Performers come from around the world and play in the widest possible range of styles.

Dance Al Fresco

Regent's Park, Marylebone, NW1 (mobile 0797 059 9445/www.dancealfresco.org). Regent's Park tube. **Date** July-Aug. **Map** p400 G3.

After a year off in 2006, it's business as usual for this outdoor dance event in 2007. Held over three weekends, it's a chance to put on your dancing shoes and tango or ballroom dance to your heart's delight. The usual format is ballroom dancing on Saturdays and tango on Sundays, both from 2pm to 6pm; novices can join the lessons at 1pm. Money raised from the small admission charge is donated to tree planting in the park.

Greenwich & Docklands International Festival

Various venues in Greenwich & Docklands (8305 1818/www.festival.org). **Date** July.

2007 will see the 11th GDIF – an exciting mix of free theatrical, musical and site-specific outdoor events, combining community arts with grander projects. Last year saw giant illuminated spheres rising over the Old Royal Naval College, a human mobile suspended from a crane in Woolwich and 30ft wheels of colour rolling through the heart of Bow.

BBC Sir Henry Wood Promenade Concerts

Royal Albert Hall, Kensington Gore, South Kensington, SW7 2AP (box office 7589 8212/www.bbc.co.uk/proms). Knightsbridge or South Kensington tube/9, 10, 52 bus. **Date** July-Sept. **Map** p399 D9.

Over the course of two months this annual event, dedicated to the late conductor Wood, brings together a wide range of mostly classical concerts. Most of the Proms are televised, but there's nothing like attending them in person. *See also p309.*

Great British Beer Festival

Earl's Court, SW5 (01727 867201/www.camra.org.uk). Earl's Court tube. **Date** 7-11 Aug.

Dust down your pewter tankards for this (not surprisingly) popular event – referred to by fans as 'the biggest pub in the world'. In 2006 some 65,000 visitors sampled over 450 real ales and over 200 foreign beers, as well as lager, cider and perry. Hiccups, belches and hangovers are guaranteed.

Fruitstock

Regent's Park, Marylebone, NW1 (8600 3939/www.fruitstock.com). Regent's Park tube. **Date** 1st wknd in Aug.

The Innocent drink company's free summer bash, established in 2003, has proved extremely popular in past years – 110,000 punters enjoyed the 2005 fest. This year will no doubt build on its success, with plenty of live music, a dance tent, posh food stalls, a farmers' market, activities for children and the chance just to laze about on the grass.

Notting Hill Carnival

Notting Hill, W10, W11 (www.lnhc.org.uk). Ladbroke Grove, Notting Hill Gate & Westbourne Park tube. **Date** 27-28 Aug.

Calling itself Europe's biggest street party, Notting Hill Carnival persuaded over a million revellers in 2006 to drink warm cans of Red Stripe, dance to thunderous sound systems loaded on to the back of trucks and watch the costume parade. Sunday is traditionally the kids' day.

Regent Street Festival

Regent Street, Soho & Mayfair, W1B 4JN (7152 5853/www.regentstreetonline.com). Oxford Circus or Piccadilly Circus tube. **Date** 2 Sept. **Map** p408 U2.

An annual themed celebration that sees the tourist-friendly promenade closed to traffic for the day to make room for fairground rides, theatre, street entertainers, storytelling, a variety of live music and, of course, shopping.

Brick Lane Festival

Brick Lane & Allen Gardens, Spitalfields, E1 (7655 0906/www.bricklanefestival.com). Aldgate East tube/Liverpool Street tube/rail. **Date** 2nd Sun in Sept. **Map** p405 S4/5.

This colourful annual celebration of Spitalfields' multicultural communities past and present is everything the Notting Hill Carnival (*see above*) isn't. Which is to say it's a festive, enjoyable combination of food, music, dance and other performances, rickshaw rides, stilt-walkers, clowns and jugglers. The main stage usually showcases world music acts, while the children's area has funfair rides, inflatables and workshops.

Great River Race

Thames, from Ham House, Richmond, Surrey, to Island Gardens, Isle of Dogs, E14 (8398 9057/www.greatriverrace.co.uk). **Date** 8 Sept.

More than 260 vessels, including everything from Chinese dragon boats to Viking longboats, vie for the UK 'traditional' boat championship over a 22-mile course. The race begins at 12.55pm and the winners will reach the finish at around 4.15pm. The best viewing points are Richmond Bridge and, along the South Bank, Millennium Bridge, Hungerford Bridge and Tower Bridge. You can also watch the action up close from the passenger boat (£25, £10 concs, under-6s free).

Mayor's Thames Festival

Between Westminster & Tower Bridges (7983 4100/www.thamesfestival.org). Blackfriars or Waterloo tube/rail. **Date** 15-16 Sept.

This increasingly popular (and often spectacular) waterfest is getting bigger and bigger each year. Festivities kick off around noon on both days and culminate in a lantern procession and firework finale on the Sunday evening. But before the pyrotechnics kick off, there are food and crafts stalls at a riverside market, environmental activities and creative workshops, and a lively assortment of dance and music performances.

Trafalgar Square: site of one-off celebrations all year round.

Open House London

Various venues across London (0900 160 0061/ www.openhouselondon.org). **Date** 15-16 Sept.
An annual event that gives lovers of architecture and the merely curious free access to more than 500 normally private or otherwise closed buildings, involving palaces, private homes and office spaces across the capital. Apply for a buildings guide from the end of August and remember that you'll need to book ahead for certain buildings.

October-December 2007

Punch & Judy Festival

Covent Garden Piazza, Covent Garden, WC2E (0870 780 5001/www.coventgardenmarket.co.uk). Covent Garden tube. **Date** Oct. **Map** p409 Y3.
This special puppet fest celebrates the shows so beloved of Samuel Pepys. Expect funny-voiced domestic incidents, a crocodile, a policeman and Mr Punch giving Judy a few slaps (and vice versa). For the May Fayre & Puppet Festival, *see p267*.

Pearly Kings & Queens Harvest Festival

St Martin-in-the-Fields, Trafalgar Square, Westminster, WC2N 4JJ (7766 1100/www.pearlysociety.co.uk). Leicester Square tube/Charing Cross tube/rail. **Date** 7 Oct. **Map** p409 X/Y4.
Pearly kings and queens – so-called because of the shiny white buttons sewn in elaborate designs on their dark suits – have their origins in the 'aristocracy' of London's early Victorian costermongers, who elected their own royalty to safeguard their interests. Now charity representatives, today's pearly monarchy gathers for this 3pm thanksgiving service in their traditional 'flash boy' outfits.

London Film Festival

National Film Theatre, South Bank, SE1 8XT (7928 3535/www.lff.org.uk). Embankment tube/Waterloo tube/rail. **Date** 18 Oct-2 Nov. **Map** p403 M8.
Attracting big-name actors and directors from right across the globe, the London Film Festival screens around 180 new British and international features, mostly at the NFT (*see p291*) and the Odeon West End (*see p288*).

London to Brighton Veteran Car Run

From Serpentine Road, Hyde Park, W2 2UH (01327 856024/www.lbvcr.com). Hyde Park Corner tube. **Date** 4 Nov. **Map** p397 E8.
If you're an early riser, you won't mind getting up at the crack of dawn to catch this parade of around 500 veteran (pre-1905) motors, none of which exceeds 20mph on the way to Brighton; they set off from the Serpentine between 7.07am and 8.30am, aiming to reach Brighton before 4pm. Otherwise, join the crowds lining the rest of the route, which wends its way south via Westminster Bridge. The vintage vehicles are also on display along Regent Street from 10am to 3pm on 3 November.

Bonfire Night

Date 5 Nov.
This annual pyrotechnic frenzy sees Brits across the country gather – usually in inclement weather – to burn a 'guy' (an effigy of Guy Fawkes, who notoriously failed to blow up James I and his Parliament in the Gunpowder Plot of 1605) on a giant bonfire and set off loads of fireworks. Most public displays are held on the weekend nearest to 5 November; among London's best are those at Battersea Park, Alexandra Palace and Crystal Palace. Alternatively, try to book a late ride on the London Eye (*see p79*).

I WANT TO LIVE IN A CITY WHERE FAITH AND NON-BELIEF ARE RESPECTED EQUAL

Diwali

Trafalgar Square, Westminster, WC2 (7983 4100/ www.london.gov.uk). Charing Cross tube/rail. **Date** 9 Nov. **Map** p409 X5.

The annual Festival of Light is celebrated in style by the capital's Hindu, Jain and Sikh communities with fireworks and group displays.

Lord Mayor's Show

Various streets in the City (7332 3456/www.lord mayorsshow.org). **Date** 10 Nov.

This is the day when, under conditions laid down by Magna Carta, the newly elected Lord Mayor of London is presented for approval to the monarch or the monarch's justices. Amid a procession of 140 floats and 6,000 people, the Lord Mayor leaves Mansion House at 11am and travels to the Royal Courts of Justice on the Strand, where he makes some vows before returning to Mansion House by 2.30pm. The procession takes around an hour and a quarter to pass, wherever you stand. At 5pm fireworks are set off from from a Thames barge.

Remembrance Sunday Ceremony

Cenotaph, Whitehall, Westminster, SW1. Charing Cross tube/rail. **Date** 11 Nov. **Map** p403 L8.

In honour of those who lost their lives in World War I, World War II and subsequent conflicts, the Queen, the prime minister and other dignitaries lay wreaths at the Cenotaph, Britain's memorial to 'the Glorious Dead'. After a two-minute silence at 11am, the Bishop of London leads a service of remembrance.

State Opening of Parliament

House of Lords, Palace of Westminster, Westminster, SW1A 0PW (7219 4272/www.parliament.uk). Westminster tube. **Date** mid-late Nov (phone for details). **Map** p403 L9.

In a ceremony that has changed little since the 16th century, the Queen officially reopens Parliament after its summer recess. You can only see what goes on inside on telly, but if you join the throngs on the streets you can watch HRM arrive and depart in the state coach, attended by the Household Cavalry.

Christmas Tree & Lights

Covent Garden (0870 780 5001/www.covent gardenmarket.co.uk); Oxford Street (7976 1123/ www.oxfordstreet.co.uk); Regent Street (7152 5853/www.regent-street.co.uk); Bond Street (www.bondstreetassociation.com); Trafalgar Square (7983 4234/www.london.gov.uk). **Date** Nov-Dec.

The Christmas lights on London's main shopping streets are an increasingly commercialised affair (they're often sponsored, with nonebrities drafted in to flick the switches), but the glittering lights of St Christopher's Place, Marylebone High Street, Bond Street and Kensington High Street continue to instil a sense of childhood wonder. The giant fir tree in Trafalgar Square is an annual gift from the Norwegian people, in gratitude for Britain's role in liberating their country from the Nazis.

New Year's Eve Celebrations

Date 31 Dec.

Celebratory events in London tend to be quite localised, although Trafalgar Square has traditionally been an unofficial (and alarmingly crowded) gathering point; no booze is permitted, which may not be a bad thing. For the cash-flash, almost all of the city's nightclubs hold ludicrously expensive New Year parties. If you're feeling up to it by noon the next day, the New Year's Day Parade starts at Parliament Square, finishes at Berkeley Square and takes in Whitehall, Trafalgar Square and Piccadilly.

Children

Capital fun for kids.

In this chapter we list the best of what the city has to offer families, but check the Around Town pages in the weekly *Time Out London* magazine for the latest shows and events, and log on to www.london.gov.uk/young-london, the mayor's website for children. Useful information can also be found on www.kidslove london.com and www.whatson4kids.com. In addition, *Time Out London for Children* (£8.99) is a comprehensive, annually updated guide.

The best way of getting around London as a family is by bus; we recommend the RV1 (Tower Hill to South Bank), the 12 (Westminster to Notting Hill) and the 52 (Kensington to Knightsbridge). Under-19s travel free on buses, while under-11s travel free on all forms of London transport; for more details, *see p361*.

Area guide

South Bank & Bankside pp78-88

The **British Airways London Eye** (*see p79*) is the best thing about the South Bank, say the kids, closely followed by the nearby **London Aquarium** (*see p81*). The programme at the **BFI London IMAX Cinema** (*see p291*) usually includes children's films. Summertime in this area is lively, thanks to the open-air entertainment laid on by the **Coin Street Festival** and the **National Theatre**'s summer fandango, Watch This Space (for both, *see p268*). A bit further east, the **Clink Prison Museum** offers ghoulish fun and the **Golden Hinde** (for both, *see p83*) is famed for its party and sleepover programme. In nearby Tooley Street, over-tens love the gory frights at the **London Dungeon** (*see p87*), while boys of all ages get a thrill from exploring floating warship museum **HMS Belfast** (*see p89*).

The City pp89-101

The **Monument** (*see p100*) offers rewarding views from the top, but will be closed for renovation until late 2007. The best day out in this area is at the **Tower of London** (*see p100*), with regular Beefeater-guided tours. The best free day out (with free activity bags for 4-11s), meanwhile, is at the excellent

We'll spell it out for you: **Blue Kangaroo** is fabulous.

Museum of London (*see p97*), but note that the entire lower level is closed for refurbishment until 2009.

Bloomsbury & Fitzrovia pp107-122

The **British Museum** (*see p109*) has more than enough to satisfy visitors of all ages; check the website for details of the more manageable highlights tours (and for memorable sleepovers in the Egyptian mummy galleries). One of London's best playgrounds, **Coram's Fields** (*see p278*), is also in this area; behind it in Brunswick Square is the affecting **Foundling Museum** (*see p110*). The newly opened **Cartoon Museum** (*see p109*) has regular children's workshops, as well as family fun days every second Saturday of the month. The enchanting **Pollock's Toy Museum** (*see p112*), however, is of far greater interest to adults than kids.

Covent Garden pp113-119

The two major child-friendly museums in this bustling tourist area are out of action: **London's Transport Museum** (*see p115*) is undergoing major refurbishment until summer 2007 and the **Theatre Museum** is to close down. However, kids always enjoy the buskers on the Piazza, who often include jugglers and acrobats.

Trafalgar Square pp137-138

The **National Gallery** (*see p137*) has year-round paper trails and audio tours for children, as well as regular kids' workshops and story-telling sessions for under-fives. For three- to 12-year-olds, the **National Portrait Gallery** (*see p138*) loans out free activity-filled rucksacks that correspond to the Tudor, Victorian and 20th-century galleries. Nearby, **St Martin-in-the-Fields** (*see p138*) has London's only brass-rubbing centre.

South Kensington pp150-154

Even grown-ups are impressed by the dinosaurs at the **Natural History Museum** (*see p153*), and there's more to this marvellous building than bones and fossils. Animatronic and interactive models fill the galleries; the Red Zone's earth galleries include an earthquake simulation, and the smaller the child the more awesome is the life-size model of the blue whale. Up the road, the **Science Museum** (*see p154*) has six play zones for different age ranges. 'Science Night' sleepovers (for children aged 8-11 years) are held once a month. Kids' facilities at the **Victoria & Albert Museum** (*see p154*) include activity backpacks and an Activity Cart on Sunday mornings (for over-3s).

Greenwich pp176-179

This World Heritage Site is a delight for kids, especially the spectacular scenery of hilly **Royal Greenwich Park** (*see p176*), where there are free children's entertainments every summer. Unfortunately, the **Cutty Sark** (*see p176*) will be closed throughout 2007, but there's plenty of seafaring adventure on offer at the **National Maritime Museum** (*see p177*).

Eating & drinking

Of the places in the **Restaurants & Cafés** chapter (*pp196-223*), **Carluccio's Caffè** (*see p201*), **Crumpet** (*see p220*) and **Wagamama** (*see p218*) are all notably child-friendly.

Blue Kangaroo

555 King's Road, Fulham, SW6 2EB (7371 7622/www.thebluekangaroo.co.uk). Fulham Broadway tube/Sloane Square tube then 11, 19, 22 bus. **Open** 9.30am-7.30pm daily. **Main courses** £8.50-£13.50. **Credit** AmEx, MC, V. **Map** p398 C13.

Parents can eat upstairs in the restaurant proper or in the midst of the basement play areas (monitored via plasma screens). The kid's menu features wholesome, well-prepared favourites such as organic sausage and mash, and own-made chicken nuggets.

London Zoo. *See p277.*

Giraffe

6-8 Blandford Street, Marylebone, W1H 3AA (7935 2333/www.giraffe.net). Baker Street or Bond Street tube. **Open** 7.45am-11pm Mon-Fri; 9am-11pm Sat; 9am-10.30pm Sun. **Main courses** £7.95-£11.95. **Credit** AmEx, MC, V. **Map** p400 G5.

Extensive kids' choices (noodles, salmon fingers, burgers) are available alongside the global main menu (stir-fries, curries, burritos, steaks). Great fruit smoothies and decent veggie choices.

Other locations: throughout the city.

Rainforest Café

20 Shaftesbury Avenue, Piccadilly, W1D 7EU (7434 3111/www.therainforestcafe.co.uk). Piccadilly Circus tube. **Meals served** noon-10pm Mon-Thur, Sun; noon-7.30pm Fri, Sat. **Main courses** £10.25-£16. **Credit** AmEx, DC, MC, V. **Map** p403 K7.

Jungle-themed and packed with animatronic creatures, this restaurant (with all-too-obvious shopping area) has a menu aimed at younger tastes (burgers, pizza, meatballs) but at adult prices.

Smollensky's on the Strand

105 Strand, Charing Cross, WC2R 0AA (7497 2101/ www.smollenskys.co.uk). Embankment tube/Charing Cross tube/rail. **Meals served** noon-11.30pm Mon-Sat; noon-10pm Sun. **Main courses** £8.95-£21.95. **Credit** AmEx, DC, MC, V. **Map** p403 L7.

Grills are the main attraction at this US steakhouse-style eaterie. It's brash and touristy, but the free kids' fun packs, weekend entertainment, friendly staff and reliably decent, well-priced food make it a good spot for families.

TGI Friday's

6 Bedford Street, Covent Garden, WC2E 9HZ (7379 0585/www.tgifridays.co.uk). Covent Garden or Embankment tube/Charing Cross tube/rail. **Open** noon-11.30pm Mon-Sat; noon-11pm Sun. **Main courses** £6.95-£17. **Credit** AmEx, MC, V. **Map** p403 L7.

Perky staff, free activity packs, weekend face painting and entertainment… kids love it here. Parents may be underwhelmed by the food (the usual chicken fingers/burger standards), but portions are generous and the elaborate puddings a sure-fire hit.

Other locations: throughout the city.

Entertainment

City farms & zoos

London Zoo (*see p128*; **photo** *p276*) has impressive walk-through monkey and exotic-bird enclosures, but if you're after something a bit more low-key there are plenty of close encounters of the furred kind to be found in the capital's many city farms. **Battersea Park Children's Zoo** (www.batterseaparkzoo.co.uk; **photo** *p279*) brings the animals closer to the kids with keeper talks and handling sessions twice daily. **Freightliners City Farm** (www.freightlinersfarm.org.uk) and **Kentish Town City Farm** (www.aapi.co.uk/cityfarm) offer weekend pony rides; in the east there's **Mudchute City Farm** (www.mudchute.org), with **Surrey Docks Farm** (www.surreydocksfarm.org) in the south-east and **Vauxhall City Farm** (7582 4204) in the south-west of the city.

Puppets

Little Angel Theatre

14 Dagmar Passage, off Cross Street, Islington, N1 2DN (7226 1787/www.littleangeltheatre.com). Angel tube/Highbury & Islington tube/rail. **Open** *Box office* 11am-6pm Mon-Fri; 10am-4.30pm Sat, Sun. **Tickets** £5-£15. Some pay-what-you-can performances; phone for details. **Credit** MC, V.

Established in 1961, this is still London's only permanent puppet theatre. Performances cover styles and stories from a wide range of cultural traditions, using just about every kind of marionette.

Puppet Theatre Barge

Opposite 35 Blomfield Road, Little Venice, W9 2PF (winter 7249 6876/summer 07836 202745/www.puppetbarge.com). Warwick Avenue tube. **Open** *Box office* 10am-9pm daily. *Children's shows* term-time Sat, Sun; school hols daily; phone for times. **Tickets** £8.50; £8 concessions. **Credit** MC, V.

High-quality puppet shows (modern twists on traditional tales alongside children's classics) and the lovely canalside location make this cosy 55-seat barge, moored between December and June, unique. Performances are held regularly on Saturday and Sunday afternoons (3pm), with a daily programme during school holidays.

Science & nature

Camley Street Natural Park

12 Camley Street, King's Cross, NW1 0PW (7833 2311/www.wildlondon.org.uk). King's Cross tube/rail. **Open** 10am-5pm Thur-Sun. *School holidays* 10am-5pm daily. **Admission** free. **Map** p401 L2.

London Wildlife Trust's flagship reserve is 87,000sq ft of wild green space on the banks of Regent's Canal, combining woods, ponds, marshes and flower meadows to lovely effect in an area that was for years just industrial wasteland. The visitors' centre has a wealth of information on urban flora and fauna, while the website lists a good programme of children's events and play activities.

Greenwich Peninsula Ecology Park

Thames Path, John Harrison Way, Greenwich, SE10 0QZ (8293 1904/www.urbanecology.org.uk). North Greenwich tube/108, 161, 422, 472, 486 bus. **Open** 10am-5pm (or dusk) Wed-Sun. **Admission** free.

A pond-dipping, birdwatching wetland haven near the Millennium Dome. Family fun days, like Frog Day in early March and tree dressing in December, are among the popular year-round activities offered.

Theatre

Half Moon Young People's Theatre

43 White Horse Road, Stepney, E1 0ND (7709 8900/ www.halfmoon.org.uk). Limehouse DLR/rail. **Open** *Box office* 10am-6pm Mon-Fri; 10am-5pm Sat. **Tickets** £4. **Credit** MC, V.

The Half Moon's inclusive policy places particular emphasis on engaging those often excluded by ethnicity and disabilities. Two studios provide a calendar of performances for children aged from six months old, and they can join one of the seven youth theatre groups (for five- to 17-year-olds).

Polka Theatre

240 The Broadway, Wimbledon, SW19 1SB (8543 4888/www.polkatheatre.com). South Wimbledon tube/Wimbledon tube/rail then 57, 93, 219, 493 bus. **Open** *Phone bookings* 9.30am-4.30pm Mon; 9am-6pm Tue-Fri; 10am-4.30pm Sat. *Personal callers* 9.30am-4.30pm Tue-Fri; 10am-4.30pm Sat. **Tickets** £4-£14. **Credit** AmEx, MC, V.

This dedicated young people's theatre has one of the best programmes of children's events in London. Touring companies stage daily shows (10.30am, 2pm) in the main auditoriums, with weekly (often puppet-based) performances for under-fours in the Adventure Theatre. There are free monthly World of Stories drop-in activities, and literature events featuring much-loved authors such as Jacqueline Wilson.

Unicorn Theatre

Tooley Street, Bankside, SE1 2HZ (7645 0560/ www.unicorntheatre.com). London Bridge tube/rail/ Tower Hill tube. **Open** *Box office* 9.30am-6pm Mon-Fri; 10am-6pm Sat; noon-5pm Sun. **Credit** MC, V.

One of Britain's leading producers of professional theatre for children, the Unicorn's £13m centre opened in 2005 after a three-year collaboration with local schoolchildren, whose thoughts are incorporated into the design. The 300-seat Weston Theatre is its large-scale performance space, the Clore a more intimate studio for education and new work. Check the website for the 2007 programme. There's a branch of family-friendly café Frizzante on site.

Spaces to play

London's parks and green spaces are plentiful and provide great escapes for little visitors bored of pounding the pavement with their parents. Many of the best are in the centre of town. These include **Regent's Park** (*see p127*), for boating and London Zoo (*see p128*); **Hyde Park** (*see p154*), for boating and the Diana Memorial Playground (*see below*); **Hampstead Heath** (*see p158*), for swimming and kite-flying; **Battersea Park** (*see p182*), for its fine adventure playground and zoo; **Greenwich Park** (*see p176*), for trees, views and deer, and **Richmond Park** (*see p185*), for the Isabella Plantation, cycling and deer.

Coram's Fields

93 Guilford Street, Bloomsbury, WC1N 1DN (7837 6138/www.coramsfields.org). Russell Square tube. **Open** *Apr-Sept* 8am-8pm Mon-Fri; 9am-8am Sat, Sun. *Oct-Mar* 8am-dusk Mon-Fri; 9am-dusk Sat, Sun. **Admission** free (adults only admitted if accompanied by child under 16). **Map** p401 L4.

This city-centre site dates back to 1747, when Thomas Coram established the Foundling Hospital. Now a wonderful children's park, it boasts lawns, sandpits, a paddling pool, football pitch, basketball court, climbing towers, play areas and an assault-course pulley over 305,000sq ft. Other draws include an outdoor café, small animal enclosures and indoor facilities for the under-fives.

Diana, Princess of Wales Memorial Playground

Nr Black Lion Gate, Broad Walk, Kensington Gardens, W8 2UH (7298 2117/recorded information 7298 2141/www.royalparks.gov.uk). Bayswater or Queensway tube. **Open** *Summer* 10am-7.30pm daily. *Winter* 10am-dusk daily. **Admission** free; adults only admitted if accompanied by under-12s. **Map** p397 E8.

Inspired by the story of Peter Pan, this commemorative playground is a youngsters' wonderland. There's a huge wooden pirate ship, mermaids' fountain, rocky outcrops, wigwams and a tree-house encampment; the equipment and facilities have mostly been designed for use by children with special needs. Unaccompanied adults may view the gardens from 9.30am to 10am daily.

Discover

1 Bridge Terrace, Stratford, E15 4BG (8536 5555/ www.discover.org.uk). Stratford tube/rail/DLR. **Open** *Term-time* 10am-5pm Tue-Sun. *School hols* 10am-5pm daily. **Admission** *Garden* free. *Story trail* £3.50; £2.50 concessions; free under-2s; half-price admission 3-5pm term-time only. **Credit** MC, V.

Discover is an interactive 'story trail' that encourages under-eights to give their imagination free rein. The creative garden includes a wet-play area, monster's-tongue slide, climbing frames and living willow hide-and-seek tunnels; indoors, children can fly on a magic carpet, cross a sparkly river, and make characters at craft tables. Weekend drop-in activities include puppet shows, as well as art, dance and music workshops.

Theme parks

Always call or check the website for special events and for opening times, which vary throughout the year. Queues are unavoidable; arrive early in the morning to at least begin your day queue-free. Also note that height and health restrictions apply on some rides.

Chessington World of Adventures

Leatherhead Road, Chessington, Surrey KT9 2NE (0870 444 7777/www.chessington.co.uk). **Getting there** *By rail* Chessington South rail then 71 bus or 10min walk. *By car* J9 off M25. **Open** times vary.

Toddler meets rooster at **Battersea Park Children's Zoo**. *See p277.*

Tot shops

There just isn't space to do justice to all the great children's retailers in London, but we know exactly where to start: our favourite all-rounder is kids' department store **Daisy & Tom** (181-183 King's Road, SW3 5EB, 7352 5000, www.daisyandtom.com). Its first floor displays an excellent range of nursery equipment, furniture and toys; its second, clothes and shoes from labels such as Timberland, Catimini and Elle. A host of attractions includes half-hourly puppet shows and mini carousel rides, plus there are all those toys for kids to try out and a central area with big beanbags to flop on to in the book department. A 'first haircut' (£16) in the hair salon includes a certificate with a photograph of your child and a lock of hair.

The UK's largest toyshop **Hamleys** (188-196 Regent Street, W1B 5BT, 0870 333 2455, www.hamleys.com) can be an overexciting experience for children, with seven floors of must-have items from Doctor Who models and high-tech gadgets to mountains of cuddly animals and dressing-up gear. Prices reflect the convenience of having everything under one roof, the store is always crowded and the queues at the tills can be long, but with over five million visitors a year Hamleys is a bona fide tourist attraction in its own right. It's certainly preferable to the flagship **Disney Store** (360-366 Oxford Street, 7491 9136, www.disneystore.co.uk), which has Mickey and Co emblazoned on everything from lunchboxes to tableware, alongside a large range of toys, stationery and clothes.

By contrast, the pleasure of blowing your pocket money on sherbet pips and jaw-locking toffee bonbons, weighed out in ounces and poured from huge glass jars into little paper bags, seems positively Dickensian. But we say retro rocks and the current fashion for nostalgic candy has seen traditional-style confectioners opening all over town. At south London's **Hope & Greenwood** (20 North Cross Road, East Dulwich, SE22 9EU, 8613 1777) Miss Hope and Mr Greenwood dress in vintage clothes to sell old-fashioned sweets over a marble-topped counter; choose from over 175 jars of cola cubes, acid drops, sarsaparilla tablets and flying saucers. In nearby Clapham, **Lollipop** (201 St John's Hill, SW11 1TH, 7585 1588) is run by Italians. Finding that their previous venture, a deli, sold more confectionery than any other item, they sold up and opened this sweet shop. It stocks 140 classic sweets. Chocs away!

Closed Nov-Feb. **Admission** £29 (accompanying under-12s free); £19.50 additional under-12s; £14.50-£18 concessions; £28-£111.50 family; free under-4s. Check website for advance bookings for fast-track entry. **Credit** MC, V.

Chessington's family-friendly policy means that most of the rides and attractions are suitable for under-12s. Highlights include the Land of the Dragons, Pirate's Cove, Beanoland, indoor foamy fun at Bubbleworks and the park's scariest ride, Rameses Revenge (height restrictions apply). Huge viewing windows in Animal Land let you get up close to gorillas and big cats, and little ones enjoy the walk-through monkey and bird garden.

Legoland

Winkfield Road, Windsor, Berkshire SL4 4AY (0870 504 0404/www.legoland.co.uk). **Getting there** *By rail* Windsor & Eton Riverside or Windsor Central rail then bus. *By car* J3 off M3 or J6 off M4. **Open** times vary. Closed late Nov-mid Mar. **Admission** *1-day ticket* £30; £23 concessions; free under-3s. *2-day ticket* £57; £45 concessions; free under-3s. **Credit** MC, V.

Legoland is a top family day out, which means you need to be prepared for long queues. Stroll through impressive scenes from Europe and Cape Canaveral in Mini Land (they have been created from nearly 40 million Lego pieces), but be sure you don't miss rides on the Dragon, Wave Surfer and Pirate Falls (a soaking is guaranteed). In addition to the rides, kids can catch a 4D movie screening, enrol for Driving School (for 6- to 13-year-olds only, although their younger siblings can enjoy a smaller version of the same thing) or take control of one of ten full-size mechanical diggers. One day isn't enough to experience it all. Note that the park is closed on selected Tuesdays and Wednesdays throughout the season.

Thorpe Park

Staines Road, Chertsey, Surrey KT16 8PN (0870 444 4466/www.thorpepark.com). **Getting there** *By rail* Staines rail then 950 bus. *By car* M25 J11 or J13. **Open** times vary. **Admission** £28.50; £14.50-£20 concessions; £78-£98 family; free for children under 1m. Check website or phone for advance bookings. **Credit** MC, V.

Europe's fastest rollercoaster, Stealth, launches thrill-seekers earthward from nought to 80mph in 2.3 gut-wrenching seconds. Other aptly named rides include Slammer, Rush, Colossus (the world's first ten-loop rollercoaster), Detonator and Vortex. There are also plenty of tamer rides for younger visitors, as well as a petting zoo.

Comedy

What's so funny – and, more importantly, where.

There's an element of seasonality to catching a comedy gig in London. Between September and December you'll get to see the countless hour-long solo shows that wowed crowds at the Edinburgh Festival the preceding August. Spring and summer is Edinburgh preview time, when you can catch acts trying new material for a bargain price (try the **Hen & Chickens** or **Lowdown at the Albany**). By contrast, August is when most comics are actually at the Festival and London is deathly short of mirth.

Clubs normally offer bills featuring three or four acts doing 20 minutes each, but there are also improv artists (the Comedy Store Players at the **Comedy Store** are the best) and satirical shows (try the Store's Cutting Edge team and the Newsrevue troupe at the **Canal Café**).

As a rule, the bigger the name, the higher the price, so don't be afraid to experiment: new act and open mic nights are cheap and sometimes throw up real gems. But if you arrive late or sit at the front, most comics ensure you become part of the show. The comedy section of *Time Out London* magazine has weekly listings.

Major venues

Bloomsbury Theatre (15 Gordon Street, WC1H 0AH, 7388 8822) and **Soho Theatre** (*see p344*) both put on great comedy.

Amused Moose

Soho *Moonlighting, 17 Greek Street, W1D 4DR (7287 3727/www.amusedmoose.com). Leicester Square or Tottenham Court Road tube.* **Shows** 8.30pm Sat. **Admission** (incl membership) £12.50. **No credit cards**. **Map** p408 W2.
Camden *The Enterprise, 2 Haverstock Hill, NW3 2BL (8341 1341/www.amusedmoose.com). Chalk Farm tube.* **Shows** 8pm Wed, Sun. **Admission** (incl membership) £5. **No credit cards**.
New talent is big on the agenda at both the older Soho branch and newer Camden joint (where there's even a comedy course), although big names such as Ricky Gervais, Bill Bailey and Graham Norton have raised many a chuckle at the original venue. Heckling is discouraged – boo hiss. The Soho venue is available for Christmas parties and secret gigs.

Banana Cabaret

The Bedford, 77 Bedford Hill, Balham, SW12 9HD (8673 8904/www.bananacabaret.co.uk). Balham tube/rail. **Shows** 9pm Fri, Sat. **Admission** £3 Tue; £12, £8 concs Fri; £15, £12 concs Sat. **No credit cards**.
Banana Cabaret has four or five stand-ups per show, usually of good quality – Mark Thomas warmed up for his politically charged TV shows here, and Omid Djalili has also graced the stage. Tuesday is the night for new acts.

Bearcat Club

Turk's Head, 28 Winchester Road, Twickenham, Middx TW1 1LF (8891 1852/www.bearcatcomedy.co.uk). St Margaret's rail. **Shows** 8.45pm Sat. **Admission** £10, £9 members. **Credit** AmEx, DC, MC, V.
The loveable Bearcat turns out strong bills of stand-up – usually four names a night – to the well-to-do denizens of Twickenham.

Canal Café Theatre

Bridge House, Delamere Terrace, Little Venice, W2 6ND (7289 6054/www.canalcafetheatre.com). Warwick Avenue tube. **Shows** *Newsrevue* 9.30pm Thur-Sat; 9pm Sun. Phone box office for details of other shows. **Admission** (incl membership) £10.50, £8.50 concs. **No credit cards**. **Map** p396 C4.
Newsrevue, the Canal Café's topical comedy sketch show, was awarded a Guinness World Record in 2004 for the longest running live comedy show (25 years); the show is updated each week. The venue also hosts comic plays and stand-up.

Chuckle Club

Three Tuns Bar, London School of Economics, Houghton Street, Holborn, WC2A 2AL (7476 1672/www.chuckleclub.com). Holborn tube. **Shows** 7.45pm Sat. **Admission** £10, £8 concs. **No credit cards**. **Map** p401 M6.
LSE's student union has been hosting this night for two decades. Slosh down beer at student prices while bonkers resident compere Eugene Cheese introduces a selection of comics and open spots.

Comedy Café

66-68 Rivington Street, Shoreditch, EC2A 3AY (7739 5706/www.comedycafe.co.uk). Liverpool Street or Old Street tube/rail. **Shows** 8pm Wed, Thur, Sat; 7pm Fri. **Admission** free Wed; £5 Thur; £12 Fri; £15 Sat. **Credit** MC, V. **Map** p405 R4.
This purpose-built Shoreditch venue usually features three to four stand-ups – expect the likes of Dan Antopolski and Friday Night Project regular Rob Rouse. Wednesday is open mic night. It's almost directly opposite Cargo (*see p321*).

Comedy Camp

Bar Code, 3-4 Archer Street, Soho, W1D 7AP (7483 2960/www.comedycamp.co.uk). Leicester Square or Piccadilly Circus tube. **Shows** 8.30pm Tue. **Admission** £10, £8 (members). **Credit** MC, V. **Map** p408 W3.

Arts & Entertainment

This Soho haunt describes itself as a 'straight-friendly lesbian and gay club'. Fun weekly nights, hosted by Simon Happily, have seen the likes of Harry Hill, Al Murray and Graham Norton on stage.

Comedy Store

1A Oxendon Street, Soho, SW1Y 4EE (Ticketmaster 0870 060 2340/www.thecomedystore.co.uk). Leicester Square or Piccadilly Circus tube. **Shows** 8pm Tue-Thur, Sun; 8pm & midnight Fri, Sat; Mon phone for details. **Admission** £14-£15, £9 concs. **Credit** AmEx, MC, V. **Map** p408 W4.

The legendary Comedy Store made its name as the home of 'alternative comedy' in the 1980s. With those radical young comics now the mainstream of British comedy, the Store is now the place every comic wants to play and it has the best bills on the circuit. The venue is purpose-built for serious punters, with its gladiatorial semi-circle of seats, and generally favours trad stand-up. Go on Tuesdays for the topical 'Cutting Edge' shows, on Wednesdays for top improv outfit the Comedy Store Players.

Downstairs at The King's Head

2 Crouch End Hill, Crouch End, N8 8AA (8340 1028/office 01920 823265/www.downstairsatthe kingshead.com). Finsbury Park tube/rail then W7 bus. **Shows** 8pm Tue, Thur, Sat, Sun. **Admission** £4, £3 concs Tue, Thur; £8, £6 concs Sat; £7, £5 concs Sun. **Credit** MC, V.

This Crouch Ender started up in 1981, when the alternative comedy scene was just beginning. Nowadays it's a favourite with many big-name comedians for trying out new material. It also showcases new talent: the long-running Thursday 'try out night' – up to 16 new acts take the mic – kick-started the careers of Mark Lamarr and Eddie Izzard.

Ha Bloody Ha

Ealing Studios, Ealing Green, St Mary's Road, Ealing, W5 5EP (8566 4067/www.headliners comedy.com). Ealing Broadway tube/rail. **Shows** 8.45pm Fri, Sat. **Admission** £10, £7.50 concs (Fri only). **No credit cards.**

In the studios where the famous Ealing Comedies were filmed, this west London institution hosts big names (Bill Bailey, Ed Byrne) twice a week. It also produces the annual Ealing Comedy festival in Walpole Park each July.

Headliners

The George IV, 185 Chiswick High Road, Chiswick, W4 2DR (8566 4067/www.headlinerscomedy.com). Turnham Green tube. **Shows** 9pm Fri, Sat. **Admission** £10, £7.50 concs (Fri only). **No credit cards.**

The unfussy younger brother of Ha Bloody Ha (*see above*) hosts stand-ups of big and middle stature.

Hen & Chickens

109 St Paul's Road, Highbury Corner, Islington, N1 2NA (7704 2001/www.henandchickens.com). Highbury & Islington tube/rail. **Shows** 7.30pm, 9.15pm; days vary. **Admission** £7-£10. **No credit cards.**

This well-established joint offers similar bills to its sister venue, Lowdown at the Albany (*see below*). There's a mix of big names (like Jimmy Carr and Daniel Kitson) and newcomers, with lots going on during the Edinburgh preview season.

Jongleurs

Battersea *The Rise, 49 Lavender Gardens, SW11 1DJ. Clapham Junction rail.* **Shows** 8.30pm Thur; 9pm Fri, Sat. **Admission** £9.50-£16.50.
Bow *221 Grove Road, E3 5SN. Mile End tube.* **Shows** 8.30pm Fri, Sat. **Admission** £14.50-£15.50.
Camden *Middle Yard, Camden Lock, Chalk Farm Road, NW1 8AB. Chalk Farm tube.* **Shows** 8.30pm Fri, Sat. **Admission** £15.50-£16.50.
All *Box office 0870 787 0707/www.jongleurs.com.* **Credit** AmEx, DC, MC, V.

Since it opened in 1983 Jongleurs has expanded to become the biggest comedy franchise in England. Although it thus attracts some of the biggest names, Jongleurs is corporate do and hen night central, with boozed-up punters who eat, drink, dance – and laugh if they happen to notice the poor soul on stage.

Lee Hurst's Backyard Comedy Club

231 Cambridge Heath Road, Bethnal Green, E2 0EL (7739 3122/www.backyardcomedyclub.moonfruit.com). Bethnal Green tube/ rail. **Shows** 8pm Thur-Sat. **Admission** £10-£15, £2-£5 concs. **Credit** MC, V.

Lee Hurst's purpose-built club features three experienced names each night, with Hurst himself usually compering. There's also a restaurant, worked to the bone on Thursday ('Curry on Comedy' night), when you get a free curry with every ticket.

Lowdown at the Albany

240 Great Portland Street, Marylebone, W1W 5QU (7387 5706/www.lowdownatthealbany.com). Great Portland Street tube. **Shows** 8pm; days vary. **Admission** £7-£10. **No credit cards.** **Map** p400 H4.

This rough-around-the-edges basement venue underneath the Albany is a simple one-man-and-his-mic set-up (there isn't even much room for the audience). Excellent for Edinburgh previews.

Red Rose

129 Seven Sisters Road, Finsbury Park, N7 7QG (7281 3051/www.redrosecomedy.co.uk). Finsbury Park tube/rail. **Shows** 9pm Sat. **Admission** £9, £5 concs. **Credit** MC, V.

This long-standing north London club was established by outspoken comic Ivor Dembina, who dedicated it to cheap nights with big names but no frills: food is available and there is a late bar.

Up the Creek

302 Creek Road, Greenwich, SE10 9SW (8858 4581/ www.up-the-creek.com). Greenwich DLR/rail. **Shows** 9pm Fri; 8.30pm Sat. **Admission** £10, £6 concs Fri; £15, £10 concs Sat. **Credit** AmEx, MC, V.

The late, great Malcolm Hardee ('To say that he has no shame is to drastically exaggerate the amount of shame that he has,' explained one journalist) established this bearpit in 1990. Although he handed over

Names to watch

Not every great comic gets their five minutes on TV; beyond the Harry Hills, Russell Brands, Ricky Gervaises and Al Murrays, the circuit has plenty of big names all its own. How do you make head or tail of these relative unknowns? You can start by checking whether they're an **if.comeddie award** winner or nominee. Awarded at the Edinburgh Festival each year, these horribly titled awards used to be the Perriers and they are still Britain's most prestigious prizes for comedy. Canadian Phil Nichol won in 2006; Josie Long, with her chipper show *Kindness and Exuberance*, nicked Best Newcomer. Nominees for the main prize included madcap sketch outfit We Are Klang, plus stand-ups Russell Howard, Paul Sinha and David O'Doherty.

Not every comic makes their name just from performances – some are behind London's more interesting and adventurous comedy nights. On Mondays Nichol runs the **Old Red Rope** club (Red, 5 Kingly Street, W1B 5PF), where leading names and good newcomers try out new material. Why Old Rope? Because the performers hold on to a noose hanging above the stage and they're only allowed to let go when they're telling new gags. Talented Irish stand-up Andrew Maxwell hosts **Maxwell's Full Mooners** (the Comedy Store, *see p282*), at which big names are encouraged to try out something unusual; Maxwell runs the night sporadically, usually starting at midnight. Also, book well in advance for Robin Ince's perennially popular **Book Club**, held monthly at Lowdown at the Albany (*see p282*) – this sees comics (frequently big names) try out new material and deliver cringeworthy readings from the club's supply of godawful literature. Those with staying power will be pleased to hear that these nights can run on and on...

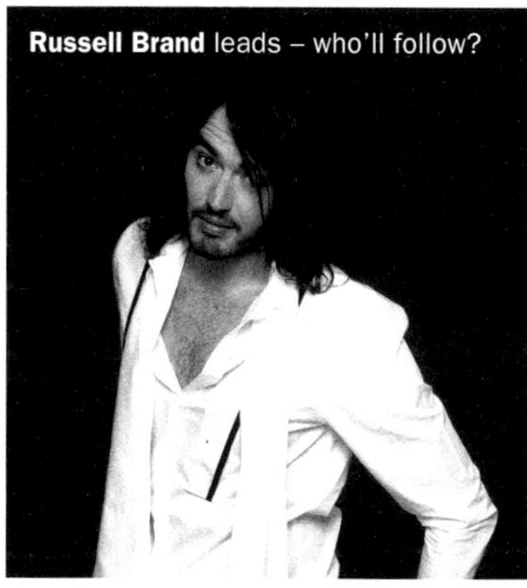
Russell Brand leads – who'll follow?

the reins long before his death in 2005, his legacy lives on. Punters are the rowdiest – some say, the most discerning – on the circuit. Expect stand-up and the odd cabaret set.

Other venues

Boat Show/Monday Club *Tattershall Castle, Kings Reach, Victoria Embankment, SW1A 7HR (mobile 07932 658895). Embankment tube.* **Shows** 8pm Fri; 8.30pm alternate Mon. **Map** p403 L8.

Comedy Brewhouse *Camden Head, 2 Camden Walk, Camden Passage, Islington, N1 8DY (7359 0851). Angel tube.* **Shows** 9pm Fri-Sat.

Covent Garden Comedy Club *The Arches, off Villiers Street, Charing Cross, WC2N 6NG (mobile 07960 071340/www.coventgardencomedy.com). Embankment tube/Charing Cross tube/rail.* **Shows** 8pm Fri, Sat. **Map** p409 Y5.

Funny Side of Covent Garden *Corner Store, 32-35 Wellington Street, WC2E 4EE (0870 446 0616/www.thefunnyside.info). Covent Garden tube.* **Shows** 8pm Wed, Fri; 7.30 Sun.

Hampstead Comedy Club *Adelaide, 143 Adelaide Road, NW3 3NL (7633 9539/ www.hampsteadcomedy.co.uk). Belsize Park or Chalk Farm tube.* **Shows** 9pm Sat.

Laughing Horse Oxford Circus *The Blue Posts, 18 Kingly Street, Soho, W1B 5PX (bookings mobile 07796 171190/www.laughinghorse.co.uk). Oxford Circus tube.* **Shows** 8.30pm Mon. **Map** p408 V2. Also in Soho, Camden, Edgeware Road, islington, Richmond, Wimbledon and Walthamstow.

Mirth Control *Lower Ground Bar, 269 West End Lane, NW6 1QS (7431 2211/www.mirthcontrol.org.uk). West Hampstead tube/rail.* **Shows** 9pm Wed.

Monkey Business Camden *Solo Bar, 20 Inverness Street, Camden, NW1 7BY (mobile 07932 338203/www.monkeybusiness comedyclub.co.uk). Camden Town tube.* **Shows** 8.30pm Fri, Sat.

Pear-Shaped in Fitzrovia *Fitzroy Tavern, 16 Charlotte Street, Fitzrovia, W1T 2LY (7580 3714). Goodge Street tube.* **Shows** 8.30pm Wed. **Map** p400 J5.

Performance Club *Inn on the Green, 3-5 Thorpe Close, Notting Hill, W10 5XL (mobile 07790 420067). Ladbroke Grove tube.* **Shows** 8.30pm Thur.

Theatre 503 *The Latchmere, 503 Battersea Park Road, SW11 3BW (7978 7040/www.theatre503.com). Clapham Junction rail.* **Shows** 8pm Sun.

Dance

We've come a long way since the 'Lambeth Walk'.

Laban Centre. *See p285.*

When you know where to look, London's vital and varied dance scene can prove a box-office bargain. The **Place** (*see p285*) presents a diverse year-round programme of rising dance companies, with no performance costing more than £15 (tickets bought well in advance are a fiver). The home base for both the Richard Alston Dance Company and the London School of Contemporary Dance, the Place also supports several choreographers-in-residence and fields an associate artists' programme for a rotating selection of emerging dance talents.

Another good deal is the **Jerwood Proms**, held at Sadler's Wells. Dubbed 'Stand Up for Dance', these performances take place during the annual **Dance Umbrella** (www.danceumbrella.co.uk), one of the world's finest dance festivals. For two weeks in September/October, the front stalls are replaced by 500 standing places, allowing people to experience up-close some of the top names in international dance for, again, only £5. Standing places for the Royal Ballet at Covent Garden's **Royal Opera House** are an even better deal, ranging from £4 to £8 (depending on the ballet), and you'll probably be standing right behind someone who has forked out up to £84 for their seat.

The scene was boosted in 2006 with the arrival of the first **Big Dance**, a week-long celebration of dance organised by the Mayor of London's office in partnership with the Arts Council. It culminated on a Saturday lunchtime with London joining 39 cities across England to present the same dance routine for two minutes in unison. Check www.london.gov.uk/bigdance for details of events in 2007.

What's more, the city is bursting with dance classes: from flamenco, Egyptian, African, street and swing to every variety of Latin dance. Check the Dance listings in the weekly *Time Out* magazine for up-to-date information on what to see and where to go. For a rundown of the latest top dance companies in London, *see p286* **Movers and shakers**.

Major venues

Barbican Centre

Silk Street, the City, EC2Y 8DS (0845 120 7553/www.barbican.org.uk). Barbican, Farringdon or Moorgate tube/rail. **Box office** *In person* 10am-8pm Mon-Sat; noon-8pm Sun. *By phone* 9am-8pm daily. **Tickets** £7-£40. **Credit** AmEx, MC, V. **Map** p404 P5.

Now in its tenth year, the Barbican International Theatre Event (BITE) has gradually helped turn this arts centre into a major London player. Dance may be just one component of BITE, but it's a crucial one. The Barbican frequently co-commissions works in collaboration with both continental and American theatre and dance companies. Michael Clark, the notorious 'bad boy' of British dance, is currently partway through a three-year residency deal, as is Cheek by Jowl.

The Place

17 Duke's Road, Bloomsbury, WC1H 9PY (7121 1000/www.theplace.org.uk). Euston tube/rail. **Box office** noon-6pm Mon-Sat; noon-8pm on performance days. **Tickets** £5-£15. **Credit** MC, V. **Map** p401 K3.
This internationally recognised dance venue provides top-notch professional training as well as classes in all genres for all levels. The 300-seat theatre presents innovative contemporary dance from around the globe. Seating isn't numbered; it's a case of first come, first served. As a result, there's sometimes a scrum when the doors are thrown open ten minutes before the show starts. Since 2005 the Place has also sponsored an annual 'Place Prize', the British contemporary dance equivalent of the literary Booker or artworld's Turner prizes.

Royal Opera House

Bow Street, Covent Garden, WC2E 9DD (box office 7304 4000/www.roh.org.uk). Covent Garden tube. **Box office** 10am-8pm Mon-Sat. **Tickets** £3-£87. **Credit** AmEx, DC, MC, V. **Map** p409 Y/Z3.
This magnificent theatre's main stage is home to the Royal Ballet, where you can see superstars of the high calibre of Carlos Acosta, Darcey Bussell, Alina Cojocaru and Sylvie Guillem. The Royal Opera House complex also houses the Linbury Studio Theatre and the Clore Studio Upstairs, used for rehearsals and workshops as well as experimental performances. Programming responsibility for both spaces, linked together under the name of ROH2, lies with ex-Royal ballerina Deborah Bull. The 'Firsts' programme, now in its fifth year, aims to bring innovative and surprising performances to the stage.The ROH's main lobby, the Vilar Floral Hall, is one of London's most handsome public spaces. It serves as the venue for afternoon tea dances, usually twice a month. *See also p115 & p309.*

Sadler's Wells

Rosebery Avenue, Finsbury, EC1R 4TN (box office 0870 737 7737/www.sadlerswells.com). Angel tube. **Box office** *In person* 9am-8.30pm Mon-Sat, times vary. *By phone* 24hrs daily. **Tickets** £10-£45. **Credit** AmEx, MC, V. **Map** p404 N3.
One of the world's premier dance venues, with the most exciting line-up in town. Top companies from Pina Bausch and William Forsythe to British troupes such as Rambert Dance Company and Birmingham Royal Ballet are showcased throughout the year. A major new initiative has brought important British dancemakers into the theatre; *see p286* **Movers and shakers**. In 2006 Sylvie Guillem was made an 'associate artist' to the theatre and, partnered with Akram Khan, wowed audiences with 'Sacred Monsters'. There is also a restaurant on-site (7863 8267).

South Bank Centre

Belvedere Road, South Bank, SE1 8XX (box office 0870 380 0400/recorded information 7921 0973/ www.rfh.org.uk). Waterloo tube/rail. **Box office** *In person* 11am-8.30pm daily (Queen Elizabeth Hall); 11am-6pm RFH Festival Riverside Foyer. *By phone* 9.30am-8pm daily. **Tickets** £5-£30. **Credit** AmEx, MC, V. **Map** p403 M8.
This multi-building complex usually presents British and international dance companies in three theatres: the huge Royal Festival Hall, the medium-sized Queen Elizabeth Hall and the pocket-sized Purcell Room. However, extensive ongoing renovations in the RFH mean it will be closed until summer 2007. This inconvenience is balanced by the promise of big improvements inside and out, to the stage as well as other facilities. In the meantime, dance and other performances continue in the other buildings.

Other venues

Circus Space

Coronet Street, Hoxton, N1 6HD (7729 9522/ www.thecircusspace.co.uk). Old Street tube/rail. **Open** 9am-10pm Mon-Thur; 9am-9pm Fri; 10.30am-6pm Sat, Sun. **Classes** phone for details. **Membership** free. **Credit** MC, V. **Map** p405 R3.
Courses and workshops in all types of circus arts, such as trapeze, juggling and high-wire walking. It also presents cabaret-style performances in its impressive space (a former power station), starting in earnest from January 2007 following renovations.

Greenwich Dance Agency

Borough Hall, Royal Hill, Greenwich, SE10 8RE (8293 9741/www.greenwichdance.org.uk). Greenwich DLR/rail. **Box office** 9.30am-5.30pm Mon-Fri. **Classes** £8. **Tickets** £7-£15. **Credit** MC, V.
Several of the country's best young companies and dance artists reside in this large art deco venue, where a variety of classes and workshops are complemented by an inventive programme of shows.

Laban Centre

Creekside, Deptford, SE8 3DZ (information 8691 8600/tickets from Greenwich Theatre 8469 9500/ www.laban.org). Deptford DLR/Greenwich DLR/rail. **Open** 10am-6pm Mon-Sat; or until start of performance. **Tickets** £1-£15. **Credit** MC, V.
This independent conservatoire for contemporary dance training and research runs undergraduate and postgrad courses. Its stunning, award-winning £22m premises – completed in 2003 and designed by Herzog and de Meuron, the architectural practice responsible for the transformation of an old power station into the Tate Modern – include an intimate 300-seat auditorium for shows by Transitions, Laban's resident company, and visiting companies, plus student showcases. **Photo** *p284.*

Dance classes

Cecil Sharp House offers fun classes in many folk dance styles, while the **London School of Capoeira** teaches the Brazilian fusion of dance, gymnastics and martial arts. The **Chisenhale** is a seminal research centre for contemporary dance and runs interesting workshops.

Cecil Sharp House English Folk Dance & Song Society

2 Regent's Park Road, Camden, NW1 7AY (7485 2206/www.efdss.org). Camden Town tube. **Phone enquiries** 9.30am-5.30pm Mon-Fri. **Classes** £4.50-£8.50. **Credit** AmEx, MC, V.

Chisenhale Dance Space

64-84 Chisenhale Road, Bow, E3 5QZ (8981 6617/ www.chisenhaledancespace.co.uk). Bethnal Green or Mile End tube. **Phone enquiries** 10am-6pm daily. **Tickets** free-£10. **No credit cards**.

Danceworks

16 Balderton Street, Mayfair, W1K 6TN (7629 6183/www.danceworks.net). Bond Street tube. **Open** 9am-10pm Mon-Fri; 9am-6pm Sat, Sun. **Classes** £4-£10. **Membership** £2.50-£5/day; £40/mth; £69-£111/yr. *Joining fee* £69. **Credit** AmEx, DC, MC, V. **Map** p400 G6.

Drill Hall

16 Chenies Street, Fitzrovia, WC1E 7EX (7307 5060/www.drillhall.co.uk). Goodge Street tube. **Open** 10am-9.30pm Mon-Sat; 10am-6pm Sun. **Classes & courses** phone for details. **Credit** AmEx, MC, V. **Map** p401 K5.

London School of Capoeira

Units 1 & 2, Leeds Place, Tollington Park, Finsbury Park, N4 3RF (7281 2020/www. londonschoolofcapoeira.co.uk). Finsbury Park tube/rail. **Classes** phone for details. *Beginners' course* £100 (8wks); concessions available. **No credit cards**.

Pineapple Dance Studio

7 Langley Street, Covent Garden, WC2H 9JA (7836 4004/www.pineapple.uk.com). Covent Garden tube. **Open** 9am-9.30pm Mon-Fri; 9am-7pm Sat; 10am-6pm Sun. **Classes** £5-£10. **Membership** £2/day; £4/evening; £25/mth; £65/quarter; £100/6mths; £140/yr; £70/yr concessions. **Credit** AmEx, MC, V. **Map** p409 Y3.

Movers and shakers

As you'd expect from a world-class city, London attracts some of the biggest names in dance, as well as being home to plenty of home-based talent. The following are the most exciting names to look out for at the moment.

Wayne McGregor's sharp and edgy **Random Dance** is the resident company at Sadler's Wells. Matthew Bourne's **New Adventures** (his reformed Adventures in Motion Pictures posse) also now has its London base at the Wells – 2006 opened with his latest work, *Edward Scissorhands*; other Bourne productions will pop up here on a regular basis. The fast-rising **Akram Khan**, hip hop guru **Jonzi D** and **George Piper Dances** (best known to TV audiences as the Ballet Boyz) are all forward-looking artists who have been invited to form ongoing creative ties with Sadler's Wells. These new partnerships promise to add extra spark to the already bustling London scene. For more information check www.sadlerswells.com.

Rambert (www.rambert.org.uk), the oldest and largest of the country's contemporary operations, is currently soaring under its new artistic director Mark Baldwin. Meanwhile, the highly regarded **Siobhan Davies** (www.sddc.org.uk) has recently, finally, acquired a home of her own – an imaginatively converted Victorian school in south London.

Other choreographers such as **Henri Oguike** (www.henrioguikedance.co.uk) and **Fin Walker** (whose company is Walker Dance Park Music; www.walkerdance.moonfruit.com) are building solid reputations for their vivid takes on contemporary dance. The excellent **Can*doco*** (www.candoco.co.uk) integrates the work of disabled and non-disabled dancers in often-stunning performances. Still irreverent rebels after more than 20 years in the game are **DV8 Physical Theatre** (www.dv8.co.uk) and the confusingly named all-female **Cholmondeleys** (pronounced 'Chumlees') and all-male **Featherstonehaughs** ('Fanshaws'; the website for both is www.thecholmondeleys.org). The two latter companies are based on the vision of their iconoclastic director Lea Anderson, a true British eccentric.

On a grander scale are the prestigious **Royal Ballet**, based at the Royal Opera House (*see p285*), and the **English National Ballet** (www.ballet.org.uk). ENB, a touring company, has two annual London seasons: in summer it fills the vast expanses of the Royal Albert Hall (*see p307*); here ballet spectaculars can see cast numbers topping the 150 mark. Over the Christmas holidays – when English National Opera (*see p308*) has a break – ENB takes up residence at the London Coliseum.

Film

London has some great cinemas, but be prepared to travel.

The bar at the **Curzon Soho**. *See p288.*

The city's film-going scene is gloriously wide and varied, at least partly due to the 50-plus film festivals that are held in the city every year, from specialist events such as the London Czech Film Festival to the all-inclusive annual London Film Festival every autumn.

For the best cinema-going experience head for one of the number of smaller first-run cinemas whose varied programmes stand out from the crowd. Chief and most central of these is the **Curzon Soho** (*see p288*), with its reliably excellent line-up of indie, foreign and arthouse fare, exquisite cakes and pastries in the lobby café (courtesy of Konditor & Cook), and the best bar on Shaftesbury Avenue, downstairs and open to all. The **National Film Theatre** down on the South Bank is London's best-appointed showcase for the cinematic treasures of the past – and it's set to get even better as a revamp of its facilities continues (*see p289* **Goodbye NFT, hello BFI**). Our other big favourite is the **Prince Charles**, which screens recent releases on rotation for as little as £1, mixing it up with singalong sessions of *The Sound of Music* and *The Rocky Horror Picture Show*.

Only if you're a Bollywood fan is it worth travelling much out of the centre. The racy potboilers unfold mostly in the suburbs: places like the Grade II-listed **Himalaya Palace** in Southall (*see p291*) justify the long journey.

Films released in the UK are classified under the following categories: **U** – suitable for all ages; **PG** – open to all, parental guidance is advised; **12A** – under-12s only admitted with an over-18; **15** – no one under 15 is admitted; **18** – no one under 18 is admitted. Unless noted, all cinemas accept major credit cards.

Programmes change on a Friday in the UK; for the latest film listings, reviews and interviews see *Time Out* magazine each week or visit www.timeout.com/film.

First-run cinemas

The closer to Leicester Square you go, the more you pay. Most cinemas charge less before 5pm from Tuesday to Friday, and a few have cheap rates all day Monday.

Central London

Apollo West End

19 Lower Regent Street, Westminster, SW1Y 4LR (0871 223 3444/www.apollocinemas.co.uk). Piccadilly Circus tube. **Screens** 5. **Tickets** £12.50; £8.50 concs. **Map** p400 J7.

Refurbished cinema that boasts a stylish bar and a modern interior, but tickets are unjustifiably pricey.

Barbican

Silk Street, the City, EC2Y 8DS (7382 7000/www.barbican.org.uk). Barbican tube/Moorgate tube/rail. **Screens** 3. **Tickets** £8.50; £4.50-£6 concs; £5.50 Mon. **Map** p404 P5.

The Barbican's three cinemas, tucked away in the complex, screen new releases with a special focus on world and independent cinema.

Chelsea Cinema

206 King's Road, Chelsea, SW3 5XP (7351 3742/www.artificial-eye.com). Sloane Square tube then 11, 19, 22, 319 bus. **Screens** 1. **Tickets** £7.50-£8.50; £5.50 concs. **Map** p399 E12.

Cosy local that is part of the Curzon Cinemas group and specialises in world cinema.

Cineworld

Chelsea *279 King's Road, Chelsea, SW3 5EW (0871 200 2000/www.cineworld.co.uk). Sloane Square tube then 11, 19, 22, 319 bus.* **Screens** 4. **Tickets** £8.80; £5.50 concs. **Map** p399 E12.

Fulham Road *142 Fulham Road, Chelsea, SW10 9QR (0871 200 2000/www.ugccinemas.co.uk). South Kensington tube.* **Screens** 6. **Tickets** £8.80; £5.20 concs. **Map** p399 D11.

Haymarket *63-65 Haymarket, Westminster, SW1Y 4RL (0871 200 2000/www.cineworld.co.uk). Piccadilly Circus tube.* **Screens** 3. **Tickets** £8.90; £4.80-£5.60 concs. **Map** p408 W4.

Shaftesbury Avenue *7-14 Coventry Street, Soho, W1D 7DH (0871 200 2000/www.cineworld. co.uk). Piccadilly Circus tube.* **Screens** 7. **Tickets** £8.90; £5.50-£6 concs. **Map** p408 W4.

Curzon

Mayfair *38 Curzon Street, Mayfair, W1J 7TY (7495 0500/www.curzoncinemas.com). Green Park or Hyde Park Corner tube.* **Screens** 2. **Tickets** £9.50; £6.50 concs; £6.50 Mon. **Map** p402 H8.

Soho *99 Shaftesbury Avenue, Soho, W1D 5DY (information 7292 1686/bookings 7734 2255/ www.curzoncinemas.com). Leicester Square tube.* **Screens** 3. **Tickets** £8.50; £5.50 concs; £6.50 Mon. **Map** p409 X3.

Both Curzons have superb programming with shorts, rarities, Sunday double bills and mini-festivals sitting alongside new fare from around the world. The Soho cinema also has a great ground-floor café and a trendy bar; arguably, London's best cinema. **Photo** *p287.*

Empire

4-6 Leicester Square, Soho, WC2H 7NA (0871 471 4714/www.empirecinemas.co.uk.) Leicester Square tube. **Screens** 3. **Tickets** £8.50-£11.50; £5.50-£7.50 concs. **Map** p409 X4.

Lowest-common-denominator programming – to the point where there is rarely anything on here we would want to watch. A shame, since the immense main auditorium is impressive.

ICA Cinema

Nash House, the Mall, Westminster, SW1Y 5AH (information 7930 6393/bookings 7930 3647/ www.ica.org.uk). Charing Cross tube/rail. **Screens** 2. **Tickets** £8; £7 concs. **Map** p403 K8.

The best in town for harder-to-find world, experimental and low-budget cinema.

Odeon

Covent Garden *135 Shaftesbury Avenue, Covent Garden, WC2H 8AH (0871 224 4007/www.odeon. co.uk). Leicester Square tube.* **Screens** 4. **Tickets** £9.50; £6 concs. **Map** p409 X2.

Leicester Square *Leicester Square, Soho, WC2H 7LQ (0871 224 4007/www.odeon.co.uk). Leicester Square tube.* **Screens** 1. **Tickets** £12.50-£17; £9-£14 concs. **Map** p409 X4.

Marble Arch *10 Edgware Road, corner of Oxford Street, W2 2EN (0871 224 4007/www.odeon.co.uk). Marble Arch tube.* **Screens** 5. **Tickets** £9.50-£11; £7.50 concs. **Map** p397 F6.

Mezzanine *next to Odeon Leicester Square, Soho, WC2H 7LP (0871 224 4007/www.odeon.co.uk). Leicester Square tube.* **Screens** 5. **Tickets** £9.50; £7.50 concs. **Map** p409 X4.

Panton Street *11-18 Panton Street, Soho, SW1Y 4DP (0871 224 4007/www.odeon.co.uk). Leicester Square or Piccadilly Circus tube.* **Screens** 4. **Tickets** £8.50; £5.50 concs. **Map** p408 W4.

Tottenham Court Road *30 Tottenham Court Road, Fitzrovia, W1T 1BX (0871 224 4007/www. odeon.co.uk). Tottenham Court Road tube.* **Screens** 3. **Tickets** £9.50; £7.50 concs. **Map** p401 K5.

West End *40 Leicester Square, Soho, WC2H 7LP (0871 224 4007/www.odeon.co.uk). Leicester Square tube.* **Screens** 2. **Tickets** £12.50; £9.50 concs. **Map** p409 X4.

Whiteleys
Whiteleys Shopping Centre, Queensway, W2 4YL (0871 224 4007/www.odeon.co.uk). Bayswater or Queensway tube. **Screens** 8. **Tickets** £8.25; £4.50-£5.50 concs. **Map** p396 C6.

Renoir

Brunswick Square, Bloomsbury, WC1N 1AW (7837 8402/www.artificial-eye.com). Russell Square tube. **Screens** 2. **Tickets** £8.50; £4.50-£6 concs. **Map** p401 L4.

A comfy little underground arthouse dedicated to top-notch world cinema.

Screen on Baker Street

96-98 Baker Street, Marylebone, W1V 6TJ (7935 2772/www.screencinemas.co.uk). Baker Street tube. **Screens** 2. **Tickets** £9; £6 concs; £6.50 Mon. **Map** p400 G5.

Good programming – the arty end of mainstream – but the screens are far too small to justify the ticket price, Mondays excepted, .

Vue West End

Leicester Square, Soho, WC2H 7AL (0871 224 0240/ www.myvue.com). Leicester Square tube. **Screens** 9. **Tickets** £12.50; £7-£9.50 concs. **Map** p409 X4.

Its Leicester Square location is the sole justification for high ticket prices, as unlike the neighbouring Odeon or Empire the screens aren't very big.

Outer London

There are **Odeons** (www.odeon.co.uk) in Camden Town, Kensington, Surrey Quays in Rotherhithe and Swiss Cottage.

Clapham Picture House

76 Venn Street, Clapham, SW4 0AT (0870 755 0061/www.picturehouses.co.uk). Clapham Common tube. **Screens** 4. **Tickets** £8; £7 concs; £5.50 Mon.

Juggles first-run titles with weekend rep double-bills, kids' clubs and parents-and-babies screenings.

Electric Cinema

191 Portobello Road, Notting Hill, W11 2ED (7908 9696/www.the-electric.co.uk). Ladbroke Grove or Notting Hill Gate tube. **Screens** 1. **Tickets** £10-£12.50; £5-£7.50 Mon.

One of London's oldest cinemas, the Electric is now one of the city's most lavish – with leather armchairs and two-seater sofas for the deep-pocketed. Just next door is the excellent Electric Brasserie.

Everyman Cinema

5 Hollybush Vale, Hampstead, NW3 6TX (0870 066 4777/www.everymancinema.com). Hampstead tube. **Screens** 2. **Tickets** £10 (luxury £15-£30); £7.50 concs.

Boasts two-seater 'club suites', complete with foot stools, wine cooler and plush upholstery.

Gate Cinema

87 Notting Hill Gate, Notting Hill, W11 3JZ (0870 755 0063/www.picturehouses.co.uk). Notting Hill Gate tube. **Screens** 1. **Tickets** £9.75; £4.50 concs. **Map** p396 A7.

Small and unpretentious, with daring programming.

Notting Hill Coronet

103 Notting Hill Gate, W11 3LB (7727 6705/ www.coronet.org). Notting Hill Gate tube. **Screens** 2. **Tickets** £7; £4.50 concs. **Map** p396 A7.

One of London's most charming local cinemas.

Phoenix

52 High Road, East Finchley, N2 9PJ (8444 6789/ www.phoenixcinema.co.uk). East Finchley tube. **Screens** 1. **Tickets** £5-£7.50; £4.50-£6 concs.

One of the country's oldest existing cinemas (1910), this attractive one-screener has good programming with Sunday reps and parent and baby screenings.

Rio Cinema

107 Kingsland High Street, Dalston, E8 2PB (7254 6677/www.riocinema.org.uk). Dalston Kingsland rail. **Screens** 1. **Tickets** £7.50; £5.50 concs.

East London's best independent cinema reflects the diversity of the Dalston area, with annual Turkish and Kurdish mini-festivals, on top of year-round choice new releases.

Ritzy

Brixton Oval, Coldharbour Lane, Brixton, SW2 1JG (0870 755 0062/www.picturehouses.co.uk). Brixton tube/rail. **Screens** 5. **Tickets** £7.75; £6.50 concs.

London's biggest independent cinema (370,000 admissions a year) programmes a good mix of mainstream and indie, with lots of rep screenings and mini-festivals.

Screen on the Green

83 Upper Street, Islington, N1 0NP (7226 3520/ www.screencinemas.co.uk). Angel tube. **Screens** 1. **Tickets** £8; £6-£6.50 concs; £6 Mon. **Map** p404 O2.

A jewel of a cinema that boasts London's best old-style neon billboard gracing its façade and super-comfy seats in the auditorium. Programming is an appealing mix of indie and mainstream.

Goodbye NFT, hello BFI

With the Royal Festival Hall and immediate South Bank surroundings currently undergoing a £90m refit, not to be left out its neighbour to the east, the National Film Theatre (*see p291*), is also investing in a bit of nip and tuck. About time. The current main entrance, which lurks in the shadows beneath Waterloo Bridge, feels more suited to a seedy all-night convenience store than the UK's leading cinema complex. That will all change in February 2007 when the revitalised NFT – to be rebranded as BFI Southbank – gets a new front door. This will take the form of a large, new glass foyer, or 'lightbox' (*see photo*), that will face the adjacent National Theatre building. There'll be a new café and bar area equipped with Wi-Fi and, at long last, the complex will get its sorely missed film and bookshop back. But that's not the half of it.

In addition to the existing three cinema auditoriums the revamped BFI Southbank will also incorporate something called the BFI Mediatheque, which will involve 14 state of the art viewing stations where visitors will be able to access hundreds of hours of film and television from the BFI archive. There will also be a new gallery space, which will be used to present exhibitions of screen-based works by contemporary artists.

The opening programme will include a themed selection of shorts, features and documentaries under the title 'London Calling'. Billed as the ultimate guide to the people and places of London, highlights are to include rare showings of London street scenes from the end of the 19th century and the sordid delights of exploitation flick *Primitive London* (1965).

Clear skies cinema

There's a lovely scene in *Cinema Paradiso* when the cinema-projectionist hero shows a film on the walls of the piazza outside his movie theatre. The sequence summons up the special charm of watching movies outside, with the gossamer-like moving images falling on to brick, turning ordinary buildings into things of silky magic.

Outdoor screenings in Britain are a riskier proposition, but a couple of strangely warm summers in England and some reckless souls have put two fingers up to the unpredictability of the British weather and challenged the heavens. Alfresco cinema is fast becoming a fixture of London's summer calendar. Whether this is one of the very few upsides of global warming we'll leave to climatologists, but there's no doubting the appeal for audiences.

Some of the most magical evenings have taken place at **Somerset House**, where in recent years Film4 Summer Screen has transformed the courtyard into a full-scale open-air cinema with a state-of-the-art giant screen, 35mm projection and surround-sound (*see photo*). In 2006 films shown included *The Shining* and *Night of the Hunter*. Just downriver, the **More Movies** season has involved outdoor screenings at the Scoop, an open-air amphitheatre just in front of the City Hall building near Tower Bridge. In 2006 there were films every Wednesday, Thursday and Friday during June.

The **Studio Artois Live Outdoor** festival, which takes place the last weekend of July in Greenwich Park, is a two-day event billed as Britain's first 'outdoor film festival'; in 2006 it revolved around two separate evening screenings: *Kill Bill Vol 1* on the first night, *Ferris Bueller's Day Off* on the second. *Time Out* itself made a contribution to the trend in 2006 hosting a couple of events in Hyde Park in tandem with the **Serpentine Gallery**. Watching Dennis Hopper exclaim 'Baby wants to fuck' on a 50-foot screen in one of London's most genteel royal parks will take some topping in the future.

One-off special events are becoming popular too: in 2004 the Pet Shop Boys and a full orchestra played a live soundtrack to director Sergei Eisenstein's *Battleship Potemkin* in **Trafalgar Square**, while in 2005 **Kensington Gardens** played host to a large screening of *Donnie Darko*. In previous years the **National Theatre** (*see p339*) has also projected silent works such as Fritz Lang's *Metropolis* on to the side of its immense riverside building during the summer months.

Screen on the Hill

203 Haverstock Hill, Belsize Park, NW3 4QG (7435 3366/www.screencinemas.co.uk). Belsize Park tube. **Screens** 1. **Tickets** £9; £5.50-£6 concs; £6 Mon.
Sister to the other Screens, with similar programming.

Tricycle Cinema

269 Kilburn High Road, Kilburn, NW6 7JR (information 7328 1900/bookings 7328 1000/ www.tricycle.co.uk). Kilburn tube. **Screens** 1. **Tickets** £8; £7 concessions; £5 Mon.
Part of an arts complex that includes the politically conscious Tricycle Theatre (*see p344*), this cinema supports small and world releases.

Repertory cinemas

Several first-run cinemas also offer a limited selection of rep-style fare. These include the **Barbican**, **Clapham Picturehouse**, the **Curzons**, **Electric**, **Everyman**, **ICA**, **Phoenix**, **Rio**, **Ritzy** and **Tricycle**.

Ciné Lumière

Institut Français, 17 Queensberry Place, South Kensington, SW7 2DT (7073 1350/www.institut-francais.org.uk). South Kensington tube. **Screens** 1. **Tickets** £7; £5 concs. **Map** p399 D10.

Launched by Catherine Deneuve in 1998, this plush cinema puts on some excellent seasons – and not all with a French focus.

National Film Theatre (NFT)

South Bank, SE1 8XT (information 7928 3535/ bookings 7928 3232/www.bfi.org.uk/nft). Embankment tube/Waterloo tube/rail. **Screens** 3. **Tickets** £8.60; £6.25 concs. **Map** p403 M8.
A London institution, with an unrivalled programme of retrospective seasons and previews, but *see p289* **Goodbye NFT, hello BFI**.

Prince Charles

7 Leicester Place, Leicester Square, WC2H 7BY (bookings 0870 811 2559/www.princecharles cinema.com). Leicester Square tube. **Screens** 1. **Tickets** £3-£4; £1-£3 members. **Map** p409 X3.
The best value in town for releases that have ended their first run elsewhere. Singalong screenings too.

Riverside Studios

Crisp Road, Hammersmith, W6 9RL (8237 1111/ www.riversidestudios.co.uk). Hammersmith tube. **Screens** 1. **Tickets** £6.50; £5.50 concs.
Double-bills, special seasons and festivals.

Bollywood cinemas

Bollywood blockbusters regularly premiere and screen at the Empire Leicester Square.

Belle-Vue Cinema, Willesden

95 High Road, Willesden Green Library, NW10 2ST (8830 0822). Willesden Green tube. **Screens** 1. **Tickets** £5; £4 Tue. *Bollywood* £6; £4 Wed.

Boleyn Cinema

7-11 Barking Road, Newham, E6 1PW (8471 4884/ www.boleyncinema.co.uk). Upton Park rail. **Screens** 3. **Tickets** £5; £3.50 Tue. **No credit cards**.

Himalaya Palace

14 South Road, Southall, Middx UB1 1RD (8813 8844/www.himalayapalacecinema.co.uk). Southall rail. **Tickets** £5.95; £4.95 concs.

Safari Cinema, Harrow

Station Road, Harrow, Middx HA1 2TU (8426 0303/www.safaricinema.com). Harrow & Wealdstone tube/rail. **Tickets** £6; £2-£4 concs.

Uxbridge Odeon

Chimes Shopping Centre, Uxbridge, Middx UB8 1GD (0871 224 4007/www.odeon.co.uk). **Screens** 9. **Tickets** £7.50; £5-£5.40 concs.

IMAX

BFI London IMAX Cinema

1 Charlie Chaplin Walk, South Bank, SE1 8XR (0870 787 2525/www.bfi.org.uk/imax). Waterloo tube/rail. **Screens** 1. **Tickets** £8.50; £5-£6.25 concs. **Map** p403 M8.
The biggest screen in the country for 3D delights.

Science Museum IMAX Theatre

Exhibition Road, South Kensington, SW7 2DD (0870 870 4868/www.sciencemuseum.org.uk). South Kensington tube. **Screens** 1. **Tickets** £7.50; £6 concs. **Map** p399 D9.
A big noise in a big museum (*see p154*).

Festivals

For the **London Film Festival**, *see p272.*

Halloween Short Film Festival

ICA, the Mall, St James's, SW1Y 5AH (7766 1407/www.shortfilms.org.uk). Piccadilly Circus tube/Charing Cross tube/rail. **Date** 6-15 Jan 2007. **Map** p403 K8.
A shorts showcase with a punk/DIY bent.

Human Rights Watch International Film Festival

Ritzy & various other venues (information 7713 2773/www.hrw.org/iff). **Date** 22-29 Mar 2007.
Fiction, documentary and animated films.

London Lesbian & Gay Film Festival

National Film Theatre, South Bank, SE1 8XT (7928 3232/www.llgff.org.uk). Embankment tube/Waterloo tube/rail. **Date** spring 2007. **Map** p403 M8.
Around 190 new and restored films from all corners of the globe.

onedotzero

ICA, Nash House, the Mall, Westminster, SW1Y 5AH (7766 1407/www.onedotzero.com). Piccadilly Circus tube/Charing Cross tube/rail. **Date** May-June 2007. **Map** p403 K8.
'Adventures in moving image' is the tagline.

Rushes Soho Shorts Festival

www.sohoshorts.com. **Date** late July.
Around 60 short films and music videos by new directors are screened for free at venues across Soho.

Portobello Film Festival

Westbourne Studios & other venues (8960 0996/ www.portobellofilmfestival.com). **Date** Aug.
An open-access neighbourhood film jamboree.

BFM International Film Festival

ICA, Prince Charles & Rio (8531 9199/ www.bfmmedia.com). **Date** Sept.
This Black Filmmaker-programmed festival shows works from inside and outside the mainstream.

Resfest

National Film Theatre, South Bank, SE1 8XT (7928 3232/www.resfest.com). Embankment tube/Waterloo tube/rail. **Date** Sept-Oct. **Map** p403 M8.
International travelling festival of new-wave digitally inflected shorts, akin to onedotzero (*see above*).

Raindance

Shaftesbury Avenue cinemas (7287 3833/www.rain dance.co.uk). Leicester Square tube. **Date** Oct.
Britain's largest indie film festival.

Galleries

Vibrant times for London's art – the east leads, but the centre is catching up.

In 2006 a wealth of expansions and relocations reflected the strength of the international contemporary art market and the bullish position of London's commercial gallery sector within it. In September the long-awaited return of **White Cube** to the West End came to fruition with the opening of White Cube Mason's Yard, half a decade after it closed the Duke Street St James's showroom that launched the careers of many Young British Artists. White Cube's operations were matched in scope by those of **Hauser & Wirth**. The Zurich-based gallery opened its first UK branch in Piccadilly in 2003 then, in summer 2006, launched Hauser & Wirth Coppermill, off Brick Lane. And, in September, the gallery announced the opening of a third branch, Hauser & Wirth Colnaghi in Mayfair. Having closed its original Heddon Street branch a couple of years ago, the mighty **Gagosian** gallery also renewed its commitment to the West End, adding a space in Davies Street, W1, to its King's Cross HQ.

This activity in central London has certainly given a boost to the traditional gallery heartland around **Cork Street** in Mayfair, but east London continues to attract the lion's share of interesting contemporary art venues. Hugging Regent's Canal, **Vyner Street** in Hackney has become the major gallery thoroughfare du jour, a small-scale version of Manhattan's Chelsea. Joining Stuart Shave's **Modern Art** are a number of smart young galleries including (at No.45) **Fred** (8981 2987), **David Risley Gallery** (8980 2202) and **One in the Other** (8983 6240) and, moving recently to No.21, **Ibid Projects** (8983 4355). With the arrival of **Wilkinson Gallery**, scheduled for March 2007, Vyner Street can justifiably claim to be the new Cork Street. It's also worth exploring north of the canal: Regent Studios at 8 Andrew's Street has smaller, artist-run spaces such as **MOT** (Unit 54, 7923 9561).

Another interesting recent development has been the appearance of large, non-profit venues like **Parasol Unit** in the east and the **Louise T Blouin Institute** in the west. Both reflect an American sort of philanthropy and are welcome additions to an increasingly mercantile scene. Before heading out we suggest you consult the weekly *Time Out* magazine (online listings at www.timeout.com) or the comprehensive free pamphlet *New Exhibitions of Contemporary Art*, available from most galleries and also online at www.newexhibitions.com.

For details of public galleries and exhibition spaces including Tate Britain, Tate Modern and the National Gallery, *see chapters* **Sightseeing**.

Hauser & Wirth London. *See p293.*

Central

Anthony Reynolds Gallery

60 Great Marlborough Street, Soho, W1F 7BG (7439 2201/www.anthonyreynolds.com). Oxford Circus tube. **Open** 10am-6pm Tue-Sat. **No credit cards. Map** p408 V2.

In a beautifully converted two-floor gallery space, Anthony Reynolds represents a mix of high-profile, established artists such as Mark Wallinger and Georg Herold, as well as some less well-known names including young Japanese sculptor Nobuko Tsuchiya.

Gagosian

6-24 Britannia Street, King's Cross, WC1X 9JD (7841 9960/www.gagosian.com). King's Cross tube/rail. **Open** 10am-6pm Tue-Sat. **No credit cards. Map** p401 M3.

US super-dealer Larry Gagosian opened his first London branch in Heddon Street in 2000, now phased out since the opening of this much more expansive site, converted from a former garage.

There's a wealth of big names, among them Jeff Koons, Francesco Clemente and Cy Twombly, plus a second tier of fashionable US and European artists including Carsten Höller and Cecily Brown. In 2006 Gagosian opened a second London gallery in Mayfair (17-19 Davies Street, W1K 3DE, 7493 3020).

Haunch of Venison

6 Haunch of Venison Yard, off Brook Street, Mayfair, W1K 5ES (7495 5050/www.haunchofvenison.com). Bond Street tube. **Open** 10am-6pm Mon-Wed, Fri; 10am-7pm Thur; 10am-5pm Sat. **Credit** AmEx, MC, V. **Map** p400 H6.

This high-ceilinged converted Georgian townhouse, formerly home (at different times) to both Lord Nelson and a car showroom, has lent itself to large-scale installations and exhibitions by major artists such as Turner Prize winners Rachel Whiteread and Keith Tyson, as well as some mid-career and emerging artists. Haunch of Venison is one of several London galleries to expand overseas with branches in Zurich and, opening in 2007, Berlin.

Hauser & Wirth London

196A Piccadilly, Mayfair, W1J 9DY (7287 2300/www.hauserwirth.com). Piccadilly Circus tube. **Open** 10am-6pm Tue-Sat. **No credit cards. Map** p408 U5.

Founded in 1992 in Zurich, this Swiss-owned gallery opened in 2003 in a former bank, complete with intact basement vaults. Hauser & Wirth represents heavyweight artists including Louise Bourgeois and Paul McCarthy, international names like Anri Sala and home-grown talents, among them Martin Creed. In 2006 the gallery expanded, opening two additional spaces. The first, Hauser & Wirth Coppermill (92-108 Cheshire Street, E2 6EJ, 7729 1252), occupies a 25,000sq ft industrial building just off Brick Lane. The second, Hauser & Wirth Colnaghi (15 Old Bond Street, W1S 4AX) in Mayfair, operates under the same roof as the Old Master paintings and drawings specialist Colnaghi, and is the focus of Hauser & Wirth's secondary art market operation. **Photo** *p292.*

Jerwood Space

171 Union Street, Bankside, SE1 0LN (7654 0171/www.jerwoodspace.co.uk). Borough or Southwark tube. **Open** 10am-6pm daily (during exhibitions; phone to check). **No credit cards. Map** p406 O8.

Part of a larger set-up of theatre and dance spaces – and a great café – the Jerwood has had an erratic presence in terms of the visual art shown there since opening in 1998. However, in late 2006 it announced plans for a much more cohesive series of exhibitions, drawing together the Jerwood Foundation's various prizes and awards (including the Jerwood Applied Arts Prize and the Jerwood Sculpture Prize), in addition to shows centred around contemporary painting and the work of emerging artists.

Lisson

29 & 52-54 Bell Street, Marylebone, NW1 5DA (7724 2739/www.lisson.co.uk). Edgware Road tube. **Open** 10am-6pm Mon-Fri; 11am-5pm Sat. **No credit cards. Map** p397 E5.

One of London's longer established contemporary art galleries, on its current site since 1991, the Lisson is a superb platform for artists including Douglas Gordon, Tony Oursler, Julian Opie and the 'Lisson Sculptors': Anish Kapoor, Tony Cragg, Richard Wentworth and Richard Deacon. A second space opened in 2002, a stone's throw away at 29 Bell Street, allowing major exhibitions to be spread across both sites.

Louise T Blouin Institute

3 Olaf Street, Shepherd's Bush, W11 4BE (7985 9600/www.ltbfoundation.org). Latimer Road tube. **Open** 10am-6pm Mon-Fri; noon-5pm Sat, Sun. **Admission** £10. **Credit** MCX, V.

CEO and President of the LTB Group of Companies, which publishes magazines *Art+Auction* and *Modern Painters* among many others, Louise T Blouin MacBain opened this 35,000sq ft non-profit space in October 2006. The inaugural show (until 28 February) is a retrospective of US artist James Turrell, who is famed for his subtle light works and installations; Marc Quinn will follow later in 2007. Housed over three storeys of a 1920s coachworks, the Institute has galleries, a conference centre, a cinema and a café. It also runs a residency programme.

Sadie Coles HQ

35 Heddon Street, Mayfair, W1B 4BP (7434 2227/www.sadiecoles.com). Oxford Circus or Piccadilly Circus tube. **Open** 10am-6pm Tue-Sat. **No credit cards. Map** p408 U3.

Sarah Lucas, Elizabeth Peyton, John Currin, Jim Lambie… Housed in an upstairs space just off Regent Street, Sadie Coles HQ represents some of the hippest artists from both sides of the Atlantic. The gallery continuously scours the globe for new talent: exhibitions for 2007 include John Bock, TJ Wilcox and Urs Fischer.

Simon Lee

12 Berkeley Street, Mayfair, W1J 8DT (7491 0100/www.simonleegallery.com). Green Park tube. **Open** 10am-6pm Mon-Fri; 11am-4pm Sat. **No credit cards. Map** p402 H7.

Formerly Sprüth Magers Lee, this smart Mayfair gallery is now run solely by Simon Lee, who kicked off his programme with work by young, London-based artist Toby Ziegler. The 2007 programme includes solo shows by respected US artists George Condo, Sherrie Levine and Stephen Shore.

Stephen Friedman

25-28 Old Burlington Street, Mayfair, W1S 3AN (7494 1434/www.stephenfriedman.com). Green Park or Piccadilly Circus tube. **Open** 10am-6pm Tue-Fri; 11am-5pm Sat. **No credit cards. Map** p408 U4.

From expanded premises Stephen Friedman shows an impressive line-up of international artists including Yoshimoto Nara, Thomas Hirschorn and David Shrigley. A highlight of 2006 was a solo show by American painter Mark Grotjahn. The 2007 programme includes new work by Yinka Shonibare.

Timothy Taylor Gallery

24 Dering Street, Mayfair, W1S 1TT (7409 3344/ www.timothytaylorgallery.com). Bond Street tube. **Open** 10am-6pm Mon-Fri; 10am-1pm Sat. **No credit cards. Map** p400 H6.

Since moving to its current location in 2003, Timothy Taylor has gone some way to filling the gap left by the closure in 2001 of the Anthony d'Offay Gallery, which occupied the same site. Among the high-profile artists shown by the gallery are Lucian Freud, Richard Patterson and Fiona Rae. In 2006 the gallery opened a second space, at 21 Dering Street, with work by US artist Kiki Smith. In 2007 the gallery is showing paintings by Sean Scully, drawings 1948-1960 by Andy Warhol and new work by Canadian artist Marcel Dzama.

Waddington Galleries

11 Cork Street, Mayfair, W1S 3LT (7437 8611/ www.waddington-galleries.com). Green Park or Piccadilly Circus tube. **Open** 10am-6pm Mon-Fri; 10am-1.30pm Sat. **No credit cards. Map** p408 U4.

If it's a selection of blue-chip stock you're after, this is your place. You're likely to find a smörgåsbord of valuable British and American modernism in the gallery's changing displays, as well as solo shows by UK and US big guns. In 2007 expect to see work by Ian Davenport, Peter Halley and a show of paintings by modernist master Josef Albers.

East

It's only possible to include a limited selection of east London's myriad galleries, so you may want explore the area yourself. Hoxton Square, Cambridge Heath Road and Vyner Street are all good places to start, but time your visit carefully: many of the smaller galleries are closed at the beginning of the week.

The Approach

Approach Tavern, 1st floor, 47 Approach Road, Bethnal Green, E2 9LY (8983 3878/www.theapproach.co.uk). Bethnal Green tube. **Open** noon-6pm Wed-Sun; also by appointment. **No credit cards.**

Occupying a converted function room above a pub, this gallery, directed by Jake Miller, has a deserved reputation for showing both emerging artists and more established names such as Michael Raedecker and Gary Webb. The location also makes it a great venue for combining an exhibition with Sunday lunch and a pint. In 2006 the gallery opened a more project-oriented space, the Reliance (336 Old Street, EC1V 9DR), above another pub, this time in Shoreditch. In 2007 the Approach is showing Martin Westwood, Mari Sunna, Michael Raedecker and Phillip Allen, while the programme at the Reliance features Eva Berendes and Florian Baudrexel.

Bloomberg Space

50 Finsbury Square, the City, EC2A 1HD (7330 7959). Moorgate tube/rail. **Open** 11am-6pm Tue-Sat. **No credit cards. Map** p405 Q5.

Instead of simply leasing or buying art for its European HQ, the financial news and media provider Bloomberg decided in 2002 to dedicate a space within its London building to art, recruiting respected art-world figures to curate an ongoing exhibition programme of contemporary pieces. Any difficulties with the corporate architecture of the space have been overcome by the quality of the exhibitions. Recent highlights have included new work by the well-respected French artist Bertrand Lavier.

Chisenhale Gallery

64 Chisenhale Road, Bow, E3 5QZ (8981 4518/ www.chisenhale.org.uk). Bethnal Green or Mile End tube/D6, 8, 277 bus. **Open** 1-6pm Wed-Sun. **No credit cards.**

Accompanied by a strong education programme, Chisenhale commissions up to five shows a year by emerging artists and has a reputation for recognising new talent. Rachel Whiteread's *Ghost*, the concrete cast of a house, and Cornelia Parker's exploded shed *Cold Dark Matter* were both Chisenhale commissions. The 2007 programme includes shows by young Argentinean painter Varda Caivano and Beck's Futures 2003 winner Rosalind Nashashibi.

Counter Gallery

44A Charlotte Road, Shoreditch, EC2A 3PD (7684 8888/www.countergallery.com). Old Street tube/rail. **Open** noon-6pm Thur-Sat. **Credit** MC, V. **Map** p405 R4.

Responsible for such seminal shows as 1990's 'Modern Medicine', Carl Freedman is an old hand at promoting Young British Art. From this smart Shoreditch gallery, he continues to focus his attention on emerging artists. Along with the gallery, Freedman co-ordinates Counter Editions, which produces prints and editions by the likes of Jake and Dinos Chapman, Tracey Emin and Gary Hume.

Flowers East

82 Kingsland Road, Hoxton, E2 8DP (7920 7777/ www.flowerseast.com). Old Street tube/rail. **Open** 10am-6pm Tue-Sat; 11am-5pm Sun. **Credit** AmEx, MC, V. **Map** p405 R3.

Flowers East might not garner the press attention of some of its neighbours but it is an admired East End institution, representing more than 40 artists including Patrick Hughes, Derek Hirst and Nicola Hicks, some since the gallery's inception as Angela Flowers Gallery in Soho in 1970. The main gallery in Hoxton also houses Flowers Graphics, while a smaller space, Flowers Central, operates from 21 Cork Street, W1. Exhibitions in 2007 include work by Bernard Cohen and Boyd & Evans.

Hales Gallery

Tea Building, 7 Bethnal Green Road, Shoreditch, E1 6LA (7033 1938/www.halesgallery.com). Liverpool Street or Old Street tube/rail. **Open** 11am-6pm Wed-Sat. **Credit** AmEx, DC, MC, V. **Map** p405 S4.

Having been instrumental in putting Deptford on the contemporary art map, Hales upscaled to these impressive, new, architect-designed premises. It is

Wapping Project.

now one of several galleries – Rocket (7729 7594) and Andrew Mummery (7729 9399) among them – that have relocated to the Tea Building, on the corner of Shoreditch High Street and Bethnal Green Road. On the schedule for 2007 are Katy Dove, Tomoko Takahashi, Adam Dant and Trevor Appleson.

Maureen Paley

21 Herald Street, Bethnal Green, E2 6JT (7729 4112/www.maureenpaley.com). Bethnal Green tube. **Open** 11am-6pm Wed-Sun; also by appointment. **No credit cards.**

Paley opened her east London gallery long before the area became the hip art mecca it is today. The gallery represents high-profile artists such as Turner Prize winners Wolfgang Tillmans and Gillian Wearing, plus Paul Noble (best known for drawings of the fictitious town Nobson) and sculptor Rebecca Warren. Highlights of 2007 include paintings by Muntean/Rosenblum and new film work by Beck's Futures 2004 winner Saskia Olde Wolbers.

Matt's Gallery

42-44 Copperfield Road, Mile End, E3 4RR (8983 1771/www.mattsgallery.org). Mile End tube. **Open** noon-6pm Wed-Sun; also by appointment. **No credit cards.**

Few galleries in town are as well respected as Matt's, named after founder/director Robin Klassnik's dog. Since 1979 Klassnik has supported artists in their often ambitious ideas for projects. Richard Wilson's sump oil installation *20:50* and Mike Nelson's *Coral Reef* were both Matt's commissions.

Modern Art

10 & 7A Vyner Street, Hackney, E2 9DG (8980 7742/www.stuartshavemodernart.com). Bethnal Green tube. **Open** 11am-6pm Thur-Sun; also by appointment. **No credit cards.**

One of the more elite spaces in east London, Modern Art was opened by Stuart Shave and Detmar Blow in 1998. It's now run by Shave and director Jimi Lee on two sites across the street from each other. The space boasts a diverse international stable of artists such as German photographer Juergen Teller, Australian artist Ricky Swallow and Brit duo Tim Noble and Sue Webster.

Parasol Unit

14 Wharf Road, Islington, N1 7RW (7490 7373). Angel tube/Old Street tube/rail. **Open** 10am-6pm Tue-Sat; noon-6pm Sun. **No credit cards. Map** p404 P3.

This former warehouse (adjacent to Victoria Miro) has been beautifully converted by architect Claudio Silverstrin to comprise exhibition spaces on two floors, accommodation for an artist residency programme and a reading area. Opened by Ziba de Weck Ardalan in 2004, the Unit shows a variety of work by emerging and major-league figures, including paintings by Michaël Borremans and videos by Yang Fudong.

Victoria Miro

16 Wharf Road, Islington, N1 7RW (7336 8109/www.victoria-miro.com). Angel tube/Old Street tube/rail. **Open** 10am-6pm Tue-Sat; Mon by appointment. **Credit** MC, V. **Map** p404 P3.

A visit to this ex-Victorian furniture factory rarely leads to disappointment – not just because it's a beautifully converted art space, but also due to the high calibre of its artists. Work shown here is both visually exciting and highly saleable. Included are Chris Ofili, Peter Doig, Tal R, Chantal Joffe and William Eggleston.

Vilma Gold

25B Vyner Street, Hackney, E2 9DG (8981 3344/www.vilmagold.com). Bethnal Green tube. **Open** noon-6pm Thur-Sun. **No credit cards.**

Steered by Rachel Williams and Steven Pippet, Vilma Gold has rapidly gained a reputation as a gallery to watch. The cognoscenti flock here for such fashionable fare as the neo-expressionist paintings of Sophie von Hellermann and the anti-heroic sculptural assemblages of Brian Griffiths. Bucking the trend, the gallery leaves Vyner Street in 2007 to open a new space nearby at 2-6 Minerva Street, where Dubossarsky and Vinogradov, Thomas Hylander, Nicholas Byrne and Daniel Guzman will be among the artists on show.

Wapping Project

Wapping Hydraulic Power Station, Wapping Wall, Wapping, E1W 3ST (7680 2080/www.thewappingproject.com). Wapping tube. **Open** noon-midnight Mon-Fri; 10am-midnight Sat; 10am-6pm Sun. **Credit** AmEx, DC, MC, V.

Under the direction of Jules Wright, the innovative creative programme of this magnificent converted hydraulic power station has included work by artists such as Elina Brotherus and Richard Wilson. Wapping has also filled its cavernous boiler room space with commissions from choreographers and designers. A recent highlight was a retrospective of fashion photographer Deborah Turbeville. The restaurant (*see p220*) in one half of the main hall is an impressive asset.

White Cube

48 Hoxton Square, Hoxton, N1 6PB (7930 5373/ www.whitecube.com). Old Street tube/rail. **Open** 10am-6pm Tue-Sat. **Credit** AmEx, MC, V. **Map** p405 R3.

White Cube may be the only East End gallery that can attract paparazzi, here to snap the A-list celebs who turn up in black cabs for openings. The reason? A-list Young British Artists, among them Tracey Emin, Damien Hirst, Jake and Dinos Chapman, and Sam Taylor-Wood. In September 2006 the gallery reasserted its West End presence by opening White Cube Mason's Yard (Nos.25-26, SW1 6BU, 7930 5373) – a double-height space offering an additional 5,000sq ft of exhibition space just a stone's throw from the original White Cube in Duke Street, St James's. Over the next year the gallery will present shows by its most famous British artists – Emin, Hurst, the Chapman brothers – as well as Andreas Gursky, Jeff Wall and Anselm Kiefer.

Wilkinson Gallery

242 Cambridge Heath Road, Bethnal Green, E2 9DA (8980 2662/www.wilkinsongallery.com). Bethnal Green tube. **Open** 11am-6pm Thur-Sat; noon-6pm Sun; also by appointment. **No credit cards**.

This space, run by Anthony and Amanda Wilkinson, has raised its profile over the past few years by showcasing fashionable German painters including Tilo Baumgartel, Matthias Weischer and Thoralf Knobloch. As a result, perhaps, in March 2007 Wilkinson is relocating to larger premises at 50-58 Vyner Street, where it will show work by David Batchelor, Joan Jonas and more Knobloch.

Beyond the galleries

If the focus of your trip to the capital is on contemporary art, it's worth considering the cultural calendar in mind. Spring and autumn provide the richest pickings. Over Christmas and New Year and, more markedly, in late July and August, many galleries shut up shop or present uninspiring shows of gallery stock. A few savvy gallerists have cottoned on to the fact that the dearth of decent exhibitions during these periods means a bonanza of media attention for those who do make the effort, but the tendency remains. If, like Charles Saatchi, you're a fan of the 'briefly new', summer is the perfect hunting season. London's colleges hold end-of-year exhibitions for graduating students, usually beginning in June with the **Royal College of Art** (www.rca.ac.uk) and ending in the second week of September with the **Chelsea College of Art & Design** (www.chelsea.arts.ac.uk). For the past five years Brick Lane's Truman Brewery has hosted **Free Range** (www.free-range.org.uk), a fast-changing display of work from final-year students, running from June to September.

By mid September the art world is gearing up for the main event: the **Frieze Art Fair** (www.friezeartfair.com), which takes place 11-14 October 2007. Since its inception in 2003, Frieze has become the centre of the art year. This year's fair has attracted New York titans Matthew Marks and Mary Boone, European stalwarts Galerie Neu and Contemporary Fine Arts from Berlin, and leading London galleries White Cube (*see above*), Maureen Paley (*see p296*) and Sadie Coles HQ (*see p293*) to a David Adjaye-designed pavilion in Regent's Park. Frieze has been the catalyst for a string of fringe events, the best of which, **Zoo Art Fair** (www.zooart fair.com), takes place concurrently across the park at London Zoo. A more relaxed and affordable version of Frieze, Zoo features the best of London's younger galleries. You might also want to check out **ScopeLondon** (www.scope-art.com), which showcases up-and-coming galleries from around the world, and the **Affordable Art Fair** (www.affordableartfair.co.uk), which is held in Battersea Park and notable for work by recent graduates. A more grass-roots alternative is **Pilot** (www.pilotlondon.org). This is a rather chaotic platform for artists without commercial representation who have been selected by well-respected curators, collectors, critics and fellow artists.

Those with a particular interest in photography should ensure that their visit coincides with **PhotoLondon** (www.photo-london.com), the annual, international photography fair held at the Royal Academy's Burlington Gardens site in May. Architecture and design buffs, meanwhile, will find much to inspire during **Architecture Week** (www.architectureweek.org.uk) in June, the **London Design Festival** (www.londondesign festival.com) in September and **Open House** (www.londonopenhouse.org; *see also p272*), the weekend in September when some of the capital's most famous and notorious buildings open their doors to the public.

South-east

Corvi-Mora/Greengrassi

1A Kempsford Road, Kennington, SE11 4NU (Corvi-Mora 7840 9111/www.corvi-mora.com/ Greengrassi 7840 9101/www.greengrassi.com). Kennington tube. **Open** 11am-6pm Tue-Sat. **No credit cards.**

These two separate galleries share a building, which comprises a ground-floor warehouse space and a smaller gallery upstairs. Greengrassi's international artists include painters Lisa Yuskavage and Tomma Abts; among those on show in 2007 are Roe Ethridge, Frances Stark and Alessandro Pessoli. Corvi-Mora's 2007 programme includes Pierpaolo Campanini, Brian Calvin and Anne Collier.

Danielle Arnaud

123 Kennington Road, Lambeth, SE11 6SF (7735 8292/www.daniellearnaud.com). Lambeth North tube. **Open** 2-6pm Fri-Sun. **Credit** AmEx, MC, V.

Established in 1995, Danielle Arnaud works with artists such as Janane Al-Ani, David Cotterell and Helen Maurer. Exhibitions are installed in the Grade II-listed Georgian premises. The gallery also curates exhibitions at off-site venues, including the Museum of Garden History (*see p81*).

Gasworks

155 Vauxhall Street, Oval, SE11 5RH (7582 6848/ www.gasworks.org.uk). Oval tube. **Open** noon-6pm Wed-Sun. **No credit cards.**

The London base of the Triangle Arts Trust, this space comprises both a gallery and artists' studios, also used for artists taking part in an international residency programme. Refurbished in 2004, the gallery provides a platform for emerging and mid-career artists and has showcased new work by Lali Chetwynd and Beagles & Ramsay.

South London Gallery

65 Peckham Road, Peckham, SE5 8UH (7703 9799/ www.southlondongallery.org). Oval tube then 436 bus/Elephant & Castle tube/rail then 12, 171 bus. **Open** noon-6pm Tue-Sun. **No credit cards.**

On this site for over a century, the South London Gallery became one of the main showcases for the emerging Young British Artists in the 1990s, giving solo shows to Tracey Emin, Marc Quinn and Gavin Turk. Still one of the capital's foremost contemporary art venues, the gallery completes its expansion into an adjacent property in 2007, creating new exhibition areas, a café and accommodation for a residency programme. Scheduled for 2007 are solo shows by Eva Rothschild and Alfredo Jaar.

Architecture & design

Architectural Association

36 Bedford Square, Fitzrovia, WC1B 3ES (7887 4000/www.aaschool.ac.uk). Tottenham Court Road tube. **Open** 10am-7pm Mon-Fri; 10am-3pm Sat. **Credit** MC, V. **Map** p401 K5.

Talks, events, discussions, exhibitions: four good reasons for visiting these elegant premises. During the summer months, the gallery shows work by students graduating from the AA School.

Crafts Council Gallery

44A Pentonville Road, Islington, N1 9BY (7278 7700/www.craftscouncil.org.uk). Angel tube. **Open** 11am-6pm Tue-Sat; 2-6pm Sun. **No credit cards. Map** p404 N2.

Alongside its shop and reference library, the Crafts Council Gallery runs a full programme of innovative exhibitions showcasing contemporary crafts, drawn from both its own collection and further afield. The gallery also organises 'Collect', the international craft fair held at the V&A (*see p154*) each February, and the Jerwood Applied Arts Prize: Jewellery, which goes on show at the Jerwood (*see p293*) in June. After refurbishment, Pentonville Road reopens in 2007 with enhanced library and resource centre.

Royal Institute of British Architects

66 Portland Place, Marylebone, W1B 1AD (7580 5533/www.architecture.com). Great Portland Street tube. **Open** 10am-6pm Mon-Fri; 10am-5pm Sat. **Credit** MC, V. **Map** p400 H5.

In 2004 RIBA opened a new Architecture Gallery at the V&A, featuring models, photographs and artefacts from historical and contemporary architecture. It still has temporary exhibitions in its Grade II-listed HQ, which houses a bookshop, café and library. In 2007 the RIBA Trust is launching a rolling programme on Architecture and Climate Change that will include exhibitions and a lecture series.

Photography

Michael Hoppen Gallery

3 Jubilee Place, Chelsea, SW3 3TD (7352 4499/ www.michaelhoppengallery.com). Sloane Square tube. **Open** noon-6pm Tue-Fri; 10.30am-4pm Sat or by appointment. **Credit** MC, V. **Map** p399 E11.

This three-storey space shows a mixture of vintage and contemporary work, including Japanese photographer Nobuyoshi Araki. A highlight of 2006 was 'Hoppé's London' – rarely seen photographs by Emil Otto Hoppé depicting the fast-changing capital during the first three decades of the 20th century.

Photographers' Gallery

5 & 8 Great Newport Street, Covent Garden, WC2H 7HY (7831 1772/www.photonet.org.uk). Leicester Square tube. **Open** 11am-6pm Mon-Sat; noon-6pm Sun. **Credit** AmEx, DC, MC, V. **Map** p409 X3.

Home of the annual £30,000 Deutsche Börse Photography Prize (9 Feb-8 Apr 2007), the Photographers' Gallery also hosts a diverse range of exhibitions, as well as running an excellent events programme. It currently occupies two almost adjacent spaces; plans are under way to relocate by 2008 to prestigious new premises in nearby Ramillies Street, designed by O'Donnell + Tuomey Architects.

Gay & Lesbian

The inside scoop on where to be out.

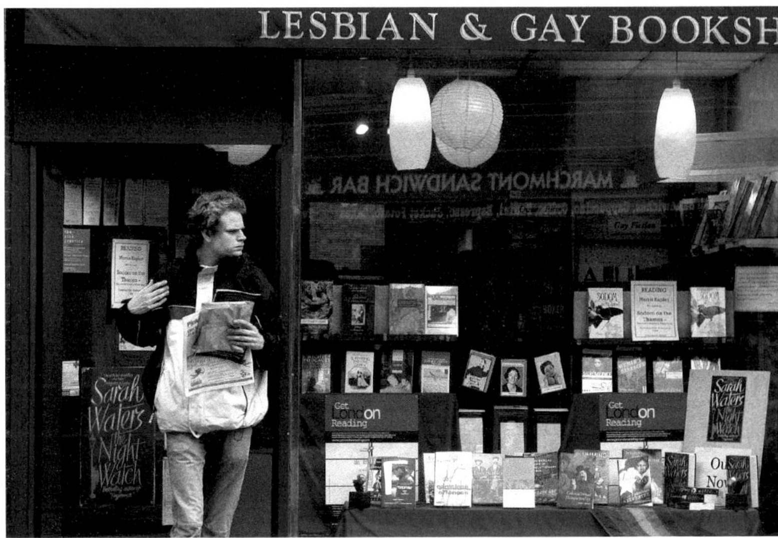

Go Wilde at **Gay's the Word**. *See p300.*

Gay Londoners have never had it so good. Or so long. Or in so many shapes and sizes. Over the past few years the gay scene has grown at such an extraordinary rate the so-called 'Vauxhall Gay Village' is fast becoming more of a market town, and the sheer number of clubs means there's more choice than ever. True, many of the most popular clubs in Vauxhall are simply variations on the familiar theme of house music, drugs and muscles, but look carefully and you'll see people dancing to a different beat.

One of the biggest successes of recent years has been **Club Caribana**. It may be located in Vauxhall, but it's a million miles away from the popular image of gay clubs with their house anthems and hordes of shirtless, predominantly white men on mind-altering chemicals. Here the men are mostly black and the music is a mixture of R&B, hip hop, reggae and ragga (or bashment, as it is now sometimes known).

Meanwhile, the indie revolution that began a decade ago with **Popstarz** has grown up and produced children of its own. In Vauxhall the **Duckie** crew provides a happy blend of queer performance art and post-punk pogo-ing. A stone's throw away is **Horse Meat Disco**, where underground disco mixes with 1980s electronica and local bears rub shoulders with visiting fashionistas. Meanwhile, up in Soho, the indie kids have taken over the **Ghetto**, producing self-consciously queer club nights like Nag Nag Nag and the Cock.

Soho is also home of the cocktail queen. Such creatures were rumoured to be extinct until a few years ago, when the **Shadow Lounge** opened its doors. This gay members' club proved so successful that soon similar venues were springing up all over Soho. Shaun & Joe came and went, but the **Element Bar** is going strong. Meanwhile, Shaun & Joe's Shaun Given has taken over the **Edge**, turning a tired old bar into one of the hottest places around. Extensive refurbishments have totally transformed the place, with the upstairs Alfresco Bar the place to go for a cocktail or two after work.

Surprisingly, it's been left to the lesbians to keep lapdancing and the spirit of old Soho alive. At **Candy Bar** punters ogle erotic dancers on a nightly basis. Attempts to launch similar nights for gay men have failed, perhaps because gay sex is just too easily available here, whether it involves a cruise around Hampstead Heath or a visit to one of the ever-increasing number of saunas. Setting the standard is the **Chariots** chain. With outlets in Waterloo, Shoreditch, Farringdon, Streatham and Limehouse, you're never too far from a steamy encounter. And with online cruising sites such as www.gaydar.com open 24 hours a day, trade really is booming.

The annual **London Lesbian & Gay Film Festival** (*see p291*) offers a round-up of the latest in lesbian and gay film and video, while the **Soho Theatre** (*see p344*) is the place to catch some of the best queer performance. Each June **Pride** (www.pridelondon.org; *see p269*) hosts a fortnight of cultural events.

The most celebrated gay shops are the excellent **Gay's the Word** bookshop (66 Marchmont Street, Bloomsbury, 7278 7654; **photo** *p299*) and the Soho 'shopping and fucking' emporiums **Clone Zone** (64 Old Compton Street, 7287 3530) and **Prowler** (3-7 Brewer Street, 7734 4031).

Under the new licensing laws introduced in November 2005, many clubs have extended their opening times, with 'after-hours' clubs proving particularly popular (*see p301* **Where'd the weekend go?**).

For a fuller take on gay London, pick up Time Out's *Gay & Lesbian London* guidebook (£9.99); for weekly listings of clubs, meetings and groups, check the Gay & Lesbian section of *Time Out* magazine or freesheets *Boyz* and *QX*. In shops, gay lifestyle is covered by *Attitude*, *Gay Times*, *Refresh* and dyke bible *Diva*.

Cafés & restaurants

Balans

60 Old Compton Street, Soho, W1D 4UG (7439 2183/www.balans.co.uk). Leicester Square or Piccadilly Circus tube. **Open** 8am-5am Mon-Thur; 8am-6am Fri, Sat; 8am-2am Sun. **Admission** £5 after midnight Mon-Thur; £7 Fri, Sat. **Credit** AmEx, MC, V. **Map** p408 W3.

This buzzing brasserie is gay central. Stop in for a steak, omelette or salad – or just eye up the beefcake over a cheesecake. The nearby Balans Café (No.34) serves up a shorter version of the menu. Both are open almost all night: good for a post-clubbing feast. **Other locations**: 249 Old Brompton Road, Earl's Court, SW5 9HP (7244 8838); 187 Kensington High Street, Kensington, W8 6SH (7376 0115); 214 Chiswick High Road, Chiswick, W4 1BD (8742 1435).

First Out

52 St Giles High Street, Covent Garden, WC2H 8LH (7240 8042/www.firstoutcafebar.com). Tottenham Court Road tube. **Open** 10am-11pm Mon-Sat; 11am-10.30pm Sun. **Credit** MC, V. **Map** p409 X1/2.

Opened in 1986, First Out was indeed London's first lesbian and gay café, with an emphasis on the lesbian. It's a right-on place, with a healthy veggie menu – if real men don't eat quiche, real lesbians surely do. Decent prices, friendly vibe and a good basement bar.

Steph's

39 Dean Street, Soho, W1D 4PU (7734 5976/www.stephs-restaurant.com). Tottenham Court Road tube. **Open** noon-3pm, 5.30-11.30pm Mon-Fri; 5.30-11.30pm Sat. **Credit** AmEx, DC, MC, V. **Map** p408 W3.

This cosy little restaurant has been a firm favourite with gay diners and other theatrical types for nigh on 20 years, and in all that time little has changed. Pink flamingos still adorn the walls, the specials still include Yorkshire puddings with a choice of fillings, the tables are still decked with a variety of board games. And Steph is still there to share a joke with customers and regale all with stories of old Soho.

Clubs

This town moves fast. This is especially true of Vauxhall, where clubs open and close more frequently than the closet door. It would, however, take an earthquake to stop scene stalwarts **G.A.Y.** or **Heaven**.

A:M

Fire, 39-41 Parry Street, Vauxhall, SW8 1RT. Vauxhall tube/rail. **Open** 11pm Fri-11am Sat. **Admission** £12; £8-£10 concessions. **No credit cards**.

This late night/early morning club has three rooms of DJs playing funky, chunky tech house.

Club Caribana

Factory, 65 Goding Street, SE11 5AW (7836 2929/mobile 07939 393971/www.caribanaclub.com). Vauxhall tube. **Open** 10.30pm-6am. **Admission** £5 before midnight, then £6. **No credit cards**.

Mixed gay Caribbean hip hop party, hosted by Bashment Barbie Celeste with DJs Alexx, Biggy C and guests.

Club Kali

The Dome, 1 Dartmouth Park Hill, Dartmouth Park, N19 5QQ (7272 8153). Tufnell Park tube. **Open** 10pm-3am 1st & 3rd Fri of mth. **Admission** £8; £5 concessions. **No credit cards**.

The world's largest Asian music lesbian and gay club echoes to the sounds of bhangra, Bollywood and plain old house music.

Club Motherfucker

Upstairs at the Garage, 20-22 Highbury Corner, Highbury, N5 1RD (7607 1818/www.meanfiddler.com). Highbury & Islington tube/rail. **Open** 9pm-3am last Fri of mth; 9pm-3am 2nd Sat of mth. **Admission** £5; £4 concessions. **No credit cards**.

The pleasantly named Club Motherfucker's polysexual party features DJs Daughters of Kaos, Vic Voltaire and Miss Alabama Cherry. DJs play dirty punk and 'bad-taste' rock. Live bands too.

Crash

66 Albert Embankment, Vauxhall, SE1 7TP (7793 9262/www.crashlondon.co.uk). Vauxhall tube/rail. **Open** 10.30pm-5am Fri; 10.30pm-6am Sat; 10pm-5am Sun. **Admission** *Fri, Sun* £5, free-£4 concessions. *Sat* £15, £12 concessions. **Credit** (bar) MC, V.

Under the arches are four bars, two dancefloors, chill-out areas… and plenty of muscle. On Sundays Joan Dairyqueen hosts Marvellous, a busy queer alternative night – punk, rock, indie and pop.

Discotec

The End, 18 West Central Street, Covent Garden, WC1A 1JJ (7419 9199/www.discotec-club.com). Holborn or Tottenham Court Road tube. **Open** 10pm-4am Thur. **Admission** £8; £6 before midnight. **Credit** (bar) MC, V. **Map** p409 Y1.

Fancy a 'midweekend' party spread across two dancefloors? With air-con, great sounds and a dressy crowd, this is one of London's classiest nights.

DTPM

Fabric, 77A Charterhouse Street, Clerkenwell, EC1M 6HJ (7749 1199). Barbican tube/Farringdon tube/rail. **Open** 11pm-late Sun. **Admission** £15; £10 concessions; £10 before midnight with flyer. **Credit** (bar) MC, V. **Map** p404 O5.

The original Sunday afternoon club, DTPM is still going strong, with three dancefloors playing house, R&B, hip hop and disco. Attracts a mixed crowd.

Duckie

Royal Vauxhall Tavern, 372 Kennington Lane, Vauxhall, SE11 5HY (7737 4043/www.duckie.co.uk). Vauxhall tube/rail. **Open** 9pm-2am Sat. **Admission** £5. **No credit cards**.

Expect 'post-gay vaudeville and post-punk pogo-ing' at this legendary dive. DJs the London Readers Wifes (*sic*) play the best retro set in town; Amy Lamé introduces bizarre cabaret.

Exilio Latino

LSE, 3 Houghton Street, off Aldwych, Covent Garden, WC2E 2AS (mobile 07931 374391/ www.exilio.co.uk). Holborn tube. **Open** 10pm-3am Sat. **Admission** £7 before 11pm; £8 after 11pm. **No credit cards. Map** p401 M6.

After several changes of venue, this popular lesbian and gay Latin music club has found its feet at the LSE and is still going strong.

Fiction

The Cross, King's Cross Goods Yard, off York Way, King's Cross, N1 0UZ (7749 1199/www.blue-cube.net). King's Cross tube/rail. **Open** 11pm-late Fri. **Admission** £15; £9 before 11.30pm; £8 before midnight with flyer, £12 after midnight with flyer. **Credit** (bar) MC, V. **Map** p401 L2.

This polysexual club may be looking a bit straight these days, but it's still a great night out. Three dancefloors, five bars and two outside terraces make it an excellent summer venue. DJs, including Fat Tony, play house grooves.

G.A.Y.

Astoria, 157 Charing Cross Road, Soho, WC2H 0EN (7434 9592/www.g-a-y.co.uk). Tottenham Court Road tube. **Open** 11pm-4am Mon, Thur, Fri; 10.30pm-4.30am Sat. **Admission** £3-£10. **No credit cards**. **Map** p409 X2.

London's largest gay venue isn't the swankiest in town any more, but that doesn't bother the hordes of disco-bunnies who congregate to dance to poppy tunes and sing along to Saturday PAs (this is where Madonna showcased her *Confessions* album). Friday's Camp Attack is a must for Kylie fans.

Ghetto

5-6 Falconberg Court (behind the Astoria), Soho, W1D 3AB (7287 3726/www.ghetto-london.co.uk). Tottenham Court Road tube. **Open** 10.30pm-3am

Where'd the weekend go?

It's the early hours of Monday morning at Fire on South Lambeth Road and after-hours club **Orange** (*see p302*) is just warming up. Some people here only got out of bed a few hours ago. Others have been hard at it since Friday. First they went to **A:M** (*see p300*). When that closed at 11am on Saturday, they rested up before the big night out at **Crash** (*see above*) or **Salvation** (*see p302*). From there it was on to the Colosseum for **Instinct** (*see p302*) or new venue Area for **Ultra** (*see p302*), then back to Fire for **Later** (*see p302*), before heading to the Vauxhall Tavern for **Horse Meat Disco** (*see p302*). Then the doors of Fire opened for Orange. In a few hours, some people will go to work, though hopefully not in a job that involves heavy machinery. Most have flexible working hours. Some are self-employed. Others will phone in sick.

Ever since Vauxhall established itself as London's gay clubbing district a few years ago, the demand has been for more clubs and longer hours. Changing licensing laws (and the impact of drugs like crystal meth) mean that as the weekend approaches Vauxhall becomes a 24-hour gay clubbing zone. The weekend used to end on Sunday. Now it stretches until Monday – or Tuesday if you're still up for **Open** (from 3am at Fire, 7820 0550).

Who knows, maybe soon someone will decide that Wednesday is the new Tuesday? If the scene at Orange is anything to go by, the possibilities are endless.

Mon-Wed; 10.30pm-4am Thur, Fri; 10.30pm-5am Sat; 10.30pm-3am Sun. **Admission** free-£7. **No credit cards**. **Map** p408 W1/2.
Leading the backlash against London's snootier venues, this gritty indie club offers Nag Nag Nag for electro fans on Wednesday and Mis-Shapes for cool lesbians on Thursdays, while the Cock puts the spunk back into Soho every Friday. Saturdays are long-running trash night Wig Out, while the disingenuously named Detox is on Sunday. **Photo** *p304*.

Heaven

The Arches, Villiers Street, WC2N 6NG (7930 2020/ www.heaven-london.com). Embankment tube/Charing Cross tube/rail. **Open** 10.30pm-late Mon, Wed, Fri, Sat. **Admission** £1-£15. **Credit** (bar) AmEx, DC, MC, V. **Map** p409 Y5.
London's most famous gay club is getting on in years, but is still a firm favourite with tourists. The best nights are Popcorn (Mon) and Fruit Machine (Wed) – both upbeat early-week fun – but attempts to revitalise Saturday nights have done little to prevent the steady migration of muscle boys to the Vauxhall Gay Village.

Horse Meat Disco

South Central, 349 Kennington Lane, Vauxhall, SE11 5QY (7793 0903/www.horsemeatdisco.co.uk). Vauxhall tube/rail. **Open** 6pm-2am Sun. **Admission** £5. **No credit cards**.
Bears and fashionistas come together at this hip but unpretentious club night, held in a traditional gay boozer. DJs spin an eclectic mix, from dance, disco and soul to new wave and punk. Join the party at 4pm, tour , then return for no extra charge.

Instinct

Club Colosseum, 1 Nine Elms Lane, SW8 5NQ. Vauxhall tube/rail. **Open** 4.30am-noon Sat. **Admission** £10 in advance, £12 with flyer. **No credit cards**.
This new after-hours club plays dirty house on the main floor and funkier sounds on the second. The venue has four bars and a cool VIP Lounge with waiter service.

Later

Fire, 39-41 Parry Street, Vauxhall, SW8 1RT (www.allthingsorange.com). Vauxhall tube/rail. **Open** from noon Sun. **Admission** £12; £8-£10 concessions. **No credit cards**.
Clubbing in the middle of the day may seem strange (and there are some messy sights to behold), but Later attracts a loyal crowd of Sunday worshippers, some of whom actually made it home last night and look all the better for it.

Orange

Fire, 39-41 Parry Street, Vauxhall, SW8 1RT (www.allthingsorange.com). Vauxhall tube/rail. **Open** 11pm Sun-11am Mon. **Admission** £10; £5 with flyer before 1am. **No credit cards**.
House music, bare torsos and poppers are what to expect at this quintessential Vauxhall Sunday night/Monday morning club. Don't you have jobs?

Popstarz

Scala, 275 Pentonville Road, King's Cross, N1 9NL (7833 2022/www.popstarz.org). King's Cross tube/ rail. **Open** 10pm-4am Fri. **Admission** £8; £5 concessions, free before 11pm with flyer. **Credit** (bar) MC, V. **Map** p401 L3.
The original indie gay party. The Love Lounge plays disco and R&B, the Common Room features indie and dance, and there's kitsch in the Trash Room. Expect a mixed, predominantly studenty crowd.

Salvation

Renaissance Rooms, off Miles Street, Vauxhall, SW8 1SD. Oval tube/Vauxhall tube/rail. **Open** 11pm-6am 1st & 3rd Sat of mth. **Admission** £15; £10 members; £12 before midnight with flyer. **No credit cards**.
A hugely popular dance party for the muscle-boy brigade, Salvation has a massive dance arena, heated outside terrace, cruise maze and chill-out rooms.

Shinky Shonky

Oak Bar, 79 Green Lanes, Newington Green, N16 9BU (7354 2791/www.oakbar.co.uk). Manor House tube. **Open** 9pm-2am 2nd Fri of mth. **Admission** £6; £5 with flyer. **Credit** AmEx, MC, V. **Map** p409 X3.
Boogaloo Stu and the gang host a camp party where it's cool to act the fool. DJs spin pop, rock and disco. Obnoxious live entertainment comes from the likes of Miss High Leg Kick and the Incredible Tall Lady.

Ultra

Area, 67-68 Albert Embankment, SE1 7TP (7091 0080. www.areaclub.info). Vauxhall tube. **Open** 5am-noon Mon. **Admission** £15; £12 with flyer. **No credit cards**.
This new superclub is open for business after next door's Crash closes, 'after hours' being the new buzz-phrase in the Vauxhall Gay Village.

Pubs & bars

Unless otherwise indicated, all the pubs and bars listed here are open to both gay men and lesbians.

Admiral Duncan

54 Old Compton Street, Soho, W1U 5UD (7437 5300). Leicester Square tube. **Open** noon-11pm Mon-Sat; noon-10.30pm Sun. **Credit** MC, V. **Map** p409 X2.
This traditional gay bar in the heart of Soho attracts a slightly older, down-to-earth crowd in a darkened setting. Having recovered after a homophobic bombing attack in 1999, this doughty old survivor is going as strong as ever.

Bar Code

3-4 Archer Street, Soho, W1D 7AP (7734 3342/ www.bar-code.co.uk). Leicester Square or Piccadilly Circus tube. **Open** 4pm-1am Mon-Sat; 4-10.30pm Sun. **Admission** £3 after 11pm Fri, Sat. **Credit** MC, V. **Map** p408 W3.
Just the ticket for those in search of a busy men's cruise bar, Bar Code also has a dancefloor down-

stairs and a late licence. Tuesday night is Comedy Camp (*see p281*), Simon Happily's popular straight-friendly gay comedy club.
Other locations: Bar Code Vauxhall, Arch 69, Goding Street, Vauxhall, SE11 5AW (7582 4180).

BJ's White Swan

556 Commercial Road, Limehouse, E14 7JD (7780 9870/www.bjswhiteswan.com). Limehouse DLR. **Open** 9pm-1am Mon; 9pm-2am Tue-Thur; 9pm-3am Fri, Sat; 5.30pm-midnight Sun. **Admission** £4 after 10pm Fri, Sat. **Credit** MC, V.
This large local attracts a loyal following, who come to savour the amateur male strip and drag shows, and to dance to commercial house music.

Black Cap

171 Camden High Street, Camden, NW1 7JY (7428 2721/www.theblackcap.com). Camden Town tube. **Open** noon-2am Mon-Thur; noon-3am Fri, Sat; noon-1am Sun. **Admission** £2-£5. **Credit** AmEx, MC, V.
This famous north London pub-club is renowned for its drag shows; it was once a second home to television's own Lily Savage.

Compton's of Soho.

The Box

Seven Dials, 32-34 Monmouth Street, Covent Garden, WC2H 9HA (7240 5828/www.boxbar.com). Leicester Square tube. **Open** 11am-11pm Mon-Sat; noon-10.30pm Sun. **Credit** MC, V. **Map** p409 X/Y2.
A popular café-bar for a mixed crowd by day, the Box transforms itself into a cruisy Muscle Mary hangout come nightfall.

Bromptons

294 Old Brompton Road, Earl's Court, SW5 9JF (7370 1344/www.bromptons.info). Earl's Court tube. **Open** 5pm-2am Mon-Sat; 5pm-12.30am Sun. **Admission** £1 10-11pm, £3 after 11pm Mon-Thur; £1 10-11pm, £5 after 11pm Fri, Sat; £1 after 10pm Mon-Sat, £2 after 10pm Sun. **Credit** MC, V. **Map** p398 B11.
This busy men's pub-club with cabaret and strippers lures a slightly older crowd with its unpretentious atmosphere.

Candy Bar

4 Carlisle Street, Soho, W1D 3BJ (7494 4041/www.thecandybar.co.uk). Tottenham Court Road tube. **Open** 5-11.30pm Mon-Thur; 5pm-2am Fri, Sat; 5-11pm Sun. **Admission** £6 after 9pm Fri, Sat; £3 after 10pm Thur. **Credit** (bar) MC, V. **Map** p408 W2.
London's best-known lesbian bar attracts a mixed clientele, from students to lipstick lesbians. Drinks aren't the cheapest, but there's a late licence at weekends, and erotic dancers in the basement bar.

Compton's of Soho

51-53 Old Compton Street, Soho, W1V 5PN (7479 7961/www.comptons-of-soho.co.uk). Tottenham Court Road tube. **Open** noon-11pm Mon-Sat; noon-10.30pm Sun. **Credit** AmEx, MC, V. **Map** p408 W3.
Popular with blokey gay men in bomber jackets, Compton's has cruisy atmosphere on both floors. The upstairs Soho Club Lounge is more comfortable and a bit less full on.

The Edge

11 Soho Square, Soho, W1D 3QE (7439 1313/www.edge.uk.com). Tottenham Court Road tube. **Open** noon-1am Mon-Sat; noon-11.30pm Sun. **Credit** MC, V. **Map** p408 W2.
This busy polysexual bar was looking a bit shabby until its recent refurb. Now it's one of the best bars in town: spread over four floors, it has the Alfresco Bar for cocktails and a top-floor club space with its own *Saturday Night Fever* dancefloor. Given the proximity to Soho Square, it's also a great place for summer drinking.

Element Bar

4-5 Greek Street, Soho, W1D 4DD (7434 3323/www.allthingsorange.com). Tottenham Court Road tube. **Open** 5pm-2am Mon-Sat; 5pm-12.30am Sun. **Admission** £5 Mon-Thur; £7 after 11pm Fri, Sat. **Credit** AmEx, MC, V. **Map** p408 W2.
This upmarket venue for the gay cocktail crowd feels almost like a private members' bar. On Fridays and Saturdays there's a lively piano singalong. Downstairs has a bar and dance area.

All I hear is Nag Nag Nag – at the **Ghetto**. *See p301.*

Escape Bar

10A Brewer Street, Soho, W1F 0SU (7734 2626). Leicester Square tube. **Open** 5pm-3am Mon-Fri, 7pm-3am Sat. **Admission** £3 after 11pm Thur; £4 after 11pm Fri, Sat. **Credit** AmEx, MC, V. **Map** p408 W3.

This intimate gay dance bar has a large screen playing music videos to a mixed crowd. It was taken over by Madame Jo Jo's (*see p324*) in late 2006.

G.A.Y. Bar

30 Old Compton Street, Soho, W1D 4UR (7494 2756/www.g-a-y.co.uk). Leicester Square tube. **Open** noon-midnight daily. **Credit** MC, V. **Map** p408 W3.

If you like the Astoria's ever-popular G.A.Y. club (*see p301*), then you'll love this cheesy bar. Girls Go Down is the women's bar in the basement.

Glass Bar

West Lodge, Euston Square Gardens, 190 Euston Road, Somers Town, NW1 2EF (7387 6184/www.southopia.com/index_glassbar.html). Euston tube/rail. **Open** 10am-11.30pm Mon-Fri; 6pm-midnight Sat. **Admission** £1 Mon-Sat. **No credit cards**. **Map** p401 K3.

This shabby-chic bar is hidden away in the westerly of the two stone lodges in Euston Square Gardens (phone if you can't find it and they'll collect you from Euston station). Strictly women-only.

The Hoist

Railway Arch, 47B&C South Lambeth Road, Vauxhall Cross, Vauxhall, SW8 1RH (7735 9972/www.thehoist.co.uk). Vauxhall tube/rail. **Open** 8.30pm-midnight 3rd Thur of mth; 10pm-3am Fri; 10pm-4am Sat; 10pm-2am Sun. **Admission** £4 Thur; £5 Fri, Sun; £10 Sat. **No credit cards**.

A popular men's fetish bar in an industrial setting. No surprise, then, that the Hoist's dress code – leather, uniform, rubber, skinhead and boots – is taken rather seriously.

King William IV

77 Hampstead High Street, Hampstead, NW3 1RE (7435 5747/www.kw4.co.uk). Hampstead tube/Hampstead Heath rail. **Open** 11am-11pm Mon-Sat; noon-10.30pm Sun. **Credit** MC, V.

Attracting a vaguely affluent crowd and a sprinkling of celebs, this old-fashioned local in swanky Hampstead turned gay in the 1930s to cater for Hampstead Heath cruisers. It is notable in the summer months for its busy beer garden.

Kudos

10 Adelaide Street, Covent Garden, WC2 4HZ (7379 4573/www.kudosgroup.com). Charing Cross tube/rail. **Open** noon-midnight Mon-Sat; noon-10.30pm Sun. **Credit** AmEx, MC, V. **Map** p409 Y4.

Close to the Oscar Wilde memorial statue and Charing Cross Station, this busy men's café-bar attracts a mixture of scene queens, tourists and men waiting for the next train back to suburbia.

Oak Bar

79 Green Lanes, Newington Green, N16 9BU (7354 2791/www.oakbar.co.uk). Manor House tube. **Open** 5pm-midnight Mon-Wed; 5pm-1am Thur; 5pm-3am Fri, Sat; 1pm-midnight Sun. **Admission** free-£5. **Credit** AmEx, MC, V.

This unpretentious venue (it hosts bingo nights on a Thursday) is a mixed gay local by day and a lesbian stronghold by night.

Retro Bar

2 George Court, off the Strand, Covent Garden, WC2N 6HH (7321 2811). Charing Cross tube/rail. **Open** noon-11pm Mon-Fri; 5-11pm Sat; 5-10.30pm Sun. **Credit** AmEx, MC, V. **Map** p409 Y4.

True to its name, this mixed gay indie/retro bar plays 1970s, '80s, goth and alternative sounds, and has a friendly atmosphere.

Rupert Street

50 Rupert Street, Soho, W1V 6DR (7292 7141). Leicester Square or Piccadilly Circus tube. **Open** noon-11pm Mon-Sat; noon-10.30pm Sun. **Credit** AmEx, MC, V. **Map** p408 W3.

This busy Soho bar has a distinctly 1990s feel and attracts a slightly smarter, after-work crowd than many of its near neighbours. It boasts large windows that are great for street-watching, or for checking out the clientele before you enter. Around dusk you'll see professionals mingling over a post-work pint; thereafter, alcopops are popped and shooters shot over pumping music.

Shadow Lounge

5 Brewer Street, Soho, W1F 0RF (7287 7988/ www.theshadowlounge.co.uk). Piccadilly Circus tube. **Open** 10pm-3am Mon-Wed; 9pm-3am Thur-Sat. **Admission** £3 after 11pm Mon, Tue; £5 Wed, Thur; £10 Fri, Sat. **Credit** AmEx, MC, V. **Map** p408 W3.

Recently refurbished, the original lounge bar and gay members' club is still popular with celebrities and gay wannabes alike. Expect funky, comfy decor, professional cocktail waiters, friendly door staff and air-conditioning. Busiest at the weekends, though Tuesday's Salon is popular.

Soho Revue Bar

11-12 Walker's Court, off Brewer Street, Soho, W1F 0ED (7734 0377). Leicester Square or Piccadilly Circus tube. **Open** 5pm-4am Tue-Sat. *Performances* 7pm. **Admission** £10; £5 concessions. **Credit** AmEx, MC, V. **Map** p408 W3.

In its former incarnation as Too2Much this was where Elton and David had their wedding reception, and in gay circles you don't get more glamorous than that, but the members' bar idea didn't really work out. The venue was duly bought in 2005 by the Soho Bar group (owners of intended rival Shadow Lounge, *see above*), renamed and relaunched. It's now more of a performance club. Trannyshack on Wednesdays attracts a multitude of cross-dressers and their admirers; Sunday's Cabaret Spectacular is also popular.

Trash Palace

11 Wardour Street, Soho, W1D 6PG (7734 0522/ www.trashpalace.co.uk). Piccadilly Circus tube. **Open** 5.30pm-1am Mon-Thur; 5pm-3am Fri, Sat; 5.30-11pm Sun. **Credit** MC, V. **Map** p408 W4.

The legendary Simon 'Popstarz' Hobart's final venture was this plastic fantastic venue, which is aimed towards the ever-growing indie crowd. Cheap drinks and regular DJs help make this the ideal warm-up spot for a night at the Ghetto (*see p301*).

Two Brewers

114 Clapham High Street, Clapham, SW4 7UJ (7498 4971/www.the2brewers.com). Clapham Common tube. **Open** 5pm-2am Mon-Thur, Sun; 5pm-4am Fri, Sat. **Admission** free-£5. **Credit** AmEx, MC, V.

This Clapham gay bar and club is a south London institution. Drag shows are usually the order of the day, and it's always packed at weekends.

Village Soho

81 Wardour Street, Soho, W1V 6QD (7434 2124/ www.village-soho.co.uk). Tottenham Court Road tube. **Open** noon-1am Mon-Sat; 3-11.30pm Sun. **Admission** £3 after 10pm Fri, Sat. **Credit** MC, V. **Map** p408 W3.

A busy boys' café-bar on two floors, Village Soho is popular with a young crowd. However, it pales in comparison with some of the glitzier venues nearby.

The Yard

57 Rupert Street, Soho, W1V 7BJ (7437 2652/www. yardbar.co.uk). Piccadilly Circus tube. **Open** *Summer* noon-11pm Mon-Sat; noon-10.30pm Sun. *Winter* 2-11pm Mon-Sat; 2-10.30pm Sun. **Credit** AmEx, MC, V. **Map** p408 W3.

Understandably popular in the summer, this gay men's bar has a coveted courtyard. The upstairs Loft bar keeps the smarter, after-work crowd interested during the colder months.

Saunas

Chariots

1 Fairchild Street, Shoreditch, EC2A 3NS (7247 5333/www.gaysauna.co.uk). Liverpool Street tube/ rail. **Open** noon-9am daily. **Admission** £14; £12 concessions. **Credit** AmEx, MC, V. **Map** p405 R4.

Decked out like a Roman bath, Chariots is London's biggest and busiest gay sauna. It comprises a swimming pool, two steam rooms, two saunas, a jacuzzi and a host of private cabins. The Waterloo branch boasts the largest sauna in the UK (with room for 50 guys) and a special baggage check for Eurostar customers – save a bundle on a hotel and get lucky at the same time! The Limehouse site (a minute from BJ's, *see p303*) is split into two sections: Heaven is filled with blue walls and soft music, whereas Hell sports sinister black walls and resonates with hard dance music.

Other locations: 57 Cowcross Street, Farringdon, EC1M 6BX (7251 5553); 292 Streatham High Road, Streatham, SW16 6HG (8696 0929); 574 Commercial Road, Limehouse, E14 7JD (7791 2808); 101 Lower Marsh, Waterloo, SE1 7AB (7247 5333).

Sauna Bar

29 Endell Street, Covent Garden, WC2H 9BA (7836 2236). Covent Garden tube. **Open** noon-midnight Mon-Thur; 24hrs from noon Fri-midnight Sun. **Admission** £14; £10 concessions. **Credit** MC, V. **Map** p409 Y2.

A comfy bar, steam room, splash pool, showers and private rooms have all been crammed together in this small men-only sauna.

Music

If you think the gigs sound good, just wait till you see the venues.

Classical & Opera

In many regards, it's all change in London's classical music world. Leading the way is the **Barbican Centre**, where a £30m programme of refurbishments has improved the acoustics in the main hall and relandscaped many of the public spaces. Not far behind is the **Royal Festival Hall** on the South Bank, due to reopen in summer 2007 following £90m worth of renovations. Add in the relatively recent opening of the **Cadogan Hall** and **LSO St Luke's**, the management changes at the **Wigmore Hall**, and the various power struggles (and financial controversies) at the **English National Opera**, and it becomes even more apparent that London's classical music scene is in a state of flux.

However, in other corners of the capital, the song remains the same. The **Proms** is still one of the highlights of the European cultural calendar, a spectacular two-month festival that offers far more variety and brilliance than is apparent from the notorious Last Night. The beautiful old churches in the City continue to welcome young musicians for lunchtime concerts. And in the ever-traditional **Royal Opera House** and the ever-excellent **London Symphony Orchestra**, or LSO (based at the Barbican), the capital retains a pair of organisations that are justly renowned around the world.

TICKETS AND INFORMATION

Tickets for most classical and opera events in London are available direct from the venues, either online or by phone. Booking ahead is advisable, especially at small venues such as the Wigmore Hall. Several venues, such as the Barbican and the South Bank, operate standby schemes, offering unsold tickets to students, seniors and others at cut-rate prices just hours before the show. Call or check online for details.

Classical venues

In addition to the venues detailed below, a handful of other spots offer less frequent classical performances. Historic **Lauderdale House** (Highgate Hill, N6 5HG, 8348 8716, www.lauderdalehouse.co.uk) in Waterlow Park stages a relaxed roster of Sunday-morning recitals as part of its arts programming, while both the **artsdepot** in North Finchley (5 Nether Street, Tally Ho Corner, N12 0GA, 8369 5454, www.artsdepot.co.uk) and the **Blackheath Halls** (*see p311*) stage occasional classical concerts. In Mayfair, the 18th-century **Grosvenor Chapel** (South Audley Street, W1K 2PA, 7499 1684, www.grosvenorchapel.org.uk) supplements its series of organ recitals with sporadic chamber concerts.

London's music schools all stage regular performances by pupils and, occasionally, visiting professionals. Check the websites of the **Royal Academy of Music** (7873 7373, www.ram.ac.uk), the **Royal College of Music** (7589 3643, www.rcm.ac.uk), the **Guildhall School of Music & Drama** (7628 2571, www.gsmd.ac.uk) and the **Trinity College of Music** (8305 4444, www.tcm.ac.uk) for details.

Barbican Centre

Silk Street, the City, EC2Y 8DS (7638 4141/ box office 7638 8891/www.barbican.org.uk). Barbican or Moorgate tube/rail. **Box office** 9am-8pm daily. **Tickets** £6.50-£45. **Credit** AmEx, MC, V. **Map** p404 P5.

The Barbican recently spent millions of pounds on a refurbishment aimed at making its labyrinthine array of public spaces more welcoming and easier to navigate. It hasn't really helped; indeed, returning visitors will take one look and wonder where on earth all the money went. Happily, a recent reworking of the acoustics in the arts centre's main concert hall has proved rather more successful, making the Barbican's already excellent music programming still more attractive.

At the core of the music roster, performing 90 concerts a year, is the London Symphony Orchestra (LSO), currently looking to consolidate its reputation as one of the world's best orchestras under the direction of principal conductor Valery Gergiev. The BBC Symphony Orchestra is a frequent visitor and the Barbican regularly welcomes soloists and ensembles from around the world as part of its Great Performers series. Occasional weekend-long festivals spotlight modern composers, a neat counterpoint to the crowd-pleasing shows promoted by Raymond Gubbay. The modern music programme takes in jazz, rock, world and country, and it's all supplemented by free performances in the foyer. Assorted special events are planned throughout 2007 to celebrate the complex's 25th birthday. For the centre's theatre, *see p339*; for its cinema, *see p287*.

Cadogan Hall

5 Sloane Terrace, Chelsea, SW1X 9DQ (7730 4500/www.cadoganhall.com). Sloane Square tube. **Box office** 10am-7pm Mon-Sat. **Tickets** £10-£65. **Credit** MC, V. **Map** p402 G10.

Built a century ago as a Christian Science church, this austere building was transformed into a light and airy auditorium in 2004. It's hard to imagine how the renovations could have been bettered: the hall is comfortable and the acoustics excellent. The somewhat erratic Royal Philharmonic Orchestra is resident, though the hall also hosts smaller-scale ensembles and serves as the venue for a handful of lunchtime BBC Proms each summer (*see p309*).

LSO St Luke's

161 Old Street, the City, EC1V 9NG (information 7490 3939/Barbican box office 7638 8891/www.lso.co.uk/lsostlukes). Old Street tube/rail. **Box office** 9am-8pm daily. **Tickets** £6.50-£45. **Credit** AmEx, MC, V. **Map** p404 P4.

Although it was designed in part by fabled architect Nicholas Hawksmoor, the Grade I-listed St Luke's church was left to decay during the latter half of the 20th century. Its recent renovation and conversion by the London Symphony Orchestra into a rehearsal room, a music education centre and a concert hall cost around £20m, but it's proving to be worth every penny. The programme takes in lunchtime recitals (some free), evening chamber concerts, and occasional jazz and rock events; many of the former are tied into the LSO's Discovery programme, which aims to make music more accessible to locals.

St Martin-in-the-Fields.

Royal Albert Hall

Kensington Gore, South Kensington, SW7 2AP (information 7589 3203/box office 7589 8212/www.royalalberthall.com). South Kensington tube/9, 10, 52 bus. **Box office** 9am-9pm daily. **Tickets** £4-£150. **Credit** AmEx, MC, V. **Map** p399 D9.

Built as a memorial to Queen Victoria's husband, this 5,000-capacity rotunda is best known as the venue for the BBC Proms each summer (*see p309*), despite acoustics that don't do orchestras any favours. Occasional classical concerts are held throughout the year (look out for recitals on the overwhelming Willis pipe organ), alongside pop and rock gigs, sporadic boxing matches and infrequent opera.

St James's Piccadilly

197 Piccadilly, St James's, W1J 9LL (7381 0441/www.sjpconcerts.org). Piccadilly Circus tube. **Open** 8am-6.30pm daily. **Admission** free-£20; tickets available at the door 30mins before performances. **No credit cards**. **Map** p408 V4.

The only Wren church outside the City to hold free lunchtime recitals (Mon, Wed, Fri at 1.10pm), programmed alongside less regular, mostly classical evening concerts. The church also has a café.

St John's, Smith Square

Smith Square, Westminster, SW1P 3HA (7222 1061/www.sjss.org.uk). Westminster tube. **Box office** 10am-5pm Mon-Fri, or until start of performance; from 1hr before performance Sat, Sun. **Tickets** £5-£45. **Credit** MC, V. **Map** p403 K10.

This elegant 18th-century church hosts a more or less nightly programme of orchestral and chamber concerts, with occasional vibrant recitals on its magnificent Klais organ. There's a wonderfully secluded restaurant in the crypt, open regardless of whether or not there are performances that evening.

St Martin-in-the-Fields

Trafalgar Square, Westminster, WC2N 4JJ (concert information 7839 8362/www.stmartin-in-the-fields.org). Charing Cross tube/rail. **Box office** 10am-5pm Mon-Sat, or until start of performance. **Admission** *Lunchtime concerts* free; donations requested. **Evening concerts** £6-£18. **Credit** MC, V. **Map** p409 X4.

As befits the church's location in the heart of tourist London, the evening concert programme at the indubitably atmospheric St Martin's is packed with crowd-pleasers: expect lashings of Mozart and Vivaldi, with many concerts performed by candlelight. The thrice-weekly lunchtime recitals (Mon, Tue & Fri) usually offer less predictable fare.

South Bank Centre

Belvedere Road, South Bank, SE1 8XX (0870 380 0400/www.rfh.org.uk). Embankment tube/Waterloo tube/rail. **Box office** *In person* 11am-8pm daily. *By phone* 9.30am-8pm daily. **Tickets** £5-£75. **Credit** AmEx, MC, V. **Map** p403 M8.

Down on the South Bank, the 3,000-capacity Royal Festival Hall is finally scheduled to reopen in the summer of 2007 after a series of renovations that's slated to cost somewhere in the region of £90m. Some of the work has already been completed: witness the new row of shops at pavement level on the river side of the buildings. But the real meat of the project is the acoustic refurbishment of the main hall itself, long criticised by both musicians and concert-goers. It'll be fascinating to see how it turns out.

Until the RFH reopens, its resident ensembles – among them the London Philharmonic Orchestra, Philharmonia and London Sinfonietta – must content themselves with the 900-capacity Queen Elizabeth Hall next door, a rather uninviting space that also houses pop and jazz gigs. Also within this building is the 360-capacity Purcell Room, for everything from chamber concerts to poetry readings. A programme of free foyer music tops things off.

Wigmore Hall

36 Wigmore Street, Marylebone, W1U 2BP (7935 2141/www.wigmore-hall.org.uk). Bond Street tube. **Box office** *In person* mid Mar-Nov 10.30am-8pm daily. Nov-mid Mar 10am-8.30pm Mon-Sat; 10.30am-8.30pm Sun. *By phone* mid Mar-Nov 10am-7pm Mon-Sat; 10.30am-7pm Sun. Nov-mid Mar 10am-7pm Mon-Sat; 10.30am-7pm Sun. **Tickets** £8-£60. **Credit** AmEx, DC, MC, V. **Map** p400 G6.

Built in 1901 as the display and recital hall for Bechstein Pianos, this is the jewel of London's music venues. With its perfect acoustics, art nouveau decor and excellent basement restaurant, it is one of the world's top concert venues for chamber music and song. A £3m refurbishment in 2004 added a new roof and ventilation system, better sight lines, new seats, improved public spaces and sympathetic lighting. Programming concentrates on the classical and Romantic periods, from some of the world's most respected performers. The Monday lunchtime recitals, broadcast live on BBC Radio 3, are excellent value, as are the Sunday morning coffee concerts.

Wigmore Hall.

Lunchtime concerts

Workers in and around the City of London are entertained throughout the year by low-key lunchtime recitals, given by young musicians (many of them students at the capital's music colleges) and staged in the city's historic churches. Regular organ recitals are held at **Temple Church** (*see p93*), **Grosvenor Chapel** (South Audley Street, Mayfair, W1K 2PA, 7499 1684) and **Southwark Cathedral** (*see p88*).

St Anne & St Agnes *Gresham Street, the City, EC2V 7BX (7606 4986). St Paul's tube.* **Performances** 1.10pm Mon, Fri. **Map** p406 P6.

St Bride's *Fleet Street, the City, EC4Y 8AU (7427 0133/www.stbrides.com). Blackfriars tube/rail.* **Performances** 1.15pm Tue, Fri (except Aug, Advent, Lent). **Map** p406 N6.

St John's *Waterloo Road, Waterloo, SE1 8TY (7928 2003/www.stjohnswaterloo.co.uk). Waterloo tube/rail.* **Performances** 1.10pm Wed, call ahead to check. **Map** p406 N8.

St Lawrence Jewry *Guildhall, the City, EC2V 5AA (7600 9478). Mansion House or St Paul's tube/Bank tube/DLR.* **Performances** 1pm Mon, Tue. **Map** p406 P6.

St Margaret Lothbury *Lothbury, the City, EC2R 7HH (7606 8330/www.stml.org.uk). Bank tube/DLR.* **Performances** 1.10pm Thur. **Map** p407 Q6.

St Martin within Ludgate *40 Ludgate Hill, the City, EC4M 7DE (7248 6054). St Paul's tube/Blackfriars tube/rail/City Thameslink rail.* **Performances** 1.15pm Wed. **Map** p406 O6.

St Mary-le-Bow *Cheapside, the City, EC2V 6AU (7248 5139/www.stmarylebow.co.uk). Mansion House tube/Bank tube/DLR.* **Performances** 1.05pm Thur. **Map** p406 P6.

Opera companies

Sadler's Wells (*see p285*), the **Peacock Theatre** (Portugal Street, Covent Garden, 0870 737 0337, www.sadlerswells.com) and the **Hackney Empire** (291 Mare Street, Hackney, 8985 2424, www.hackneyempire.co.uk) all stage occasional opera performances.

English National Opera

The Coliseum, St Martin's Lane, Covent Garden, WC2N 4BR (box office 7632 8300/fax 7379 1264/www.eno.org). Leicester Square tube/Charing Cross tube/rail. **Box office** *By phone* 9.45am-8.30pm Mon-Sat. *In person* day tickets can be purchased from 10am on day of performance or by phone from 12.30pm on day of performance. **Tickets** £8-£85. **Credit** AmEx, DC, MC, V. **Map** p409 X4.

English National Opera. *See p308.*

The Coliseum's auditorium, built in 1904 by the renowned architect Frank Matcham, was restored to its former glory in 2004 as part of a restoration that cost around £80m. Now all the English National Opera needs is a similarly impressive programme. The company has endured a torrid few years, culminating in the resignations of popular music director Paul Daniel, deeply unpopular artistic director Sean Doran and, eventually, chairman Martin Smith. Ironically, some of the productions Doran set in motion before he quit went on to meet with approval from the critics who helped force him out, but an ill-conceived and poorly received opera based on the life of Colonel Gaddafi didn't exactly ease new artistic director John Berry into his job. Daniel is due to be replaced in spring by Edward Gardner, at which point the new era at ENO will really begin. Fingers crossed. Unlike at the Royal Opera House (*see below*), all works are performed in English.

Royal Opera House

Royal Opera House, Covent Garden, WC2E 9DD (7304 4000/www.royaloperahouse.org.uk). Covent Garden tube. **Box office** 10am-8pm Mon-Sat. **Tickets** £4-£175. **Credit** AmEx, DC, MC, V. **Map** p409 Z3.

While the ENO has spent the last few years being bashed from pillar to post by critics, staff at the ROH have been keeping their heads down, grateful to be out of the spotlight for a change. After all, they were in the firing line not so very long ago, hammered in the press for the venue's perceived exclusivity and humiliated by the public after a fly-on-the-wall documentary showed the chaos that reigned behind the scenes at this venerable old warhouse. These days, though, the controversy has more or less died down, leaving the ROH to quietly resume its position as one of the world's great opera houses. A massively expensive renovation in 2000 gave the largely traditional productions the setting they deserve: the discreetly air-conditioned auditorium and comfortable seating make a night here an appetising prospect, whatever the performance. For behind-the-scenes tours, *see p115.*

Festivals

In addition to the major annual events listed below, the **Barbican** (*see p306*), the **South Bank Centre** (*see p307*) and the **Wigmore Hall** (*see p308*) present regular one-off classical events throughout the year. There are also concerts of classical crowd-pleasers as part of the Picnic Concerts festivals at Hampstead's **Kenwood House** (*see p160*) and **Marble Hill House** (*see p188*) each summer; for details, call 8233 7435 or visit www.picnicconcerts.com.

BBC Proms

Royal Albert Hall, Kensington Gore, South Kensington, SW7 2AP (7589 8212/www.bbc.co.uk/proms). South Kensington tube/9, 10, 52 bus. **Date** 13 July-8 Sept 2007. **Box office** (May-Sept) 9am-9pm daily. **Tickets** £5-£45. **Credit** AmEx, MC, V. **Map** p399 D9.

The BBC Sir Henry Wood Promenade Concerts, as they're officially known, together comprise arguably the world's finest orchestral music festival. Running annually from mid July until mid September, the event features around 70 concerts that take in a huge amount of the classical repertoire, with special dispensation given to composer anniversaries: Mozart and Shostakovich featured heavily in 2006.

The Proms began in 1895 with twin aims: occupying idle musicians during the summer holidays, and informally educating Londoners who couldn't afford to take holidays. Audiences paid a minimal ticket price provided they were prepared to do without a seat. The tradition continues today: you can buy reserved seats in advance, but many prefer to queue on the day for £5 tickets for the seatless promenade area in front of the stage (or the gallery at the top of the auditorium, where the sound is far better). Tickets for the hilariously over-the-top Last Night, when normally well-behaved grown-ups act like schoolchildren, are only available to those attending a number of other concerts throughout the summer; a second and considerably more populist event is staged simultaneously in Hyde Park.

City of London Festival

Venues in & around the City (information 7796 4949/Barbican box office 0845 120 7502/www.colf.org). **Date** 25 June-12 July 2007. **Box office** 9am-8pm daily. **Tickets** free-£50. **Credit** AmEx, MC, V.

This adventurously programmed annual event continues to expand, but the core of its programme remains the chamber music concerts held in beautiful halls of ancient livery companies that are ordinarily closed to the public. Concerts, talks and exhibitions are also staged in small local churches, as well as in venues such as the Barbican and even St Paul's Cathedral. A terrific festival.

Hampton Court Palace Festival

Hampton Court, East Molesey, Surrey KT8 9AU (See Tickets, Ticketmaster, see p311/www.hamptoncourtfestival.com). Hampton Court rail/riverboat from Westminster or Richmond to Hampton Court Pier (Apr-Oct). **Date** 5-23 June. **Tickets** phone for details. **Credit** AmEx, MC, V.

Cardinal Wolsey built himself this vast luxury home but later gave it to Henry VIII, who frolicked here with Anne Boleyn before he cut off her head. The air of idle pleasure persists in the palace's annual summer festival, where overtures and operatic arias have supper intervals during which audiences picnic on the grass or loiter in champagne tents.

Opera Holland Park

Holland Park, Kensington High Street, Kensington, W8 6LU (0845 230 9769/www.operahollandpark.com). High Street Kensington or Holland Park tube. **Date** 5 June-11 Aug. **Tickets** £10-£46. **Credit** MC, V. **Map** p396 A8.

This outdoor, canopied theatre hosts a season of opera each summer, with around a half-dozen productions each receiving a limited run. Book ahead or be disappointed: many of the performances sell out. The cries emanating from the unseen peacocks beyond the theatre wall add a surreal touch.

Spitalfields Festival

Christ Church Spitalfields, Commercial Street, E1 6LY (7377 1362/www.spitalfieldsfestival.org.uk). Liverpool Street tube/rail. **Dates** 5-22 June, 11-19 Dec 2007. **Box office** 10am-5.30pm Mon-Fri. **Tickets** free-£30. **Credit** MC, V. **Map** p405 S5.

This enchanting festival, which takes place twice a year, is staged in Hawksmoor's stunning Christ Church (with the odd event elsewhere), offering a spread of music by well-known and neglected composers, and usually boasting a particularly strong line-up of early music and baroque works. The concerts are supplemented by walks and talks in and around the Spitalfields area.

Rock, Pop & Roots

The problem with live music in London is the complacency of a number of the town's top venues. Safe in the knowledge there's never any shortage of bands wanting to play, and that large audiences for them are essentially guaranteed, many major venues get away with wretched sound, surly staff, overpriced drinks and ridiculously expensive tickets. Through little fault of the acts up on the stage, seeing a big show here can be a frustrating experience.

Bad news duly dispatched, we can move on to the good stuff. Fortunately, there's a lot of it. The range of acts passing through this music industry hub is unparalleled anywhere in the world: from Scandinavian death-metallers to Appalachian banjo-pickers, more or less everyone plays here at some time or other. Every bit as exciting are the home-grown acts: not since the oft-derided Britpop boom of the mid 1990s has there been such a healthy grassroots scene, dealing in such disparate genres as rockabilly, dubstep and folk. And with smaller venues such as the **Luminaire**, **Bush Hall** and the **Spitz** keen to show the big boys how to do it, mixing personable service with brilliantly eclectic booking policies and fair pricing, there's plenty to enjoy.

TICKETS AND INFORMATION

Your first stop should be *Time Out London* magazine, which lists hundreds of gigs each week. Most venues have websites detailing future shows. Look out too for the free signings/in-store shows at **Virgin Megastore**, **HMV**, **Fopp** and **Rough Trade** (*see pp238-241*).

Always check ticket availability for shows before setting out: venues, large and small, can sell out weeks in advance. The main exceptions are small pub venues such as the Bull & Gate, which generally don't sell tickets in advance. Prices vary wildly: on any given night, you could pay £150 for the privilege of watching Madonna at Earl's Court, or catch a perfectly serviceable singer-songwriter for free. Likewise, call ahead to check stage times. Some venues run club nights after the gigs, which generally means the show has to be wrapped up by 10.30pm; at other venues, though, the main act won't even come on until nearer 11pm.

Many venues offer tickets online via their websites, but beware: the majority of these online box offices are operated by ticket agencies, which add booking fees and service charges that can raise the ticket price by as much as 30 per cent. If you're going to a gig at any of the Mean Fiddler venues (the Astoria, the Mean Fiddler, the Jazz Café or the Forum), you can cut out these ridiculous fees by paying in cash at the Astoria or Jazz Café box offices. Similarly, tickets for the Shepherd's Bush Empire, the Carling Academy Brixton and the Carling Academy Islington can be bought at face value with cash from the Islington Academy's box office. However, if you absolutely must, there are four main ticket agencies: **Ticketmaster** (0870 534 4444, www.ticketmaster.co.uk), **Stargreen** (7734 8932, www.stargreen.com), **Ticketweb** (0870 060 0100, www.ticketweb.co.uk) and **See Tickets** (0871 220 0260, www.seetickets.com).

Rock & dance venues

Major venues

In addition to the venues below, the **Barbican** (*see p306*), the **South Bank Centre** (*see p307*) and the **Royal Albert Hall** (*see p307*) all stage regular pop and rock gigs, with the **Alexandra Palace** (*see p162*) and the **Roundhouse** (*see p161*) also occasionally getting in on the act. The **Coronet** (26-28 New Kent Road, tickets 0870 600 100, information 0870 055 6611) is primarily a club, but does sometimes host rock shows. UCL's **Bloomsbury Theatre** (15 Gordon Street, Bloomsbury, WC1H 0AH, 7388 8822, www.thebloomsbury.com) and the **Blackheath Halls** (23 Lee Road, Blackheath, SE3 9RQ, 8463 0100, www.blackheathhalls.com) both run cultured music programmes.

Astoria

157 Charing Cross Road, Soho, WC2H 0EL (information 8963 0940/box office 0870 060 3777/ www.meanfiddler.com). Tottenham Court Road tube. **Box office** *In person* 10am-6pm Mon-Sat. *By phone* 24hrs daily. **Tickets** £10-£20. **Credit** MC, V. **Map** p408 W2.

Rumours that this historic old 2,000-capacity alt-rock sweatbox may close in 2008 have been greeted with outrage, proof that not even rock music is immune from pathetic, dewy-eyed sentimentality. The sound system is atrocious, the bar prices are outrageous, the decor is shabby (and not in a good way), the sight lines are poor, the staff are rude and the room is habitually packed to the point where breathing is difficult. Apart from that, it's great.

Carling Academy Brixton

211 Stockwell Road, Brixton, SW9 9SL (information 7771 3000/box office 0870 771 2000/www.brixton-academy.co.uk). Brixton tube/rail. **Box office** *By phone* 24hrs daily. **Tickets** £10-£40. **Credit** MC, V.

The 51st state

Everywhere you look in central London, builders are hard at work. Old structures are getting replenished with new façades, sparkling skyscrapers are springing up like weeds. But while construction teams work hard to transform the capital into a 21st-century city, a sizeable minority of local music lovers seem convinced that they're living in the 1950s... and roughly 4,000 miles to the east. How else to explain the plethora of gigs offering vintage American music?

A couple of monthly Sunday sessions provide country and Americana fans with a place to have a hoedown. And when we say country, we're talking Hank not Shania. The long-running **Come Down & Meet the Folks** is held on the last Sunday of the month at the Apple Tree in Clerkenwell (45 Mount Pleasant, WC1X 0AE, 0871 984 3540, www.comedownandmeetthefolks.co.uk), while relative newcomer **Honky Tonkin' Sunday** is staged on the first Sunday of the month at the Gloucester Arms in Kentish Town (59-61 Leighton Road, NW5 2QH, 7482 3227, www.honkytonkinsunday.co.uk). Both mix live acts with DJs spinning the finest in old-school country tunes.

There's more where that pair came from at **Health & Happiness** (The Social, 5 Little Portland Street; *see p328*), the third Tuesday of the month. A little further out in Leytonstone, **What's Cookin'** (The Sheepwalk, 692 High Road, E11 3AA, 8556 1131, www.whatscookin.co.uk) offers a similar grab-bag of transatlantic fare on Wednesdays and Saturdays. Cowboy boots are optional, but nonetheless favoured by many.

The music is slightly more raucous at the **Hillbilly Hop** (www.hillbillyhop.com). Held on the second Friday of the month at the **Bethnal Green Working Men's Club** (42-44 Pollard Row; *see p321*), the evening hosts rockabilly and (if you're lucky) western swing acts. You might recognise a few faces among the crowd from the **Virginia Creepers Club** (www.virginiacreepersclub.co.uk), a monthly festival of jump jive, rockabilly and other good-time tunes held at the Water Rats (328 Gray's Inn Road; *see p317*). And if you time your visit right, you can complete the hat-trick with **Stompin'** (www.swingdanceuk.com) at the 100 Club (100 Oxford Street; *see p315*), which bills itself as the city's foremost swing-dance club. It's like punk never happened.

That's all folk

In the last year or two, folk music has made a comeback in the capital. Acid folk nights have sprung up here and there on the back of some prescient CD reissues. Regular clubs such as **In the Pines** (every other Sunday at the Harrison, 28 Harrison Street, King's Cross, WC1H 8JF, 7278 3966, www.inthepines.org) and **Tapestry** (on the last Friday of the month at the St Aloysius Social Club, 20 Phoenix Road, Euston, NW1 1TA, 7388 4026, www.tapestry club.co.uk) have revived hippie-folk records unheard since the 1970s. And then there's the antifolk circuit, a loose collective of like-minded songwriters, rebels and general mischief-makers that convenes regularly at the **Blang** nights at the 12 Bar Club (22-23 Denmark Place; *see p317*).

Amid all these fleetingly fashionable trends, the old-school folk scene has rather slipped between the cracks. But it's still there, defiantly maintained by a clutch of old-timers and an increasing number of younger converts. There are occasional folky shows at, again, the **12 Bar Club**, as well as at the **Green Note** (106 Parkway; *see p315*) and November's **Folk in the Fall** festival (www.mrscasey.co.uk) on the South Bank, but you're best off starting at **Cecil Sharp House** in Camden (2 Regent's Park Road, NW1 7AY, 7485 2206, www.efdss.org). The home of the English Folk Dance & Song Society stages a variety of events in its somewhat ascetic surroundings; check online for details of its barn dances, ceilidhs and folk dance classes. Sharp's Folk Club on Tuesdays occasionally welcomes special guest musicians, but leans mostly on its members to provide the songs.

There's even more frequent folky fare at London's weekly folk clubs, dotted around the capital and scattered throughout the week. Among the best are the often irreverent **Islington Folk Club**, held on Thursdays (except in the summer) at 8pm at the Horseshoe in Clerkenwell (www.islington folkclub.co.uk), the largely traditional **Cellar Upstairs**, which takes place each Saturday at 8.15pm at Euston's Exmouth Arms (http://hometown.aol.co.uk/cellarupstairs), and the eclectic **Walthamstow Folk Club**, staged at 7.30pm every Sunday at the Plough Inn (www.walthamstowfolk.co.uk). All are welcome, with membership always available on the door.

Built in the 1920s as a cinema, the Brixton Academy is a little ragged around the edges these days, worn and torn by two decades of use as a rock venue. You'd never call the 5,000-capacity space intimate: indeed, the echo can be off-putting, especially at shows that are less than a sell-out. Compared to the Hammersmith Apollo (*see p313*), its similar-sized rival across town, the programming leans more to metal and alt-rock, but you can also expect to see more mainstream names such as Corinne Bailey Rae and DJ Shadow.

Carling Academy Islington

N1 Centre, 16 Parkfield Street, Islington, N1 0PS (information 7288 4400/box office 0870 771 2000/ www.islington-academy.co.uk). Angel tube. **Box office** *In person* noon-4pm Mon-Sat. *By phone* 24hrs daily. **Tickets** £3-£20. **Credit** MC, V. **Map** p404 N2.

Located in a shopping mall and decorated with the flair and pizzazz you'd expect of a multi-storey car park, this relatively new operation is never going to be one of London's more atmospheric music venues. Still, the line-up of gigs is pretty decent (you can expect mostly fast-rising indie bands and cultured singer-songwriters), and the solid sound system ensures that the acts get their message across with ease. The adjacent Bar Academy hosts shows by smaller names.

Earl's Court & Olympia

Warwick Road, Earl's Court, SW5 9TA (7385 1200/ box office 7370 8078/www.eco.co.uk). Earl's Court tube. **Box office** *In person* 9am-6pm Mon-Fri. *By phone* 24hrs daily. **Tickets** £17-£50. **Credit** MC, V. **Map** p398 A11.

By the time an act has made it to vast aircraft hangars like these, they're probably not worth seeing. You think we're being too harsh? Perhaps so, but it's pretty much unarguable that even the best rock bands and pop performers get the sting taken out of their acts by the crummy acoustics and less-than-intimate seating arrangements that are the norm at venues like this. All the cons of massive outdoor shows, with precisely none of the pros.

Electric Ballroom

184 Camden High Street, Camden, NW1 8QP (7485 9006/www.electricballroom.co.uk). Camden Town tube. **Box office** 9am-5pm Mon-Thur; 10.30am-1am Fri, Sat; 10.30am-5pm Sun. **Tickets** £7-£20. **No credit cards**.

Threatened with redevelopment for years, this scuzzy yet spacious hall looks to have secured its future after next-door neighbour London Underground dropped plans to expand Camden Town tube station. The weekend clubs are still its main money-spinner, but the venue does stage occasional gigs by indie acts on their way up or mainstream rock groups taking a break from bigger arenas (the Killers played here in 2006).

Forum

9-17 Highgate Road, Kentish Town, NW5 1JY (information 7284 1001/box office 0870 060 3777/www.meanfiddler.com). Kentish Town tube/rail. **Box office** *In person* from the Astoria (*see p311*) or the Jazz Café (*see p315*). *By phone* 24hrs daily. **Tickets** £10-£30. **Credit** (phone bookings only) MC, V.

After a spell in the doldrums while the Astoria (*see p311*), its similarly proportioned but infinitely worse sibling, got all of the trade, this grand old theatre is once more staging several shows a week from alt-rock acts young and old. Like most Mean Fiddler venues, it's in desperate need of a little TLC, but the sound system has held up pretty well and the sight lines are decent from almost anywhere in the hall.

Hammersmith Apollo

Queen Caroline Street, Hammersmith, W6 9QH (information 8748 8660/0870 616 3413/box office 0870 606 3400/www.getlive.co.uk). Hammersmith tube. **Box office** *In person* 4pm-event starts on performance days only. *By phone* 24hrs daily. **Tickets** £10-£40. **Credit** AmEx, MC, V.

Older readers may remember this capacious theatre as the scruffy old Hammersmith Odeon. However, following a refit several years ago, the space now works double duty as an all-seater theatre popular with comedy acts (the *Little Britain* tour pulled in here for an astonishing 35 nights last year), and a standing-room-only space hosting shows by the likes of Feeder and Primal Scream.

Koko

1A Camden Road, Camden, NW1 OJH (0870 432 5527/www.koko.uk.com). Mornington Crescent tube. **Box office** phone ahead for details. **Tickets** £3-£15. **Credit** MC, V.

The erstwhile Camden Palace has scrubbed up very nicely after its refit a few years back, and has built up a roster of events to match. The 1,500-capacity venue stages a fair few club nights alongside an indie-heavy (but still interesting) gig programme.

Shepherd's Bush Empire

Shepherd's Bush Green, W12 8TT (8354 3300/box office 0870 771 2000/www.shepherds-bush-empire.co.uk). Shepherd's Bush tube. **Box office** *In person* 4-6pm; 6.30-9.30pm show nights only. *By phone* 24hrs daily. **Tickets** £10-£40. **Credit** MC, V.

This former BBC theatre remains London's best mid-sized venue. The sound is decent (with the exception of the alcove behind the stalls bar) and the staff are among London's friendliest, resulting in a booking policy that takes in everything from the Roots to the Bonzo Dog Doo-Dah Band. The only irritation is the lack of decent sight lines from the stalls (occasionally seated but usually standing-room only) for concert-goers less than 6ft tall; things are a lot more comfortable on the all-seated balconies. **Photo** *p314*.

Union Chapel

Compton Terrace, Islington, N1 2XD (7226 1686/www.unionchapel.org.uk). Highbury & Islington tube/rail. **Box office/credit** varies with event; check website for details. **Tickets** free-£40.

For years one of London's more characterful music venues, this grand old church (which still holds services) was forced to pull the plug on its concert programme in 2005. However, the closure was temporary: as of mid 2006, it's been open for business once more. The acoustics are great for a church organ but rubbish for an electric guitar: generally speaking, the larger the line-up, the worse the sound. Thankfully, the programmers here seem to be big fans of all-acoustic singer-songwriters.

Wembley Arena

Arena Square, Engineers Way, Wembley, Middx HA9 0DH (0870 060 0870/www.livenation.co.uk/wembley). Wembley Park tube. **Box office** *In person* 10.30am-5pm Mon-Sat. *By phone* 24hrs daily. **Tickets** £5-£100. **Credit**, MC, V.

A £30m refurbishment (finished more or less on time, unlike the stadium just down the road) has improved this much-derided 12,500-capacity venue no end, but below-par acoustics and above-price concessions mean it'll never be the most enjoyable place to see a show.

Club & pub venues

In addition to the venues detailed below, a handful of nightclubs stage regular gigs. Chief among them is the fabulously eclectic **Cargo** (*see p321*), whose programme is one of the most consistently interesting in London. Elsewhere, **93 Feet East** and the **Notting Hill Arts Club** (for both, *see p324*) both stage decent programmes of alternative music. Venerable cabaret hangout **Madame Jo Jo's** (*see p324*), the impossibly fashionable **Bethnal Green Working Men's Club** (*see p321*) and the all-encompassing **ICA** (*see p144*) also host sporadic gigs, as does the raucous **On the Rocks** (25 Kingsland Road, Shoreditch) and the rather mellower **Enterprise** (2 Haverstock Hill, Camden, NW3 2BL, 7485 2659). Fans of garage rock should make a point of visiting the **Boston Arms** for Friday's Dirty Water Club (178 Junction Road, Tufnell Park, N19 5QQ, 7272 8153, www.dirtywaterclub.com).

The **Bull & Gate** (*see p314*) is by no means London's only venue to stage primarily new bands. Camden's **Dublin Castle** (94 Parkway, NW1 7AN, 7485 1773, www.bugbearbookings.com) and the **Hope & Anchor** in Islington (207 Upper Street, N1 1RL, 7354 1312, www.bugbearbookings.com) both cram their rosters with unsigned guitar bands, who can otherwise be found playing out east at the **Pleasure Unit** (359 Bethnal Green Road, Bethnal Green,

E2 6LG, 7729 0167, www.pleasureunitbar.com) or the **Rhythm Factory** (16-18 Whitechapel Road, Whitechapel, E1 1EW, 7375 3774, www.rhythmfactory.co.uk), or in Clerkenwell in the tiny basement room of the **Betsey Trotwood** (56 Farringdon Road, EC1R 3BL, 7253 4285).

Bardens Boudoir

38-44 Stoke Newington Road, N16 7XJ (7249 9557/www.bardensbar.co.uk). Dalston Kingsland rail/67, 76, 149, 243 buses. **Box office** phone for details. *Gigs* 8pm. **Tickets** £4-£5. **No credit cards.**
Having resolved a few licensing issues (it turned out that it didn't have one), this basement space is back open for business once more. In truth, the space is something of a shambles: the room is at least three times wider than it is deep, and the stage isn't really a stage at all. But none of that bothers the often out-there line-ups and the hipsters that love them.

Barfly

49 Chalk Farm Road, Chalk Farm, NW1 8AN (7691 4244/box office 0870 907 0999/www.barflyclub.com). Chalk Farm tube. **Open** 7.30pm-1am Mon-Thur; 7.30pm-3am Fri, Sat; 7-10.30pm Sun. *Gigs* 7.30pm daily. **Admission** £6-£8. **No credit cards.**
The website of this nationwide chain (seven cities and counting) promises 'The stars of tomorrow'. Fair enough: the planet-conquering likes of Keane and Coldplay played the pokey but by no means unpleasant upstairs venue early in their careers. Less well documented are the dozens of no-hoper indie acts who make up the majority of the programme. New sister venue the Fly (36-38 New Oxford Street, Fitzrovia, WC1A 1EP) stages a similar mix of up-and-comers and never-will-bes.

Borderline

Orange Yard, off Manette Street, Soho, W1D 4JB (7734 5547/box office 0870 060 3777/www.meanfiddler.com). Tottenham Court Road tube. **Box office** *In person* 10am-6pm Mon-Fri; 10am-5pm Sat. *By phone* 24hrs daily. **Tickets** £10-£25. **Credit** MC, V. **Map** p399 K6.
The Americana trend has cooled considerably in the last couple of years, but the Borderline is still flying the flag. When acts such as Fred Eaglesmith and the Sadies visit the capital, they usually play at this likeable basement spot on the edge of Soho. Otherwise, the venue welcomes a pretty shrug-inducing selection of rock and indie acts. Shows usually finish by 10.30pm to make room for the nightly clubs.

Buffalo Bar

259 Upper Street, Islington, N1 1RU (7359 6191/www.buffalobar.co.uk). Highbury & Islington tube/rail. **Open** 8.30pm-2am Mon-Thurs, Sun; 8pm-4am Fri, Sat. **Admission** free-£6. **Credit** MC, V.
Depending on your taste, this Highbury Corner hangout is cosy or cramped, relaxed or chaotic. Either way, you don't come here for a quiet night. The somewhat precious Artrocker organisation hosts a popular Tuesday-night shindig; look out too for the always messy gigs staged by Guided Missile.

Shepherd's Bush Empire. See p313.

Bull & Gate

389 Kentish Town Road, Kentish Town, NW5 2TJ (7093 4820/www.bullandgate.co.uk). Kentish Town tube/rail. **Box office** from 8pm daily. **Tickets** £5 (weekdays), £6 (weekends). **No credit cards.**
A number of venues around London concentrate on unsigned bands (for others, *see p313*), but this venerable old boozer is perhaps the best. Expect to find groups with names such as Two Bear Mambo and Dancing With Henry playing for the benefit of friends, family and the occasional A&R scout who took a wrong turning on the way to Camden.

Bush Hall

310 Uxbridge Road, Shepherd's Bush, W12 7LJ (8222 6933/0870 060 0100/www.bushhallmusic.co.uk). Shepherd's Bush tube. **Box office** 10am-5pm Mon-Sat. **Tickets** £6-£25. **Credit** AmEx, MC, V.
Built as a dance hall in 1904, this west London building was used as a bingo hall, a rehearsal room and a snooker club before receiving a beautiful refurbishment a few years ago. It's now perhaps the most handsome small venue in London, albeit with an acoustic more suited to classical chamber concerts (which it also stages) than to the rock and pop events that dominate its programme.

Dingwalls

11 East Yard, Camden Lock, Chalk Farm Road, Camden, NW1 8AB (7428 5929/Ticketmaster 7344 4040/www.dingwalls.com). Camden Town or Chalk Farm tube. **Open** *Gigs* 7.30pm-2am; nights vary. **Admission** £5-£15. **Credit** AmEx, DC, MC, V.

The range of concerts staged at this long-standing Camden staple has always been agreeably eclectic, but it's spread its net even wider of late: expect to find everything from country rock to obscure jazz. Unfortunately, the long, multi-level space is patently unsuitable for gigs, nor does the sound system seem to be up to the task.

Garage

20-22 Highbury Corner, Islington, N5 1RD (information 8963 0940/box office 0870 060 3777/ www.meanfiddler.com). Highbury & Islington tube/ rail. **Box office** *In person* at the Astoria (*see p311*). *By phone* 24hrs daily. **Open** *Gigs* 8pm-midnight Mon-Thur, occasional Sun; 8pm-3am Fri, Sat. **Admission** £5-£15. **Credit** MC, V.

This low-ceilinged sweatbox (and its smaller sibling, Upstairs at the Garage) have historically concentrated on fast-breaking indie acts. Both venues are currently closed for refurbishment, but are expected to reopen in 2007.

Green Note

106 Parkway, Camden, NW1 7AN (7485 9899/ www.greennote.co.uk). Camden Town tube. **Open** 6pm-12.30am Wed-Fri; noon-midnight Sat, Sun. **Tickets** £3-£8. **Credit** MC, V.

Roots music and vegetarian food make for a winning combination at this Camden newcomer. Neither is particularly daring: the music comes from a string of folkies, blues musicians and singer-songwriters, while the menu contains a variety of earthy dishes served tapas-style. But it all hangs together nicely at what is clearly, not to say charmingly, a labour of love on the part of the young owners. A regular open mic event (1-6pm Sun) was due to start in late 2006.

Half Moon Putney

93 Lower Richmond Road, Putney, SW15 1EU (8780 9383/www.halfmoon.co.uk). Putney Bridge tube/Putney rail. **Open** noon-11.30pm Mon-Thur; noon-midnight Fri, Sat; noon-11pm Sun. *Gigs* 8.15pm daily. **Tickets** £2.50-£12. **Credit** MC, V.

This highly personable Young's boozer close to the Thames has long staged shows in its smallish back room: the walls of the main pub are lined with mementoes from those who've graced its stage. These days, the schedule is a well-meaning jumble of cover bands, ageing rockers and folk legends (Martin Carthy and Dave Swarbrick both played in 2006).

Jazz Café

5 Parkway, Camden, NW1 7PG (information 7916 6060/box office 0870 060 3777/www.jazzcafe.co.uk). Camden Town tube. **Open** 7pm-1am Mon-Thur; 7pm-2am Fri, Sat; 7pm-midnight Sun. *Gigs* 9pm daily. **Admission** £10-£30. **Credit** MC, V.

The name doesn't tell the whole story. There is some jazz on the schedules here, but this Mean Fiddler-operated two-floor club deals more in soul, R&B and hip hop these days, performed by well-known and fast-rising acts from home and abroad. A word of warning: tickets can cost substantially more on the door than they do in advance.

Luminaire

307-311 Kilburn High Road, Kilburn, NW6 7JR (7372 8668/www.theluminaire.co.uk). Kilburn tube/ Brondesbury rail. **Open** 7pm-midnight Mon-Wed, Sun; 7pm-1am Thur; 7pm-2am Fri, Sat. **Tickets** £5-£12. **Credit** AmEx, MC, V.

This newcomer won *Time Out* magazine's Live Venue of the Year award for 2006, and with good reason. The booking policy is fantastically broad, taking in everything from country legend Billy Joe Shaver to hyper-hip electro-poppers Junior Boys; the sound system is well up to scratch; the decor is stylish (with seated areas away from the stage); the drinks are fairly priced, and the staff are actually approachable, even friendly. If only all venues were built this way.

Mean Fiddler

165 Charing Cross Road, Soho, WC2H 0EL (7434 9592/box office 0870 060 3777/www. meanfiddler.com). Tottenham Court Road tube. **Box office** *In person* at the Astoria (*see p311*). *By phone* 24hrs daily. **Tickets** £10-£25. **Credit** MC, V. **Map** p399 K6.

This basement space sits in the shadow of the Astoria (*see p311*), its larger and more storied neighbour, but is a rather more agreeable place to see a show: both sound and sight lines are better, although the staff are just as apathetic. On Saturdays, the venue is home to student-indie night Frog, which hosts a live band each week. If the music's terrible, head upstairs to the glassed-off bar to the left of the balcony.

Metro

19-23 Oxford Street, Soho, W1D 2DN (7437 0964/ www.blowupmetro.com). Tottenham Court Road tube. **Open** *Box office* from 5pm Mon-Fri. *Club* 11pm-3am Tue-Thur; 11pm-4am Fri, Sat. **Admission** £3-£12. **No credit cards. Map** p408 W1.

This shambolic dive earned a reputation as *the* place to play during the garage-rock boom of 2002/3. The line-ups these days are considerably less attention-grabbing, but it can still get enjoyably messy; expect to be drenched with both sweat and beer by the time you eventually leave.

100 Club

100 Oxford Street, Soho, W1D 1LL (7636 0933/ www.the100club.co.uk). Oxford Circus or Tottenham Court Road tube. **Open** *Gigs* 7.30pm-midnight Mon; 7.30-midnight Tue-Thur; 7.30pm-midnight Fri, Sat; 7.30-11pm Sun. **Tickets** free-£20. **Credit** MC, V. **Map** p399 K6.

Perhaps the most adaptable venue in London, the basement room of the 100 Club has provided a home at various points for the city's jazz, blues, northern soul and punk communities (the venue staged a historic show in 1976 that featured the Sex Pistols, the Clash and the Damned). These days, the jazz gigs are supplemented by swing-dance nights, a variety of indie shows and regular turns by the old rockers hosted by Club Bang! Bang! (for more details, see www.bangbang-live.com).

Clean air gets in your eyes

Does life begin at 40? Theatrical impresario Sally Greene hopes so. That said, it's not as if **Ronnie Scott's** (*see p318*) has had a quiet first four decades. Arguably the most famous music venue in Europe, the dimly lit Soho hangout has hosted a veritable A-to-Z of jazz greats since saxophonist Scott and business partner Pete King moved it to 47 Frith Street from its original Gerrard Street location in 1965. Few jazz joints can match it for history.

However, since Scott's death in 1996, the club's past has increasingly looked like overtaking its present. When King finally sold the place to Greene in 2005, he handed over a club that can scarcely have been redecorated since it opened. Woozy on whisky, head fugged by a billion cigs, with hard-earned character emanating from every tear in the tablecloths, it was a club literally decades out of time.

Greene soon shut the place for a subtle yet character-altering renovation. The tables are no longer held together with gum and duct tape. The lights are a little brighter. The food and drinks menu has received a total overhaul. And, in direct contravention of jazz law, smoking is banned. The club hasn't quite been reborn, but it's had a heart transplant.

Of course, someone has to pay for all this, and it's the customers. Ticket prices have risen under the new regime, with the added irritation that seats are guaranteed only to diners. The food has improved, but whether it's improved enough to merit a charge of £24 for two courses is another matter. And £2.20 for half a lager is just silly.

Yet, from the monochrome photos on the wall to the heart-of-Soho location, the place retains its mystique. Purists grumble about the cheesification of the music programme, which reached a nadir when fabulous New York pianist Benny Green was bumped from headliner to support act in order to make room for the Blues Brothers Band. But the booking policy under the old management had long since lost its spark, hamstrung by an insistence on weekly residencies and a reliance on a handful of bankable acts.

In much the same way that the new decor pays tribute to the club's history while unsentimentally looking to the future, Greene and her team have broadened the programming remit. There's still room for long-time favourites such as Georgie Fame and George Melly, but the intimate space has also welcomed the likes of Wynton Marsalis and Christian McBride. Sure, it's not the club it once was. But had nothing changed then it's likely that rather than writing this eulogy, we'd be penning an obituary.

Pigalle Club

215 Piccadilly, St James's, W1J 9HN (office 7734 8142/reservations 0845 345 6053/www.vpmg.net/pigalle). Piccadilly Circus tube. **Open** 7pm-2am Mon-Wed; 7pm-3am Thur-Sat. **Tickets** free. **Credit** AmEx, DC, MC, V. **Map** p408 V4.

Vince Power may have sold his stake in the Mean Fiddler, the company he founded in 1982, but he's not ready to retire just yet. The Pigalle is chalk to the cheese of his previous venues: located right by Piccadilly Circus, it's an old-fashioned supper club where the prices demand – or, at least, imply – a certain measure of sophistication. Acts are generally jazzy, with the occasional big-name singer thrown in to keep things interesting.

Scala

275 Pentonville Road, King's Cross, N1 9NL (7833 2022/www.scala-london.co.uk). King's Cross tube/rail. **Box office** 10am-6pm Mon-Fri. **Tickets** £8-£25 (cash only). **Credit** MC, V (bar). **Map** p401 L3.

Built as a cinema shortly after World War I, this surprisingly capacious building in King's Cross now stages a laudably broad range of shows: 2006 saw appearances by everyone from Scritti Politti to the Melvins. Unlike many venues of a similar size (capacity is around 1,145), the sound quality is decent and the staff are extremely personable. The venue also stages regular club nights.

Spitz

Old Spitalfields Market, 109 Commercial Street, Spitalfields, E1 6BG (7392 9032/box office 0871 220 0260/www.spitz.co.uk). Liverpool Street tube/rail. **Open** 11am-midnight Mon-Sat; 10am-10.30pm Sun. **Box office** 24hrs daily. **Tickets** £4-£17.50. **Credit** MC, V. **Map** p405 R5.

The Spitz tries to be all things to all people, and more or less succeeds. Downstairs there's a bar, café-restaurant and small gallery space, while upstairs sits a larger-than-expected music venue, staging folk, jazz and rock gigs alongside shows by rather more uncategorisable acts: the Necks and Damo Suzuki both played recently, though sadly not together.

12 Bar Club

22-23 Denmark Place, Soho, WC2H 8NL (office 7240 2120/box office 7240 2622/www.12barclub.com). Tottenham Court Road tube. **Open** *Café* 9am-9pm Mon-Sat. *Gigs* 7.30pm; nights vary. **Admission** £5-£15. **Credit** MC, V. **Map** p408 W4.

This minuscule and much-cherished hole-in-the-wall books a real grab-bag of stuff. Its size (the stage is barely big enough for three people) dictates a predominance of singer-songwriters, but that doesn't stop the occasional full band from trying their luck.

ULU (University of London Union)

Malet Street, Bloomsbury, WC1E 7HY (7664 2000/www.ulu.lon.co.uk). Goodge Street tube. **Box office** 8.30am-11pm Mon-Fri; 9am-11pm Sat; 9am-7pm Sun. **Open** *Gigs* 7.30-11pm; nights vary. **Admission** £8-£15. **No credit cards. Map** p401 K4.

This 800-capacity hall was redecorated in 2005, when it also had a new sound system installed. However, while the venue has improved, it's no more characterful than it was before. This being a student venue, two things are guaranteed: the programme of gigs will rely heavily on dodgy major-label guitar bands, and the drinks will be invitingly cheap.

Underworld

174 Camden High Street, Camden, NW1 0NE (information 7482 1932/box office 0870 060 0100/7734 8932/www.theunderworldcamden.co.uk). Camden Town tube. **Open** *Gigs* 7-10.30pm; nights vary. **Admission** £5-£20. **No credit cards.**

A dingy maze of pillars and bars in the bowels of Camden, this subterranean oddity is an essential for punk, metal and hardcore fans. Its insalubrious interior is enlivened by friendly, youthful audiences and a real community feel. If you can tell friends you're going to see Pickled Dick support Necrophagist while maintaining a straight face, you'll fit in fine.

Water Rats

328 Gray's Inn Road, King's Cross, WC1X 8BZ (7837 7269/www.monto.com). King's Cross tube/rail. **Open** *Gigs* 8.30-11pm Mon-Sat. **Admission** £3-£6. **Credit** MC, V. **Map** p401 M3.

Long-time bookers Plum Promotions left the Water Rats in the middle of 2006 with a fair amount of acrimony, throwing the future of this agreeably uncomplicated pub venue into doubt. The new promoters are apparently due to take over the space in due course, but it remains to be seen whether they'll stick to the same indie-schmindie policy as their aggrieved predecessors.

Windmill

22 Blenheim Gardens, Brixton, SW2 5BZ (8671 0700/www.windmillbrixton.co.uk). Brixton tube/rail. **Open** *Gigs* 8-11pm Mon-Thur; 8pm-midnight Fri, Sat; 5-11pm Sun. **Admission** free-£3/£4. **No credit cards.**

If you can live with the frankly iffy sound system and the amusingly taciturn local barflies, you might think this pokey little pub is one of the best venues in London, thanks to an adventurous bookings policy (anything goes, from country to techno to punk to folk to metal), cheap admission and friendly staff.

Festivals & outdoor venues

Outdoor music festivals come and go like the wind in London: events are launched in a blaze of publicity one year, then mysteriously fail to appear the next. That said, a few festivals return each summer without fail. Chief among them is the series of pop and rock shows held in the courtyard of **Somerset House** (*see p119*), where the handsomeness of the surroundings just about wins out over the ugliness of the obligatory sponsor's branding. There are also regular concerts by big names in **Hyde Park** (*see p154*), some of them under the banner of the Wireless Festival.

Other events last only a weekend. Held in Victoria Park, July's **Lovebox Weekender** (www.loveboxweekender.com) supplements dance-oriented headliners with a broad range of support acts, while **Get Loaded in the Park** (www.getloadedinthepark.co.uk) presents indie and dance acts over two August days on Clapham Common. Clapham is also the home of **Ben & Jerry's Summer Sundae** in early August (www.benjerry.co.uk), two days of alt-rock and ice-cream held around the same time as mellow freebie **Fruitstock** (www.fruitstock.co.uk). Finsbury Park is home to a pair of weekenders: the **Big Gay Out** (www.biggayout.com), scheduled to return in July 2007 after a year off, and **Rise** (www.london.gov.uk/rise), a GLA-staged anti-racism event that in 2006 brought together unlikely bedfellows Roy Ayers and the Buzzcocks.

New festivals will certainly spring up in 2007, so keep an eye on *Time Out London* magazine for details. Music is also a big component of **Pride London** (*see p269*), the **Notting Hill Carnival** and the **Brick Lane Festival** (for both, *see p271*).

Jazz

Jazz venues

In addition to the venues listed below, the **100 Club** (*see p315*) and the **Spitz** (*see p317*) both stage regular jazz, the former concentrating on trad and the latter dealing in more modern material. The **Jazz Café** (*see p315*) lives up to its name four or five times a month, and the **Pigalle Club** (*see p316*) also offers regular jazz nights. Both the **Barbican** (*see p306*) and the **South Bank Centre** (*see p307*) host jazz events from time to time.

Bull's Head

373 Lonsdale Road, Barnes, SW13 9PY (8876 5241/www.thebullshead.com). Barnes Bridge rail. **Open** 11am-11pm Mon-Sat; noon-11pm Sun. *Gigs* 8.30pm Mon-Sun; 1-3.30pm, 8.30-11pm Sun. **Admission** £5-£12. **Credit** AmEx, DC, MC, V.

For a time, it looked like this venerable old riverside pub would have to curtail its long-running music programme after complaints about noise. Happily, closure was averted, and a refurbishment of sound and lighting systems have left the Yamaha Jazz Room, as it's now known, in better shape than ever. Look out for the regular sets from ever-thrilling pianist Stan Tracey, sax maestro Peter King and the almost legendary Humphrey Lyttleton.

Pizza Express Jazz Club

10 Dean Street, Soho, W1D 3RW (restaurant 7437 9595/jazz club 7439 8722/www.pizzaexpress.co.uk). Tottenham Court Road tube. **Open** *Restaurant* 11.30am-midnight daily. *Club* 7.45pm-midnight daily. *Gigs* 9pm daily. **Admission** £15-£20. **Credit** AmEx, DC, MC, V. **Map** p408 W2.

Rather like the pizzas dished up by the busy kitchen (the upstairs restaurant is jazz-free), the acts at this small Soho basement range from the appetising to the bland, and are perhaps priced a little higher than their qualities merit. Still, the room is agreeably intimate and the sound is well up to snuff.

Pizza on the Park

11 Knightsbridge, Belgravia, SW1X 7LY (7235 5273/www.pizzaonthepark.co.uk). Hyde Park Corner tube. **Open** 7.30-11.15pm Mon-Sat; 7-10.45pm Sun. **Admission** £12-£20. **Credit** AmEx, DC, MC, V. **Map** p402 G8.

It's not quite as sophisticated as it thinks it is, but this basement music room is nonetheless nicely atmospheric. The programme is mostly made up of well-mannered young men and women singing the Great American Songbook in front of a piano trio, but does throw out the occasional curveball.

Ronnie Scott's

47 Frith Street, Soho, W1D 4HT (7439 0747/ www.ronniescotts.co.uk). Leicester Square or Tottenham Court Road tube. **Open** 6pm-3am Mon-Sat; 6pm-midnight Sun. *Gigs* 6.30pm Mon-Sat; 6.30pm Sun. **Admission** (non-members) £26 Mon-Sat; students & musicians' union members free after 11.30 Mon-Wed. **Credit** AmEx, DC, MC, V. **Map** p408 W2.

See p316 **Clean air gets in your eyes**.

606 Club

90 Lots Road, Chelsea, SW10 0QD (7352 5953/ www.606club.co.uk). Earl's Court or Fulham Broadway tube/11, 211 bus. **Open** 7.30pm-1.30am Mon-Wed; 8pm-1.30am Thur; 8pm-2am Fri, Sat; 8pm-midnight Sun. *Gigs* 8pm-1am Mon-Wed; 9pm-1am Thur; 9.30pm-1.30am Fri, Sat; 9-11.30pm Sun. **Admission** *Music charge* (non-members) £8 Mon-Thur; £10 Fri, Sat; £9 Sun. **Credit** AmEx, MC, V. **Map** p398 C13.

On the face of it, the music policy at the 606 (only British-based jazz musicians play here) seems expressly designed to haemorrhage cash. However, it's testament to the talents of both management and musicians that the 150-capacity club celebrated its 30th birthday in 2006. There's no entry fee: instead, the band are funded from a music charge that's added to your bill at the end of the night. Alcohol can only be served with food.

Vortex Jazz Club

11 Gillet Street, Dalston, N16 8JN (7254 4097/ www.vortexjazz.co.uk). Dalston Kingsland rail. **Open** 8pm-midnight daily. *Gigs* 8.30pm. **Admission** free-£12. **Credit** MC, V.

A fixture in Stoke Newington for many years before a dispute with the landlord, the Vortex reopened in 2005 in the handsome new Dalston Culture House building. It's still finding its feet: the upstairs space feels a little sterile, and the promised café has yet to open. However, the line-ups remain as good as ever, packed with talent from Britain, Europe and the US.

Festivals

The big event on London's jazz calendar each year is the **London Jazz Festival** (7324 1880, www.serious.org.uk). Held over ten days each November, the creatively curated event spans many genres and venues, from the Vortex to the Wigmore Hall. Tickets for most shows are available online.

It's not, though, the only jazz festival in the city. July alone sees two annual events, both of which are entirely free. **Jazz on the Streets** (www.jazzonthestreets.co.uk) offers a week's worth of low-key music in cafés and bars in and around Soho, while the **Ealing Jazz Festival** (8825 6640, www.ealing.gov.uk) stages a variety of generally mainstream acts over five late July evenings in Walpole Park, W5. And in late September, the **Riverfront Jazz Festival** in Greenwich (8921 4456, www.riverfront jazz.co.uk) dishes up a spread of small-scale shows in the area's pubs and cafés; the same organisers run a mini-festival in mid May.

Nightlife

There's a whole other world out there.

The winning element of London's 2012 Olympic bid was, it's said, the bid's focus on the kids. And the kids, gushed our mayor, all want to come to London. He doesn't know the half of it. When it comes to clubbing, London is the most happening place on the planet. Judging by the number of people who would happily sell their grandmothers to DJ and dance here, the whole world knows it too.

Fresh off the boat? It doesn't matter if you arrive at 10pm on Friday or 6am on Monday, there's a party to be had. The only issue is that with ever more DJs playing more types of music in ever more clubs every night of the week, it's easy to be overwhelmed.

Work out what you simply have to do (perhaps the legendary **Fabric** is number one on your list? maybe you couldn't possibly do London without rinsin' out at Grace, Grooverider's epic Sunday session at **Herbal**?), but then make time for lots more nights and venues that you haven't heard of. DJs moan that Londoners are a hard bunch to play to, but that's because we're used to mega-quality. Wherever you end up, the odds are it will be a blinder.

So what's new? Indie rave kids, for one. With their skinny jeans riding low in a hip-hop style, they've been taking over warehouses and abandoned buildings in London's East End, particularly Whitechapel and Dalston, and mashing up guitar records with rave anthems. Although early hardcore purists should note that their take on 'rave' is a pretty loose one: anything from acid house through to mid-1990s handbag house gets thrown down and cheered. Fancy it? **Barfly** and the **333** are great places to start, but also check out the Myspace sites of leading protagonists such as Teens of Thailand, Shitdisco and the Klaxons for the details of cheeky warehouse parties.

The minimal scene has grown from an underground trend to a fully blown scene: experience its pared-down electronic sounds at much-loved parties like **Secretsundaze** (a secret Sunday session, held throughout the summer and easily located with a little online sleuthing) and DDD (monthly at the **Key**).

Revellers have been stepping out in an explosion of retro glamour at cabaret and burlesque clubs (*see p323* **Frocking up**), while the ultra-raw, bass-fuelled sounds of grime and dubstep have stopped being all about media hype and now tear out speaker stacks at FWD at **Plastic People**.

London rewards those who are willing to chance something new. Not all risks are worth taking, however. If you can't walk home from the club, find out which night bus gets you home and (more importantly) where you get it from before you head out. You'll never regret

Bethnal Green Working Men's Club

Raid your granny's wardrobe and dress up for quirky, kooky and downright hilarious retro and cabaret nights. *See p321.*

EGG

With its central, astroturfed terrace, EGG is perfect for finding a vacant sun lounger and pretending that you were anywhere but King's Cross. *See p321.*

The End

Owned and run by music bods who care a whole lot about the important stuff: crystal sound, clean toilets and cool security. *See p321.*

Fabric

The queues, the crowds, the superstar DJs from open to close in every room – still world renowned and still adored by punters and DJs alike. *See p323.*

The Key

It's a bit of a bleak and lonely trek to get here (and whatever you do, don't turn up before midnight) but once you find this perfect dark little rave space then everything's just disco-tastic. *See p323.*

333

Old Street's beacon for kids in skinny jeans. The queues outside are testament to the fact that you can rely on this club for some of the most exciting nights in London. *See p325.*

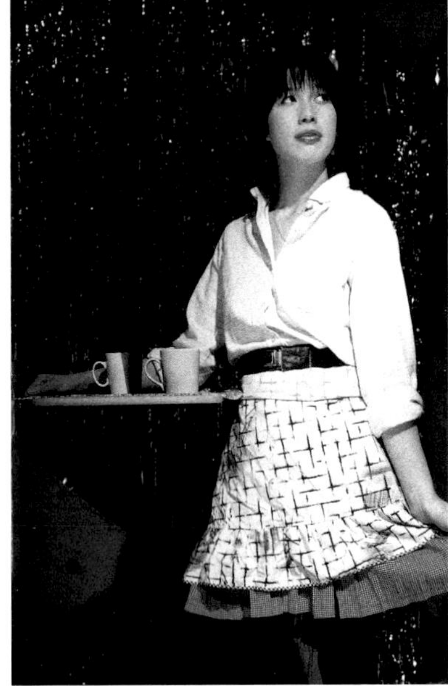

London's best club? **Bethnal Green Working Men's Club**. *See p321*.

working out the night-bus system: the tube doesn't start until around 7am on Sundays, black cabs are expensive and rare. If you must take a minicab, make sure it's an official one.

Clubs

Aquarium

256 Old Street, Hoxton, EC1V 9DD (7251 6136/ www.clubaquarium.co.uk). Old Street tube/rail. **Open** 10pm-3am Thur; 10pm-4am Fri, Sat; 10am-4am Sun. **Admission** £7-£20. **Map** p405 Q4.

The only nightclub in the UK with a swimming pool and a six-person jacuzzi, Aquarium is proud of its aquatic status. Despite being in the ultra-hip vicinity of Old Street, it hosts nights that are strictly tongue-in-cheek – 1970s funkfest Carwash still rules the roost on Saturdays – although local promoters have taken to using the stunning rooftop terrace for their summer after-parties. It's not always open, so check before you make a special trip.

Bar Rumba

36 Shaftesbury Avenue, Soho, W1D 7EP (7287 6933/www.barrumba.co.uk). Piccadilly Circus tube. **Open** 9pm-3.30am Mon; 6pm-3am Tue; 7pm-3am Wed; 6pm-3.30am Thur, Fri; 9pm-5am Sat; 8pm-2am Sun. **Admission** £3-£10; free before 9pm Tue; free before 8pm Thur; free before 10pm Fri. **Map** p408 W4.

Offering pretty much every flavour going (bar rumba, geddit?), this basement space has long been a fave haunt for proper music bods despite its West End locale. The superstar junglist line-up of Movement still reigns on Thursdays, while Fridays feature the heavyweight hip hop of Get Down.

Bethnal Green Working Men's Club

42-44 Pollard Row, Bethnal Green, E2 6NB (7739 2727/www.workersplaytime.net). Bethnal Green tube. **Open** check website for details. **Admission** £4-£10.

What was once a run-down East End working men's club threatened with closure is now one of London's coolest clubs, thanks to a canny local boy turned promoter. The sticky red carpet and broken lampshades perfectly suit the quirky lounge, retro rock'n'roll and fancy-dress burlesque parties, like Whoopee presents Hip Hip (a monthly try-out night) and Get in the Ring, for which a circus tent is put up inside the club. The mood is friendly, the playlist upbeat and the air one of playful mischief. **Photo** *p320*. *See also p323* **Frocking up**.

Canvas

King's Cross Goods Yard, off York Way, King's Cross, N1 0UZ (7833 8301/www.canvaslondon.net). King's Cross tube/rail. **Open** 8pm-midnight Thur; 8pm-2am Fri; 10pm-6am Sat. **Admission** £10-£20. **Map** p401 L2.

Old ravers know this former warehouse as Bagley's, but now it's a beautifully revamped three-room club that's even got a pretty, Ibiza-flavoured terrace for summer sunnin'. Roller Disco every Thursday and Friday is the best fun on wheels, while irregular one-offs fill out the rest of the year. **Photo** *p324*.

Cargo

Kingsland Viaduct, 83 Rivington Street, Shoreditch, EC2A 3AY (7739 3440/www.cargo-london.com). Old Street tube/rail. **Open** 11am-1am Mon-Thur; 11am-1am Fri; 6pm-3am Sat; 1pm-midnight Sun. **Admission** free-£12. **Map** p405 R4.

Located down a side street and under some arches, Cargo has cemented its position as an essential East End music space hosting some terrific gigs. The restaurant serves yummy tapas-style street food, while the bar and club hosts everything from Manchester's Friends&Family hip-hop crew to Oscar Fullone's Mish Mash – which offers pretty much what it says on the label.

The Cross

The Arches, 27-31 King's Cross Goods Yard, off York Way, King's Cross, N1 0UZ (7837 0828/ www.the-cross.co.uk). King's Cross tube/rail. **Open** 10pm-6am Fri, Sat. **Admission** £12-£15. **Map** p401 L2.

This stylish bricks 'n' arches space was the first of the trio of clubs currently lodged in the Goods Yard. It's still a firm fave with a beautiful international crowd who love lolling in the palm-filled garden pretending they're really in Ibiza. The focus is on house music: Fridays are for polysexual Fiction, while the roster of Saturday parties includes X-Press 2's Muzikism and legendary northern club Renaissance. **Photo** *p325*.

EGG

200 York Way, King's Cross, N7 9AP (7609 8364/www.egglondon.net). King's Cross tube/rail. **Open** 10pm-10am Fri; 10pm Sat-2pm Sun; phone for weekday openings. **Admission** £8-£15. **Map** p401 L2.

Need another reason to head to King's Cross? We give you EGG. With its Mediterranean-styled three floors, garden and enormous terrace (complete with a pool), it's big enough to lose yourself in but still manages to retain an intimate atmosphere. The upstairs bar in red ostrich leather is particularly elegant, while the main dancefloor downstairs has a warehouse rave feel. Club nights range from dark electro synth raves to house; the most famous is Jaded, every Sunday morning.

The End

18 West Central Street, Holborn, WC1A 1JJ (7419 9199/www.endclub.com). Holborn or Tottenham Court Road tube. **Open** 10pm-3am Mon, Wed; phone for details Tue; 10pm-4am Thur; 10pm-5am Fri; 10pm-7am Sat; phone for details Sun. **Admission** £4-£15. **Map** p409 Y1.

Sure, it's in the uncool environs of the West End, but the End continues to get queues around the block and then some by maintaining a club list that includes Erol Alkan's brilliant indie pop party Trash, plus Fabio's Swerve, Bugged Out!, Layo & Bushwacka,

owner Mr C's minimal tech house session Superfreq, Darren Emerson's Underwater… All attract an international and super-friendly crowd. **Photo** *p326*.

Fabric

77A Charterhouse Street, Clerkenwell, EC1M 3HN (7336 8898/advance tickets for Fri & Sat 0870 902 0001/www.fabriclondon.com). Farringdon tube/rail. **Open** 9.30pm-5am Fri; 10pm-7am Sat. **Admission** £12-£15. **Map** p404 O5.

Seven years old and still going strong, Fabric is the club that most party people come to see in London. Fridays belong to the bass: guaranteed highlights include DJ Hype when he takes over all three rooms once a month for his drum'n'bass True Playaz, and the Plump DJs' Eargasm party is a sure-fire sell-out every other month. Saturdays descend into techy, minimal, deep house territory.

The Fridge

1 Town Hall Parade, Brixton, SW2 1RJ (7326 5100/ www.fridgerocks.com). Brixton tube/rail. **Open** 8.30pm-4am Mon-Thur, Sun; 8.30pm-5am Fri, Sat. **Admission** £8-£20.

The legendary Fridge hasn't had a great time of it lately, with its doors shut more times than we can remember. Licensing problems and a singling out of the club for drugs offences (expect serious and multiple bodysearches at the door) have been the cause of the problems. As we go to press, there's a question mark hanging over the future of the club following a fatal shooting. Here's hoping that if all the hard-dance peeps who worship at the altar of the Fridge pray hard enough the venue will pull through.

Herbal

10-14 Kingsland Road, Hoxton, E2 8DA (7613 4462/www.herbaluk.com). Old Street tube/rail. **Open** 8pm-2am Tue; 9pm-2am Tue-Thur, Sun; 9pm-3am Fri, Sat. **Admission** free-£10. **Map** p405 R3.

A genuine pose-free zone in the middle of Hoxton, two-floored Herbal is all about the music. Grooverider's Grace is *the* weekly drum 'n' bass party in town, causing roadblocks on Sunday nights. Soul II Soul's Jazzi B hosts a monthly party too.

Jamm

261 Brixton Road, Brixton, SW9 6LH (7274 5537/ www.brixtonjamm.org). Brixton tube/rail. **Open** 5pm-2am Mon-Thur; 5pm-6am Fri; 2pm-6am Sat; 2pm-2am Sun. **Admission** £5-£10.

This busy road isn't the classiest location for a club, but then this place is more about slamming parties than swanky soirées. Spoken word and open mic nights like Speakerscorner get slotted next to whopping house parties like Throb.

The Key

King's Cross Freight Depot, King's Cross, N1 0UZ (7837 1027/www.thekeylondon.com). King's Cross tube/rail. **Open** 11pm-5am Fri; 10pm-6am Sat. **Admission** £7-£15. **Map** p401 L2.

The flashing disco dancefloor of this intimate space is typically filled with cracking house, electro and minimal parties, such as DDD, Chicken Nickers and the after-hours, never-say-die Formulate. The newly opened chandelier room upstairs has trebled the club's capacity. It's down a cobbled alley, so watch your step if it's been raining. **Photo** *p327*.

Frocking up

Not too long ago, donning an old trilby and stepping out in a sharp 1950s suit or stringing pearls around your neck and layering on the red lipstick was strictly fancy-dress fare, but now Soho clubs, indie dancefloors and Whitechapel warehouse raves are full of girls in sweet tea dresses and guys in brogues. Wearing battered Converse and a record label T-shirt – clubland's late 1990s uniform – seems positively retro.

Fashion has embraced retro glamour with both arms. The cabaret and burlesque scenes, bubbling underground for years now, have burst into the mainstream with itinerant club nights like **Whoopee** (www.thewhoopeeclub.com), the **Flash Monkey** (www.theflashmonkey.biz) and **Lost Vagueness** (www.lostvagueness.com) selling out London spaces throughout the year. Clubs like **Lady Luck** (monthly Thursdays at Soho Revue Bar, *see p326*), the **Rakehell's Revels** (every Tuesday at a 'secret' West End location – easily discovered by a quick online search) and **Virginia Creepers Club** (www.virginiacreepersclub.co.uk), all of which have been running largely unnoticed for years, are suddenly some of the coolest nights in town.

Best club of 2006 has to be the **Bethnal Green Working Men's Club** (*see p321*), a tatty East End venue very much in danger of closing due to crippling debts until it was given a new lease of life when a local promoter started booking retro lounge and kooky nights. Girls on rollerskates serving Earl Grey tea or students dressing the tired 1970s room as a circus tent have made it the only place to be. Other clubs are opening on the back of its success, notably **Volupte** (*see p326*) in the otherwise club-free zone of Chancery Lane. The ripple effect has also seen a boom in dance classes (lindy hop and swing lessons are full to bursting throughout the week) and the emptying of London's second-hand clothes stores.

Canvas – doesn't look like a roller disco does it? *See p321.*

KoKo

1A Camden High Street, Camden, NW1 7JE (0870 432 5527/www.koko.uk.com). Camden Town or Mornington Crescent tube. **Open** 10pm-3am Fri; call for opening hours for the rest of the week. **Admission** £7; £5 before 11.30pm.

After struggling to find its niche, the former Camden Palace has become a fixture for indie fans thanks to Club NME and live bands most nights of the week. It's also a regular haunt for those seeking a serious dose of retro cheese courtesy of Sean Rowley's immensely popular Guilty Pleasures.

Madame Jo Jo's

8 Brewer Street, Soho, W1F 0SE (7734 3040/ www.madamejojos.com). Leicester Square or Piccadilly Circus tube. **Open** 10pm-3am Tue-Sat. **Admission** £5-£8. **Map** p408 W3.

Calling itself the heart of Soho's darkness, Jo Jo's is a beacon for those seeking to escape the All Bar Ones and post-work drinkers. The indie kids glam up and pose at White Heat every Tuesday or apply the heavy eyeliner and glitter shapes for Glitz on Thursday. Electrogogo and Keb Darge's legendary soul and funkfest take care of Friday.

Ministry of Sound

103 Gaunt Street, off Newington Causeway, Newington, SE1 6DP (0870 060 0010/www.ministry ofsound.com). Elephant & Castle tube/rail. **Open** 10pm-3am Wed (term-time only); 10.30pm-5am Fri; 11pm-7am Sat. **Admission** £12-£17. **Map** p406 O10.

Cool it ain't, home to a killer sound system it most certainly is. DJs tell us that they play the Ministry to hear what records should really sound like. Also, being the Microsoft of the club world, this is pretty much the only outfit that can afford the likes of Masters At Work or Danny Tenaglia.

Neighbourhood

12 Acklam Road, Ladbroke Grove, W10 5QZ (8960 9331/www.neighbourhoodclub.net). Ladbroke Grove or Westbourne Park tube. **Open** 8pm-2am Wed-Sun; call for weeknight events. **Admission** free-£15.

Neighbourhood used to be the sterling Subterrania, and the inside has changed surprisingly little since. The varied repertoire includes live music, one-off week-night events and house music on weekends.

93 Feet East

150 Brick Lane, Spitalfields, E1 6QL (7247 3293/ www.93feeteast.co.uk). Shoreditch or Aldgate East tube or Liverpool Street tube/rail. **Open** 5-11pm Mon-Thur; 5pm-1am Fri; noon-1am Sat; noon-10.30pm Sun. **Admission** free-£5. **Map** p405 S5.

With three rooms, a balcony and a giant, wrap-around courtyard that's just made for summer barbecues, 93 Feet East manages to overcome the otherwise crippling lack of a late licence. There are plenty of good nights: It's Bigger Than is just like a student house party only without the puking on the carpets and we love the winter season of Rock 'n' Roll Cinema with local ska and rockabilly bands.

Notting Hill Arts Club

21 Notting Hill Gate, Notting Hill, W11 3JQ (7460 4459/www.nottinghillartsclub.com). Notting Hill Gate tube. **Open** 6pm-1am Mon-Wed; 6pm-2am Thur, Fri; 4pm-2am Sat; 4pm-1am Sun. **Admission** £5-£8; free before 8pm. **Map** p396 A7.

This small basement club almost single-handedly keeps west London on the cool clubbing radar with nights such as YoYo, the weekly Thursday soul- and funkfest that kept booking Lily Allen in 2006 resulting in queues practically across town, and Radio Gagarin, doing for Balkan music what Pete Doherty did for the Priory.

Pacha London

Terminus Place, Victoria, SW1V 1JR (7833 3139/www.pachalondon.com). Victoria tube/rail. **Open** 10pm-6am Fri, Sat. **Admission** £15-£20. **Map** p402 H10.

This lavish outpost of the global club giant that has dominated Ibiza for years was truly made for lording it. A heady mix of chandeliers, oak panels and a stained-glass ceiling guarantees a chic clubbing experience and almost enables you to forget that the place is located in a bus depot.

Plan B

418 Brixton Road, Brixton, SW9 7AY (7733 0926/ www.plan-brixton.co.uk). Brixton tube/rail. **Open** 5pm-6am Fri, Sat; 7pm-4am Thur, Sun; call venue for Mon-Wed. **Admission** prices vary, call for details.

It may be small, but Plan B punches well above its weight thanks to a constant flow of hip hop and funk stars at Fidgit on Fridays and plenty of soulful house fare on Saturdays, with Norman Jay a regular behind the decks.

Plastic People

147-149 Curtain Road, Shoreditch, EC2A 3QE (7739 6471/www.plasticpeople.co.uk). Old Street tube/rail. **Open** 10pm-2am Mon-Thur; 10pm-3.30am Fri, Sat; 7.30pm-midnight Sun. **Admission** £3-£8. **Map** p405 R4.

Plastic People subscribes to the old-school line that says all you need for a kicking party is a dark basement and a sound system. But what it lacks in size and decor it makes up for in sound quality (the rig embarrasses those in many larger clubs) and some of London's most progressive club nights. Sounds range from Afro-jazz and hip hop to Latin at Balance, and dubstep and grime at regular forward-thinking urban night FWD.

The Telegraph

228 Brixton Hill, Brixton, SW2 1HE (8678 0777). Brixton tube/rail. **Open** noon-2.30am Mon-Thur; noon-4am Fri; noon-6am Sat; noon-12.30am Sun. **Admission** £5-£10.

A one-time haunt of the Clash (Strummer's 101ers played their first gig here), the Telegraph gained city-wide fame a few years ago thanks to the infamous Basement Jaxx Rooty parties. It's never looked back. The enormous room at the rear gets filled with reggae fans every Thursday, and hedonistic party people at weekends.

333

333 Old Street, Hoxton, EC1V 9LE (7739 5949/ www.333mother.com/www.myspace.com/333mother). Old Street tube/rail. **Open** *Bar* 8pm-3am Mon-Wed; 8pm-4am Thur; 8pm-4am Fri-Sun. *Club* 10pm-5am Fri, Sat; 10pm-4am Sun. **Admission** *Club* £5-£10. **Map** p405 Q4.

This pivotal East End venue houses a no-frills three floors of indie mash-up rave sounds (Troubled Minds is particularly popular), while Friday and Saturdays mix jungle with electro and live guitars with early 1990s acid house. The Mother bar up top also hosts its own nights.

The Cross. *See p321.*

This is the **End**. *See p321.*

Soho Revue Bar

11-12 Walker's Court, off Brewer Street, Soho, W1F 0ED (7734 0377). Leicester Square or Piccadilly Circus tube. **Open** 5pm-4am Tue-Sat. *Performances* 7pm. **Admission** £10; £5 concs. **Credit** AmEx, MC, V. **Map** p408 W3.

Soho's grooviest club (which isn't saying much). Formerly Too2Much, it has two grand rooms that host the popular, monthly retro-rock rolling grind-fest Lady Luck, plus there's cabaret most Sundays in a supper-club style. *See also p323* **Frocking up**.

Turnmills

63B Clerkenwell Road, Clerkenwell, EC1M 5PT (7250 3409/www.turnmills.com). Farringdon tube/rail. **Open** 9pm-2am Thur; 10.30pm-7.30am Fri; 10pm-6am Sat; 9pm-3am Sun. **Admission** £8-£15. **Map** p404 N4.

A legend in its own lifetime, Turnmills is a true hedonists' playground. The Gallery draws the hard dance and trance kids every Friday, thanks to the likes of Paul Van Dyk and Armin van Buuren, while Saturdays bill more credible fare, including the bi-monthly, festival-inspired Together, the super-friendly Smartie Partie and superstar DJs like Roger Sanchez and Bob Sinclar.

Volupte

9 Norwich Street, Holborn, EC4A 1EJ (7831 1622/ www.volupte-lounge.com). Chancery Lane tube. **Open** noon-late Tues-Sat. **Admission** £8-£12. **Credit** MC, V. **Map** p406 N5.

Expect to suffer extreme wallpaper envy as you enter the ground-floor bar then descend to the club proper. Here tables are set beneath absinthe-inspired vines, surrounded by lush curtains and plenty of red, from where punters enjoy some of the best cabaret talent in town. Wednesday nights are Cabaret Salon and once a month the Black Cotton Club turns back the clock to the 1920s.

DJ bars

The line between DJ bar (pubs with decks and late licences) and club has become so blurred that *Time Out* magazine's Nightlife section dropped the distinction altogether in 2006. When the T Bar gets Ivan Smagghe and Andy Weatherall down for free parties does that make it a DJ bar or a club? As a rule of thumb, DJ bars are usually small, free to get in, serve drinks at lower prices than clubs and close earlier.

AKA

18 West Central Street, Holborn, WC1A 1JJ (7836 0110/www.akalondon.com). Holborn or Tottenham Court Road tube. **Open** 10pm-3am Tue; 6pm-3am Thur; 6pm-4am Fri; 7pm-5am Sat; 10pm-4am Sun. **Admission** £5 after 11pm Tue, Thur; £7 after 11pm Fri; £10 after 9pm Sat. **Credit** AmEx, MC, V. **Map** p409 Y1.

Joined – physically as well as musically – to the End (*see p321*) next door, this popular pre-club hangout attracts top international DJs to entertain punters who have been loosened up by good food and cocktails. The venue is incorporated into the End's club nights on Saturdays; be prepared to queue.

Barfly

49 Chalk Farm Road, Camden, NW1 8AN (7691 4244/www.barflyclub.com). Chalk Farm tube. **Open** 7pm-1am Mon-Thur; 7pm-3am Fri, Sat; midday-11pm Sun. **Admission** £6-£15. **Credit** MC, V.

Barfly is a big part of the reason why indie guitar-meets-electro parties are doing so well at the moment. Kill Em All, Let God Sort It Out held every couple of weeks on a Saturday features bands guaranteed to get the crowd going; Adventures Close to Home packs out the dancefloor once a month.

Big Chill Bar

Dray Walk, Brick Lane, E1 6QL (7392 9180/ www.bigchill.net). Aldgate East tube or Liverpool Street tube/rail. **Open** noon-midnight Mon-Thurs; noon-1am Fri, Sat; noon-11.30pm Sun. **Admission** £5 after 11pm. **Credit** MC, V. **Map** p405 S5.

A big box of a bar with a helpfully long bartop running down the left-hand side, and plenty of comfy sofas, this is the place to head when the famous Big Chill festival seems just too far away. It attracts top DJs and the atmosphere is as kicking as the tunes.

Big Chill House

257-259 Pentonville Road, King's Cross, N1 9NL (7427 2540/www.bigchill.net). Kings Cross tube/rail. **Open** 11am-midnight Mon-Wed; 11-1am Thurs; 11am-4am Fri; noon-4am Sat; noon-midnight Sun. **Admission** £5 after 11pm. **Credit** MC, V.

A festival, a record label, a bar and now also a house, the Big Chill empire rolls on. And a good thing that is too, if it keeps offering such interesting things as this three-floor space. It boasts an enormous sun-catching terrace – perfect for the Sunday papers and brunch – while the likes of Sean Rowley and owner Pete Lawrence regularly handle deck duties.

Cherry Jam

58 Porchester Road, Bayswater, W2 6ET (7727 9950/www.cherryjam.net). Royal Oak tube. **Open** 7pm-1.30am Wed-Sat; phone to check times Sun. **Admission** £5-£8 after 10pm, depending on night; phone for details. **Credit** MC, V. **Map** p396 C5.

Combines an elevated area for sitting and supping cocktails (or nursing a beer), and a proper dancefloor – which sadly doesn't get as much use as it did when Cherry Jam was more clubby. Best bet? The monthly Book Slam, a blistering spoken word soirée.

Dogstar

389 Coldharbour Lane, Brixton, SW9 8LQ (7733 7515/www.thedogstar.com). Brixton tube/rail. **Open** 4pm-2am Mon-Thur; noon-4am Fri, Sat; noon-2am Sun. **Admission** £3 after 10pm Fri, Sat; £5 after 11pm Fri, Sat. **Credit** MC, V.

A Brixton institution, Dogstar is a big street-corner pub that exudes the urban authenticity loved by clubbers. The atmosphere can be intense, but it's never less than vibrant. The music varies from night to night but the quality stays high. It's something of a training ground for the DJ stars of tomorrow.

Lock Tavern

35 Chalk Farm Road, Chalk Farm, NW1 8AJ (7482 7163). Chalk Farm tube. **Open** noon-11pm Mon-Sat; noon-10.30pm Sun. **Admission** free.

Excellent bar-pub (*see p233*) with DJs most nights of the week, although Sundays are the musical staples, with off-duty DJs stumbling through the doors and splashing their pints over the turntables.

The Key. *See p323.*

The Macbeth

70 Hoxton Street, N1 6LP (7739 5095). Old Street tube/rail. **Open** 11am-11pm Mon-Sat; noon-10.30pm Sun. **Admission** Varies. **Credit** MC, V. **Map** p405 R3.

Sean McClusky runs his Secret Door indie party here every Friday, and it's now a firm favourite for kids in super-skinny jeans and Corey Haim highlights. Essentially, it's still a tattered old boozer with really cheap drinks and the odd bemused old-timer at the end of the bar.

Salmon & Compass

58 Penton Street, Islington, N1 9PZ (7837 3891/ www.salmonandcompass.com). Angel tube. **Open** 5pm-1am Mon-Thur; 5pm-4am Fri, Sat; 5pm-midnight Sun. **Admission** free; £3 after 9pm Fri; £5 after 9pm Sat. **Credit** MC, V. **Map** p404 N2.

Islington's no-nonsense DJ bar still packs in an up-for-it crowd on weekends with a rotating series of theme nights. Early in the week, it's chilled.

The Social

5 Little Portland Street, Marylebone, W1W 7JD (7636 4992/www.thesocial.com). Oxford Circus tube. **Open** noon-midnight Mon-Fri; 1pm-midnight Sat. **Admission** free; £3 acoustic nights. **Credit** AmEx, MC, V. **Map** p408 U1.

The same (and as great) as it ever was, despite these days being surrounded by flashier venues – note the opulent Annex 3 bar-restaurant next door. An unnoticeable, opaque front still hides this daytime diner and DJ bar of supreme quality, established by Heavenly Records in 1999. It remains popular with music industry workers, minor alt-rock celebs and other sassy trendies who, after drinks upstairs descend to an intimate basement space rocked by DJs six nights a week. Monthly Hip Hop Karaoke (www.hiphopkaraokelondon.com) is a giggle.

T Bar

Tea Building, 56 Shoreditch High Street, Shoreditch, E1 6JJ (7729 2973/www.tbarlondon.com). Liverpool Street tube/rail. **Open** times vary, call for details. **Admission** free. **Credit** MC, V. **Map** p405 R4.

Straddling the DJ bar/club divide, the T's upped the ante in London by offering stellar DJs for no money whatsoever. Damian Lazarus hosts his filthy electro party Stink here, while the hilarious Gay Bingo takes over the bunker warehouse space one Sunday a month.

Vibe Bar

Old Truman Brewery, 91-95 Brick Lane, Shoreditch, E1 6QL (7426 0491/www.vibe-bar.co.uk). Aldgate East tube or Liverpool Street tube/rail. **Open** 11am-11.30pm Mon-Thur, Sun; 11am-1am Fri, Sat. **Admission** £3.50 after 8pm Fri, Sat. **Credit** AmEx, MC, V. **Map** p405 S5.

Rotating DJs and a full book of live acts play diverse styles (reggae to hip hop, proper songs to experimental leftfield). In the summer folk hang in the fairy-lit courtyard, a convenient stumble across the road from 93 Feet East (*see p324*).

AKA. *See p327.*

Sport & Fitness

Fork out for football or rake it in at the dogs – and lots more besides.

Arsenal's new **Emirates Stadium**. *See p330.*

Check the Sport section of the weekly *Time Out* magazine for a comprehensive guide to the main action during your visit. For a more in-depth approach to keeping fit in the capital, pick up the *Time Out Health & Fitness Guide* (£4.99). For information on the new facilities being built for the Olympics (www.london2012.org), *see p171*. For seasonal sporting events such as the London Marathon, *see pp266-273*.

Major stadiums

Crystal Palace National Sports Centre

Ledrington Road, Crystal Palace, SE19 2BB (8778 0131/www.gll.org). Crystal Palace rail.

This Grade II-listed building has been in need of repair for some time now, though in 2006 the site was given a new lease of life after a period of uncertainty when the Mayor of London and the London Development Agency took it over. That means the popular summer Grand Prix athletics events will continue here for now, although the 2012 Olympic stadium being built in Stratford will supersede Crystal Palace as the main home of British Athletics.

Wembley Stadium/Wembley Arena & Conference Centre

Stadium Way, Wembley, Middx HA9 0DW (www.wembleystadium.com). Wembley Park tube/Wembley Stadium rail.

The rebuilding of Wembley Stadium – long one of Britain's iconic sporting landmarks, host to the national football team, cup, play-off and rugby league finals, as well as countless huge pop concerts – has been an interminable, at times impenetrable, saga over recent years. The old stadium, with its famous twin towers, staged its last major football match in October 2000, when England lost to Germany. Since then the extensive rebuilding process has been plagued by contractors' disputes, legal wrangles, political infighting and delay after delay. Due to reopen in 2003, the stadium still isn't quite finished at the time of writing, though it should be completed in 2007. The new 90,000-seat venue, designed by Lord Norman Foster, will certainly be impressive – the huge steel arch that loops over the stadium is already an established feature of the local landscape. But boy has it been a long wait.

Snooker and basketball tournaments, international boxing and showjumping events, as well as pop concerts, take place infrequently at the adjacent, refurbished Wembley Arena (8902 8833, box office 0800 600 0870, www.whatsonwembley.com).

Spectator sports

Basketball

London United are the capital's sole representatives in the ten-strong British Basketball League. For more information, including a list of indoor and outdoor courts, contact the **English Basketball Association** (0870 7744 225, www.englandbasketball.co.uk).

London United

Hackney Space Sports Centre, Falkirk Street, N1 6HF (7613 9525/www.london-united.co.uk). **Admission** £8; £4 concs.

Cricket

Test cricket, that most glorious of games, can still result in a draw after five day's play, so Tests are not for those with busy schedules. If you're pushed for time, catch a one-day match in the C&G Trophy or Pro40 League or, shorter still, the increasingly popular Twenty20 matches (20 overs per side, played in the evening). **Lord's** (home to Middlesex) and the **Brit Oval** (Surrey's home ground) also host Test matches and one-day internationals. Interest in the game has revived in recent years, most notably in 2005 when England's thrilling Test series victory over the mighty Australians sparked widespread euphoria. The season runs from April to September. On the best approach to getting tickets, *see p332* **Getting a ticket**.

Brit Oval

Kennington Oval, Kennington, SE11 5SS (7582 6660/7764/www.surreycricket.com). Oval tube. **Tickets** *County* £10-£20. *Test* £40-£65.

Lord's

St John's Wood Road, St John's Wood, NW8 8QN (MCC 7289 1611/tickets 7432 1000/www.lords.org). St John's Wood tube. **Tickets** *County* £12-£15. *Test* £40-£65.

Cycling

The sport does not have the public profile it has in many other European countries, but 2007 is set to be a big year, with London chosen to host the opening stage of the **Tour de France**. In September, the capital also hosts the closing stages of the annual **Tour of Britain**. Since being granted world championship ranking status in 2004, the Tour of Britain has drawn up to 100,000 people to the capital's streets to watch the sprint finishes.

Football

Arsenal and Chelsea have taken over from Manchester United as the standard-setters in the Premiership over the last few seasons. **Chelsea** secured their first league title for 50 years in 2005 and retained it with ease the following year. They owe their success in considerable part to the largesse of Russian oil tycoon Roman Abramovich, who has lavished millions on the club, and their astute and charismatic Portuguese manager, Jose Mourinho. **Arsenal**, though they lack the vast resources of their west London rivals, have won the Premiership three times (going unbeaten through the 2003/2004 season, something no club had done since Preston won the league without a single defeat in 1888/89) and the FA Cup twice during French manager Arsène Wenger's reign, as well as reaching a Champions League final. As a consequence of their success they moved to a sparkling 60,000-capacity new ground at Ashburton Grove in 2006 (**photo**, *see p329*).

Chelsea aren't the only London club to have received the attentions of foreign tycoons – overseas investors led by Iranian businessman Kia Joorabchian engineered the arrival of Argentinian superstars Carlos Tevez and Javier Mascherano at **West Ham United** in September 2006, which may or may not lead to a fully fledged takeover. The capital's other top-flight clubs – **Tottenham** (Arsenal's near neighbours and traditional rivals), **Charlton** and **Fulham** (Chelsea's key rivals) – can only look on enviously as the gap between the game's mega-wealthy elite and the rest widens.

Tickets for league games in the Barclays Premiership are extremely difficult to get your hands on, especially for Chelsea and Arsenal; for a how-to guide, *see p332* **Getting a ticket**. For London clubs in the Coca-Cola Championship and both divisions of the Coca-Cola Football League tickets are cheaper and easier to obtain. For information, try www.thefa.com. Prices quoted are for adult non-members.

Arsenal

Emirates Stadium, Ashburton Grove, N7 7AF (7704 4040/www.arsenal.com). Arsenal tube. **Tickets** £13-£94.

Barnet

Underhill Stadium, Barnet Lane, Barnet, EN5 2DN (8441 6932/www.barnetfc.com). High Barnet tube. **Tickets** *Standing* £13-£15. *Seated* £16-£20.

Brentford

Griffin Park, Braemar Road, Brentford, Middx TW8 0NT (0845 345 6442/www.brentfordfc.co.uk). South Ealing tube/Brentford rail. **Tickets** *Standing* £15; £5-£8 concs. *Seated* £19-£20; £14-£20 concs.

Charlton Athletic

The Valley, Floyd Road, Charlton, SE7 8BL (0871 226 1905/www.cafc.co.uk). Charlton rail. **Tickets** £25-£45.

Chelsea

Stamford Bridge, Fulham Road, Chelsea, SW6 1HS (0870 300 1212/www.chelseafc.co.uk). Fulham Broadway tube. **Tickets** £35-£55.50. **Map** p398 B13.

Crystal Palace

Selhurst Park, Whitehorse Lane, Selhurst, SE25 6PU (0871 200 0071/www.cpfc.co.uk). Selhurst rail/468 bus. **Tickets** £37-£50.

Fulham

Craven Cottage, Stevenage Road, Fulham, SW6 6HH (0870 442 1234/www.fulhamfc.com). Putney Bridge tube. **Tickets** £25-£55.

Leyton Orient

Matchroom Stadium, Brisbane Road, Leyton, E10 5NF (8926 1111/tickets 0870 310 1883/www.leyton orient.com). Leyton tube/Leyton Midland Road rail. **Tickets** £18-£35.

Millwall

The Den, Zampa Road, Bermondsey, SE16 3LN (7232 1222/tickets 7231 9999/www.millwallfc.co.uk). South Bermondsey rail. **Tickets** £19-£26.

Queens Park Rangers

Loftus Road Stadium, South Africa Road, Shepherd's Bush, W12 7PA (0870 112 1967/ www.qpr.co.uk). White City tube. **Tickets** £22-£30.

Tottenham Hotspur

White Hart Lane Stadium, 748 High Road, Tottenham, N17 0AP (0870 420 5000/www. tottenhamhotspur.com). White Hart Lane rail. **Tickets** £39-£71.

West Ham United

Upton Park, Green Street, West Ham, E13 9AZ (0870 112 2700/www.whufc.com). Upton Park tube. **Tickets** £23-£57.

Greyhound racing

For a cheap night out that could end up paying for itself (and more), head to one of the capital's four greyhound tracks. For an admission fee that's never more than £6, you can enjoy the art deco glories of **Walthamstow** (Chingford Road, 8531 4255, www.wsgreyhound.co.uk), the decent restaurants at **Wimbledon** (Plough Lane, 8946 8000, www.lovethedogs.co.uk), the chirpy charms of **Romford** (London Road, 01708 762345, www.trap6.com/romford) or the relaxed atmosphere at **Crayford** (Stadium Way, 01322 557836, www.trap6.com). Small stakes (coins rather than ten pound notes) are accepted at most venues and a single judicious punt could keep you in drinks all evening. For more information visit www.thedogs.co.uk.

Horse racing

The racing year is divided into the flat racing season, which runs from April to September, and the National Hunt season (races over jumps), from October to April. For more information about the 'sport of kings', visit www.discover-racing.com.

The Home Counties (those immediately surrounding London) are sprinkled with a fine variety of courses, which make for fine and unusual days out from the city.

Epsom

Epsom Downs, Epsom, Surrey KT18 5LQ (01372 726311/www.epsomderby.co.uk). Epsom Downs or Tattenham Corner rail. **Open** *Box office* 9am-5pm Mon-Fri. **Admission** £5-£35.

The Derby, held here each June, is one of the great events in Britain's social and sporting calendar, attracting around 15,000 spectators every year. The impressive Queen's Stand and grandstand both offer fine viewing and restaurants.

Kempton Park

Staines Road East, Sunbury-on-Thames, Middx TW16 5AQ (01932 782292/www.kempton.co.uk). Kempton Park rail (race days only). **Open** *Box office* 9am-5pm Mon-Fri. **Admission** £11-£20.

The Londoner's local haunt, this course is far from glamorous but the year-round meetings are well attended, especially in summer.

Royal Ascot

Ascot Racecourse, Ascot, Berks SL5 7JX (01344 622211/www.ascot.co.uk). Ascot rail. **Open/admission** phone for details.

The famous Royal Meeting takes place in 2007 on 19-23 June. Get your top hats, posh frocks and credit cards ready for this society bash masquerading as a sporting event. Tickets to the public enclosure are usually available on the day, but it's always wiser to book in advance.

Sandown Park

Portsmouth Road, Esher, Surrey KT10 9AJ (01372 463072/www.sandown.co.uk). Esher rail. **Open** *Box office* 9am-5pm Mon-Fri. **Admission** £15-£26. Phone for details on Gold Cup and Coral Eclipse.

Most famous for hosting the Whitbread Gold Cup in April and the Coral Eclipse Stakes in July. Sandown pushes horses to the limit with a hill finish.

Windsor

Maidenhead Road, Windsor, Berks SL4 5JJ (01753 498400/tickets 0870 220 0024/www.windsor-race course.co.uk). Windsor & Eton Riverside rail. **Open** *Box office* 9.30am-5.30pm Mon-Fri. **Admission** £6-£20.

A pleasant Thameside location in the shadow of Windsor Castle helps to make this a lovely spot for first-timers and families, especially for the three-day May festival or a summer evening Monday meeting.

Getting a ticket

As top-level sport morphed into bigger business (in some instances showbusiness), the once-simple act of getting in to watch the action became a lot more complicated – and costly. A couple of decades back it was relatively easy to merely turn up on the day for a big football match or cricket test and, provided you didn't mind queuing and the risk of a cramped view, you'd more than likely get in. Sadly, it's not that simple any more.

Football's elite clubs know that demand will always outstrip supply, and ticketing arrangements and admission prices reflect that. But a trip to a big match is highly recommended and, with a little patience and luck, it can be done.

The majority of the seats at most Premiership grounds are allocated to season-ticket holders (clubs such as Chelsea, Arsenal and Tottenham have lengthy waiting lists even of aspiring season-ticket holders). However, all clubs sell a proportion of their tickets on a match-by-match basis: club members tend to get priority on these, alongside season-ticket holders offered the chance to buy additional seats. Then, after these needs have been met, clubs sell any remaining tickets to the general public, usually around a fortnight before the match in question. They often sell out (even at mid-ranking – and smaller-capacity – clubs such as Charlton), but there is a decent chance that, if you get your application in quick enough, you'll get a ticket. Keep an eye on club websites for details; the Chelsea website runs a ticket-exchange scheme under which people with individual tickets to sell or buy can advertise them through the club.

Some clubs also use the agency Ticketmaster (*see p337*) to sell tickets to matches, and the company would certainly be one useful port of call for fans looking to snap up tickets on spec, although booking fees apply. Other ticket agencies, of which there are many in London, also often offer match tickets for sale, though prices charged can be exorbitant.

Visitors will find it much easier to get in to see London's smaller clubs, in the Football League Championship, League One and League Two, though it is also worth checking prices and availability in advance here too, as some clubs have small grounds that are easily filled.

Big match tickets are also difficult to come by in the other major spectator sports – rugby union, cricket and tennis. Six Nations **rugby union** internationals at Twickenham sell out very quickly – the major autumn Tests against the likes of New Zealand and Australia are hardly less popular – but renovations to the south stand at Twickenham (currently under way) will increase capacity to 82,000, making the ticket hunt marginally less difficult.

The capital's **cricket** venues, Lord's and the Oval, have in recent years sold out the first four days of almost every Test match – mostly months in advance – leaving only fifth-day tickets available on the day. However, the Oval in 2006 sold tickets in advance even for the final day of England versus Pakistan, tickets that proved to be no use as the game was abandoned on the fourth day after a row erupted when the Pakistan team were accused of cheating by umpire Darrell Hair.

It is still possible to gain admission on the day to the **Wimbledon Tennis Championships**, via the traditional method of queuing from the early hours of the morning (or even the previous night). The All England Club makes 6,000 ground admission tickets available each day to punters paying at the gate, although these tickets do not secure entry to the showpiece Centre Court (*see below*) or Courts One and Two. For seats at these courts, you'll need to enter your name in the public ballot for tickets (www.wimbledon.org).

Motorsport

Wimbledon Stadium (8946 8000, www.wimbledonstadium.co.uk) is the place to come for pedal-to-the-metal entertainment: speedway motorbike racing takes place on Wednesdays; every other Sunday bangers, hot rods and stock cars come together for family-oriented mayhem. **Rye House Stadium** (01992 440400, www.ryehouse.com) in Hoddesdon, on the northern edge of London near the M25, also hosts speedway as home to the Rye House Rockets. Matches are usually on Saturday evenings.

Rugby league

The heartland of rugby league remains the north of England, but the capital's one Super League club, **Harlequins RL**, have remained at the highest level of the game despite leading a somewhat nomadic existence that has seen changes of home ground and of name.

Harlequins Rugby League

Stoop Memorial Ground, Langhorn Drive, Twickenham (0871 871 8877/www.quins.co.uk). Twickenham rail. **Admission** £15-£30.

Rugby union

Fans come out in force to watch the annual **Six Nations Championship** (Jan-Mar). Tickets for these games – which take place at **Twickenham** (Rugby Road, Twickenham, Middx, 8892 2000), the home of English Rugby Union – are virtually impossible to get hold of, but other matches are more accessible (*see p332* **Getting in**). The Guinness Premiership, in which London and its immediate environs are well represented, and the three-division National League run from early September to May; most games are played on Saturday and Sunday afternoons.

Here we list only Premiership clubs; contact the **Rugby Football Union** (8892 2000, www.rfu.com) for other divisions.

Harlequins

Stoop Memorial Ground, Langhorn Drive, Twickenham, Middx TW2 7SX (0871 871 8877/www.quins.co.uk). Twickenham rail. **Admission** £15-£18; £12-£15 in advance.

London Irish

Madejski Stadium, Shooters Way, Reading, RG2 0SL (0870 999 1871/www.london-irish.com). Reading rail then shuttle bus to ground (£2). **Tickets** £8-£32.

London Wasps

Causeway Stadium, Hillbottom Road, High Wycombe, HP12 4HJ (8993 8298/tickets 0870 414 1515/www.wasps.co.uk). High Wycombe rail. **Tickets** £12-£44.

Saracens

Vicarage Road Stadium, Watford, Herts WD18 0EP (01923 475222/www.saracens.com). Watford High Street rail. **Open** *Box office* 9am-5.30pm Mon-Fri. **Tickets** £6-£35.

Tennis

Getting to see the action at the Wimbledon Championships at the **All England Lawn Tennis Club** (25 June-8 July 2007) requires forethought (*see p332* **Getting a ticket**). Or try the Stella Artois tournament at the **Queen's Club**, where stars from the men's circuit warm up for the main event (11-17 June 2007).

All England Lawn Tennis Club

PO Box 98, Church Road, Wimbledon, SW19 5AE (8944 1066/tickets 8971 2700/information 8946 2244/www.wimbledon.org). Southfields tube.

Queen's Club

Palliser Road, West Kensington, W14 9EQ (7385 3421/ticket information 0870 890 0518/www.queensclub.co.uk). Barons Court tube.

Participation sports & fitness

Cycling

Speed merchants can pedal round the **Herne Hill Velodrome** (Burbage Road, Herne Hill, SE24 9HE, 7737 4647, www.hernehillvelodrome.org.uk), the oldest cycle circuit in the world. The **Lee Valley Cycle Circuit** (Quartermile Lane, Stratford, 8534 6085, www.leevalleypark.org.uk) was due to close temporarily at the end of 2006 while a new Olympic velodrome, BMX track and fencing hall are built. Those wanting to hire a bike and zip around town, *see p365*.

Golf

You don't have to be a member to tee off at any of these public courses – but book in advance. For more clubs, see www.englishgolfunion.org.

Dulwich & Sydenham Hill

Grange Lane, College Road, Dulwich, SE21 7LH (8693 8491/www.dulwichgolf.co.uk). Sydenham Hill rail. **Open** 8am-dusk daily. *Green fee* £30; £20 members' guests Mon-Fri.

A fine course. Members and guests only at weekends.

North Middlesex

Manor House, Friern Barnet Lane, Arnos Grove, N20 0NL (8445 3060/www.northmiddlesexgc.co.uk). Arnos Grove or Totteridge & Whetstone tube. **Open** 8am-dusk Mon-Fri; 1pm-dusk Sat, Sun. *Green fee* £15-£29 Mon-Fri; £25-£32 Sat, Sun.

An undulating course that's not for beginners.

Health clubs & sports centres

Many clubs and centres admit non-members and allow them to join classes. You can get a list of venues in Camden by calling 7974 4456; in Westminster on 7641 1846. Last entry is normally 45-60 minutes before the closing time. **Hyde Park**, **Kensington Gardens** and **Battersea Park** all have terrific jogging trails.

Central YMCA

112 Great Russell Street, Bloomsbury, WC1B 3NQ (7343 1700/www.centralymca.org.uk). Tottenham Court Road tube. **Open** 6.30am-10.30pm Mon-Fri; 10am-8.30pm Sat; 10am-7.30pm Sun. **Map** p401 K5.

Conveniently located and user-friendly, the Y has a good range of cardiovascular and weight-training equipment, a pool and a squash court, as well as a full timetable of excellent classes.

Jubilee Hall Leisure Centre

30 The Piazza, Covent Garden, WC2E 8BE (7836 4835/www.jubileehallclubs.co.uk). Covent Garden tube. **Open** 7am-10pm Mon-Fri; 9am-9pm Sat; 10am-5pm Sun. **Map** p409 Z3.

Cardiovascular workouts in calm surroundings.

Queen Mother Sports Centre

223 Vauxhall Bridge Road, Victoria, SW1V 1EL (7630 5522/www.courtneys.co.uk). Victoria tube/rail. **Open** 6.30am-10pm Mon-Fri; 8am-8pm Sat, Sun. **Map** p402 J10.

A busy venue with a pool, the QM has plenty of decent sweating and lifting facilities.

Seymour Leisure Centre

Seymour Place, Marylebone, W1H 5TJ (7723 8019/www.courtneys.co.uk). Edgware Road tube. **Open** 6.30am-10pm Mon-Fri; 7am-8pm Sat; 8am-8pm Sun. **Map** p397 F5.

Unglamorous but central, the Seymour has a pool and sufficient weights.

Soho Gym

12 Macklin Street, Holborn, WC2B 5NF (7242 1290/www.sohogyms.com). Holborn tube. **Open** 7am-10pm Mon-Fri; 8am-8pm Sat; noon-6pm Sun. **Map** p409 Y2.

Busy and well-equipped, Soho Gym is particularly notable for its gay-friendly atmosphere.

Westway Sports Centre

1 Crowthorne Road, Ladbroke Grove, W10 6RP (8969 0992/www.westway.org). Ladbroke Grove or Latimer Road tube. **Open** 8am-10pm Mon-Fri; 8am-8pm Sat; 10am-10pm Sun.

A smart, diverse activity centre, with all-weather pitches, tennis courts and the largest indoor climbing facility in the country.

Ice skating

Broadgate is London's only permanent outdoor rink. For getting on the ice over the winter, *see p270* **Air play**.

Alexandra Palace Ice Rink

Alexandra Palace Way, Muswell Hill, N22 7AY (8365 4386/www.alexandrapalace.com). Wood Green tube/W3 bus. **Open** 11am-1.30pm, 2-5.30pm Mon-Fri; 10.30am-12.30pm, 2-4.30pm, 8.30-11pm Sat, Sun. **Admission** £6; £5 concs.

Riding

The following run classes for all ages and abilities on a horse; for stables in the city approved by the **British Horse Society**, see www.bhs.org.uk.

Hyde Park & Kensington Stables

63 Bathurst Mews, Lancaster Gate, W2 2SB (7723 2813/www.hydeparkstables.com). Lancaster Gate tube. **Open** 7.15am-5pm daily. *Fees* £49-£85/hr. **Map** p397 D6.

Wimbledon Village Stables

24 High Street, Wimbledon, SW19 5DX (8946 8579/www.wimbledonvillagestables.co.uk). Wimbledon tube/rail. **Open** 9am-5pm Tue-Sun. *Fees* £38-£43/hr.

Street sports

Under the Westway, **Baysixty6 Skate Park** (Acklam Road, W10, 8969 4669, www.baysixty6.com) has a large street course and four halfpipes, all wooden and covered. Though **Stockwell Skate Park** (www.stockwellskatepark.com) is the city's most popular outdoor park, it's about to be rivalled by **Cantelowes Gardens** on Camden Road, NW1, due to be finished by the end of 2006. Favourite unofficial street spots include the South Bank under the Royal Festival Hall. Skaters also collect every July at the **Sprite Urban Games** (www.spriteurbangames.com) on Clapham Common.

Inline skaters and BMXers tend to use the same skate parks. Inliners should keep an eye on www.londonskaters.com for a diary of inline events across the city, including free lessons, mass skates and extreme exhibitions.

Swimming

To find the swimming pool nearest to you check the Yellow Pages. Listed below we give three of the best centrally located pools. For pools particularly well suited to children, check www.britishswimming.co.uk. If alfresco swimming is more your thing, London still has **open-air lidos** at venues such as Parliament Hill Fields, the Serpentine, Tooting Bec and Brockwell Park. The survival of such pools, and the reopening of some that had previously closed, is testament to the tireless work of the **London Pools Campaign**; its website (www.londonpoolscampaign.com) has a list of lidos.

Highbury Pool

Highbury Crescent, Highbury, N5 1RR (7704 2312/ www.aquaterra.org). Highbury & Islington tube/rail. **Open** 6.30am-10pm Mon-Fri; 7.30am-7.30pm Sat; 7.30am-10pm Sun. *Women only* 7.30-10pm Tue. **Admission** £3.40; £1.50; free under-4s.

Hidden away at the bottom of Highbury Fields, this compact pool building is light, airy and has laudably clean facilities.

Ironmonger Row Baths

Ironmonger Row, Finsbury, EC1V 3QF (7253 4011/www.aquaterra.org). Old Street tube/rail. **Open** 6.30am-9pm Mon; 6.30am-8pm Tue-Thur; 6.30am-7pm Fri; 9am-5.30pm Sat; 10am-6pm Sun. **Admission** £3.40; £1.50 concs; free under-3s. **Map** p404 P3.

A 31m (100ft) pool with excellent lane swimming; the site also features good-value Turkish baths.

Oasis Sports Centre

32 Endell Street, Covent Garden, WC2H 9AG (7831 1804). Holborn tube. **Open** *Indoor pool* 6.30am-6.30pm Mon, Wed; 6.30am-7.15pm Thur; 6.30am-4pm Tue, Fri; 9.30am-5pm Sat, Sun. *Outdoor pool* (lane swimming only) 6.30am-9.30pm Mon-Fri; 7.30am-8.30pm Thur; 9.30am-5pm Sat, Sun. **Admission** £3.45; £1.35 concs; free under-5s. **Map** p409 Y2.

A central London gem renowned for its sun terrace and outdoor pool; adjacent is an indoor version.

Tennis

Many city parks have council-run courts that cost little or nothing to use. For lessons, try the **Regent's Park Golf & Tennis School** (7724 0643, www.rpgts.co.uk). For grass courts, phone the Information Department of the **Lawn Tennis Association** (7381 7000, www.lta.org.uk). The **Westway Sports Centre** (*see p334*) has indoor and outdoor courts available for hire.

Islington Tennis Centre

Market Road, Islington, N7 9PL (7700 1370/www. aquaterra.org). Caledonian Road tube/Caledonian Road & Barnsbury rail. **Open** 7am-11pm Mon-Thur; 7am-10pm Fri; 8am-10pm Sat, Sun. **Court hire** *Indoor* £18.00; £11.50 concs. *Outdoor* £8.50; £6.30 concs. **Credit** MC, V.

Offers both indoor and outdoor courts. Membership card holders qualify for a £1 discount per session, as well as booking privileges. Non-members can only book a maximum of five days in advance.

Ten-pin bowling

A useful first stop when looking for lanes is the **British Ten-pin Bowling Association** (8478 1745, www.btba.org.uk).

All-Star Lanes

Victoria House, Bloomsbury Place, Bloomsbury, WC1B 4DA (7025 2676/www.allstarlanes.co.uk). Holborn tube. **Open** 5-11.30pm Mon-Wed; 5pm-midnight Thur; noon-2am Fri, Sat; noon-11pm Sun. **Rates** £7.50-£8.50/game. **Lanes** 6. **Map** p401 L5.

Boutique bowling alley that also devotes commendable attention to food and drink.

Bloomsbury Bowling Lanes

Tavistock Hotel, Bedford Way, Bloomsbury, WC1H 9EU (7691 2610/www.bloomsburybowling.com). Russell Square tube. **Open** noon-1am Mon-Weds, noon-2am Thur-Sat; noon-midnight Sun. **Rates** From £36 a lane per hr. **Lanes** 8. **Map** p401 L4.

Central, so will save a journey to the sticks.

Rowans Bowl

10 Stroud Green Road, Finsbury Park, N4 2DF (8800 1950/www.rowans.co.uk). Finsbury Park tube/rail/Crouch Hill rail. **Open** 10.30am-12.30am Mon-Thur, Sun; 10.30am-2.30am Fri, Sat. **Charges** £1-£4.50/game. **Lanes** 24.

Easy to get to from central London by tube.

All-Star Lanes.

Theatre

The stages are alive with the sound of music.

Menier Chocolate Factory. *See p337.*

London has a full hand when it comes to theatre, with Hollywood aces, a run of great musicals and all the serious trump cards an intellectually proud city could hope for.

This is not merely a lucky streak but an ongoing improvement in the quality of drama on offer, underpinned by a renewed public sense that theatre is relevant. Politically conscious plays continue to have a big influence in this respect, with several productions last year showing the trouble and moral strife that Westerners get into in political crises abroad.

My Name is Rachel Corrie at the Royal Court told the true story of an American student who went on a crusade to help the Palestinians in Gaza and ended up crushed by an Israeli bulldozer. Meanwhile, *The Overwhelming* at the National Theatre made its naïve academic protagonists squirm with unflattering self-revelations in the early stages of the Rwandan genocide. The docudrama formula pioneered by the Tricycle theatre in Kilburn found another headline-grabbing success with *Blackwatch*, the National Theatre of Scotland's 'unauthorised biography' of the famous Scottish regiment. The play is due to transfer to central London in 2007, even though the NTS showed the director of their English counterpart, Nicholas Hytner, who's boss by turning down his offer to put on the play at the National's Olivier theatre.

Now that the British public has chosen a Maria for Andrew Lloyd Webber (voted into the role as part of a TV reality show), London will soon be alive with *The Sound of Music*. And it's not just music by Rodgers and Hammerstein. Monty Python's jokey song-filled *Spamalot* is currently following the Arthurian trail across the West End; Oz's witches are abroad in Victoria in *Wicked*; and an influx of orcs and hobbits is due in spring 2007 courtesy of the all-singing, all-dancing stage adaptation of *The Lord of the Rings*. That's not to mention the countless other musical long-runners that continue to draw the crowds. In fact, figures supplied by the Society of London Theatres show that 60 per cent of West End theatre-goers chose a musical over a play.

For all the latest developments, reviews and information, check the theatre section of the weekly *Time Out* magazine. It offers a brief but pertinent critique of every West End show running, and has useful 'book ahead' listings.

WHERE TO GO AND WHAT TO SEE

The West End, when speaking about London's theatre, is not a strictly geographical term, but for most Londoners it is synonymous with the traditional theatre district centred on Shaftesbury Avenue. Venues in this area tend to host transfers of successful smaller-scale productions, plus the usual blockbusting fare. More polished and more innovative are venues such as the **National Theatre** on the South Bank or the **Royal Court** in Chelsea – considered West End, despite their location, because of their importance.

Off-West End denotes smaller budgets and smaller capacity. These theatres – many of which are sponsored or subsidised – push the creative envelope with new, experimental writing, often brought to life by the cream of acting and directing talent. The **Soho Theatre** and the **Bush** are good for up-and-coming playwrights, while the **Almeida** and **Donmar Warehouse** are safe bets for classy production values, sometimes with big international names.

Lurking under the Fringe moniker are dozens of smaller theatres, not always guaranteed to deliver quality, but nevertheless mobbed by hopefuls looking for their London stage debut.

The **Menier Chocolate Factory** (51-53 Southwark Street, SE1 1TE, 7907 7060), which is housed, unsurprisingly, in a former chocolate factory, is an attractive new Fringe venue with reliable, mainstream fare and a restaurant attached – great for a glass of wine and food post-play. The accomplished **Arcola Theatre** (27 Arcola Street, E8 2DJ, 7503 1646) in Dalston, meanwhile, is worth the trek for fresh writing.

TICKETS AND INFORMATION

The first rule to observe when buying tickets for London performances is to book ahead. The second rule is to bypass agents and, whenever possible, go direct to the theatre's box office.

Booking agencies such as **Ticketmaster** (7344 4444, www.ticketmaster.co.uk) and **First Call** (7420 0000, www.firstcalltickets.com) sell tickets to many shows, but you'll get hit with booking fees that could top a whopping 20 per cent. In a late bid to fill their venues, many West End theatres offer reduced-price tickets for shows that have not sold out. These seats, available only on the night, are known as 'standby' tickets, and usually sell for about half of what a top-priced ticket would cost. Always call to check the availability and the conditions: some standby deals are limited to those with student ID, and when tickets go on sale varies. Or try **tkts**' cut-price tickets (*see p339*).

Forever young

The Young Vic opened in 1970 aiming a spirited two fingers at the traditional theatre establishment. It was built on a bombsite in under a year and founded on egalitarian, class-free principles, with a remit to nurture young talent among aspiring directors. That philosophy carried it through three successful decades, but by the time we got to the millennium the cheaply knocked-together building and shabby industrial stage – originally intended to last only five years – were beginning to look a bit crumpled.

The Young Vic promptly booked itself in for a comprehensive makeover, shutting its doors while the builders moved in. Meanwhile, the company took off on a 'Walkabout' tour of the UK and Europe. The refurbishment took more than two years, slowed considerably by lack of funds.

Progress would have been even slower without the help of poster-boy Jude Law, who fronted the fundraising effort (£12.5m was needed) as a gesture of loyalty to the place where he cut his theatrical chops.

David Lan, the theatre's artistic director since 2000, has overseen the relaunch and has ambitious plans for the theatre's new season. It includes a new play, *Generations*, by rising star Debbie Tucker Green, exploring the discontents of a South African family. And for Brecht fans there is a resurrection of his early plays in 'The Big Brecht Fest', with new versions by Rory Bremner and Martin Crimp. Later in 2007 comes the stage adaptation of DBC Pierre's *Vernon God Little*.

The new building itself is a massive improvement on the old. To the former main stage, it adds two new theatres, the 160-seater Maria and 80-seater Clare. The spruce-up also includes the Cut Bar & Restaurant, which has an outdoor terrace and serves tasty grub from Hampstead's Holly Bush pub.

One question still hangs over the Young Vic, however. Will Jude Law, as has long been rumoured, take to the stage as the troubled Dane in David Lan's *Hamlet*? Fingers are crossed. But in the meantime there is much else to celebrate.

Tom Stoppard's *Rock 'n' Roll.*

tkts

Clocktower building, Leicester Square, WC2H 7NA (www.officiallondontheatre.co.uk). Leicester Square tube. **Open** 10am-7pm Mon-Sat; noon-3pm Sun. **Credit** AmEx, DC, MC, V. **Map** p409 X4.

This non-profit-making organisation is run from Leicester Square by the Society of London Theatre, selling cut-price tickets for West End shows on a first-come, first-served basis on the day of the performance. The Canary Wharf branch opens 11.30am-6pm Mon-Sat.

Other locations: Canary Wharf DLR, platforms 4/5.

West End

Barbican Centre

Silk Street, the City, EC2Y 8DS (0845 120 7550/ www.barbican.org.uk). Barbican tube/Moorgate tube/rail. **Box office** 9am-8pm daily. **Tickets** *Barbican* £7-£50. *Pit* £15. **Credit** AmEx, MC, V. **Map** p404 P5.

The Barbican Centre hits the quarter-century mark in 2007, and thanks to a recent £14m facelift it isn't really showing its age. The venue's year-long birthday bash is billed to include some excellent theatre – with the National Theatre of Iceland staging Ibsen's *Peer Gynt* and Cheek By Jowl taking on Chekhov's *Three Sisters*. The annual BITE season (Barbican International Theatre Events) continues to cherry-pick exciting and eclectic theatre companies from around the globe.

National Theatre

South Bank, SE1 9PX (information 7452 3400/ box office 7452 3000/www.nationaltheatre.org.uk). Embankment or Southwark tube/Waterloo tube/rail. **Box office** 10am-8pm Mon-Sat. **Tickets** *Olivier & Lyttelton* £10-£36. *Cottesloe* £10-£27.50. **Credit** AmEx, DC, MC, V. **Map** p403 M8.

Under the aegis of Nicholas Hytner as artistic director, the National has blossomed, with landmark successes such as Alan Bennett's *History Boys* showing that the venue can turn out quality drama at a profit. The 2007 season looks set for more starry alliances, with Deborah Warner directing Fiona Shaw in Beckett's *Happy Days*, Ben Chaplin directed by Richard Eyre in Nicholas Wright's new play *The Reporter* and, for 2008, Ralph Fiennes tentatively booked for *Oedipus*. A new play by David Hare has also been commissioned. The Travelex season, for which two-thirds of the seats are offered for £10, is set to continue for another year. During the summer the free outdoor performing arts stage is a great way to see booty-shaking bhangra or fire-swallowing avant-garde dancers by the Thames.

Old Vic

Waterloo Road, Waterloo, SE1 8NB (0870 060 6628/ www.oldvictheatre.com). Waterloo tube/rail. **Box office** 9am-9pm Mon-Sat; 10am-6pm Sun. **Tickets** £10-£45. **Credit** AmEx, MC, V. **Map** p406 N9.

The combination of double-Oscar winner Kevin Spacey and top producer David Liddiment at this 200-year-old theatre continues to be a commercial success, if not a critical one, pulling almost half a million people in its first two seasons. The eclecticism of theatre that has so far been offered – from high- to lowbrow, via Shakespeare – continues with the 2007 season, set to include Robert Lindsay starring in John Osborne's *The Entertainer* and the Propellor company with blokes-only versions of *Twelfth Night* and *The Taming of the Shrew*.

Open Air Theatre

Regent's Park, NW1 4NR (7935 5756/box office 0870 060 1811/www.openairtheatre.org). Baker Street tube. **Repertory season** June-Sept; phone for details. **Tickets** £10-£32. **Credit** AmEx, DC, MC, V. **Map** p400 G3.

The lovely verdant setting of this alfresco theatre lends itself perfectly to summery Shakespeare romps. Standards are far above village green dramatics, with last year's delightful resurrection of old-school musical *The Boyfriend* showing that the diminutive stage need not cramp a production's style. Book well ahead and take an extra layer to fight chills during Act 3. Buy good-value, tasty grub on-site, or eat at the funkily refurbed Garden Café.

Backstage pass

'Who wants a squeeze of my big juicy oranges?' shouts the woman on the steps of London's oldest theatre. A bloke from across the street volunteers his services, but he's out of luck because this is Nell of Drury Lane, orange seller and king's mistress, and she's being played by an actress as part of a tour of the **Theatre Royal Drury Lane** (tours 2.15pm & 4.45pm Mon, Tue, Thur, Fri; 10.15am & noon Wed, Sat; £9, £7 concessions). A vital but often-overlooked element of the city's theatre scene are the theatre buildings. Many offer daytime tours. At the Theatre Royal groups get to see underground tunnels that once connected the building to the Thames, to explore under the largest stage in London and to sit in the Royal Room, whose walls are decorated in 24-carat gold leaf.

'In the original theatre, the audience would be drinking, shouting and chatting, and prostitutes would be "doing business" in the upper circle, all during a performance,' explains the guide at **Shakespeare's Globe** (tours every 30mins 9.30am-12.30pm daily; £7.50). Eating and drinking is still allowed during shows, he continues, although lobbing vegetables at actors is now frowned on.

A tour of the **National Theatre** (five times daily, phone 7452 3400 for details; £5, £4 concs) offers an excellent insight into how major productions are developed – plus you learn what Laurence Olivier's favourite colour was. It also takes a tour to appreciate just how vast is Covent Garden's **Royal Opera House** (tours 10.30am, 12.30pm & 2.30pm Mon-Fri, and on the half-hour 10.30am-1.30pm Sat; £9, £8/£7 concessions). Visitors are led up and down some of the eight floors and get to nose around some of workshops that produce the masses of costumes required for each production. The 10.30am tour also includes 10 minutes spent watching the ballerinas in rehearsal.

Other worthwhile tours include the **Old Vic** (11.20am Wed; £3), where you can peek in at Kevin Spacey's warm-up room, and Soho's **Prince Edward** (call 0870 850 9191 for details), home of *Mary Poppins*, and **Prince of Wales** (call 0870 850 0393 for details), currently hosting *Mamma Mia!*

Arts & Entertainment

Royal Court Theatre

Sloane Square, Chelsea, SW1W 8AS (7565 5000/ www.royalcourttheatre.com). Sloane Square tube. **Box office** 10am-6pm Mon-Sat. **Tickets** 10p-£25; all tickets £7.50 Mon. **Credit** AmEx, MC, V. **Map** p402 G11.

A hard-hitting theatre in a well-heeled location. The emphasis here has always been on new voices in British theatre – from John Osborne's *Look Back in Anger* in the inaugural year, 1956, to numerous discoveries over the past decade: Sarah Kane, Joe Penhall and Conor McPherson among them. The theatre turned 50 in style in 2006, with a sell-out run of Tom Stoppard's latest play, *Rock'n'Roll*, which subsequently transferred to the West End. The 2007 season includes a new play by Caryl Churchill, plus the unlikely pairing of Mackenzie Crook and Kristen Scott Thomas in Chekhov's *The Seagull*.

Royal Shakespeare Company

Novello Theatre (previously Strand Theatre), Aldwych, WC2B 4CD (0870 950 0940/www.delfont mackintosh.co.uk/www.rsc.org.uk). Charing Cross tube/rail/Temple tube. **Box office** *In person* 10am-8pm Mon-Sat. *By phone* 24hrs daily. **Tickets** £10-£45. **Credit** AmEx, MC, V. **Map** p411 Z3.

While the RSC ploughs on with its project to perform Shakespeare's Complete Works in a year at Stratford-upon-Avon, its London residency at Sir Cameron Mackintosh's newly renovated Novello Theatre continues at a less frenetic pace. The 2007 season sees two appearances by Patrick Stewart, in *Antony and Cleopatra* and *The Tempest*.

Shakespeare's Globe

21 New Globe Walk, Bankside, SE1 9DT (7401 9919/ www.shakespeares-globe.org). Mansion House tube/ London Bridge tube/rail. **Box office** *Off season* 10am-5pm Mon-Fri. *Theatre* 10am-8pm daily. **Tickets** £5-£29. **Credit** AmEx, MC, V. **Map** p406 O7.

Sam Wanamaker's dream – to recreate the Bankside theatre where Shakespeare first staged many of his plays – has become a very successful reality, underpinned in part by the theatre's accomplished exhibition centre. The all-important artistic director role has recently changed hands from Mark Rylance to Dominic Dromgoole, an old hand of British theatre who is adamant that the Globe should showcase new writers alongside the Bard. The free-standing pit tickets are excellent value, but the Heathrow flight path overhead can interrupt the peerless iambics.

Long-runners & musicals

Billy Elliot the Musical

Victoria Palace Theatre, Victoria Street, Victoria, SW1E 5EA (0870 895 5577/www.victoriapalace theatre.co.uk). Victoria tube/rail. **Box office** 10am-8.30pm Mon Sat. **Tickets** £17.50-£55. **Credit** AmEx, MC, V. **Map** p402 H10.

Set during the miner's strike of 1984, this story of a working-class northern boy with balletic talent burning in his shoes transfers well from screen to stage. Scored by Elton John and directed by Stephen Daldry.

Chicago

Cambridge Theatre, Earlham Street, Covent Garden, WC2H 9HU (0870 890 1102/www.cambridge theatre.co.uk). Covent Garden or Leicester Square tube. **Box office** *Seetickets* 24hrs daily. **Tickets** £17.50-£49. **Credit** MC, V. **Map** p409 Y2.

The jailbird roles are passed at regular intervals from one blonde TV star to the next, but this production still razzle-dazzles 'em with high spirits.

Daddy Cool

Shaftesbury Theatre, 210 Shaftesbury Avenue, Covent Garden, WC2H 8DP (7379 5399). Holborn or Tottenham Court Road tube. **Box office** *In person* 10am-8pm Mon-Sat. *By phone* 24hrs daily. **Tickets** £17.50-£45. **Credit** AmEx, MC, V. **Map** p409 Y1.

A tale of star-crossed lovers Rose and Sunny, set to the music of Boney M, Milli Vanilli and No Mercy.

Evita

Adelphi Theatre, Strand, Covent Garden, WC2R 0NS (Ticketmaster 0870 403 0303/www.adelphi theatre.co.uk). Charing Cross tube/rail. **Box office** *In person* 10am-8pm Mon-Sat. *By phone* 24hrs daily. **Tickets** £15-£55. **Credit** AmEx, MC, V. **Map** p409 Y4.

Andrew Lloyd Webber and Tim Rice's version of the Argentinian's life manages to grasp the darker complexities of her character, albeit using upbeat music and infectious tango dancing.

Guys & Dolls

Piccadilly Theatre, Denman Street, Soho, W1V 8DY (0870 060 0123/www.piccadillytheatre.co.uk). Piccadilly Circus tube. **Box office** *By phone* 9am-10pm Mon-Sat; 10am-8pm Sun. *In person* 10am-6pm Mon Sat. **Tickets** £20-£60. **Credit** MC,V. **Map** p408 V4.

Gamblers, lovers and losers in 1940s New York. Currently with Patrick Swayze.

Les Misérables

Queen's Theatre, Shaftesbury Avenue, Soho, W1D 6BA (7494 5040/www.lesmis.com). Leicester Square or Piccadilly Circus tube. **Box office** *In person* 10am-8pm Mon-Sat. *Seetickets* 24hrs daily. **Tickets** £12.50-£52. **Credit** AmEx, MC, V. **Map** p408 W3.

The RSC's version of Boublil and Schönberg's musical has played 21 years on the London stage. It's still raking in the crowds with Victor Hugo's vision of the poor and destitute in revolutionary Paris.

Mamma Mia!

Prince of Wales Theatre, 31 Coventry Street, Soho, W1D 6AS (0870 850 0393/www.mamma-mia.com). Leicester Square or Piccadilly Circus tube. **Box office** *In person* 10am-8pm Mon-Sat. *By phone* 24hrs daily. **Tickets** £27.50-£55. **Credit** AmEx, MC, V. **Map** p408 W4.

This feel-good musical links Abba's hits into a continuous but spurious story. Deathlessly popular.

Mary Poppins

Prince Edward Theatre, Old Compton Street, Soho, W1D 4HS (0870 850 9191). Leicester Square tube. **Box office** *In person* 10am-8pm Mon-Sat. *By phone* 24hrs daily. **Tickets** £27.50-£55. **Credit** AmEx, MC, V. **Map** p408 W3.

Something **Wicked** this way comes to the Apollo Victoria. *See p343.*

Chipper chimney sweeps and spoonfuls of magic in this enchanting take on the evergreen children's classic, directed by Richard Eyre.

Spamalot

Palace Theatre, Cambridge Theatre, Soho, W1D 5AY (0870 895 5579/www.montypythons spamalot.com.co.uk). Leicester Square tube. **Box office** *In person* 10am-8pm Mon Sat. *By phone* 24hrs daily. **Tickets** £15-£60. **Credit** AmEx, MC, V. **Map** p409 X3.

The Tony Award-winning musical based on the lunacy that is *Monty Python and the Holy Grail.* All together now: 'We're knights of the Round Table/We dance whene'er we're able/We do routines and chorus scenes/With footwork impec-cable...'.

Wicked

Apollo Victoria, Wilton Road, Victoria, SW1V 1LL (0870 400 0751/www.wickedthemusical.co.uk). Victoria tube/rail. **Box office** *In person* 10am-8pm Mon-Sat. *By phone* 24hrs daily. **Tickets** £15-£55. **Credit** AmEx, MC, V. **Map** p402 H10.

Transfer of the smash-hit Broadway musical that tells the untold back story of the Wicked Witch of the West and Glinda the Good Witch from *The Wizard of Oz.* **Photo** *p341.*

Off-West End

Almeida

Almeida Street, Islington, N1 1TA (7359 4404/ www.almeida.co.uk). Angel tube. **Box office** *In person* 10am-7.30pm Mon-Sat. *By phone* 24hrs daily. **Tickets** £6-£29.50. **Credit** AmEx, MC, V. **Map** p404 01.

A well-groomed venue with a funky bar attached and a Conran restaurant opposite, the Almeida turns out thoughtfully crafted theatre for grown-ups. Under the reign of artistic director Michael Attenborough it has commanded loyalty from top directors such as Howard Davies and Richard Eyre, and it has the clout to attract world premières such as Frank McGuiness's new play *There Came a Gypsy Riding*, due to open in January 2007.

BAC (Battersea Arts Centre)

Lavender Hill, Battersea, SW11 5TN (7223 2223/ www.bac.org.uk). Clapham Common tube/Clapham Junction rail/77, 77A, 345 bus. **Box office** *In person* 10am-6pm Mon; 10.30am-7pm Tue-Fri; 5.30-7pm Sat; 4-7pm Sun. *By phone* 10.30am-6pm Mon-Fri; 4.30-7pm Sat, Sun. **Tickets** £5-£10; 'pay what you can' Tue (phone ahead). **Credit** MC, V.

The forward-thinking BAC, which inhabits the old Battersea Town Hall, plays alma mater to new writers and theatre companies. Expect the very latest in quirky, fun and physical theatre, particularly after the Edinburgh festival when excited BAC talent scouts return to the south with their next big things in tow. Artistic director David Jubb's track record includes starting up the now-infamous Scratch programme, which shows a work in progress to progressively larger audiences until it's finished and polished. In 2007 the Battersea Arts Centre celebrates its 25th birthday with a 'theatre summit' that is hoping to inspire the next quarter-century.

The Bush

Shepherd's Bush Green, Shepherd's Bush, W12 8QD (7610 4224/www.bushtheatre.co.uk). Goldhawk Road or Shepherd's Bush tube. **Box office** *In person* 5-8pm Mon-Sat (performance nights only). *By phone* 10am-7pm Mon-Sat. **Tickets** £10-£15. **Credit** AmEx, MC, V.

A small, cash-poor champion of new writers and performers, the Bush has over 30 years' experience under its belt. Alumni include Stephen Poliakoff, Mike Leigh and Jim Broadbent, so watch that space.

Donmar Warehouse

41 Earlham Street, Covent Garden, WC2H 9LX (0870 060 6624/www.donmarwarehouse.com). Covent Garden or Leicester Square tube. **Box office** *In person* 10am-7.30pm Mon-Sat. *By phone* 9am-9pm Mon-Sat; 10am-6pm Sun. **Tickets** £15-£26. **Credit** AmEx, MC, V. **Map** p409 Y2.

Less warehouse, more intimate chamber, the Donmar is another favourite crossover spot for actors more often seen on screen. Artistic director Michael Grandage has kept the venue on a fresh, intelligent path, with inventive collaborations such as the forthcoming *Don Juan in Soho*, Patrick Marber's new riff on Molière's lothario.

In the queue for the **Donmar Warehouse**.

Arts & Entertainment

Drill Hall

16 Chenies Street, Fitzrovia, WC1E 7EX (7307 5060/www.drillhall.co.uk). Goodge Street tube. **Box office** 10am-9.30pm Mon-Sat; 10am-6pm Sun. **Tickets** £5-£17.50. **Credit** AmEx, MC, V. **Map** p401 K5.

Polyfunctional (it's a theatre, cabaret, gig venue and photo studio) and polysexual, Drill Hall is London's biggest gay and lesbian theatre.

Gate Theatre

Above the Prince Albert, 11 Pembridge Road, Notting Hill, W11 3HQ (7229 0706/www.gatetheatre.co.uk). Notting Hill Gate tube. **Box office** 10am-6pm Mon-Fri. **Tickets** £15; £10 concs. **Credit** MC, V. **Map** p396 A7.

A doll's house of a theatre, with rickety wooden chairs as seats, the Gate devotes itself entirely to foreign drama, often performed in specially commissioned translations.

Hampstead Theatre

Eton Avenue, Swiss Cottage, NW3 3EU (7722 9301/www.hampsteadtheatre.com). Swiss Cottage tube. **Box office** 9am-7pm Mon-Sat. **Tickets** £10-£22. **Credit** MC, V.

This purpose-built space, opened in 2004, gave a home to one of the city's most reliable theatres. Its programme of fresh British and international playwrights is astute but accessible. One of its latest experiments was a bold adaptation of Jonathan Safran Foer's *Everything is Illuminated*. For new artists, it organises Start Nights in which performers have 15 minutes to show off a slice of rehearsed material in its 80-seater Michael Frayn Space.

King's Head Theatre

115 Upper Street, Islington, N1 1QN (7226 1916/www.kingsheadtheatre.org). Angel tube. **Box office** noon-7.30pm daily. **Tickets** £12-£20. **Credit** MC, V. **Map** p404 N2.

London's first pub theatre, started in the 1970s on a spectacularly lean budget, is a tiny space at the back of a charming, if ramshackle, Victorian boozer. In the past it has launched a raft of wannabe stars, among them Hugh Grant. But with the juicy controversy of recent plays such as Toby Young and Lloyd Evans's *Who's the Daddy?*, an acidic satire of the Blunkett–*Spectator* entanglements, the King's Head has proved it is still worth talking about.

Lyric Hammersmith

Lyric Square, King Street, Hammersmith, W6 0QL (0870 050 0511/www.lyric.co.uk). Hammersmith tube. **Box office** 10am-6pm Mon-Sat; 10am-8pm performance nights. **Tickets** £10-£27. **Credit** DC, MC, V.

The Lyric has a knack for vibrant, offbeat scheduling and it also offers good kids' theatre. The hideous façade, built when concrete was still regarded as the architectural panacea for all building ills, hides a 19th-century gem of an auditorium, conceived by Victorian theatre-design supremo Frank Matcham. The smaller Lyric Studio houses short-run shows.

Roundhouse

Chalk Farm Road, Camden Town, NW1 8EH (0870 389 1846/www1.roundhouse.org.uk). Chalk Farm tube. **Box office** 11am-6pm Mon-Sat. **Tickets** phone for details. **Credit** MC, V.

We love the sleek makeover (*see p161* **Right round, baby, right round**). The reincarnation began with a stomach-punch of visceral dance-theatre, courtesy of the impossibly energetic Fuerzabruta group, and continues with the staging of top-notch music and other performance arts.

Soho Theatre

21 Dean Street, Soho, W1D 3NE (7478 0100/box office 0870 429 6883/www.sohotheatre.com). Tottenham Court Road tube. **Box office** *In person* 10am-6pm Mon-Sat; 10am-7.30pm performance nights. **Tickets** £5-£20. **Credit** AmEx, MC, V. **Map** p399 K6.

Its cool blue neon lights, newly refurbished front-of-house café and occasional late-night performances may blend it into the Soho landscape, but since taking up its Lottery-funded residence on Dean Street in 2000, the theatre has made quite a name for itself. It encourages playwrights to submit their work by offering a free script-reading service and runs regular workshops.

Theatre Royal Stratford East

Gerry Raffles Square, Stratford, E15 1BN (8534 0310/www.stratfordeast.com). Stratford tube/rail/DLR. **Box office** 10am-7pm Mon-Sat. **Tickets** £10-£20. **Credit** MC, V.

A community theatre with many shows written, directed and performed by black or Asian artists. Musicals are big here – whether about hip hop culture or the Windrush generation of immigrants.

Tricycle

269 Kilburn High Road, Kilburn, NW6 7JR (7328 1000/www.tricycle.co.uk). Kilburn tube. **Box office** 10am-9pm Mon-Sat; 2-9pm Sun. **Tickets** £8-£22. **Credit** MC, V.

Passionate and political, the Tricycle has been freewheeling over the past few years with its 'tribunal' docudramas investigating Stephen Lawrence's murder, the Hutton Inquiry and Guantanamo Bay. It consistently finds original ways into difficult subjects – in *An Arab-Israeli Cookbook* characters told stories of West Bank traumas while making houmous, meatballs and other dishes live on stage. The centre has a loyal local following and a buzzy bar.

Young Vic

66 The Cut, Waterloo, SE1 8LZ (7928 6363/www.youngvic.org). Waterloo tube/rail. **Box office** 10am-6pm Mon-Sat. **Tickets** £10-£24.50. **Credit** MC, V. **Map** p406 N8.

The Young Vic is finally back at its old residence on the Cut; its peripatetic 'Walkabout' programme had seen it performing across Europe while the old home was given a needed makeover. Artistic director David Lan has firm plans to reintegrate the venue as a community theatre (*see p337* **Forever young**).

Trips Out of Town

Features

Maps

Thermae Bath Spa. *See p351.*

Trips Out of Town

London's even better if you can get away from it now and again.

Engrossing and exhilarating as London is, it's very different from the rest of the country. Centuries as the capital and 94 years (from 1831 to 1925) as the world's largest city have set it apart. Thus locals and visitors alike sometimes hanker for something different – most often a change of pace from hare to tortoise. Fortunately, there are a number of interesting towns, easily accessible from London, that meet that desire. We've listed the best destinations, with details of local tourist information centres that can provide further information. For the main attractions, we've included details of opening times, admission and transport, but be aware that these can change without notice: always phone to check. Major sights are open all through the year, but many of the minor ones close from November to March. Before setting out, drop in on the **Britain & London Visitor Centre** (*see p377*).

Getting there

By train

For information on train times and ticket prices, call National Rail Enquiries on **0845 748 4950**. Ask about the cheapest ticket for the journey you are planning, and be aware that for long journeys the earlier you book, the cheaper the ticket. If you need extra help, there are rail travel centres in London's main-line stations, as well as Heathrow and Gatwick airports. These can give you guidance for things like timetables and booking. We specify the departure station(s) in the 'Getting there' section for each destination; the journey times cited there are the fastest available.

The website **www.virgintrains.co.uk** gives online timetable information for any British train company. You can buy your tickets online for any train operator in the UK via **www.thetrainline.com**.

By coach

National Express (0870 580 8080, www.nationalexpress.com) coaches travel throughout the country and depart from Victoria Coach Station (*see below*), five minutes' walk from Victoria rail and tube stations. **Green Line Travel** (0870 608 7261) also runs coaches.

Victoria Coach Station

164 Buckingham Palace Road, Victoria, SW1W 9TP (7730 3466/www.tfl.gov.uk). Victoria tube/rail. **Map** p402 H11.

Britain's most comprehensive coach company, National Express (*see above*), is based at Victoria Coach Station, as are many other companies that operate to and from London (some depart from Marble Arch) and Europe.

By car

If you're in a group of three or four, it may be cheaper to hire a car (*see p365*), especially if you plan to take in several sights within an area. The road directions given in the listings below should be used in conjunction with a proper map.

By bicycle

Capital Sport (01296 631671, www.capital-sport.co.uk) offers gentle cycling tours along the Thames from London. Leisurely itineraries include plenty of time to explore royal palaces, parks and historic attractions. Or you could try **Country Lanes** (www.country lanes.co.uk), whose representatives lead you on cycling tours of the New Forest in Hampshire (01590 622627/0845 370 0668).

Bath

There are two early myths about Bladud, who became ninth king of the Britons in 863 BC, that seek to explain the origins of this ancient spa town's healing properties. In one 'the king who learnt to fly' used necromancy to create the hot springs for which the town is famous. In the later, more sophisticated version of the fable, the heir-apparent returned home a leper, after an eleven-year visit to Athens, and was duly confined to prevent the disease spreading. Escaping, he disguised himself as a swineherd. In cold weather, his pigs would wallow in the warm mud, and Bladud noticed how their diseases vanished. Testing the waters himself, he was duly healed, and subsequently inherited the throne.

Bath's ability to restore and revive officially dates from Roman times – and extends beyond mere livestock. It was, however, not until the 18th century that things really took off, with a

Trips Out of Town

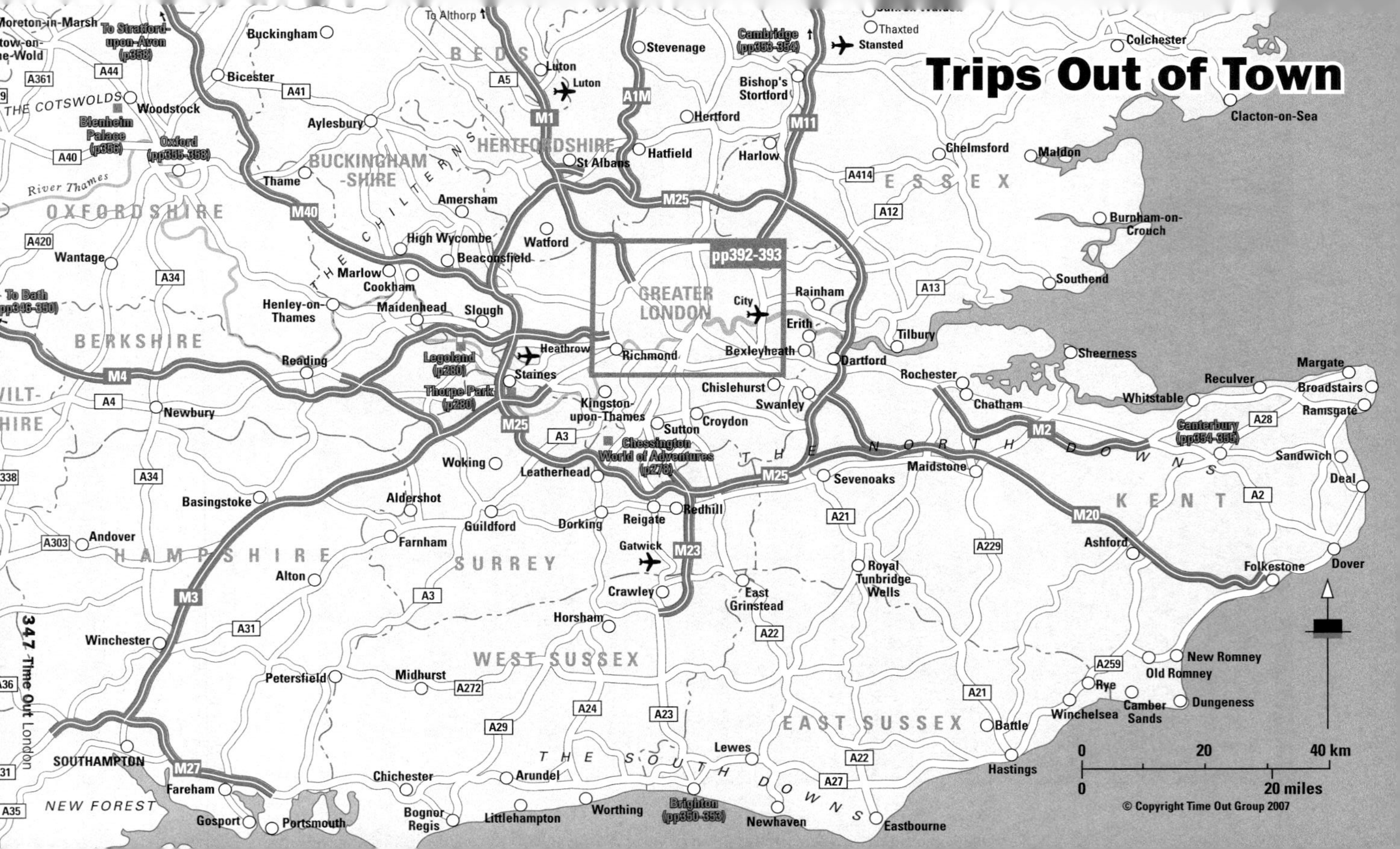

housing boom signalling the rise of Georgian Bath. The visionary architect John Wood the Elder (1704-54) was, together with his son, responsible for the extraordinary unity of the architecture still on view, an elegant expression of English Palladianism.

Bath's heyday lasted almost a century, until Jane Austen's time (she lived here from 1800 to 1805), after which it declined until after World War II, when the current revival began. The city is as beautiful as ever now, although it can be stiflingly crowded in the summer when it often seems as if all of the three million annual visitors have descended at once.

Most head first for the wonderful, steam-enshrouded **Roman Baths** museum (*see below*). Once a temple to Sulis Minerva, this is now the city's most famous attraction. The hot water bubbles up at a rate of 250,000 gallons a day, filling a pool surrounded by classical statues. You can taste sulphuric water in the adjoining Pump Room, if you're so inclined. Opening behind schedule, **Thermae Bath Spa** on Hot Bath Street (01225 335 678/331 234, www.thermaebathspa.com, open daily) welcomed its first visitors in 2006. For details, *see p351* **Bath time**.

Adjacent to the Roman baths are the noble towers of **Bath Abbey** (Abbey Churchyard, 01225 422462). It was built on the site of the Saxon church where Edgar, first king of a united England, was crowned back in 973. If the crypt is open, you can trace the building's history back through the centuries in its stones and artefacts.

Bath has close to 20 museums, including the **Building of Bath Museum** (*see below*) and the **Museum of East Asian Art** (12 Bennett Street, 01225 464640, www.bath.co.uk/museumeastasianart), which contains a fine collection of Chinese jade carvings. Opposite, in the Assembly Rooms (which were the social focus of high society in Georgian times), there's the renowned **Museum of Costume** (*see below*), where the oldest posh togs displayed date back to the 1660s. On Bridge Street, the **Victoria Art Gallery** (01225 477233/www.victoriagal.org.uk; closed Mon) houses a collection of British and European art from the 15th century to the present. The **American Museum in Britain** (*see below*) contains reconstructed US domestic interiors from the 17th, 18th and 19th centuries.

The grandest street in Bath is the much-photographed **Royal Crescent**, a curl of 30 stately white houses designed by John Wood the Younger between 1767 and 1775. The house at **No.1** (*see below*) is furnished in period style with a restored Georgian garden that you can visit (closed Dec-mid Feb). Nearby is the **Circus**, designed by the elder John Wood and finally completed by John Wood the Younger in 1767.

The **River Avon**, spanned by the Italianate, shop-lined **Pulteney Bridge**, adds to the city's appeal. There are walks beside the river and the Kennet and Avon Canal; in summer boats can be hired from the Victorian **Bath Boating Station** (Forester Road, 01225 312900).

American Museum in Britain

Claverton Manor, BA2 7BD (01225 460503/www.americanmuseum.org). **Open** *Mid Mar-late Oct* noon-5pm Tue-Sun (last entry 4pm). *Mid Nov-mid Dec* noon-4.30pm. Also bank holidays and Mon Aug noon-5pm. **Admission** £7.50; £4-£6.50 concs; free under-5s. **Credit** AmEx, MC, V.

Building of Bath Museum

The Countess of Huntingdon's Chapel, The Vineyards, BA1 5NA (01225 333895/www.bath-preservation-trust.org.uk). **Open** 10.30am-5pm Tue-Sun (last entry 4.30pm). Closed Dec-mid Feb. **Admission** £4; £1.50-£3 concs; free under-5s. **Credit** AmEx, MC, V.

Museum of Costume

The Assembly Rooms, Bennett Street, BA1 2QH (01225 477789/www.museumofcostume.co.uk). **Open** *Mar-Oct* 11am-6pm daily. *Nov-Feb* 11am-5pm daily. **Admission** £6.50; £5.50 concs; free under-6s. **Credit** MC, V.

No.1 Royal Crescent

1 Royal Crescent, BA1 2LR (01225 428126/www.bath-preservation-trust.org.uk). **Open** *Mid Feb-Oct* 10.30am-5pm Tue-Sun. *Nov* 10.30am-4pm Tue-Sun. *1st 2wks Dec* 10.30am-4pm Sat, Sun. Closed mid Dec-mid Feb. **Admission** £5; £3.50 concs; £2.50 under-16s; £12 family; group bookings £3pp (phone in advance); schools £2.50 (adults free); free under-5s. **Credit** MC, V.

Roman Baths

Abbey Churchyard, BA1 1LZ (01225 477785/www.romanbaths.co.uk). **Open** *Nov-Feb* 9.30am-5.30pm daily. *Mar-June, Sept, Oct* 9am-6pm daily. *July, Aug* 9am-9pm daily. Last entry 1hr before closing. **Admission** £10.25; £6.60-£8.75 concs; free under-6s. **Credit** MC, V.

Where to eat & drink

Bath has a formidable gourmet reputation. Three of the best restaurants are the classic and Mediterranean **Pimpernel's** (Royal Crescent Hotel, 16 Royal Crescent, 01225 823333, set lunch £18 2 courses, £25 3 courses), **Olive Tree** (Queensbury Hotel, Russell Street, 01225 447928, main courses £15.50-£21.50, lunch £15 2 courses, £17.50 3 courses) and the **Priory** (Bath Priory Hotel, Weston Road, 01225 331922, main courses £26), where you'll find country house dining that dreams are made of.

At **Sally Lunn's Refreshment House & Museum** (4 North Parade Passage, 01225 461634, main courses £8-£9) you can tuck into some history by sampling the buns that were first made fashionable in the 1680s.

Popular pubs in Bath include the **Bell Inn** (01225 460426) in Walcot Street, the **Old Green Tree** (01225 448259) on 12 Green Street, and the historic, 300-year-old inn, **Crystal Palace** (01225 482666), on Abbey Green, complete with its walled garden.

Where to stay

Harington's Hotel (8-10 Queen Street, 01225 461728, www.haringtonshotel.co.uk, doubles £88-£114) is the best-value central hotel in Bath. **Haydon House** (9 Bloomfield Park, 01225 444919, doubles £85-£135) is a classy guesthouse perched high above the city. The **Queensberry Hotel** (Russell Street, 01225 447928, www.thequeensberry.co.uk, doubles £110-£300) provides elegance in the centre of town, while to really live the life of a Jane Austen character the **Royal Crescent** (16 Royal Crescent, 01225 823333, www.royal crescent.co.uk, doubles £290-£390) is the place to stay, assuming money is no object.

Getting there

By train

Trains to Bath Spa leave hourly from Paddington most days (1hr 25mins; map p397 D5/6).

By coach

National Express coaches to Bath leave from Victoria Coach Station (3hrs 20mins).

By car

Take Junction 18 off the M4, then follow the A46 to Bath. Use park & rides to get into the centre.

Tourist information

Tourist Information Centre

Abbey Chambers, Abbey Churchyard, BA1 1LY (0906 711 2000/http://visitbath.co.uk). **Open** *June-Sept* 9.30am-6pm Mon-Sat; 10am-4pm Sun. *Oct-Apr* 9.30am-5pm Mon-Sat; 10am-4pm Sun.

Brighton

Brighton began life as Brighthelmstone, a small fishing village, and so it remained until 1783, when the future George IV transformed it into a fashionable retreat. He kept the architect John Nash busy converting a modest abode into a faux-oriental pleasure palace. That building is now the elaborate-to-the-point-of-gaudy **Royal Pavilion** (*see below*). Next door, the **Brighton Museum & Art Gallery** (Royal Pavilion Gardens, 01273 292882) has entertaining displays and a good permanent art collection.

Only two of Brighton's three Victorian piers are still standing. Lacy, delicate **Brighton Pier** is a clutter of hot-dog stands, karaoke and fairground rides, filled with customers in the summertime. But sadly, the **West Pier** is now a spooky, twisted ruin.

With seven miles of coastline, Brighton has all the traditional seaside resort trappings, hence the free **Brighton Fishing Museum** (201 King's Road Arches, on the lower prom between the piers, 01273 723064) and the **Sea-Life Centre** (*see below*), the world's oldest functioning aquarium.

Perhaps reflecting its singular character, the town has a huge number of independent shops, boutiques and art stores. The best shopping for clothes, records and gifts is found in and around **North Laine** and in the charming network of narrow cobbled streets known as the **Lanes**.

The town that seems to be on a perpetual holiday received a further boost (to visitor numbers, at least) when it was announced that Frank Gehry – about to redesign the £250m King Alfred residential and leisure complex along adjoining Hove seafront – would be helped by none other than Brad Pitt, who is charged with designing a restaurant and a penthouse as part of the controversial plan.

Royal Pavilion

Brighton, BN1 1EE (01273 292820/www.royal pavilion.org.uk). **Open** *Apr-Sept* 9.30am-5.45pm daily. *Oct-Mar* 10am-5.15pm daily. *Tours* by appointment. Last entry 45mins before closing. **Admission** £7.50; £5.70 concs; £5 under-16s; £6.50 groups 20+; free under-5s. **Credit** AmEx, MC, V.

Sea-Life Centre

Marine Parade, BN2 1TB (01273 604234). **Open** 10am-6pm daily (last admission 5pm). **Admission** £10.95; £6.50-£9.50 concs; free under-3s. **Credit** AmEx, DC, MC, V.

Where to eat & drink

There's a menu of beautifully presented, wholly authentic French fare at **La Fourchette** (105 Western Road, 01273 722556, set lunch £10-£14, set dinner £23-£29).

One of England's most celebrated vegetarian restaurants is also here: **Terre à Terre** (71 East Street, 01273 729051, main courses £12-£16) is known for its innovative menu. The newly opened **Real Eating Company** (86-87 Western Road, Hove, 01273 221444, main courses £8-£14) is a great place for lunch, while the fantastic food and considerate

Bath time

The biggest thing to happen to Bath since John Wood the Elder, the town's new **Thermae Bath Spa** has drawn praise and condemnation in about equal measure. Not only was it four years late in opening (due to complete in 2002, the doors opened in August 2006), but the initial projected cost of £13m ended up being £45m. According to press reports, £4.3m of that was wasted on the wrong paint. A local Member of Parliament calculated that every constituent in his area was paying £200 for the spa. However, now it is finally finished, there's no denying that the place is a looker. Architect Nicholas Grimshaw (best known for London's Waterloo Station international terminus) has combined a listed Georgian building with an ultra-modern glass-fronted shell. At the corners the glass curves smoothly round, while inside huge pillars support four floors of treatment rooms and a rooftop pool with stunning views of the city's honey-coloured houses.

You'd expect England's quintessential spa town to know a thing or two about therapeutic water remedies, and when it comes to the treatments themselves, the spa doesn't disappoint. For a start, it's the only spa in the country to use natural hot springs as part of the treatments. There's an extensive range available, with plenty of options geared for detox. Body wraps use everything from moor mud to Arizona sand and seaweed to firm skin and blitz water retention. Wraps start from £38 for 50 minutes, while thermal treatments start from £32 for 30 minutes. If your detox stretches to doing something energetic, then there are Pilates and yoga classes available too.

Thermae Bath Spa *The Hetling Pump Room, Hot Bath Street, Bath, BA1 1SJ (01225 331 234/www.thermaebathspa.com).* **Open** *New Royal & Hot Bath* 9am-10pm daily (last entry 8pm). *Cross bath* 9am-9pm daily (last entry 7.30pm). *Spa visitors' centre* 9.30am-5pm daily. *Spring Café & restaurant* 10.30am-9.30pm daily. *Shop* 10am-6pm daily. **Credit** AmEx, MC, V.

Weavers House, **Canterbury**.
See p354.

staff combine to make **Seven Dials** (1-3 Buckingham Place, 01273 885555, set lunch £10) an excellent choice for dinner.

This city's laid-back attitude makes it ideal for café culture and many coffeeshops have sprung up; two excellent choices are **Nia Café Bar** (87 Trafalgar Street, 01273 671371) and **Alfresco** (Milkmaid Pavilion, King's Road Arches, 01273 206523).

Of the traditional pubs, the **Cricketers** (15 Black Lion Street, 01273 329472), the **Heart in Hand** (75 North Road, 01273 683320) and the **Colonnade Bar** (10 New Road, 01273 328728) all have the most charm.

The **Sidewinder** (65 Upper St James Street) is a pre-club bar with DJs. **Ali-Cats** (80 East Street), the **Hampton** (57 Upper North Street) and **Riki-Tik** (18A Bond Street) are also reliable bets for a good night out.

Of the gay bars, the most fun is to be had at the **Amsterdam Hotel** (11-12 Marine Parade). **Doctor Brighton's** (16 King's Road), on the seafront, is also worth a punt, with DJs playing house and techno. And for the ladeeez... the **Candy Bar** (129 St James Street) is a strictly women-only lesbian hangout.

Where to stay

Given Brighton's popularity with tourists, it's perhaps not surprising that hotel prices can be on the high side. An interesting choice is the **Alias Hotel Seattle** (01273 679799, www.aliasseattle.com, doubles £100-£160), which is situated on the recently developed Brighton Marina and feels much like a state-of-the-art liner. For other good quality stops, try **Hotel du Vin** (2-6 Ship Street, 01273 718588, www.hotelduvin.com, doubles £140-£400), or **Blanch House** (17 Atlingworth Street, 01273 603504, www.blanchhouse.co.uk, doubles £125-£220), which is unassuming from the outside, but highly chic. **Nineteen** (19 Broad Street, 01273 675529, www.hotelnineteen.co.uk, doubles £120-£250) has just seven rooms in a stylish townhouse. **Hotel Pelirocco** (10 Regency Square, 01273 327055, www.hotelpelirocco.co.uk, doubles £100-£145) is funky, with themed decor in the bedrooms. **Hotel Twenty One** (21 Charlotte Street, 01273 686450, doubles £65-£99) is a well-run bed and breakfast a few minutes' walk from the Palace Pier and town centre. **Oriental Hotel** (9 Oriental Place, 01273 205050, doubles Mon-Thur, Sun £60-£100; Fri, Sat £80-£125) is calm and centrally located. For a clean, cheap, central but otherwise rather bland chain, you could try **Brighton Premier Lodge** (144 North Street, 0870 990 6340, www.premierlodge.com, doubles £60-£65).

Getting there

By train

Trains for Brighton leave from Victoria (50mins; map p402 H10) or King's Cross/London Bridge (1hr 10mins; map p401 L2/3).

By coach

National Express coaches for Brighton leave from Victoria Coach Station (1hr 50mins).

By car

Take the M23, then the A23 to Brighton.

Tourist information

Tourist Information Centre

10 Bartholomew Square, BN1 1JS (0906 711 2255/ www.visitbrighton.com). **Open** *Summer* 10am-5pm Mon-Sat; 10am-4pm Sun. *Winter* 10am-5pm Mon-Sat.

Cambridge

Gorgeous, intimidating Cambridge has the feel of an enclosed city. With its narrow streets and tall old buildings blocking out the sun in the town centre, it has a way of conveying disapproval to visitors architecturally as well as intellectually (before you even reach the 'Keep off the Grass' signs). But once you pluck up the courage to pass through the imposing gates and stone walls, you discover a pretty little town of green parks and streams where time seems to have stopped back in the 18th century.

Cambridge first became an academic centre when a fracas at Oxford – involving a dead woman, an arrow and a scholar holding a bow, apparently – led to some of the learned monks bidding a hasty farewell to Oxford and a hearty how do you do to Cambridge. Once the dust settled, the monks needed somewhere to peddle their knowledge: the first college, **Peterhouse**, was established in 1284. The original hall survives, though most of the present buildings are 19th century. Up the road is **Corpus Christi College**, founded in 1352. Its Old Court dates from that time and is linked by a gallery to its original chapel, the 11th-century **St Bene't's Church** (Bene't Street, www.stbenets.com), the oldest surviving building in Cambridge.

Down Silver Street is 15th-century **Queens' College**; most of its original buildings remain, including the timbered president's lodge. The inner courts are wonderfully picturesque. Further up on King's Parade, grand **King's College** was founded by Henry VI in 1441 and is renowned for its **chapel** (01223 331155), built between 1446 and 1515. It has a breathtaking interior with the original stained glass. Attend a service in term-time to hear its choirboys.

Further north, pretty **Trinity College** was founded in 1336 by Edward III and then refounded by Henry VIII in 1546. A fine crowd of Tudor buildings surrounds the Great Court where, legend has it, Lord Byron was known to bathe naked in the fountain with his pet bear. Wittgenstein studied and taught here, and the library (designed by Wren) is open to visitors at certain times (noon-2pm Mon-Fri all year, 10.30am-12.30pm Sat term-time, 01223 338488).

Further on, at the corner of Bridge and St John's streets, is the 12th-century **Round Church** (Church of the Holy Sepulchre, Bridge Street, 01223 311602), the oldest of only four remaining round churches in the country.

Behind the main colleges, the beautiful meadows bordering the willow-shaded River Cam are known as the **Backs**. This is idyllic for summer strolling, or 'punting' (pushing flat boats with long poles). Punts can be hired; **Scudamore's Boatyard** (01223 359750) is the largest operator. If you get handy at the surprisingly difficult skill of punting, you could boat down to the **Orchard Tea Rooms** (Mill Way, Grantchester, 01223 845788) where Rupert Brooke lodged when he was a student. There's a small museum dedicated to the poet (rather prosaically) in the car park outside.

Among Cambridge's relatively few non-collegiate attractions, the **Fitzwilliam Museum** on Trumpington Street (01223 332900) has an outstanding collection of antiquities and Old Masters; **Kettle's Yard** (Castle Street, 01223 352124) has fine displays of 20th-century art; and the **Botanic Gardens** (01223 336265) on Bateman Street offer a relaxing place to watch the grass grow.

Where to eat & drink

Graffiti (Hotel Felix, Whitehouse Lane, Huntingdon Road, 01223 277977, main courses £15-£22) has a beautiful terrace for outdoor dining during the summer months, and a fine Mediterranean menu. **Midsummer House** (Midsummer Common, 01223 369299, à la carte £55, tasting menu £75) is where chef-patron Daniel Clifford creates posh and inventive French dishes in a bid to earn a second Michelin star. For superlative (but pricey) Chinese food, try **Peking** (21 Burleigh Street, 01223 354755, main courses £7-£14).

Cambridge has many creaky old inns in which to settle down and enjoy one of the city's decent local ales. The **Eagle** on Bene't Street (01223 505020) is the most famous, but there are many others, including the **Pickerel Inn** (30 Magdalene Street, 01223 355068), **Fort St George** by the river on Midsummer Common (01223 354327), the **Mill** (14 Mill Lane, 01223 357026) and the **Anchor** (Silver Street, 01223 353554), which is on the riverbank. A stroll along the Cam from Midsummer Common will take you to the picturesque **Green Dragon** (5 Water Street, 01223 505035), with its beer garden by the river.

Where to stay

Because of the university, there are plenty of guesthouses in town. The **Cambridge Garden House Hotel** (Granta Place, Mill Lane, 01223 259988, doubles £139-£174) on the banks of the Cam is lovely. A mile out of town, the **Hotel Felix** (Whitehouse Lane, Huntingdon Road, 01223 277977, www.hotelfelix.co.uk, doubles £168-£275) has a great restaurant, landscaped gardens and stylishly elegant rooms. For budget travellers, the simple modern **Sleeperz Hotel** betrays minimalist Scandinavian and Japanese influences (Station Road, 01223 304050, doubles £59).

Getting there

By train

Trains to Cambridge leave from King's Cross (50mins; map p401 L2/3) or Liverpool Street (map p407 R5; 1hr 15mins).

By coach

National Express coaches to Cambridge leave from Victoria Coach Station (1hr 50mins).

By car

Take Junction 11 or Junction 12 off the M11.

Tourist information

Visitor Information Centre

Old Library, Wheeler Street, CB2 3QB (0870 226 8006/www.visitcambridge.org). **Open** *Easter-mid Oct* 10am-5.30pm Mon-Fri; 10am-5pm Sat; 11am-4pm Sun. *Mid Oct-Easter* 10am-5.30pm Mon-Fri; 10am-5pm Sat.

Canterbury

The home of the Church of England since St Augustine was based here in 597, the ancient city of Canterbury is rich in atmosphere. Gaze up at its soaring spires, or around you at the enchanting medieval streets, and you'll soon feel blessed, even if you're not an Anglican.

Its busy tourist trade and large university provide a colourful counterweight to the brooding mass of history present in its old buildings and, of course, the glorious **Canterbury Cathedral** (*see p355*). Be prepared to shell out at every step, even to enter the close: this is one of the country's most money-grabbing attactions. However, it is, quite simply, well worth it. The cathedral has superb stained glass, stone vaulting and a vast Norman crypt. A plaque near the altar marks what is believed to be the exact spot where Archbishop Thomas à Becket was murdered. Trinity Chapel contains the site of the original shrine, plus the tombs of Henry IV and the Black Prince.

A pilgrimage to Becket's tomb was the focus of Chaucer's *Canterbury Tales* written in the 14th century. At the exhibition named after the book (*see below*), visitors are given a device that they point at tableaux inspired by Chaucer's tales of a knight, a miller and others, enabling them to hear the stories.

Eastbridge Hospital (25 High Street, 01227 471688), founded to provide shelter for pilgrims, retains the smell of ages past. The **Roman Museum** (*see below*) has the remains of a townhouse and mosaic floor among its treasures.

Canterbury Cathedral

The Precincts, CT1 2EH (01227 762862/ www.canterbury-cathedral.org). **Open** *Easter-Sept* 9am-5pm Mon-Sat; 12.30-2.00pm Sun. *Oct-Easter* 9am-4.30pm Mon-Sat; 12.30-2.00pm Sun. Admission restricted during services and special events. **Admission** £6; £5 concs; free under-5s. **Credit** MC, V.

Canterbury Tales

St Margaret's Street, CT1 2TG (01227 454888/ 479227/www.canterburytales.org.uk). **Open** *Mid Feb-June, Sept, Oct* 10am-5pm daily. *July, Aug* 9.30am-5pm daily. *Nov-mid Feb* 10am-4.30pm daily. **Admission** £7.25; £5.25-£6.25 concs; free under-4s. **Credit** MC, V.

Roman Museum

Butchery Lane, CT1 2JR (01227 785575/www. canterbury-museums.co.uk). **Open** *Nov-May* 10am-5pm Mon-Sat. *June-Oct* 10am-5pm Mon-Sat; 1.30-5pm Sun. Last entry 1hr before closing. **Admission** £3; £1.85 concs; free under-5s. **Credit** MC, V.

Where to eat & drink

The Goods Shed (Station Road West, 01227 459153, main courses £10-£17) is perfect for a leisurely lunch or dinner, while **Café des Amis du Mexique** (93-95 St Dunstan's Street, 01227 464390, main courses £7.95-£24.95) is upbeat and popular. Stop for a drink in the peaceful **Unicorn** (61 St Dunstan's Street, 01227 463187) with its kitsch garden.

Where to stay

Prices are good at the 19th-century **Acacia Lodge & Tanglewood** B&B (39-40 London Road, 01227 769955, www.acacialodge.co.uk, doubles £58-£70). Mid-range is the **Coach House** B&B (34 Watling Steet, 01227 784324, doubles £60-£70). At the other end of the scale, the **Falstaff** is a lovely historic hotel (8-10 St Dunstan's Street, 01227 462138, doubles £130).

Getting there

By train

From Victoria Station to Canterbury East (1hr 20mins; map p402 H10), or from Charing Cross (map p401 L7) to Canterbury West (1hr 30mins).

By coach

National Express from Victoria (1hr 50mins).

By car

Take the A2, the M2, then the A2 again.

Tourist information

Tourist Information Centre

12-13 Sun Street, Buttermarket, CT1 2HX (01227 378100/www.canterbury.co.uk). **Open** *Easter-Oct* 9.30am-5pm Mon-Sat. *Jan-Easter, Nov-Dec* 10am-4pm Mon-Sat. *Easter-Dec* 10am-4pm Sun.

Oxford

With its medieval churches, domed library and narrow old streets, Oxford has a noble, ancient beauty. The city's stateliness remains intact, mercifully, despite the packs of continental schoolchildren roaming its streets and giggling while robed students glumly trudge off to take their formal exams. The myriad colleges that make up **Oxford University** have defined this town since the middle of the 12th century. Nearly everything else in town – the galleries and museums, the good restaurants, the expansive green parks – stems from them.

This wasn't always the way. Oxford arose as a Saxon burg built to defend Wessex from the dastardly Danes, who repeatedly attacked the region (the 11th-century **St Michael's Tower** in Cornmarket Street is the only survivor of this period). In the years 1348-50 a great plague hit Oxford. While all the academics moved to safe country retreats, the majority of the population remained, and huge numbers died. Shrewd, if not exactly sympathetic, university magnates promptly bought up the residences of the deceased, vastly expanding college property holdings.The dissolution of the monasteries under Henry VIII meant that much of Oxford's land and money passed from the Church to the colleges, setting the town's course.

Most of Oxford's many colleges are open to the public, and the chapel at **Christ Church** also serves as Oxford's cathedral. **Magdalen College** (pronounced 'maudlin') has a lovely meadow and deer park. Nearby **Merton College**, founded in 1264, has a medieval library and garden. Scorch marks can still be discerned on the doors of **Balliol College**, where Bloody Mary burned leading Protestants Latimer and Ridley alive for refusing to recant.

Other centres of academia include the grand **Bodleian** (*see below*), the university's huge, reference-only library. It is housed in a spectacular building, with the oldest part dating back to 1488, and contains every book published in the United Kingdom and Ireland.

The **University Botanic Gardens** (Rose Lane, 01865 286690) are the oldest in Great Britain and have occupied this spot by the River Cherwell for more than 375 years.

Oxford's non-university sights include **Carfax Tower** (01865 792653), the only surviving part of the 14th-century church of St Martin, with its two 'quarter-boy' clocks (they chime every quarter-hour). Climb the 99 steps to the top for fantastic views.

A wealth of museums ranges from the quirky (and free) **Pitt Rivers** (South Parks Road, 01865 270927), with its voodoo dolls, shrunken heads and other ethnological delights, to the all-embracing **Ashmolean** (Beaumont Street, 01865 278000; free), the country's oldest museum, which houses the university's extraordinary collection of art and antiquities. **Modern Art Oxford** (30 Pembroke Street, 01865 722733; free) has established an international reputation for pioneering exhibitions of contemporary work.

Central Oxford, with its sweet covered market (opened in 1774) linking Market Street to the High Street, its car-unfriendly streets and bicycling youth, is a wonderful place to wander around in. It can get uncomfortably clogged with tourists at times, but then that's the ideal time to explore the neighbourhoods of Jericho, Summertown and Cowley. Beyond Jericho, wild horses roam on the vast expanse of lovely **Port Meadow**.

Eight miles north-west of Oxford, near the pretty town of Woodstock, **Blenheim Palace** (0870 060 2080, www.blenheimpalace.com) is the only non-royal residence in England grand enough to be given the title 'palace'. It was designed by Sir John Banbrugh, and its grounds include a butterfly house, a maze, an adventure playground, a boating and fishing lake, and a miniature railway.

Bodleian Library

Broad Street, OX1 3BG (01865 277000/tours 01865 277224/www.bodley.ox.ac.uk). **Open** *Library* term-time 9am-10pm Mon-Fri, 9am-5pm Sat; vacations 9am-7pm Mon-Fri, 9am-1pm Sat. *Shop* 9am-4.45pm Mon-Sat. *Tours* 10.30am, 11.30am, 2pm, 3pm Mon-Sat. **Admission** £2; *Groups + teacher* £1. *Tours* £6-£12. Children under 11 not permitted on tours. **Credit** AmEx, MC, V.

St John's College and the Bridge of Sighs, **Cambridge**. *See p353.*

Where to eat & drink

Enjoy excellent lunchtime dim sum at **Liaison** (29 Castle Street, 01865 242944, main courses £7-£28). **Branca** (111 Walton Street, 01865 556111, main courses £8-£17) is perfect for those seeking a zippy atmosphere with their pasta. Popular diner **Joe's** (21 Cowley Road, 01865 201120/260 Banbury Road, 01865 554484, main courses £6.95-£12.50) is renowned for its excellent burgers and brunches. **Cherwell Boat House** (Bardwell Road, 01865 552746, midweek lunch £12.50 2 courses, set lunch £21.50, set dinner £24) is a riverside favourite.

Oxford has loads of pubs, but few are cheap or quiet – the 16th-century **King's Arms** in Holywell Street (01865 242369) is studenty with good beer; the **Turf Tavern** (01865 243235) between Hertford and New Colleges is Oxford's oldest inn; and the **Perch** (01865 728891) on Binsey Lane has a garden with play area.

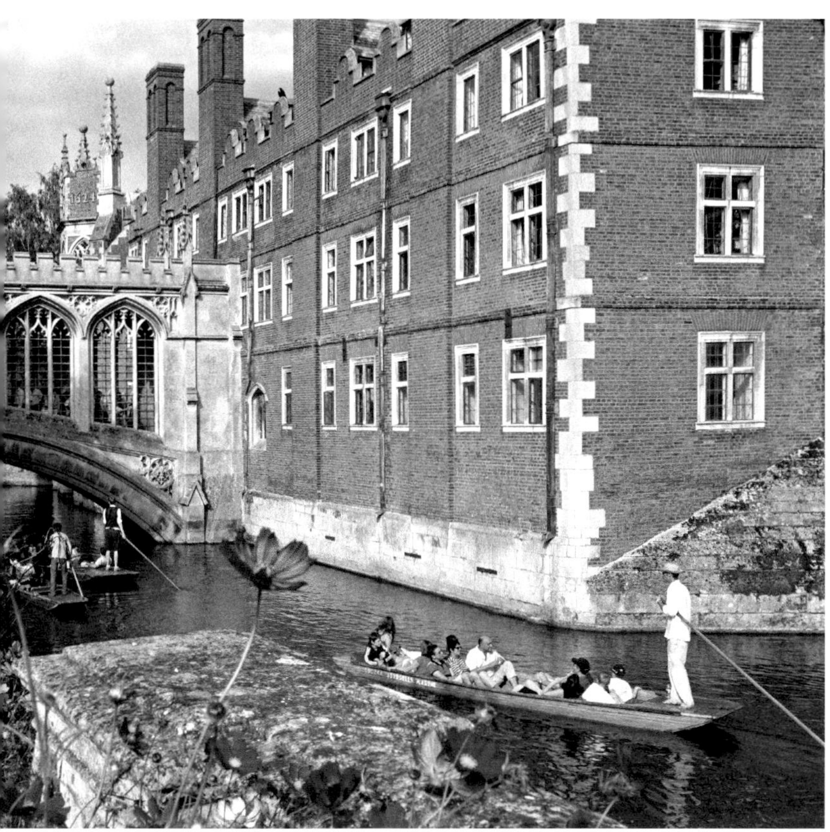

Where to stay

Burlington House (374 Banbury Road, 01865 513513, doubles £85-£95) is an outstanding small hotel with good value, bed-and-breakfast prices, but it is a little way out of town. More centrally, the **Old Parsonage** (1 Banbury Road, 01865 310210, www.oldparsonage-hotel.co.uk, doubles £155-£195) is classy and ancient, and the **Old Bank Hotel** (92-94 High Street, 01865 799599, doubles £165-£325) is sleek, modernist and arty. Next to the station is the prosaic **Royal Oxford Hotel** (Park End Street, 01865 248432, doubles £140).

Getting there

By train

There are regular trains from Paddington (1hr; map p397 D5/6); your rail ticket qualifies you for a free ride into the centre on an electric bus (every 10mins).

By coach

There are frequent, cheap, fast services from several London departure points; details from National Express (1hr 40mins), Stagecoach (01865 772250) and Oxford Bus Company (01865 785400).

By car

Take Junction 8 off the M40, and then the A40 into town. Park at the edge and use the park & rides.

Tourist information

Oxford Information Centre

15-16 Broad Street, OX1 3AS (01865 726871/ www.visitoxford.org). **Open** 9.30am-5pm Mon-Sat; 10am-4pm Sun.

Daily tours of Oxford run from the centre at 11am and 2pm, with additional departures at busy times, every day except 25 and 26 December. Tickets are sold at the information centre during opening hours, otherwise you can buy them directly from the guide. There's a maximum of 19 people on all tours.

Inspector Morse tours
Depart from information centre. **Time** 1.30pm Sat.
Follow the footsteps of the celebrated TV detective.

Ghost tours
Depart from information centre. **Time** *June-Oct* 7.45pm Fri, Sat.
Take a walk on the dark side of Oxford's streets and alleyways in search of the city's ghoulish past.

Stratford-upon-Avon

This chocolate-box of a town is England's second biggest tourist draw (after London), and for good reason. Yes, it's the birthplace of the most marketed author of all time, but it's also charming, historic and filled with interesting little sights. The problem is that unless you visit in the off-season you won't get much chance to appreciate any of that: it gets almost unbearably crowded in the summertime, which can make it hard to enjoy its beauty.

Don't be put off by the aggressive marketing of 'Shakespeare Country' – half-timbered architecture overkill, over zealous cobbling and teashops everywhere. It can all be forgiven if you're one of Will's fans. There's never a shortage of his works to see, and the **Royal Shakespeare Theatre** is the place to see them. If you can't get a ticket, take a backstage tour and visit the **RSC Collection** museum of props and costumes (for both, *see below*).

Stratford has been a market town since 1169 and, in a way, that's still what it does best. See the market on a Friday, when locals flock in from outlying villages to the colourful stalls at the top of Wood Street. In the town centre, with its medieval grid pattern, many fine old buildings survive, among them **Harvard House** (High Street, 01789 204507, open May-Oct), which dates from 1596. It was home to Katharine Rogers, mother of John Harvard, founder of Harvard University, and now houses a pewter collection.

In the town centre are **Shakespeare's Birthplace** (01789 204016) on Henley Street; **Hall's Croft** (01789 292107) on Old Town, named after Dr John Hall, who married the Bard's daughter Susanna; and **Nash's House** (01789 292325) on Chapel Street, which once belonged to the first husband of Shakespeare's granddaughter, Elizabeth. In the garden of the latter are the foundations of **New Place**, the writer's last home, demolished in 1759. Shakespeare was educated at **Stratford Grammar School**, on Church Street, and buried in **Holy Trinity** church.

A mile and a half away at **Shottery**, and accessible from Stratford by public footpath or public sightseeing bus, is **Anne Hathaway's Cottage** (01789 292100), where Shakespeare's wife lived before she married him. The girlhood home of his mother, **Mary Arden's House** (01789 293455), is at **Wilmcote**, a pleasant four-mile stroll along the Stratford Canal. Both may also be reached by bus; there are also trains to Wilmcote.

Stratford's charms are enhanced by the **River Avon** and the **Stratford Canal**, and the walks alongside them. Spend some time on the water by hiring a boat at **Stratford Marina**. The long-established **Avon Boating** (01789 267073, open April-Oct) has punts and rowing boats for hire.

Royal Shakespeare Company
Waterside, CV37 6BB (box office 0870 609 1110/ tours 01789 403492/www.rsc.org.uk). **Tickets** *Tour* £5; £4 concs or groups of 10 or more. *Performances* prices vary. **Credit** MC, V.

Where to eat & drink

The **Fox & Goose Inn** (Armscote, off A3400, 01608 682293, main courses £9.95-£15) may be off the beaten track but is worth the journey for its boudoir-style dining room and great food. Drink with thesps at the **Dirty Duck** (aka the **Black Swan**, Waterside, 01789 297312).

Where to stay

Caterham House Hotel (58-59 Rother Street, 01789 267309, doubles £80-£90) is close to the Royal Shakespeare Theatre and popular with both audience and actors. The **Falcon Hotel** (Chapel Street, 0870 609 6122, doubles £80-£140) is very olde-worlde: at least 20 of the 84 en suite rooms are in a 16th-century inn. Another good choice, **Victoria Spa Lodge** (Bishopton Lane, 01789 267985, single £55, doubles/twin £70) has the feel of a grand country house; Princess Victoria stayed here in 1837.

Tourist information

Tourist Information Centre
Bridgefoot, CV37 6GW (0870 160 7930/www. shakespeare-country.co.uk). **Open** *Early Apr-Sept* 9am-5.30pm Mon-Sat; 10am-4pm Sun. *Oct-early Apr* 9am-5pm Mon-Sat; 10am-3pm Sun.

Getting there

By train
Regular service from Paddington (2hrs 10mins).

By coach
National Express runs regular coaches to Stratford (2hrs 45mins).

By car
Take Junction 15 off the M40, then A46 into town.

Directory

Features

Directory

Getting Around

Arriving & leaving

For London's domestic rail and coach stations, *see p346*.

By air

Gatwick Airport

0870 000 2468/www.baa.co.uk/gatwick. About 30 miles south of central London, off the M23.
Of the three rail services that link Gatwick to London, the quickest is the **Gatwick Express** (0845 850 1530, www.gatwickexpress.co.uk) to Victoria Station, which takes about 30 minutes and runs from 3.30am to 12.30am daily. Tickets cost £14 single, £13.20 day return (after 9.30am) and £24 for an open period return (valid for 30 days). Under-15s are £6.50 single, half-price open and cheap day returns; under-5s go free.

Southern (0845 748 4950, www.southernrailway.com) also runs a rail service between Gatwick and Victoria, with trains every 15-20 minutes (or around hourly 1-4am). It takes about 35 minutes, at £9 for a single, £9.30 for a day return (after 9.30am) and £18 for an open period return (valid for one month). Under-16s get half-price tickets; under-5s go free.

If you're staying in the King's Cross or Bloomsbury area, consider the **Thameslink** service (0845 748 4950, www.firstcapitalconnect.co.uk) via London Bridge, Blackfriars, Farringdon and King's Cross; journey times vary. Tickets cost £10 single (after 9.30am), £10.10 day return and £20.20 for a 30-day open return.

Hotelink offers a shuttle service (01293 532244, www.hotelink.co.uk) at £19 each way (£22 online). A taxi costs about £100 and takes ages.

Heathrow Airport

0870 000 0123/www.baa.co.uk/heathrow. About 15 miles west of central London, off the M4.
The **Heathrow Express** (0845 600 1515, www.heathrowexpress.co.uk) runs to Paddington every 15 minutes 5.10am-23.25am daily, and takes 15-20 minutes. The train can be boarded at either of the airport's two tube stations. Tickets cost £14.50 single or £27 return; under-16s go half-price. Many airlines have check-in desks at Paddington.

A longer but cheaper journey is by tube. Tickets for the 50- to 60-minute **Piccadilly Line** ride into central London cost £4 one way (£2 under-16s). Trains run every few minutes from about 5am to 11.57pm daily except Sunday, when they run from 6am to 11pm.

National Express (0870 580 8080, www.nationalexpress.com) runs daily coach services to London Victoria between 7am and 0.15am daily, leaving Heathrow Central bus terminal around every 30 minutes. For a 90-minute journey to London, you can expect to pay £4 for a single (£2 under-16s) or £8 (£4 under-16s) for a return.

As at Gatwick, **Hotelink** (*see above*) offers an airport-to-hotel shuttle service for £17 per person each way. A taxi into town will cost roughly £100 and take an hour or more, depending on traffic.

London City Airport

7646 0000/www.londoncityairport.com. About 9 miles east of central London.
The Docklands Light Railway (DLR) now includes a stop for London City Airport. The journey to Bank in the City takes around 20 minutes, and trains run 5.30am-12.30am Mon-Sat or 7am-11.30pm Sun. A taxi costs around £20 to central London; less to the City or to Canary Wharf.

Luton Airport

01582 405100/www.london-luton.com. About 30 miles north of central London, J10 off the M1.
Luton Airport Parkway Station is close to the airport, but not in it: there's still a short shuttle-bus ride. The **Thameslink** service (*see above*) calls at many stations (King's Cross and City, on Ludgate Hill, among them); it has a journey time of 35-45 minutes. Trains leave every 15 minutes or so and cost £11.10 single one-way and £20.60 return, or £11.20 for a cheap day return (after 9.30am Monday to Friday, weekends). Trains from Luton to King's Cross run at least hourly through the night.

The Luton to Victoria journey takes 60-90 minutes by coach. **Green Line** (0870 608 7261, www.greenline.co.uk) runs a 24-hour service every 30 minutes or so at peak times. A single is £10.50, £7 for under-16s, while returns cost £15 and £11. A taxi costs upwards of £50.

Stansted Airport

0870 000 0303/www.stanstedairport.com; www.baa.co.uk/stansted. About 35 miles north-east of central London, J8 off the M11.
The quickest way to get to London is on the **Stansted Express** train (0845 748 4950) to Liverpool Street Station; the journey time is 40-45 minutes. Trains leave every 15-45 minutes depending on the time of day, and tickets cost £15 single, £25 return; under-16s travel half-price, under-5s free.

The **Airbus** (0870 580 8080, www.nationalexpress.com) coach service from Stansted to Victoria takes at least an hour and 20 minutes and runs 24 hours. Coaches run roughly every 30 minutes, more frequently at peak times. A single is £10 (£5 for under-16s), return is £16 (£8 for under-16s). A taxi is about £80.

By rail

Eurostar

Waterloo International Terminal, SE1 (0870 518 6186/www.eurostar.com). Waterloo tube/rail. **Map** p403 M8.

Public transport

Information

Details on public transport times and other information can be found online at www.tfl.gov.uk, or by calling 7222 1234. Alternatively, see www.journeyplanner.org to help you find the best route.

Travel Information Centres

TfL's Travel Information Centres provide maps and information about the tube, buses and Docklands Light Railway (DLR; *see p363*). You can find them in the stations listed below. Call 7222 5600 for more information.

Heathrow Airport Terminals 1, 2 & 3 Underground station 6.30am-10pm daily.

Liverpool Street 7.15am-9pm Mon-Sat; 8.15am-8pm Sun.

Victoria 7.15am-9pm Mon-Sat; 8.15am-8pm Sun.

Travelcards

A flat cash fare of £4 per journey applies across zones 1-6 on the tube; customers save up to £2.50 per journey with an pre-pay Oyster card (*see below*). Tube and DLR fares are based on a system of six zones, stretching 12 miles out from the centre of London. Anyone caught without a valid ticket or Oyster card is subject to a £20 on-the-spot fine.

Oyster card

Oyster is the cheapest way of getting around on buses, tubes and the DLR. It's a pre-paid travel smart-card that you can charge up at tube stations, London Travel Information Centres (*see p360*), some national rail stations and at newsagents. Oyster cards speed up passage through tube station ticket gates as they need only be touched on a special yellow card reader. There is a £3 refundable deposit payable for the card and you can put up to £90 on it.

Any tube journey within zone 1 using Oyster to pay-as-you-go costs £1.50 (50p for under-16s). A single tube journey within zone 2, 3, 4, 5 or 6 costs £1 (50p for under-16s). Single tube journeys from zones 1-6 using Oyster to pay-as-you-go are £3.50 (7am-7pm Mon-Fri); £2 at other times and £1 for children.

If you make a number of journeys on the tube, DLR, buses or trams, Oyster fares to pay-as-you-go will always be capped at 50p less than the price of an equivalent Day Travelcard, no matter how many journeys are made. If you only make one journey using Oyster to pay-as-you-go, you will only be charged a single Oyster fare. You can put up to £90 on your Oyster card to pay as you go.

You can also get up to three 7-Day, monthly or longer period (including annual) Travelcards and Bus Passes put on your Oyster card. For more details visit www.tfl.gov.uk/oyster or cal 0870 849 9999.

Day Travelcards

If you are only using the tube, DLR, buses and trams, using Oyster to pay as you go will always be 50p cheaper than the equivalent Day Travelcard. If you are also using National Rail services, Oyster may not be accepted: opt for a Day Travelcard. Peak Day Travelcards can be used all day, Monday to Friday (except public holidays). They cost from £6.20 for zones 1-2 (£3.10 child), up to £12.40 for zones 1-6 (£6.20 child). All tickets are valid for journeys started before 4.30am the next day. Most people are happy with the Off-Peak Day Travelcard, which allows you to travel from 9.30am (Mon-Fri) and all day Saturday, Sunday and public holidays. They cost from £5.10 for zones 1-2, rising to £6.70 for zones 1-6.

1-Day Family Travelcards

Up to four under-11s can travel free on the tube (from 9.30am Monday to Friday, all day Saturday, Sunday and public holidays) as long as they are accompanied by a fare-paying adult. Another four can travel with an adult for £1 each (a Day Travelcard is issued) at the same times.

3-Day Travelcards

If you plan to spend a few days charging around town, you can buy a 3-Day Travelcard. Again the off-peak version will meet most visitors' needs. It can be used from 9.30am Monday to Friday and all day on Saturday and Sunday, and public holidays on the start date through to any journey that starts before 4.30am on the morning following the expiry date. It costs £20.10 for zones 1-6. The peak version can be used all day Monday to Friday on the start date and for any journey that starts before 4.30am on the day following the expiry date; it's available for £16.40 (zones 1-2) or £39.60 (zones 1-6).

Children

Under-14s travel free on buses and trams without the need to provide any proof of identity. 14- and 15-year-olds can also travel free, but need to get an Under-16 Oyster photocard. For details of how to get this, visit www.tfl.gov.uk/fares or call 0845 330 9876.

A 14-15 Oyster photocard is needed by 11- to 15-year-olds to pay as they go on the tube or DLR or to buy 7 -Day, monthly or longer period Travelcards and by 11- to 15-year-olds if using the tram to/from Wimbledon.

Photocards

Photocards are not required for adult rate 7 Day Travelcards, Bus Passes or for any adult rate Travelcard or Bus Pass charged on an Oyster card. For details of how to obtain under-14, 14-15 or 16-17 Oyster photocards visit www.tfl.gov.uk/fares or call 0845 330 9876.

London Underground

Delays are common. Escalators are often out of action. Some lines close at weekends for engineering. It's hot, smelly and crowded in rush hour (approximately 8am to 9.30am and 4.30pm to 7pm Mon-Fri). Nevertheless, the underground rail system – also known as 'the tube' – is still the quickest way to get around London.

Using the system

You can get Oyster cards from www.tfl.gov.uk/oyster, by calling 0870 849 9999, at tube stations, London Travel Information Centres, some National Rail stations and newsagents. Single or day tickets can be purchased from a ticket office or from self-service machines.
You can buy most tickets and top up Oyster cards at self-service machines at most stations. Ticket offices in some stations close early (around 7.30pm), so carrying a charged-up Oyster card is a good way to avoid being stranded.

To enter and exit the tube using an Oyster card, simply touch it to the yellow reader, which will open the gates. Make sure you also touch the card to the reader when you exit the tube, otherwise you will be charged a higher fare when you next use your Oyster card to enter a station.

To enter using a paper ticket, place it in the slot with the black magnetic strip facing down, then pull it out of the top to open the gates. Exiting the system at your destination is done in much the same way, though if you have a single journey ticket, it will be retained by the gate as you leave.

There are 12 tube lines, colour-coded on the tube map (*see p416*).

Underground timetable

Tube trains run daily from around 5.30am (except Sunday, when they start an hour or two later, depending on the line). The only exception is Christmas Day, when there is no service. Generally, you should not have to wait more than ten minutes for a train, and during peak times services should run every two or three minutes. Times of last trains vary, though they're usually around 11.30pm-1am daily except Sunday, when they finish 30 minutes to an hour earlier. Other than on New Yera's Eve, when the tubes run all night, the only all-night public transport is by night bus (*see p363*). There are occasional debates about whether to run the tube an hour later at weekends, but as this would mean starting later it's not a popular idea with early shift workers. Watch this space – and learn your night buses!

Fares

The single fare for adults across the network is £4. Using Oyster pay-as-you-go the fare varies by zone: zone 1 costs £1.50; zones 1-2 costs £1.50 or £2, depending on the time you travel; the zones 1-6 single fare is £2 or £3.50. The single fare for children is

£2 for any journey that includes travel in zone 1 and £1.50 for any journey not including zone 1.

Docklands Light Railway (DLR)

DLR trains (7363 9700, www.tfl.gov.uk/dlr) run from Bank (where they connect with the tube sytem's Central and Waterloo & City lines) or Tower Gateway, which is close to Tower Hill tube (Circle and District lines). At Westferry DLR the line splits east and south via Island Gardens to Greenwich and Lewisham; a change at Poplar can take you north to Stratford. The easterly branch forks after Canning Town to either Beckton or London City Airport. Trains run from 5.30am to 12.30am Monday to Saturday and 7am to 11.30pm Sunday.

Fares

The adult single fares on DLR are the same as for the tube (*see p361*), except for a DLR-only zones 2-3 journey, which costs £1.50 (£1 using Oyster pay-as-you-go) or, for children, 70p (Oyster pay-as-you-go 50p).

The DLR also offers one day 'Rail & River Rover' tickets, which combine unlimited DLR travel with a boat trip between Greenwich, Tower and Westminster piers (riverboats run 10am-6pm; call City Cruises on 7740 0400 for round-trip times). Starting at Tower Gateway, trains leave on the hour (from 10am), with a DLR guide giving a commentary as the train glides along. Tickets cost £10.50 for adults, £5.25 for kids and £26 for a family pass (two adults and up to three under-16s); under-5s free.

Family tickets can only be bought in person from the piers; prices will change from 1 April 2007.

Buses

In the past couple of years hundreds of new buses have been introduced to the network as the old Routemasters have been phased out. All buses are now low-floor and easily accessible to wheelchair-users and passengers with buggies, and they run 24 hours. The only exceptions are Heritage routes 9 and 15, which are operated by the world-famous and much-loved open-platform Routemaster buses (*see p140* **Room for one more on top**). The introduction of 'bendy buses' with multiple-door entry and the fact that you *must* have a ticket or valid pass before getting on has at least contributed to speeding up boarding times at bus stops. Inspectors patrol and board buses at random; they can fine you £20 if you're on a bus and you haven't paid. You can buy a ticket (or 1-Day Bus Pass) from pavement ticket machines, although, frustratingly, they're often out of order. Better to travel armed with an Oyster card or some other pass (*see p361*).

Fares

Using Oyster pay-as-you-go costs £1 a trip and the most you will pay a day will be £3. Paying with cash at the time of travel costs £2 for a single trip. Under-16s travel for free (using an Under-14 or 14-15 Oyster photocard as appropriate; *see p361*). A 1-Day Bus Pass gives unlimited bus and tram travel for £3.50.

Bus Savers

A book of six Saver tickets costs £6 (under-16s travel free as above) and can be bought at some newsagents and tube station ticket offices.

Night buses

Many buses run 24 hours a day, seven days a week. There are also some special night buses with an 'N' prefix to the route number, which operate from about 11pm to 6am. Most night services run every 15 to 30 minutes, but many busier routes have a bus around every ten minutes. Fares for night buses are the same as for daytime buses. Travelcards and Bus Passes can be used on night buses at no additional charge – and until 4.30am of the morning after they expire. Oyster Pre Pay and bus Saver tickets are also valid on night buses.

Green Line buses

Green Line buses (0870 608 7261, www.greenline.co.uk) serve the suburbs and towns within a 40-mile radius of London. Their main office can be found opposite Victoria Coach Station (164 Buckingham Palace Road, Victoria, SW1W 9TP; Victoria tube/rail), and they run 24-hour services.

Rail services

Independently run commuter services leave from the city's main rail stations. Travelcards are valid on these services within the right zones. One of the most useful is **Silverlink** (0845 601 4867, www.silverlink-trains.com; or National Rail Enquiries on 0845 748 4950), which runs from Richmond in the south-west through north London to Stratford in the east. Trains run about every 20 minutes daily except Sunday, when they run every half-hour.

Tramlink

A tram service runs between Beckenham, Croydon, Addington and Wimbledon in south London. Travelcards that include zones 3, 4, 5 or 6 and all Bus Passes can be used on trams. Cash single fares are £2 (Oyster pay-as-you-go are £1 or 50p for 16-17 Oyster photocard holders who are ineligible for free bus travel). A 1-Day Bus Pass gives unlimited tram and bus travel at £3.50 for adults. Bus Saver tickets cannot be used on the tram network.

Water transport

The times of London's various river services differ, but most operate every 20 minutes to one hour between 10.30am and 5pm. Services may be more frequent and run later in summer. Call the operators listed below for schedules and fares, or see www.tfl.gov.uk. **Thames Clippers** (www.thamesclippers.com) runs a reliable commuter boat service. Piers to board the Clippers from are: Savoy (a short walk east of Embankment tube), Blackfriars, Bankside (for the Globe), London Bridge and St Katharine's (Tower Bridge). The names in bold below are the names of piers.

Embankment–Tower (25mins)–**Greenwich** (40mins); Catamaran Cruises 7987 1185/www.bateaux london.com.

Royal Arsenal Woolwich–Greenwich (15mins)–**Masthouse Terrace** (5mins)–**Greenland Dock** (4mins)–**Canary Wharf** (8mins)–**St Katharine's** (7mins)–**London Bridge City** (4mins)–**Bankside** (3mins)–**Blackfriars** (3mins)–**Savoy** (4mins); Collins River Enterprises 7252 3018/ www.thamesclippers.com.

Westminster–Festival (5mins)–**London Bridge City** (20mins)–**St Katharine's** (5mins); Crown River 7936 2033/www.crownriver.com.

Westminster–Greenwich (1hr); Thames River Services 7930 4097/ www.westminsterpier.co.uk.

Westminster–Kew (1hr 30mins)–**Richmond** (30mins)–**Hampton Court** (1hr 30mins); Westminster Passenger Service Association 97930 2062/www.wpsa.co.uk.

Westminster–Tower (40mins); City Cruises 7740 0400/ www.citycruises.com.

Taxis

Black cabs

Licensed London taxis are known as 'black cabs' – even though they often come in a variety of colours – and are a much-loved feature of London life. Drivers of black cabs must pass a test called 'the Knowledge' to prove they know every street in central London, and the shortest route to it.

If a taxi's orange 'For Hire' sign is switched on, it can be hailed. If a taxi stops, the cabbie must take you to your destination, if it's within seven miles. It can be hard to find a free cab, especially just after the pubs close, and the minute it rains. Expect to pay slightly higher rates after 8pm on weekdays and all weekend.

You can book black cabs in advance. Both **Radio Taxis** (7272 0272) and **Dial-a-Cab** (7253 5000; credit cards only) run 24-hour services (booking fee £2). Enquiries or complaints about black cabs should be made to the Public Carriage Office. Note the cab's badge number, which should be displayed in the rear of the cab and on its back bumper. For lost property, *see p371*.

Public Carriage Office

15 Penton Street, Islington, N1 9PU (0845 602 7000/www.tfl.gov.uk/pco). **Open** *Phone enquiries* 9am-8pm Mon-Fri. **Map** p404 N2.

Minicabs

Minicabs (saloon cars) are generally cheaper than black cabs, but only use licensed firms (look for the yellow disc in the front and rear windows) and avoid those who tout for business. They'll be unlicensed and uninsured, possibly dangerous, almost certainly won't know how to get around, and will charge huge rates.

There are, happily, plenty of trustworthy and licensed local minicab firms. Londonwide firms include **Lady Cabs** (7272 3300), which employs only women drivers, and **Addison Lee** (7387 8888). If you're on the move and want to find a licensed minicab firm, just text HOME to 60835 – Transport of London will send you the phone numbers of the two nearest. Always ask the price when you book and confirm it with the driver.

Driving

Congestion charge

The Congestion Charging zone operates across eight square miles of central London, bounded by the 'inner ring road' linking Euston Road, Pentonville Road, Tower Bridge, Elephant & Castle, Vauxhall Bridge Road, Park Lane and Marylebone Road. This road provides a route around the charging zone; charges apply only to vehicles inside it, not those travelling on the border roads.

From 19 February 2007, the Congestion Charging zone will be extended westward to include Bayswater, Notting Hill, High Street Kensington, north and South Kensington, Knightsbridge, Chelsea, Belgravia and Pimlico.

There is an £8 daily charge for driving on public roads within this zone 7am-6.30pm Monday to Friday. You'll know when you're about to drive into the charging zone from the red 'C' signs painted on the road. There are no tollbooths; instead you pay to register your vehicle registration number on a database. Cameras read your number plate as you enter or drive within the zone and check to see that you have paid the charge. Register and pay online (www.cclondon.com) or by calling 0845 900 1234; the charge can also be paid at newsagents, garages and NCP car parks. You can pay any time during the day of entry, even after your journey, and up to the following day, but it costs £2 extra between 10pm and midnight of the day following travel. Expect a fine of £100 (£50 if paid within 14 days) if you fail to pay by midnight on the day of travel (rising to £155 if you delay payment). For more details call 0845 900 1234 or go to www.cclondon.com. Apart from its most westerly extent, the zone is indicated on our **Central London by Area** map; *see pp394-395*.

Breakdown services

If you're a member of a motoring organisation in another country, check to see if it has a reciprocal agreement with a British organisation. Both the AA and the RAC offer schemes that cover Europe in addition to the UK.

AA (Automobile Association) *Information 0870 550 0600/ breakdown 0800 87766/membership 0800 444999/www.theaa.com.* **Open** 24hrs daily. **Credit** MC, V.

ETA (Environmental Transport Association) *68 High Street, Weybridge, Surrey KT13 8RS*

(0845 389 1010/www.eta.co.uk). **Open** *Membership* 8am-6pm Mon-Fri; 9am-4pm Sat. *Breakdown service* 24hrs daily. **Credit** MC, V.

RAC (Royal Automobile Club) *RAC House, 1 Forest Road, Feltham, Middx TW13 7RR (breakdown 0800 828282/office & membership 0870 572 2722/www.rac.co.uk).* **Open** *Office* 8am-8pm Mon-Fri; 8.30am-5pm Sat. *Breakdown service* 24hrs daily. **Credit** AmEx, DC, MC, V.

Parking

Central London is scattered with parking meters, but free ones are rare, they'll cost you up to £1 for every 15 minutes, and you'll be limited to two hours on the meter. Parking on a single or double yellow line, a red line or in residents' parking areas during the day is illegal, and you may end up being fined, clamped or towed.

However, in the evening (from 6pm or 7pm in much of central London) and at various times at weekends, parking on single yellow lines is legal and free. If you find a clear spot on a single yellow line during the evening, look for a sign giving the regulations for that area. Meters also become free at certain times during evenings and weekends. Parking on double yellow lines and red routes is illegal at all times.

NCP 24-hour car parks (0870 606 7050, www.ncp.co.uk) around London are numerous but pricey (£6-£10 for two hours). Central ones include Arlington House, Arlington Street; St James's, W1; Snowsfield, Southwark, SE1; and 4-5 Denman Street, Soho, W1.

Clamping

The immobilising of illegally parked vehicles with a clamp is commonplace in London. There will be a label on the car telling you which payment centre to phone or visit. You'll have to stump up an £80 release fee and show a valid licence.

The payment centre will de-clamp your car within the next four hours, but they won't say exactly when. If you don't remove your car at once, they might clamp it again, so wait by your vehicle.

Vehicle removal

If your car has disappeared, the chances are (assuming it was legally parked) it's been nicked; if not, it's probably been taken to a car pound. A release fee of £200 is levied for removal, plus £25 per day from the first midnight after removal. To add insult to injury, you'll also probably get a parking ticket of £60-£100 when you collect the car (which will be reduced by a 50% discount if paid within 14 days). To find out how to retrieve your car, call the Trace Service hotline (7747 4747).

Vehicle hire

To hire a car, you must have at least one year's driving experience with a full current driving licence; in addition, many car hire firms refuse to rent vehicles out to people under 23. If you're an overseas visitor, your driving licence is valid in Britain for a year.

Prices vary wildly; always ring several competitors for a quote. **Easycar**'s online-only service, at www.easycar.com, offers competitive rates, just so long as you don't mind driving a branded car around town.

Alamo *0870 400 4508/www.alamo.com.* **Open** 8am-6pm Mon-Fri; 9am-5pm Sat; 10am-3pm Sun. **Credit** AmEx, MC, V.

Avis *0870 590 0500/www.avis.co.uk.* **Open** 6am-10pm daily. **Credit** AmEx, MC, V.

Budget *0844 581 9999/www.budget.co.uk.* **Open** 8am-8pm daily. **Credit** AmEx, DC, MC, V.

Enterprise *0870 607 7757/www.enterprise.com.* **Open** 7am-midnight Mon-Fri; 8am-midnight Sat, Sun. **Credit** AmEx, DC, MC, V.

Europcar *0870 607 5000/www.europcar.co.uk.* **Open** 24hrs daily. **Credit** AmEx, DC, MC, V.

Hertz *0870 599 6699/www.hertz.co.uk.* **Open** 24hrs daily. **Credit** AmEx, DC, MC, V.

Motorbike hire

HGB Motorcycles *69-71 Park Way, Ruislip Manor, Middx HA4 8NS (01895 676451/www.hgbmotorcycles.co.uk). Ruislip Manor tube.* **Open** 9am-6pm Mon-Sat. **Credit** MC, V.

Rental prices include 250 miles a day (with excess mileage at 10p a mile), AA cover, insurance and VAT. Bikes can only be hired with a valid credit card and you'll have to leave a deposit (£350-£850). You'll also need your own helmet.

Cycling

London isn't the friendliest of towns for cyclists, but the **London Cycle Network** (see www.londoncyclenetwork.org) and **London Cycling Campaign** (7234 9310, www.lcc.org.uk) help make it better. Call **Transport for London** (7222 1234) for cycling maps that indicate designated cycle paths and quieter routes.

Cycle hire

OY Bike (www.oybike.com) has 28 bike stations in west London from which you can rent a bike for a reasonable cost 24/7 by calling in on a mobile phone (the lock is electronically released). You do have to pre-register with £10 credit. Hire rates begin at 30p for 15 minutes.

London Bicycle Tour Company
1A Gabriel's Wharf, 56 Upper Ground, South Bank, SE1 9PP (7928 6838/www.londonbicycle.com). Southwark tube, Blackfriars or Waterloo tube/rail. **Open** 10am-6pm daily. **Hire** £3/hr; £16/1st day; £8/day thereafter. **Deposit** £150 cash or £1 by credit card. **Credit** AmEx, DC, MC, V. **Map** p406 N7.
Bikes, tandems and rickshaw hire; bicycle tours Sat, Sun.

Go Pedal!
07850 796320/www.gopedal.co.uk.
Delivers a bicycle and accessories to where you want them, and collects when you're done. The website offers good advice about cycling in London.

Walking

The best way to see London is on foot, but the city is very complicated in its street layout – even locals carry maps around with them. We've included street maps of central London in the back of this book (starting on p392), but the standard Geographers' *A–Z* and Collins' *London Street Atlas* are both very good. Nonetheless, expect to get lost – and enjoy finding your way back again.

Resources A-Z

Addresses

London postcodes are less helpful than they could be for locating addresses. The first element starts with a compass point – out of N, E, SE, SW, W and NW, plus the smaller EC (East Central) and WC (West Central) – which at least gives you a basic idea. However, the number that follows bears no relation to geography (unless it's a 1, which indicates that the address is central), though they apparently follow a rough alphabetical order. So N2, for example, is way out in the boondocks (East Finchley), while W2 includes the very central Bayswater.

Age restrictions

You must be 17 or older to drive in the United Kingdom, and 18 to buy cigarettes or to buy or be served alcohol (to be safe, carry photo ID if you look younger). The age of heterosexual and homosexual consent is 16.

Business

Conventions & conferences

Visit London
7234 5800/www.visitlondon.com. Visit London runs a venue enquiry service for conventions and exhibitions. Call or email for an information pack that lists the facilities offered by various venues, or follow the links from the website.

Queen Elizabeth II Conference Centre
Broad Sanctuary, Westminster, SW1P 3EE (7222 5000/www.qeiicc.co.uk). Westminster tube. **Open** 8am-6pm Mon-Fri. *Conference facilities* 24hrs daily. **Map** p403 K9.
This purpose-built centre has some of the best conference facilities in the capital. Rooms have capacities ranging from 40 to 1,100, all with wireless LAN technology installed.

Couriers & shippers

DHL and FedEx (both with drop-off points all over London) offer courier services both locally and internationally; Excess Baggage is the UK's largest shipper of luggage.

DHL *St Alphage House, 2 Fore Street, the City, EC2Y 5DA (7562 3000/www.dhl.co.uk). Moorgate tube/rail.* **Open** 9am-5.45pm Mon-Fri. **Credit** AmEx, DC, MC, V. **Map** p404 P5.

Excess Baggage *168 Earl's Court Road, Earl's Court, SW5 9QQ (7373 1977/www.excess-baggage.com). Earl's Court tube.* **Open** 8am-6pm Mon-Fri; 9am-1pm Sat. **Credit** AmEx, MC, V. **Map** p398 B10.

FedEx *08456 070809/www.fedex.com.* **Open** 7.30am-7.30pm Mon-Fri. **Credit** AmEx, DC, MC, V.

Office hire & business centres

ABC rents office equipment, while British Monomarks offers communications services.

ABC Business Machines
17 Nottingham Street, Marylebone, W1U 5EW (7486 5634/www.abcbusiness.co.uk). Baker Street tube. **Open** 9am-5pm Mon-Fri; *Sat* phone for details. **Credit** MC, V. **Map** p400 G5.

British Monomarks
Monomarks House, 27 Old Gloucester Street, Holborn, WC1N 3XX (7419 5000/www.britishmonomarks.co.uk). Holborn tube. **Open** *Mail forwarding* 9.30am-5.30pm Mon-Fri. *Telephone answering* 9am-6pm Mon-Fri. **Credit** AmEx, MC, V. **Map** p401 L5.

Customs

See also www.hmrc.gov.uk.

From inside the EU

You may bring in the following quantities of tax-paid goods, as long as they are for your own consumption (there are some exceptions when coming from Eastern European countries).

- 3,200 cigarettes or 400 cigarillos or 200 cigars or 3kg (6.6lb) tobacco;
- 90 litres wine plus either ten litres of spirits or liqueurs (more than 22% alcohol by volume) or 20 litres of fortified wine (under 22% ABV), sparkling wine or other liqueurs.

From outside the EU

These are total allowances, whether or not the goods were purchased duty-free.

- 200 cigarettes or 100 cigarillos or 50 cigars or 250g of tobacco;
- 2 litres of still table wine plus either 1 litre of spirits or strong liqueurs over 22% volume or two litres of fortified wine, sparkling wine or other liqueurs;
- £145 worth of all other goods including gifts and souvenirs.

Travel advice

For current information on travel to a specific country – including the latest news on health issues, safety and security, local laws and customs – contact your home country's government department of foreign affairs. Most have websites with useful advice for would-be travellers.

Australia
www.smartraveller.gov.au

Republic of Ireland
http://foreignaffairs.gov.ie

Canada
www.voyage.gc.ca

UK
www.fco.gov.uk/travel

New Zealand
www.safetravel.govt.nz

USA
http://travel.state.gov

Disabled

As a city that evolved long before the needs of disabled people were considered, London is a difficult place for disabled visitors, though legislation is gradually improving access and general facilities. In 2004 anyone who provides a service to the public was required to make 'reasonable adjustments' to their properties, and the capital's bus fleet is now more wheelchair accessible. The tube, however, remains extremely escalator-dependent and can therefore be of only limited use to wheelchair users. The *Tube Access Guide* booklet is available free of charge by calling the Travel Information line for more information (7222 1234).

Most major visitor attractions and hotels offer good accessibility, though provisions for the hearing- and sight-disabled are patchier. Call businesses in advance to enquire about facilities, and use your judgement in interpreting their response. *Access in London* is an invaluable reference book for disabled travellers, available for a £10 donation (sterling cheque, cash US dollars or online via PayPal to gordon.couch@virgin.net) from Access Project (www.accessproject-phsp.org), 39 Bradley Gardens, West Ealing, W13 8HE.

Artsline

54 Chalton Street, Somers Town, NW1 1HS (tel/textphone 7388 2227/www.artslineonline.com). Euston tube/rail. **Open** 9.30am-5.30pm Mon-Fri. **Map** p401 K3.
Information on disabled access to arts and entertainment events in and around London.

Can Be Done

11 Woodcock Hill, Harrow, Middx HA3 0XP (8907 2400/www.canbedone.co.uk). Kenton tube/rail. **Open** 9.30am-5pm Mon-Fri.
This company runs disabled-adapted holidays and tours in London, around the UK and worldwide.

DAIL (Disability Arts in London)

20-22 Waterson Street, Hackney, E2 8HE (7739 1133/www.ldaf.org). Liverpool Street tube/rail then 149, 242 bus/Old Street tube/rail then 243 bus. **Enquiries** 11am-4pm Mon-Fri.
DAIL produces a bimonthly magazine (£15/yr waged, £9/yr unwaged). DAIL is part of LDAF (London Disability Arts Forum, 7916 5484), which organises events for disabled people in London.

Greater London Action on Disability

1st floor, Downstream Buildings, 1 London Bridge, SE1 9BG (7022 1890/textphone 7378 1686/www.glad.org.uk). London Bridge tube/rail. **Open** *Phone enquiries* 9am-5pm Mon-Fri. **Map** 407 Q8.
A valuable resource for disabled visitors and residents.

Royal Association for Disability & Rehabilitation

12 City Forum, 250 City Road, Islington, EC1V 2AF (7250 3222/textphone 7250 4119/www.radar.org.uk). Old Street tube/rail. **Open** 9am-5pm Mon-Fri. **Map** p404 P3.
A national organisation for disabled voluntary groups that also publishes books and the bimonthly magazine *New Bulletin* (£35/yr).

Tourism for All

0845 124 9971/www.tourismforall.org.uk. **Open** *Helpline* 9am-5pm Mon-Fri.
Information for older people and people with disabilities in relation to accessible accommodation and other tourism services.

Wheelchair Travel & Access Mini Buses

1 Johnston Green, Guildford, Surrey GU2 9XS (01483 233640/www.wheelchair-travel.co.uk). **Open** 9am-5.30pm Mon-Fri; 9am-noon Sat.
Hires out converted vehicles (driver optional), plus cars with hand controls and wheelchair-adapted vehicles.

Electricity

The UK uses the standard European 220-240V, 50-cycle AC voltage. British plugs use three pins, so travellers with two-pin European appliances should bring an adaptor, as should anyone using US appliances, which run off 110-120V, 60-cycle.

Embassies & consulates

American Embassy *24 Grosvenor Square, Mayfair, W1A 1AE (7499 9000/www.usembassy.org.uk). Bond Street or Marble Arch tube.* **Open** 8.30am-5.30pm Mon-Fri. **Map** p402 G7.

Australian High Commission *Australia House, Strand, Holborn, WC2B 4LA (7379 4334/www.australia.org.uk). Holborn or Temple tube.* **Open** 9.30am-3.30pm Mon-Fri. **Map** p403 M6.

Canadian High Commission *38 Grosvenor Street, Mayfair, W1K 4AA (7258 6600/www.canada.org.uk). Bond Street or Oxford Circus tube.* **Open** 8-11am Mon-Fri. **Map** p402 H7.

Embassy of ireland *17 Grosvenor Place, Belgravia, SW1X 7HR (7235 2171/passports & visas 7225 7700). Hyde Park Corner tube.* **Open** 9.30am-1pm, 2.30-5pm Mon-Fri. **Map** p402 G9.

New Zealand High Commission *New Zealand House, 80 Haymarket, St James's, SW1Y 4TQ (7930 8422/www.nzembassy.com). Piccadilly Circus tube.* **Open** 9am-5pm Mon-Fri. **Map** p408 W4.

South African High Commission *South Africa House, Trafalgar Square, St James's, WC2N 5DP (7451 7299/www.southafricahouse.com). Charing Cross tube/rail.* **Open** 9am-5pm Mon-Fri. **Map** p409 X5.

Emergencies

In the event of a serious accident, fire or other incident, call **999** – free from any phone, including payphones – and ask for an ambulance, the fire service or police. For addresses of Accident & Emergency departments, *see p369*; for helplines, *see p370*; and for city police stations, *see p373*.

Gay & lesbian

For a complete gay guide to the capital, purchase the *Time Out Gay & Lesbian London Guide* (£9.99). The phonelines below offer help and information.

London Friend *7837 3337/www.londonfriend.org.uk.* **Open** 7.30-10pm daily.

London Lesbian & Gay Switchboard *7837 7324/www.queery.org.uk.* **Open** 24hrs daily.

Health

Free emergency medical treatment under the National Health Service (NHS) is available to the following:

- European Union nationals, plus those of Iceland, Norway and Liechtenstein. They may also be entitled to treatment for a non-emergency condition on production of form E112 or E128.
- Nationals of Bulgaria, Romania, the Czech and Slovak Republics, Gibraltar, Hungary, Malta, New Zealand, Russia, most former USSR states and the former Yugoslavia.
- Residents, irrespective of nationality, of Anguilla, Australia, Barbados, British Virgin Islands, Channel Islands, Falkland Islands, Iceland, Isle of Man, Montserrat, Poland, Romania, St Helena and Turks & Caicos Islands.
- Anyone who has been in the UK for the previous 12 months.
- Anyone who has come to the UK to take up permanent residence.
- Students and trainees whose courses require more than 12 weeks in employment during the first year.
- Refugees and others who have sought refuge in the UK.
- People with HIV/AIDS at a special clinic for the treatment of STDs. The treatment covered is limited to a diagnostic test and counselling associated with that test.

There are no NHS charges for services including:

- Treatment in Accident & Emergency departments.
- Emergency ambulance transport to a hospital.
- Diagnosis and treatment of certain communicable diseases, including STDs.
- Family planning services.
- Compulsory psychiatric treatment.

Accident & emergency

Below are listed most of the central London hospitals that have 24-hour Accident & Emergency departments.

Charing Cross Hospital *Fulham Palace Road, Hammersmith, W6 8RF (8846 1234). Barons Court or Hammersmith tube.*

Chelsea & Westminster Hospital *369 Fulham Road, Chelsea, SW10 9NH (8746 8000). South Kensington tube.* **Map** p398 C12.

Guy's Hospital *St Thomas Street (entrance Snowsfields), Borough, SE1 9RT (7188 7188). London Bridge tube/rail.* **Map** p406 P8.

Homerton University Hospital *Homerton Row, Homerton, E9 6SR (8510 5555). Homerton rail/242 bus.*

Royal Free Hospital *Pond Street, Hampstead, NW3 2QG (7794 0500). Belsize Park tube/ Hampstead Heath rail.*

Royal London Hospital *Whitechapel Road, Whitechapel, E1 1BB (7377 7000). Whitechapel tube.*

St Mary's Hospital *Praed Street, Paddington, W2 1NY (7886 6666). Paddington tube/rail.* **Map** p397 D5.

St Thomas's Hospital *Lambeth Palace Road, Lambeth, SE1 7EH (7188 7188). Westminster tube/ Waterloo tube/rail.* **Map** p403 L9.

University College Hospital *Grafton Way, Fitzrovia, WC1E 3BG (7387 5798). Euston Square or Warren Street tube.* **Map** p400 J4.

Whittington Hospital *Highgate Hill, Archway, N19 5NF (7272 3070). Archway tube.*

Complementary medicine

For a full list of alternative health centres, see the *Time Out Health & Fitness Guide* (£4.99).

British Homeopathic Association

0870 444 3950/www.trust homeopathy.org. **Open** *Phone enquiries* 9am-5pm Mon-Fri.
The BHA will refer you to the nearest homeopathic chemist/doctor.

Contraception & abortion

Family planning advice, contraceptive supplies and abortions are free to British citizens on the NHS; also to EU residents and foreign nationals living in Britain. Phone the Contraception Helpline on 0845 310 1334 or visit www.fpa.org.uk for your local **Family Planning Association**. The 'morning after' pill (around £25), effective up to 72 hours after intercourse, is available over the counter at pharmacies.

British Pregnancy Advisory Service

0845 730 4030/www.bpas.org.
Callers are referred to their nearest clinic for treatment. Contraceptives are available, as is pregnancy testing.

Brook Advisory Centre

7284 6040/helpline 0800 018 5023/ www.brook.org.uk). **Open** *Helpline* 9am-5pm Mon-Fri.
Information on sexual health, contraception and abortion, plus free pregnancy tests for under-25s. Call for your nearest clinic.

Marie Stopes House

Family Planning Clinic/ Well Woman Centre

108 Whitfield Street, Fitzrovia, W1P 6BE (0845 300 8090/www.marie stopes.org.uk). Warren Street tube. **Open** *Clinic* 8.30am-4.30pm Mon-Fri. *Termination helpline* 7am-10pm Mon-Fri. **Map** p400 J4.
For contraceptive advice, emergency contraception, pregnancy testing, an abortion service, cervical and health screening or gynaecological services. Fees may apply.

Dentists

Dental care is free for resident students, under-18s and people on benefits. All other patients must pay. NHS-eligible patients pay on a subsidised scale. To find an NHS dentist, get in touch with the local Health Authority or a Citizens' Advice Bureau (*see p370*), or the following:

Dental Emergency Care Service

Guy's Hospital, St Thomas Street, Bankside, SE1 9RT (7188 0511). London Bridge tube/rail. **Open** 9am-5pm Mon-Fri. **Map** p406 Q8.
Queues start forming at 8am; arrive by 10am if you're to be seen at all.

Doctors

If you're a British citizen or working in the United Kingdom, you can go to any general practitioner (GP). If you're not visiting your usual GP, you'll need to give their details so your records can be updated. People ordinarily resident in the UK, including overseas students, are also permitted to register with an NHS doctor. If you fall outside these categories, you can still see a GP but will have to pay. Your hotel concierge should be able to recommend a suitable one.

Great Chapel Street Medical Centre

13 Great Chapel Street, Soho, W1F 8FL (7437 9360). Leicester Square, Oxford Circus or Tottenham Court Road tube. **Open** *Drop in* 11am-12.30pm, 2-4pm Mon, Tue, Thur; 2-4pm Wed, Fri. **Map** p408 W2.
A drop-in centre for homeless single people without a doctor. Phone before you go, as it operates different clinics each day.

Hospitals

For a list of hospitals with A&E departments, *see p369*; for other hospitals, see the Yellow Pages directory.

Pharmacies

Also called 'chemists' in the UK. Larger supermarkets and all branches of Boots (*see p258*) have a pharmacy, and there are independents on the high street. Staff are qualified to advise on over-the-counter medicines. Most pharmacies keep shop hours (9am-6pm, closed Sun).

Prescriptions

A pharmacist will dispense medicines on receipt of a prescription from a GP. NHS prescriptions cost £6.65; under-16s and over-60s are exempt from charges. Contraception is free for all. If you're not eligible to see an NHS doctor, you'll be charged cost price for medicines prescribed by a private doctor.

STDs, HIV & AIDS

NHS Genito-Urinary Clinics (such as the Centre for Sexual Health, *see below*) are affiliated to major hospitals. They provide free, confidential treatment of STDs and other problems, such as thrush and cystitis; offer counselling about HIV and other STDs, and can conduct blood tests.

The 24-hour **Sexual Healthline** (0800 567123, www.playingsafely.co.uk) is free and confidential. Check the website to find your nearest clinic. For other helplines, *see below*; for abortion and contraception services, *see p369*.

Ambrose King Centre

Royal London Hospital, Whitechapel Road, Whitechapel, E1 1BB (7377 7306/www.bartsandthelondon.nhs.uk). Whitechapel tube. **Open** 9am-4pm Mon, Thur; 9am-3pm Tue, Fri; noon-4pm Wed.
Screening for and treatment of STDs, HIV testing and counselling. Services are provided on a walk-in basis. Doors open 30 minutes before clinic hours.

Centre for Sexual Health

Genito-Urinary Clinic, Jefferiss Wing, St Mary's Hospital, Praed Street, Paddington, W2 1NY (7886 1697). Paddington tube/rail. **Open** *Walk-in clinic* 8.45am-6.15pm Mon, Tue, Thur; 11.45am-6.15pm Wed; 8.45am-1.15pm Fri. **Map** p397 D5.
A free and confidential walk-in clinic. New patients must arrive at least 30 minutes before closing.

Mortimer Market Centre for Sexual Health

Mortimer Market, off Capper Street, Bloomsbury, WC1E 6JB (7530 5050). Goodge Street or Warren Street tube. **Open** *Bloomsbury clinic* 9am-5.30pm Mon, Tue, Thur; 1-4pm Wed; 9am-noon Fri. *GUM clinic (appointments only)* 10.30am-3pm Mon; 9am-4.30pm Tue, Thur; 1-4pm Wed; 9am-noon Fri. *Walk-in clinic* (men over 24; women over 22) 3.45-6pm Mon. **Map** p400 J4.

Terrence Higgins Trust Lighthouse

314-320 Gray's Inn Road, Holborn, WC1X 8DP (office 7812 1600/ helpline 0845 122 1200/www.tht.org.uk). King's Cross tube. **Open** *Office* 9.30am-5.30pm Mon-Fri. *Helpline* 10am-10pm Mon-Fri; noon-6pm Sat, Sun. **Map** p401 M5.
This well-known charity advises and counsels those with HIV/AIDS, their relatives, lovers and friends. It also offers free leaflets about AIDS and safer sex.

Helplines

Sexual health helplines are listed under **STDs, HIV & AIDS** (*see above*).

Alcoholics Anonymous

0845 769 7555/www.alcoholics-anonymous.org.uk.

Citizens' Advice Bureaux

The council-run CABs offer free legal, financial and personal advice. Check the phone book or see www.citizensadvice.org.uk for your nearest office.

NHS Direct

0845 4647/www.nhsdirect.nhs.uk. **Open** 24hrs daily.
NHS Direct is a free, first-stop service for medical advice on all subjects.

National Missing Persons Helpline

0500 700 700/www.missingpersons.org. **Open** 24hrs daily.
The volunteer-run NMPH publicises information on anyone reported missing, and helps to find missing persons. Its 'Message Home' freephone service (0800 700 740) allows runaways to reassure friends or family of their wellbeing without revealing their whereabouts.

Rape & Sexual Abuse Support Centre

8683 3300/www.rapecrisis.org.uk. **Open** *Helpline* noon-2.30pm, 7-9.30pm Mon-Fri; 2.30-5pm Sat, Sun.
Provides support and information for victims and families.

Samaritans

0845 790 9090/www.samaritans.org.uk. **Open** 24hrs daily.
The Samaritans listen to anyone with emotional problems. It's a busy service, so persevere when phoning.

Victim Support

Head office: Cramner House, 39 Brixton Road, Brixton, SW9 6DZ (0845 303 0900/www.victimsupport.com). **Open** *Support line* 9am-9pm Mon-Fri; 9am-7pm Sat, Sun.
Volunteer provides emotional and practical support to victims of crime, including information and advice on legal procedures. Interpreters can be arranged where necessary.

Insurance

Insuring personal belongings is very important. It can be difficult to arrange once you have arrived in London, so do so before you leave home.

Medical insurance is usually included in travel insurance packages. Unless your country has a reciprocal medical treatment arrangement with Britain (*see p369*), it's very important to ensure you have adequate health cover.

Internet

Most hotels have at least a modem plug-in point (dataport) in each room, if not broadband or wireless access. Those that don't have either usually offer some other form of surfing.

There are lots of cybercafés around town, including the **easyInternetCafé** chain (*see below*). You'll also find terminals in public libraries (*see below*). For more, check www.cybercafes.com.

Wireless access has taken off slowly in Britain, but if your machine is properly equipped Islington has a 'technology mile' of free Wi-Fi access that stretches along Upper Street from Angel to Highbury & Islington. Some major railway stations, including London Bridge and Charing Cross, parts of the major airports and many Starbucks locations also offer access, usually for a fee. For locations, check with your provider or visit www.wi-fi hotspotlist.com.

Internet access

easyInternetCafé *456-459 Strand, Trafalgar Square, WC2R ORG (www.easyinternetcafe.com). Charing Cross tube/rail.* **Open** 8am-11pm daily. **Terminals** 393. **Map** p409 Y5.
Other locations: throughout the city.

Left luggage

Airports

Gatwick Airport *South Terminal 01293 502014/North Terminal 01293 502013.*
Heathrow Airport *Terminal 1 8745 5301/Terminals 2-3 8759 3344/Terminal 4 8897 6874.*
London City Airport *7646 0162.*
Stansted Airport *01279 663213.*

Rail & bus stations

The threat of terrorism has meant that London stations tend to have left-luggage desks rather than lockers; to find out whether a train station offers this facility, call 0845 748 4950.

Legal help

Those in difficulties can visit a Citizens' Advice Bureau (*see p370*) or contact the groups below. Try the Legal Services Commission (7759 0000, www.legalservices.gov.uk) for information. If you are arrested, your first call should be to your embassy (*see p368*).

Community Legal Services Directory

0845 345 4345/www.clsdirect.org.uk. **Open** 9am-5pm Mon-Fri.
Telephone service providing free information for those with legal problems.

Joint Council for the Welfare of Immigrants

115 Old Street, Hoxton, EC1V 9RT (7251 8706/www.jcwi.org.uk). **Phone enquiries** 2-5pm Tue, Thur.
JCWI's telephone-only legal advice line offers guidance and referrals.

Law Centres Federation

Duchess House, 18-19 Warren Street, Fitzrovia, W1T 5LR (7387 8570/www.lawcentres.org.uk). Warren Street tube. **Open** *Phone enquiries* 9.30am-5pm Mon-Fri.
Local law centres offer free legal help for people who can't afford a lawyer. and are living or working in the immediate area; this central office connects you with the nearest.

Libraries

Unless you're a London resident, you won't be able to join a lending library. Only the British Library's exhibition areas are open to non-members; other libraries listed can be used for reference.

Barbican Library *Barbican Centre, Silk Street, the City, EC2Y 8DS (7638 0569/www.cityoflondon.gov.uk/barbicanlibrary). Barbican or Moorgate tube/rail.* **Open** 9.30am-5.30pm Mon, Wed; 9.30am-7pm Tue, Thur; 9.30am-2pm Fri; 9.30am-4pm Sat. **Map** p404 P5.
British Library *96 Euston Road, NW1 2DB (7412 7000/www.bl.uk). King's Cross tube/rail.* **Open** *Reading room* 10am-8pm Mon; 9.30am-8pm Tue-Thur; 9.30am-5pm Fri, Sat. *Admissions office* 9.30am-6pm Mon, Wed, Thur; 9.30am-8pm Tue; 9.30am-4.30pm Fri, Sat. **Map** p401 L3.
Holborn Library *32-38 Theobald's Road, Bloomsbury, WC1X 8PA (7974 6345). Chancery Lane tube.* **Open** 10am-7pm Mon, Thur; 10am-6pm Tue, Wed, Fri; 10am-5pm Sat. **Map** p401 M5.
Kensington Central Library *12 Philimore Walk, Kensington, W8 7RX (7937 2542/www.rbkc.gov.uk/libraries). High Street Kensington tube.* **Open** 9.30am-8pm Mon, Tue, Thur; 9.30am-5pm Wed, Fri, Sat.
Marylebone Library *109-117 Marylebone Road, Marylebone, NW1 5PS (7641 1041/www.westminster.gov.uk/libraries). Baker Street tube/Marylebone tube/rail.* **Open** 9.30am-8pm Mon, Tue, Thur, Fri; 10am-8pm Wed; 9.30am-5pm Sat; 1.30-5pm Sun. **Map** p397 F4.
Victoria Library *160 Buckingham Palace Road, Belgravia, SW1W 9UD (7641 4287/www.westminster.gov.uk/ libraries). Victoria tube/rail.* **Open** 9.30am-8pm Mon; 9.30am-7pm Tue, Thur, Fri; 10am-7pm Wed; 9.30am-5pm Sat. *Music library* 11am-7pm Mon-Fri; 10am-5pm Sat. **Map** p402 H10.
Westminster Reference Library *35 St Martin's Street, Westminster, WC2H 7HP (7641 4636/www.westminster.gov.uk/libraries). Leicester Square tube.* **Open** 10am-8pm Mon-Fri; 10am-5pm Sat. **Map** p409 X4.

Lost property

Always inform the police if you lose anything, if only to validate insurance claims. *See p373* or the Yellow Pages for your nearest police station. Only dial 999 if violence has occurred. Report lost passports both to the police and to your embassy (*see p368*).

Airports

For property lost on the plane, contact the relevant airline; for items lost in a particular airport, contact the following:

Gatwick Airport *01293 503162.*
Heathrow Airport *8745 7727.*
London City Airport *7646 0000.*
Luton Airport *01582 395219.*
Stansted Airport *01279 663293.*

Public transport

If you've lost property in an overground station or on a train, call 0870 000 5151, and give the operator the details.

Transport for London

Lost Property Office, 200 Baker Street, Marylebone, NW1 5RZ (7918 2000/www.tfl.gov.uk). Baker Street tube. **Open** 8.30am-4pm Mon-Fri. **Map** p400 G4.

Allow three working days from the time of loss. If you lose something on a bus, call 7222 1234 and ask for the phone numbers of the depots at either end of the route. If you lose something on a tube, pick up a lost property form from any station.

Taxis

Taxi Lost Property

200 Baker Street, Marylebone, NW1 5RZ (7918 2000/www.tfl.gov.uk). Baker Street tube. **Open** 8.30am-4pm Mon-Fri. **Map** p400 G4.

This office deals only with property found in registered black cabs. You are advised to allow seven days from the time of loss. For items lost in a minicab, contact the office of the relevant company.

Media

Magazines

Time Out remains London's only quality magazine, widely available every Tuesday in central London, and gives listings for the week from the Wednesday. If you want to know what's going on and whether it's going to be any good, this is where to look.

Nationally, *Loaded, FHM* and *Maxim* are big men's titles, while women read handbag-sized *Glamour* and glossy weekly *Grazia* alongside *Vogue, Marie Claire* and *Elle*. The appetite for celebrity magazines like *Heat, Closer* and *OK* doesn't seem to have abated, while style mags like *i-D* and *Dazed and Confused* have found a profitable niche.

The *Spectator, Prospect,* the *Economist* and the *New Statesman* are at the serious, political end of the market, while the satirical *Private Eye* brings a little levity to the subject. The applaudable *Big Issue* is sold across the capital by registered homeless vendors – a good read for a good cause.

Newspapers

London's main daily paper is the dull, right-wing *Evening Standard*, published Mon-Fri. *Metro*, an *Evening Standard* spin-off, led what in 2006 became a deluge of free dailies: *London Lite* (the *Standard* again) and the *London Paper* are overpriced at gratis – pick up one of the copies discarded on the tube or a bus to see what we mean.

Quality national dailies include, from right to left, the *Daily Telegraph* and *The Times* (which is best for sport), the *Independent* and the *Guardian* (best for arts). All have bulging Sunday equivalents bar the *Guardian*, which has a sister Sunday paper, the *Observer*. The pink *Financial Times* (daily except Sunday) is the best for business. In the middle market, the leader is the right-wing *Daily Mail* (and *Mail on Sunday*); the *Daily Express* (and *Sunday Express*) tries to compete. Tabloid leader is the *Sun* (and Sunday's *News of the World*). The *Daily Star* and *Mirror* are the main lowbrow contenders.

Radio

The stations listed below are broadcast on standard wavebands as well as digital, where they are joined by some interesting new channels, particularly from the BBC. The format is not yet widespread, but you might just be lucky enough to have digital in your hotel room or hire car.

BBC Radio 1 *97-99 FM.* Standard mix of youth-oriented pop, indie, metal and dance.

BBC Radio 2 *88-91 FM.* Bland during the day, but good after dark.

BBC Radio 3 *90-93 FM.* Classical music dominates, but there's also discussion, world music and arts.

BBC Radio 4 *92-95 FM, 198 LW.* The BBC's main speech station. News agenda-setter *Today* (6-9am Mon-Fri, 7-9am Sat) exudes self-importance.

BBC Radio 5 Live *693, 909 AM.* Rolling news and sport. Avoid the morning phone-ins, but *Up All Night* (1-5am nightly) is terrific.

BBC London *94.9 FM.* Robert Elms (noon-3pm Mon-Fri) is good.

BBC World Service *648 AM.* A distillation of the best of all the other BBC stations; transmitted worldwide.

Capital FM *95.8 FM.* London's best-known station: chat and music.

Classic FM *100-102 FM.* Easy-listening classical.

Heart FM *106.2 FM.* Capital for grown-ups.

Jazz FM *102.2 FM.* Smooth jazz (aka elevator music) now dominates.

LBC *97.3 FM.* Phone-ins and features. The cabbies' favourite.

Resonance *104.4 FM.* Arts radio – an inventively oddball mix.

Xfm *104.9 FM.* Alternative rock.

Television

With a multiplicity of formats, there are plenty of pay-TV options. However, the relative quality of free TV (most notably the BBC's new digital channels) keeps subscriptions from attaining US levels.

Network channels

BBC1 The Corporation's mass-market station. Relies too much on soaps, game shows and lifestyle TV, but has quality offerings too, notably in nature and drama. As with all BBC stations, there are no commercials.

BBC2 A reasonably intelligent cultural cross-section and plenty of documentaries, but upstaged by the BBC's digital arts channel, BBC4 (*see below*).

ITV1 Carlton provides monotonous weekday mass-appeal shows, with oft-repeated successes for ITV. LWT (London Weekend Television) takes over at the weekend with more of the same. ITV2 is on digital.

Channel 4 C4's output includes a variety of extremely successful US imports (*Desperate Housewives, ER, Lost, The Sopranos* and so on – many now on E4), but it still comes up with some gems of its own, particularly documentaries.

Five Sex, TV movies, rubbish comedy and the occasional good documentary.

Selected satellite, digital & cable

BBC3 *EastEnders* reruns and other light fare, quality comedy.

BBC4 Highbrow stuff, including earnest documentaries and dramas.

BBC News 24 Rolling 24hr news.

BBC Parliament Live debates and highlights from Parliament.

Discovery Channel Science and nature documentaries.

E4/Film4 C4's entertainment and movie channels.
Five US US sport, drama and documentaries.
ITV4 'Challenging' drama, comedy and film.
Sky News Rolling news.
Sky One Sky's version of ITV.
Sky Sports There are also Sky Sports 2 and Sky Sports 3.

Money

Britain's currency is the pound sterling (£). One pound equals 100 pence (p). Coins are copper (1p, 2p), silver (round: 5p, 10p; seven-sided: 20p, 50p), yellowy-gold (£1) or silver in the centre with a yellowy-gold edge (£2). Paper notes are blue (£5), orange (£10), purple (£20) or red (£50). You can exchange foreign currency at banks, bureaux de change and post offices; there's no commission charge at the last of these (for addresses of the most central *see p374*). Many large stores also accept euros.

Western Union

0800 833833/www.westernunion.co.uk. The old standby for bailing out cash-challenged travellers. Chequepoint (*see below*) also offers this service.

ATMs

As well as inside and outside banks, cash machines can be found in some supermarkets and in larger tube and rail stations. Some commercial premises have 'pay-ATMs', which charge for withdrawals. If you are visiting from outside the UK, your cash card should work via one of the debit networks, but check charges in advance. ATMs also allow you to make withdrawals on your credit card if you know your PIN number; you will be charged interest plus, usually, a currency exchange fee. Generally, getting cash with a card is the cheapest form of currency exchange but increasingly there are hidden charges, so do your research. Bank of America customers can use Barclays ATMs free.

Britain has moved over to the Chip and PIN system, whereby you are required to enter your PIN number rather than sign a credit or debit card slip. You will usually not be allowed to make a purchase with your card without your PIN. For more information, see www.chipandpin.co.uk.

Banks

No commission is charged for cashing sterling travellers' cheques if you go to one of the banks affiliated with the issuing company. You do have to pay to cash travellers' cheques in foreign currencies, and to change cash. You will always need to produce ID to cash travellers' cheques.

Bureaux de change

You'll be charged for cashing travellers' cheques or buying and selling foreign currency at bureaux de change. Commission varies. Major rail and tube stations have bureaux, and there are many in tourist areas and on major shopping streets. Most open 8am-10pm.

Chequepoint *550 Oxford Street, Marlyebone, W1C 1LY (7724 6127). Marble Arch tube.* **Open** 8am-10pm Mon-Sat; 10am-6pm Sun. **Map** p400 G6. **Other locations**: throughout the city.
Garden Bureau *30A Jubilee Market Hall, Covent Garden, WC2E 8BE (7240 9921). Covent Garden tube.* **Open** 9.30am-6pm daily. **Map** p409 Z3.
Thomas Exchange *13 Maddox Street, Mayfair, W1S 2QG (7493 1300/www.thomasexchange.co.uk).* **Open** 8.45am-5.30pm Mon-Fri. **Map** p408 U3.

Credit cards

Credit cards are accepted in pretty much every shop (except small corner shops) and restaurant (except caffs), particularly MasterCard and Visa. American Express and Diners Club tend to be accepted at more expensive outlets and multiples.

Report **lost/stolen credit cards** immediately to both the police and the services below.

American Express *01273 696933.*
Diners Club *01252 513500.*
MasterCard/Eurocard *0800 964767.*
Switch *0870 600 0459.*
Visa/Connect *0800 895082.*

Tax

With the exception of food, books, newspapers, children's clothing and a few other items, UK purchases are subject to VAT – Value Added Tax, aka sales tax – of 17.5 per cent. Unlike in the US, this is included in prices quoted in shops. In hotels, always check that the room rate quoted includes tax.

Opening hours

The following are general guidelines. Government offices all close on every bank (public) holiday (*see p377*); shops are increasingly remaining open. Only Christmas Day seems sacrosanct. Most attractions remain open on the other public holidays, but always call first.

Banks 9am-4.30pm (some close at 3.30pm, some 5.30pm) Mon-Fri; sometimes also Saturday mornings.
Businesses 9am-5pm Mon-Fri.
Post offices 9am-5.30pm Mon-Fri; 9am-noon Sat.
Pubs & bars 11am-11pm Mon-Sat; noon-10.30pm Sun.
Shops 10am-6pm Mon-Sat; some to 8pm. Many are also open on Sunday, usually 11am-5pm or noon-6pm.

Police stations

The police are a good source of information about the area and are used to helping visitors. If you've been robbed, assaulted or involved in an infringement of the law, go to your nearest police station. (We've listed a handful in central London; look under 'Police' in Directory Enquiries or call 118 118/500/888 for more). If you have a complaint, ensure that you take the offending officer's identifying number (it should be displayed on his or her epaulette). You can then register a complaint with the **Independent Police Complaints Commission** (90 High Holborn, WC1V 6BH, 0845 300 2002).

Belgravia Police Station
202-206 Buckingham Palace Road, Pimlico, SW1W 9SX (7730 1212). Victoria tube/rail. **Map** p402 H10.

Camden Police Station *60 Albany Street, Fitzrovia, NW1 4EE (7404 1212). Great Portland Street tube.* **Map** p400 H4.

Charing Cross Police Station
Agar Street, Covent Garden, WC2N 4JP (7240 1212). Charing Cross tube/rail. **Map** p409 Y4.

Chelsea Police Station *2 Lucan Place, Chelsea, SW3 3PB (7589 1212). South Kensington tube.* **Map** p399 E10.

Islington Police Station
2 Tolpuddle Street, Islington, N1 0YY (7704 1212). Angel tube. **Map** p404 N2.

Kensington Police Station
72-74 Earl's Court Road, Kensington, W8 6EQ (7376 1212). Earl's Court tube. **Map** p398 B11.

Marylebone Police Station
1-9 Seymour Street, Marylebone, W1H 7BA (7486 1212). Marble Arch tube. **Map** p397 F6.

Paddington Green Police Station *2-4 Harrow Road, Paddington, W2 1XJ (7402 1212). Edgware Road tube.* **Map** p397 E5.

West End Central Police Station *27 Savile Row, Mayfair, W1X 2DU (7437 1212). Piccadilly Circus tube.* **Map** p408 U3.

Postal services

You can buy stamps at all post offices and many newsagents and supermarkets. Current prices are 32p for first-class and 23p for second-class letters and small items weighing less than 100g, or 42p for letters to the EU and 50p to the United States. Postcards cost 50p to anywhere in the world. Rates for other letters and parcels vary with weight, size and destination.

Post offices

Post offices are usually open 9am to 5.30pm Monday to Friday and 9am to noon Saturday, with the exception of **Trafalgar Square Post Office** (24-28 William IV Street, WC2N 4DL, 0845 722 3344), which opens 8.30am to 6.30pm Monday to Friday and 9am to 5.30pm on Saturday. Listed below are the other main central London offices. For general enquiries, call 0845 722 3344 or consult www.postoffice.co.uk.

43-44 Albemarle Street *Mayfair, W1S 4DS (0845 722 3344). Green Park tube.* **Map** p408 U5.

111 Baker Street *Marylebone, W1U 6SG (0845 722 3344). Baker Street tube.* **Map** p400 G5.

54-56 Great Portland Street
Fitzrovia, W1W 7NE (0845 722 3344). Oxford Circus tube. **Map** p400 H4.

1-5 Poland Street *Soho, W1F 8AA (0845 722 3344). Oxford Circus tube.* **Map** p408 V2.

181 High Holborn *Holborn, WC1V 7RL (0845 722 3344). Holborn tube.* **Map** p409 Y1.

Poste restante

If you want to receive mail while you're away, you can have it sent to Trafalgar Square Post Office (*see above*), where it will be kept for a month. Your name and 'Poste Restante' must be clearly marked on the letter. You'll need ID to collect it.

Religion

Times may vary; always phone to check.

Anglican

St Paul's Cathedral *For listings details, see p93.* **Services** 7.30am, 8am, 12.30pm, 5pm Mon-Fri; 8am, 8.30am, 12.30pm, 5pm Sat; 8am, 10.15am, 11.30am, 3.15pm, 6pm Sun. **Map** p406 O6.

Westminster Abbey *For listings details, see p141.* **Services** 7.30am, 8am, 12.30pm, 5pm Mon-Fri; 8am, 9am, 12.30pm, 3pm Sat; 8am, 10am, 11.15am, 3pm, 5.45pm Sun. **Map** p403 K9.

Baptist

Bloomsbury Central Baptist Church *235 Shaftesbury Avenue, Covent Garden, WC2H 8EP (7240 0544/www.bloomsbury.org.uk). Tottenham Court Road tube.* **Open** 10am-4pm Mon-Fri. *Friendship Centre Oct-June* noon-2.30pm Tue. **Services & meetings** 11am, 6.30pm Sun. **Classical concerts** phone to check. **Map** p401 Y1.

Buddhist

Buddhapadipa Thai Temple
14 Calonne Road, Wimbledon, SW19 5HJ (8946 1357/www.buddhapadipa.org). Wimbledon tube/rail then 93 bus. **Open** *Temple* 9-6pm Sat, Sun. *Meditation retreat* 7-9pm Tue, Thur; 4-6pm Sat, Sun. *See also p185.*

Catholic

Oratory Catholic Church *For listings, see p150.* **Services** 7am, 8am (Latin mass), 10am, 12.30am, 6pm Mon-Fri; 7am, 8.30am, 10am, 6pm Sat; 7am, 8.30am, 10am (tridentine), 11am (sung Latin), 12.30pm, 3.30pm, 4.30pm, 7pm Sun. **Map** p399 E10.

Westminster Cathedral
For listings, see p143. **Services** 7am, 8am, 9am, 10.30am, 12.30pm, 5pm Mon-Fri; 8am, 9am, 12.30pm, 6pm Sat; 7am, 8am, 9am, 10.30am, noon, 5.30pm, 7pm Sun. **Map** p402 J10.

Islamic

Islamic Cultural Centre & London Central Mosque
146 Park Road, Marylebone, NW8 7RG (7724 3363/ www.iccuk.org). Baker Street tube/74 bus. **Open** dawn-dusk daily. **Services** phone 7725 2213 to check.

East London Mosque *82-92 Whitechapel Road, Whitechapel, E1 1JQ (7650 3000). Aldgate East or Whitechapel tube.* **Open** 10am-10pm daily. **Services** *Friday prayer* 1.30pm (1.15pm in winter). **Map** p407 S6.

Jewish

Liberal Jewish Synagogue
28 St John's Wood Road, St John's Wood, NW8 7HA (7286 5181/ www.ljs.org). St John's Wood tube. **Open** 9am-5pm Mon-Thur; 9am-1pm Fri. **Services** 6.45pm Fri; 11am Sat.

West Central Liberal Synagogue *21 Maple Street, Fitzrovia, W1T 4BE (7636 7627/ www.wcls.org.uk). Warren Street tube.* **Services** 3pm Sat. **Map** p400 J4.

Methodist

Methodist Central Hall *Central Hall, Storey's Gate, Westminster, SW1H 9NH (7222 8010/www.c-h-w.co.uk). St James's Park tube.* **Open** *Chapel* 8am-6pm daily. **Services** 12.45pm Wed; 11am, 6.30pm Sun. **Map** p403 K9.

Quaker

Religious Society of Friends (Quakers) *173-177 Euston Road, Bloomsbury, NW1 2BJ (7663 1000/ www.quaker.org.uk). Euston tube/rail.*

Open 8.30am-9.30pm Mon-Fri; 8.30am-4.30pm Sat. **Meetings** 6.30pm Mon; 11am Sun. **Map** p401 K3.

Safety & security

There are no 'no-go' areas in London as such, but thieves haunt busy shopping areas and transport nodes as they do in all cities. Use common sense and follow these basic rules.

- **Keep** wallets and purses out of sight, and handbags securely closed.
- **Don't** leave briefcases, bags or coats unattended; even if they aren't stolen, they might well trigger a bomb alert.
- **Don't** leave bags or coats beside, under or on the back of a chair.
- **Don't** put bags on the floor near the door of a public toilet.
- **Don't** take short cuts through dark alleys and car parks.
- **Don't** keep your passport, money, credit cards, etc together.
- **Don't** carry a wallet in your back pocket.
- **Be aware** of your surroundings.

Smoking

From summer 2007 a new law comes into force that prohibits smoking in all enclosed public spaces, which means all pubs, bars, clubs, restaurants and shops, as well as on public transport. Even prior to the ban, many places have already decided to prohibit smoking – phone ahead if this is important to you.

Study

Being a student in London is as expensive as it is exciting. Certain places do offer student admissions; in this guide, entry prices for students are designated 'concs' (concessions). Show ID (an NUS or ISIC card) to qualify.

Language classes

Aspect College London *3-4 Southampton Place, Covent Garden, WC1A 2DA (7404 3080/ www.aspectworld.com). Holborn tube.* **Map** p409 Z1.

Central School of English *1 Tottenham Court Road, Bloomsbury, W1T 1BB (7580 2863/ www.centralschool.co.uk). Tottenham Court Road tube.* **Map** p408 W1.

Frances King School of English *77 Gloucester Road, South Kensington, SW7 4SS (7870 6533/ www.francesking.co.uk). Gloucester Road tube.* **Map** p397 F9.

London Study Centre *Munster House, 676 Fulham Road, Fulham, SW6 5SA (7731 3549/ www.londonstudycentre.com). Parsons Green tube.*

Sels College *64-65 Long Acre, Covent Garden, WC2E 9SX (7240 2581/www.sels.co.uk). Covent Garden tube.* **Map** p409 Y3.

Shane Global Language Centre *59 South Molton Street, Mayfair, W1K 5SN (7499 8533/www.shane global.com). Bond Street tube.* **Map** p400 H6.

Students' unions

Many unions will only let in students with ID, so always carry your NUS or ISIC card with you. We've listed those with the best bars, all of which offer a good night out. Call for opening times and specific events, which vary with the academic year.

Imperial College *Beit Quad, Prince Consort Road, South Kensington, SW7 2BB (7594 8060/ www.imperialcollegeunion.org). South Kensington tube.* **Map** p399 D9.

International Students House *229 Great Portland Street, Marylebone, W1W 5PN (7631 8300/ www.ish.org.uk). Great Portland Street tube.* **Map** p400 H4.

King's College *Macadam Building, Surrey Street, Covent Garden, WC2R 2NS (7836 7132/www.kcl.ac.uk). Temple tube.* **Map** p403 M7.

London Metropolitan University *166-220 Holloway Road, Holloway, N7 8DB (7423 0000/ www.londonmet.ac.uk). Holloway Road tube.*

University of London Union (ULU) *Malet Street, Bloomsbury, WC1E 7HY (7664 2000/www.ulu. co.uk). Goodge Street tube.* **Map** p401 K4.

Universities

Brunel University *Cleveland Road, Uxbridge, Middx UB8 3PH (01895 274000/students' union 01895 269269/www.brunel.ac.uk). Uxbridge tube.*

City University *Northampton Square, Clerkenwell, EC1V 0HB (7040 5060/students' union 7040 5600/www.city.ac.uk). Angel tube.* **Map** p404 O3.

London Metropolitan University *166-220 Holloway Road, Holloway, N7 8DB (7607 2789/students' union 7133 2769/www.londonmet.ac.uk). Holloway Road tube.*

South Bank University *Borough Road, Borough, SE1 0AA (7815 7815/students' union 7815 6060/ www.lsbu.ac.uk). Elephant & Castle tube/rail.* **Map** p406 O10.

University of Greenwich *Old Royal Naval College, Park Row, Greenwich, SE10 9LS (8331 8000/ students' union 8331 7629/www. gre.ac.uk). Greenwich DLR/rail.*

University of Middlesex *Trent Park, Bramley Road, Cockfosters, N14 4YZ (8411 5968/students' union 8411 6450/www.mdx.ac.uk). Cockfosters tube.*

University of Westminster *309 Regent Street, Mayfair, W1B 2UW (7911 5000/students' union 7915 5454/www.wmin.ac.uk). Oxford Circus tube.* **Map** p400 J5.

University of London

The university consists of 34 separate colleges, spread across the city, of which the seven largest are listed below. All except Imperial College are affiliated to the National Union of Students (NUS; 0871 221 8221, www.nusonline.co.uk).

Goldsmiths' College *Lewisham Way, New Cross, SE14 6NW (7919 7171/students' union 8692 1406/ www.goldsmiths.ac.uk). New Cross tube/rail.*

Imperial College *Exhibition Road, Kensington, SW7 2AZ (7589 5111/ students' union 7594 8060/www. imperial.ac.uk). South Kensington tube.* **Map** p399 D9.

King's College *The Aldwych, Strand, Covent Garden, WC2R 2LS (7836 5454/students' union 8481 5588/www.kcl.ac.uk). Temple tube.* **Map** p403 M7.

Kingston University *Penrhyn Road, Kingston, Surrey KT1 2EE (8547 2000/students' union 8547 8868/www.kingston. ac.uk). Kingston rail.*

London School of Economics (LSE) *Houghton Street, Holborn, WC2A 2AE (7405 7686/students' union 7955 7158/www.lse.ac.uk). Holborn tube.* **Map** p401 M6.

Queen Mary, University of London *327 Mile End Road, Stepney, E1 4NS (7882 5555/ students' union 7882 5390/www. qmul.ac.uk). Mile End or Stepney Green tube.*

University College London (UCL) *Gower Street, Bloomsbury, WC1E 6BT (7679 2000/students' union 7387 3611/www.ucl.ac.uk). Euston Square, Goodge Street or Warren Street tube.* **Map** p401 K4.

Useful organisations

More useful organisations for students, including BUNAC and the Council on International Educational Exchange, can be found on p378.

National Bureau for Students with Disabilities *Chapter House, 18-20 Crucifix Lane, Bermondsey, SE1 3JW (7450 0620/www.skill.org.uk).* **Open** 9am-5pm Mon-Fri.

Telephones

London's dialling code is 020; standard landlines have eight digits after that. You don't need to dial the 020 from within the area, so we have not given it in this book. If you're calling from outside the UK, dial your international access code, then the UK code, 44, then the full London number, omitting the first 0 from the code. For example, to make a call to 020 7813 3000 from the US, dial 011 44 20 7813 3000. To dial abroad from the UK, first dial 00, then the relevant country code from the list below. For more international dialling codes, check the phone book or www.kropla.com/dialcode.htm.

Australia 61; **Canada** 1; **New Zealand** 64; **Republic of Ireland** 353; **South Africa** 27; **USA** 1.

Public phones

Public payphones take coins or credit cards (sometimes both). The minimum cost is 20p, which buys you a 110-second local call. Some payphones, such as the counter-top ones found in many pubs, require more. International calling cards, offering bargain minutes via a freephone number, are widely available.

Operator services

Operator

Call **100** for the operator if you have difficulty in dialling; for an alarm call; to make a credit card call; for information about the cost of a call; and for help with international person-to-person calls. Dial **155** for the international operator if you need to reverse the charges (call collect) or if you can't dial direct, but be warned that this service is very expensive.

Directory enquiries

This service is now provided by various six-digit 118 numbers. They're pretty pricey to call: dial (free) 0800 953 0720 for a rundown of options and prices. The best known is 118 118, which charges 49p per call, then 14p per minute thereafter. 118 888 charges 49p per call, then 9p per minute. 118 180 charges 25p per call, then 30p per minute. Online, use the free www.ukphonebook.co.uk.

Yellow Pages

This 24-hour service lists the numbers of thousands of businesses in the UK. Dial **118 247** (49p/min) and say what type of business you require, and in what area of London.

Telephone directories

There are several telephone directories for London, divided by area, which contain private and commercial numbers. Available at post offices and libraries, these hefty tomes are also issued free to all residents, as is the invaluable Yellow Pages directory (also online at www.yell.com), which lists businesses and services.

Mobile phones

Mobile phones in the UK work on either the 900 or 1800 GSM system. If you're a US traveller, your home service provider will use the GSM system, and your phone probably runs on the 800 or 1900 MHz band, so you'll need to acquire a tri- or quad-band handset.

The simplest option may be to buy a 'pay as you go' phone (about £50-£200); there's no monthly fee, you top up talk time using a card. Check before buying whether it can make and receive international calls.

Alternatively, you can rent a mobile phone from the AmEx offices at Terminals 3 and 4 at Heathrow Airport.

Telegrams

To send telegrams abroad, call 0800 190190. This is also the number to call to send an international telemessage: phone in your message and it will be delivered by post the next day. Alternatively, go to www.telegramonline.co.uk.

Time

London operates on Greenwich Mean Time (GMT), which is five hours ahead of the US's Eastern Standard time. In spring (25 March 2007) the UK puts its clocks forward by one hour to British Summer Time. In autumn (28 October 2007) the clocks go back to GMT.

Tipping

In Britain it's accepted that you tip in taxis, minicabs, restaurants (some waiting staff rely heavily on tips), hotels, hairdressers and some bars (not pubs). Ten per cent is normal, with some restaurants adding as much as 15 per cent. Always check if service has been included in your bill: some restaurants include service, then leave the space for a gratuity on your credit card slip blank.

Toilets

Public toilets are few and far between in London, and pubs and restaurants reserve their toilets for customers only. However, all mainline rail stations and a few tube stations – Piccadilly Circus, for one – have public toilets (you may be charged a small fee). Department stores, too, usually have loos that you can use free of charge.

Tourist information

Visit London (7234 5800, www.visitlondon.com) is the city's official tourist information company. There are also tourist offices in Greenwich, Leicester Square and next to St Paul's (www.cityoflondon.gov.uk; *see p90*).

Britain & London Visitor Centre *1 Lower Regent Street, Piccadilly Circus, SW1Y 4XT (8846 9000/ www.visitbritain.com). Piccadilly Circus tube.* **Open** 9.30am-6.30pm Mon-Sat; 10am-4.30pm Sun. **Map** p408 W4.

London Information Centre *Leicester Square, WC2H 7BP (7292 2333/www.londontown.com). Leicester Square tube.* **Open** 8am-11pm Mon-Fri; 10am-6pm Sat, Sun. Info and booking services.

London Visitor Centre *Arrivals Hall, Waterloo International Terminal, SE1 7LT.* **Open** 8.30am-10.30pm Mon-Sat; 9.30am-10.30pm Sun. **Map** p403 M8.

Visas & immigration

EU citizens do not require a visa to visit the UK; citizens of the USA, Canada, Australia, South Africa and New Zealand can also enter with only a passport for tourist visits of up to six months as long as they can show they can support themselves during their visit and plan to return. Use www.ukvisas.gov.uk to check your visa status well before you travel, or contact the British embassy, consulate or high commission in your own country. You can arrange visas online at www.fco.gov.uk. For work permits, *see p378*.

Home Office *Immigration & Nationality Bureau, Lunar House, 40 Wellesley Road, Croydon, Surrey CR9 2BY (immigration info 0870 606 7766; nationality info 0845 010 5200/www.ind.homeoffice.gov.uk).* **Open** *Phone enquiries* 9am-4.45pm Mon-Thur; 9am-4.30pm Fri.

Weights & measures

It has taken quite some time but the UK is slowly moving towards full metrication. Distances are still measured in miles but all goods are now officially sold in metric quantities, with no legal requirement for the imperial equivalent to be given.

Some useful conversions:

1 centimetre (cm) = 0.39 inches (in)
1 inch (in) = 2.54 centimetres (cm)
1 yard (yd) = 0.91 metres (m)
1 metre (m) = 1.094 yards (yd)
1 mile = 1.6 kilometres (km)
1 kilometre (km) = 0.62 miles
1 ounce (oz) = 28.35 grammes (g)
1 gramme (g) = 0.035 ounces (oz)
1 pound (lb) = 0.45 kilogrammes (kg)
1 kilogramme (kg) = 2.2 pounds (lb)
1 US pint = 0.8 UK pints
1 UK pint = 0.57 litres (l)
1 litre (l) = 1.76 UK pints

When to go

Climate

The British climate is famously unpredictable, but Weathercall on 0906 850 0401 (60p per min) can offer some guidance. *See also below* **Weather report**. The best websites for weather news and features include www.metoffice.com; www.weather.com; and www.bbc.co.uk/london/weather, which all offer good detailed long-term forecasts and are easily searchable.

Spring extends from March to May, though frosts can last into April. March winds and April showers may be a month early or a month late, but May is often very pleasant.

Summer (June, July and August) can be unpredictable, with searing heat one day followed by sultry greyness and violent thunderstorms the next. There are usually pleasant sunny days, too, though they vary greatly in number from year to year. High temperatures, humidity and pollution can create problems for those with hay fever or breathing difficulties, and temperatures down in the tube can reach horrible levels in rush hour.

Autumn starts in September, although the weather can still have a mild, summery feel. Real autumn comes with October, when the leaves start to fall. When the November cold, grey and wet sets in, you'll be reminded that London is situated on a fairly northerly latitude.

Winter can have some delightful crisp, cold days, but don't bank on them. The usual scenario is for a disappointingly grey, wet Christmas, followed by a cold snap in January and February, when London may even see a sprinkling of snow – and immediate public transport chaos.

Public holidays

On public holidays (bank holidays), many shops remain open, but public transport services generally run to a Sunday timetable. On Christmas Day almost everything, including public transport, closes down.

New Year's Day Mon 1 Jan 2007.
Good Friday Fri 6 Apr 2007.
Easter Monday Mon 9 April 2007.
May Day Holiday Mon 7 May 2007.

Weather report

Average daytime temperatures, rainfall and hours of sunshine in London

	Temp (°C/°F)	**Rainfall** (mm/in)	**Sunshine** (hrs/dy)
Jan	6/43	54/2.1	1.5
Feb	7/44	40/1.6	2.3
Mar	10/50	37/1.5	3.6
Apr	13/55	37/1.5	5.3
May	17/63	46/1.8	6.4
June	20/68	45/1.8	7.1
July	22/72	57/2.2	6.4
Aug	21/70	59/2.3	6.1
Sept	19/66	49/1.9	4.7
Oct	14/57	57/2.2	3.2
Nov	10/50	64/2.5	1.8
Dec	7/44	48/1.9	1.3

Spring Bank Holiday Mon 28 May 2007.
Summer Bank Holiday Mon 27 Aug 2007.
Christmas Day Tue 25 Dec 2007.
Boxing Day Wed 26 Dec 2007.

Women

London is home to dozens of women's groups and networks, from day centres to rights campaigners; www.gn.apc.org and www.wrc.org.uk provide information and many links.

Women visiting London are unlikely to be harassed. Bar the very occasional sexually motivated attack, London's streets are no more dangerous for women than for men if you follow the usual precautions (*see p375*).

The Women's Library

25 Old Castle Street, Whitechapel, E1 7NT (7320 2222/www.thewomenslibrary.ac.uk). Aldgate or Aldgate East tube. **Open** *Reading room* 9.30am-5pm Tue, Wed, Fri; 9.30am-8pm Thur; 10am-4pm Sat. **Map** p407 S6.
Europe's largest women's studies archive, with changing exhibitions and an upstairs café.

Working in London

Finding temporary work in London can be a full-time job. Those with a reasonable level of English, who are EU citizens or have work permits, should be able to find work in catering, labouring, bars/pubs, coffee bars or shops. Graduates with an English or foreign-language degree could try teaching. Ideas can be found in *Summer Jobs in Britain*, published by Vacation Work, 9 Park End Street, Oxford OX1 1HJ (£10.99 plus £1.75 p&p); their website is www.vacationwork.co.uk.

Good sources of job information are the *Evening Standard*, local/national newspapers and newsagents' windows. Vacancies for temporary and unskilled work are often displayed on Jobcentre noticeboards; your nearest Jobcentre can be found under 'Employment Agencies' in the Yellow Pages. If you have good typing (over 40 wpm) or word processing skills, you could sign on with some temp agencies. Many have specialist areas beyond the obvious administrative or secretarial roles, such as translation.

For shop, bar and restaurant work, just go in and enquire.

Work permits

With few exceptions, citizens of non-European Economic Area (EEA) countries have to have a work permit before they can legally work in the United Kingdom. Employers who are unable to fill particular vacancies with a resident or EEA national must apply for a permit to the Department for Education and Employment (DfEE; *see below*). Permits are issued only for high-level jobs.

Au Pair Scheme

Citizens aged 17 to 27 from the following non-EEA countries (along, of course, with EEA nationals) are permitted to make an application to become au pairs: Andorra, Bosnia-Herzegovina, Bulgaria, Croatia, Faroe Islands, Greenland, Macedonia, Monaco, Romania, San Marino, Turkey. A visa is sometimes required, so make sure you check. See the appropriate page of www.workingintheuk.gov.uk for details, or contact the **Immigration & Nationality Directorate** (*see below* **Home Office**).

Sandwich students

Approval for course-compulsory sandwich placements at recognised UK colleges must be obtained for potential students by their home country college from the DfEE's **Overseas Labour Service** (*see below* **Work Permits UK**).

Students

Visiting students from the US, Canada, Australia or Jamaica can sign up for the BUNAC programme, which allows them to work in the UK for up to six months. Contact the Work in Britain Department of the **Council on International Educational Exchange** (from the US, call 1-800 407 8839 or visit www.ciee.org) or call **BUNAC** direct (*see below*). Students should get an application form OSS1 (BUNAC) from BUNAC, and submit it to a UK Jobcentre to obtain permission to work. Students may not exceed 20 hours' work during term-time.

Working holidaymakers

Citizens of Commonwealth countries aged from 17 to 27 are allowed to apply to come to the UK as a working holidaymaker. Start by contacting your nearest British diplomatic post in advance. You are then allowed to take part-time work without a DfEE permit. Contact the **Immigration & Nationality Directorate** (*see below* **Home Office**) for more information.

Useful addresses

BUNAC

16 Bowling Green Lane, Clerkenwell, EC1R 0QH (7251 3472/www.bunac.org.uk). Farringdon tube/rail. **Open** 9.30am-5.30pm Mon-Thur; 9.30am-5pm Fri. **Map** p404 N4.

Council on International Educational Exchange

3rd floor, 7 Custom House Street, Portland, Maine, ME 04101, USA (7553 7600/www.ciee.org). **Open** 9am-5pm Mon-Fri.
The Council on International Educational Exchange helps young people to study, work and travel abroad.

Home Office

Immigration & Nationality Directorate, Lunar House, 40 Wellesley Road, Croydon, Surrey CR9 2BY (0870 606 7766/www.ind.homeoffice.gov.uk). **Open** *Phone enquiries* 9am-4.45pm Mon-Thur; 9am-4.30pm Fri.
The Home Office is able to provide advice on whether or not a work permit is required; application forms can be downloaded from the website.

Overseas Visitors Records Office

180 Borough High Street, Borough, SE1 1LH (7230 1208). Borough tube. **Open** 9am-4pm Mon-Fri. **Map** p406 P9.
The Overseas Visitors Records Office charges £34 to register a person if they already have a work permit.

Work Permits UK

0114 207 4074/www.workingintheuk.gov.uk. **Open** *Phone enquiries* 9am-5pm Mon-Fri.
Information for UK-based employers about the various routes open to foreign nationals who want to come and work in the UK.

Further Reference

Books

Fiction

Peter Ackroyd *Hawksmoor*; *The House of Doctor Dee*; *Great Fire of London*; *The Lambs of London* Intricate studies of arcane London.
Monica Ali *Brick Lane* Arranged marriage in Tower Hamlets.
Martin Amis *London Fields* Darts and drinking way out east.
Jonathan Coe *The Dwarves of Death* Mystery, music, mirth, male violence and the like.
Norman Collins *London Belongs to Me* Witty saga of 1930s Kennington.
Sir Arthur Conan Doyle *The Complete Sherlock Holmes* Reassuring sleuthing shenanigans.
Joseph Conrad *The Secret Agent* Anarchism in seedy Soho.
Charles Dickens *Oliver Twist*; *David Copperfield*; *Bleak House*; *Our Mutual Friend* Four of the master's most London-centric novels.
Maureen Duffy *Capital* The bones beneath us and the stories they tell.
Christopher Fowler *Soho Black* Walking dead in Soho.
Anthony Frewin *London Blues* One-time Kubrick assistant explores 1960s Soho porn movie industry.
Graham Greene *The End of the Affair* Adultery and Catholicism during the Blitz.
Patrick Hamilton *Twenty Thousand Streets Under the Sky* Dashed dreams at the bar of the Midnight Bell in 1950s Fitzrovia.
Alan Hollinghurst *The Swimming Pool Library*; *The Line of Beauty* Gay life around Russell Square; beautiful, ruthless look at metropolitan debauchery – won the 2004 Booker.
Hanif Kureishi *The Buddha of Suburbia* Sexual confusion and identity crisis in the 1970s.
Colin MacInnes *City of Spades*; *Absolute Beginners* Coffee 'n' jazz, Soho 'n' Notting Hill. Tour of rock history's blue plaque sites.
Derek Marlowe *A Dandy in Aspic* A capital-set Cold War classic.
Michael Moorcock *Mother London* A love letter to London.
Ferdinand Mount *Heads You Win* Tale of East End headhunting scam.
George Orwell *Keep the Aspidistra Flying*; *Nineteen Eighty-Four* Saga of a struggling writer; bleak vision of totalitarian takeover.
Derek Raymond *I Was Dora Suarez* The blackest London noir.
Nicholas Royle *The Matter of the Heart*; *The Director's Cut* Abandoned buildings and secrets.
Edward Rutherfurd *London* A city's history given a novel voice.
Iain Sinclair *Downriver*; *Radon Daughters*; *White Chappell/Scarlet Tracings* The Thames's *Heart of Darkness*; William Hope Hodgson; Ripper murders/book dealers.
Evelyn Waugh *Vile Bodies* Shameful antics in 1920s Mayfair.
Virginia Woolf *Mrs Dalloway* A kind of London *Ulysses*.
HG Wells *War of the Worlds* Early SF classic with a suburban London setting and Primrose Hill finale.

Non-fiction

Peter Ackroyd *London: The Biography* Wilfully obscurantist history of the city.
Nicholas Barton *The Lost Rivers of London* Fascinating studies of old watercourses and their legacy.
James Boswell *Boswell's London Journal 1762-1763* Rich account of a ribald literary life.
Geoffrey Fletcher *The London Nobody Knows* Long out of print discourse on the capital by a great forgotten London writer.
Ed Glinert *A Literary Guide to London; The London Compendium* Two essential London reference volumes full of capital minutiae.
Peter Guillery *The Small House in 18th-Century London* Social and architectural history.
Sarah Guy (ed) *Time Out Book of London Walks volumes 1 & 2* Writers, cartoonists, comedians and historians walk the capital.
Neil Hanson *The Dreadful Judgement* The embers of the Great Fire raked over.
Sarah Hartley *Mrs P's Journey* Biography of Phyllis Pearsall, the woman who created the *A–Z*.
Stephen Inwood *A History of London* Straightforward reading of the city's history.
Edward Jones & Christopher Woodward *A Guide to the Architecture of London* What it says on the cover. A brilliant work.
Jack London *The People of the Abyss* Poverty in the East End.
Tim Moore *Do Not Pass Go* Hilarious Monopoly addict's London.
George Orwell *Down and Out in Paris and London* Waitering, begging and starving.
Samuel Pepys *Diaries* Fires, plagues, bordellos and more.
Liza Picard *Dr Johnson's London*; *Restoration London* London past, engagingly revisited.
Patricia Pierce *Old London Bridge* The story of the world's longest inhabited bridge.
Roy Porter *London: A Social History* An all-encompassing history.
Iain Sinclair *Lights Out for the Territory*; *London Orbital* Time-warp visionary crosses London; time-warp visionary circles it on the M25.
Iain Sinclair (ed) *London: City of Disappearances* Scraps, clippings and faded post-it notes from a host of contemporary city mythologisers.
Stephen Smith *Underground London: Travels Beneath the City Streets* Absorbing writing on the subterranean city.
Judith Summers *Soho: A History of London's Most Colourful Neighbourhood* Great local history, although weakest on recent times.
Richard Tames *Feeding London*; *East End Past* Eating history from coffee houses onwards; a close look at the East End.
William Taylor *This Bright Field* Spitalfields in enjoyable detail.
Adrian Tinniswood *His Invention So Fertile* Illuminating biography of Sir Christopher Wren.
Richard Trench and Ellis Hillman *London Under London: A Subterranean Guide* Tunnels, lost rivers, disused tube stations, military bunkers – one of the most fascinating London books ever.
Ben Weinreb & Christopher Hibbert (eds) *The London Encyclopaedia* Fascinating, thorough, indispensable reference guide.
Jerry White *London in the 20th Century: A City and Its People.* How London became a truly global city.

Films

Alfie *dir. Lewis Gilbert* (1966) What's it all about, Michael?
Blow-Up *dir. Michelangelo Antonioni* (1966) Swinging London captured in an unintentionally hysterical fashion.
Breaking and Entering *dir. Anthony Minghella* (2006) Star-studded thievery in Kings Cross.
A Clockwork Orange *dir. Stanley Kubrick* (1971) Kubrick's vision still shocks – but so does Thamesmead, location for many Orange scenes.
Closer *dir. Mike Nichols* (2004) Infidelity and emotional uncertainty in and around Clerkenwell.
Da Vinci Code *dir. Ron Howard* (2006) Film version of Dan Brown's blockbuster novel, partly filmed in London (Inner Temple gets a look-in).
Death Line *dir. Gary Sherman* (1972) Cannibalism on the tube. Yikes.
Dirty Pretty Things *dir. Stephen Frears* (2002) Drama centred on immigrant hotel workers.
The Krays *dir. Peter Medak* (1990) The life and times of the most notorious of East End gangsters.

Life is Sweet; Naked; Secrets & Lies; Career Girls; All or Nothing; Vera Drake *dir. Mike Leigh* (1990; 1993; 1996; 1997; 2002; 2004) An affectionate look at Metroland; study of misanthropy; familial tensions; old friends meet; family falls apart; problems of post-war austerity.
Lock, Stock & Two Smoking Barrels; Snatch *dir. Guy Ritchie* (1998; 2000) Mr Madonna's pair of East End faux-gangster flicks.
London; Robinson in Space *dir. Patrick Keiller* (1994; 1997) Fiction meets documentary.
The Long Good Friday *dir. John MacKenzie* (1989) Bob Hoskins stars in the classic London gangster flick.
Match Point *dir. Woody Allen* (2005) He should have stuck with *Manhattan* – Woody's postcards from England.
Mona Lisa; The Crying Game *dir. Neil Jordan* (1986; 1992) Prostitution, terrorism, transvestism.
Notting Hill *dir. Roger Michell* (1999) Hugh Grant and Julia Roberts get it on in west London.
Peeping Tom *dir. Michael Powell* (1960) Powell's creepy murder flick: a young man films his dying victims.
Performance *dir. Nicolas Roeg, Donald Cammell* (1970) This cult movie to end all cult movies made west London cool for life.
28 Days *dir. Danny Boyle* (2002) Post-apocalyptic London.
Wonderland *dir. Michael Winterbottom* (1999) A mix of love, loss and deprivation in Soho and south London.

In the bloghouse

A weblog gives intimacy through anonymity, bringing a city's thoughts and secrets to your desktop. Check out www.lights.com/weblogs/searching for a list of blog-searching sites, and find your own area of interest.

Belle de Jour
www.belledejour-uk.blogspot.com
Elegant diary of a London call girl.

Hackney Lookout
www.hackneylookout.blogspot.com
Keeping tabs on local eccentrics.

In the Aquarium
www.intheaquarium.blogspot.com
Poetic observations and life drawings.

London
www.lndn.blogspot.com
Lists, guides and photos of out-of-the-way London landmarks from Diamond Geezer.

Londonist
www.londonist.com
London photos, gossip and goings-on.

Route 79
www.route79.com/journal
A second-generation Indian on London life and aloo gobi.

Sashinka
www.sashinka.blogspot.com
Sharp stories from a Jewish girl-about-town.

Music

Lily Allen *Alright, Still* (2006) Her feisty, urban reggae-pop was the sound of summer 2006.
Babyshambles *Down in Albion* (2005) Pete Doherty's adherence to a vision of an idealised England oddly takes in unglamorous Deptford and Catford.
Blur *Modern Life is Rubbish* (1993); *Parklife* (1994) Modern classics by the Essex exiles.
Billy Bragg *Must I Paint You a Picture? The Essential Billy Bragg* (2003) Greatest hits from the bard of Barking.
Chas and Dave *Don't Give a Monkey's* (1979) Pioneers of the cockney sound.
The Clash *London Calling* (1979) Epoch-making punk classic.
Ian Dury *New Boots and Panties* (1977) Named for the only clothes thrifty Dury wouldn't buy from charity shops.
The Good, the Bad and the Queen *The Good, the Bad and the Queen* (2007) Damon Albarn, Paul Simonon, Simon Tong and Tony Allen: the first London-centric supergroup of the 21st century.
The Jam *This is the Modern World* (1977) Weller at his splenetic finest.
Madness *Rise and Fall* (1982) The nutty boys wax lyrical.
Morrissey *Vauxhall & I* (1994) His finest solo album.
The Rolling Stones *December's Children (and Everybody's)* (1965) Moodily cool evocation of the city.
Saint Etienne *Tales from Turnpike House* (2005) Kitchen-sink opera by London-loving indie dance band named for a French football team.
Small Faces *Ogdens' Nut Gone Flake* (1968) Concept album by band fronted by East End-born Steve Marriott.
Squeeze *Greatest Hits* (1994) Lovable south London geezer pop.
The Streets *Original Pirate Material* (2001) Geezer pop for a new millennium: garage meets Madness.

Websites

All in London *www.allinlondon.co.uk* London links site.
BBC London *www.bbc.co.uk/london* Online capital news, travel, weather, sport etc.
Classic Cafés *www.classiccafes.co.uk* London's 1950s and '60s caffs.
Greater London Authority *www.london.gov.uk* A wealth of information.
Gumtree *www.gumtree.com* Online community noticeboard.
Hidden London *www.hiddenlondon.com* The city's undiscovered gems.
London Active Map *www.uktravel.com* Click on a tube station and find out which attractions are nearby.
London Footprints *www.london-footprints.co.uk* Free walks to print out.
Pubs.com *www.pubs.com* London's traditional boozers.
River Thames Guide *www.riverthames.co.uk* Places along the riverbank.
Street Map *www.streetmap.co.uk* Grid references and postcodes.
Time Out *www.timeout.com* A vital source. From here you can access our eating and drinking guides, as well as a host of features and listings from the weekly magazine.
Transport for London *www.tfl.gov.uk/tfl* Journey planners, maps, information.

Index

Note: page numbers in **bold** indicate section(s) giving key information on topic; *italics* indicate illustrations.

n

p

Hotels & hostels

Restaurants & cafés

Pubs & bars

Advertisers' Index

Please refer to the relevant sections for addresses / telephone numbers

Where To Stay

Sightseeing

Eat, Drink, Shop

Shops & Services

Arts & Entertainment

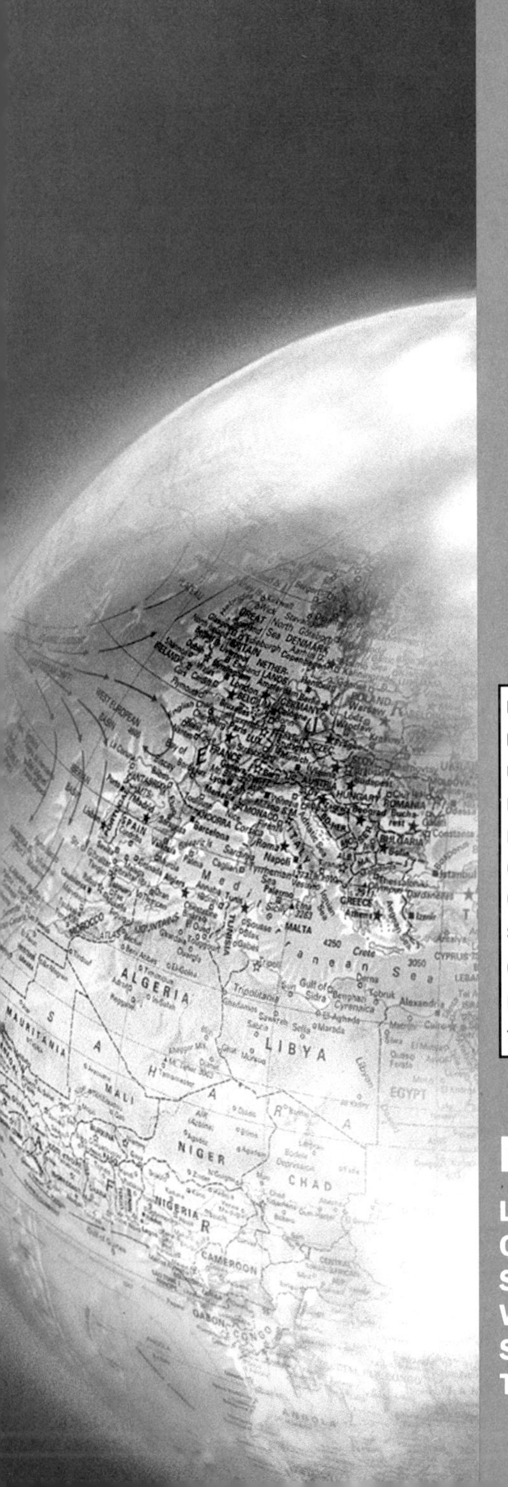

Places of interest or entertainment
Railway stations
Underground stations
Parks
Hospitals
Casualty units
Churches
Synagogues
Congestion Zone
Districts — MAYFAIR
Theatre

Maps

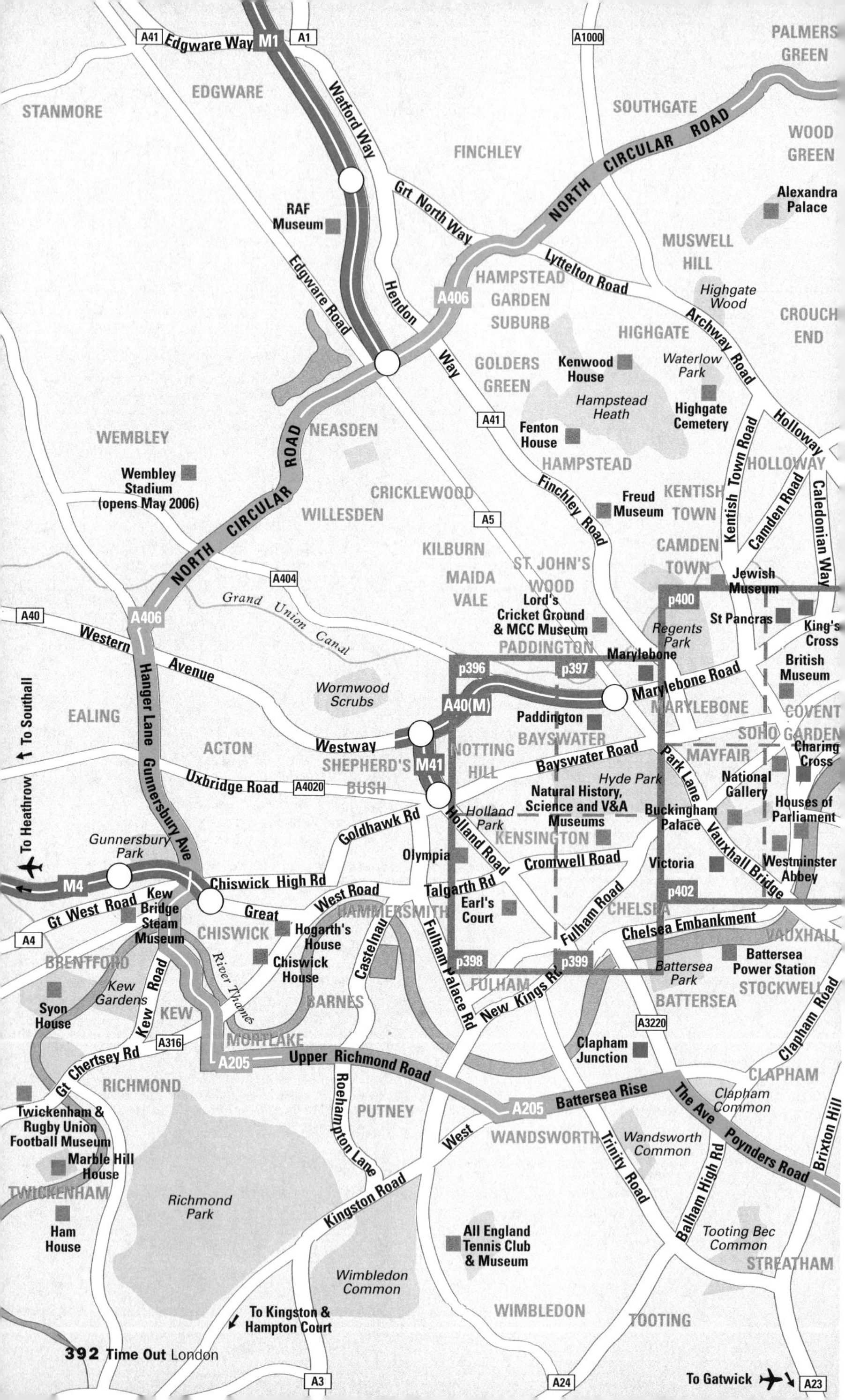

PALMERS GREEN
EDGWARE
STANMORE
SOUTHGATE
WOOD GREEN
FINCHLEY
Alexandra Palace
MUSWELL HILL
RAF Museum
HAMPSTEAD GARDEN SUBURB
Highgate Wood
CROUCH END
HIGHGATE
GOLDERS GREEN
Kenwood House
Waterlow Park
Hampstead Heath
Highgate Cemetery
NEASDEN
Fenton House
WEMBLEY
HAMPSTEAD
HOLLOWAY
Wembley Stadium (opens May 2006)
CRICKLEWOOD
Freud Museum
KENTISH TOWN
WILLESDEN
CAMDEN TOWN
KILBURN
ST JOHN'S WOOD
MAIDA VALE
Jewish Museum
Lord's Cricket Ground & MCC Museum
St Pancras
King's Cross
Regents Park
PADDINGTON
Marylebone
British Museum
Wormwood Scrubs
MARYLEBONE
COVENT GARDEN
EALING
Paddington
SOHO
ACTON
BAYSWATER
Charing Cross
NOTTING HILL
MAYFAIR
SHEPHERD'S BUSH
Hyde Park
National Gallery
Natural History, Science and V&A Museums
Holland Park
Buckingham Palace
Houses of Parliament
Gunnersbury Park
KENSINGTON
Olympia
Westminster Abbey
Victoria
Earl's Court
Kew Bridge Steam Museum
HAMMERSMITH
CHELSEA
Hogarth's House
CHISWICK
VAUXHALL
Chiswick House
BRENTFORD
Battersea Power Station
Kew Gardens
Battersea Park
FULHAM
STOCKWELL
Syon House
KEW
BARNES
BATTERSEA
MORTLAKE
Clapham Junction
CLAPHAM
RICHMOND
Clapham Common
PUTNEY
Twickenham & Rugby Union Football Museum
WANDSWORTH
Wandsworth Common
Marble Hill House
TWICKENHAM
Richmond Park
Ham House
Tooting Bec Common
All England Tennis Club & Museum
STREATHAM
Wimbledon Common
WIMBLEDON
TOOTING
To Kingston & Hampton Court
To Heathrow
To Southall
To Gatwick
Edgware Way
Watford Way
Grt North Way
NORTH CIRCULAR ROAD
Lyttelton Road
Edgware Road
Hendon Way
Archway Road
Holloway
Kentish Town Road
Camden Road
Caledonian Way
Finchley Road
Grand Union Canal
Western Avenue
Hanger Lane
Gunnersbury Ave
Marylebone Road
Westway
Bayswater Road
Uxbridge Road
Park Lane
Goldhawk Rd
Holland Road
Vauxhall Bridge
Cromwell Road
Chiswick High Rd
Talgarth Rd
Gt West Road
Great West Road
Fulham Road
Chelsea Embankment
Castelnau
Fulham Palace Rd
River Thames
Kew Road
New Kings Rd
Gt Chertsey Rd
Upper Richmond Road
Clapham Road
Roehampton Lane
Battersea Rise
The Ave
Poynders Road
Brixton Hill
West
Trinity Road
Balham High Rd
Kingston Road
M1
A1
A41
A1000
A406
A5
A404
A40
A40(M)
M41
A4020
M4
A4
A316
A205
A3220
A3
A24
A23
p396
p397
p398
p399
p400
p402

London Overview

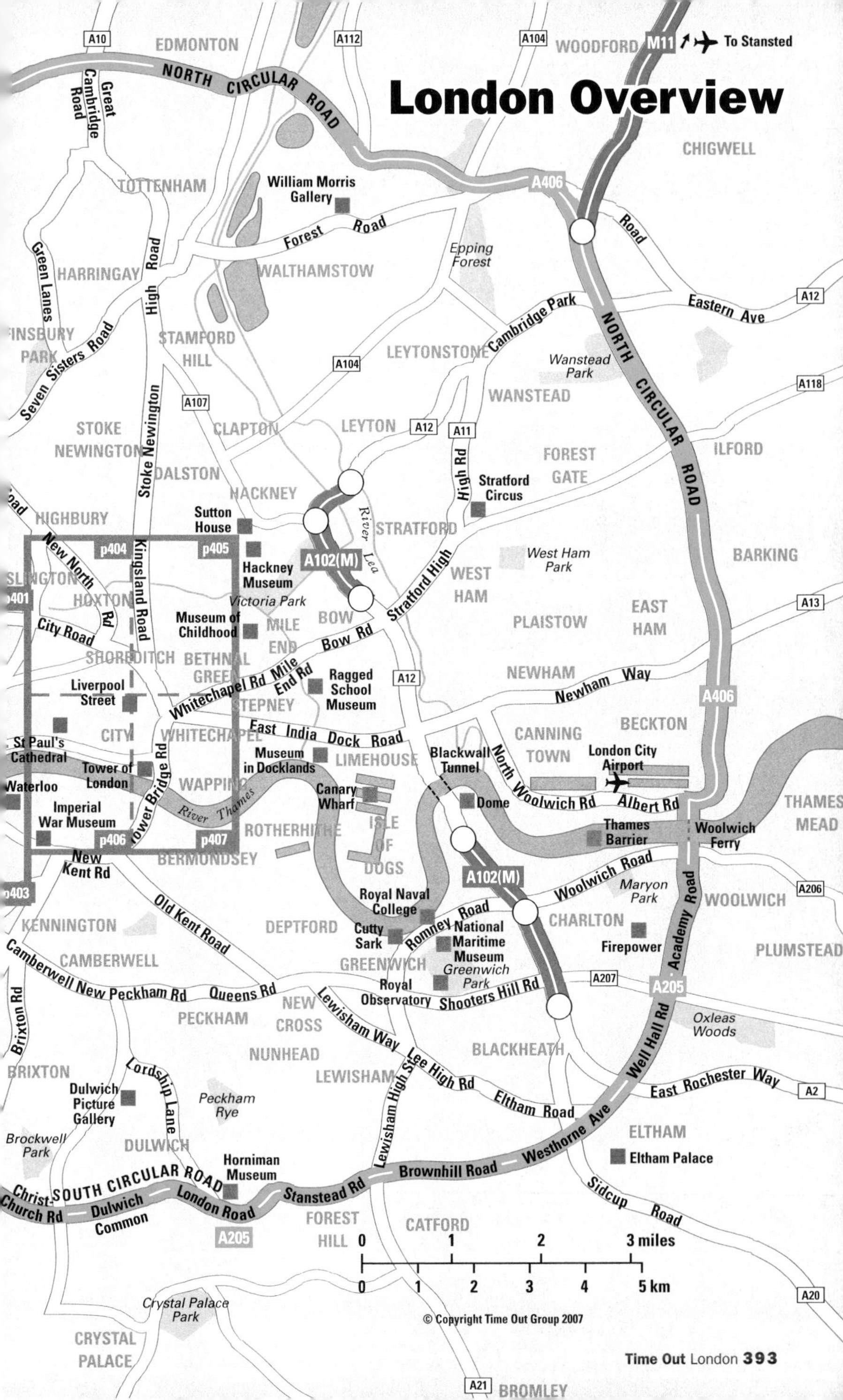

Central London by Area

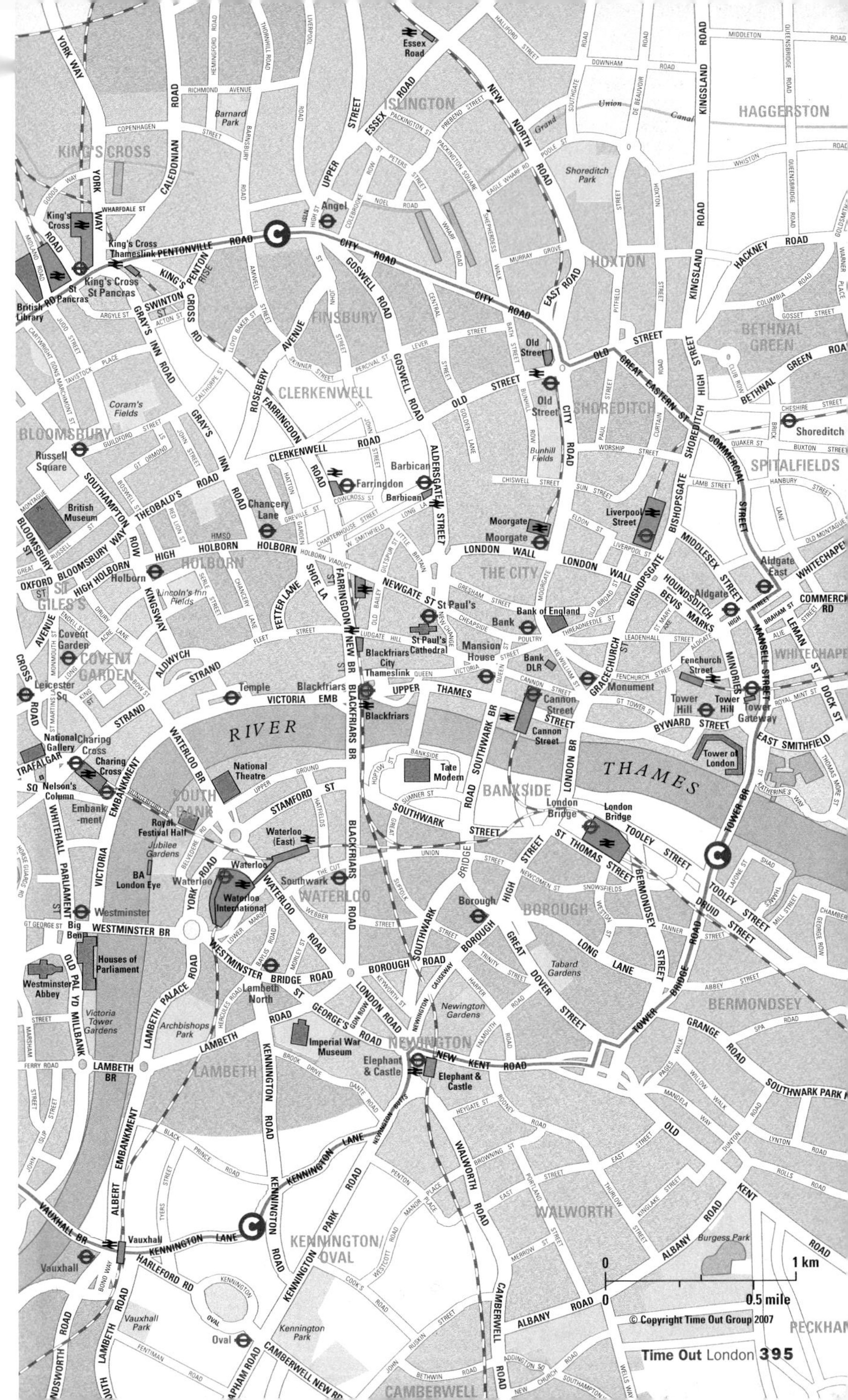

ISLINGTON
HAGGERSTON
KING'S CROSS
HOXTON
FINSBURY
BETHNAL GREEN
CLERKENWELL
SHOREDITCH
BLOOMSBURY
SPITALFIELDS
HOLBORN
THE CITY
ST GILES'S
COVENT GARDEN
WHITECHAPEL
RIVER
THAMES
SOUTH BANK
BANKSIDE
WATERLOO
BOROUGH
BERMONDSEY
LAMBETH
NEWINGTON
WALWORTH
KENNINGTON/ OVAL
CAMBERWELL
PECKHAM
Essex Road
Angel
King's Cross
King's Cross Thameslink
King's Cross St Pancras
St Pancras
British Library
Barnard Park
Shoreditch Park
Old Street
Shoreditch
Coram's Fields
Russell Square
British Museum
Farringdon
Barbican
Chancery Lane
Moorgate
Liverpool Street
Aldgate East
Aldgate
Holborn
Lincoln's Inn Fields
St Paul's
St Paul's Cathedral
Bank
Bank of England
Bunhill Fields
Mansion House
Bank DLR
Monument
Fenchurch Street
Tower Hill
Tower Gateway
Covent Garden
Leicester Sq
Temple
Blackfriars
City Thameslink
Cannon Street
Charing Cross
National Gallery
Nelson's Column
Embankment
National Theatre
Tate Modern
Tower of London
London Bridge
Royal Festival Hall
Jubilee Gardens
BA London Eye
Waterloo
Waterloo (East)
Waterloo International
Southwark
Westminster
Big Ben
Houses of Parliament
Westminster Abbey
Victoria Tower Gardens
Archbishops Park
Lambeth North
Imperial War Museum
Borough
Tabard Gardens
Newington Gardens
Elephant & Castle
Vauxhall
Vauxhall Park
Oval
Kennington Park
Burgess Park
YORK WAY
CALEDONIAN ROAD
PENTONVILLE ROAD
CITY ROAD
UPPER STREET
ESSEX ROAD
NEW NORTH ROAD
KINGSLAND ROAD
HACKNEY ROAD
GOSWELL ROAD
GRAY'S INN ROAD
ROSEBERY AVENUE
FARRINGDON ROAD
CLERKENWELL ROAD
OLD STREET
GREAT EASTERN ST
COMMERCIAL STREET
SHOREDITCH HIGH STREET
BISHOPSGATE
LONDON WALL
HOLBORN
HIGH HOLBORN
NEW OXFORD ST
THEOBALD'S ROAD
SOUTHAMPTON ROW
KINGSWAY
ALDWYCH
STRAND
FLEET STREET
NEWGATE ST
CHEAPSIDE
UPPER THAMES STREET
VICTORIA EMB
WATERLOO BR
BLACKFRIARS BR
SOUTHWARK BR
LONDON BR
TOWER BR
TOOLEY STREET
SOUTHWARK STREET
STAMFORD ST
UNION STREET
BOROUGH HIGH STREET
GREAT DOVER STREET
LONG LANE
BOROUGH ROAD
WESTMINSTER BRIDGE ROAD
WESTMINSTER BR
LAMBETH PALACE ROAD
KENNINGTON ROAD
KENNINGTON LANE
KENNINGTON PARK ROAD
WALWORTH ROAD
NEW KENT ROAD
OLD KENT ROAD
ALBANY ROAD
CAMBERWELL ROAD
ALBERT EMBANKMENT
MILLBANK
WHITEHALL
VAUXHALL BR
LAMBETH BR
0
1 km
0.5 mile
© Copyright Time Out Group 2007

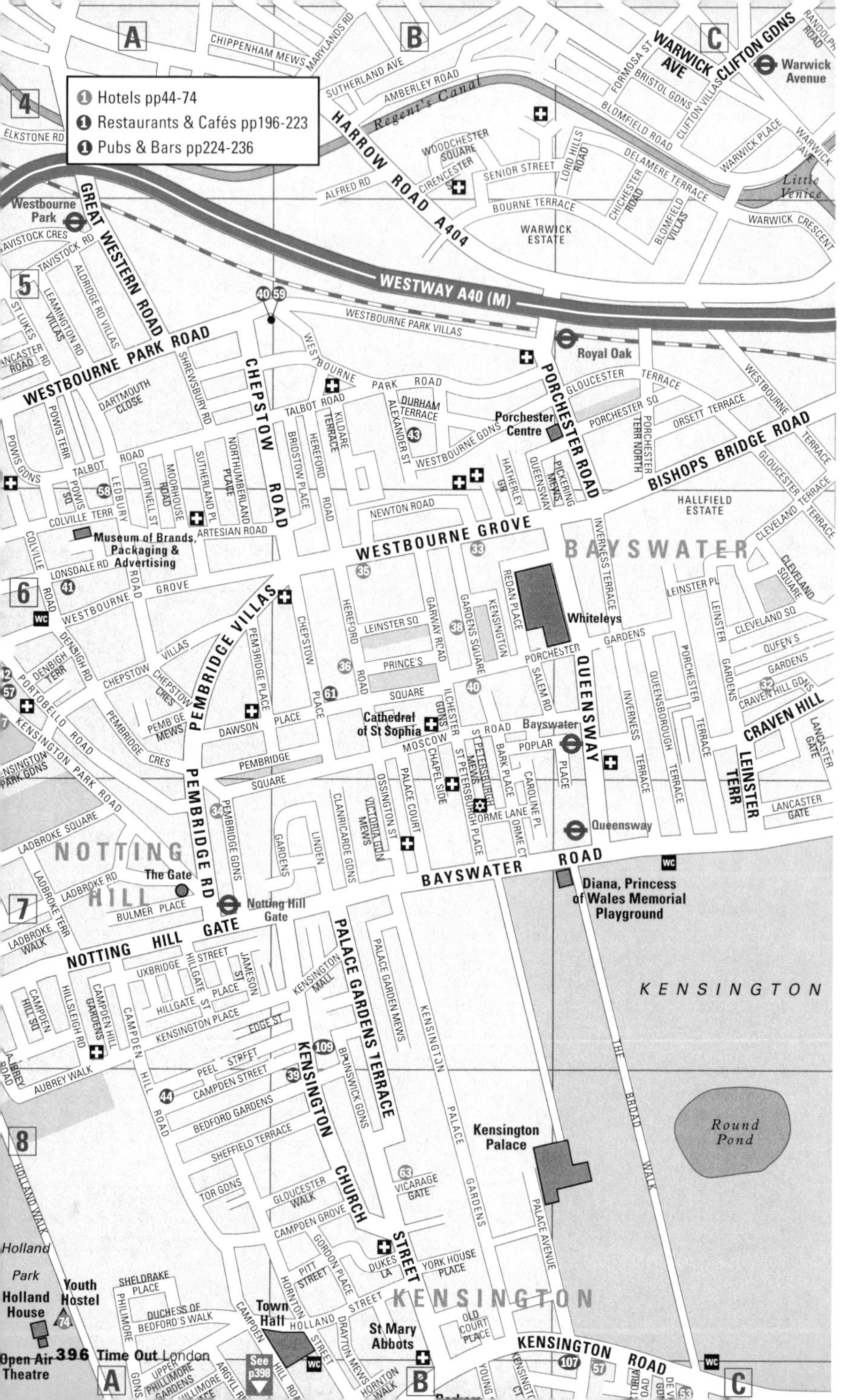

A
B
C
4
5
6
7
8
Hotels pp44-74
Restaurants & Cafés pp196-223
Pubs & Bars pp224-236
CHIPPENHAM MEWS
MARYLANDS RD
SUTHERLAND AVE
AMBERLEY ROAD
Regent's Canal
HARROW ROAD A404
WARWICK AVE
FORMOSA ST
BRISTOL GDNS
CLIFTON GDNS
CLIFTON VILLAS
RANDOLPH ROAD
Warwick Avenue
BLOMFIELD ROAD
DELAMERE TERRACE
WARWICK PLACE
WARWICK AVE
Little Venice
WARWICK CRESCENT
ELKSTONE RD
WOODCHESTER SQUARE
CIRENCESTER ST
ALFRED RD
SENIOR STREET
LORD HILLS ROAD
BOURNE TERRACE
CHICHESTER ROAD
BLOMFIELD VILLAS
WARWICK ESTATE
Westbourne Park
GREAT WESTERN ROAD
TAVISTOCK CRES
TAVISTOCK RD
ALDRIDGE RD VILLAS
LEAMINGTON RD VILLAS
ST LUKES RD
LANCASTER ROAD
WESTWAY A40 (M)
WESTBOURNE PARK VILLAS
WESTBOURNE PARK ROAD
Royal Oak
SHREWSBURY RD
CHEPSTOW ROAD
DARTMOUTH CLOSE
TALBOT ROAD
KILDARE TERRACE
DURHAM TERRACE
ALEXANDER ST
PORCHESTER ROAD
GLOUCESTER TERRACE
PORCHESTER SQ
PORCHESTER TERR NORTH
ORSETT TERRACE
WESTBOURNE TERRACE
Porchester Centre
WESTBOURNE GDNS
BISHOPS BRIDGE ROAD
POWIS GDNS
POWIS TERR
POWIS SQ
LEDBURY ROAD
COURTNELL ST
MOORHOUSE ROAD
SUTHERLAND PL
NORTHUMBERLAND PLACE
BRIDSTOW PLACE
HEREFORD ROAD
HATHERLEY GR
QUEENSWAY MEWS
PICKERING MEWS
NEWTON ROAD
HALLFIELD ESTATE
GLOUCESTER TERRACE
CLEVELAND TERRACE
COLVILLE TERR
ARTESIAN ROAD
Museum of Brands, Packaging & Advertising
WESTBOURNE GROVE
BAYSWATER
INVERNESS TERRACE
COLVILLE ROAD
LONSDALE RD
WESTBOURNE GROVE
PEMBRIDGE VILLAS
CHEPSTOW PLACE
HEREFORD ROAD
GARWAY ROAD
GARDENS SQUARE
KENSINGTON
REDAN PLACE
Whiteleys
LEINSTER PL
CLEVELAND SQUARE
LEINSTER GARDENS
CLEVELAND SQ
QUEEN'S GARDENS
LEINSTER SQ
PRINCE'S SQUARE
DENBIGH RD
DENBIGH TERR
PORTOBELLO ROAD
CHEPSTOW VILLAS
CHEPSTOW CRES
PEMBRIDGE PLACE
ILCHESTER GDNS
PORCHESTER GARDENS
QUEENSWAY
SALEM RD
INVERNESS TERRACE
QUEENSBOROUGH TERRACE
PORCHESTER TERRACE
CRAVEN HILL GDNS
CRAVEN HILL
LANCASTER GATE
KENSINGTON PARK GDNS
KENSINGTON PARK ROAD
PEMBRIDGE CRES
PEMB'GE MEWS
DAWSON PLACE
Cathedral of St Sophia
MOSCOW ROAD
Bayswater
POPLAR PLACE
LEINSTER TERR
PEMBRIDGE SQUARE
CHAPEL SIDE
ST PETERSBURGH MEWS
ST PETERSBURGH PLACE
BARK PLACE
CAROLINE PL
ORME LANE
ORME CT
LANCASTER GATE
OSSINGTON ST
PALACE COURT
VICTORIA GDN MEWS
CLANRICARDE GDNS
LINDEN GARDENS
PEMBRIDGE GDNS
PEMBRIDGE RD
LADBROKE SQUARE
NOTTING HILL
Queensway
BAYSWATER ROAD
The Gate
LADBROKE RD
LADBROKE TERR
BULMER PLACE
Notting Hill Gate
Diana, Princess of Wales Memorial Playground
LADBROKE WALK
NOTTING HILL GATE
UXBRIDGE STREET
HILLGATE ST
JAMESON ST
KENSINGTON MALL
PALACE GARDENS TERRACE
PALACE GARDEN MEWS
KENSINGTON PALACE GARDENS
KENSINGTON
HILLGATE PLACE
CAMPDEN HILL SQ
HILLSLEIGH RD
CAMPDEN HILL GARDENS
CAMPDEN HILL ROAD
KENSINGTON PLACE
EDGE ST
PEEL STREET
CAMPDEN STREET
KENSINGTON CHURCH STREET
BRUNSWICK GDNS
THE BROAD WALK
AUBREY WALK
AUBREY ROAD
BEDFORD GARDENS
SHEFFIELD TERRACE
Kensington Palace
Round Pond
HOLLAND WALK
TOR GDNS
GLOUCESTER WALK
VICARAGE GATE
PALACE AVENUE
CAMPDEN GROVE
GORDON PLACE
YORK HOUSE PLACE
DUKES LA
PITT STREET
Holland Park
Youth Hostel
Holland House
SHELDRAKE PLACE
PHILLIMORE GDNS
DUCHESS OF BEDFORD'S WALK
HORNTON STREET
Town Hall
HOLLAND STREET
DRAYTON MEWS
St Mary Abbots
KENSINGTON
OLD COURT PLACE
KENSINGTON ROAD
Open Air Theatre
UPPER PHILLIMORE GARDENS
ARGYLL RD
See p398
HORNTON WALK
YOUNG ST

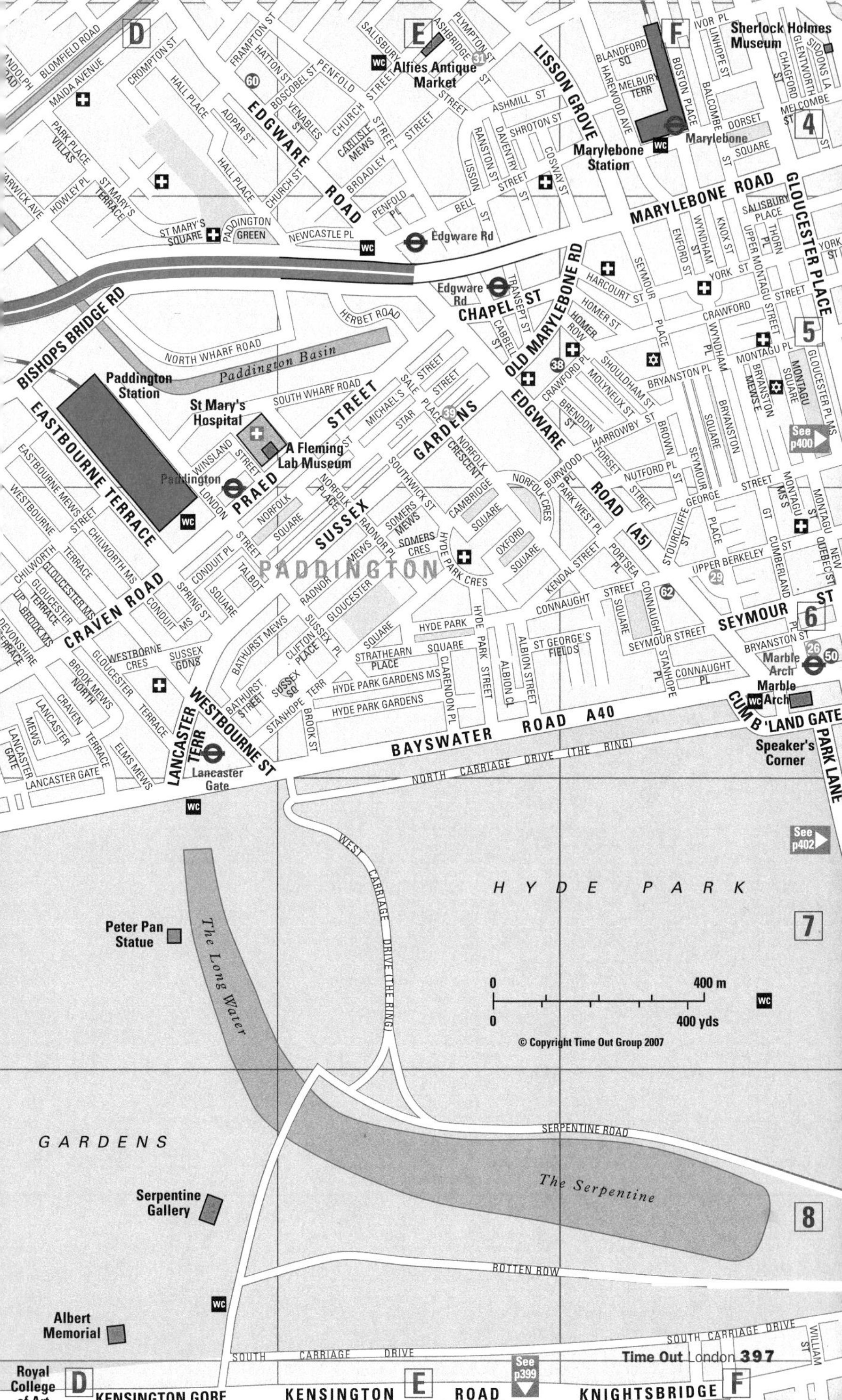
D
E
F
4
5
6
7
8
Sherlock Holmes Museum
Alfies Antique Market
Marylebone Station
Marylebone
Edgware Rd
Paddington Station
Paddington
St Mary's Hospital
A Fleming Lab Museum
Paddington Basin
PADDINGTON
Lancaster Gate
Marble Arch
Speaker's Corner
HYDE PARK
GARDENS
The Long Water
The Serpentine
Peter Pan Statue
Serpentine Gallery
Albert Memorial
Royal College
LISSON GROVE
MARYLEBONE ROAD
GLOUCESTER PLACE
EDGWARE ROAD
OLD MARYLEBONE RD
BISHOPS BRIDGE RD
NORTH WHARF ROAD
SOUTH WHARF ROAD
EASTBOURNE TERRACE
PRAED STREET
SUSSEX GARDENS
CRAVEN ROAD
WESTBOURNE ST
LANCASTER TERR
BAYSWATER ROAD A40
NORTH CARRIAGE DRIVE (THE RING)
WEST CARRIAGE DRIVE (THE RING)
SERPENTINE ROAD
ROTTEN ROW
SOUTH CARRIAGE DRIVE
KENSINGTON GORE
KENSINGTON ROAD
KNIGHTSBRIDGE
CUMB'LAND GATE
PARK LANE
SEYMOUR ST
CHAPEL ST
(A5)
See p400
See p402
See p399
0
400 m
0
400 yds
© Copyright Time Out Group 2007

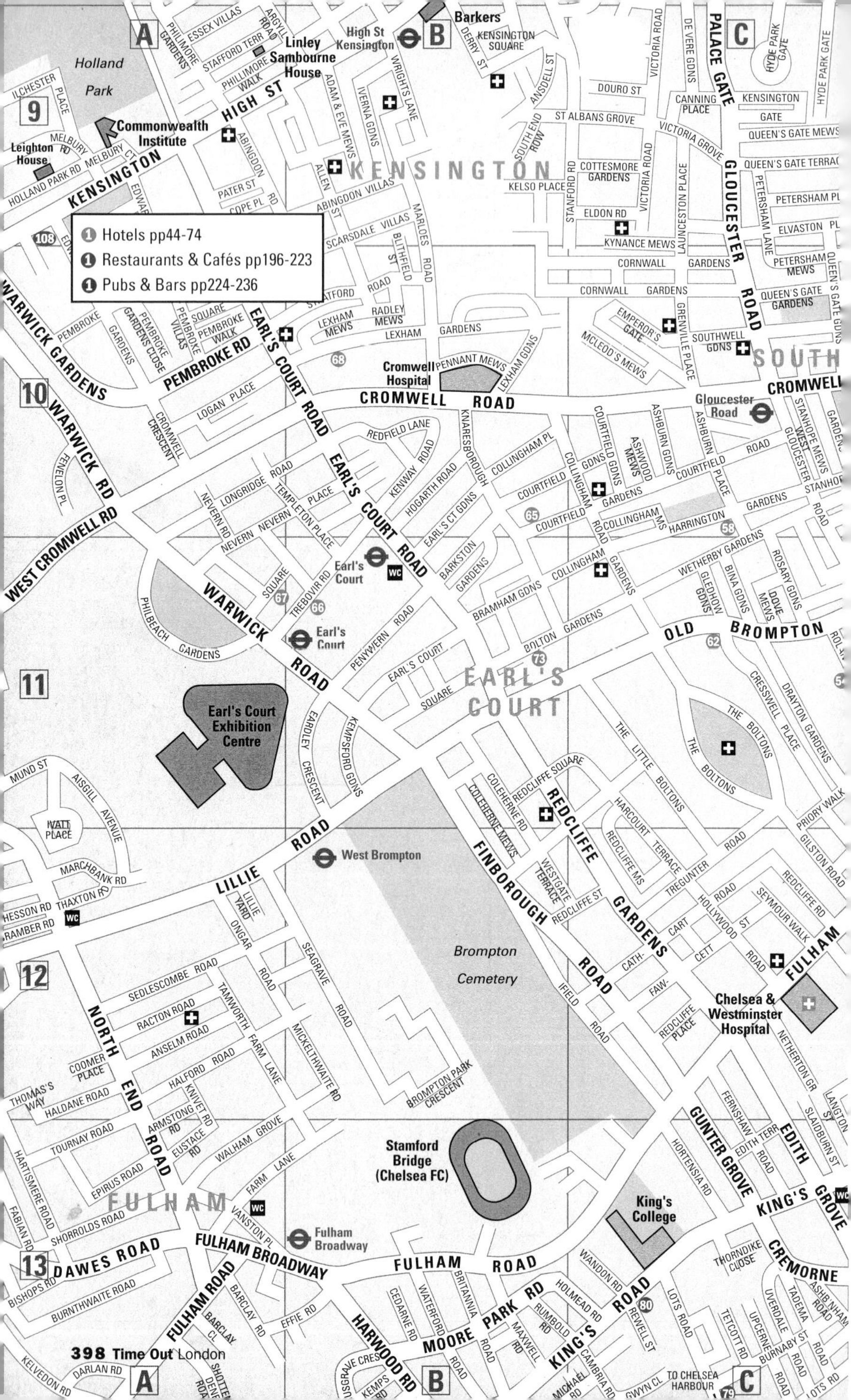

A
B
C
9
10
11
12
13
Holland Park
Commonwealth Institute
Leighton House
Linley Sambourne House
High St Kensington
Barkers
KENSINGTON SQUARE
KENSINGTON
Hotels pp44-74
Restaurants & Cafés pp196-223
Pubs & Bars pp224-236
108
68
65
58
67
66
73
62
54
80
79
ILCHESTER PLACE
MELBURY RD
MELBURY CT
HOLLAND PARK RD
KENSINGTON HIGH ST
PHILLIMORE GARDENS
ESSEX VILLAS
ARGYLL ROAD
STAFFORD TERR
PHILLIMORE WALK
ADAM & EVE MEWS
IVERNA GDNS
WRIGHTS LANE
DERRY ST
ANSDELL ST
VICTORIA ROAD
DE VERE GDNS
PALACE GATE
HYDE PARK GATE
DOURO ST
CANNING PLACE
KENSINGTON GATE
ST ALBANS GROVE
VICTORIA GROVE
QUEEN'S GATE MEWS
QUEEN'S GATE TERRAC
SOUTH END ROW
ABINGDON ROAD
ALLEN ST
ABINGDON VILLAS
PATER ST
COPE PL
EDWARDES SQUARE
SCARSDALE VILLAS
MARLOES ROAD
BLITHFIELD ST
COTTESMORE GARDENS
KELSO PLACE
STANFORD RD
ELDON RD
KYNANCE MEWS
LAUNCESTON PLACE
GLOUCESTER ROAD
PETERSHAM LANE
PETERSHAM PL
ELVASTON PL
PETERSHAM MEWS
QUEEN'S GATE GARDENS
CORNWALL GARDENS
STRATFORD ROAD
LEXHAM MEWS
RADLEY MEWS
LEXHAM GARDENS
EMPEROR'S GATE
GRENVILLE PLACE
SOUTHWELL GDNS
MCLEOD'S MEWS
SOUTH
WARWICK GARDENS
PEMBROKE GARDENS
PEMBROKE GARDENS CLOSE
PEMBROKE VILLAS
PEMBROKE SQUARE
PEMBROKE WALK
PEMBROKE RD
EARL'S COURT ROAD
Cromwell Hospital
PENNANT MEWS
LEXHAM GDNS
CROMWELL ROAD
Gloucester Road
LOGAN PLACE
CROMWELL CRESCENT
WARWICK RD
FENELON PL
REDFIELD LANE
KENWAY ROAD
KNARESBOROUGH PL
HOGARTH ROAD
COLLINGHAM PL
COURTFIELD GDNS
ASHWOOD MEWS
ASHBURN GDNS
ASHBURN PLACE
COURTFIELD ROAD
STANHOPE MEWS WEST
GLOUCESTER MEWS
STANHOPE GARDENS
LONGRIDGE ROAD
TEMPLETON PLACE
NEVERN RD
NEVERN PLACE
NEVERN SQUARE
EARL'S CT GDNS
COLLINGHAM ROAD
COURTFIELD GARDENS
COLLINGHAM MS
HARRINGTON ROAD
WEST CROMWELL RD
Earl's Court
BARKSTON GARDENS
COLLINGHAM GARDENS
WETHERBY GARDENS
BINA GDNS
GLEDHOW GDNS
DOVE MEWS
ROSARY GDNS
TREBOVIR RD
BRAMHAM GDNS
BOLTON GARDENS
OLD BROMPTON ROAD
PHILBEACH GARDENS
WARWICK ROAD
PENYWERN ROAD
EARL'S COURT SQUARE
EARL'S COURT
CRESSWELL PLACE
DRAYTON GARDENS
THE BOLTONS
THE LITTLE BOLTONS
Earl's Court Exhibition Centre
EARDLEY CRESCENT
KEMPSFORD GDNS
REDCLIFFE SQUARE
COLEHERNE RD
COLEHERNE MEWS
REDCLIFFE GARDENS
HARCOURT TERRACE
REDCLIFFE MS
PRIORY WALK
GILSTON ROAD
MUND ST
AISGILL AVENUE
IVATT PLACE
MARCHBANK RD
THAXTON RD
HESSON RD
RAMBER RD
LILLIE ROAD
LILLIE YARD
West Brompton
FINBOROUGH ROAD
WESTGATE TERRACE
REDCLIFFE ST
TREGUNTER ROAD
HOLLYWOOD ROAD
SEYMOUR WALK
REDCLIFFE RD
CATHCART ROAD
FAWCETT ST
FULHAM ROAD
Chelsea & Westminster Hospital
ONGAR ROAD
SEAGRAVE ROAD
Brompton Cemetery
SEDLESCOMBE ROAD
RACTON ROAD
TAMWORTH
ANSELM ROAD
NORTH END ROAD
COOMER PLACE
HALFORD ROAD
FARM LANE
MICKLETHWAITE RD
IFIELD ROAD
REDCLIFFE PLACE
NETHERTON GR
THOMAS'S WAY
HALDANE ROAD
KNIVET RD
ARMSTRONG RD
EUSTACE RD
WALHAM GROVE
BROMPTON PARK CRESCENT
FERNSHAW ROAD
EDITH TERR
HORTENSIA RD
GUNTER GROVE
EDITH GROVE
LANGTON ST
SLAIDBURN ST
TOURNAY ROAD
HARTISMERE ROAD
EPIRUS ROAD
Stamford Bridge (Chelsea FC)
FULHAM
SHORROLDS ROAD
VANSTON PL
Fulham Broadway
King's College
KING'S ROAD
FABIAN RD
DAWES ROAD
BISHOPS RD
FULHAM BROADWAY
THORNDIKE CLOSE
CREMORNE ROAD
BURNTHWAITE ROAD
FULHAM ROAD
BARCLAY ROAD
BARCLAY CL
EFFIE RD
HARWOOD RD
CEDARNE RD
WATERFORD ROAD
BRITANNIA ROAD
MOORE PARK RD
MAXWELL RD
RUMBOLD RD
HOLMEAD RD
WANDON RD
REWELL ST
LOTS ROAD
TETCOTT RD
UPCERNE RD
UVERDALE ROAD
TADEMA ROAD
ASHBURNHAM ROAD
BURNABY ST
CAMBRIA RD
TO CHELSEA HARBOUR
GWYN CL
KEMPS RD
MUSGRAVE CRES
KELVEDON RD
DARLAN RD
SHOTTENDANE ROAD
WC

Royal College of Art
Royal Albert Hall
D
E
F
See p397
Knightsbridge
Harrods
KNIGHTSBRIDGE
Royal College of Music
Imperial College of Science and Technology
Goethe Institute
Science Museum
Victoria & Albert Museum
Brompton Oratory
Natural History Museum
KENSINGTON
BROMPTON
South Kensington
Michelin House
Royal Marsden Hospital
Royal Brompton Hospital
CHELSEA
Chelsea Old Town Hall
Chelsea Antiques Market
Carlyle's House
Chelsea Old Church
Crosby Hall
Chelsea Physic Garden
Chelsea Royal Hospital
National Army Museum
Sloane Square
River Thames
Peace Pagoda
Zoo
BATTERSEA PARK
Chelsea Wharf
Lots Road Power Station
9
10
11
12
13
0
400 m
400 yds
PRINCE CONSORT ROAD
EXHIBITION ROAD
CROMWELL ROAD
BROMPTON ROAD
FULHAM ROAD
KING'S ROAD
SLOANE STREET
SYDNEY STREET
OAKLEY STREET
CHEYNE WALK
CHELSEA EMBANKMENT
ROYAL HOSPITAL ROAD
ALBERT BRIDGE
BATTERSEA BRIDGE
BATTERSEA BRIDGE ROAD
ALBERT BRIDGE ROAD
BEAUFORT ST
PONT ST
BEAUCHAMP PL
LOTS ROAD

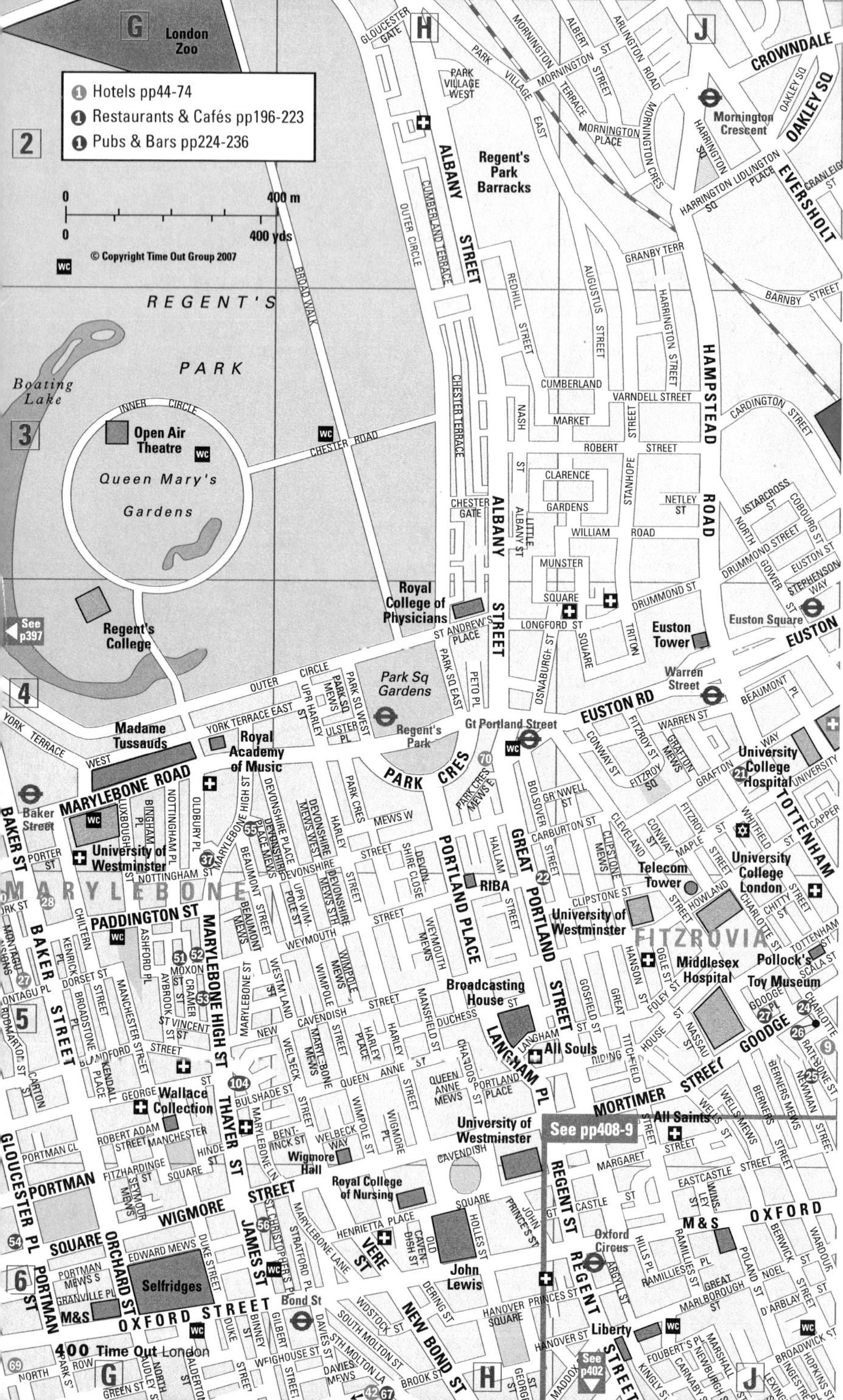

G
H
J
London Zoo
Hotels pp44-74
Restaurants & Cafés pp196-223
Pubs & Bars pp224-236
2
3
4
5
6
0
400 m
0
400 yds
© Copyright Time Out Group 2007
WC
REGENT'S PARK
Boating Lake
INNER CIRCLE
Open Air Theatre
Queen Mary's Gardens
CHESTER ROAD
BROAD WALK
Regent's College
See p397
OUTER CIRCLE
YORK TERRACE WEST
YORK TERRACE EAST
Madame Tussauds
Royal Academy of Music
MARYLEBONE ROAD
Baker Street
BAKER ST
University of Westminster
MARYLEBONE
PADDINGTON ST
MARYLEBONE HIGH ST
Wallace Collection
THAYER ST
Wigmore Hall
WIGMORE STREET
PORTMAN SQUARE
GLOUCESTER PL
PORTMAN ST
ORCHARD ST
Selfridges
M&S
OXFORD STREET
JAMES ST
Bond St
NEW BOND ST
Royal College of Nursing
John Lewis
HANOVER SQUARE
CAVENDISH SQUARE
Oxford Circus
REGENT ST
REGENT STREET
Liberty
See p402
See pp408-9
University of Westminster
All Saints
MARGARET STREET
EASTCASTLE STREET
OXFORD
M & S
MORTIMER STREET
GOODGE STREET
All Souls
LANGHAM PL
Broadcasting House
PORTLAND PLACE
GREAT PORTLAND STREET
RIBA
University of Westminster
FITZROVIA
Middlesex Hospital
Pollock's Toy Museum
Telecom Tower
University College London
University College Hospital
TOTTENHAM
Warren Street
EUSTON RD
EUSTON
Euston Square
Euston Tower
Gt Portland Street
Regent's Park
PARK CRES
Park Sq Gardens
Royal College of Physicians
ALBANY STREET
HAMPSTEAD ROAD
Regent's Park Barracks
PARK VILLAGE WEST
PARK VILLAGE EAST
Mornington Crescent
CROWNDALE
OAKLEY SQ
EVERSHOLT
GLOUCESTER GATE
CUMBERLAND TERRACE
CHESTER TERRACE
OUTER CIRCLE
CUMBERLAND MARKET
ROBERT STREET
CLARENCE GARDENS
WILLIAM ROAD
MUNSTER SQUARE
DRUMMOND ST
CARDINGTON STREET
GRANBY TERR
BARNBY STREET

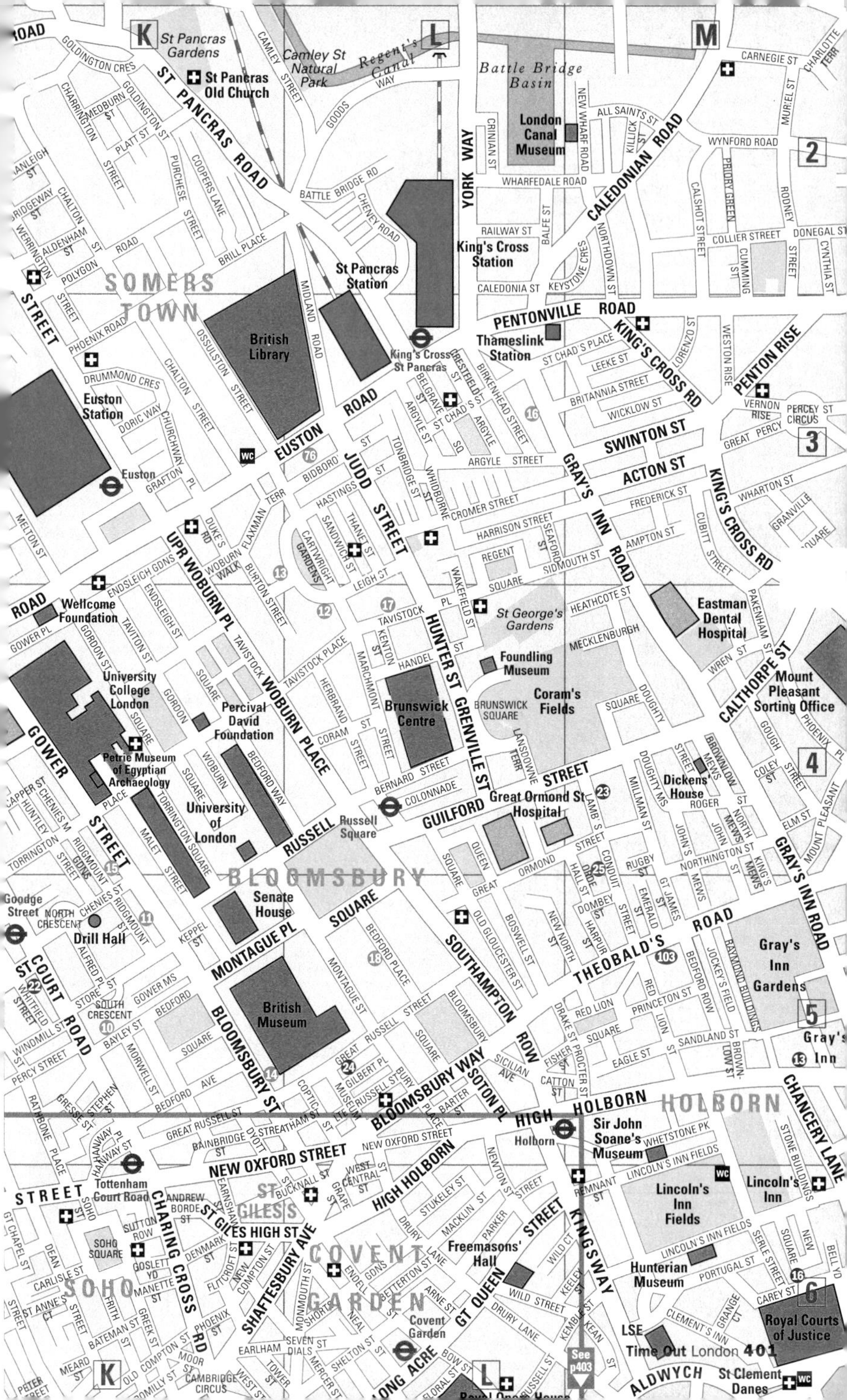
K
L
M
2
3
4
5
6
St Pancras Gardens
St Pancras Old Church
Camley St Natural Park
Regent's Canal
Battle Bridge Basin
London Canal Museum
St Pancras Road
Goldington Cres
Camley Street
Goods Way
York Way
Crinian St
New Wharf Road
All Saints St
Killick St
Caledonian Road
Carnegie St
Charlotte Terr
Muriel St
Wynford Road
Priory Green
Rodney
Calshot Street
Collier Street
Donegal St
Cynthia St
Cumming St
Wharfedale Road
Railway St
Balfe St
Northdown St
Keystone Cres
King's Cross Station
Caledonia St
Battle Bridge Rd
Cheney Road
St Pancras Station
Midland Road
Somers Town
British Library
Ossulston Street
Chalton Street
Phoenix Road
Drummond Cres
Euston Station
Doric Way
Churchway
Euston
Grafton Pl
Melton St
Medburn St
Charrington
Goldington St
Platt St
Purchese Street
Coopers Lane
Brill Place
Polygon Road
Aldenham St
Werrington
Chalton
Ridgeway St
Pentonville Road
Thameslink Station
King's Cross St Pancras
St Chad's Place
Leeke St
Britannia Street
Wicklow St
King's Cross Rd
Lorenzo St
Weston Rise
Penton Rise
Vernon Rise
Percy Circus
Great Percy St
Swinton St
Acton St
Frederick St
Wharton St
Granville Square
Cubitt Street
King's Cross Rd
Gray's Inn Road
Ampton St
Sidmouth St
Regent Square
Heathcote St
Mecklenburgh Square
Eastman Dental Hospital
Pakenham St
Wren St
Calthorpe St
Mount Pleasant Sorting Office
Phoenix Pl
Gough St
Coley St
Elm St
Mount Pleasant
Euston Road
Judd Street
Bidborough St
Tonbridge St
Whidborne St
Argyle Street
Argyle Sq
Belgrave St
Crestfield St
Birkenhead Street
St Chad's St
Argyle St
Cromer Street
Harrison Street
Seaford St
Hastings St
Sandwich St
Thanet St
Cartwright Gardens
Leigh St
Flaxman Terr
Burton Street
Duke's Rd
Woburn Walk
Upr Woburn Pl
Endsleigh Gdns
Endsleigh St
Wellcome Foundation
Gower Pl
Gordon St
Taviton St
Tavistock Place
Tavistock Sq
Kenton St
Handel St
Hunter St
Wakefield St
St George's Gardens
Foundling Museum
Coram's Fields
Brunswick Square
Lansdowne Terr
Marchmont Street
Herbrand Street
Coram St
Brunswick Centre
Bernard Street
Colonnade
Grenville St
Guilford Street
Great Ormond St Hospital
Lamb's Conduit Street
Doughty St
Doughty Ms
Millman St
Dickens' House
Brownlow Mews
Roger St
John's Mews
John St
North Mews
Northington St
King's Mews
Rugby St
Gt James St
Emerald St
Dombey St
Harpur St
New North St
Boswell St
Old Gloucester St
Queen Square
Great Ormond Street
Orde Hall St
University College London
Gordon Square
Percival David Foundation
Petrie Museum of Egyptian Archaeology
Woburn Square
Bedford Way
University of London
Woburn Place
Russell Square
Gower Street
Torrington Square
Malet Street
Capper St
Chenies M
Huntley St
Torrington Pl
Ridgmount Gdns
Ridgmount St
Chenies St
North Crescent
Goodge Street
Drill Hall
Keppel St
Senate House
Montague Pl
Bloomsbury
Bedford Place
Montague St
British Museum
Southampton Row
Theobald's Road
Red Lion Square
Red Lion St
Princeton St
Bedford Row
Jockey's Field
Raymond Buildings
Gray's Inn Gardens
Gray's Inn
Sandland St
Eagle St
Brownlow St
Drake St
Procter St
Fisher St
Catton St
Sicilian Ave
Gower Ms
Bedford Square
Store St
South Crescent
Alfred Pl
Court Road
Whitfield Street
Windmill St
Percy Street
Bayley St
Morwell St
Bloomsbury St
Bloomsbury Way
Bloomsbury Square
Great Russell Street
Gilbert Pl
Museum St
Bury Pl
Barter St
Southampton Pl
Coptic St
High Holborn
Holborn
Sir John Soane's Museum
Whetstone Pk
Lincoln's Inn Fields
Lincoln's Inn
Chancery Lane
Stone Buildings
Rathbone Place
Gresse St
Stephen St
Bedford Ave
Hanway Pl
Hanway St
Great Russell St
Bainbridge St
Dyott St
Streatham St
New Oxford Street
West Central St
Bucknall St
Grape St
Earnshaw St
Tottenham Court Road
Andrew Borde St
St Giles High St
St Giles
Shaftesbury Ave
Stukeley St
Macklin St
Drury Lane
Parker St
Newton St
Remnant St
Kingsway
Freemasons' Hall
Great Queen Street
Wild Ct
Keeley St
Wild Street
Kemble St
Kean St
Hunterian Museum
Portugal St
Serle Street
New Square
Bell Yd
Carey St
Clement's Inn
Grange Ct
Royal Courts of Justice
LSE
Aldwych
St Clement Danes
Soho Square
Soho St
Sutton Row
Goslett Yd
Manette St
Denmark St
Flitcroft St
New Compton St
Charing Cross Rd
Covent Garden
Monmouth St
Shorts Gdns
Endell St
Neal St
Betterton St
Arne St
Drury Lane
Seven Dials
Earlham St
Shelton St
Mercer St
Long Acre
Bow St
Floral St
Russell St
Carlisle St
Dean St
Frith Street
Greek St
Bateman St
St Anne's Ct
Meard St
Old Compton St
Moor St
Romilly St
Cambridge Circus
Phoenix St
Tower St
West St
Soho
Gt Chapel St
Street
See p403

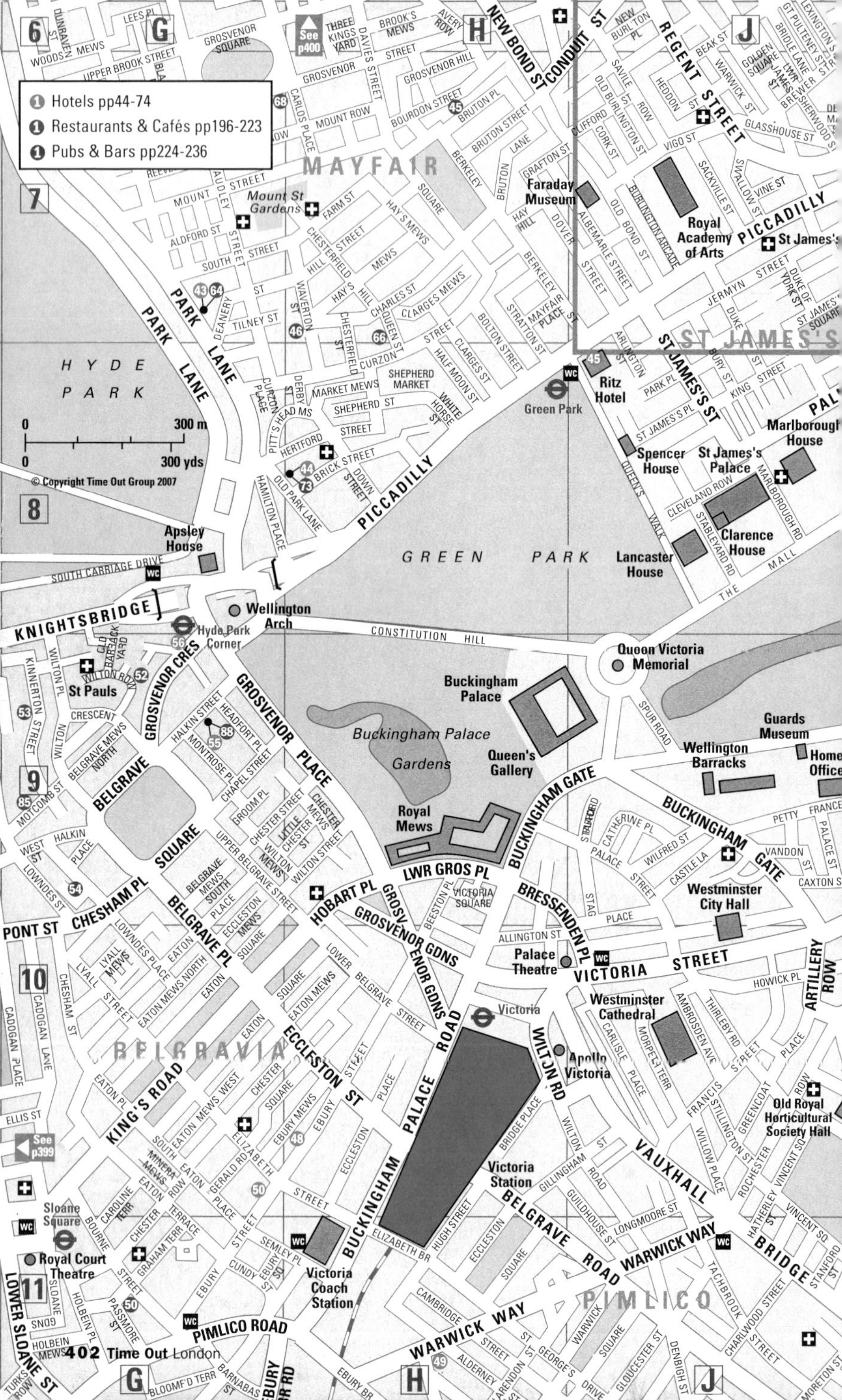
Hotels pp44-74
Restaurants & Cafés pp196-223
Pubs & Bars pp224-236
MAYFAIR
HYDE PARK
GREEN PARK
BELGRAVIA
PIMLICO
ST JAMES'S
Buckingham Palace Gardens
Buckingham Palace
Victoria Station
Victoria Coach Station
Westminster Cathedral
Royal Academy of Arts
© Copyright Time Out Group 2007

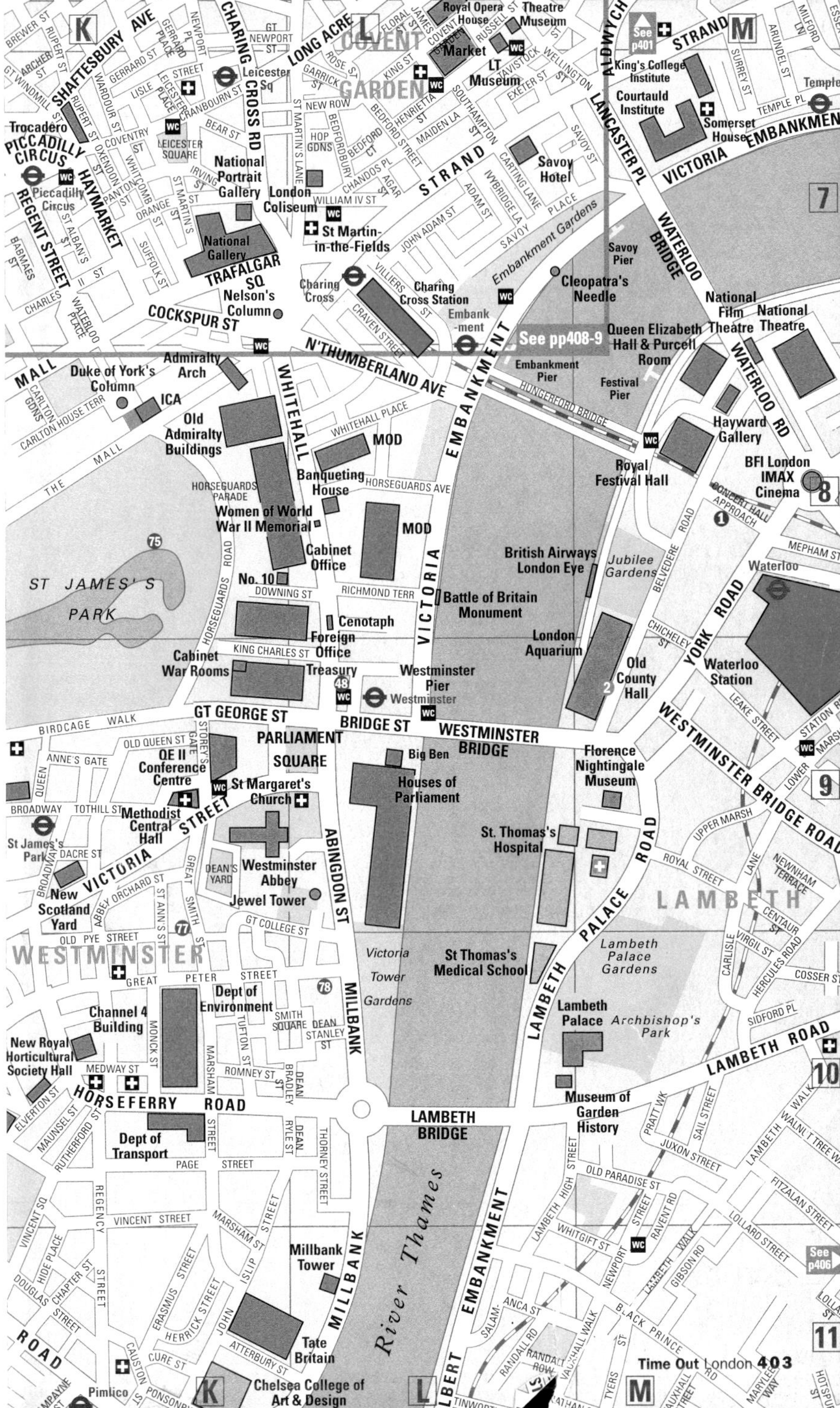
K
L
M
COVENT GARDEN
Royal Opera House
Theatre Museum
Market
LT Museum
ALDWYCH
See p401
STRAND
King's College Institute
Courtauld Institute
Somerset House
Temple
TEMPLE PL
VICTORIA EMBANKMENT
SHAFTESBURY AVE
CHARING CROSS RD
LONG ACRE
Leicester Sq
LEICESTER SQUARE
Trocadero
PICCADILLY CIRCUS
Piccadilly Circus
HAYMARKET
REGENT STREET
National Portrait Gallery
London Coliseum
National Gallery
TRAFALGAR SQ
Nelson's Column
St Martin-in-the-Fields
Charing Cross
Charing Cross Station
Embankment
STRAND
Savoy Hotel
Embankment Gardens
Savoy Pier
Cleopatra's Needle
LANCASTER PL
WATERLOO BRIDGE
National Film Theatre
National Theatre
Queen Elizabeth Hall & Purcell Room
See pp408-9
COCKSPUR ST
N'THUMBERLAND AVE
Embankment Pier
Festival Pier
HUNGERFORD BRIDGE
MALL
Duke of York's Column
Admiralty Arch
ICA
Old Admiralty Buildings
WHITEHALL
MOD
Banqueting House
HORSEGUARDS AVE
HORSEGUARDS PARADE
Women of World War II Memorial
THE MALL
CARLTON HOUSE TERR
Hayward Gallery
Royal Festival Hall
BFI London IMAX Cinema
WATERLOO RD
ST JAMES'S PARK
Cabinet Office
MOD
No. 10
DOWNING ST
RICHMOND TERR
VICTORIA EMBANKMENT
Battle of Britain Monument
British Airways London Eye
Jubilee Gardens
Waterloo
YORK ROAD
Cenotaph
Foreign Office
KING CHARLES ST
Cabinet War Rooms
Treasury
London Aquarium
Old County Hall
Waterloo Station
Westminster Pier
Westminster
GT GEORGE ST
BRIDGE ST
WESTMINSTER BRIDGE
BIRDCAGE WALK
PARLIAMENT SQUARE
QE II Conference Centre
Big Ben
Houses of Parliament
Florence Nightingale Museum
WESTMINSTER BRIDGE ROAD
St Margaret's Church
Methodist Central Hall
VICTORIA STREET
St James's Park
Westminster Abbey
Jewel Tower
ABINGDON ST
St. Thomas's Hospital
LAMBETH PALACE ROAD
LAMBETH
New Scotland Yard
WESTMINSTER
Victoria Tower Gardens
St Thomas's Medical School
Lambeth Palace Gardens
GREAT PETER STREET
Dept of Environment
MILLBANK
Lambeth Palace
Archbishop's Park
Channel 4 Building
New Royal Horticultural Society Hall
HORSEFERRY ROAD
LAMBETH BRIDGE
Museum of Garden History
LAMBETH ROAD
Dept of Transport
River Thames
ALBERT EMBANKMENT
Millbank Tower
See p406
Tate Britain
Chelsea College of Art & Design
Pimlico
7
8
9
10
11

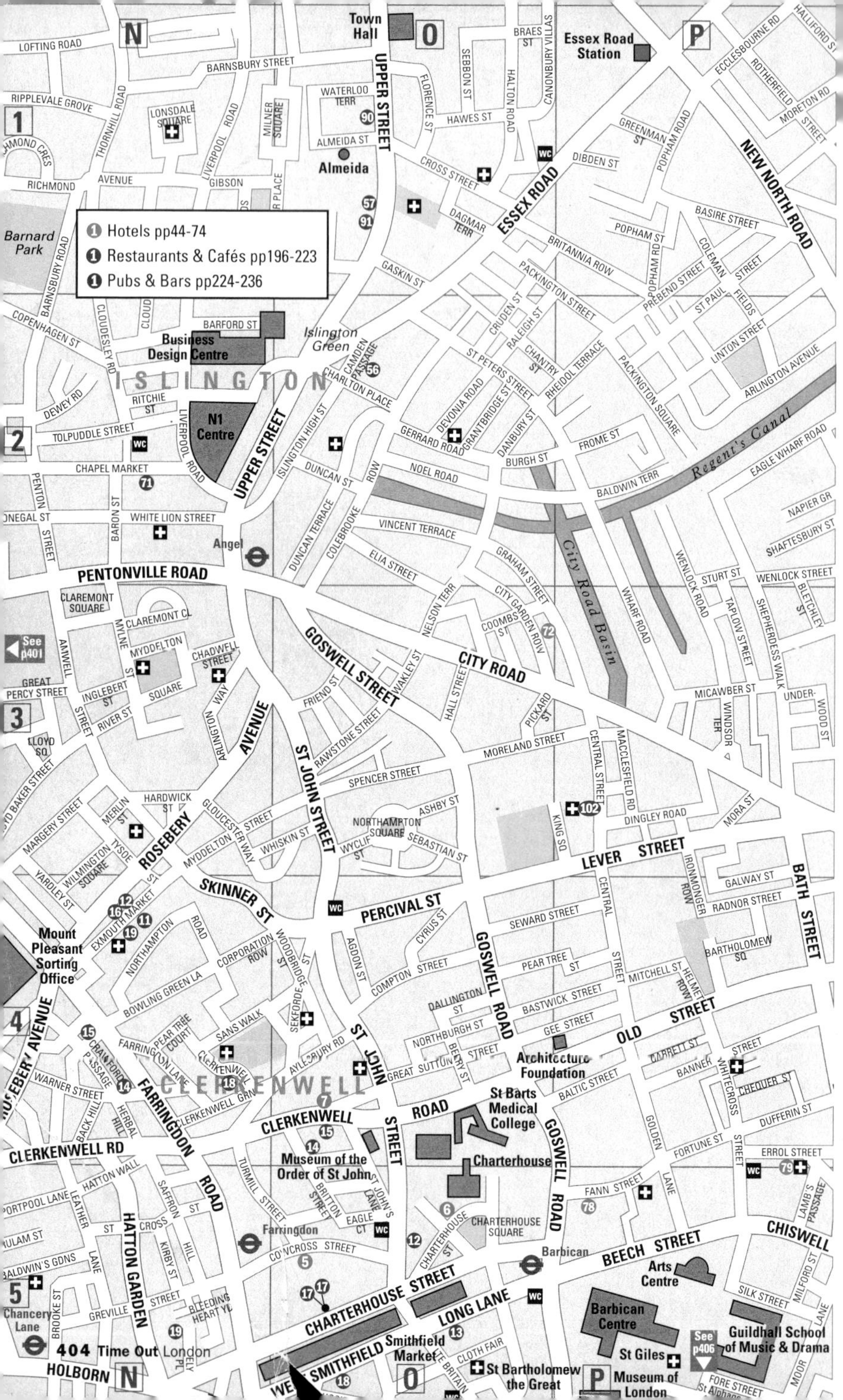

N
O
P
1
2
3
4
5
Town Hall
Essex Road Station
Hotels pp44-74
Restaurants & Cafés pp196-223
Pubs & Bars pp224-236
Barnard Park
Almeida
Islington Green
Business Design Centre
ISLINGTON
N1 Centre
Angel
Regent's Canal
City Road Basin
Mount Pleasant Sorting Office
CLERKENWELL
Museum of the Order of St John
Farringdon
Architecture Foundation
St Barts Medical College
Charterhouse
Charterhouse Square
Barbican
Arts Centre
Barbican Centre
Guildhall School of Music & Drama
St Giles
Museum of London
St Bartholomew the Great
Smithfield Market
Chancery Lane
See p401
See p406
LOFTING ROAD
BARNSBURY STREET
RIPPLEVALE GROVE
THORNHILL ROAD
LONSDALE SQUARE
LIVERPOOL ROAD
MILNER SQUARE
WATERLOO TERR
ALMEIDA ST
UPPER STREET
FLORENCE ST
SEBBON ST
BRAES ST
HALTON ROAD
CANONBURY VILLAS
HAWES ST
CROSS STREET
DAGMAR TERR
ESSEX ROAD
DIBDEN ST
GREENMAN ST
POPHAM ROAD
ECCLESBOURNE RD
ROTHERFIELD ST
MORETON RD
NEW NORTH ROAD
RICHMOND AVENUE
GIBSON
BARNSBURY ROAD
COPENHAGEN ST
CLOUDESLEY RD
BARFORD ST
GASKIN ST
BRITANNIA ROW
PACKINGTON STREET
POPHAM ST
BASIRE STREET
PREBEND STREET
COLEMAN FIELDS
ST PAUL STREET
LINTON STREET
ARLINGTON AVENUE
CAMDEN PASSAGE
CHARLTON PLACE
CRUDEN ST
RALEIGH ST
CHANTRY ST
RHEIDOL TERRACE
ST PETERS STREET
PACKINGTON SQUARE
DEVONIA ROAD
GRANTBRIDGE ST
DANBURY ST
GERRARD ROAD
FROME ST
BURGH ST
NOEL ROAD
BALDWIN TERR
EAGLE WHARF ROAD
DEWEY RD
RITCHIE ST
TOLPUDDLE STREET
CHAPEL MARKET
PENTON STREET
WHITE LION STREET
BARON ST
ISLINGTON HIGH ST
DUNCAN ST
DUNCAN TERRACE
COLEBROOKE ROW
VINCENT TERRACE
ELIA STREET
GRAHAM STREET
NAPIER GR
SHAFTESBURY ST
WENLOCK ROAD
STURT ST
WENLOCK STREET
BLETCHLEY ST
TAPLOW STREET
SHEPHERDESS WALK
PENTONVILLE ROAD
CLAREMONT SQUARE
CLAREMONT CL
MYLNE ST
MYDDELTON SQUARE
CHADWELL STREET
AMWELL STREET
GREAT PERCY STREET
INGLEBERT ST
RIVER ST
ARLINGTON WAY
AVENUE
GOSWELL STREET
FRIEND ST
WAKLEY ST
NELSON TERR
CITY GARDEN ROW
COOMBS ST
CITY ROAD
HALL STREET
PICKARD ST
WHARF ROAD
MICAWBER ST
WINDSOR TER
UNDERWOOD ST
LLOYD SQ
LLOYD BAKER STREET
RAWSTONE STREET
ST JOHN STREET
SPENCER STREET
MORELAND STREET
CENTRAL STREET
MACCLESFIELD RD
HARDWICK ST
MARGERY STREET
MERLIN ST
ROSEBERY
GLOUCESTER WAY
MYDDELTON STREET
WHISKIN ST
NORTHAMPTON SQUARE
ASHBY ST
SEBASTIAN ST
WYCLIF ST
KING SQ
DINGLEY ROAD
MORA ST
WILMINGTON SQUARE
TYSOE ST
YARDLEY ST
SKINNER ST
PERCIVAL ST
LEVER STREET
IRONMONGER ROW
GALWAY ST
RADNOR STREET
BATH STREET
EXMOUTH MARKET
NORTHAMPTON ROAD
CORPORATION ROW
WOODBRIDGE ST
AGDON ST
CYRUS ST
COMPTON STREET
GOSWELL ROAD
SEWARD STREET
PEAR TREE ST
MITCHELL ST
HELMET ROW
BARTHOLOMEW SQ
BOWLING GREEN LA
SEKFORDE ST
DALLINGTON ST
BASTWICK STREET
GEE STREET
OLD STREET
ROSEBERY AVENUE
PEAR TREE COURT
SANS WALK
FARRINGDON LANE
CRAWFORD PASSAGE
WARNER STREET
BACK HILL
HERBAL HILL
FARRINGDON ROAD
CLERKENWELL GRN
AYLESBURY RD
NORTHBURGH ST
BERRY ST
GREAT SUTTON STREET
CARRETT ST
BANNER STREET
WHITECROSS STREET
CHEQUER ST
DUFFERIN ST
BALTIC STREET
CLERKENWELL RD
CLERKENWELL ROAD
GOLDEN LANE
FORTUNE ST
ERROL STREET
HATTON WALL
PORTPOOL LANE
LEATHER LANE
SAFFRON HILL
TURNMILL STREET
BRITTON STREET
ST JOHN'S LANE
FANN STREET
LAMB'S PASSAGE
CHISWELL STREET
EAGLE CT
HATTON GARDEN
CROSS ST
KIRBY ST
ULAM ST
BALDWIN'S GDNS
COWCROSS STREET
BEECH STREET
MILFORD LANE
SILK STREET
BROOKE ST
GREVILLE STREET
BLEEDING HEART YD
ELY PL
CHARTERHOUSE STREET
LONG LANE
CLOTH FAIR
LITTLE BRITAIN
WEST SMITHFIELD
HOLBORN
FORE STREET
MOOR LANE
St Alphage

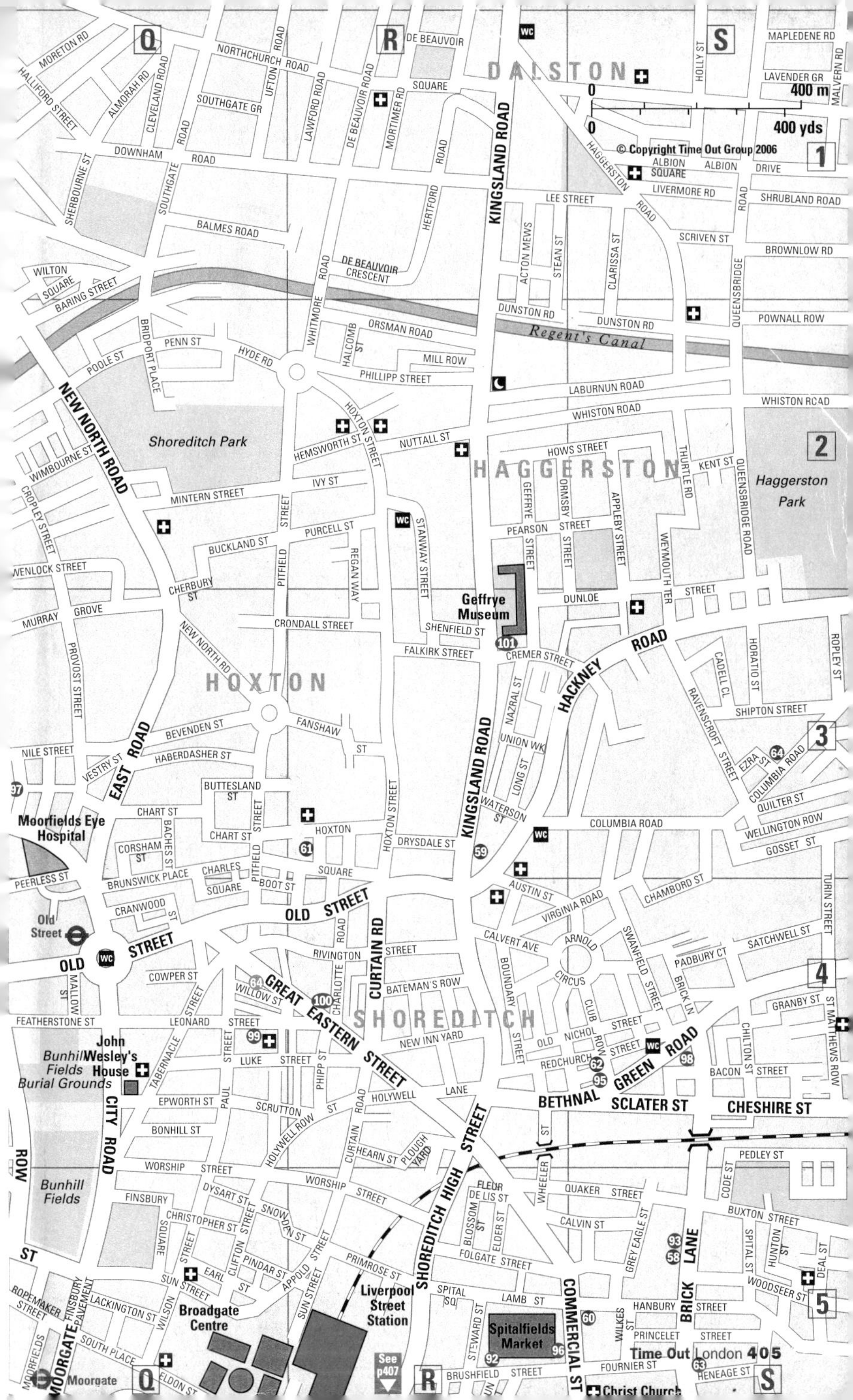
Q
R
S
DE BEAUVOIR
DALSTON
MORETON RD
HALLIFORD STREET
ALMORAH RD
CLEVELAND ROAD
NORTHCHURCH ROAD
UFTON ROAD
SOUTHGATE GR
LAWFORD ROAD
DE BEAUVOIR ROAD
SQUARE
MORTIMER RD
KINGSLAND ROAD
HOLLY ST
MAPLEDENE RD
LAVENDER GR
MALVERN RD
0
400 m
0
400 yds
© Copyright Time Out Group 2006
1
DOWNHAM
ROAD
SHERBOURNE ST
SOUTHGATE ROAD
HERTFORD ROAD
HAGGERSTON ROAD
ALBION SQUARE
ALBION DRIVE
LIVERMORE RD
SHRUBLAND ROAD
LEE STREET
BALMES ROAD
ACTON MEWS
STEAN ST
CLARISSA ST
SCRIVEN ST
BROWNLOW RD
WILTON SQUARE
BARING STREET
DE BEAUVOIR CRESCENT
WHITMORE ROAD
QUEENSBRIDGE ROAD
DUNSTON RD
DUNSTON RD
POWNALL ROW
Regent's Canal
BRIDPORT PLACE
PENN ST
HYDE RD
ORSMAN ROAD
HALCOMB ST
MILL ROW
POOLE ST
PHILLIPP STREET
LABURNUN ROAD
WHISTON ROAD
WHISTON ROAD
NEW NORTH ROAD
Shoreditch Park
HOXTON STREET
HEMSWORTH ST
NUTTALL ST
HOWS STREET
HAGGERSTON
2
KENT ST
THURTLE RD
Haggerston Park
WIMBOURNE ST
CROPLEY STREET
MINTERN STREET
IVY ST
GEFFRYE STREET
ORMSBY STREET
APPLEBY STREET
WEYMOUTH TER
PURCELL ST
STANWAY STREET
PEARSON STREET
BUCKLAND ST
PITFIELD STREET
REGAN WAY
WENLOCK STREET
CHERBURY ST
Geffrye Museum
DUNLOE STREET
MURRAY GROVE
CRONDALL STREET
SHENFIELD ST
101
FALKIRK STREET
CREMER STREET
HACKNEY ROAD
PROVOST STREET
NEW NORTH RD
HOXTON
NAZRAL ST
CADELL CL
HORATIO ST
RAVENSCROFT STREET
ROPLEY ST
SHIPTON STREET
BEVENDEN ST
FANSHAW ST
UNION WK
3
EZRA ST
64
COLUMBIA ROAD
NILE STREET
VESTRY ST
EAST ROAD
HABERDASHER ST
LONG ST
QUILTER ST
97
BUTTESLAND ST
WATERSON ST
COLUMBIA ROAD
WELLINGTON ROW
Moorfields Eye Hospital
CHART ST
CHART ST
BACHES ST
HOXTON SQUARE
61
DRYSDALE ST
59
GOSSET ST
CORSHAM ST
PEERLESS ST
BRUNSWICK PLACE
CHARLES SQUARE
BOOT ST
AUSTIN ST
CHAMBORD ST
TURIN STREET
CRANWOOD ST
OLD STREET
VIRGINIA ROAD
Old Street
RIVINGTON STREET
CALVERT AVE
ARNOLD CIRCUS
SWANFIELD STREET
SATCHWELL ST
PADBURY CT
OLD STREET
CURTAIN RD
COWPER ST
64
GREAT EASTERN STREET
BATEMAN'S ROW
BOUNDARY STREET
CLUB ROW
BRICK LN
4
MALLOW ST
WILLOW ST
100
CHARLOTTE ROAD
SHOREDITCH
GRANBY ST
ST MATTHEWS ROW
FEATHERSTONE ST
LEONARD STREET
99
NEW INN YARD
OLD NICHOL STREET
REDCHURCH STREET
62
95
GREEN ROAD
98
CHILTON STREET
BACON STREET
John Wesley's House
Bunhill Fields Burial Grounds
TABERNACLE STREET
LUKE STREET
PHIPP ST
BETHNAL
SCLATER ST
CHESHIRE ST
CITY ROAD
EPWORTH ST
PAUL STREET
SCRUTTON ST
HOLYWELL LANE
BONHILL ST
HOLYWELL ROW
CURTAIN ROAD
SHOREDITCH HIGH STREET
HEARN ST
PLOUGH YARD
PEDLEY ST
WORSHIP STREET
WORSHIP STREET
WHEELER ST
FLEUR DE LIS ST
QUAKER STREET
CODE ST
ROW
Bunhill Fields
FINSBURY SQUARE
DYSART ST
CHRISTOPHER ST
SNOWDEN ST
BLOSSOM ST
ELDER ST
CALVIN ST
BUXTON STREET
GREY EAGLE ST
93
58
BRICK LANE
SPITAL ST
HUNTON ST
DEAL ST
ST
CLIFTON STREET
PINDAR ST
PRIMROSE ST
FOLGATE STREET
WOODSEER ST
EARL ST
APPOLD STREET
SUN STREET
Liverpool Street Station
SPITAL SQ
LAMB ST
COMMERCIAL ST
5
ROPEMAKER STREET
FINSBURY PAVEMENT
LACKINGTON ST
WILSON STREET
Broadgate Centre
SUN STREET
STEWARD ST
Spitalfields Market
60
WILKES ST
HANBURY STREET
PRINCELET STREET
96
92
FOURNIER ST
63
HENEAGE ST
MOORFIELDS
MOORGATE
SOUTH PLACE
Moorgate
ELDON ST
BRUSHFIELD STREET
Christ Church
See p407

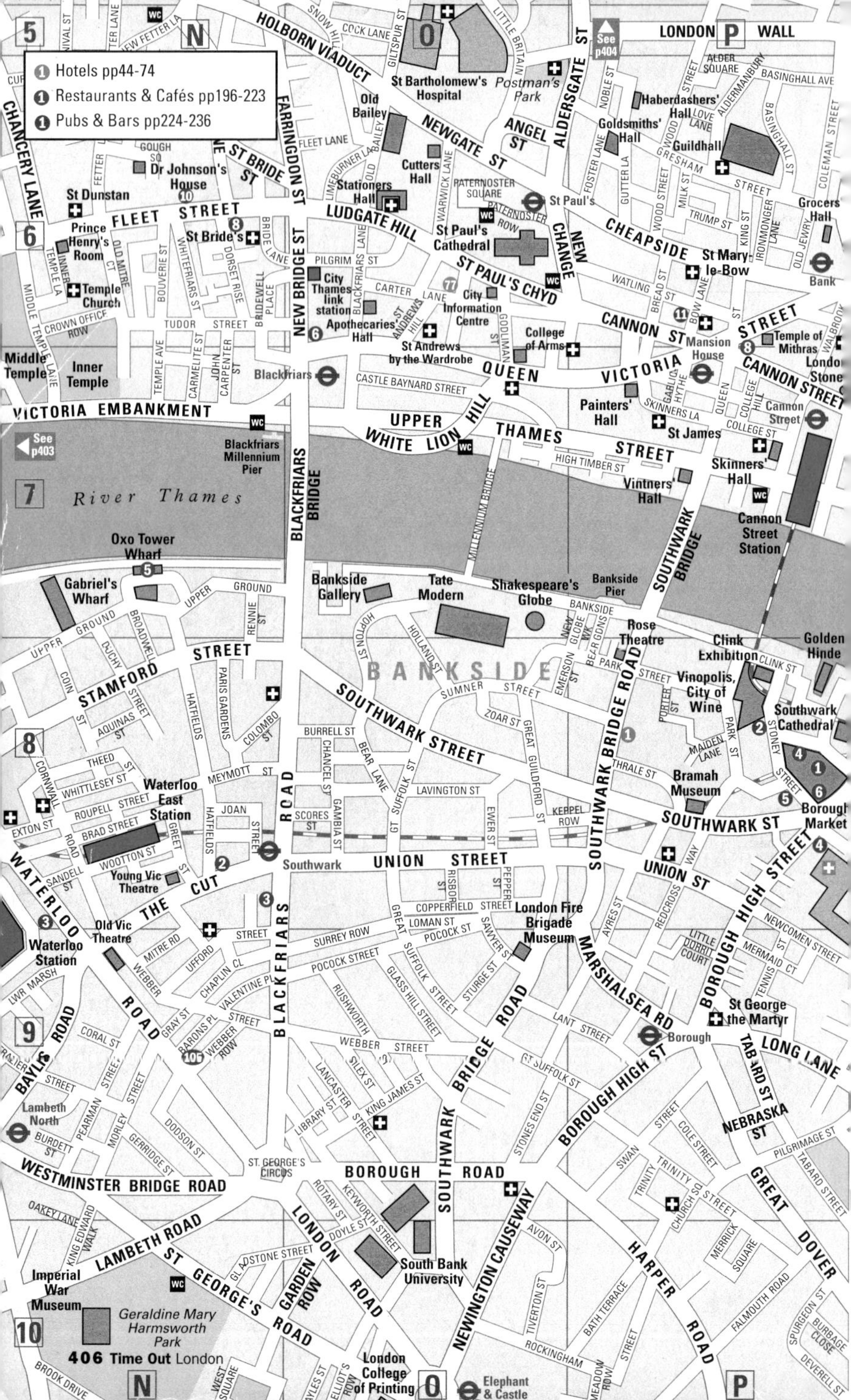

Hotels pp44-74
Restaurants & Cafés pp196-223
Pubs & Bars pp224-236
See p404
See p403
LONDON WALL
HOLBORN VIADUCT
St Bartholomew's Hospital
Postman's Park
ALDERSGATE ST
Old Bailey
NEWGATE ST
ANGEL ST
FARRINGDON ST
CHANCERY LANE
Dr Johnson's House
ST BRIDE ST
Cutlers Hall
Stationers Hall
Guildhall
Haberdashers' Hall
Goldsmiths' Hall
GRESHAM STREET
St Paul's
PATERNOSTER SQUARE
LUDGATE HILL
St Paul's Cathedral
NEW CHANGE
CHEAPSIDE
Grocers Hall
St Mary-le-Bow
Bank
St Dunstan
FLEET STREET
St Bride's
Prince Henry's Room
Temple Church
NEW BRIDGE ST
City Thames link station
Apothecaries' Hall
ST PAUL'S CHYD
City Information Centre
College of Arms
CANNON ST
Mansion House
Temple of Mithras
London Stone
CANNON STREET
St Andrews by the Wardrobe
Blackfriars
QUEEN VICTORIA STREET
Middle Temple
Inner Temple
CASTLE BAYNARD STREET
Painters' Hall
Cannon Street
VICTORIA EMBANKMENT
UPPER THAMES STREET
WHITE LION HILL
St James
Skinners' Hall
Blackfriars Millennium Pier
HIGH TIMBER ST
Vintners' Hall
Cannon Street Station
River Thames
BLACKFRIARS BRIDGE
MILLENNIUM BRIDGE
SOUTHWARK BRIDGE
Oxo Tower Wharf
Gabriel's Wharf
Bankside Gallery
Tate Modern
Shakespeare's Globe
Bankside Pier
UPPER GROUND
Rose Theatre
Clink Exhibition
Golden Hinde
BANKSIDE
STAMFORD STREET
SOUTHWARK STREET
SUMNER STREET
Vinopolis, City of Wine
Southwark Cathedral
SOUTHWARK BRIDGE ROAD
Bramah Museum
Borough Market
Waterloo East Station
BLACKFRIARS ROAD
SOUTHWARK ST
Southwark
UNION STREET
UNION ST
Young Vic Theatre
THE CUT
Old Vic Theatre
London Fire Brigade Museum
BOROUGH HIGH STREET
Waterloo Station
WATERLOO ROAD
MARSHALSEA RD
St George the Martyr
Borough
LONG LANE
BAYLIS ROAD
LANT STREET
TABARD ST
Lambeth North
NEBRASKA ST
WESTMINSTER BRIDGE ROAD
BOROUGH ROAD
SOUTHWARK BRIDGE ROAD
GREAT DOVER STREET
LAMBETH ROAD
ST GEORGE'S ROAD
LONDON ROAD
NEWINGTON CAUSEWAY
South Bank University
HARPER ROAD
Imperial War Museum
Geraldine Mary Harmsworth Park
London College of Printing
Elephant & Castle

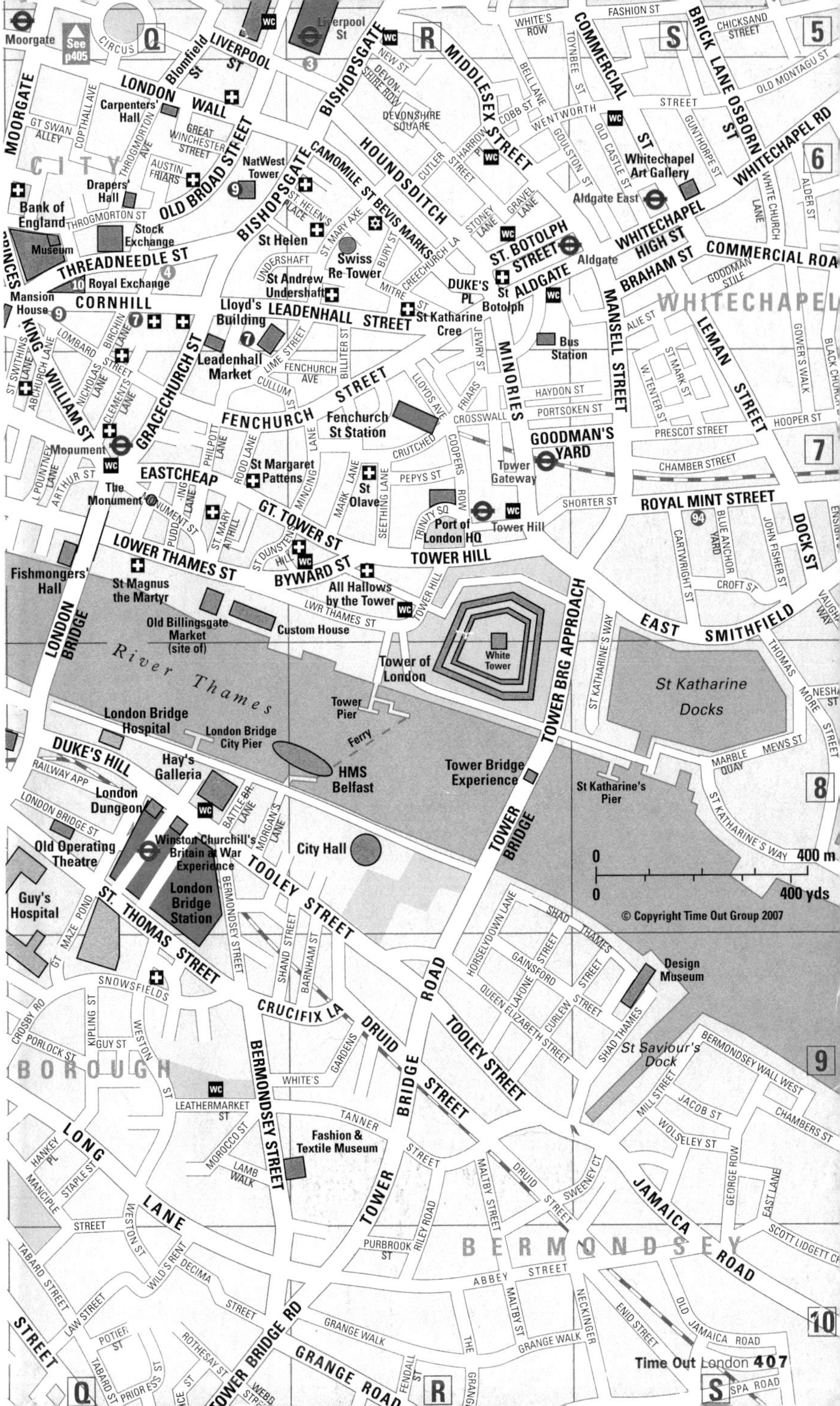
Q
R
S
5
6
7
8
9
10
Moorgate
See p405
CIRCUS
Blomfield St
LIVERPOOL ST
Liverpool St
BISHOPSGATE
MIDDLESEX STREET
WHITE'S ROW
FASHION ST
COMMERCIAL ST
TOYNBEE ST
BRICK LANE
OSBORN ST
CHICKSAND STREET
OLD MONTAGU ST
MOORGATE
LONDON WALL
Carpenters' Hall
COPTHALL AVE
GT SWAN ALLEY
THROGMORTON AVE
GREAT WINCHESTER STREET
OLD BROAD STREET
AUSTIN FRIARS
NatWest Tower
NEW ST
DEVONSHIRE ROW
DEVONSHIRE SQUARE
HOUNDSDITCH
CAMOMILE ST
CUTLER ST
HARROW PL
COBB ST
BELL LANE
WENTWORTH
GOULSTON ST
OLD CASTLE ST
STREET
GUNTHORPE ST
Whitechapel Art Gallery
WHITECHAPEL RD
CITY
Drapers' Hall
Bank of England
THROGMORTON ST
Stock Exchange
Museum
PRINCES
THREADNEEDLE ST
Royal Exchange
Mansion House
CORNHILL
ST HELEN'S PLACE
St Helen
ST MARY AXE
Swiss Re Tower
BEVIS MARKS
BURY ST
UNDERSHAFT
St Andrew Undershaft
Lloyd's Building
LEADENHALL STREET
MITRE ST
CREECHURCH LA
St Katharine Cree
DUKE'S PL
St Botolph
ST. BOTOLPH STREET
ALDGATE
Aldgate
Aldgate East
WHITECHAPEL HIGH ST
STONEY LANE
GRAVEL LANE
COMMERCIAL ROAD
WHITE CHURCH LANE
ALDER ST
BRAHAM ST
GOODMAN STILE
WHITECHAPEL
MANSELL STREET
ALIE ST
LEMAN STREET
KING WILLIAM ST
LOMBARD ST
BIRCHIN LANE
ST SWITHINS LANE
ABCHURCH LANE
NICHOLAS LANE
CLEMENTS LANE
GRACECHURCH ST
Leadenhall Market
LIME STREET
FENCHURCH AVE
BILLITER ST
JEWRY ST
MINORIES
Bus Station
CULLUM ST
FENCHURCH STREET
Fenchurch St Station
LLOYDS AVE
FRIARS
CROSSWALL
HAYDON ST
PORTSOKEN ST
ST MARK ST
W. TENTER ST
GOWER'S WALK
BLACK CHURCH
HOOPER ST
PRESCOT STREET
CHAMBER STREET
Monument
PHILPOT LANE
ROOD LANE
MINCING LANE
St Margaret Pattens
CRUTCHED
COOPERS ROW
GOODMAN'S YARD
Tower Gateway
PEPYS ST
EASTCHEAP
L POUNTNEY LANE
ARTHUR ST
The Monument
MONUMENT ST
PUDDING LANE
ST. MARY AT HILL
MARK LANE
St Olave
SEETHING LANE
TRINITY SQ
Port of London HQ
Tower Hill
SHORTER ST
ROYAL MINT STREET
CARTWRIGHT ST
BLUE ANCHOR YARD
JOHN FISHER ST
DOCK ST
GT. TOWER ST
ST DUNSTAN'S HILL
BYWARD ST
TOWER HILL
LOWER THAMES ST
St Magnus the Martyr
Fishmongers' Hall
All Hallows by the Tower
LWR THAMES ST
CROFT ST
TOWER BRG APPROACH
ST KATHARINE'S WAY
EAST SMITHFIELD
VAUGHAN WAY
LONDON BRIDGE
Old Billingsgate Market (site of)
Custom House
River Thames
Tower of London
White Tower
THOMAS MORE STREET
St Katharine Docks
Tower Pier
London Bridge Hospital
London Bridge City Pier
Ferry
HMS Belfast
Tower Bridge Experience
St Katharine's Pier
MARBLE QUAY
MEWS ST
DUKE'S HILL
RAILWAY APP
Hay's Galleria
London Dungeon
LONDON BRIDGE ST
BATTLE BR. LANE
MORGAN'S LANE
TOWER BRIDGE
ST KATHARINE'S WAY
0
400 m
400 yds
Old Operating Theatre
Winston Churchill's Britain at War Experience
City Hall
TOOLEY STREET
Guy's Hospital
London Bridge Station
BERMONDSEY STREET
© Copyright Time Out Group 2007
ST. THOMAS STREET
MAZE POND
SHAD THAMES
HORSELYDOWN LANE
GAINSFORD STREET
LAFONE STREET
QUEEN ELIZABETH STREET
CURLEW STREET
Design Museum
SHAND STREET
BARNHAM ST
ROAD
SNOWSFIELDS
CRUCIFIX LA
DRUID ST
GARDENS
BRIDGE
TOOLEY STREET
St Saviour's Dock
CROSBY RD
KIPLING ST
PORLOCK ST
GUY ST
WESTON ST
BOROUGH
WHITE'S
MILL STREET
BERMONDSEY WALL WEST
JACOB ST
CHAMBERS ST
LEATHERMARKET ST
TANNER
STREET
WOLSELEY ST
LONG LANE
Fashion & Textile Museum
MOROCCO ST
HANKEY PL
STAPLE ST
LAMB WALK
MALTBY STREET
DRUID STREET
SWEENEY CT
JAMAICA ROAD
GEORGE ROW
EAST LANE
MANCIPLE
RILEY ROAD
TOWER BRIDGE RD
SCOTT LIDGETT CR
BERMONDSEY
PURBROOK ST
WILD'S RENT
DECIMA STREET
ABBEY STREET
MALTBY ST
NECKINGER
TABARD STREET
LAW STREET
GRANGE WALK
ENID STREET
OLD JAMAICA ROAD
POTIER ST
ROTHESAY ST
THE GRANGE
GRANGE ROAD
FENDALL ST
PRIOR ESS ST
WEBB ST
SPA ROAD

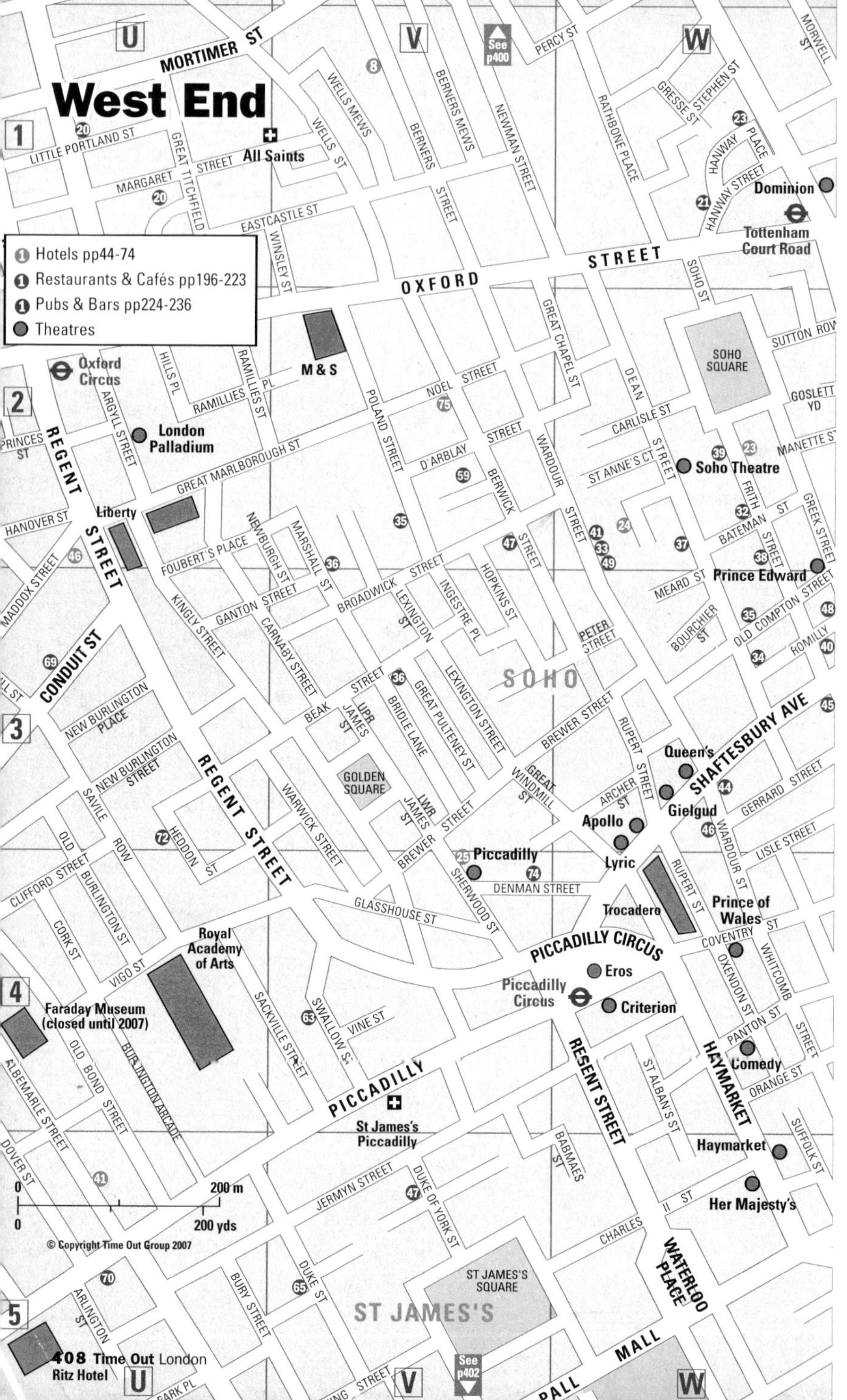
West End
U
V
W
1
2
3
4
5
See p400
See p402
Hotels pp44-74
Restaurants & Cafés pp196-223
Pubs & Bars pp224-236
Theatres
MORTIMER ST
LITTLE PORTLAND ST
MARGARET STREET
GREAT TITCHFIELD
All Saints
WELLS MEWS
WELLS ST
BERNERS MEWS
BERNERS STREET
NEWMAN STREET
PERCY ST
RATHBONE PLACE
GRESSE ST
STEPHEN ST
HANWAY PLACE
HANWAY STREET
MORWELL ST
Dominion
Tottenham Court Road
EASTCASTLE ST
WINSLEY ST
OXFORD STREET
SOHO ST
SOHO SQUARE
SUTTON ROW
GOSLETT YD
MANETTE ST
Oxford Circus
M & S
HILLS PL
RAMILLIES PL
RAMILLIES ST
ARGYLL STREET
PRINCES ST
REGENT STREET
London Palladium
GREAT MARLBOROUGH ST
POLAND STREET
NOEL STREET
D'ARBLAY STREET
BERWICK STREET
WARDOUR STREET
GREAT CHAPEL ST
DEAN STREET
CARLISLE ST
ST ANNE'S CT
Soho Theatre
FRITH STREET
BATEMAN ST
GREEK STREET
Prince Edward
MEARD ST
BOURCHIER ST
OLD COMPTON STREET
ROMILLY
HANOVER ST
Liberty
MADDOX STREET
FOUBERT'S PLACE
NEWBURGH ST
MARSHALL ST
GANTON STREET
KINGLY STREET
CARNABY STREET
BROADWICK STREET
LEXINGTON ST
INGESTRE PL
HOPKINS ST
PETER STREET
SOHO
CONDUIT ST
NEW BURLINGTON PLACE
NEW BURLINGTON STREET
BEAK STREET
UPR JAMES ST
BRIDLE LANE
GREAT PULTENEY ST
LEXINGTON STREET
BREWER STREET
RUPERT STREET
Queen's
SHAFTESBURY AVE
GOLDEN SQUARE
WARWICK STREET
GREAT WINDMILL ST
ARCHER ST
Gielgud
Apollo
Lyric
GERRARD STREET
LISLE STREET
SAVILE ROW
OLD BURLINGTON ST
HEDDON ST
LWR JAMES ST
Piccadilly
DENMAN STREET
SHERWOOD ST
CLIFFORD STREET
CORK ST
GLASSHOUSE ST
Trocadero
RUPERT ST
Prince of Wales
COVENTRY ST
WHITCOMB ST
Royal Academy of Arts
VIGO ST
PICCADILLY CIRCUS
Eros
Piccadilly Circus
Criterion
OXENDON ST
Faraday Museum (closed until 2007)
OLD BOND STREET
BURLINGTON ARCADE
SACKVILLE STREET
SWALLOW ST
VINE ST
REGENT STREET
ST ALBAN'S ST
HAYMARKET
PANTON ST
Comedy
ORANGE ST
ALBEMARLE STREET
PICCADILLY
St James's Piccadilly
Haymarket
SUFFOLK ST
DOVER ST
BABMAES ST
JERMYN STREET
DUKE OF YORK ST
Her Majesty's
0
200 m
0
200 yds
© Copyright Time Out Group 2007
CHARLES II ST
WATERLOO PLACE
ST JAMES'S SQUARE
ARLINGTON ST
BURY STREET
DUKE ST
ST JAMES'S
PALL MALL
Ritz Hotel
PARK PL

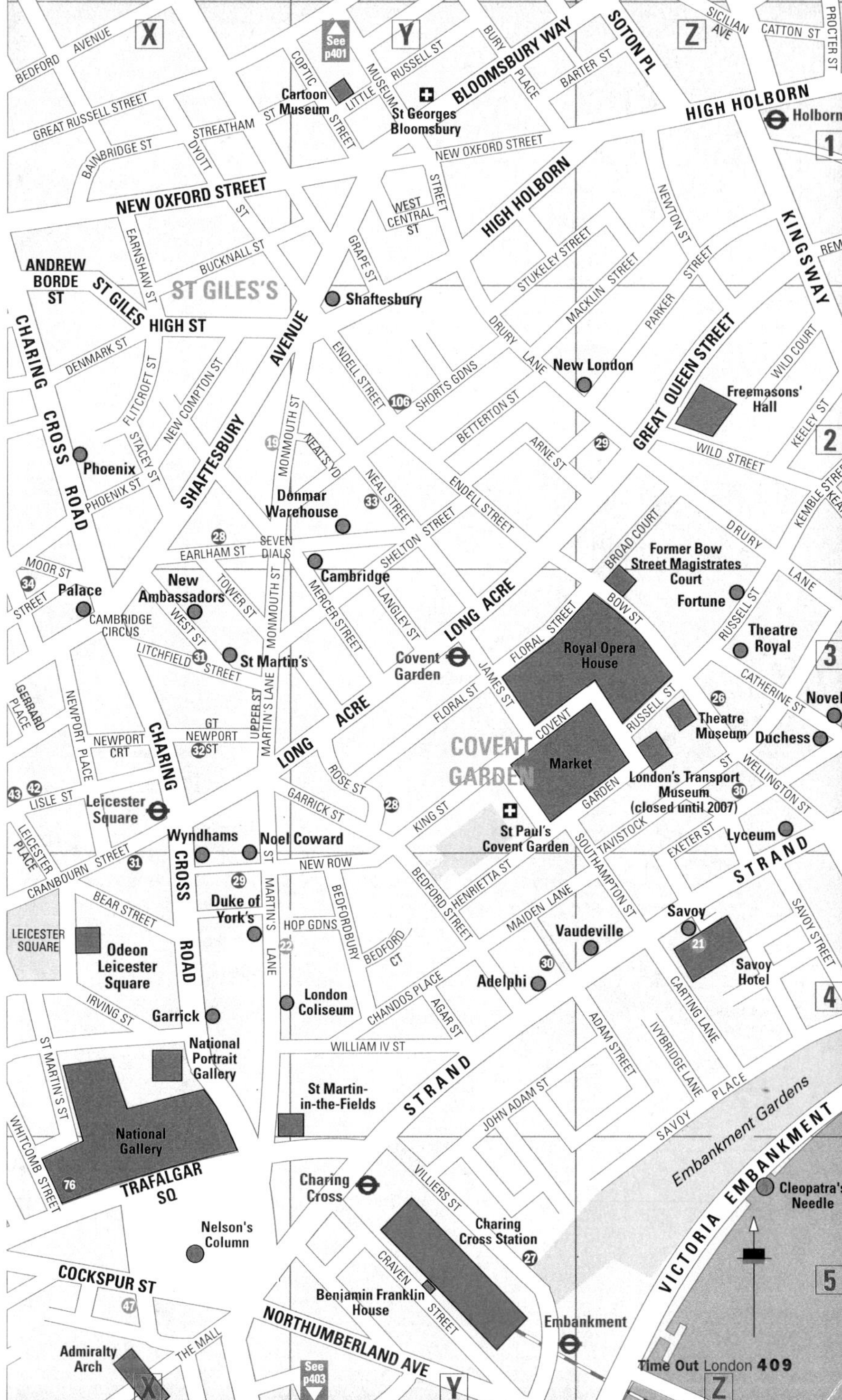

X
Y
Z
See p401
1
2
3
4
5
ST GILES'S
COVENT GARDEN
Cartoon Museum
St Georges Bloomsbury
Holborn
Shaftesbury
New London
Freemasons' Hall
Phoenix
Donmar Warehouse
Cambridge
Palace
New Ambassadors
St Martin's
Covent Garden
Former Bow Street Magistrates Court
Fortune
Royal Opera House
Theatre Royal
Novello
Theatre Museum
Duchess
Market
London's Transport Museum (closed until 2007)
Leicester Square
St Paul's Covent Garden
Lyceum
Wyndhams
Noel Coward
Duke of York's
Savoy
Vaudeville
Savoy Hotel
Odeon Leicester Square
Adelphi
London Coliseum
Garrick
National Portrait Gallery
St Martin-in-the-Fields
National Gallery
Embankment Gardens
Charing Cross
Charing Cross Station
Cleopatra's Needle
Nelson's Column
Benjamin Franklin House
Embankment
Admiralty Arch
See p403

Street Index

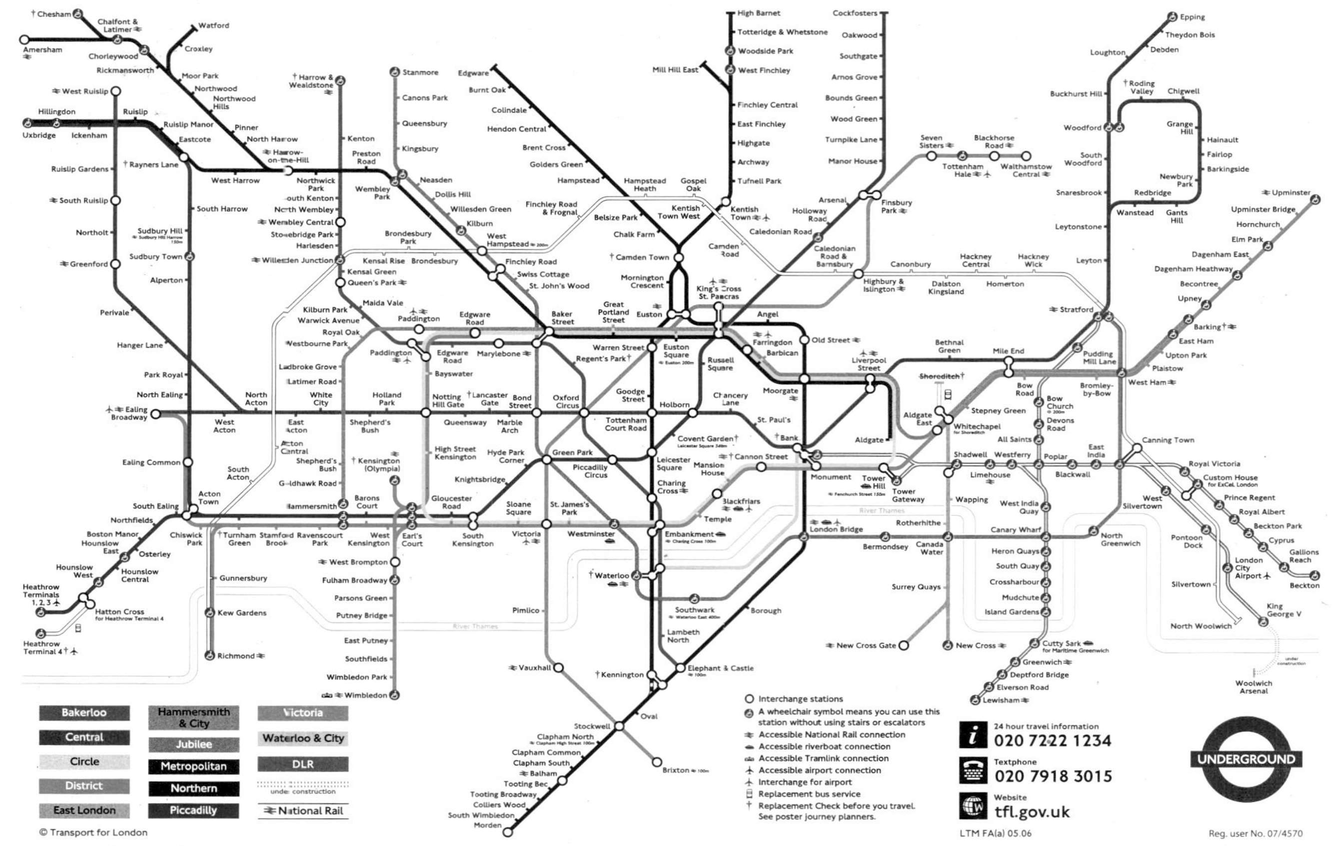

Chesham
Chalfont & Latimer
Amersham
Chorleywood
Rickmansworth
Watford
Croxley
Moor Park
Northwood
Northwood Hills
Pinner
North Harrow
Harrow-on-the-Hill
West Ruislip
Ruislip
Hillingdon
Uxbridge
Ickenham
Ruislip Manor
Eastcote
Rayners Lane
Ruislip Gardens
South Ruislip
Northolt
Greenford
Perivale
Hanger Lane
Park Royal
North Ealing
Ealing Broadway
Ealing Common
South Ealing
Northfields
Boston Manor
Hounslow East
Hounslow Central
Hounslow West
Heathrow Terminals 1, 2, 3
Hatton Cross for Heathrow Terminal 4
Heathrow Terminal 4
West Harrow
South Harrow
Sudbury Hill
Sudbury Hill Harrow 150m
Sudbury Town
Alperton
Harrow & Wealdstone
Kenton
Preston Road
Northwick Park
South Kenton
North Wembley
Wembley Central
Stonebridge Park
Harlesden
Willesden Junction
Wembley Park
Stanmore
Canons Park
Queensbury
Kingsbury
Neasden
Dollis Hill
Willesden Green
Kilburn
West Hampstead 200m
Finchley Road
Swiss Cottage
St. John's Wood
Edgware
Burnt Oak
Colindale
Hendon Central
Brent Cross
Golders Green
Hampstead
Belsize Park
Chalk Farm
Camden Town
Mornington Crescent
Finchley Road & Frognal
Hampstead Heath
Gospel Oak
Kentish Town West
Kentish Town
Camden Road
Caledonian Road & Barnsbury
Highbury & Islington
Canonbury
Dalston Kingsland
Hackney Central
Hackney Wick
Homerton
High Barnet
Totteridge & Whetstone
Woodside Park
West Finchley
Mill Hill East
Finchley Central
East Finchley
Highgate
Archway
Tufnell Park
Cockfosters
Oakwood
Southgate
Arnos Grove
Bounds Green
Wood Green
Turnpike Lane
Manor House
Arsenal
Holloway Road
Caledonian Road
Finsbury Park
Seven Sisters
Tottenham Hale
Blackhorse Road
Walthamstow Central
Brondesbury Park
Brondesbury
Kensal Rise
Kensal Green
Queen's Park
Kilburn Park
Maida Vale
Warwick Avenue
Royal Oak
Westbourne Park
Ladbroke Grove
Latimer Road
Paddington
Edgware Road
Marylebone
Baker Street
Great Portland Street
Euston
King's Cross St. Pancras
Angel
Old Street
Farringdon
Barbican
Moorgate
Liverpool Street
Warren Street
Regent's Park
Euston Square
Euston 200m
Russell Square
Goodge Street
Tottenham Court Road
Holborn
Chancery Lane
St. Paul's
Bank
Aldgate
Bayswater
Notting Hill Gate
Lancaster Gate
Bond Street
Oxford Circus
Queensway
Marble Arch
Holland Park
Shepherd's Bush
White City
East Acton
North Acton
West Acton
Acton Central
South Acton
Acton Town
Shepherd's Bush
Goldhawk Road
Hammersmith
Kensington (Olympia)
High Street Kensington
Hyde Park Corner
Knightsbridge
Green Park
Piccadilly Circus
Leicester Square
Covent Garden
Leicester Square 240m
Mansion House
Cannon Street
Monument
Tower Hill
Fenchurch Street 150m
Tower Gateway
Charing Cross
Blackfriars
Temple
Embankment
Charing Cross 100m
Westminster
Waterloo
Southwark
Waterloo East 400m
Lambeth North
Elephant & Castle
100m
Borough
London Bridge
Gloucester Road
Sloane Square
St. James's Park
Victoria
South Kensington
Barons Court
Earl's Court
West Kensington
Ravenscourt Park
Stamford Brook
Turnham Green
Chiswick Park
Gunnersbury
Kew Gardens
Richmond
West Brompton
Fulham Broadway
Parsons Green
Putney Bridge
East Putney
Southfields
Wimbledon Park
Wimbledon
Pimlico
Vauxhall
Kennington
Oval
Stockwell
Brixton 100m
Clapham North
Clapham High Street 100m
Clapham Common
Clapham South
Balham
Tooting Bec
Tooting Broadway
Colliers Wood
South Wimbledon
Morden
Bethnal Green
Mile End
Shoreditch
Aldgate East
Whitechapel
for Shoreditch
Stepney Green
Bow Road
Bow Church
200m
Devons Road
All Saints
Shadwell
Westferry
Limehouse
Poplar
Blackwall
East India
Wapping
Rotherhithe
Canada Water
Bermondsey
Surrey Quays
New Cross Gate
New Cross
West India Quay
Canary Wharf
Heron Quays
South Quay
Crossharbour
Mudchute
Island Gardens
Cutty Sark for Maritime Greenwich
Greenwich
Deptford Bridge
Elverson Road
Lewisham
North Greenwich
Canning Town
West Silvertown
Pontoon Dock
London City Airport
Silvertown
North Woolwich
King George V
Woolwich Arsenal
under construction
Royal Victoria
Custom House for ExCeL London
Prince Regent
Royal Albert
Beckton Park
Cyprus
Gallions Reach
Beckton
Stratford
Pudding Mill Lane
Bromley-by-Bow
West Ham
Plaistow
Upton Park
East Ham
Barking
Upney
Becontree
Dagenham Heathway
Dagenham East
Elm Park
Hornchurch
Upminster Bridge
Upminster
Leyton
Leytonstone
Wanstead
Redbridge
Gants Hill
Newbury Park
Barkingside
Fairlop
Hainault
Grange Hill
Chigwell
Roding Valley
Snaresbrook
South Woodford
Woodford
Buckhurst Hill
Loughton
Debden
Theydon Bois
Epping
River Thames
Bakerloo
Central
Circle
District
East London
Hammersmith & City
Jubilee
Metropolitan
Northern
Piccadilly
Victoria
Waterloo & City
DLR
under construction
National Rail
© Transport for London
Interchange stations
A wheelchair symbol means you can use this station without using stairs or escalators
Accessible National Rail connection
Accessible riverboat connection
Accessible Tramlink connection
Accessible airport connection
Interchange for airport
Replacement bus service
Replacement Check before you travel. See poster journey planners.
24 hour travel information
020 7222 1234
Textphone
020 7918 3015
Website
tfl.gov.uk
LTM FA(a) 05.06
UNDERGROUND
Reg. user No. 07/4570